D0768641

STUDENT PROTESTS IN
TWENTIETH-CENTURY CHINA

THE VIEW FROM SHANGHAI

STUDENT PROTESTS IN TWENTIETH-CENTURY CHINA

THE VIEW FROM SHANGHAI

JEFFREY N. WASSERSTROM

STANFORD UNIVERSITY PRESS

Stanford, California

1991

Stanford University Press
Stanford, California

© 1991 by the Board of Trustees
of the Leland Stanford Junior University

CIP data are at the end of the book

PRINTED IN THE UNITED STATES OF AMERICA

 *To Anne, who listened to my ideas, helped me put my thoughts in order, and kept me sane in China, and Sam, who gave me something to smile about even in the darkest days of 1989*

ACKNOWLEDGMENTS

MANY FRIENDS, TEACHERS, COLLEAGUES, foundations, and institutions have helped make this book possible. Although none of them should be held responsible for either my views or my mistakes, they have all shaped the pages that follow, and it is a pleasure now to thank them for their support, beginning with the organizations that provided me with funding. Fellowships from the Harvard University Grants-in-Aid Program, the Foreign Languages and Area Studies Program, and the University of California at Berkeley helped me begin work on the dissertation from which this book evolved. The Fulbright-Hayes Doctoral Dissertation Research Abroad Program made it possible for me to spend the 1986–87 academic year doing research in China; a grant from the American Council of Learned Societies allowed me to continue on from there to libraries and archives in Geneva, Paris, and London; and the Committee for Scholarly Communication with the People's Republic of China and the Shanghai Academy of Social Sciences made a short return visit to Shanghai in 1988 possible. The Charlotte Newcombe Foundation generously supported a year of dissertation writing, and awards from the University of Kentucky's Summer Fellowship Program and the National Academy of Education's Spencer Fellowship Program provided me with time to make final revisions.

Archivists and librarians on three continents assisted me in numerous ways. I am most grateful to those at Berkeley's East Asian and Chinese Studies libraries; the Hoover Institution's Library and Archive; the Fudan University Library; the Shanghai Municipal Library; and the Shanghai Municipal Archive. Librarians and archivists at the British Foreign Office, Harvard University (especially Eugene Wu), the International Labor Organization Archive, the Library of Congress's Prints and Photographs Division, the New York Public Library, and the U.S. National Archive were also particularly helpful, as were the school history archivists at the Jiaotong, Tongji, and Fudan campuses. I owe a special debt of gratitude to Liu Ding and the other members of the Shanghai branch of the Communist Youth League's Youth Movement Research Group, who shared their knowledge of local history with me and allowed me to use their collection of unpublished memoirs.

Both before and after entering graduate school, I had the good fortune to study under a variety of gifted teachers, all of whom indirectly or directly shaped the pages that follow. Of those I encountered early in my academic career, I owe the biggest debts to Peter Sawaya, Olive Anderson, Donald Sasoon, Buchanon Sharpe, and most of all Michael Freeman, my senior thesis adviser and the person who inspired me to become a Chinese historian. Of those I studied with or met at Harvard, I am most grateful to Hue-Tam Tai, Josh Fogel, and Paul Cohen (all of whom have continued to comment and advise me on my work ever since); Philip Kuhn (under whose supervision I wrote a master's thesis that laid the foundation for some of the arguments in this book); and, above all, Liz Perry (whose generosity with ideas, sources, criticism, encouragement, and time has been greater than any student, colleague, or even friend has a right to expect). In Shanghai, I had able *laoshi* and helpful advisers in Huang Meizhen, Wang Min, Xie Shengzhi, Yu Zidao, and Zhao Shaoquan.

The debt I owe to those I worked with at Berkeley should be obvious, at least to them, in the pages that follow. Lynn Hunt, David Keightley (who was a diligent dissertation committee member as well as teacher), Tom Laqueur, and Irwin Scheiner have all influenced profoundly the way I think about and do history. Tom Gold gave my dissertation a close and careful reading, and Yeh Wen-hsin and David Johnson did the same for individual chapters. Most of all, I am grateful to Fred Wakeman for supervising my dissertation work, showing me the virtues of steering clear of the easy way out when confronting a theoretical or historical problem, and, among other reasons too numerous to mention, paying me to read all 67 reels of the Shanghai Municipal Police files.

A wide variety of people either read individual chapters, shared their observations of Chinese protests with me, made comments that led me to rethink specific sections, pointed me to new sources, provided me with opportunities to present my ideas to critical audiences, supplied me with copies of their unpublished papers, and/or gave me emotional support at some point during this project. For reasons such as these, I am grateful to Bill and Nettie Adams, Bill Alford, Ming Chan, Marie-Claire Bergère, Lucian Bianco, Chris Borstel, Tim Cheek, Yves Chevrier, Chow Tse-tsung, Nick Clifford, Parks Coble, Sherm Cochran, Arif Dirlik, George Doyle, Art Ford, Dru Gladney, Ellen Goldberg, Merle Goldman, Bryna Goodman, Richard Gordon, Sebastian Heilmann, Gail Hershatter, James Hevia, Emily Honig, Peter Hoffenberg, Yasheng Huang, Sandra Hutchinson, Bill Kirby, Tracey Lee, Dave Macauley, Melissa Macauley, Doug Merwin, Kristen Parris, Don Price, Julie Strauss, Lynn Struve, Su Shaozhi, Sun Sibai, Jonathan Spence, Jonathan Unger, Phyllis and Richard Wasserstrom, Woody Watson, Tim Weston, George Wilson, Eddie Yuen, Zhang Jishun, and the two anonymous readers Stanford University Press selected.

Several people and groups deserve special thanks. Patty Stranahan and John Israel were both extremely generous with their time and expertise. Liu Xinyong and Joe Esherick collaborated with me on articles and in the process changed my thinking on key points. Frank Pieke's willingness to exchange works in progress and thoughts on 1989 helped clarify my image of the Beijing protests leading up to the June 4th Massacre, and Deborah Pellow supplied me with photographs from and a firsthand account of her time at Fudan that gave me important insights into related Shanghai events. Years of conversations with Dan Letwin have shaped the way I view popular protests. The Chinese informants who spoke with me about their experiences as student protesters in the 1930's, 1940's, and 1980's (whose identities I have withheld for their own protection) provided me with insights and data I could not have gotten from other sources. Muriel Bell and John Ziemer of Stanford University Press have earned my sincerest gratitude; the first by skillfully steering the manuscript through its various stages, and the second by carefully copyediting the finished product. My colleagues at the University of Kentucky, and George Herring in particular, helped me survive—and even get some thinking and revising done during—my first year of teaching. The Chinese and foreign participants in the International Symposium on Modern Shanghai collectively shaped my vision of the city's social and cultural peculiarities. Last but not least, I would like to thank the members of the Berkeley History Department Dissertation Group, whose support and criticism were equally valuable to me, and Anne Bock, for the reasons stated in the dedication and much more.

J.N.W.

 CONTENTS

STUDENT PROTESTS IN TWENTIETH-CENTURY CHINA

THE VIEW FROM SHANGHAI

INTRODUCTION

THROUGHOUT THE TWENTIETH CENTURY the streets of Shanghai have been more than just the thoroughfares of China's biggest city: they have also served as battlefields for a variety of conflicts. Some of the battles fought on these streets, such as those that accompanied the Japanese invasions of the 1930's, have been military ones. Others, such the Three Workers' Uprisings of 1926 and 1927, have been violent rebellions. Still others have been symbolic in nature, playing themselves out in terms of political theater rather than warfare and temporarily transforming the streets into stages. During these theatrical battles, in which students have most often played the leading roles, brigades of demonstrators have marched through the city, usually armed only with banners and flags. At times these youths have paraded unopposed. On other occasions they have struggled with other marchers for control of the stage. In still other cases they have confronted detachments of police or soldiers armed with much deadlier weapons, and the drama has become a tragedy and the street a bloodstained stage.

Although students have most often preferred symbols and slogans to guns and have only rarely tried to acquire territory or wrest control of the political apparatus, theatrical street battles involving educated youths have played as crucial a role as military confrontations in shaping Shanghai's political history. Both the actors involved in student protests and the authorities who have served as audiences for and targets of this subversive street theater have viewed demonstrations as extremely serious events. The theatrical battles staged on the city's streets have been part of life-and-death struggles over crucial issues of how power should be exercised and who should be allowed to rule. Youthful martyrs have not been the only ones hurt during these clashes: officials, policies, and in some cases regimes have also been among the casualties.

PROTEST AS WARFARE

I do not use metaphors of battle and theater here simply as stylistic conventions. In important ways the actions of Shanghai student protesters are best conceptualized as acts of struggle and dramatic performances.[1] Presenting protests as battles requires little special explanation: terms such as "march" and "strike" evoke images of warfare, and Western political theorists and commentators often explicitly treat demonstrations in martial terms.[2] Chinese writers have also found military metaphors useful for describing events of this sort; for example, Mao Zedong depicted the protests against Jiang Jieshi (Chiang K'ai-shek) in cities under Guomindang (GMD) rule as conflicts being waged on the "second battlefront."[3]

Moreover, Shanghai student protesters themselves have consistently seen and portrayed their actions in martial terms. This is in part because, as later chapters show, they have at times literally fought for control of symbolically or strategically important locations: this occurred in 1931 (when educated youths seized municipal government buildings), 1947 (when protesters turned their flags and banner poles into staffs to fight mounted policemen), and 1989 (when students and workers blockaded the streets of the city to protest, and to prevent a local replication of, the Beijing massacre of June 4). In addition, whenever foreign foes have threatened China's territorial integrity, educated youths have responded by forming or joining special "student armies," whose members have donned military uniforms and vowed to travel to the front to fight for their homeland (see Chapters 1 and 7). But even when "student armies" have not been necessary, angry educated youths have routinely utilized martial imagery, organizing themselves into "brigades" (*duiwu*) and calling their leaders "generals" (*zhihui*). During the anti–Civil War demonstrations of 1946 and 1947, for example, even though students were working toward a pacifist end, they still turned to symbols and terms linked to battle: marching songs from the War of Resistance against Japan (1937–45) were popular among these youths, and one of their key slogans was "fighting for peace" (*zheng heping*).

PROTEST AS THEATER

Treating student demonstrations as acts of political theater requires more explanation, since the connections between drama and protest may seem more tenuous at first than those between military maneuvers and marches. Ultimately, however, theatrical metaphors often prove even more appropriate and interpretively powerful than martial ones.[4] It has become commonplace in recent decades for journalists in the West to speak of politics and theater as analogous and related genres of activity.[5] This is only natural; from Classical Greece on, dramatic performances have played crucial roles in political life as reflections or critiques of systems of power relations, and political philosophers beginning with Plato and Aristotle have taken tragedy and other dramatic forms seriously.[6] Contemporary idiom makes connections between theater and politics difficult to avoid: we speak of "staging" demonstrations and political "actors."

The connection between theater and politics is not, however, a mere fluke of language: as scholars in a variety of fields have shown, treating political acts as a genre of performance can enrich our understanding of how power is wielded and contested. The anthropologist Victor Turner has argued convincingly that many forms of collective action with political consequences can best be understood as "social dramas."[7] Clifford Geertz has demonstrated the degree to which symbolic performances and politics can become intertwined in the ceremonies of "theater states" such as Bali.[8]

Whereas Geertz and other authors stress the role of theater in maintaining the political status quo, other writers focus on the subversive potential of both formal dramas and street theatrics, such as parades that mock official ceremonies or satirize governmental leaders. The "guerrilla theater" so central to the American youth movement of the 1960's is one clear example of drama with this potential.[9] But the phenomenon is by no means either a strictly contemporary or a uniquely American one, as recent work on English and French history illustrates. Studies of Hanoverian London by John Brewer and Nicholas Rogers are filled with examples of the way in which both formal theatrical productions and improvised mockeries of authorized rituals performed on the streets challenged officials and their institutions.[10] And E. P. Thompson argues persuasively that all acts of popular protest in eighteenth-century England can usefully be interpreted as part of a subversive "counter-theatre of threat and sedition" that challenged the deference-based "theatre of hegemony" that the British gentry employed to legitimate its uses of power.[11] Natalie Davis, in a similar vein, stresses that the street theater accompanying French festivals of misrule could "act both to reinforce order and to suggest alternatives to the existing order."[12]

Thus far I have stressed the linking of theater and politics by Western writers, but to speak of Chinese student protests as "performances" is not to impose a foreign terminology upon the events. Classical Chinese philosophers were as concerned with the political implications of performances as their Greek counterparts, although they tended to focus solely on that most rule-bound and conservative genre of performance, orthodox ritual (*li*), rather than on more creative, less predictable, and (at least potentially) more subversive forms such as tragedy and street theater.[13] For Confucians the correct performance of sacrifices and other rituals at court and in local seats of power was crucial to the maintenance of both natural and sociopolitical harmony and order.[14] And during the imperial period, theatrical performances, ranging from operas sponsored by powerful lineages to puppet shows and tales told by itinerant storytellers, helped reaffirm existing hierarchies by reinforcing Confucian values and thus supported the hegemony of the state and its institutions.[15] Theatrical performances have continued to be important to China's post-imperial rulers as well: the Chinese Communist Party (CCP), for example, has used everything from operas glorifying revolutionary heroes and heroines to skits celebrating the joys of small families to carefully orchestrated pageants staged to mark revolutionary anniversaries in its efforts to inculcate a new set of values.[16]

In China as in the West, however, the theater has always had a subversive side: dramatic performances have often disrupted instead of buttressed the social order, undermined instead of reinforced orthodox values, and served counter-hegemonic instead of hegemonic ends. The Qing Dynasty (1644–1911), for example, banned certain operas with seductive performances by female impersonators on moral grounds and tried to prevent the staging of dramatic works that touched on politically sensitive issues such as official corruption or Manchu-Chinese relations.[17] Joseph Esherick's analysis of the Boxer Uprising illustrates another way in which Chinese drama could serve subversive ends during the final decades of imperial rule; he argues that some Boxers found models for their activities in the folk heroes celebrated in the dramas performed at village festivals.[18] And throughout the first half of the twentieth century, successive generations of Chinese revolutionaries discovered that plays could serve as important "vehicles of propaganda" in their struggles against native and foreign powerholders.[19] Despite the periodic efforts of the CCP to make drama serve narrowly defined "revolutionary" goals, dissident artists have produced a number of powerful plays and movies that have used historical analogies and thinly disguised references to political figures to attack leaders and orthodox policies.[20] Finally, as later chapters illustrate, throughout the twentieth century Shanghai's student protesters have consistently used self-consciously theatrical performances—improvised skits, group singing, and pageants—to gain popular support.

Theater is also an important source of political metaphor in modern China, as it is in the West. The first character in the word for "giving a speech" (*yanjiang*) is used to describe the "acting" (*biaoyan*) of an actor in the theater, for example, and both political meetings and operas begin with a "curtain raising" (*kaimushi*). And in Chinese as in English the word for "stage" (*tai*) has political as well as dramatic usages: politicians speak from "stages," Mao Zedong wrote of the early twentieth century as the time when the Chinese proletariat mounted the historical "stage," and in 1989 two favorite slogans of student protesters called for Deng Xiaoping and his hardline protégé Li Peng to "get off the stage" (*xiatai*). Protesters and their critics have also frequently used theatrical terms to describe political events associated with student movements: for example, cynics have wondered about the identity of "backstage managers" (*houtai*) directing certain demonstrations; and students have called shootings of protesters by policemen or soldiers "tragedies" (*beiju*).

Describing Chinese student demonstrations in theatrical terms is in no way meant to trivialize these events as mere playacting. As I argue in Chapter 10, what made these protests so powerful was their efficacy as *symbolic performances* that questioned, subverted, and ultimately undermined official rituals and spectacles. Lacking economic clout and generally shunning violence, students had to rely primarily upon their ability to move an audience. This they did through the use of oratory, song, gestures, and other forms of symbolic actions. In short, they made all the techniques actors use in aesthetic forms of drama serve the purposes of the *political theater* of the street.

STUDENTS AS POLITICAL ACTORS

I continue to invoke and explore the implications of martial and theatrical metaphors throughout the following pages, as part of my larger effort: to show how one important urban social group, Shanghai students, have experienced and helped shape the course of the Chinese Revolution. In light of the events of 1989, the significance of this particular social group, and of student movements as a genre of collective action, hardly needs underlining. Nonetheless, since China's Revolution is so often dubbed a "peasant revolution," it is worth pointing out that student strikes, streetside lecture campaigns, and demonstrations have played a vital role not just in recent political upheavals but in every phase of the revolutionary process. Although the CCP won its final victory in the countryside in 1949, members of urban classes played crucial parts in bringing each of China's twentieth-century revolutionary regimes to power. Student movements of the Republican era (1911–49) contributed to this process by, among other ways, making people both inside and outside the nation aware of wrongs committed by foreign and domestic authorities; mobilizing and politicizing workers and merchants; and serving as a form of basic training for many future leaders of armed struggles, including Mao Zedong himself. Most important of all, throughout both the Republican period and the period of CCP rule, student movements have consistently challenged the legitimacy of existing political arrangements.

Since all the great youth movements of this century, from the May 4th Movement of 1919 to the People's Movement of 1989, have involved the students of more than one city, no local study can provide a fully comprehensive picture of the history of Chinese student protest. Focusing on a single city unavoidably leads the historian to emphasize some events at the expense of other equally significant ones. Thus, for example, because Shanghai students played central roles in the Anti-Japanese Movement of 1931 but only peripheral ones in the more famous December 9th Movement of 1935, I devote an entire chapter to the former and refer to the latter only in passing. Similarly, although I spend a great deal of time discussing the young protesters shot by members of the Shanghai Municipal Police force on May 30, 1925, I have little to say about the more than 50 demonstrators British troops killed in Guangzhou on June 23 of the same year or about the dozens of unarmed student marchers who died from shots fired by warlord troops in Beijing's March 18th Tragedy of 1926. Furthermore, because of various factors—the city's size, cosmopolitan character, unique political structure—Shanghai was an atypical Chinese metropolis in many regards. Although local student activists were much like their counterparts in other cities in terms of the tactics they used and the texts they produced, the city's special features gave the Shanghai youth movement a distinctive rhythm and style.

This said, there are good reasons for using the experience of a single city to explore the history of Chinese student protest; the most important is that the complexity of events makes it impossible to do justice to them without narrowing either one's chronological sweep or one's geographical scope. There are also good reasons why, if one city is to be chosen, that city should be either Shanghai or Beijing. These have been China's two leading educational centers throughout the past century. Most of the nation's earliest modern institutions of higher learning were established in one of these two cities, and Shanghai and Beijing continue to be home to many of China's most prestigious universities. One indication of the extent of their domination of Chinese higher education throughout the twentieth century is that in 1930 of China's 59 colleges and universities, twelve were located in Shanghai and seven in Beijing. During that same year nearly 60 percent of the nation's 34,000 undergraduate and graduate students were studying in one or the other of the two cities.[21]

Beijing and Shanghai have not only been key cities in educational terms but have also been the dominant centers of student activism. The educated youths of other cities have played key roles in particular periods of campus unrest: some of the most important protests of 1931 and 1947 took place in Nanjing, the December 1st Movement of 1945 began in Kunming, and important early pro-democracy protests occurred in Changsha in 1980 and Hefei in 1986. Nonetheless, to quote John Israel, the history of Chinese student protest has remained "to a considerable extent a tale of two cities." [22] In some cases, the youths of one of these cities clearly played the dominant role: the May 30th Movement of 1925 began and remained based in Shanghai; Beijing campuses were the main centers for student activism in spring 1926 and throughout the December 9th Movement. In other cases, the students of the two cities have traded the vanguard position within a given struggle. The May 4th Movement of 1919, for example, began in Beijing but reached its peak in Shanghai. And during the democracy protests of the late 1980's, the most important student demonstrations of 1986 occurred in Shanghai, but Beijing's Tiananmen Square became the main rallying point during the struggle's resurgence in spring 1989.

Although both Beijing and Shanghai have strong attractions for the scholar interested in student unrest, there is one compelling reason for choosing the latter as the focus for a local history of this type: the abundance of source materials available for the study of the Republican period (1911–49). Journals and books published in the People's Republic provide numerous memoirs concerning campus unrest in Shanghai and Beijing alike, and these materials are invaluable sources for reconstructing the history of mass movements of the Republican era. Because these materials were written with an eye toward serving political purposes as well as simply recording historical events, however, they are problematic. To get a full picture of student protests in the first half of the twentieth century, it is necessary to play these accounts off as wide a variety of other types of primary sources as possible, particularly those written by people such as foreign observers and GMD supporters who, though by no means "objective," had very different political agendas and biases than do the authors of PRC memoirs. This is much easier to do for Shanghai, thanks to the availability of a rich variety of documents dealing with that city. The historian working on either city can compare and contrast materials written by former protesters with official accounts of popular unrest. Thanks to the unusually cosmopolitan nature of Republican Shanghai, however, the historian interested in this metropolis can also test the descriptions in PRC memoirs against accounts written by a broad variety of other kinds of observers, ranging from French journalists to British police sergeants to American diplomats to Chinese novelists. (For further discussion of sources and their biases, see the Bibliographic Essay.)

METHODOLOGY AND APPROACH

Given the important role that student movements have played in the politics of twentieth-century Shanghai and the history of the Chinese Revolution as a whole, it is not surprising that many scenes in the drama that I reconstruct and interpret in the following chapters have already been treated (and in many cases treated well) by others. My study is, nevertheless, unlike any to date in several important ways. First, my interest in continuities and discontinuities in patterns of protest over time has led me to adopt a larger time frame than that found in most extant works on Chinese student unrest, the vast majority of which limit themselves to a specific year or at most a decade.[23]

The second factor that sets the present work apart from important works on the topic done outside China in the 1960's and the 1970's—such as John Israel's pioneering study of youth activism during the Nanjing Decade (1927–37), *Student Nationalism in China*, and Joseph Chen's case study of mass activism in 1919, *The May 4th Movement in Shanghai*—is the use I make of recently published or newly available materials. For example, many of the memoirs I rely upon were gathered by the Youth Movement Research Group of the Shanghai branch of the Communist Youth League during the 1980's. Some of these have been published; others are held in manuscript copies at the League's Shanghai archive. None were available in any form until after Israel and Chen had completed their studies. The same is true of some of the most important document collections dealing with Republican student movements and of the records of the Shanghai Municipal Police (SMP) held at the U.S. National Archives, which have only recently been declassified and contain a number of files dealing with campus unrest. (See the Bibliographic Essay for more details on these and other source materials on Chinese student movements inaccessible to earlier foreign scholars.)

Also distinguishing the present study are the kinds of questions it asks. Most scholars of Chinese youth movements—whether working in the PRC, Taiwan, Japan, or the West—have approached the subject of student unrest from the perspective of intellectual or political history fairly narrowly defined. Previous Western works on Chinese student unrest have tended to focus on questions such as How did political organizations, such as the CCP and the GMD, try to manipulate or suppress youth protests of the Republican era, and to what degree were these attempts successful?

Which ideologies had the most appeal to members of China's intellectual community and why? What impact did foreign ideas have on student beliefs?[24] Chinese scholars in Taiwan and the PRC, though attempting to place the events in question within very different frameworks, have likewise tended to focus on the nature of student beliefs and the activities of political parties.[25]

Obviously no serious study of Chinese mass movements can wholly ignore the issues these scholars have emphasized, and I build upon their work continually in the pages that follow. Nonetheless, their emphasis upon ideologies and political parties has meant that there are, to borrow the term Arif Dirlik uses in a critique of scholarship on the May 4th Movement, important "silences" in the literature on student unrest, relating to such things as the links between ideas and social practice.[26] This study attempts to address two of the most significant of these silences: the symbolic meanings of student protests and the process by which students were able to translate collective anger into effective collective action. To address these silences, I draw upon methodologies and approaches pioneered by social and cultural historians, sociologists, anthropologists, and theorists in other fields concerned with the symbolism of group action. These modes of analysis lead me to argue that, to be fully understood, Shanghai student movements must be placed within a new interpretive framework. We must put less emphasis upon tracing the relationship between student protesters and political parties or upon analyzing the attractions of specific ideologies and much more upon locating student protests within the context of their social milieu and the dynamic revolutionary political culture of which they were part.

SOCIAL HISTORY AND POLITICAL CULTURE

The first step toward placing student unrest in this new framework is to resist the temptation to view educated youths primarily as intellectuals (or at least intellectuals in the making) who should be analyzed first and foremost in terms of their beliefs and ideas. Although aware of the importance that intellectual commitments to concepts of nationalism and democracy have played in inspiring Shanghai's educated youths throughout this century, in the chapters that follow I generally take these commitments for granted and view the city's student protesters primarily as political actors who band together to try to gain redress for common grievances. Thus I often treat youth movements as just one more genre of mass action, and apply the techniques that the "new" social historians and theorists of collective violence—such as Eric Hobsbawm, George Rudé, and Charles

[handwritten margin note: What questions does he ask?]

Tilly—have used to explain European labor strikes, food riots, and peasant rebellions.[27] How did students organize themselves for demonstrations? What types of people became leaders and why? Which protest tactics did students favor? These kinds of questions, which social historians routinely ask of labor movements and peasant insurrections and need to be asked of Shanghai student struggles, are seldom addressed in the literature on Chinese youth movements.*

The unique qualities of student protesters—their exceptional articulateness, the largely theatrical and generally nonviolent nature of their acts—allow (and at times force) me to ask a different set of questions concerning the symbolic side of student activism that takes me from the realm of social history to that of "political culture." This second term requires some explanation, since it is a tendentious one within sinology, where it has often been linked with the socio-psychological approach to comparative politics pioneered by Gabriel Almond and Sydney Verba, who link patterns of political behavior to deeply embedded cultural characteristics associated with specific national groups.[28] The most influential proponents of this approach within sinology, Lucian Pye and Richard Solomon, use psychoanalytic categories to argue that deeply entrenched patterns of dependency and attitudes toward hierarchy and consensus, embedded in such things as childhood socialization techniques, have had a profound impact on the Chinese Revolution.[29]

My use of the term does not follow that of Pye and Solomon; rather, it looks to a quite different tradition of studying the connections between revolutionary politics and culture pioneered in important recent studies of late-eighteenth-century France. My working definition of "political culture," which builds upon those Lynn Hunt and Keith Baker—two leading scholars of the French Revolution—propose in recent works,[30] treats the term as encompassing "all of the discourses, values, and implicit rules that express and shape collective action and intentions, determine the claims

---

*The tendency to approach student protests from the perspective of intellectual and political history is not limited to Chinese studies. Despite the great influence scholars such as Thompson and Tilly have had on studies of Western collective action, there have been few serious attempts to subject campus unrest to serious social-historical scrutiny. Instead, most scholars of Western student movements have been interested less in collective action per se than in such questions as why some youths become radicalized and others do not. For illustrations of this, see Molly Levin and John Speigel's overview of dominant themes in studies of the campus unrest of the 1960's, "Point and Counterpoint in the Literature on Student Unrest," and the extensive bibliography appended to Donald Phillips, *Student Protest, 1960–1970*. Recently, some scholars interested in European and American student movements have taken a more social-historical approach. Two important examples are Konrad Jarausch, *Students, Society, and Politics in Imperial Germany*, and Samuel Kassow, *Students, Professors, and the State in Tsarist Russia*. (For complete citations of these and other works cited in the footnotes, see the Bibliography, pp. 391–412.)

groups may (and may not) make upon one another, and ultimately provide the logic of revolutionary action." Pye and Solomon would probably have no objection to most or all of this working definition, but in practice studies of revolutionary political culture by Hunt, Baker, and other scholars with similar concerns such as François Furet and Mona Ozouf differ from those of these two sinologists in at least three important ways. First, although the four French historians cited above differ among themselves regarding how best to interpret the interplay between politics and culture in the French Revolution, all stress the fluid nature and creative possibilities of revolutionary political culture. Whereas, in other words, Solomon and Pye argue that a deeply entrenched set of cultural relations determined the course of the Chinese Revolution, French historians not only acknowledge the role that the ancien régime played in shaping the succeeding revolutionary one, but also stress the ways in which the revolutionary process itself transformed existing power relations and forms of discourse. Second, historians of the French Revolution such as Furet do not rely upon psychoanalytical notions of authority and dependency to explain the ways that power is exercised and contested. Third, unlike Pye and Solomon, who are interested in describing *the* political culture of a national group, historians such as Ozouf leave open the question of whether people in different parts of a country have differing values and subscribe to varying sets of implicit rules when acting collectively.*

If one advantage of the interpretive tradition I follow here is the room it leaves for regional variation—which means that one can treat Shanghai students not as part of a unified national political culture but as people whose beliefs and actions were shaped in many ways by the political and cultural peculiarities of their city—another benefit of the approach is that it does not require one to posit a sharp distinction between "elite" and "popular" culture. In fact, it leads one to assume that the boundary lines between these two cultural realms are fuzzy at best. Whereas some "discourses" may be the special province of specific social groups and used only or mainly to advance their interests, many of the "implicit rules" that shape collective behavior are likely to be widely shared throughout any given society. In other words, certain cultural forms and values are likely to be hegemonic. Thanks to attempts by the elite to justify its rule by im-

---

*Several recent studies of modern Chinese history either use the term "political culture" similarly or show a similar sensitivity to the variety of ways in which culture and politics influence each other. David Strand's *Rickshaw Beijing*, Elizabeth Perry's "Shanghai on Strike," and Prasenjit Duara's *Culture, Power, and the State: Rural North China, 1900–1942* are examples of sinological studies of the intersections between culture and politics, which either explicitly challenge or diverge in important ways from the political culture tradition associated with Pye and Solomon.

posing a particular worldview upon the populace at large and to the common patterns of daily life that shape the existence of wide segments of the population, "high" and "low" alike are bound to view some ideas and patterns of behavior simply as part of the natural landscape.* These traditional values and forms of behavior then serve as blinders or "blinkers" (to use E. P. Thompson's term) that limit actors' views of what is possible, even during the most subversive and counter-hegemonic of acts of political theater, such as demonstrations and revolutionary uprisings.[31]

This blurring of the lines between elite and popular culture is one of the great attractions of a political culture approach. A variety of important recent studies of modern Chinese history, dealing with everything from sectarian religion and village rituals to labor movements, have argued in one way or another that scholars have tended to differentiate too sharply between China's elite and popular, and even rural and urban, cultural spheres.[32] According to these studies, the overlaps and interconnections and gray areas between these spheres are as important as the distinctions between them. This insight is important for anyone interested in the student protesters of Republican Shanghai, since they continually participated in and were influenced by both "high" and "low" cultural forms. For example, although they studied elite texts in school—the Chinese classics, translations of Western scientific and social scientific works, and so forth—many of them grew up attending village festivals and even in Shanghai continued to listen to the folktales of streetcorner storytellers.[33] In addition, as Chapter 8 shows, student protesters, as activists interested in building broad-based mass movements, also quite self-consciously set out to cross the boundary lines between the elite and popular cultural spheres during their publicity campaigns.

My concern with political culture, and the problems and possibilities created by the position of student protesters as elite figures interested

---

*Here and elsewhere I use "hegemony" and "hegemonic" in two related senses derived from the prison writings of Antonio Gramsci and more recent studies by Marxist critics such as Raymond Williams. First, hegemony is one of two means by which elites (or, to use Gramsci's term, "historical blocs") assert their authority over the rest of society; unlike domination, the other means, hegemony does not require force but relies on the manipulation of cultural forms (media, religious services, public ceremonies) to impose a consensus concerning how power should be wielded and by whom. Hegemony in this sense is a process: there are always counter-hegemonic tendencies within society, and elites must continually work to reimpose their vision of how power should be distributed upon the populace at large. Hegemonic values and practices, by contrast, are those that are pervasive throughout society, usually because they have been part of this hegemonizing process for long periods of time. For valuable discussions of hegemony, see Gramsci, *Prison Notebooks*; Williams, *Marxism and Literature*; Thompson, "Eighteenth Century English Society"; Adamson, *Hegemony and Revolution*; Sassoon, *Approaches to Gramsci*; and Lears, "The Concept of Cultural Hegemony." For some important recent attempts to use concepts of hegemony to understand Chinese politics and culture, see the various contributions to the Symposium on Hegemony and Chinese Folk Ideologies, special issues of *Modern China*, 13, nos. 1 and 2 (1987).

in creating popular movements, leads me to ask the following questions about student activism. What kinds of political rituals did educated youths take part in on a regular basis, what other groups of people joined in these performances, and how did participation in such rites affect the behavior of educated youths when they took to the streets? What audiences did student protesters hope to move with their street theater? And did these youths alter the content or style of these performances when trying to appeal to specific groups of observers and listeners? The work of some historians concerned with crowd behavior provides insights into problems of this sort.[34] In this case, however, studies of the symbolism of revolutionary festivals, as well as general theoretical works on public performance, are also of value.[35]

FORMAT

In order to answer these questions about Chinese student protests, I break away from a strictly chronological format in the pages that follow. Instead, I alternate between chapters that look at specific time periods or movements and chapters that explore general themes relevant to all of Shanghai's twentieth-century student struggles.[36] The text is divided into two main parts focusing upon the Warlord era (1911–27) and Nationalist period (1927–49), respectively, and concludes with an Epilogue, which places the protests of 1986–89 in historical perspective. Although each concentrates on the events of a specific period, the two main sections of the book are not completely narrative in structure. Each contains three distinctly different types of chapters: contextual ones, which provide general information concerning Shanghai and its students during the era in question; case studies of the most important student-led mass movements of the time; and thematic chapters that explore general features of campus unrest throughout the Republican era. In other words, to return to the language of the theater, I alternate between descriptions of specific dramatic episodes and chapters that do such things as set the stage, examine the repertoire of student protest scripts, look at how casts evolved, and explore the techniques students used to communicate with specific audiences.

Part I begins with a brief overview of Shanghai culture, society, and politics through 1927. This chapter discusses such topics as the city's division into foreign concessions and a Chinese district, the government of each part of the metropolis, and the role missionaries and radical intellectuals played in Shanghai's cultural development. Chapter 1 also introduces several of the academic institutions that served as centers of political activism during the period and surveys some of the main political struggles the students of the city took part in before 1927.

Chapter 2 is a case study of the contribution Shanghai's educated youths made to one of the most important of these early struggles, the May 4th Movement of 1919. The first great twentieth-century youth movement, this dramatic struggle was named for the date police officers in Beijing arrested and beat up student protesters, who had taken to the streets over provisions in the Treaty of Versailles that ceded control of China's Shandong Province to Japan. The May 4th Movement soon grew to be national in scope. Protesters in cities throughout the country staged mass actions to call attention to Japanese encroachments upon Chinese territory, the failure of native officials to fight this "national humiliation," and the repressive measures these same officials were using to try to silence Beijing's students. The high point of Shanghai's May 4th Movement took the form of a *sanba* (a "triple stoppage" or general strike of students, workers, and merchants), which paralyzed the city for a week in early June.

Chapter 3, the book's first thematic chapter, analyzes the genesis of the protest repertoire of Shanghai students. It begins by asking why the May 4th protesters decided to stage particular types of demonstrations and rallies, and how they arrived at a common vision of the way a given action should be performed. In answering these questions, the chapter highlights the stylistic and structural similarities between protest events and other types of collective actions the city's youths routinely took part in or observed, ranging from funeral processions to Boy Scout reviews, and argues that these familiar forms of group activity provided educated youths with a common pool of well-practiced "scripts" from which to improvise their street theater. The chapter then looks at the way protest tactics evolved in later youth movements, whose participants frequently modeled their actions on those of the May 4th students.

Chapter 4 returns to a narrative format with a case study of the May 30th Movement of 1925, a series of anti-imperialist strikes and demonstrations. Named for the day a British officer ordered his men to fire into an unarmed crowd of protesters amassed outside a Shanghai police station, the May 30th Movement, like its predecessor of 1919, culminated in a sanba that brought Shanghai to a standstill. My case study of the upheaval traces the events that led up to and accompanied this general strike, paying special attention to the continuities and discontinuities between 1919 and 1925 in terms of student activities. It shows that although the May 30th students did many of the same things their May 4th counterparts had done—they too carried out publicity campaigns, organized boycotts, and staged mass rallies—the mass movement of 1925 was by no means simply a replay of that of 1919, thanks to changes in such things as the role organized political parties played within the academic community.

Chapter 5 breaks away from narrative once again to focus on the dynamics of student mobilization and leadership: it looks, in other words, at how the casts for acts of political theater evolved, and at the kinds of people who tended to take on starring roles. Using examples from the May 30th Movement as well as other Republican mass movements, this chapter tries to explain why students were consistently so much more successful than workers at organizing themselves for large-scale coherent collective action. It argues that the best way to account for the speed and ease with which students were able to organize themselves throughout the Republican era is to focus on the highly organized nature of campus daily life. The differing aims of students and workers, as well as their contrasting statuses within Chinese society, undeniably affected their ability to take collective action on a grand scale. Nonetheless, if we want to understand why Shanghai's students rather than workers so frequently led the mobilization drives that accompanied urban mass movements, Chapter 5 concludes, we must also look closely at the contrasts between the social world of the factory and that of the university.

Even though Chapters 3 and 5 use examples drawn from post-1927 movements to illustrate their points, there is a rationale for placing these two thematic studies in the opening section of the book. Although students continued to refine their tactics and organizational strategies throughout later years, all the main elements in the student protest repertoire and all the main features of campus life that contributed to the youth mobilization process were squarely in place by the end of the Warlord era. Chapters 3 and 5 also share a common concern with basic questions relating to the mechanics of campus unrest. And in both cases I argue that the key to answering queries of this sort, which despite (or, perhaps, because of) their apparent obviousness are seldom directly addressed in the scholarly literature, lies in looking closely at the dynamics of everyday campus life. Student movements may have been breaks in ordinary routines, but Chapters 3 and 5 show that they were disjunctures structured and shaped by ordinary patterns of social organization and previous life experiences.*

Part II, which covers the Nationalist era, also contains five chapters and is structured much like the first: it begins with a stage-setting overview of

---

*Whereas the first "scientific" studies of popular protest and "crowd psychology"—e.g., Le Bon's *The Crowd* and *The Psychology of Revolution*—viewed mass actions such as riots and demonstrations as radical departures from "normal" patterns of behavior, social historians have recently begun to emphasize the ways in which even unruly events tend to be structured by pre-existing routines. This theme is implicit or explicit in various works by E. P. Thompson, Eric Hobsbawm, Charles Tilly, Natalie Davis, and George Rudé. It also figures in one form or another in recent studies of Chinese social unrest, such as Elizabeth Perry, *Rebels and Revolutionaries in North China*; Gail Hershatter, *The Workers of Tianjin*; and Joseph Esherick, *The Origins of the Boxer Uprising*, as well as in some earlier works on the topic, such as Frederic Wakeman, Jr., *Strangers at the Gate*.

Shanghai and its students from 1927 to 1949 and then alternates between case studies of specific movements and thematic chapters. The main difference is that whereas the non-chronological chapters in the first section focus on the mechanics of youth movements, the thematic essays in this second section are more concerned with the symbolic aspects of student unrest. These themes take on a special importance in protests of the Nationalist era, because Jiang Jieshi based his bid for political legitimacy upon the claim that he would fight for the May 4th ideals of creating a rejuvenated nation free from imperialism, and because throughout the Nationalist era he depended heavily upon mass ceremonies involving students to demonstrate that his party was still a revolutionary and popular one representing "new" China. This made Jiang's regime unusually vulnerable to the symbolic threat posed by radical student movements, which by their very existence challenged the legitimacy of the GMD.

Chapter 6 traces some of the ways in which the GMD's rise to power affected governmental arrangements and campus politics in Shanghai. It also examines the impact major events such as the Japanese occupation of the city during World War II had on the development of the local student movement. And, like Chapter 1, it concludes with a brief overview of some of the main political struggles of Shanghai students throughout the period as a whole.

Chapter 7 presents a detailed analysis of one of the most important but least studied youth movements of the Republican era: the anti-Japanese agitation of fall 1931, during which students took to the streets to protest Japan's military activities in North China and the GMD's failure to go to war to protect China's national honor. This youth movement was triggered by the Japanese invasion of the Manchurian city of Shenyang (Mukden), in what Chinese came to call the September 18th Incident. As soon as educated youths in Shanghai and other cities heard news of the events in Shenyang, they started to organize rallies to publicize the event. They also mounted mass petition drives, during which large groups of students traveled to Nanjing (which replaced Beijing as the nation's capital during this period) to call on the government to take a more forceful stance against imperialism.

Chapter 8, the first thematic chapter of Part II, is devoted to the monologues and dialogues that accompanied or supplemented student street theater, the various forms of propaganda work produced by educated youths.* Here I survey the various media student activists used to commu-

---

*The Chinese term for propaganda, *xuanchuan*, has none of the pejorative connotations of its English-language equivalent and means simply communication intended to persuade. Whenever "propaganda" is used in this text, it is used in this value-free sense of "persuasive communication."

nicate political messages to their classmates and members of other social groups, and I highlight some of the dominant symbols educated youths used to express their ideas and influence others. This chapter pays particularly close attention to the special problems student propagandists faced in trying to make their message intelligible and compelling to one particularly important yet difficult to reach audience: the uneducated peasants, workers, and coolies who made up the great bulk of the Chinese population of Republican Shanghai.

Chapter 9 moves away from the texts students produced to return to the performances they staged and presents case studies of some of the main protests of the Civil War era (1945–49). The protest parade that radical youths held to greet U.S. special envoy George C. Marshall on his arrival in Shanghai in late 1945; the enormous Peace Petition demonstration of June 23, 1946; the anti-American march of New Year's Day, 1947, which local youths staged to protest the alleged rape of a Beijing coed by two U.S. marines—these are but a few of the events examined in Chapter 9. The chapter ends with a brief look at Shanghai student involvement in the largest urban protest of the Civil War period: the Anti-Hunger, Anti–Civil War Movement of 1947.

Throughout this overview of popular unrest during the Civil War years, I focus on one special feature of the post–World War II era: the extreme polarization of the Shanghai student movement during these years. Before 1945, even though there were often important divisions within the ranks of campus activists, it was generally possible to speak of the Shanghai youth movement as a single entity. From the Japanese surrender until the Communist victory in 1949, however, two distinctly different youth movements (which for convenience I refer to as "radical" and "loyalist" ones) competed with each other for control of the public stage. Each was determined to show that it alone was the one "true" representative of student opinion. Thanks to the activities of participants in these two movements, throughout the Civil War years Shanghai's citizens watched and were forced to try to make sense of a bewildering pageant of student mass actions, including not only government-sponsored youth parades and radical demonstrations, but also anti-radical "protests" against Communism that were carried out with GMD backing. What made the situation so complex was that, as different as the political intents of these various forms of ritual and political theater were, they were so similar in terms of style, format, staging, and in some cases even slogans that it was often hard to tell at first glance whether a given event was meant to uphold or to challenge the status quo.

Chapter 10 tries to decode the meaning of this complex contest between loyalist and radical symbolic actions involving educated youths. Building upon the discussion of the 1940's in Chapter 9, I argue that loyalist and radical marches are best read as part of an ongoing struggle for legitimacy. Both ruling elites intent upon reimposing their hegemony and protesters equally intent upon challenging that hegemony used similar genres of street theater to try to show that they alone could speak for "the people" and hence had the right to wield power. Each student parade was an effort by one side or the other to identify itself as closely as possible with what Clifford Geertz refers to as the "political center," the core set of values and "symbolic forms" their society held most sacred.[37] A close look at the structural similarities between such seemingly disparate events as the pro-government rally of February 1946 held to celebrate Jiang Jieshi's first post–World War II Shanghai visit and the giant marches of the following year protesting the GMD's domestic policies provides a rare opportunity to figure out just what symbols and ideals were most "central" in late Republican China.

I do more in this final thematic chapter, however, than simply try to place the student marches of the 1940's in this new framework; I argue that the student protests of the Republican era as a whole are best understood as attempts by educated youths to assert and challenge claims to political legitimacy. The key to this argument, I stress, lies in the tendency of pro-testing youths to appropriate roles and forms of discourse ordinarily re-served for officials. The subversive power of such usurpations helps to explain why Shanghai's foreign and native authorities frequently viewed these unarmed youths with alarm. Even when youth movements did not constitute *physical* threats to the status quo, student protesters posed very real *symbolic* threats. Through their words and deeds, they raised doubts in the mind of the audience about the right of those in power to rule.

The Epilogue brings the story of student protest in Shanghai up to 1989 and tries in the process to highlight the extent to which the basic patterns of campus unrest explored in earlier chapters survived forty years of Com-munist rule essentially intact. It does so by presenting a case study of the post-1949 protests most equivalent in terms of style, scope, and intent to the mass movements treated in earlier narrative chapters: the demonstra-tions of 1986–89. I argue that these events, which like their precursors of the Republican era succeeded in raising serious questions about the legit-imacy of China's rulers, need to be seen as a continuation of traditions of student activism stretching back to 1919 and beyond. The students of the mid- to late 1980's in fact took pains to present themselves as direct de-scendents of the May 4th activists. This was clearest exactly one month before the June 4th Massacre, when Beijing students chose the seventieth anniversary of the 1919 student movement as the day to stage one of their largest demonstrations.

STUDENT MOVEMENTS DEFINED

My use of the terms "student movement" and "youth movement" to refer to the popular unrest of 1919, 1925, and other years requires some clarification, because students were not the only ones involved in any of the mass movements discussed in later chapters, nor were all participants in these events young. In the case of the May 30th Movement of 1925, some scholars argue that workers played the vanguard role and students were only of secondary importance, although, as Chapter 4 shows, this view is problematic. But even in those struggles clearly led by students, members of other social groups always played crucial parts. Sympathy strikes by workers often helped student activists achieve their aims, and merchant boycotts gave a much-needed economic punch to many of the patriotic movements of the 1910's through 1930's. In addition, ever since the first decades of the century, Shanghai's professoriate has included many former student activists, and these teachers as well as others have often shared the same concerns as their students about corruption, limitations on freedom of expression, and foreign threats to China's national sovereignty. Throughout the Republican era, there were always older intellectuals ready and willing to advise student activists and to transmit their knowledge of the scripts used in earlier episodes of street theater to new generations of educated youths. This was still true in the 1980's. The dissident Su Shaozhi, who had a good deal of influence over some student leaders of the People's Movement of 1989, for example, was a veteran of anti-GMD youth movements of the 1940's.

But despite the importance of other social groups, I still consider the terms "student movement" and "youth movement" to be valid descriptions of all the mass movements treated here. Although protesters from other classes played key parts in the drama both as actors and as backstage directors, educated youths were the main driving force behind all the struggles in question. It was they who usually took the lead in organizing, publicizing, and enforcing general strikes and anti-imperialist boycotts, as well as providing many (and in some case most) of the march brigades for popular demonstrations. In many cases an awkward term such as "student-led multi-class mass movement" might be more accurate, but as long as one remembers that all the struggles involved people other than students, simpler phrases are preferable.

Although this is a study of student movements, I am not equally concerned with all "movements" that involved students. For example, Shanghai's educated youths were involved in a number of different "movements" that were either nonpolitical in intent (e.g., the Christian Student Movement missionaries led in the 1920's) or spearheaded by officials within the ruling regime (as was the case with Jiang Jieshi's New Life Movement). My main concern is with student *protests*, however; even though the following chapters touch upon many of these nonpolitical and overtly loyalist movements, I devote most of my attention to events that challenged the way the city or the nation was being ruled. The Red Guard Movement of the 1960's, though it certainly involved protests of a sort, likewise receives only limited attention in the Epilogue, because the devotion to a leading member of the ruling regime, Mao Zedong, gave this struggle a decidedly loyalist tone.

COLLEGE STUDENTS AS A SOCIAL GROUP

Just as I am not equally concerned with all genres of student movements, I am also not equally interested in all types of students. My main concern is with those youths—usually between approximately age 17 and 27 (though thanks to the disruptions caused by wars and other factors sometimes a few years older) and before 1949 usually male—who attended Shanghai's leading colleges and universities, such as Fudan, Jiaotong, St. John's, and Tongji.[38] Secondary school students and youths studying at vocational and professional schools also played important roles in many of the events discussed below, but their activities will be referred to only in passing. As active as these students were, it was the young men and women* studying at the city's leading institutes of higher education who most often led the way in rallying Shanghai's citizens to action in times of crisis. Before 1949, it was they who most frequently took to the streets in the name of "saving the nation" (*jiuguo*) and used their banners and slogans as weapons to fight the twin threats of imperialist aggression and domestic tyranny. And it is

---

*The role of gender-related issues in Chinese student movement history is an important topic to which scholars have thus far given little attention (for rare discussions of the subject, see Ono, *Chinese Women*, pp. 106–111; Chow, *May 4th Movement*, pp. 258–59; and Borthwick, "Changing Concepts"). Below I refer in passing to individual female students who took on leadership roles in specific protests (see, e.g., Chapter 4) and to marches in which groups of women figured prominently (see Chapter 9). Because of the small number of women in Shanghai colleges and universities (in 1923, a mere 2.3 percent of all students in insitutions of higher learning nationally were female, and by 1947 the figure had only risen to 17.8 percent; MacKerras, "Education," pp. 170–73) and the paucity of sources dealing with their political activities, however, I do not directly address gender-related issues in any detail, except for in isolated comments on the division of labor within May 4th–era student associations (Chapter 2) and the role of women in the People's Movement of 1989 (Epilogue). Since a far richer supply of primary sources concerning the political activism of middle-school as opposed to college-level female students exists (including a special issue of *Shanghai qingyunshi ziliao* [vol. 16, 1986] devoted to memoirs of former underground organizers at Shanghai girls' schools in the 1940's), the importance of gender as a factor in youth movements can be better understood by focusing on students younger than those with whom I am primarily concerned.

they who, in recent years, have once more taken the lead in the fight against new forms of oppression.

What kind of people were these youths, what types of institutions did they attend, and how did they see their role in society and politics? Information that helps answer each of these questions is revealed in the chapters that follow, but it is worth making some preliminary comments here. To begin with, the students at Shanghai's leading Republican colleges and universities came from a variety of backgrounds: they were usually, though not always, the children of elite parents—officials, landlords, merchants— and they were frequently from places other than Shanghai (a fact whose implications for student activism are explored in later chapters).[39] They were also a diverse lot in terms of their studies: Fudan was known for training humanists; Jiaotong was famous for training engineers. Schools such as St. John's had a large percentage of foreign missionary teachers and required pupils to receive religious instruction; others were purely secular and native-run. Some students studied abroad for a period in their academic career; others received Western ideas secondhand through books and Western-trained professors. The future prospects of college and university students varied just as widely: some would go on to teach or serve in the professions, others would become soldiers or spend years seeking employment, and still others would go from playing leading roles in student protests to becoming revolutionaries or serving as officials in one or another regime (another fact whose implications are treated later).

Though diverse, these Republican college and university students had certain things in common. One of the most important for our purposes, and something that has carried over into the Communist period as well, is that these students viewed themselves as an elite group who had a right and duty to speak out on political issues because in due course the next generation of high officials would come from their ranks. Such an assumption grew naturally from the fact that only a minute percentage of China's populace attended institutions of higher learning: in 1931, high school students constituted approximately 0.1 percent of the population, college students 0.01 percent.[40] The elite status of college students was further reinforced by the nation's long tradition of prizing education and viewing learning as the most legitimate path to political power for all except the emperor himself. The students who attended colleges and universities in Republican Shanghai differed from the examination candidates of earlier generations in many ways: their education was not limited primarily to study of the Confucian classics, there was more ambiguity concerning the career paths open to them, and the institutions in which they studied were quite unlike imperial academies. Nonetheless, when it came to their political rights and duties, these twentieth-century youths made the same assumptions as their imperial predecessors. At times, as Chapter 3 shows, participants in Republican youth movements explicitly connected their own actions with those of dissident examination candidates of the past, who had demanded the attention of the nation's rulers during pre–twentieth century student movements.

What is perhaps more extraordinary than the students' own image of themselves as an elite with special privileges and a right to take part in politics is that officials and ordinary citizens so often accepted this image, at least in part, a response that differs sharply from the view of educated youths in many industrialized Western nations.[41] As later chapters show, Shanghai's citizens have continually demonstrated a willingness to let educated youths speak in the name of the people, by following students out onto the streets and supporting them with gifts of money and food. China's twentieth-century rulers have often been either ambivalent or overtly hostile toward the political activism of educated youths, as later chapters show only too clearly, but they too have consistently viewed college and university students as an elite group worthy of special treatment. Thus, even during the crackdown on political dissent in summer and fall 1989, the government often punished student activists less severely than members of dissident labor unions; most of those who were beaten or executed during this period were workers rather than educated youths.[42]

The self-image of these college and university students as an elite political group, and the acceptance of this image by members of other classes, has had a number of important consequences for their political activism. As Chapter 4 argues, it has limited the risks involved in taking to the streets. It has also meant that, in contrast to students in other contexts, Chinese students have been able to frame their protests as routine assertions of the political rights and social duties traditionally accorded their class, rather than as attempts to secure a new corporate identity within society or a new role in politics.[43]

Finally, it has meant that these Shanghai youths have tended to think in national rather than in either strictly academic or local terms. Purely academic or campus-based issues, ranging from complaints about teachers and grading systems to the poor quality of dormitory food, have inspired China's college and university students to protest. Nonetheless, most of the major student movements of the twentieth century were triggered by incidents with broader political implications, and struggles that began as conflicts over internal matters often quickly escalated into protests that involved social issues and social groups far beyond the walls of individual campuses. Thus in contrast to some of the most important American conflicts involving educated youths—such as the Berkeley Free Speech Movement of 1964, during which issues relating to campus rules and policies remained at the forefront and most protest activity remained confined to the university itself—in each of the major Shanghai youth movements of the Republican era, academic issues quickly fused with patriotic ones, and educated youths used school campuses primarily as organizational bases and dressing rooms for acts of political theater performed on more public stages.[44]

And, as the Epilogue shows, the same pattern carried over into the Communist era. The student unrest of 1986 was triggered largely by specifically student concerns over school governance and the quality of campus life, but it soon evolved into a much more generalized attack on the way power was being exercised in society at large. By 1989, even though no foreign power threatened China's sovereignty or territorial integrity, students once again took to calling their struggle a battle to "save the nation," claiming that official corruption and oppression were destroying their homeland. And, as in all the great mass movements of the Republican era, the students of 1989 performed their most important acts not in campus yards but on much more public stages, such as Beijing's Tiananmen Square and Shanghai's People's Square.

I

THE WARLORD ERA
1911-1927

ONE

SHANGHAI AND
ITS STUDENTS,
1900–1927

ON JUNE 19, 1842, A SMALL FLEET of British warships steamed up the Huangpu River, the waterway that links the port of Shanghai to the Yangzi River, as some thousand infantry and artillery troops approached the city by land. Local Chinese defense forces fired on the invading fleet from riverbank batteries, but the warships succeeded in entering the harbor almost completely unscathed. The British land forces met with even less resistance on their march toward the old walled city of Shanghai, which was then a medium-sized market town and port with a population of around a hundred thousand. Before the end of the day, the foreign troops had entered the city, and Shanghai's officials had surrendered to the invaders.[1] Although the British forces held the city captive for only a few days before moving on, the 1842 skirmish (one of the shortest battles of the Opium War) turned out to be the first in a long line of military, diplomatic, economic, cultural, and political invasions Shanghai would face, invasions that would ultimately transform the market town into a cosmopolitan metropolis and center for international trade.[2]

By the turn of the century the city's transformation was nearly complete, and the Shanghai of 1900 would have been almost unrecognizable to any pre-1842 resident of the port. The main event responsible for this change occurred in 1843, when the British government forced representatives of the Qing Dynasty (1644–1911) to sign the Treaty of Nanjing to end the Opium War. One of its main terms was that the Chinese would allow the British to live and conduct business in five special "treaty port" cities, including Shanghai; other foreign nations soon forced the Qing to

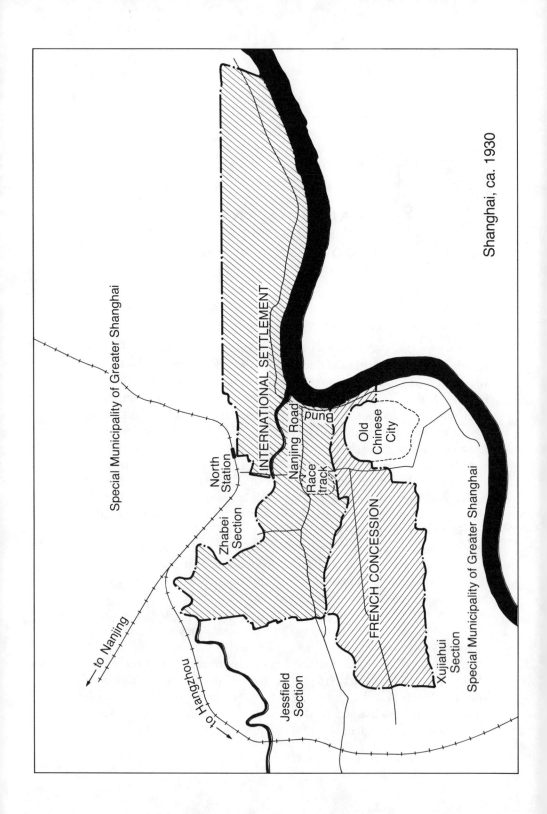

Shanghai, ca. 1930

sign similar agreements allowing their nations to trade in these ports. The treaty port system did more, however, than simply allow foreigners to reside in Chinese cities. It also granted foreigners special privileges of extraterritoriality that placed their personal behavior and most of their business activities as well under Western as opposed to Chinese laws.

TREATY PORT POLITICS

Extraterritoriality created a complex set of legal and administrative problems, which the foreign and Chinese residents and officials in each treaty port solved in different ways. In the case of Shanghai, the city was eventually divided into three separate administrative districts: the International Settlement; the French Concession; and Chinese territory (see Map 1). Each of the two foreign territories began at the Huangpu and extended due west, with the International Settlement (the larger of the two and the one with the best river frontage) farther north than the French Concession.[3] The Chinese territory consisted of several separate parts. The first was the old city of Shanghai, an area often referred to as Nanshi (meaning "South City"), because it lay near the Huangpu River just south of the eastern arm of the French Concession. Rural areas situated directly across the Huangpu from Shanghai proper were also under Chinese rule. So, too, were the metropolitan and suburban areas such as Zhabei that lay to the north and west of the foreign concession boundaries.

There was some ambiguity to these territorial arrangements. For example, because of the high concentration of Catholic buildings (including a cathedral and seminary) in the Xujiahui section of the city, this neighborhood was often treated as part of foreign Shanghai, even though it was technically located outside the concession borders. St. John's University (a missionary establishment discussed in more detail below) was something of a special case as well, since it was located in the Jessfield section of the city several miles west of the International Settlement border, yet the school was for all intents and purposes protected by extraterritoriality. Despite these special cases and even though throughout the late nineteenth and early twentieth century the administrators of the foreign concessions tried continually (and often successfully) to extend their respective jurisdictions beyond the original concession boundaries established in the mid-nineteenth century, the basic tripartite division described above remained essentially intact for almost a century.

The Chinese territory was by far the largest of the three districts, even after the concession authorities succeeded in wresting control of extra bits of land around the turn of the century. When the boundaries of the three districts finally became fairly well fixed by 1914, the Chinese authorities were responsible for administering over 300 square miles, and both foreign concessions were less than 10 square miles in size.[4] This contrast in size is misleading in economic terms, however, since most of the city's commercial activity took place in the concessions. The Huangpu Harbor, the Bund (headquarters to most of the major local financial institutions), and Nanjing Road (the hub of local commerce)—foreigners controlled all these key parts of the city.

Each of Shanghai's three districts was governed in a different way. The International Settlement, for example, was administered by the Shanghai Municipal Council (SMC), a body that often functioned as if it were the parliament of a small independent republic. The residents of the Settlement retained close personal and economic ties with their homelands, and SMC members were perfectly ready (when threatened) to ask Western governments to provide troops and warships to protect the people and business interests of the foreign enclave. Nonetheless, the Council was an independent body, beholden not to any foreign government or consular group but to the local ratepayers who elected it. Since English business interests played the central economic role in the International Settlement, British members of the community tended to dominate the nine-member SMC, which not only collected taxes, passed laws, and maintained public roads and parks, but also ran the Shanghai Municipal Police and a number of public schools.[5] The British domination was not, however, absolute. The Council always contained members from other nations, and for much of the Warlord era an American named Sterling Fessden served as president of the SMC. In addition, although the SMC often seemed to take its lead from London when dealing with the Chinese authorities, it occasionally took actions at odds with British policies.

The French Concession was governed by a council superficially much like the SMC. It too was originally composed of nine members who, like those of the SMC, were elected by landowning ratepayers and performed a wide variety of legislative and administrative duties. There was, however, one crucial difference between the French Concession's Municipal Council and the SMC: the former was directly responsible to a foreign government. The French consul-general in Shanghai served as ex-officio chairman of the body, and even though he generally let an acting chairman selected by the council members oversee day-to-day business, he had veto power over all legislation. It was also he, not the Council members, who controlled the concession police force.

There were other important differences between the SMC and the French body. The French Council was quicker to allow Chinese residents

some say in municipal affairs, when in 1914 it made provisions for two native representatives to sit on the Council. These Chinese representatives
were just honorary members, since no Chinese were granted full voting
rights on either foreign municipal council until after the GMD takeover of
1927. But the administrators of the International Settlement did not even
allow Chinese residents to serve on the SMC in an advisory capacity until
1921, even though Chinese taxpayers provided the Council with much of
its revenue.[6] In contrast to these and other differences between the two
foreign municipal councils, judicial arrangements were handled much the
same way in both the International Settlement and the French Concession. In both enclaves foreign diplomatic officials generally took charge of
trying cases that did not involve Chinese defendants or plaintiffs. Each
concession also established a special Mixed Court to resolve conflicts between Chinese and foreigners. A board composed of a specially appointed
Chinese judge and a foreign assessor presided over each Mixed Court, but
both were run along Western rather than Chinese legal principles.[7]

Throughout the late Imperial and Warlord eras, Shanghai's Chinese
territory was administered much more haphazardly than were the foreign
concessions. Before 1911, a number of imperial officials with overlapping
jurisdictions, including the governor of Jiangsu (the province of which the
city was then considered part), had some authority in Chinese Shanghai.[8]
The local intendant (*daotai*) played the dominant role in dealing with foreigners, and the magistrate of Shanghai administered justice within the old
city.[9] From 1911 until 1927, a succession of revolutionary and warlord regimes took power in Beijing, and each of these central governments continued to appoint officials to administer Chinese Shanghai, but these
officials seldom wielded much power in the city. In 1895 members of
Shanghai's Chinese elite began to experiment with new forms of municipal administration modeled largely upon the foreign municipal councils,
and by the Warlord era these local gentrymen and business leaders had
succeeded in wresting control of such things as the police department and
road upkeep from centrally appointed officials.[10] Nonetheless, no fully
developed system of municipal government was established in Chinese
Shanghai until the GMD took control of the city in 1927; up until that
point real power generally lay with one or another of the local warlords
battling for control of the provinces of Zhejiang and Jiangsu.

TREATY PORT SOCIETY

By the early twentieth century, all three sections of the city had extremely
diverse populations. The International Settlement was originally designed

to house only foreigners, particularly nationals from a core group of
Western countries, such as Britain (whose forces played the leading role
in opening Shanghai to Western business interests) and the United States
(whose representatives abandoned an early attempt to establish their own
settlement in Shanghai and joined the British). The French Concession
was designed at its inception to serve as a haven for businessmen and consular officials from France and their families. By the end of the nineteenth
century, however, neither foreign enclave was anything like the homogeneous community its founders had envisioned.

Not only did an increasingly diverse group of foreigners flock to the
two concessions to take advantage of the treaty port system in the late
nineteenth century, but Chinese (many of them refugees from the popular
rebellions endemic to the period) poured into the foreign enclaves as well.
By the early decades of the twentieth century, Chinese residents far outnumbered Westerners in both concessions, and the foreign country with
the largest number of nationals in the concessions was neither Britain nor
the United States nor France. It was Japan. A 1918 survey found 21,000
foreigners living in Shanghai; of these 7,169 were Japanese, 4,822 were
British, 1,323 were Portuguese, 1,307 were Americans, and 1,155 were
Germans. The Chinese population within the foreign enclaves had already
topped half a million by 1918.[11]

The sections of Shanghai under native control were, comparatively
speaking, much more homogeneous, since few Westerners lived outside
the foreign enclaves. This image of homogeneity is illusory, however; although there was little national diversity in the Chinese sections of the
metropolis, there was a great deal of cultural heterogeneity. Shanghai's
rapid growth from a market town of only regional importance into a metropolitan trading center of over a million inhabitants meant that by the
first decades of the twentieth century it was a city of immigrants, native as
well as foreign. Thus the Chinese sections of Shanghai were filled with
people who were born in other parts of the country, spoke different dialects, favored different foods, and clung to different customs. Immigrants
from other parts of Jiangsu and from Zhejiang, the province to the south
of Shanghai, had traveled only a short distance to come to the city. In
other cases (for example, those who had come from the southern province
of Guangzhou), the geographical distance was much greater. In cultural
terms, however, even sojourners whose birthplaces were less than a hundred miles away often thought of themselves as "foreigners" of a sort in
Shanghai.

As a result, Shanghai's social and economic life was structured around a
wide range of (sometimes overlapping) formal and informal associations
based upon place of origin. Thus English residents socialized and trans-

acted business with fellow nationals at the St. George's Society, those from the United States gathered at the American Association of China, and foreigners from various lands met together at the Shanghai Club.[12] The Chinese gathered at one or another of the city's native-place guilds and societies, groups in which they claimed membership by right of either their own place of birth or that of one of their parents or even grandparents. These native-place associations (known as *bang, huiguan,* or *tongxianghui*) performed social, economic, and ritual functions, ranging from running schools to providing funeral services. Like foreign associations such as the Shanghai Club, membership in these Chinese societies also established important informal ties between businessmen. But whereas groups such as the Shanghai Club seldom played formal roles in political affairs, Chinese guilds were often at the center of power struggles. For example, the city's powerful Ningbo Guild played the leading role in the riots of 1874 and 1896. Both were triggered by attempts of the French Concession authorities to run a road through a tract of land that served as the Ningbo Guild's burial ground.[13]

Most of those who filled the city's clubs and native-place guilds came to the city to work or to seek their fortune. Others, however, came for very different reasons: to teach or to foment revolution. Shanghai's unusual political structure made it an attractive location for both Western missionaries and radical Chinese intellectuals, groups who despite their differences shared a desire to spread their ideas as widely as possible through schools and publications. These two groups deserve special attention here, because together they helped make Shanghai a cultural and educational (as well as economic) center, and this in turn laid the groundwork for the city's rise as a center of student activism.

MISSIONARIES AND TREATY PORT EDUCATION

Shanghai's treaty port society proved attractive to Western missionaries for various reasons. There, a foreign-run police force provided protection from anti-foreign violence, and printing and publishing facilities were close at hand, as were Western schools for their children to attend. From Shanghai, as opposed to many Chinese cities, they could travel abroad with ease, and while resident in the city they could enjoy the society of others of their own nationality. Thanks to attractions such as these, throughout the last decades of the Imperial era and the first years of the Republic, many missionaries chose to settle in the city, and the dozens of churches, schools, and clubs they established to serve the foreign community and spread the gospel to Shanghai's Chinese residents were soon central fixtures in local society.

The most important of Shanghai's missionary schools was St. John's University, an institution founded in 1879 on 49 acres of land in the Jessfield section of the city.[14] Run by Episcopal missionaries from the United States, St. John's University (like most of the city's major institutions of higher education) contained a middle school as well as a college for more advanced students. In 1916 over 500 Chinese youths were studying at St. John's, learning from a faculty that (like that of other Christian schools) consisted of Western preachers and Chinese converts.[15] The goals at St. John's (again like those at most other missionary schools) were twofold. The university's administrators sought to convert Chinese youths to Christianity and train them in Christian practices (thus chapel services were an important part of school life). In addition, however, these administrators also had a genuine interest in providing Chinese youths with a general education comparable to that students in Western schools received.

St. John's was the most prominent, but by no means the only, important Shanghai institution of higher education run by foreigners. In fact, with the exceptions of the Imperial Nanyang College (which the Chinese compradore Sheng Xuanhuai established in 1896 with government sponsorship and which later evolved into Jiaotong University) and Fudan University (whose founding is described below), before the 1920's the city's major colleges and middle schools were administered by foreigners.[16] Not all these foreign schools were religious institutions; neither the German-run Tongji University nor the Japanese-run Dongwen College was directly affiliated with religious groups. Nevertheless, missionary colleges (such as the Shanghai Baptist College, which an American group established in 1912) and Christian middle schools (such as the famous McTyeire Girls' School) dominated the local educational scene during the first decades of the century. Adding further to the missionary impact upon Shanghai's Chinese students, the YMCA and YWCA maintained active branches in the city. These branches not only provided services for the foreign community but ran a number of programs aimed at native youths as well. The YMCA, for example, sponsored a middle school for Chinese students and played an active part in the growth of the city's Chinese Boy Scout league.[17]

RADICAL INTELLECTUALS AND SHANGHAI CULTURE

Ironically, some of the same features of civic life that made Shanghai attractive to foreign missionaries also drew radical intellectuals (including ardent opponents of imperialism) to the city throughout the first decades of the twentieth century. For those intellectuals who had studied abroad in their own youth, as part of the earliest delegations of Chinese students to travel to Japan or the West, and even for those who had never left China but found inspiration in the works of foreign philosophers (Darwin and Mill, and later Marx), Shanghai's cosmopolitanism was one of its main attractions. Another (and in many cases even more compelling) attraction was the relative freedom in the enclaves to speak out against the Chinese government. Throughout the first decades of the century, the Western treaty port authorities had a much firmer commitment to a free press than did their Chinese counterparts, and the principle of extraterritoriality protected native as well as foreign residents of the concessions to a certain extent. Thus those who preached the gospel of revolution had as good cause to feel safe within foreign enclaves as did the Westerners who came to China to preach the gospel of Christ. Not surprisingly, therefore, Shanghai's concessions were among the main places to which dissident intellectuals under first the Qing and later the warlords came to open newspapers, flee persecution, and (in the case of the CCP, whose first national congress was held in the city's French Concession) even to found new political parties.

The concessions were not perfect havens for revolutionaries by any means, since the foreign councils did at times take repressive actions against Chinese radicals. In 1903, for example, the *Subao*, an International Settlement newspaper, carried articles by the revolutionaries Zou Rong and Zhang Binglin that openly advocated the violent overthrow of the Qing Dynasty. The Chinese government immediately demanded that the Settlement authorities shut the paper down and turn its writers and editors over to the imperial government for punishment, which would have meant execution at least for Zou and Zhang. The SMC vacillated for a time but refused from the outset to hand those involved over to the Chinese authorities, since this would set a dangerous precedent in terms of extraterritoriality. The Council did eventually bow to Chinese pressure to the extent of sending members of its own police force to close the paper. The Settlement authorities also arrested Zou and Zhang, as well as several other people connected with the paper. The revolutionaries were brought to trial before the Mixed Court and convicted of sedition.[18] Zou was sentenced to two years' imprisonment in a foreign-run prison and Zhang to three years.

Even when, as happened in 1903, one or the other of Shanghai's foreign councils decided to crack down on radical activity, the city's division into three separate districts still worked to the advantage of Chinese revolutionaries. Thanks to the lack of communication between the Shanghai Municipal Police and the French Concession Police, each enclave's jealous protection of its own autonomy, and other factors (such as the notorious corruption of the French force), a radical wanted by the police in one part of Shanghai could often simply move to another area and continue his or her political activities. In some cases, an entire protest league transferred its base of operations from one part of the city to another when one district's police force became interested in the group's activities.

Political developments in the late 1910's and early 1920's made Shanghai's foreign authorities much less tolerant of the activities of Chinese radicals. The founding of the CCP in 1921, which came at a time when "red scares" were sweeping the West; the GMD's decision to work with Soviet advisers and to allow native Communists to join its ranks in 1924; and the rise of anti-imperialist popular movements—all these phenomena made foreigners in Shanghai warier of Chinese revolutionaries, who now seemed to pose a direct threat to the entire concession system. As a result, throughout the 1920's Shanghai's two foreign police forces became increasingly concerned with ridding the concessions of "reds" (a category that often included members of the GMD as well as the CCP; before 1927 Jiang Jieshi was often called a "red general") and emphasized suppressing all "anti-foreign" movements (a similarly loose term used by many in Shanghai's Western and Japanese communities to refer both to xenophobic riots and nonviolent protests against imperialism). In the mid- to late 1920's, however, Shanghai's status as a divided city continued to work to the advantage of even the most overtly anti-imperialist of Communists. Bribes to the right people could frequently guarantee the "reddest" agents safety in the French Concession. In addition, during periods of intense nationalist agitation (such as the May 30th Movement), radicals could often avoid arrest by crossing into Chinese Shanghai, since the police in the native city were generally more sympathetic to attacks on foreign privilege and since even the most despotic of warlords preferred (at times) to tolerate disorder rather than to risk appearing unpatriotic.

The intellectuals who came to Shanghai during the first decades of the twentieth century did not establish as strong an institutional presence as their missionary counterparts. Their activities were often centered, in fact, around one or two local schools and an equal number of newspapers and publishing houses. Nonetheless, their writings and teachings had a strong impact upon Shanghai's student population, and their institutional bases, even though few in number, played central roles in youth movements. Revolutionary publications (such as the *Subao* and its successors) did so by inspiring students to take political action and then by keeping information flowing among individual campuses. Schools with clusters of radical faculty members played an even more important role in youth movements, because (not surprisingly) pupils at these campuses tended to take the lead in forming and then directing citywide student protest organizations.

It is possible, in fact, in the case of each wave of campus unrest that swept the nation during the first three decades of the century, to single out one or two core publications and schools that together served as the nucleus for local student activism.[19] Since the members of these institutions often had close ties, and the founders of new core groups often emerged directly from the ranks of earlier ones, radical intellectuals helped provide continuity to the Shanghai student movement. Because of this, it is worth taking time here to sketch some of the institutions (most of which were located within parts of the city under foreign control: see Map 2), that served as organizational focal points for student activists in the first decades of the century.

CORE GROUPS, 1902–1903

The earliest radical institutions to serve as student protest centers were the newspaper *Subao* and the Patriotic Academy (Aiguo gongxue), which included among its teachers Zhang Binglin and other contributors to the *Subao*.[20] The Patriotic Academy was founded in 1902 in the wake of Shanghai's first modern "student strike." This strike took place at Nanyang College and began with a seemingly trivial affair known as the Ink Bottle Incident. When school administrators disciplined two members of the school's fifth form for tampering with a hated teacher's bottle of ink, the entire fifth form began a boycott of all classes. The troubles at Nanyang had much deeper roots, however. For some time members of the fifth form (many of whom were partisans of revolutionary and reformist ideas and avid readers of progressive publications) had battled with conservative school administrators over what they should and should not be allowed to read and discuss (translations of Rousseau were among the works considered inflammatory). Some of the school's more radical faculty members supported the students. When the fifth form finally withdrew completely from Nanyang in protest, one of these teachers, Cai Yuanpei, founded the Patriotic Academy to accommodate the youths. This school had both a college for male students and a school for young women.[21]

Thanks in part to their example, as well as to the *Subao*'s efforts in 1902 and 1903 to publicize this protest and air other student grievances, school strikes became common occurrences in the early years of the century.[22] Strikes were not, however, the only protest activities of the time in which Shanghai students and their teachers were involved. As early as the spring of 1901, progressive teachers and their students joined with members of

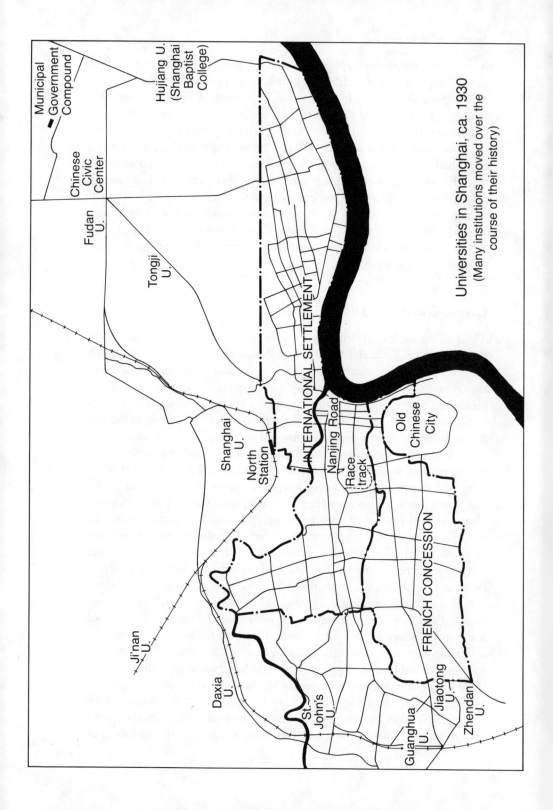

Universities in Shanghai, ca. 1930
(Many institutions moved over the course of their history)

Municipal Government Compound

Chinese Civic Center

Fudan U.

Hujiang U. (Shanghai Baptist College)

Tongji U.

Ji'nan U.

Daxia U.

Shanghai U.

North Station

INTERNATIONAL SETTLEMENT

Nanjing Road

Race track

Old Chinese City

St. John's U.

Guanghua U.

Jiaotong U.

Zhendan U.

FRENCH CONCESSION

other classes to take part in public meetings denouncing Russia for refusing to cede control of Manchuria to China.[23] Information on the background of the intellectuals and educated youths who took part in these
early protests is hard to find, since most records of intelligentsia participation are fragmentary at best. Some of the tidbits of information that survive are, however, fascinating—according to some accounts, for example,
the highlight of one of the 1901 rallies was a patriotic speech by a girl of
seventeen, who moved the audience to tears.[24]

Another significant aspect of the 1901 protest is the organizers' decision
to hold their meetings in the Zhang Gardens, a decision that highlights
some peculiarities of Shanghai politics. The rallies protesting Russian
military activities had an anti-Qing slant, since the protesters held the
imperial authorities responsible for China's inability to protect its sovereignty. Thus it would have been extremely dangerous for the demonstrators to gather anywhere in Shanghai's native city. Public parks run by
the concession councils were, however, generally off-limits to all Chinese
(except servants). The Zhang Gardens, a privately owned space within the
International Settlement, which included a theater for performances of
Beijing opera and other recreational facilities (at one point a photo studio
and tennis court could be found on the premises), was one of the few
places in which Chinese protesters could freely assemble in greater Shanghai. Soon after the overthrow of the Qing Dynasty, Shanghai's new native
authorities built a public stadium (known as the Gonggong tiyuchang or
Public Recreation Ground) just outside the West Gate of the old walled
city, and beginning in the late 1910's this replaced the Zhang Gardens as
the favorite site of Chinese protesters.[25] Before this, however, thanks to the
willingness of the landlords of the Zhang Gardens to rent their space to
the proponents of radical causes, many important political events (including several relating to the Revolution of 1911) were held in this unusual
amusement park cum protest arena.[26]

The Zhang Gardens served, for example, as the setting for the second
series of protests against Russian imperialism, which took place in spring
1903 at the instigation of people affiliated with the *Subao* newspaper and
the Patriotic Academy. The newspaper took the lead in publicizing this
new patriotic struggle.[27] Both male and female students at the Academy
filled the audiences and spoke at the public meetings that were the movement's highlights.[28] Student activism at the Patriotic Academy is hardly
surprising, since the school's chief administrator, Cai Yuanpei, organized
and presided over the largest rally of 1903, an April 30 meeting attended
by over 1,200 people. Cai began the rally with a passionate speech calling on the Chinese government to take stronger steps to protect their nation's sovereignty. After he finished speaking, someone read aloud a Chi-

nese translation of an English-language set of rules for public meetings (Robert's *Rules of Order?*), more speeches were given, the assembly joined together to sing "The Patriots' Song" ("Aiguo ge"), and then those present agreed to form a political association known as the Chinese Citizens' Union (Zhongguo guomin gonghui).[29]

Teachers and pupils of the Patriotic Academy showed their commitment to the cause of patriotism in other ways as well in 1903. Under Professor Cai's supervision, for example, over 90 of the Academy's male pupils began military training, forming themselves into a "student army" composed of eight small brigades (*xiaodui*) whose avowed purpose was to prepare to defend the nation's sovereignty.[30] Students from the Patriotic Academy and a couple of other local schools also founded what was probably Shanghai's first student union that year, the Chinese Students' Alliance (Zhongguo xuesheng tongmenghui).[31] And, finally, teachers and students from the Patriotic Academy were in the vanguard during the rallies protesting the closure of the *Subao* near the end of 1903. These rallies were, however, the last protests in which the Patriotic Academy performed a core function; the school disbanded soon afterward.

Zhendan as a Core Group, 1903–1905

The political vacuum created by the closure of *Subao* and the Patriotic Academy was filled almost immediately by Aurora University (Zhendan daxue), which welcomed the pupils of the defunct Patriotic Academy. Zhendan was founded in 1902 by Ma Xiangpo, who had connections with a diverse group of Shanghai intellectuals. He had close ties with the radical intellectuals in the Patriotic Academy and *Subao*, thanks in large part to his teaching of Latin to scholars connected with these institutions, including Academy founder Cai Yuanpei. But, as a former priest who had been educated by Jesuits in a local religious school and later spent time in Europe and America, Ma also had many friends among Shanghai missionaries, particularly among French Catholics. The Catholic church provided Zhendan with the school's first classrooms, in fact, when it let Ma use some of the rooms it owned in Xujiahui.[32] Despite Ma's ties to the church and foreign missionaries, however, he was as devout a patriot as he was a Christian and actively supported popular struggles against imperialism.

Ma's commitment to patriotic causes became clearest in 1905, when he took an active role in two struggles that pitted him and his students directly against foreigners. The most famous of these struggles was the anti-American boycott that Chinese businessmen launched to protest discriminatory American immigration policies.[33] This boycott (unlike those discussed in later chapters) remained essentially a merchant affair and never evolved into a broad-based popular movement. In Shanghai and a few other cities, however, citizens did hold mass meetings to publicize the boycott of American goods. Shanghai students also engaged in streetside propaganda work, and youths at two American-run schools withdrew en masse. Ma Xiangpo, for his part, was a leading speaker at boycott rallies.[34]

The other 1905 struggle that pitted Ma and his students against foreigners involved Zhendan's internal politics. Just after the spring term began, a dispute broke out between the foreign missionaries, who taught many of the school's language classes, and the Zhendan student body. The dispute originally centered around the question of how much time pupils should devote to various Western languages, with the Jesuits on the staff insisting that students spend less time studying English and more time studying French. The conflict was part of a more general struggle over the governance of the school, with the foreign teachers insisting that the powers of the student government association be curbed. Ma Xiangpo, as head of the school, tried to mediate between the two sides, but it quickly became clear that his sympathies lay with the students. He had insisted from the beginning that the school be responsive to students' needs and that students play an active role in its governance. When students went on strike to protest the imperialist activities of the French Jesuits on the Zhendan faculty, who seemed to be using the school's dependence on Catholic sponsorship to take over the school, Ma sided with the youths against the foreign teachers. The end result was that he and all but two of the school's 132 students withdrew from Zhendan in protest.[35]

The French Jesuits eventually found new students to replace the protesters, and the reconstituted Zhendan became one of Shanghai's most important missionary schools, although it would never again be a center for radical student activism. As had happened in 1903 after the closure of the Patriotic Academy, however, the youths who withdrew from Zhendan soon found a new academic home, which quickly took the place of their old school as a center for political activism. This new home was the Fudan Academy (Fudan gongxue), which Ma Xiangpo founded in late 1905. Once again, his goal was to establish a school that would have high academic standards, encourage free thinking, be free from foreign control, and grant its pupils a high degree of self-government.

FUDAN AS A CORE INSTITUTION, 1905–1919

Ma's new school, whose name was a pun on that of his earlier one (whereas Zhendan means "dawn," Fudan means "new dawn" or "dawn again"), would later evolve into Fudan University (Fudan daxue), recognized today as Shanghai's premier institution of higher learning. Despite the grandeur of its later history, the school's beginnings were humble indeed. Several leading progressive thinkers and activists came to Ma's aid in Fudan's early years: for example, Yan Fu (the noted translator of Western philosophical works) joined the faculty just after the school was founded, and Ceng Shaoqing (one of the leading organizers of the anti-American boycott of 1905) not only agree to teach at the school but raised much of the money that Ma used to get the institution started. Despite the help these and other intellectuals provided, when Fudan opened its doors in late 1905 many of its introductory courses and business affairs were handled not by trained teachers and administrators but by students active in the Zhendan protest earlier that year.

Luckily for Fudan, these former protesters were an unusually talented group of young men, who would go on to become newspaper editors, college administrators, and high government officials. Thanks largely to the activities of several key members of this group, such as Yu Youren and Shao Lizi, Fudan was able to remain Shanghai's main academic center for progressive student activities throughout the political upheavals of the decade and a half that followed the school's founding. Not only did young professors like Yu and Shao encourage their students to become involved in political affairs, they also edited and wrote for some of the Shanghai newspapers that served as major conduits for the transmission of revolutionary ideas and information about protest activities. Thus, for example, Yu founded the *Minli bao* (People's strength) in 1909, and in 1916 Shao became editor of *Minguo ribao* (Republican daily news), Shanghai's leading revolutionary daily of the Warlord era.[36]

The ties of these two professors and others of their generation with the leading radical political parties and social organizations of the day also helped keep Fudan at the center of local revolutionary politics. Shao Lizi is again a revealing and important case in point: not only did he join the Revolutionary Alliance (Tongmenghui), which Sun Zhongshan (Sun Yat-sen) formed in Tokyo in 1905, and this organization's successor, the GMD, but he was also an early member of the CCP. Thanks in large part to Shao's connections with these parties, Fudan students regularly heard speeches by the leading radical politicians of the time, and no less a personage than Sun Zhongshan himself served as chairman of the school's board of regents in 1913.[37]

Besides the political parties alluded to above, Shao was a leading member of the Chinese World Students Association (Huanqiu Zhongguo xueshenghui). This name is misleading in a sense since members were not students but Chinese educators and officials who had studied abroad at some point in the past and were committed to helping youths travel to Japan and the West to study. Not all the members of this Shanghai-based association were revolutionaries by any means, but from 1905 (when the group supported the anti-American boycott) to 1919 (when it supported the May 4th Movement), it consistently championed patriotic causes. Members of Fudan played a special role in this organization: not only was Shao Lizi (who left Fudan for a few years soon after its founding to study in Japan) one of its most active members, but the man who served as Fudan's president for most of its early years, Li Denghui (an overseas Chinese who came to Shanghai after graduating from Yale), was a co-founder and the first chairman of the World Chinese Students Association.[38]

The impact of people like President Li and Professor Shao on the development of the May 4th Movement in Shanghai, as well as the central role the Fudan student body played in the events of 1919, are dealt with at length in the next chapter. Although the dramatic protests that accompanied the May 4th Movement overshadow other student political struggles during Fudan's early years, they were by no means the only political activities in which local youths took part during this period.

For example, Shanghai students did not play a decisive role in the Revolution of 1911, but the city's educated youths did show their support for the event in various ways, including forming student armies that vowed to fight for the new regime if necessary.[39] Two years later, after agents of General Yuan Shikai (the warlord who ruled China from 1913 to 1916) shot one of the Revolution's most important leaders, Song Jiaoren, students from Fudan and other schools took part in funeral parades and rallies (at which Li Denghui and Shao Lizi were leading speakers) held to honor the martyred leader.[40] In 1915 the city's students again took political action as supporters of that year's anti-Japanese boycott, which patriotic merchants and intellectuals called to protest the Japanese government's attempts to force Yuan Shikai to agree to its notorious Twenty-one Demands, under which Japan would gain control of large parts of northern China.[41] Then, in 1917, when Yuan Shikai's warlord successors in Beijing began to talk of restoring the imperial system by placing former emperor Pu Yi back on the Dragon Throne, a group of Fudan youths formed an anti-monarchical protest league to undercut these plans.[42]

As important as these and other early struggles were for giving students from Fudan and other local schools a taste for political activity, the anti-Japanese protests of late spring and summer 1918 were the first ones that deserve to be thought of as a full-fledged "student movement." These protests were triggered by rumors that the Beijing government was planning to enter into (or had already signed) a secret treaty of mutual cooperation with the Japanese government that would give Japan control over Chinese territory in return for economic aid. Chinese students in Tokyo took the lead in protesting this newest threat to China's sovereignty by holding rallies and demonstrations in the Japanese capital and by forming a special association called the National Salvation Corps of Chinese Students Studying in Japan (Liuri xuesheng jiuguotuan—hereafter "Jiuguotuan"). In late May, as a further sign of protest, members of the Jiuguotuan returned en masse to China, where they immediately began to call on students in Beijing and other cities to take collective action to fight Japanese imperialism and warlord treachery. This agitation quickly bore fruit: 2,000 Beijing students staged a mass march on May 21 and youths in Shanghai (where the Jiuguotuan set up its Chinese headquarters) as well as other cities quickly followed suit.[43]

Neither Shanghai's students nor their counterparts in Beijing capitalized on the momentum of these late May demonstrations by holding additional marches or launching classroom strikes. Political activities that, like the late May marches, set a precedent and helped lay the foundation for the much larger anti-Japanese movement of the following year did, however, continue to take place during the following months. During June and July, for example, students at several Shanghai schools sent telegrams of protest to government officials, and Jiuguotuan representatives visited dozens of local schools and arranged for noted local intellectuals to give public speeches as part of its effort to keep the issue of Japanese aggression alive.[44] In addition, representatives of a newly formed Beijing student protest organization came to Shanghai in summer 1918 to meet with local activists, as part of a drive to form China's first national student union.[45] Fudan and people affiliated with the institution played a key role in all of these activities: the school's students were among those to draft petitions of protest to send to Beijing; the school's administrators allowed the Jiuguotuan to hold many of its meetings and congresses in Fudan classrooms and assembly halls; Shao Lizi spoke at Jiuguotuan-sponsored public lectures; and Shao's newspaper, *Minguo ribao*, carried dozens of articles about and proclamations by the Jiuguotuan and the fledgling national student association formed in Beijing.

THE RISE OF SHANGDA, 1922–1924

Fudan remained a center for political activity after 1919, thanks to the continued presence of many of the same pupils and faculty members active in the May 4th Movement and to an influx of new students and professors with radical leanings attracted by the school's growing reputation for militancy. This influx began during summer 1919, when Li Denghui granted a request for admission from ten former students of the St. John's University Middle School, who had been expelled because of their May 4th political activities.[46] During the next several years, other students entered the school for similar reasons. Many noted political figures also came to Fudan to teach in the early 1920's, including both GMD theoreticians such as Dai Jitao and important early members of the CCP such as Chen Wangdao (the first translator of the Communist Manifesto into Chinese).[47]

Although Fudan continued to attract radical students and professors throughout the early 1920's, around 1922 it began to lose its position as a core institution within the local student movement. Two factors contributed to this decline. The first was a geographical one: in 1920 the school's administrators began constructing a new campus far removed from the heart of the city in the largely rural Jiangwan section north of Shanghai, and by 1922 the college had relocated from its more centrally located Xujiahui site to the new buildings (see Map 2). The other factor was the founding of new schools expressly devoted to the cause of revolution, the most important of which was Shanghai University (Shanghai daxue or Shangda for short).

Shangda, like the Patriotic Academy and Fudan before it, was established as the result of a classroom strike. The students of Southeastern Teachers College began to boycott classes in November 1922 to protest a trip by school president Wang Litang to Japan funded by tuition fees. In the midst of this strike, the heads of the school's main student organizations demanded that the college be reorganized, put under the leadership of Yu Youren and other progressive intellectuals, and renamed Shanghai University. By the time Wang Litang returned from Japan, after receiving an urgent telegram from one of Southeastern's teachers, he found Shangda in operation on his school's former premises. Wang took the matter before the local Chinese court, and eventually the two sides reached a settlement. Shangda was allowed to take possession of the school buildings and Southeastern Teachers College ceased to exist. By the end of 1922, Shangda was formally established with Yu Youren as president and several of his old colleagues from Fudan as professors.[48]

Shangda was closely linked with the GMD and the CCP from its inception, and its faculty was filled with leading theoreticians (such as Dai Jitao), literary figures (such as Mao Dun), and journalists (such as Shao Lizi) affiliated with one or both parties. During its first years, these ties grew closer still, as the GMD began to allocate funds to Shangda to support the school's operations, and key figures of the two parties ranging from Wang Jingwei (the GMD leader) to Chen Duxiu (one of the cofounders of the CCP) became involved in running Shangda. By 1923 the school had, in fact, begun to evolve into a training ground for party cadres. Although instruction in academic subjects continued throughout the school's existence, Shangda's students (who, in contrast to those of most local colleges, were drawn from diverse social backgrounds rather than almost exclusively from the ranks of the elite) were also given practical training in such subjects as labor organizing by Communist leaders like Deng Zhongxia. In addition, they were continually exposed to works of political philosophy by Marx and Sun Zhongshan (in classes taught by theorists such as CCP leader Qu Qiubai). And they were given frequent opportunities to do radical propaganda work of their own, since the school served as the publishing headquarters for two of China's leading radical journals: *Xinqingnian* (New youth) and *Xiangdao zhoubao* (The guide).

Shangda's faculty roster, close ties to revolutionary political parties, and publishing activities made the school's students well suited to act as core figures in the local student movement. Although Shandga students took part in political activities on and around their campus from the moment they helped found the school, they did not get an opportunity to perform this core function in a citywide movement of any size until the anti-Christian movement of 1924.[49] Shanghai's students were never completely quiescent between the end of the May 4th Movement and the beginning of this new wave of patriotic activities. Throughout the early 1920's in any given semester a *bake* (school strike) of some sort took place at a local school. Between 1920 and 1924, a number of threats to China's national sovereignty inspired Shanghai's students to hold mass meetings, call for boycotts on foreign goods, or march through the city's streets in protest.[50] The anti-Christian agitation of 1924 was, however, the first post-1919 struggle in which students throughout Shanghai banded together in a sustained series of political activities.

Shangda as a Core Group, 1924–1927

The 1924 movement, during which students from Shangda and other local schools rallied around the slogan "Restore educational rights" and demanded that all institutions of higher learning be brought under Chinese control, had its roots in the abortive anti-Christian agitation of 1922. This earlier fight against Christianity, though an important chapter in Chinese intellectual history, produced few concrete results in terms of mass actions, since it remained essentially an elite rather than a popular movement. In 1922 small bands of protesters in Shanghai and other cities did disrupt (or attempt to disrupt) gatherings sponsored by Christian groups, and some local anti-Christian activists tried to gain support for their cause outside the ranks of the intelligentsia.[51] For the most part, however, the agitation played itself out in a series of polemics written by New Culture

Movement scholars influenced by Western rationalism, who argued that China's only hope for becoming a strong nation lay in abandoning all "superstitions" (Christian and Confucian alike) and embracing "science" and "democracy" (terms that Chinese writers of the time invoked with an almost millenarian fervor).*

The revived anti-Christian movement of 1924, although it did not grow into a struggle on par with the May 4th or May 30th movements, was a quite different affair from its predecessor of 1922 for three basic reasons. First, propagandists trying to discredit missionary activities in China made much more use of explicitly Marxist and Leninist terminology in 1924 than had their predecessors in 1922. Thus whereas the 1924 protesters continued to denounce missionaries as purveyors of superstition, they also stressed that members of the church were the handmaids of capitalist exploitation and that Chinese converts were "running dogs" willing to do the bidding of foreign imperialist masters. Similar language had appeared in some of the polemics written during the anti-Christian movement of 1922.[52] Moreover, one of the most notable aspects of the anti-missionary agitation of 1922 is that it seems to have been the first youth movement in which members of groups linked to the CCP, such as branches of the Socialist Youth League (Shehuizhuyi qingniantuan, the forerunner of the Communist Youth League [CYL], or Gongqingtuan, of later years), played a prominent role.[53] Nonetheless, when taken as a whole, the anti-missionary propaganda of 1922 is much less colored by Marxist concepts and images than the tracts of 1924, and the Communist Youth League (which had a very strong presence at Shangda) played an even more central role in the anti-Christian activities of 1924 than the Socialist Youth League had played in those of two years before.[54]

Second, many more mass actions took place in 1924. Students at missionary campuses throughout the nation went on strike in 1924 and 1925 to protest such things as required Bible classes, or in the case of later classroom strikes (such as the strike at St. John's during the May 30th Movement) to protest attempts by school administrators to limit student participation in patriotic protests.[55] Third, participants in the 1924 protests made serious efforts to spread their message to ordinary Chinese citizens. The

---

*Some authors use the terms New Culture Movement and May 4th Movement to encompass both the political struggles and the cultural debates that preoccupied Chinese intellectuals throughout the late 1910's and early 1920's. Throughout this study, however, in order to avoid confusion, I reserve the second term to describe the protest actions of late spring and summer 1919. The anti-religious and, in particular, anti-Confucian emphasis in the New Culture Movement, as well as the tendency of many intellectuals of the time to idealize the concepts of science and democracy, is treated well in Chow Tse-tsung, *The May 4th Movement*, pp. 58–60; and Vera Schwarcz, *The Chinese Enlightenment.*

highlight of these anti-Christian publicity activities came during the days following Christmas, which the protesters dubbed "anti-Christian propaganda week" and celebrated in a variety of creative ways. They filled the pages of radical newspapers (including Shanghai's *Minguo ribao*) with anti-Christian diatribes written in a colloquial style.[56] They held public rallies to discuss the threat missionary dominance of Chinese institutions of higher learning posed to the nation (the Shanghai one lasted three days and drew a crowd of some 300, most of them students).[57] They gave streetside lectures outside of churches and school chapels where Christmas services were being held. And, finally, they mocked the foreign custom of exchanging Christmas cards by sending greeting cards inscribed with anti-Christian messages.[58]

Shanghai, though not the main center for mass actions during the anti-Christian Movement of 1924, was the chief hub for anti-missionary organizational and propaganda activities. Shangda students took the lead in both these areas.[59] In February 1924 Shangda became the first local school to form an "anti-Christian alliance," and when teachers and students from schools throughout Shanghai formed a citywide protest league that summer, three of the five people selected to lead the organization were affiliated with Shangda. The university's domination of the movement went beyond this concentration of power in the protest league's central committee, however. The two co-editors of the movement's leading journal, *Fei Jidujiao* (The non-Christian), were classmates in the school's sociology department. The head of that department was CCP leader Qu Qiubai, a fact that helps account for the increasing importance of Marxist terminology in the anti-Christian propaganda pieces of the time.[60] In addition, Shangda professors (including leading Communists such as Cai Hesen) wrote many of *Fei Jidujiao*'s articles, and students from the school held key posts in Shanghai's Great Anti-imperialist Alliance (Fan diguozhuyi datongmeng), a group that worked together closely with the city's Anti-Christian Federation.

Shangda continued to function as the main core group in local student politics throughout the anti-imperialist and anti-warlord protests that followed the struggles of 1924, although other schools such as Southern University (Nanfang daxue) and Great China University (Guanghua daxue, which was formed during the May 30th Movement itself) were also notable centers of radical activity.[61] Shangda's central role in the May 30th Movement of 1925 is examined in Chapter 4, but two aspects of Shangda's May 30th activities are relevant to the current discussion. First, many of the same students and teachers at the center of the anti-Christian Movement of 1924 ended up playing similar roles in the more broadly based struggle of the following year. Gao Erbai, a co-editor of *Fei Jidujiao* in

1924, for example, helped to found and wrote one of the keynote pieces for the magazine *Shangda wusa tekan* (Shanghai University May 30th special), which students at his school put out in 1925 to publicize the May 30th Incident.[62] And Liu Yiqing, Shangda's main representative to the Great Anti-Imperialist Alliance in 1924, led one of the most important demonstrations of the entire May 30th Movement, the march staged on May 31 to call attention to the previous day's tragic events.[63]

Second, the political activities of Shangda students and professors during 1925 led the authorities of the International Settlement (where Shangda was then located) to become increasingly antagonistic toward the school, which they considered a hotbed of "red" activity and a danger to the foreign community. The first step by the Shanghai Municipal Police against the school was to arrest Shao Lizi, the acting president of Shangda, in February 1925.[64] Then, in early June, after the school took the lead in protesting the May 30th tragedy, the Shanghai Municipal Police raided the university, ordered all students to leave, and stationed American troops on the premises. Thanks to Shanghai's tripartite structure, however, this police occupation did not succeed in destroying the university. Shangda relocated to the Chinese-controlled Zhabei section of the city and continued to function much as usual.[65]

One aspect of Shangda life that did not change because of the school's relocation was the activism of its students. These youths continued to exert a great deal of influence upon local political struggles, both through their participation in marches and through their activities as officers in protest leagues such as the Shanghai Student Union. Some Shangda students also played leading roles in the national youth movement during the mid-1920's, thanks to their positions as Shanghai representatives to the Nationwide Student Union (Quanguo xuelian). Shangda students also played major roles in one other national organization, the CYL. Membership in this organization, like that in both the CCP and the GMD (see Chapter 4), swelled in the immediate aftermath of the May 30th Movement. According to internal party documents, by late 1925 the CYL had established cells within nine local schools. Of these, by far the strongest was that in Shangda, where 120 (or approximately one-fourth of the school's students) were members.[66]

Shangda's students took leading roles in several struggles during the school's first year in Zhabei, such as the new anti-Christian propaganda drive of late 1925, the gatherings held to protest the March 18th Tragedy of 1926 (named for the day on which police in Beijing fired on unarmed students taking part in an anti-warlord demonstration), and the demonstrations staged to mark the first anniversary of the May 30th killings.[67] In late 1926 and early 1927, however, students from the school participated in

a much more important series of political struggles: the three armed uprisings that overthrew warlord rule in Chinese Shanghai and delivered the
city to Jiang Jieshi.[68] These uprisings are known as workers' revolts, and
laborers did indeed play the central roles in the Communist-engineered
events. But Shanghai's educated youths also contributed to each of the uprisings, notably by helping to organize laborers and doing propaganda
work at factories. Youths from various institutions including Fudan, Nanfang, and Guanghua took part in these activities, but once again students
from one school—Shangda—stood out as the main agitators.[69]

The main goal of this chapter has been to provide a framework for looking at the student movements of the Warlord era. It has stopped short,
however, of providing a detailed analysis of any one of these struggles or a
nuanced picture of the evolution of student-led protest movements. The
following chapter does just that, as it traces the development in Shanghai of one of China's most important student-led struggles, the May 4th
Movement of 1919.

 TWO

THE MAY 4TH MOVEMENT

SCHOLARS OF THE CHINESE REVOLUTION invariably single out the May 4th Movement as one of the great turning points in the history of twentieth-century China. Just what kind of turning point they consider it varies, however, depending largely upon their particular political and ideological orientation. Their evaluation also depends upon whether they use the term "May 4th" to refer to the whole range of cultural and political developments that occurred between 1915 and 1922—including the campaign to get authors to use "plain speech" (*baihua*) rather than classical or literary Chinese (*wenyan*) (see Chapter 8)—or simply to refer to the popular anti-Japanese protests of 1919, as the term is used here. Thus some scholars focus on the May 4th era as a pivotal period of intellectual ferment comparable to the European Enlightenment or Renaissance.[1] Others emphasize the part the political struggles of 1919 played in laying the groundwork for the rise of the CCP.[2] But for both intellectual and social historians, and for scholars working in Taiwan as well as for their counterparts in the People's Republic, the May 4th Movement stands out as a crucial point of origin, a transformative series of events that shaped much that followed.[3] This is especially true of historians of student protest, almost all of whom point to 1919 as the year the modern youth movement began.

There is good reason to treat the May 4th Movement as just such a turning point and moment of origin in this study as well. Even though (as the preceding chapter shows) Shanghai students participated in a variety of political activities before 1919, the anti-Japanese demonstrations in Shanghai and other cities in May and June of that year were of a different order than previous ones. They were, however, like many that would follow. The May 4th demonstration, itself—which began as an orderly parade by patriotic Beijing students, but ended in violence as students attacked the house of a hated official and police attacked students—became the prototype for numerous incidents that triggered later youth movements.[4] And the protesters' responses to news of the Beijing incident set a pattern that nearly all subsequent youth movements copied closely: governmental attempts to disrupt student activities and arrest student leaders led to telegrams of outrage from students and members of other social groups; next came classroom strikes, streetside lecture campaigns, and additional demonstrations; finally, youths formed a nationwide student union and began organizing multi-class protest actions.[5]

May 4th Comes to Shanghai

It is seldom possible to pinpoint the exact time and place a student struggle starts in a given city, but the May 4th Movement in Shanghai is an exception: it began at around 8 A.M. on the morning of May 6 on the Fudan campus.[6] The city's leading merchants and educators had met to discuss the Paris peace negotiations long before May 6. Various civic associations sent telegrams to Beijing early in spring 1919 to express concern over rumors that the World War I victors were planning to give the Japanese control of China's Shandong Province. And at the very beginning of May, the heads of the Jiangsu Province Educational Association and other concerned civic leaders began preparations to hold a "citizens' assembly" (guomin dahui) on May 7 to mark the fourth anniversary of the date the Japanese government had issued its infamous Twenty-one Demands and to publicize the new threat Japan posed to China's sovereignty.[7] As important as these developments were for laying the groundwork for Shanghai's May 4th Movement, May 6 still stands out as the starting point of the popular movement to resist Japanese imperialism and warlord oppression.

On that morning Shanghai students first heard that their counterparts in Beijing had held a march on May 4 and that the police had beaten and arrested some of the participants in this demonstration. Shao Lizi reported this news at a special early morning school assembly at Fudan, which he convened by ringing the school bell with his own hands. Shao had been one of the first people in Shanghai to hear of the May 4th Incident, in a telegram received at the *Minguo ribao* offices late the previous night. He began the special school assembly by waving this telegram in the air, telling the Fudan students what it said, and then calling on them to show their mettle by responding to the example set by Beijing's youths.

Taking his words to heart, the students selected messengers to transmit the news of the May 4th Incident to Shanghai's other schools and began to make plans for coordinating citywide protest actions.[8]

By the evening of May 6, students at campuses across Shanghai were holding meetings to discuss ways of expressing their anger over the Beijing arrests, as well as forming special committees to take charge of protest activities.[9] The first positive step local students took was to send a joint telegram that very night to the national government in Beijing in the name of the student bodies of 33 Shanghai campuses; the text decried both the general handling of the Shandong question and the May 4th arrests.[10] Their second step was to organize themselves to take part in the Citizens' Assembly scheduled for the following day. Some 3,000 youths attended this gathering, held at the Recreation Ground outside the West Gate of the old city. The meeting began with a series of short speeches and ended with a march.[11]

Several things are worth noting about this initial stage of Shanghai's May 4th Movement. The first is the central role Fudan students and faculty members played in mobilizing youths at other campuses, since people affiliated with this school would play major roles in protest activities throughout the following months.* A Fudan student, He Baoren, would become the first president of the Shanghai Student Union (SSU), and his classmates would fill a disproportionate number of the highest offices in the organization.[12] In addition, Fudan president Li Denghui would become one of the SSU's most trusted advisers and patrons and would use his influence as head of the Chinese World Students Association to provide the student league its first meeting place.[13]

Li's role as a backer of the SSU is exemplary of another noteworthy aspect of the events of early May: the leadership roles non-students played in protests involving students. Joseph Chen highlights this phenomenon in his study *The May 4th Movement in Shanghai* and claims that local students were unusually slow to respond to the national crisis precipitated by the Treaty of Versailles, since they did not "organize themselves for direct political action" until May 8. He argues, therefore, that an important difference between the unfolding of the May 4th Movement in Shanghai and its evolution in Beijing was that in the capital students took the lead from the very beginning, whereas members of the local elite (and especially what he

---

*One factor in the campus's growing importance as a center of student activism was that when youths were expelled from or simply decided to leave other (usually missionary) institutions for political reasons, Fudan took them in. For examples, see Li Yuji, "Shanghai xuesheng," p. 60; and Zhang Yi, "Fudan shisheng," a memoir by a former student of St. John's Middle School who transferred to Fudan in summer 1919.

about national politics city

calls the "educated elite") seized the initiative in Shanghai. To reinforce this claim, Chen notes that elite groups in Shanghai were more active than student organizations in sending telegrams protesting the Treaty of Versailles in March and April, and that non-student organizations played the leading roles in Shanghai's first May 4th Movement mass action: the Citizens' Assembly of May 7.[14]

There is certainly some validity to Chen's claim; merchants and educators undeniably played vital roles in the earliest Shanghai protests of 1919, and in general the city's May 4th Movement was more a multi-class affair than was its Beijing counterpart.[15] Chen's argument is, however, problematic. First, by stressing the political and organizational activities of members of other social groups, he obscures the basic fact that in Shanghai as well as in Beijing students were the driving force behind the development of the patriotic mass movement of May and June. Second, Chen draws a sharp line between the actions of "the educated elite" and those of "the students," when in fact there was a great deal of overlap; educated youths were often the main participants in events Chen views as "elite" protests.

The best way to illustrate this is to look at contemporary accounts of the Citizens' Assembly of May 7, which Chen presents as an "elite" event that took place before Shanghai's students entered the mass movement. These reports do note, as Chen stresses, that the Jiangsu Province Educational Association and other non-student groups planned this earliest of Shanghai's May 4th mass actions. But unlike him, they highlight the key role students played in the events of May 7. The Shanghai Municipal Police report on the Citizens' Assembly claims, for example, that "the majority" of those attending this first great mass meeting were students.[16] Almost all local newspapers described the march that followed the meeting as a "student parade" or "student demonstration" and pointed out that most brigades taking part in the event were composed of youths from local campuses, many of whom marched behind banners emblazoned with the names of their school.[17] According to some accounts, the entire student bodies of several schools turned out for this march, an indication that a good deal of organizational activity had taken place on Shanghai campuses before Chen's May 8 starting date.* Press reports also show that a student provided the day's most dramatic moment when he bit his fingers so that

---

*These claims of full turnouts are probably slight exaggerations, intended to play up the patriotic fervor of a given school's students, but the vast majority of students enrolled on some campuses do seem to have turned out. The claim made in Shi Wenxiang et al., *Jiaotong daxue xiaoshi*, p. 116, that the "whole school, over 600 people" took part in the Citizens' Assembly may be excessive, but a contemporary account does say that there were some 500 people in the Jiaotong march brigade (*WY*, 1: 257).

he could write "Return our Qingdao" (one of the day's main slogans) with his own blood.[18]

Although his choice is misleading, it is easy to see why Chen singles out May 8 as the starting point for local student activism: this was the day representatives from local schools first met to form a citywide protest league, and this meeting played a key role in laying the groundwork for the inauguration of the SSU on May 11. Here again, however, it is inappropriate to think of a clear-cut split between members of the "educated elite" and "students," for just as students provided the bodies that made the "elite" protest of May 7 a success, non-students played central roles in the founding of the SSU. Li Denghui's role in this process has already been mentioned, but non-student contributions to the SSU went beyond patronage: some delegates at the initial meetings of the newly formed "student" union were not students at all, but teachers or even principals chosen by the student body of their school to represent the pupils at committee meetings.[19]

This said, it is true that as the movement developed in Shanghai the role of students began to change and increase in importance. After May 8, students would never again be passive participants in a show directed by their elders, as they had been in the Citizens' Assembly of May 7.* By mid-May, middle-school and college students were not only taking charge of their own protest activities but also acting as the main group responsible for publicizing and mobilizing support for the anti-Japanese boycott among the population at large. Educated youths continued to work closely with, and listen to the counsel of, sympathetic teachers and other respected intellectuals until the very end of the movement. This relationship grew more tenuous, however, as the youths adopted more militant tactics, of which all but the most progressive of their older patrons disapproved. The question of whether to launch a general classroom strike was particularly divisive in this regard: at least one principal serving as his school's representative to the SSU was expelled from the group in mid-May for agitating against such a strike.[20] By the end of the movement, thanks to the growing militancy of the students, only one teacher and no administrators remained in the SSU.[21]

Three main turning points in the Shanghai May 4th Movement after

---

*Despite the claim made by a Chinese youth in a lengthy letter to the American-owned *China Press* (published June 10, p. 8) that students "spontaneously" decided to join the Citizen's Assembly, there is clear evidence that the day's main events were carefully planned in advance by groups such as the Jiangsu Province Educational Association. Specific directions relating to when pupils from each school were to gather at the Recreation Ground and even to the kinds of flags they should carry were printed in the May 7 editions of *Minguo ribao* (p. 10), and *Shen bao* (reprinted in *WS*, pp. 178–81).

the Citizens' Assembly of May 7 led students to adopt new (and, in all but the last case, more militant) tactics.[22] The first came on May 19, when news reached Shanghai that the central authorities had stepped up their campaign to suppress the popular movement and that Beijing students had responded by calling for a citywide classroom strike. This news inspired a renewed burst of activism on the part of the SSU, which called on its members to refuse to attend classes beginning May 26. The student league also called for and led two massive demonstrations during this period: one on May 26 (to celebrate the inauguration of this strike) and one on May 31 (to commemorate a Beijing student martyr who died from injuries received during the May 4th Incident).

The second turning point came two weeks later and was also triggered by word that the Beijing government was taking new repressive measures against the students of the capital. The news this time was that the Beijing police had arrested scores of students on June 2; as before, Shanghai's youth responded by calling for a strike. This new strike was not, however, to be simply a *bake* (stopping of classes) but rather a sanba (a "triple stoppage," of work and market activity as well as academic work). This general strike, which began on June 5 and paralyzed the city for the ensuing week, was by definition a multi-class protest. It was nonetheless a student-led mass action, since educated youth took the lead both in agitating for the sanba at the outset and in enforcing compliance with the closing of shops that was the strike's crucial component.

The end of this general strike on June 12 marked the third great turning point of Shanghai's May 4th Movement, and once again news from the capital triggered the start of a new phase. The news this time was that the Beijing government had given in to one of the students' key demands and dismissed from office the "three traitorous officials" whom the students held responsible for the nation's "humiliation" at Versailles.* Shanghai protesters marked this victory by holding celebratory parades and calling off the sanba. These celebrations did not signal the end of all patriotic activity by any means; throughout the following weeks students and members of other social groups maintained the anti-Japanese boycott and held a series of public protest meetings to pressure the Chinese delegates in Paris to refuse to sign any treaty that compromised the nation's sovereignty. In addition, students used this period to capitalize on their victory, by organizing the National Student Union, whose members convened for

---

*The other demands most consistently voiced throughout the movement were that all Beijing students arrested for protesting be released; that the Treaty of Versailles be renounced; and that Shandong be restored to China. According to some reports, the students originally demanded that the "traitorous officials" not only be dismissed but also executed; see *Shanghai Times*, May 9, 1919, p. 7.

the first time in Shanghai in mid-June. Nonetheless, the sanba was clearly the highpoint of local protest activities, and the June 12 victory parades marked the beginning of the end, if not the end, of the May 4th Movement proper in Shanghai.

Since detailed chronologies of each phase of Shanghai's May 4th Movement already exist, this chapter does not attempt to present a day-to-day account of local protest activities.[23] Rather, it focuses on three distinctive roles—bureaucrats, strikers, and policemen—that student protesters played between May 7 and June 12, each of which was particularly important during a specific stage of the movement.

MAY 7 – MAY 19: STUDENTS AS BUREAUCRATS

During the first weeks of May, students devoted much of their energy to forming scores of specialized and often highly bureaucratized protest leagues to coordinate local patriotic activities. For example, during the week immediately following the Citizens' Assembly of May 7, pupils at several schools formed "exhortation corps" to direct the streetside lecture drives in their respective neighborhoods, and students at several schools in the northern section of the city joined together to found a Cooperative National Salvation Society (Gongtong jiuguohui) to supervise propaganda work in their area. As noted earlier, during this same week representatives from campuses throughout Shanghai laid the foundation for the first citywide May 4th student protest league, the SSU.[24]

What kinds of people formed and then led the new student protest groups, and How, precisely, were these associations constituted and structured? The nature of the available sources makes it impossible to answer these questions for most Shanghai student groups, since many are mentioned only in passing in press reports. Thanks to the existence of several memoirs by former members and a number of relevant contemporary documents, however, the SSU is an exception.[25]

The SSU grew out of two meetings at Fudan of delegates from local middle schools and colleges. Eighty-one people representing 31 schools attended the first meeting on May 8. By the next day, when the follow-up meeting began, the number of delegates had risen to 96, and the total of participating campuses had grown to 44.[26] These two planning meetings, during which the students chose a temporary chairman and assigned three people to draft bylaws, laid the groundwork for the organization's first general meeting, which was held at the Chinese World Students Association headquarters on May 11 and attended by representatives from 61 schools.[27]

How exactly delegates were chosen is unclear in most cases and no doubt varied from campus to campus. Existing information suggests, however, that representatives tended to have had experience in a leadership role, either within their schools or in extracurricular organizations.[28] The fact that teachers and even school principals were chosen as "student representatives" is an obvious case in point. Another example is the Tongji University delegates, who were chosen by (and presumably from the ranks of) the school's Class Monitors' Association (Banzhang huiyi).* At least two Fudan delegates also had previous experience in leadership roles: Zhu Zhonghua, the first, temporary chairman of the SSU, had been a leading figure within his school's Students Self-governing Society in previous years; and Cheng Tianfang, who later served in several important positions within the SSU, had helped found a short-lived anti-monarchical association in 1917.[29] Representatives of the Jiuguotuan, the group that had spearheaded the anti-Japanese protests of 1918 (see Chapter 1), were also invited to join the SSU.

Many of the representatives to the SSU, therefore, were far from novices in holding meetings and drafting petitions, and this helped speed the organization process. So, too, did the fact that many individual representatives knew each other and in some important cases had worked together in the past. The schoolteachers and principals who served as SSU representatives are again an obvious case in point, since most were members of the Jiangsu Province Educational Association. More important still was the Fudan connection. Not only were an inordinate number of SSU leaders classmates at this college, but many of the representatives from other colleges who rose to prominence within the union had studied together at the middle school connected with Fudan.[30]

Most important of all, in terms of providing experience for and establishing connections among student leaders, was the popular lecture campaign Fudan students organized in March and April 1919 to present the ideas of the New Culture Movement to the masses. The participants in this drive, which was led by Fudan study societies, spent their spring vacation traveling to nearby towns and cities giving speeches on "morality, hygiene, and all kinds of scientific knowledge."[31] The campaign was thus similar to the activities of the much better known Beijing University student association, the Mass Education Speech Corps. And just as many of

---

*The institution of class monitors, which still exists in China, has no real American equivalent. Class monitors remain with a "class" of students—usually defined as a group of youths who enter a school in a given year and have the same major—throughout the four years of college. They can both serve social control functions (e.g., a teacher may depend upon them to keep order among the students or to collect assignments) and represent the class vis-à-vis teachers and administrators (e.g., they present class grievances to the relevant authorities). The role of Tongji's class monitors in the May 4th Movement is alluded to in passing in Tu Tingxiang et al., *Tongji daxue*, pp. 3–4.

the most prominent figures in the Beijing May 4th Movement (for example, Xu Deheng, Deng Zhongxia, and Zhang Guotao) came out of the Speech Corps, many SSU leaders had taken part in the Shanghai lecture campaign that ended just a few weeks before the May 4th Incident.[32] The SSU's director of communications, the vice-chairman of its discussion committee, its first, temporary chairman, and the member of its documentation department who chose the wording for the Union's first public statement—all of these youths had worked together during the speechmaking drive of March and April.[33]

The list of posts in the preceding paragraph highlights an important feature of the SSU: its highly bureaucratized nature. No mere ad hoc working group of student activists, the Union was composed of specialized departments, many of which had two vice-directors as well as a director. The SSU also formed special task forces as the need arose, such as a group to process the gifts of food, clothing, and money donated by community members to aid the Union. How exactly duties were assigned within this bureaucratic structure remains obscure, but assignments depended on a mixture of factors: sometimes a school would delegate a person to join a specific task force, in other cases personal interests and talents (or lack thereof) played a decisive role.[34] A memoir by Jiaotong University student Wu Daoyi draws attention to this second factor in a blunt description of what happened when he and a classmate joined the SSU. Wu's classmate "had the gift of gab" (*nengyan shandao*) and hence was assigned to liaison work, "but I was no good with words [*bushan yanci*], so all I could do in the organization was keep track of the money, as a 'cashier.'"[35]

The centralized bureaucracy of the SSU—with its departments, department directors, and assistant department directors—had its "local" counterparts in the branch unions (*fenhui*) the league required each member-school to form.[36] These campus associations usually simply called themselves chapters of the SSU, but in some cases they took more original names. Thus Jiaotong and Fudan students referred to their organizations as SSU branches, but Tongji youths called their association the Consciousness Society (Zijuehui).[37] Whatever name they chose, these chapters tended to be almost as bureaucratized as their citywide counterpart.[38] The Fudan branch office, for example, devoted its first meeting to selecting someone to draft a complete set of bylaws. Its second meeting was then spent approving these bylaws and choosing a president, vice-president, secretary, assistant secretary, and treasurer.[39] The Jiaotong association had not only a president, vice-president, Chinese-language secretary, and Western-language secretary but also four separate specialized bureaus for such things as publishing pamphlets.[40]

Organizational activities extended to an even lower level; below these school branches were groups that were smaller and even more specialized.

The lecture teams, which took to the streets surrounding each school almost every day during late spring 1919 to exhort local merchants and shoppers to boycott Japanese products, are an important case in point. In this case four or five students could constitute themselves a special "team."[41] Branch unions also organized "investigation groups," which could have as few as three people, to make sure that neighborhood shops did not stock Japanese products.[42]

Student activists thus established a complex hierarchy of interconnected organizations, all of which played some role in coordinating youth protest activities. The SSU stood at the top of this organizational pyramid, acting as a maker of general policies, which the school branch unions were in charge of implementing. Internal chains of command also existed at each level of the pyramid, with nearly every organization and bureau, from the SSU itself to the propaganda department of one of the union's branch offices, having a designated leader, who in turn often had one or two chief assistants.[43] The weeks immediately following the Citizens' Assembly, in other words, saw the birth not only of a mass movement but also of a protest bureaucracy run almost exclusively by students.

MAY 19–JUNE 4: STUDENTS AS STRIKERS

If the middle of May was a time for building organizations, the next few weeks were most notable for the great student strike that began on May 26. The classroom boycott or strike is probably the single most fundamental and commonly used tactic of student protesters throughout the world and throughout history. Its only close competitors are the demonstration parade and the mass petition drive, actions that often accompany and are facilitated by a cessation of classes.* However, not all student strikes are the same. Just as features of the organization process outlined above (such as the emphasis upon hierarchy and bureaucratization) reveal the imprint of a particular historical and above all cultural context, the May 4th classroom strike was similar to but not the same as, say, the massive (but little

---

*Alexander DeConde, *Student Activism*, refers to student strikes in such disparate times and places as Tsarist Russia (p. 127), Franco's Spain (p. 6), post–World War II Japan (p. 194) and Burma (p. 7), as well as during the 1960's in Portugal (p. 6), Turkey (p. 151), Italy (p. 87), and of course the United States (p. 325). There are obviously some contexts in which classroom boycotts do not figure in the student protest repertoire for fairly obvious reasons. The pre–twentieth century Chinese student movements are a clear case in point: petition drives rather than classroom strikes were the most fundamental tactic in Song times because participation in "classes" was not what defined one's identity as a student. As the DeConde volume again illustrates, petitioning and demonstrating have also been used by very disparate student populations; see, e.g., the contributions by Priscilla Robertson, "Students on the Barricades: Germany and Austria, 1848," pp. 59–71; and William Douglas, "Korean Students and Politics," pp. 221–34.

remembered) American student strike of 1935 or its much better known successors of the 1960's.* The Chinese classroom strike of 1919 also differed sharply in terms of style as well as goals from the much bloodier Argentinean student strike of the same year.[44] To understand the May 4th student strike, we must go beyond simply stating that youths refused to attend classes and try to present a "thick description" of how the strike was carried out and what it meant to those involved.[45]

Since the first planning meeting of the SSU on May 8, student activists had struggled with the problem of how best to make the Beijing government take a stronger stance against Japan and a more tolerant one toward the youth movement. And throughout mid-May, although students were concentrating on composing telegrams and petitions of complaint to send to officials, many educated youths were already aware that such actions alone would not bring enough pressure on the Beijing authorities.[46] Thus from the very first days of the SSU, some students suggested the need for a citywide classroom strike, which would both demonstrate that Shanghai's educated youths were unhappy with official policies and free these youths to spend more of their time promoting the patriotic movement within the city.[47] Thus when Shanghai students heard in late May that their counterparts in Beijing had decided to hold a general student strike, the SSU was ready to call almost immediately for its membership to walk out as well. The inauguration of this citywide student strike was delayed for several days, as a result of successful efforts by the Jiangsu Province Educational Association to persuade the SSU leadership to postpone such a potentially precipitous action. When it finally started on May 26, however, it did so on a grand scale: press accounts estimated initial student participation at anywhere from 12,000 to over 20,000.[48]

The strike did not, however, begin with students simply staying away from classes; the SSU marked the strike's inauguration with what Joseph Chen aptly describes as a "solemn and colorful ceremony."[49] Representatives of 52 local schools took part in this ceremony, which was held at the Recreation Ground, where the Citizens' Assembly had met almost three weeks previously. The highlight of the day came when the assembled youths swore a collective oath to do all they could to "relieve and save [the

---

*These American strikes were in turn dissimilar from each other, just as later Chinese classroom boycotts would not be quite like the one of 1919, a fact that will become clear in later chapters. The most basic difference between the American strikes of the 1930's and the 1960's is the absence of building occupations and sit-ins as a basic part of the strike process during the earlier period. James Wechsler, "Revolt on the Campus: April 13, 1934–April 12, 1935," gives a good sense of the special set of dramatic performances (from prayer meetings to the disruption of Army Day parades) and symbolic gestures (from gathering together to listen to "Taps" to planting white crosses in honor of those who died in earlier wars) that accompanied the American peace strikes of the 1930's.

Chinese nation] from danger and destruction" no matter what the consequences to their own personal safety.[50]

The May 26 program, which also included a parade through the city and
a flag-raising ceremony involving a Chinese Boy Scout, reveals much
about the general mood of the student striker, and the aims of the participants. The public nature of the day's events, for example, shows that the
students intended their boycott of classes to affect more than just the academic community; in their eyes it was to go hand in hand with renewed
efforts to convert the city's entire population to the patriotic cause.[51] The
oath-taking ritual illustrates the extreme seriousness with which Shanghai's educated youths viewed the task of national salvation. The complete
orderliness of the day's rally and march, which is emphasized in press accounts of the May 26 protest, is indicative of the stress student strikers put
on organization and self-discipline.[52] These three features of the strike—a
concern with reaching out to the public, a solemn purposefulness, and a
desire to behave at all times in a disciplined way—continued to shape the
events of the following weeks.

For example, when groups of youths poured onto the streets to hand out
leaflets, paste up posters, act out patriotic plays, and make speeches to anyone who would listen, this was a clear sign that the members of the SSU
were determined to spread their message outside the walls of academic institutions. Some students had engaged in similar activities since news of
the May 4th Incident first reached Shanghai, but the strike freed many
more to take part in the streetside propaganda work. It also provided
youths assigned to the publicity departments of branch unions more time
to write and print protest pamphlets and posters. Soon the streets were
flooded not only with bodies but also with paper; according to one newspaper report, the Fudan branch union's publicity department alone was responsible for printing over 10,000 copies each of five different pamphlets.[53]

Students also used the opportunity provided by the strike to spread
news of the patriotic movement outside Shanghai and establish connections with protesting youths in other cities. Thus the branch unions of
various local schools sent lecture teams to outlying areas to let the people
of nearby towns and villages know what had happened in Beijing on May 4
and June 2 and to explain why all patriotic Chinese should stop buying and
selling Japanese products.[54] The SSU dispatched delegates to Guangdong,
Hangzhou, and other cities, in an effort to lay the groundwork for the formation of a national student union.[55] The arrival of these delegates served
another purpose as well: just as the arrival in Shanghai of representatives
from Beijing and Tianjin had helped spur Shanghai students on to greater
militancy in mid-May, the SSU's traveling delegations similarly inspired

educated youths in other areas. In short, as would often occur in later youth movements, student *mobility* played a crucial role in national student *mobilization*.

Finally, the Shanghai student strikers demonstrated their concern with public relations in the week following the May 26 ceremony and march by staging additional mass displays. The most impressive of these was the SSU's May 31 memorial service for Guo Qinguang, a Beijing student who died from wounds received during the May 4th melee between protesters and policemen.[56] Attended by representatives from even more schools than its predecessor of May 26, this gathering at the Recreation Ground was equally dramatic. One interesting feature of the demonstration was that all the student-participants wore special white caps instead of the straw hats local educated youths had formerly favored, which were now shunned because they were imported from Japan. The lavish assortment of wreaths and banners, which stood beside a portrait of Guo on the speakers' podium, added to the visual impact of the May 31 gathering. This mass memorial, like the oath-taking rally five days previously, served two main purposes: as a ritual act, it solidified and sanctified student commitment to the cause of patriotism; and as an event, it impressed members of other social groups. The May 31 parade, which followed the singing of a specially written mourning song and other funeral rites, went to much greater lengths in the second regard than had its predecessor of May 26; this time students not only marched through the native city but also sent special groups of demonstrators to each of Shanghai's three main commercial organizations.[57]

The orderly events of May 31 bore witness to the strikers' continuing concern with publicity, as well as to the seriousness with which the youths viewed their mission. However, this seriousness of purpose did not influence ceremonial events alone; it also informed day-to-day student behavior during the strike, as the rules branch unions drafted as guidelines for campus life illustrate. The notion that the strike was not to be viewed as a carefree holiday period shows up clearly in the emphasis of student rulemakers on the need for students to engage in "self-cultivation" (*zixiu*) and in their stipulation that students not leave school grounds except when engaged in protest activities.[58] These rules, and other evidence provided in memoirs and newspaper accounts, indicate that students felt a great need to show that they were not motivated by frivolous concerns, such as a wish to avoid classwork.[59]

The day of the typical student striker was in fact supposed to be anything but frivolous, since he or she was likely to be called upon to spend a good part of the day on such arduous tasks as printing leaflets or (in the case of female students) making some of the 20,000 special white hats students wore on May 31.* Branch union rules also required strikers at many schools to spend four hours a day studying on their own and an extra hour in a military training program.[60] The following schedule formulated by one branch union may be idealized and unusually strict, but it does provide an insight into the mood of the time:

> After the strike is called, the daily schedule will be as follows: 6:00, wake up; 6:30 to 7:20, group military calisthenics and limbering up; 7:30, eat breakfast; 8:00 to 9:00, self-cultivation; 9:00 to 11:00, assemble in the auditorium for reports on the situation at the general union [by student leaders]—teachers from our campus and noted figures from outside the university with things of practical value to say will also be invited to give lectures; 11:00 to 12:00, read newspapers; 12:00, eat lunch; 1:00 to 5:00, the four departments [in charge of military training, streetside lecturing, investigating local shops, and printing propaganda materials—every student had to join at least one] independently carry out activities; 5:00 to 6:00, rest; 6:00, eat dinner; 7:00 to 9:30, self-cultivation; 10:00, lights out and quiet.[61]

As the preceding paragraphs show, student leaders envisioned the strike as a serious affair. But the leaders of the SSU and campus branch unions did not fool themselves into thinking that all students would be sufficiently self-disciplined and committed to the May 4th cause to follow all rules without supervision. This brings us to the final distinguishing feature of the strike: the specific mechanisms Shanghai student groups developed to enforce regulations and ensure that order was maintained during the strike. Ideally, individual self-discipline was supposed to ensure that the movement did not degenerate into mere "anarchy," a term of opprobrium favored by Japanese journalists to denigrate the student strike.[62] School protest groups decided, nonetheless, to form special brigades of "monitors" (*jiucha*, sometimes translated as "pickets"), whose main task was to step in when self-discipline failed.

The guidelines for organizing these disciplinary corps reveal the same influence of bureaucratic principles seen in the formation of other student

---

*For the SSU's assigning of the task of hat-making to specific girls' schools, see *WY*, 2:263. Various sources, such as Quanguo fulian fuyunshi yanjiushi, "Wusi yundong," rightfully emphasize the strides made by women during the May 4th Movement, but they were often strides that remained structured by traditional types of divisions of labor. Of course, for a social group that normally played virtually an invisible role in Chinese political struggles, even an act such as making hats to be worn in a memorial service could take on profound implications, especially since some of those wearing the new headgear were girls and young women. See *China Press*, June 1, 1919, p. 2, for a letter from a Chinese girl who cites the hat-making efforts with pride and suggests that it should serve as a first step toward such things as the formation of a girls' student federation.

protest associations and task forces. At Jiaotong University, for example, the school's branch union instructed each class (*ban*) to select two of its number to be monitors.[63] These monitors then constituted themselves a "disciplinary department" (*jiuchabu*), enacted a complete set of bylaws, and selected a director and vice-director to oversee operations. Individual monitors then took responsibility for five specific tasks, including "keeping track of their fellow students." They also monitored a sign-in procedure under which each student was required to write his name (to prove that he was on the school premises) four times a day: "once at breakfast, once at lunch, once at dinner, and once at 9:30 in the evening."[64]

Cheng Tianfang notes, in a memoir of his student days at Fudan, that thanks to the efforts of these monitors intraschool discipline actually became *stricter* during the strike than it had been in ordinary times. According to Cheng, the protesters at Fudan were so intent upon proving that the strike was not being undertaken for "personal pleasure" that monitors were assigned to guard the school gates to prevent those "few who viewed a strike as simply an opportunity to go eat seeds and watch movies" from leaving the campus.[65] Unlike some of the American campus strikes of the 1960's, which were carried out in an intentionally playful spirit, Shanghai's students were determined to show that their boycott of classes was a serious affair.*

JUNE 4–JUNE 12: STUDENTS AS POLICEMEN

During late spring 1919, educated youths went far beyond merely enforcing order among themselves and began to assume civic peacekeeping functions ordinarily taken care of by municipal officials and employees. This usurpation of official roles, which became most pronounced during the week of the sanba, was in a sense the final and logical step in the evolution of bureaucratically minded student activists. These youths, who had begun mimicking the authorities by forming protest bureaucracies, decided in early June to formulate and enforce municipal policy as well.

---

*Not all American student strikes were accompanied by a holidaylike mood: in the aftermath of Kent State, for example, the mood during such events was often very serious. Nonetheless, the classroom boycotts of the 1960's influenced by counterculture ideas were clearly intended to be more celebratory and anarchic than their May 4th counterparts. See, e.g., Gitlin, *The Sixties*, pp. 209–10, for a description of a mass meeting to decide on a university strike during which participants ended up singing "Yellow Submarine." Not all Chinese student strikes have been without their festive side; various firsthand observers of the 1989 protests with whom I have talked have referred to the "carnival-like" atmosphere in Beijing during the early phases of the strike there. On a related theme, Perrot, *Workers on Strike*, notes that some nineteenth-century French labor strikes were carried out in a self-consciously festive spirit.

Students had begun to take the law into their own hands long before the general strike began on June 5 by forming the school investigation teams mentioned above. These early student attempts to ensure that Chinese merchants complied with the anti-Japanese boycott were not piecemeal efforts. By late May, according to the *China Press*, the students in Shanghai were determined "to investigate all shops and firms" and "appoint teams of censors" to "remain on the premises of stores" to make sure no Japanese goods were sold.[66] The students also began, long before the sanba started, to organize their own version of the most basic of all Chinese social control apparatuses: the household registration (*baojia*) system.[67] This alternative baojia system deserves a detailed look, both because of its intrinsic importance within the movement and because its operation illustrates the extent to which the May 4th protesters modeled their methods of social control upon traditional institutions.

The basic unit in the students' social control system was the "group of ten" (*shirentuan*).[68] Students were not the only protesters to form these ten-person mutual responsibility groups equivalent to the ten-household *bao* of the baojia system in 1919;* in fact, the first groups of ten seem to have been established by merchants. As with so many other aspects of the May 4th Movement, however, students took to the idea with greater enthusiasm than did members of other social groups.[69] The basic premise of the groups of ten, as described in an SSU circular issued May 11, was simple: ten people swore a collective oath to boycott Japanese products and promised to make sure that the other nine members of the group remained true to their word. All ten also swore to try to convert others outside the group to the patriotic cause. Ideally, each member of a newly formed unit would convince nine others to join in the effort, thereby creating ten new groups of ten, which together would constitute a group of 100. If possible, ten of these groups of 100 would later come together to form a brigade, the 1,000-member organizations that were to be the largest in the system.

Although each person who joined a social control unit was responsible both for his or her own behavior and for that of others within the group, not all members were equal. Each group nominated one person to represent and take responsibility for the group as a whole, much as the chiefs in

---

*Both Joseph Chen's pioneering study of the May 4th Movement in Shanghai and Chow Tse-tsung's seminal work on the national movement discuss the "groups of ten" in some detail, but neither author explicitly draws attention to the similarities between this stucture and the household registration system. As the following paragraphs show, these similarities are obvious: like the household registration system, the "groups of ten" system was built around units based on decimals, relied on mutual supervision to ensure compliance with rules, and made specially selected people responsible for the behavior of a unit as a whole.

the baojia system took responsibility for the actions of their subordinates. In addition, each unit was supposed to appoint one inspector, to monitor local shops; one head of publicity, to oversee the composition of propaganda materials; one disciplinarian, to enforce the rules; one treasurer, to keep track of the group's finances; and five speechmakers, to deliver streetside lectures on behalf of the group. Actual groups probably never functioned in quite the way outlined in the SSU's circular and other such idealized plans. There is no proof that any fully functional brigade of 1,000 ever existed, for instance, or that the precise division of labor and responsibility described above became the rule in smaller units. There is solid evidence, however, that groups of ten not only existed but played an important function as watchdog structures that made their own members and outsiders stick to the "laws" of the anti-Japanese boycott.[70]

If in May students were already acting like official shop inspectors and baojia chiefs, in June they began to play still more daring roles, acting as leaders of multi-class associations, legislators, and even surrogate policemen. The sanba was by definition a multi-class affair, and the general strike would never have come about if merchants and laborers had not been genuinely angered by the same causes that inspired student protesters.[71] It took more than love of country, however, to make shopkeepers forgo potential profits day after day; nor was a shared desire to protect China's national sovereignty enough to keep the sanba from degenerating into anarchy. The leaders of the SSU quickly realized this. They knew that the success of the general strike depended on making sure that shopkeepers kept their shutters down and that coolies and workers refrained from violence against Japanese nationals.

Every contemporary account attests that students played the leading role in starting the triple strike, keeping it going, and maintaining order. SSU president He Baoren headed the coalition of educational and commercial leaders that coordinated the strike in its first days. Students went from store to store en masse on June 5 and "persuaded" or "coerced" (different sources use different terms) merchants to join the sanba.[72] And students wrote and posted most of the thousands of proclamations, which appeared on virtually every wall and pole during the strike, reminding people of the causes behind the movement and of the need to maintain order.

It is easy to understand why the need to prevent disorder figured so prominently in student posters and lectures of the time: violence could all too easily have ended the general strike almost as soon as it began, by convincing the hitherto relatively tolerant foreign authorities who ran the Shanghai Municipal Council (SMC) to use force to suppress the mass movement. The issue of violence was more than a theoretical one; from the beginning of the Shanghai May 4th Movement, crowds roughed up Japanese residents of the city, as well as Koreans and even Chinese nationals mistakenly thought to be Japanese. Having spent weeks trying to stir up hatred for Japan and occasionally taking violent actions themselves against Japanese property if seldom against people, the students now confronted a situation in which success depended upon keeping the masses calm.[73] This was no easy task on city streets that were suddenly even more crowded than usual, thanks to the presence of striking workers.

The students approached the problem of keeping order on the streets much as they had approached the problems of spreading the news of the May 4th Incident and maintaining discipline among themselves: they formed special task forces and divided up responsibilities. Boy Scout troops were assigned to take charge in designated sections of the city, and local colleges and middle schools organized additional brigades of monitors and volunteers to aid in this task. Propaganda workers joined in the effort, by switching from printing notices that explained the need to boycott Japanese goods to ones that stressed the necessity of nonviolent tactics; hitting foreign nationals, the propaganda corps explained, would end up hurting the patriotic cause, not the Japanese.

The foreigners on the SMC were happy, at first, to let the students help keep order within the city's International Settlement. Editorials in English-language papers noted how "pleased" at least some Westerners were "at the sight of Chinese Boy Scouts and others doing what they could to maintain order."[74] The moment the market strike began, however, relations between the foreign authorities and the SSU grew increasingly strained, and this inevitably affected the way Westerners viewed student efforts to keep the peace. As long as the students confined themselves to streetside lectures denouncing domestic traitors and calling for a boycott of Japanese goods, Westerners in Shanghai were willing to let the movement run its course. Once the sanba began, however, although some Westerners remained wholeheartedly sympathetic toward the movement and its goals, others began to be irritated at the protest's effect on their life. It was one thing to put up with student speeches, but quite another to find one's servants unable to buy fresh vegetables at the local market or, worse still, to have one's chauffeur go on strike.[75]

Within this context of increasing tension, important members of the foreign community began to see the Boy Scout troops and the newly formed student "peace-keeping brigades" (bao'andui) in a negative light. Rather than viewing these student peacekeepers as civic-minded youths, Western journalists and officials now saw them as upstarts intent upon usurping the prerogatives of the duly constituted authorities. The degree to which Shanghai youths were acting like "policemen," as well as the concerns these activities raised in the minds of some Westerners, is attested in English-language editorials. These referred to "bands of Chinese" who were "wearing uniforms and badges, functioning generally as if they had been armed by the authorities with full powers," and asked rhetorically what right Chinese youths had to set themselves up as keepers of the peace.[76]

Official pronouncements and government dispatches reveal a similar fear that Chinese protesters were usurping roles better reserved for foreigners. Fear of usurpation was not, however, the only cause of the shift in policy toward the movement in the second week of June and the active measures to end the strike that foreign volunteers and police began to take. Despite the efforts of Boy Scouts and other student peacekeepers, there were frequent (though usually minor) outbursts of violence. A desire to prevent riots, as well as general displeasure over the inconveniences imposed by the strike, helped motivate the foreign authorities to adopt increasingly repressive measures toward the mass movement after the sanba began.[77] The leaders of the foreign community seem, however, to have been as galled by the militancy of student attempts to maintain *order* as they were by any *disorder* that accompanied the strike. For example, among the first items on the SMC's list of stringent regulations against the sanba was a rule forbidding unauthorized people from "appearing in the streets or in any public place, in uniform or wearing any distinctive dress or badge or headgear signifying membership in any particular organization, association or body."[78] A June dispatch from Shanghai's most senior British consular official is even more revealing. Referring to criticisms by Americans of the calling up of British volunteers to quell disturbances on June 6, Acting Consul-General Phillips wrote that "it must not be forgotten that had not some counter-demonstration been made on their [the SMC's] part, they would have had to sit by and watch the Students' Union usurp the duties of the police of the Settlement."[79]

Fear of usurpation, according to Phillips, also lay behind the SMC's June 8 decision to force the SSU to move its headquarters out of the International Settlement. The foreign concessions were a key factor in the evolution of the May 4th Movement in Shanghai, since the native authorities would probably not have allowed the SSU to operate unmolested until as late as June 8. Shanghai's peculiar political arrangements remained important even after the SMC clamped down on the Union, since the SSU simply moved its operations to the even laxer French Concession, which was already providing a safe haven for Sun Zhongshan. Even so, the Council's decision was a harsh blow to SSU leaders, who had spent much time and energy trying to convince the foreign community that the student league deserved to be treated as a legitimate organization. In the end,

even the SSU's repeated assurances that the strike and boycott were aimed
at the Japanese and pro-Japanese officials and its apologies for any inconvenience its protests caused its Western "friends" were not enough to convince the authorities that the student movement posed no threat to foreign
privilege.[80] Such promises notwithstanding, according to Phillips, the
SMC felt the need to close down the Union to show "that students would
not be allowed to usurp the duties of the regular administration by patrol-
ling the streets."[81]

Despite the efforts of SMC members and local Chinese authorities to
end the popular movement when it began to prove too militant, it was the
protesters themselves who decided to halt the general strike after the Beijing government dismissed the "three traitorous officials" from office.
Flushed with victory, protesters spent June 12 setting off firecrackers and
holding parades, giving the hitherto relatively somber protest movement a
festive air.[82]

The victory that Shanghai's students, workers, and merchants celebrated on June 12 was only a partial one, since the forced resignations of
the three traitorous officials did nothing to alter the Treaty of Versailles.
Not surprisingly, therefore, Shanghai's streets and meeting halls continued to serve as venues for a wide range of anti-Japanese and anti-warlord activities throughout the following months. Some of these activities
were less protests than outbursts of mob violence: for example, a series of
violent attacks on Japanese nationals (triggered by rumors that these foreigners were poisoning local food and water supplies) took place in June.*
Most events, however, were orderly gatherings reminiscent of those of
May and early June. Thus, for example, in late June Shanghai served as the
site of the inaugural meetings of China's first full-fledged national student
union.[83] And in late June and early July, the SSU and other groups staged
several impressive mass demonstrations to protest the news that the Beijing government was planning to tell its representatives in Paris to sign the
Treaty of Versailles.†

---

*Unsavory incidents such as this are usually omitted from accounts on the May 4th Move-
ment, many of which tend to idealize the students' motives and activities, but outbursts of
anti-Japanese violence (though condemned by many campus leaders) did occur throughout
China. For citations of relevant sources and a full discussion of both the Shanghai poison
scare itself and the reasons events such as this are downplayed in the literature, see Wasserstrom, "Taking It to the Streets," chap. 1.
†The largest of these anti-treaty rallies took place on July 1; some 80,000 people attended the
gathering, at which SSU president He Baoren presided. In the end, these protests and similar
ones in other cities helped convince the Beijing authorities to change their position on the
Treaty of Versailles, which the Chinese delegates to the conference did not sign. See Joseph
Chen, May 4th Movement, pp. 184–92, for additional details.

Despite the significance of these and later events (including the revival of patriotic protests in December 1919 and March 1920, triggered by new incidents related to Sino-Japanese affairs), June 12 is a fitting date to end this narrative of Shanghai's May 4th Movement. The sanba that ended on that day was unquestionably the highlight of the local movement, as well as one of the most impressive events in the nation as a whole in 1919. The SSU's role in initiating and coordinating this event, moreover, marked the coming of age of the local student movement as a potent political force. During the few short weeks between the May 4th march in Beijing and the end of the general strike in Shanghai, Chinese students proved that they were capable not only of organizing themselves for disciplined political action, but also of bringing citizens of all classes together in common cause to fight imperialist aggression and domestic misgovernment.

THREE

STUDENT TACTICS

THE PRECEDING CHAPTER DESCRIBES various techniques Shanghai students used to express their anger and try to gain redress for their grievances during the May 4th Movement; it does not, however, confront the basic question of why they chose these particular tactics. Nor does it examine the equally important question of how, once a given tactic was selected, the participants came to share a common vision of the specific way they should perform the action. Why did the protesters of 1919 feel that the best way to draw attention to their cause was to send or present petitions to local and national officials and to stage the kinds of streetside lecture campaigns, rallies, boycotts, strikes, and marches analyzed in the previous pages? And why did even those youths new to mass actions seem to have a clear sense of how they should behave? These are the two main questions this chapter seeks to answer.

Surprisingly, these kinds of issues are rarely addressed directly in the literature on campus unrest. Scholars have tended to take student tactical choices for granted, preferring to look instead at quite different topics. For example, in the case of the American campus upheavals of the 1960's, social scientists have paid more attention to the question of why some students rebelled and others remain quiescent than they have to the question of why radical youths turned again and again to specific types of protest techniques. Thus many articles, with titles such as "Some Sociopsychological Characteristics of Student Political Activists," seek to explain why certain youths became radicalized, but few focus on the popularity of, say, occupying university facilities as a form of protest.[1] Previous students of Chinese youth movements have likewise tended to be interested more in ideology and motivation than in tactics per se.[2] As a result sinologists working in China, Japan, and the West have written volumes about the factors that led students to take to the streets, highlighting such causes as the rise of nationalism on campuses,[3] the economic hardships of student life,[4] agitation by underground members of the CCP,[5] and generational tensions between educated youths and their parents.* They have had little to say, however, about the meaning of the tactics students turned to once mobilized.

Existing works, in fact, generally take student tactics for granted, as if there were certain things that students just *naturally* do when protesting. This assumption is problematic, however, because student protesters in different times and places have found it "natural" to do different things. Students in Republican-era Shanghai, for example, almost never employed certain protest techniques Western youths relied on heavily during the student movements of the 1960's, such as occupying school buildings. Conversely, European and American youths have seldom involved themselves in boycotts, as their Shanghai counterparts frequently did during the first decades of this century. Nor did Western youths of the 1960's routinely bite their fingers and write out slogans in blood, something Chinese students participating in both the anti-Japanese agitations of 1915 and 1919 and the popular protests of 1989 did to prove their commitment to a patriotic cause.[6]

Furthermore, even in the case of tactics that students in different cultural settings have found effective, youths in different times and places often find it "natural" to carry them out in quite dissimilar ways. The case of parades illustrates this. Marches of one sort or another have accompanied most modern student movements, but the specific way they are carried out varies considerably, depending on the historical and cultural

---

*Analyses of student movements worldwide, in terms of generational conflict, such as Lewis Feuer's influential *Conflict of Generations*, were popular during the late 1960's and early 1970's. The extreme version of this theory, which essentially reduces all youthful activism to attacks upon symbolic father figures and attempts to resolve oedipal crises, has been effectively discredited. Critics have stressed such things as the frequent links between student unrest and broader social forces beyond the university; the difficulty of delineating "historical generations" with any precision; the many cases of shared values and political orientation of student activists and their parents (at least in the United States, where a significant number of campus radicals came from left-wing families); and the tendency of Feuer and others to use psychological theories associated with adolescence to interpret the actions of people in their twenties. All these points are relevant to the Chinese case. Despite the problems with Feuer's theory, some sinologists have used generational tensions as a partial explanation of Chinese student movements. See, e.g., the persuasive discussion of the role of such tensions in early-twentieth-century campus unrest in Sally Borthwick, *Education and Social Change in China*. For trenchant and generally convincing attacks on Feuer's work, see Statera, *Death of a Utopia*, pp. 22–24; and Miles, *Radical Probe*, pp. 85–86; for a summary of the literature, see Jarausch, *Students, Society, and Politics*, p. 15.

context. Just as the student strike that accompanied the May 4th Movement was a more serious and a more disciplined affair than some American strikes of the 1960's (see Chapter 2), typical Shanghai student marches of the Republican era differed stylistically from those held in other contexts. They were generally more subdued, for example, than the violent processions that Argentinean youths staged during their campus reform movement of 1918[7] or the equally unruly marches that students held periodically in Tsarist Russia.[8] In addition, Chinese students have found it "natural" to end parades by presenting petitions asking the government to change specific policies by kneeling outside government buildings holding their petitions above their heads.[9] Youthful protesters in radically different political cultures would view such acts as anything but routine. In other words, although students may indeed use tactics that come "naturally" to them, youths in different cultural and historical contexts often find it most "natural" to carry out quite dissimilar protests.

Some analysts prefer a "conspiratorial" approach to student tactics to the "naturalistic" one described above. In the case of Shanghai youth movements, those who favor this kind of approach generally use the activities of CCP campus organizers to account for the methods students employed, as well as for the general coherence of youth actions.* Both pro- and anti-Communist historians in China often give CCP organizers much of the credit for student tactics, although scholars in the PRC differ markedly from their counterparts in Taiwan (for obvious reasons) on the issue of whether these underground activists used simple persuasion or trickery and deceit to get other students to go along with the CCP plans.[10] But such explanations, though popular with critics and defenders of the CCP alike, are ultimately problematic. Even memoirs by former student activists that claim CCP members guided the youth movement often reluctantly admit that underground activists frequently had to follow the lead of other students in order to avoid "alienating themselves from the masses."[11] Still more damning to any theory based on the role of the CCP are three simple facts. First, many of the same tactics used in party-led (or suppos-

---

*Other kinds of conspiracy theories have been used to explain Chinese student protests. For instance, in 1919, contemporary Japanese observers and officials claimed that Chinese youths were the "puppets" of American missionaries (Shanhai Nihon Shōkō Kaigisho, *Santō mondai*, pp. 430–59). And in 1989, China's leaders insisted that spies from Taiwan, foreign news agencies such as the Voice of America, and a handful of domestic conspirators, including remnants of the Gang of Four, were the main instigators and directors of that year's popular unrest. Thus, for example, the official report of Beijing mayor Chen Xitong on the demonstrations in his city argued that "the turmoil was premeditated and prepared for a long time," and referred to the role "reactionary forces in Hong Kong, Taiwan, the United States and other Western countries" played in the movement. For this report, as well as other official documents that advance conspiracy theories, see Appendix 1 of Yi and Thompson, *Crisis at Tiananmen*, pp. 155–238.

edly party-led) movements were used in 1919, two years before the CCP was founded. Second, as the Epilogue to this book illustrates, many of those tactics reappeared during protests of the 1980's that challenged instead of supported the Communist Party. And finally and most important, conspiracy theories centering on the role of CCP agitators do not adequately explain how small groups of underground organizers communicated their visions of what given protest actions should be like to their fellow students.

This chapter argues that both the nature of student tactics and the high degree of coordination seen in even the most spontaneous of student mass actions can be explained without reference to conspiracy theories. CCP activists played a vital role in some protests, a lesser one in many more, and none at all in still others. Yet the similarities between these events, in terms of the kinds of mass actions involved and the orderliness of the actions themselves, are much more striking than the differences. This is because, whether or not *agents provocateurs* were involved, neither the choice of what to do nor decisions regarding how to do it were ever made from scratch. Instead, tactics were usually chosen because they were in some way already familiar to the youths involved, because they were part of what Charles Tilly calls a distinctive "repertoire of collective action." [12]

REPERTOIRES AND SCRIPTS

This notion of "repertoire" is based on the assumption that protest, like acting, is a form of learned behavior that grows out of a lifetime of observing and participating in various social activities. It also assumes that effective protest gatherings, like other genres of theatrical performances, are usually carried out by groups that follow closely or improvise from a common set of familiar "scripts." Some of the scripts in a group's collective action repertoire come directly from past actions that members of the group have used to express their grievances. In this case, the coherence of a protest can come from the fact that the people involved have quite literally rehearsed their part at an earlier time and thus familiarized themselves in advance with all the stage directions and speeches required. More often, however, street theater involves variations upon familiar types of collective action, some of which are unrelated to protest per se. In these cases, the shared past experiences of the protesters serve not as "rehearsals," but rather as the sort of "preparations" that performance theorist Richard Schechner argues are essential for improvisational theater troupes and sports teams. According to Schechner, whereas "rehearsals" set an "exact sequence of events," "preparations" make members of a group ready to "do something appropriate" at a given moment and give them a sense of how to work together as a unit.[13] The common "preparations" of Shanghai students, their improvisation upon familiar scripts, allowed their street theater to seem both spontaneous and organized, just as even the most novel skits of a skilled improv troupe have an internal coherence, thanks to the way in which they build upon routines used in previous workshops and practice sessions.

To what kinds of familiar scripts are protesters drawn when improvising on the streets? The most obvious ones are, of course, those that worked for them in the past. Studies by scholars interested in Western popular movements suggest, however, that protesters are also drawn to tactics familiar for quite different reasons. For example, an awareness of the collective action strategies used by other groups can have a significant impact upon the tactics a set of protesters uses. This point is clear in Todd Gitlin's recent study, *The Sixties*, a book that is part historical narrative and part memoir. Throughout his work Gitlin draws attention to the ways in which American student protesters were attracted by tactics derived from the Civil Rights movement, contemporaneous French campus struggles, and Third World guerrilla insurrections.[14]

The use Russian student protesters made of *skhodki* (assemblies) is another case in point. The calling of these free-form group meetings to air grievances, reaffirm the corporate identity of the student class, and (in some cases) plan strikes or marches, signaled the start of many campus movements in the late nineteenth century, and the subversive quality and power of the skhodki are attested by the many official pronouncements outlawing them.[15] Despite such bans by the early twentieth century skhodki had become a routine part of campus political life, and students knew how these exercises in direct democracy worked from firsthand experience. Even when the campus skhodki were first called in the mid-nineteenth century, however, students already had a familiar script from which to improvise, since this style of meeting was an adaptation of the assemblies traditionally held in peasant communes, which were also known as skhodki. Although the participants in the peasant and student versions of the gatherings may have had little else in common, both shared, in Daniel Brower's words, "egalitarian sentiments" and "a disdain for all authority but that emanating from the group."[16] As both the Russian and American student movements illustrate, familiarity often derives simply from observing, hearing of, or reading about the collective actions of other groups.

Events that have nothing at all to do with protest or the expression of grievances can also help introduce new scripts into a group's repertoire, as Charles Tilly's study *The Contentious French* illustrates. Tilly argues that most of the tactics seventeenth-century French protesters used were simply variations upon familiar, everyday routines, rituals, and ceremonies.[17] Recent works by other European social historians similarly point to connections between protest marches and riots, on the one hand, and such routine events as annual festivals and charivari, on the other.[18] Thus a wide range of different experiences, ranging from earlier protests to the most ordinary of daily activities, can provide protesters with a viable repertoire from which to draw inspiration in times of trouble.

Working from this premise, I devote the rest of this chapter to examining some of the basic scripts from which Shanghai students worked, the familiar events and activities that prepared these youths to protest effectively and that lent coherence to mass actions that might otherwise have dissolved into chaotic gatherings. I do not try to *prove* that students self-consciously modeled their behavior during a given protest upon a particular past event or a certain ceremony. This would be impossible, because for many events the only sources available are newspaper accounts. In addition, even in those cases where memoirs by former participants exist, few directly address the issue of why a particular action was chosen.* What this chapter tries to do instead is to highlight similarities between Shanghai student protests and other events and to pinpoint some of the people who (often unintentionally) helped teach youths how to carry out these protests by encouraging or even forcing them to perform preparatory exercises. Its overall goal is to show how the city's youth created a unique protest tradition by putting already acquired skills to new uses and by improvising upon familiar patterns of activity.

It is fairly easy to show that the various mass movements that followed the May 4th Movement relied heavily upon familiar scripts, since this struggle served as a model for much that would come after it. Many participants in the May 4th Movement remained on university campuses—first as students and then as professors—and passed on their protest tradition to later generations. Many of those who took part in subsequent movements self-consciously claimed to be re-enacting the events of 1919. The real challenge in understanding the evolution of Shanghai student strategies thus lies in figuring out where the tactics used in the May 4th Movement came from. This chapter concentrates, therefore, on the events of

---

*During my interviews in Shanghai between 1986 and 1988 with participants in various pre-1949 student protests, I also found it hard to get meaningful answers to questions concerning the tactics protesters used. Interview subjects often accounted for their actions with the same naturalistic ("we just did what you did during mass movements") or conspiratorial ("we just followed the direction of underground party members") explanations critiqued above. Conspiratorial explanations, in part for political reasons, likewise predominate in memoirs published in the People's Republic. The prevalence of naturalistic explanations in my interviews had less to do with politics, however, than with the limits the hegemony of certain cultural forms can place upon one's vision of the possible: to participants in any movement, many tactics will indeed be chosen because they simply seem the appropriate and hence in a sense the "natural" thing to do.

1919. It tries to show that even during the May 4th Movement Shanghai students already had a number of useful scripts with which to work and hence seldom did things that were wholly new to them.

THE REPERTOIRE IN ACTION: MAY 26, 1919

One can get a good feel for the range of scripts youths of the May 4th era had at their disposal by looking closely at the first important student-led protest in Shanghai in 1919: the rally and parade the Shanghai Student Union (SSU) staged on May 26. Held to mark the Union's decision to launch a citywide general student strike, the event attracted some 12,000 youths.[19] The day began with a mass rally at the Recreation Ground outside the West Gate of the city, during which youths from each participating school stood together and listened to a brief opening speech by SSU president He Baoren. Following a musical interlude, a Boy Scout raised the national flag, to which the assembled youths bowed. These preliminaries completed, the students swore a solemn oath to persevere until they achieved their patriotic goals. They then filed out of the park in an orderly fashion to march through the city. The demonstration ended with the youths returning to the Recreation Ground to hear more speeches, after which they shouted "Long live the Republic" three times and dispersed.

Shanghai's students had never before staged anything comparable to this protest in terms of size, scope, or elaborateness, but every step in the ceremony had roots in familiar activities. To begin with, as mentioned in Chapter 2, some of the youths who took part in the May 26 gathering had participated in a similar event nineteen days earlier: the Citizens' Assembly of May 7 organized by some of the city's leading educators and merchant groups. Then, too, people had gathered at the Recreation Ground to listen to speeches by representatives of organizations; then, too, marchers (many of whom were students) had divided up into brigades and paraded through the city. Holding a meeting at the Recreation Ground would also have been nothing new, however, even to those students who had never before taken part in a political gathering, since this was the site of Boy Scout reviews and citywide intermural sporting competitions. These competitions often began with educators giving speeches to groups of youths from various educational institutions, who stood under banners emblazoned with school names, very like those used in protest marches to identify campus brigades.[20]

If gatherings such as sports meets provided potential models for part of the day's program, other phases of the May 26 protest more closely resembled quite different events. Chinese rebels and revolutionaries had long used the swearing of sacred oaths, for example, as a way of demon-strating a group's solidarity and seriousness of purpose, and the youths who gathered on May 26 would have been familiar with the ritualized script involved. Each would have encountered such events in popular novels such as *Water Margin* and seen dramatic re-enactments of famous oath-taking ceremonies in theatrical productions, such as the popular *Three Kingdoms*.[21] At least some would have read about a more recent perfor-mance of a similar rite by a group of Shanghai tobacco workers in 1918.[22] This worker oath-taking is particularly interesting because, like that of the students, it was used to mark the beginning of a strike, though in this case a labor stoppage (*bagong*) rather than a classroom boycott (*bake*).

The raising of the national flag, in contrast, was reminiscent not of ear-lier Chinese protests but of the civic rituals carried out by Shanghai's Brit-ish community on holidays. Just two days before the May 26 rally, for example, British residents of Shanghai had begun their Empire Day festivities by having a Western Boy Scout hoist the Union Jack.[23] At the May 26 rally, the only novelties were the nationality of the flag and of the scout who raised it. With the musical interlude, however, we are back within the Chinese protest tradition, since such songs had been a standard part of patriotic rallies involving students since at least as far back as the anti-Russian agitation of 1903 described in Chapter 1. Finally, much of the day's program as a whole would have seemed familiar to any veterans of the anti-Japanese agitation of the previous year: the highlight of the 1918 struggle had been a mass march of 2,000 youths that closely resembled those of May 1919 in terms of format and style, though much smaller in size.[24]

The preceding paragraphs do not exhaust the topic of familiar elements found in the May 26 program. One could, for example, also draw links between the bowing to the flag and the bowing to Confucius that began the traditional school day and so forth.[25] The preceding comments should suffice, however, to indicate the types of people and events that helped teach youths how to protest and the kinds of scripts from which May 4th students improvised. Youths could learn from educators and folk heroes, as well as from earlier generations of student protesters. Parts of the day's program were much like the events of past student protests; others were variations upon official ceremonial forms.

AUTHORIZED ACTIVITIES AS PROTEST SCRIPTS

It requires nothing more than common sense to assume that protesters model their behavior upon that of other protesters, but the similarities between protests and official ceremonies alluded to above deserve some explanation, since these would seem to be disparate types of events. Recent work on the history of popular unrest in England and France, however, shows strong connections between authorized and unauthorized gatherings. Studies by Natalie Davis, E. P. Thompson, and others suggest that many (if not most) of the basic tactics used by European protesters—ranging from the burning of effigies to grain stoppages and religious riots—are best treated as inverted versions of authorized rituals, radical rearrangements of official scripts in which ordinary people temporarily usurp roles normally played by powerholders.[26]

The street theater students performed during the mourning parade of May 31 and the victory parade of June 12, two 1919 processions briefly described in Chapter 2, shows clearly that this same tendency toward inversion and usurpation helped shape May 4th marches.* Ironically, both of these marches held to protest imperialist aggression and the actions of domestic authorities owed much in terms of style and basic format to earlier events organized or sponsored by foreigners or members of the Chinese elite.

The parade following the memorial meeting of May 31, for example, was strikingly like the public processions that traditionally followed funeral services for high Chinese officials. The most recent mourning ceremony of this type, a procession honoring the famous compradore and official Sheng Xuanhuai, had been held less than two years before. According to the *North China Herald*, this late 1917 event—in which students from Nanyang College (a school Sheng had helped to found that later changed its name to Jiaotong) and "children carrying banners" as well as other youths took part—comprised seventeen different sections of marchers (each headed by its own band) and cost an estimated $300,000.[27] The May 31 memorial march in honor of the student protester, Guo Qinguang, was not nearly as elaborate as Sheng's, but in other ways the two events were much alike: the main difference between the two processions was that in the protest march the crowd elevated one of its own to a position of public respect.[28] Both the memorial services for the official and the protest martyr involved large contingents of mourners; music (school bands played and groups of students sang before and during the May 31 march); banners (made of silk and peacock's feathers in the one case, cloth in the other);

---

* Philip Kuhn's analysis of "orthodox" and "heterodox" military hierarchies in *Rebellion and Its Enemies* is of interest here. Although Kuhn does not deal explicitly with parallels between official rituals and protest actions, he does draw attention to a comparable kind of "script" sharing between rebels and their enemies in regard to organizational activities.

marchers who wore distinctive clothing (various costumes were worn in the 1917 procession; in 1919 students wore special black armbands and white hats); and a representation of the deceased (a statue of Sheng, a picture of Guo).

Events such as Sheng's funeral were bound to influence the way student protesters marked the deaths of martyrs. Educated youths had other experiences to draw upon as well. For example, many would have taken part in smaller services for deceased family members; since music and mourning clothing are generic parts of Chinese funeral rites, these rituals would have been similar in many ways to the memorial honoring Guo.[29] In addition, since the college students who took part in the 1919 memorial services for Guo Qinguang would have been in middle school in 1913, some of them might well have taken part in the protests held that year to honor Song Jiaoren, which also took the form of a memorial service and march (see Chapter 1). Nonetheless, mourning services for officials such as the march held to honor Sheng Xuanhuai or the ceremonies involving schoolchildren performd to honor the Empress Dowager and the Guangxu emperor after their deaths in 1908,[30] stand out as key events that provided student protesters with ready-made scripts to follow, and in some cases active preparation as well, when the time came to mourn their own dead.

The student victory march of June 12 was inspired by a much more joyous event than the memorial parade of May 31, and it is not surprising to find that it was a different type of affair. Like the procession honoring Guo, however, the victory march can also be read as a protest variation upon an official script, although in this case the dramaturgy was borrowed from celebratory rather than funeral parades. Joseph Chen has already noted some of the similarities between the events of June 12 and annual New Year's celebrations, such as the use of fireworks.[31] The victory march that greeted news of the traitors' dismissal from office also resembled the gatherings each year on October 10 (Double Ten) to honor the anniversary of the 1911 Revolution, as the following quotations from articles in the *Shanghai Times*, describing the 1918 Double Ten celebrations and the June 12 victory parade of 1919, respectively, indicate:

> In the Settlement the Chinese flag was profusely displayed. . . . Chinese school children took part in a procession in Nantao [the South City]. . . . Chinese bands livened up the procession and as the children went along they either sang or shouted cheers for the Republic. (Oct. 11, 1918, p. 7)

> There was a procession of about 4,000 students in the native city. . . . The procession which included 1,000 girls paraded all the streets, with flying banners. . . . The Lungwha [Longhua] Orphanage Band dis-

coursed the usual "patriotic" airs we are accustomed to hear, while
the national flag was displayed from many shops. (June 13, 1919, p. 7)

Annual festivities were not, however, the only potential celebratory
models familiar to students. Just a little more than six months before the
June 12 student procession, Shanghai had been the scene of a series of special victory parades celebrating the end of World War I, and youth groups
had played central parts in these events.[32] The Armistice celebrations, like
those held to mark the dismissal of the "traitorous" officials, included mass
meetings, fireworks, and parades by troops of schoolchildren, Boy Scouts,
college students, and others.[33] The 1918 victory parades differed from
those of the following June in certain respects. Most notably, the earlier
ones were much more elaborate, and Shanghai's Western authorities were
the main organizers of the former but tried to prevent the latter. However, the basic similarities in form between these different events remain
striking.* Thus, ironically, foreigners inadvertently provided students with
a gestural vocabulary for their anti-imperialist demonstrations.

This theme of Westerners unintentionally training Chinese students in
protest techniques becomes even more apparent if one focuses on a youth
group that played a key role in the May 4th Movement: the Chinese Boy
Scouts. This organization, originally affiliated with local foreign Boy
Scout troops, was founded in 1913. By 1916 it had some 500 members, and
by 1919 there were thirteen Chinese troops in Shanghai proper.[34] These
Boy Scouts, like their counterparts in other countries, engaged in a variety
of activities, some purely recreational and others geared toward public service. At first glance, this organization seems an unlikely trainer of participants in a radical movement, since its leaders expressly claimed that scout-
ing was "not intended to lead youths to interfere in the government of the
country." Their only goal was to encourage boys to be "honourable, useful
and pure," "live a healthy open air life," and fill "every moment with
useful and health giving hobbies."[35] Nonetheless, when the May 4th
Movement broke out, Chinese Boy Scouts immediately began to put their
special skills to use in the new cause of protest.[36] Since troop leaders were

---

*I am not the first to call attention to the Armistice day marches as models for May 4th
parades. In an editorial entitled "Students 1919" published on Dec. 24, 1935, the *China Press*
claimed that the parades the Allies sponsored in Beijing in fall 1918 had convinced radicals of
the value mass displays could have in drawing attention to a political cause. This argument is
plausible, if unprovable, since some of the main speakers at the Beijing rallies celebrating the
Armistice were radical young intellectuals who would play important parts in the May 4th
Movement. The photographs in Spence, *Search for Modern China*, following p. 388, lend further plausibility to this argument. Two of these show a crowd armed with signs gathering in
Beijing in November 1918 to "celebrate the armistice" and "press for China's territorial
rights," and a third shows a May 4th Movement march that looks very similar.

often students or instructors at local secondary schools or universities, this transition from being part of a Western-run organization to being an anti-imperialist vanguard was quite logical.*

What specifically did Boy Scouts do during the May 4th Movement that can be traced back to their earlier troop activities? Forming ranks and marching is the first thing that comes to mind, since this was a skill they practiced as part of regular reviews.[37] In addition, the Boy Scouts often performed important functions as monitors during assemblies and processions, keeping order among the protesters themselves and between protesters and outsiders, as part of the peacekeeping brigades described in the preceding chapter.[38] Scout training had prepared them to perform these policing functions. Just the previous March, for instance, troops of Chinese Boy Scouts had helped the Shanghai Municipal Police keep order when it was arranging for the deportation of German subjects back to Europe.[39] Thus when Chinese Boy Scouts began to act like a shadow police force to enforce the sanba two months later, behavior whose implications greatly troubled the leaders of the foreign community (see Chapter 2), the youths were doing nothing more than applying previously acquired skills in a new context.[40]

The preceding overview suggests some ways in which official ceremonies could inadvertently teach youths how to protest by training them in routines and providing them with scripts easily adapted to suit radical purposes. Many other related ideas could be explored here, such as the connection between campus military training and the style of protest marches.[41] Much more could be said about some issues brought up in passing in the preceding pages, since topics such as the connections between yearly festivals and protest behavior could themselves be the focus of entire essays.[42] Some of these themes receive more attention below (e.g., the subject of military training is treated briefly later in this chapter and then examined at length in Chapter 7). Now, however, let us examine another set of activities that provided youths with scripts for action and trained them in the skills they would use during the May 4th Movement: the routines of campus life.

---

*A March 15, 1919, article in the *North China Herald*, p. 712, which listed the organizations that sponsored and provided the scout masters for several troops, interestingly included the names of two of the Shanghai colleges (Fudan and Jiaotong, then known as Nanyang) that were most active in the May 4th Movement. It also mentioned troops belonging to two other bodies (the YMCA and the Chinese World Students Association) that were centers of radical student activity during the struggle. The local head of the Chinese Boy Scout Association expressly directed troop leaders to mobilize their scouts to assist May 4th protesters (*WY*, 2:136).

CLASSROOM ACTIVITIES AS PROTEST SCRIPTS

There is an obvious link between ordinary classroom activities and some of the main student protest techniques used in 1919, such as streetside lecture drives and the writing of pamphlets and petitions. Whereas in the previous examples, municipal authorities and even police officers were shown inadvertently playing the role of "teachers," in these cases it was professors and middle-school instructors themselves who trained students (though again often inadvertently) in protest tactics. Youths interested in publicizing the arrest of Beijing students and convincing members of other social groups to join the patriotic movement began by simply turning to things they either did or had watched their instructors do in the classroom. Whether they had ever given a speech before, all members of May 4th speechmaking corps[43] were intimately familiar with what went into lectures from listening to them daily in class.* It was likewise a short jump from composing essays to composing pamphlets, from reading memorials in dynastic histories to writing petitions, from acting in school pageants to performing patriotic plays on the streets.[44]

The case of one May 4th protester, SSU leader Cheng Tianfang, illustrates just how well ordinary campus activities could prepare a youth to take part in a political movement. In Cheng's memoir of his life at Fudan, he notes that before 1919 he participated in debating competitions held at the school and worked on one of the campus newspapers, two activities that obviously facilitated his activities as an orator at protest rallies and editor of an SSU propaganda sheet in 1919.[45]

LEARNING FROM OTHER PROTESTERS

The preceding pages focus on ways in which activities essentially unrelated to protest helped prepare students for collective action, but in some cases May 4th students found models for action in techniques other groups had used effectively in the past.[46] The most important tactic students borrowed from another social class was probably the boycott, a form of merchant protest to achieve economic and political ends that long predated the May 4th Movement and other twentieth century anti-imperialist struggles.[47] Other tactics of different social classes during the period im-

---

*Classroom lectures were, however, not the only activites that provided students with models for their streetside speechmaking activites. As Chapter 8 suggests, student lecturers were also likely to have been influenced by many other kinds of oratorical performances to which they had been exposed, ranging from officially sponsored talks on Confucian morality to performances by storytellers to sermons by missionaries.

mediately preceding May 1919 may also have served as scripts for May 4th actions. For example, there was at least a tenuous connection between the Hongkou Riots of 1918 (during which Chinese mobs in the Hongkou section of Shanghai attacked Japanese nationals) and May 4th activities. Although youth leaders took great pains to deny that the May 4th Movement as a whole was just another "anti-foreign" outburst, students did harass Japanese nationals and Chinese considered "pro-Japanese" in 1919. If such harassment can qualify as a "tactic," it is one that needs to be understood in relation to previous anti-Japanese riots.

Students, although occasionally looking to scripts provided by members of other social classes, more frequently looked to their own tradition of mass action, which even in 1919 was already a rich one.[48] One finds precursors of many May 4th tactics in the early-twentieth-century upsurges surveyed in Chapter 1. Student strikes, for example, were nothing new in 1919. Local youths had also participated in patriotic assemblies long before 1919, since such actions had accompanied the anti-Russian struggles of 1901 and 1903, as well as the anti-American boycott movement of 1905 and the anti-Japanese protests of 1915 and spring 1918. Some of these pre-1919 struggles, such as those of 1915 and 1918, provided May 4th youths with firsthand experience in specific tactics.[49] Even nonparticipants in these earlier protests had many ways of learning about them: student struggles quickly became a part of school lore (Fudan students of 1919 knew, for example, that their school had been founded after the Zhendan strike of 1905); and (as the partial life histories of Shao Lizi and Yu Youren given in Chapter 1 illustrate) many May 4th–era teachers were former student strikers ready to share their memories with a new generation of protesters.[50]

There is also good reason to think that Shanghai's May 4th activists inherited some of their scripts from student protests that took place long before either they or their teachers were born. The students who took to the streets in 1919 were concerned with turning China into a nation that was "modern" and "scientific" (two terms they invested with powerful positive connotations) and insisted that their fight against Japanese imperialism and warlord oppression was in many ways a distinctly new one. However, May 4th youths were also keenly aware and proud of the fact that throughout the preceding millennia militant intellectuals—from petitioners of the Han Dynasty (206 B.C.–A.D. 220) who had spoken out against corrupt officials to scholars of the late seventeenth century who refused to serve China's Manchu conquerors when the Ming Dynasty (1368–1642) fell—had continually been at the forefront of similar struggles to save the nation from foreign invaders and domestic tyrants.[51]

This sense of continuity of purpose with intellectuals of the past, particularly with examination candidates (the closest imperial equivalents to modern college students) who had taken part in protests, is clearest in a speech Duan Xipeng, one of the leaders of Beijing's May 4th Movement, gave in Shanghai in June 1919 at the inaugural meetings of the National Student Union. Duan called on his listeners to emulate the actions of the Song Dynasty (960–1279) martyr Chen Dong, a twelfth-century examination candidate who spoke out against traitorous officials and whose exploits are recounted in a dynastic history students routinely studied.[52] During the months before Duan's speech, educated youths in Shanghai and other cities had begun to use many of the same tactics that Chen Dong and other pre-twentieth-century protesters had routinely used. One of the reasons the rulers of China decided to execute Chen Dong, for example, was that the scholar had been an ardent writer of petitions of complaint denouncing evil ministers, a protest technique that scholars had been using for centuries before Chen himself was born.[53] If the types of petitions May 4th students wrote were nothing new, neither were the posters they pasted up denigrating hated officials—examination candidates had done the same thing early in the Qing Dynasty.[54]

TRANSMITTING THE REPERTOIRE

The influence student movement history had upon campus activists increased dramatically after 1919 because of the high regard successive generations of students have had for the participants in the May 4th Movement. Viewing the protesters of 1919 as heroic and successful (since they had brought about the dismissal of the three traitorous officials), new generations have faithfully kept the May 4th protest scripts alive. From the 1920's through the 1940's, in fact, Shanghai youth movements generally followed May 4th patterns quite closely. First, students angered by an incident (usually involving a threat to national sovereignty) held mass meetings, drafted telegrams of complaint, and pasted up wall posters; then, they called classroom strikes and mounted streetside lecture campaigns; finally, they promoted labor strikes and boycotts of foreign goods, staged parades, and (when there were martyrs, as there usually were) held mass memorial services to honor the dead.

This May 4th pattern was far from unique to Shanghai. Shanghai's social, political, and cultural peculiarities gave special twists to some local May 4th actions (for example, not all student unions succeeded in launching effective sanba) and gave special meaning to some protest events (see the discussion below of the foreign community's reaction to the SSU's policing activities). Nonetheless, local protesters were much like their counterparts in other cities when it came to basic tactics; youths in other cities drafted similar petitions, formed similar unions, and established groups of ten to enforce the anti-Japanese boycott in 1919. This is hardly surprising, since not only were students in other cities likely to be influenced by the same kinds of pre-existing scripts, but protest leaders in different locales were in close contact with each other throughout the May 4th Movement. The nationalization of the student protest repertoire increased during the decades after 1919, moreover, as campus activists from different regions met together in national unions to trade information concerning the tactics they had found most effective, and the May 4th Movement evolved into a model for action for youths throughout China.[55]

This model has continued to shape student protests in Shanghai and elsewhere in recent years, since, as the Epilogue shows, many of the tactics alluded to above reappeared in 1986 and 1989. Ironically, whereas veterans of the May 4th Movement who had become professors played key roles in transmitting their tactical repertoire to new generations of protesters during the Republican era, since 1949 a different set of teachers has inadvertently performed the same function: party history instructors. Because the official CCP line traces the party's birth to the May 4th Movement, history textbooks used in the PRC are filled with detailed accounts of student protests of the past. Thanks to such texts and the lectures of history professors, both of which are supplemented by a profusion of propaganda materials issued on the anniversaries of May 4 and December 9, contemporary youths are intimately familiar with the tactics their predecessors used. The irony of this situation became strikingly clear to me in December 1986. At the beginning of the month, bulletin boards at Fudan University were covered with officially authorized posters celebrating the anniversary of the December 9th Movement, which detailed the protests students from the school had participated in 51 years earlier. As the month of December wore on, however, student protesters involved in the new December 19th Movement (see the Epilogue for details), covered these official posters with new ones of their own describing the very similar events in which they themselves had just taken part.

As regular as the May 4th pattern of student activism became, however, neither Republican protesters nor their PRC equivalents have simply reenacted the events of 1919. Students have continually refined, adjusted, and modified May 4th scripts. This has occurred even when youths have explicitly identified their actions with those of 1919. For example, when students carried banners honoring "Mr. Science" and "Mr. Democracy" on May 4, 1989, they were symbolically linking themselves with New Culture ideals but not replicating an action performed 70 years before, since on that date student slogans had focused exclusively upon anti-imperialist themes.

In addition to improvising upon historically transmitted scripts, each new generation has also introduced new tactics of its own. The following chapters provide many examples of improvisation and innovation, often inspired by such things as changes in campus life, student exposure to new kinds of official rituals, or an awareness of techniques protesters in other countries have found effective. The Popular Tribunal Incident (described in Chapter 7) and the hunger strikes of 1989 (discussed in the Epilogue) are but two of the most obvious cases. Perhaps the best way to show how new experiences and political exigencies led later protesters to modify the most familiar forms of May 4th street theater and in the process continually recombine protest scripts associated with religious and political rituals to create new hybrid genres of collective action is to look at the evolution of petition drives of the 1930's and 1940's.

Both the petition drives of 1919 and those that accompanied the anti-Japanese struggle of 1931 were intended to pressure the Chinese authorities to take a stronger stance against Japan, but in other ways they were quite dissimilar. An obvious contrast lies in the distance between the protesters and the authorities. In 1919 Shanghai students were content to present their demands to local officials and send telegrams of complaint to Beijing. Their counterparts in 1931 began by sending representatives to Nanjing (which had by then replaced Beijing as the national capital) to present their requests to top officials in person and ended up traveling en masse by the thousands to argue their case before the authorities.[56]

This use of extensive travel as part of the petitioning process gave the 1931 events something of the air of a religious pilgrimage to a holy spot such as Mount Tai. Such pilgrimages—like so many rituals associated with both "orthodox" Confucian religion and "folk" Buddhist and Taoist cults—have usually involved petitioning, though of the gods rather than of temporal rulers.[57] As in protests, in some religious pilgrimages selected representatives would present a collective petition, whereas in others entire groups would go to the sacred spot en masse. And pilgrims, like the protesters of 1931, typically used banners emblazoned with their place of origin (a village in the one case, a city or school in the other) to mark themselves off from other supplicants.[58] Since such pilgrimages continued to be a common part of Chinese religious life well into the twentieth century, students would have been well acquainted with the script involved, although most would have denied that their trips to Nanjing were comparable.

They would have been more likely to admit that another type of script, that provided by military exercises, distinguished their petition drives from those of 1919; indeed, some memoirs of 1931 point proudly to the martial quality of the trips to Nanjing.[59] Military exercises had become an increasingly common part of ordinary school life after 1927.[60] And, in part because of this, students treated their journeys to Nanjing as military campaigns, forming themselves into brigades, selecting generals, enforcing a militaristic discipline among themselves, and in many cases even dressing in quasi-military school uniforms (see Chapter 7).

If the 1931 campaigns revealed the effects a change in the location of the capital (Nanjing was a few hours away by train from Shanghai, Beijing at least a 24-hour ride) and changes in campus routines could have on the implementation of traditional techniques, the petition presentation students organized to greet General Marshall's arrival in Shanghai in December 1945 showed that the introduction of new official ceremonies could also lead to variations in the performance of protest scripts. The aim of this petition (see Chapter 9) was not unusual: like many earlier ones, it complained about the presence of foreign (in this case American) troops on Chinese soil and called for an increase in domestic freedoms. The mass gathering planned to accompany the petition's presentation was also not unusual, since it was to be a parade along one of Shanghai's main streets. The style of this parade, however, was atypical in at least one regard: students marched behind standard-bearers carrying American and Chinese flags. This and other details indicate that there was more to the event than simply a revival of a traditional student protest technique. It was also an imitation of the official reception local GMD leaders had organized to mark Marshall's arrival, which included marching bands playing the two countries' national anthems and prominent displays of both nations' flags.[61] As these two examples indicate and later chapters show, the May 4th Movement set a pattern for later youth movements, but this pattern was continually being modified by student exposure to other scripts.

COMPARING CAMPUS REPERTOIRES

So far this chapter has focused on why Shanghai students used particular tactics and why they so often seemed to share a vision of how to carry out a given mass action. Tracing the connections between student tactics and other forms of social activity is, however, important for reasons that go beyond the basic questions posed at the beginning of this chapter. For example, close attention to the scripts from which a given group of student protesters works is useful for the comparativist, since this exercise can help account for some of the tactical differences between youth movements at different times and places.

For instance, although both Shanghai youths of the Republican era and American students of the 1960's found imitating their professors a useful method for drawing attention to their cause, thanks to differences in the basic scripts for classroom behavior, the typical Chinese streetside lecture drive was quite unlike its closest American counterpart: the "teach-in." Shanghai student propaganda campaigns of the Republican era, like Republican classrooms themselves, were structured around one person imparting knowledge and moral dictums to a group; American "teach-ins," for which seminars and discussion groups rather than lectures served as the models, often took the form of debates or dialogues.[62]

Differences in patterns of campus life, as well as in the festive and ritual traditions of a culture, also go a long way toward accounting for the fact that some student demonstrations are orderly parades by brigades with specially designated group leaders and others are much more unruly affairs. Here it is worth returning to the contrast between Russian and Chinese marches noted earlier in this chapter. Because of personal inclination, geographic placement (in school compounds often miles away from the centers of popular amusement), the strictures of campus disciplinarians (some of whom were missionaries intent upon protecting the souls of their charges as well as educating their minds), and the youths' self-image as members of a serious scholarly elite, Shanghai students of the Republican era seldom participated in raucous gatherings. And outside of warfare and protest movements, in fact, few of their collective activities involved violence. In contrast, Russian students of the late nineteenth century were notoriously rowdy. Celebrations of holidays and academic anniversaries, such as that of the founding of St. Petersburg University, not infrequently ended with drunken outbursts and public brawls with local workers or confrontations with the police.[63] In light of these contrasts, it makes sense to see the more boisterous style of Russian marches as opposed to those of the Chinese students as in part a reflection of two contrasting patterns of campus life.

The Power of Particular Scripts

A second reason it is worth taking the time to isolate collective action scripts is that similarities between student protests and other kinds of events can have implications for the efficaciousness of the tactics youths employ. For example, student reliance upon a tactic familiar to another group can make members of that group more sympathetic to the youth movement. During the May 4th Movement, for instance, the linguistic and other points of commonality—for example, the similar uses of oaths noted above—between student strikes (*bake*) and labor strikes (*bagong*) may have helped bridge the large cultural gap separating educated youths from factory workers. And bridging this gap was crucial, since students were most powerful when allied with workers in actions such as sanba.

Basing a protest upon an authorized activity or a script favored by those in power can increase the action's chances for success for a different reason: because it can make the event harder to suppress. Charles Tilly argues that this was, in fact, one of the main reasons protesters in seventeenth-century France so frequently modeled their actions on officially approved ceremonies.[64] Through mimicry, protesters were often able to disguise (for a time at least) the fact that what they were doing threatened the government. And, even when the challenge was explicit, by following official patterns French protesters gave their actions an air of legality that made official interference more difficult than it would have been otherwise.

These observations concerning pre-industrial France have direct relevance for Republican Shanghai, where disguise and apparent legality also made imitative protests particularly troublesome for the authorities. When May 4th activists staged a march similar in form to the parades Shanghai's foreign authorities regularly allowed and in some cases (for example, the Armistice marches of November 1918) even sponsored, this placed the Westerners in a difficult position. Banning such an event could make the authorities appear hypocritical or unjust in the eyes of the native population. This point is brought out clearly in a memoir by Zhou Peiyuan, a St. John's Middle School student who participated in the May 4th Movement. Zhou argues that when his school's principal claimed in spring 1919 that to "stop classes and demonstrate" (*bake youxing*) was against campus rules, this was nothing but hypocrisy. Less than six months previously, the author points out, the school's administration had in fact *required* students to do just that, when it suspended classes and ordered youths to participate in World War I victory parades.[65] Similarly, any attempt by the Shanghai Municipal Council to disrupt the memorial service for May 4th martyr Guo Qinguang would have risked angering not only student activists but also many ordinary Chinese citizens, who viewed the event less as a protest per se than as an accepted form of honoring the dead.

Events that looked like official ceremonies were often even more troublesome for the GMD officials who governed Shanghai after 1927, as the case of the Welcome Marshall petition march mentioned above illustrates. The local police were aware that the march was meant to embarrass the regime, but direct interference could have created serious problems for the Chinese government, since outwardly the student protest looked like a simple attempt by Shanghai students to greet a foreign dignitary.

Overt steps to punish the participants might have created a diplomatic incident, with General Marshall wondering why his hosts had stopped a group of youths from presenting their own equivalent of the official welcoming parade.

And even when international issues were not involved, student protests of the Civil War era (1945–49) often placed the authorities in the awkward position of trying to justify suppressing events much like the gatherings the GMD itself routinely sponsored (see Chapter 9). Throughout these years radical youths habitually staged protests on political anniversaries— such as March 8 (International Women's Day) and May 4 itself—that were dates the GMD claimed *should* be celebrated with mass gatherings. These protests were often similar in form to the government-sponsored ceremonies held on those days, despite their radical intent of challenging instead of supporting the GMD. Hence they presented the authorities with a difficult dilemma: officials could either allow the events to take place (and take the chance that the protesters' slogans would bring new converts to the opposition) or take repressive action and risk appearing hypocritical (which could also alienate popular support).

Even in the late 1980's, Chinese students continued to stage protests that resembled or took place at the same time as official celebrations or ceremonies, and thus presented the rulers of the People's Republic with dilemmas similar to those the GMD once faced. This phenomenon is examined in more detail in the Epilogue. For now it is enough simply to mention three key instances of protests in the popular struggle of spring 1989 that resembled or competed with CCP-sponsored mass actions.[66] First, in mid-April students in various cities held mourning ceremonies for former party leader Hu Yaobang that looked much like officially sanctioned funeral marches but were accompanied by calls for more democracy. Second, on the seventieth anniversary of the May 4th Movement, a crowd gathered outside the Great Hall of the People—where the government was simultaneously performing its own ceremony to honor the heroes of 1919—to chant slogans critical of official corruption and the lack of political freedom. Third, in mid-May, as Mikhail Gorbachev visited China for summit meetings with Chinese leaders, Chinese students in Beijing and Shanghai staged contemporary equivalents to the alternative Welcome Marshall ceremonies of 1945, which in this case effectively upstaged the official receptions planned for the Soviet leader.

This chapter has called attention to some of the main scripts from which Shanghai student protesters worked and to some reasons why it is important to understand the connections between youth movement tactics and other kinds of actions. The topic of how the student protest repertoire

developed is such a large and complex one, however, that it is impossible
to deal with all aspects in detail in a single chapter. Thus the present chapter has been able only to touch upon or had to ignore several topics that
warrant further discussion. The role of popular religious practices in shaping the style of political demonstrations, and the extent to which educated
youths were able to adapt actions seen in operatic performances and other
theatrical events into protest scripts are two subjects that deserve attention.* The influence of Japanese and Korean protests of the May 4th era is
another issue that would need to be addressed before we had a comprehensive picture of how the student tactical repertoire evolved.[†]

The present chapter has been even less exhaustive on two other subjects: the evolution of the May 4th repertoire after 1919, and the ways
in which similarities between protest tactics and other kinds of actions
affected the meaning of student demonstrations. These shortcomings are,
however, remedied to a certain extent in the chapters that follow. All the
case studies of specific mass movements to come pay close attention to the
contribution each new generation of educated youths made to the development of the student protest repertoire. The final chapters return to the
issue of connections between protests and officially sponsored mass actions and focus on their implications for the legitimacy of different ruling
groups.

Despite these limitations, I will consider this chapter successful if it
convinces scholars to pay as much attention to what students *did* when
angered, as they have traditionally devoted to understanding why they be-

---

*The relevance of operatic performances as models for student action was first suggested to
me by David Johnson; recently several commentators on the events of 1989 have drawn similar connections. David Strand, for example, describes Beijing protests of the 1920's and 1980's
alike as possessing an operatic quality. He cites comments by Perry Link (an observer of the
1989 demonstrations) comparing the marches and petition presentations that accompanied
the People's Movement to scenes of "morally charged Beijing opera" (Strand, "Popular
Movement," p. 30), and also highlights the stylistic and rhetorical similarities between the
speeches given by student propagandists of the Republican era and the orations of actors
playing "loyal official" roles in Beijing opera (p. 17).

[†]Political events in Japan and Korea are of special interest. Although Chinese students
seemed largely unaware of contemporaneous student struggles in Latin America, they were
well aware of Japanese and Korean events. Many leaders of anti-Japanese marches in the late
1910's had themselves been students in Japan at some point and had hence observed or at
least heard about Japanese student rallies (for one such rally, see *Japan Advertiser*, Feb. 12,
1918, p. 1). Few would have witnessed Korean student protests firsthand, but almost all would
have read about such events, since Shanghai newspapers such as *Minguo ribao* were filled with
stories about the Korean March 1st Movement during late winter and early spring 1919.
Many of the things Korean students did—e.g., marching en masse to police stations to demand the release of their arrested comrades—were similar to May 4th actions. See the report
in *Shanghai Times*, Mar. 15, 1919, p. 7, and the comprehensive analysis of the Korean unrest
in Frank Baldwin, "The March First Movement: Korean Challenge and Japanese Response"
(Unpublished Ph.D. diss., Columbia University, 1969).

came angry. It is obviously important to know what triggered student unrest, but it is equally clear that we must also try to find out as much as possible about how participants chose their tactics, as well as about the significance of these choices for those who observed or were challenged by youth movements.

The need to look at more than just the causes of student unrest is particularly clear in the case of Shanghai student movements of the Republican era. Patriotic outrage stands out so prominently as the main factor that drove youths to take to the streets that studies focusing upon the specific events and ideas behind campus outbursts run the risk of falling into the same trap as those who use Rostow's "social tension charts" (indexes designed to calibrate such things as unemployment rates and food prices) to explain English bread riots. E. P. Thompson, whose seminal work "The Moral Economy of the English Crowd in the 18th Century" was in large part a response to the Rostow approach, admits that these charts do indeed prove "a self-evident truth (people protest when they are hungry)." By constructing a "national tension chart" (calibrating incidents of foreign aggression and the introduction of new concepts, such as Lenin's theory of imperialism), one could no doubt prove a comparable "truth" (that Chinese students of the Republican era protested when they felt nationalistic). The problem, according to Thompson, is that "if used unwisely," these kinds of charts "conclude investigation at the exact point at which it becomes of serious sociological and cultural interest: being hungry [or in our case feeling patriotic], what do people do? How is their behavior modified by custom, culture, and reason?"[67] The main aim of this chapter has been to answer Thompson's last question. If it has succeeded, its analysis of the collective action scripts of the May 4th era will have given useful insights into at least some ways in which customary procedures, culturally specific patterns of group behavior, and simple reason structured the actions of Shanghai student protesters.

FOUR

THE MAY 30TH MOVEMENT

SHANGHAI STUDENTS WERE SELDOM completely quiescent for more than a month or two during the years immediately following the May 4th Movement. Classroom strikes and other types of campus disturbances known as "student storms" (*xuechao*), inspired by a wide variety of causes (some trivial, some of broad political import), were endemic to academic life throughout the early 1920's.[1] So too were other kinds of political activities, for throughout these years educated youths came together to publicize new incidents of foreign aggression, take part in protest rallies, and commemorate politically charged dates, such as May 4 and May 9 (the day Yuan Shikai accepted Japan's Twenty-one Demands in 1915).[2] As important as these various student struggles and gatherings of the early 1920's were for keeping the May 4th spirit of patriotic engagement alive on Shanghai campuses, the city's educated youths did not take part in a comparable struggle until the May 30th Movement of 1925, which gave them a second chance to use all the tactics in their newfound repertoire in the cause of patriotism.

The story of the May 30th Movement reinforces the thesis, presented in Chapter 3, that protesters tend to rely upon strategies proved successful in the past; many of the techniques the students of 1925 used to express their anger were strikingly similar to those used in 1919. Outraged by new threats to China's national sovereignty and by police repression of the protesters, student participants in the May 30th Movement once again turned to such familiar activities as streetside lecture drives, boycotts, rallies, parades, and mass memorial services to publicize their grievances and to gain redress. Once again, as in 1919, they formed campus unions and citywide

protest leagues, drafted telegrams of complaint, and covered the walls of
the city with handbills and proclamations. And, again as in the May 4th
Movement, their actions culminated in a sanba, which paralyzed the
Shanghai business world and terrified the foreign community.

The events that followed the bloodshed of May 30 were not simply a
replay of those precipitated by the May 4th Incident of 1919, however, either in terms of student activities or in terms of overall accomplishments.
There were important (though in some cases quite subtle) differences between the two upheavals, relating to such things as the ideological tenets
of the students and the influence of party politics on youth protest activities. These contrasts are treated in some detail at the end of this chapter,
but first let us examine the events that led up to the Nanjing Road shooting of May 30, 1925, and those that resulted from it.

STUDENTS AS ALLIES:
THE LABOR UPSURGE OF FEBRUARY 1925

There are several places one can logically begin the story of the May 30th
Movement. For example, one can start with the anti-Christian agitation of
1924 (see Chapter 1), since this struggle to regain control of China's educational system helped pave the way for the fight in 1925 to force the foreign community to return the concessions to Chinese rule. Some leaders
of the May 30th Movement, such as Gao Erbai and Liu Yiqing, gained
their first real experience as organizers and publicists during the anti-
Christian agitation. Many of the propaganda pamphlets of the May 30th
Movement were similar in form to tracts published in December 1924 as
part of Anti-Christian Propaganda Week. The May 30th writers simply
emphasized economic and political as opposed to cultural imperialism and
substituted stories of foreign bosses mistreating native workers or accounts of members of the foreign-run police forces killing unarmed protesters for tales of missionary teachers misleading their Chinese pupils.

The roots of the May 30th Movement can also be traced to attempts,
contemporaneous with the anti-Christian agitation, by Shanghai students
to organize and form alliances with local workers by volunteering to teach
at "people's night schools" and helping to establish recreational clubs for
laborers.[3] The alliances students from Shangda and other schools established through these activities helped lay the foundation for the various
joint worker-student actions of spring 1925 that were so central to the success of the May 30th Movement. These alliance-building activities are
important for another reason: many of the youths who led the mass
movement of 1925—such as the printer Liu Hua (a *bangong, banxue,* or

"part-time work, part-time study," student at Shangda Middle School) and Zhu Yiquan (a sociology student who became principal of a Shangda-run worker night school)—served their political apprenticeship teaching laborers to read and write in 1924.

The idea behind the people's night schools that sprang up throughout the city in 1924 was nothing new. The notion that intellectuals had a special mission to educate the untutored masses dates back at least to the late 1910's, when youths in Shanghai and other cities formed "popular lecture corps" to spread new ideas to illiterate and semiliterate members of the community. The May 4th Movement stimulated new efforts, and in its aftermath groups of progressive students and professors established a number of special schools for workers, which, like their counterparts of 1924, emphasized literacy training. Other New Culture intellectuals organized mass literacy campaigns directed at the inhabitants of nearby towns and villages.[4] The YMCA and other religious organizations sponsored similar schools and campaigns in the late 1910's and early 1920's, and the successes of foreign-run organizations in this field probably inspired the renewed efforts at mass education of 1924, by convincing non-Christian intellectuals that inaction would soon give missionary groups a monopoly of popular education in addition to their virtual monopoly of higher education in China.

However, the proliferation in 1924 of institutions promoting the welfare of the lower classes was rooted in more than simple altruism or a desire to compete with Christian organizations. Some intellectuals had a more explicitly political purpose in mind when they founded night schools and recreational clubs; they intended to use these organizations to promote class and national consciousness and thereby lay the foundation for a revolutionary labor movement. This was certainly true of many Shangda students who took part in the popular education drive of 1924. Often members of the CCP and/or the Socialist Youth League, these youths were committed to the idea that the proletariat was the class best suited to lead the national revolution. They hoped that these clubs and schools would evolve from places where workers came to socialize and take classes into places where workers came to be politicized and mobilized.

The workers in the Japanese-owned mills of the western section of the city—exploited by both imperialism and capitalist economic relationships—seemed an ideal target group for these young organizers. Several Shangda students focused exclusively upon this special population, taking an active role in the newly established West Shanghai Workers' Club. This club, which sponsored a special night school, began as a gathering place where the textile workers of the district came to relax, practice martial arts, and occasionally listen to lectures on economics or contemporary events. However, thanks in large part to the efforts of Liu Hua—who not only lectured at the club's night school but also was one of the organization's chief officers—and of other students from Shangda and Southern University, it quickly evolved into something much more akin to a labor union.

The mill strike of February 1925 served as the catalyst for the transformation of the club into a fully functional union and of students such as Liu Hua (who withdrew from Shangda to devote all his time to the labor movement) from night-school teachers and social workers into full-fledged organizers. The strike grew out of the early February firing by Japanese managers at the Nagai Wata Company's Cotton Mill No. 8 of 40 Chinese adult male employees without warning.[5] Allegedly dismissed for "disobedience of orders," these men were replaced immediately by *yangchenggong* (youths trained by the company who would accept a lower wage and be more docile), an act that angered many of the mill's employees. This dissatisfaction increased when on February 4 the police arrested six of the laborers in question on a charge of "intimidation," after attempts to collect their final wages ended in a fracas with company officials. The workers at Mill No. 8 walked off their jobs that very day and were soon joined by the employees at ten other Nagai Wata factories, in a strike that lasted for almost a month and ultimately affected somewhere between 17,000 and 40,000 workers. The strike was accompanied by outbreaks of *dachang* (literally "hitting the factory," a traditional term for machine-breaking riots) and daily mass meetings, as well as a series of militant demonstrations aimed at preventing scabs from entering the factories. The *North China Herald* criticized the Chinese-controlled police force in western Shanghai for its laxness in suppressing these activities, but before workers returned to their jobs during the final week of February and the first week of March the police had arrested more than 50 people for strike-related activities.

The dispute was a bitter one, and although the violence never got out of hand the way it would in May and June, one confrontation between protesters and police officers almost ended in bloodshed.[6] This confrontation took place in mid-February and began, like the May 30th Incident, with a crowd of protesters marching on a police station to secure the release of a group of their comrades. Even though initial attempts by the Chinese police protecting the station to disperse the mob by shooting into the air proved ineffectual, tragedy was averted (as it would not be on May 30th) when a party of reinforcements from a nearby station broke up the crowd.

The February strike gave students the chance to deepen their alliances with workers at Japanese mills and to refine the propaganda themes, organizational skills, and protest techniques they would use in the May 30th

Movement three months later. Views of the role students played in the events of February vary considerably: some praise student involvement as an act of patriotism; others condemn it as inappropriate youthful meddling.[7] All sources agree, however, that the role was an important one: police reports, newspaper accounts, and memoirs alike testify that educated youths took an active part in unionizing workers, raising funds to support the strike, publicizing the strikers' grievances, and working to gain the release of arrested laborers. Shanghai Municipal Police (SMP) reports claim, in addition, that many participants in the "worker" demonstrations that accompanied the dispute—parades by "strikers" with flags threatening violence to scabs—were in fact members of what the SMP calls the "student class."

One student in particular, Liu Hua, became a central figure in the strike, emerging as the textile workers' chief spokesman and one of the top leaders of their new union. That a young Communist like Liu played so powerful a role in the labor struggle gives some credence to the idea, which newspapers like the *North China Herald* and the *Shishi xinbao* (Current affairs) championed, that the strikes were the work of "bolshevik agitators" connected with radical universities who were determined to use the masses of "peacefully disposed" mill workers for their own selfish purposes.[8] This conspiracy theory is at least partially true: Liu Hua did indeed try to radicalize the laborers he taught and met with, and once the strike wave began, he tried to work his way into a position of authority.[9] So too did other Shangda students who belonged to the CCP, such as Yang Zhihua, who would later marry one of her Shangda professors, party leader Qu Qiubai. According to Mao Dun, Yang not only actively tried to organize female workers throughout the strike wave, but also gave a keynote speech to some 10,000 laborers at a February 9 rally.[10]

Despite these case histories, a purely conspiratorial explanation of the strikes and student involvement is misleading. First, the CCP did not plan the initial protest at Mill No. 8. Communist organizers had been trying for months to sow unrest among workers, but their efforts bore fruit only when management gave the laborers a specific cause around which to rally. Even foreign police officers, who tended to see bolshevik conspiracies everywhere, had to admit that the SMP's "investigation failed to disclose any proof that the strike in question in the primary stage was anything but the result of a real or imaginary grievance."[11]

Second, although people like Yang Zhihua and Liu Hua may have been following party directives, many of the youths involved in organizing and supporting labor strikes were not. A wide range of student groups became involved in the February strike, either by issuing statements criticizing the Nagai Wata management for its treatment of workers or by joining the

consortium of clubs and societies in the Strikers Support Committee (Bagong gongren houyuanhui; hereafter Houyuanhui). Some of these youth
groups were admittedly closely tied to the CCP or its affiliated Youth
League. Others—such as the National Student Union, which issued a
proclamation calling the Nagai Wata strikes a response to the same kinds
of indignities that had inspired the May 4th Movement—contained at
least some members committed to Marxism-Leninism. Most of the dozens
of youth groups that came to the aid of the strikers, however, were not
directly controlled by Communists.*

The Houyuanhui, which took charge of the mammoth task of collecting
funds for strike pay and distributing it daily to a target population of
30,000 workers, was a coalition of more than 40 political, social, and cultural organizations.[12] These groups were very diverse in nature, ranging
from Shanghai's most politically active women's league and the local
branch of the Seamen's Union to an association known as the West Shanghai Four Roads Merchant Alliance. A wide range of student groups also
joined the organization, including both associations (like the Shanghai
Student Union) with roots in earlier mass movements and essentially apolitical clubs. Thus, for example, a group called the Chinese National Salvation Youth Corps was represented at the committee's February 15 meeting, as was the Union of Anhui Province Students Sojourning in Shanghai.
In addition, some Shangda youths came to the meeting as representatives
of the Anti-Christian Federation, but others came because they were
members of one of the school's native-place societies (tongxianghui).[13]
Memoirs claim that a number of the explicitly political groups that joined
the Houyuanhui (e.g., the Anti-Christian Federation and the Shanghai
Student Union), as well as at least some of the nonpolitical associations
(e.g., the Shangda Sichuan Native-place Society), had Communist members. These same memoirs have nothing to say about the majority of the
Houyuanhui's constituent groups, however, and no documentary evidence suggests that more than a handful of the youth associations in-

---

*The clearest indication of this is that the names of most of the youth groups that joined the
Houyuanhui do not appear in any of the memoirs on the May 30th Movement published in
the PRC. These memoirs, most of which were written by people who claim to have been
underground party members at the time, paint an optimistic picture of the influence of Communist cadres in local political circles. These memoirists admit that before the May 30th
Movement no more than a few dozen Shanghai youths were committed to Communism.
They argue, nonetheless, that these youths managed to infiltrate and work their way up to
leadership positions within a wide range of local student groups, and they take pains to document these claims by listing the names of organizations that members of the CCP or the
Socialist Youth League had joined. Whether or not all these claims are valid, references to
youth associations that no memoirist has even tried to present as a Communist front group
are a stong indication that the organization was quite independent of the CCP.

volved had any allegiance to or even connection with the CCP or its Youth League.

Reports concerning Houyuanhui activities suggest, in fact, that the February strike played a crucial role in radicalizing students who had until then not been committed to any political party or ideology. Thanks to the work of CCP organizers and propagandists, the strike was presented from the start as much more than a simple economic struggle. The mill workers' spokesmen, by playing up the fact that the strikers were *Chinese* who were being treated like chattel by greedy foreign industrialists, appealed to the nationalist ideals and sensitivities of all Shanghai students.[14] The experience of the Houyuanhui indicates that this appeal was successful in inspiring at least some of these youths to take militant action. Angered at the thought of Japanese managers mistreating Chinese employees and moved by the economic plight and bravery of laborers willing to risk their jobs for a cause, these newly radicalized youths joined longtime agitators in taking to the streets in support of the strike at the Japanese mills. Thus the February strike gave not only Communist students like Liu Hua a chance to put their training into practice and hone their skills in organizing mass actions, but also many noncommitted youths who would go on to experience in the May 30th Movement their first taste of radical political activity.

STUDENTS AS MOURNERS: MAY 1925

The February strike petered out at the end of the month in compromise settlements, which accorded both sides enough concessions to be able to claim some measure of victory but left workers and employers alike nursing their wounds and feeling unsatisfied. It was no surprise, therefore, when a new round of labor disputes broke out two months later. This strike wave, like its predecessor, began with a walkout at Nagai Wata Mill No. 8 inspired by a specific grievance, in this case a demand for a wage increase. As in February, workers at nearby factories soon joined the strike, labor leaders presented what had started as a simple economic struggle as a battle for national salvation, and students left their campuses to support what they saw as the patriotic efforts of Chinese workers to fight foreign exploitation.

The similarities between the strikes of February and May ended on May 15, however, when several Chinese were injured during a scuffle between mill workers armed with iron bars and Japanese managers armed with pistols. The death two days later of one of the Chinese workers, a young man named Gu Zhenghong, gave the Shanghai labor movement its first important martyr and completed the strike wave's transformation from an economic dispute to a full-fledged nationalist movement. Gu's death also played a vital role in bringing students out in force. The foreign authorities pressured Chinese newspapers to refrain from printing potentially inflammatory accounts of strike-related activities, and when most local press organs ignored the May 15 shooting, educated youths responded in a by-now familiar way—they blanketed the city with streetside lecture teams.

Many students were not content to honor Gu's memory through speeches alone, however, and began to work with labor leaders to plan mass memorial meetings to draw attention to this hero's martyrdom. The first such gathering, which was attended by approximately 2,000 people, took place outside a workers' club on May 18. Liu Hua, who arrived carrying a white flag bearing the slogan "The Chinese people will have revenge for this brutal killing by the Japanese," presided. The main speakers were the martyr's wife and a youth from Wen Zhi University, who began by telling the crowd how cruelly Japanese professors had treated him when he had been in Japan as an exchange student and ended with a cry that Gu's death be avenged.[15]

This gathering was not enough, however, to satisfy Liu Hua and other organizers. They immediately began making plans for a larger and more elaborate memorial service for Gu, to further publicize the mistreatment of Chinese workers in Japanese mills (many of whom were still on strike) and the general injustice of imperialism.[16] The organizers' first step was to publish a notice in the May 22 issue of Shanghai's leading newspaper, *Shen bao*, inviting all associations and schools to send representatives to a memorial on May 24. This announcement gave few details, but two days later *Minguo ribao* published a detailed schedule for the gathering, as well as the names of the people in charge of specific aspects of the rally, such as overall coordination, monitors, and so forth.

This careful planning helped bring between 5,000 and 10,000 people to the gathering, for which the organizers had erected a special speaker's platform, on which a picture of the martyr Gu stood surrounded by wreaths of flowers and plaques supplied by various labor unions. The service proceeded according to plan, beginning with a welcoming address by Liu Hua and the singing of funeral songs. Next came ritual bows to Gu's portrait, more music, some shouting of slogans, additional ritual bows, the taking of a group picture, and a speech on the meaning of Gu's life and tragic death. When the formal service ended after a final musical interlude, representatives of various groups gave speeches to small bands of lingering spectators and passed out leaflets.

A journalist from *Minguo ribao* claimed that "nine out of ten people at the gathering were workers," but, though outnumbered, the students' presence was important for symbolic and pragmatic reasons.[17] Their attendance showed that Gu's death was more than just a labor issue and gave strikers a feeling that they were not alone. A postal worker's account of how he and his co-workers were greeted at the gathering gives a sense of the latter point: "Seeing that we had on long gowns and seemed comparatively refined, [the crowd] took us for 'students,' and excitedly passed the word in whispers 'the students have come.' Their enthusiasm and hope deeply moved us."[18] Students did more, however, than simply show by their attendance that some wearers of "long gowns" were disturbed by Gu's death. They also took an active part in the day's events, particularly those following the close of the formal service; many of those who made speeches and handed out literature during this period were delegates from youth groups.

Students became even more active during the days that followed the May 24 mass memorial, as they mounted publicity drives to spread news of Gu's death and began to give speeches on two related issues that had recently stirred their anger. The first of these side issues was the Shanghai Municipal Council's plan to vote on four controversial bylaws on June 2, including new restrictions on Chinese and Western publications distributed within the International Settlement. Many radical and non-radical intellectuals alike viewed these new bylaws as an affront to China's sovereignty. The second side issue was the SMP's arrest of six student protesters, including four seized while leading a brigade of pupils from the Shangda workers' night school to the May 24 memorial service.[19]

The plight of these arrested students soon grew to be more than an issue of peripheral concern. The foreign authorities turned a deaf ear to attempts by students and professors to negotiate the release of the youths, a decision that would have fateful (and fatal) consequences on the day the prisoners were scheduled to be tried before the Mixed Court: May 30. The first hint that something serious might occur on this date came on the night of May 27, when 32 student representatives from twenty local schools gathered at Tongji to discuss the arrests. The participants in this meeting decided that if the student prisoners had "still not been freed by May 30, then other methods would have to be used to secure their release."[20] They concluded that the best way to pressure the authorities would be to fill the central district of the International Settlement with student lecture teams.[21]

Choosing a stage within the Settlement for their political theater had a strong symbolic appeal: not only would the crowds that regularly thronged downtown streets such as Nanjing Road provide student lecturers with an enormous ready-made audience, but the speechmaking teams would directly challenge the right of the Shanghai Municipal Council to regulate the flow of information among Chinese. As attractive as the idea of lecturing against imperialism in the very heart of the foreigners' lair may have been, however, such an event was full of potential pitfalls. The foreign authorities had already shown themselves less tolerant of student propagandists than their Chinese counterparts, and student speakers, no matter how eloquent and persuasive, would accomplish nothing if they were jailed as soon as they crossed into the Settlement.

The students, well aware of this problem, took careful precautions to make sure that their demonstration was not crushed at the outset. They were aided in these efforts by members of the CCP Central Committee, which included a number of Shangda professors, who decided at an emergency meeting on May 28 to do all they could to help make the events of May 30 a success. Student organizers and their professorial advisers devised detailed plans, which included everything from using special code words to staggering the times lecture teams entered the Settlement, all of which were intended to frustrate any SMP effort to keep student lecturers from gathering en masse in the center of the city in the early afternoon.

Protest leaders spent May 29 and the early hours of May 30 in feverish preparation. They split their time between writing banners and pamphlets, picking people to fill each school's bicycle liaison brigades (the groups in charge of spreading information between lecture teams), and dividing students up into "large," "mid-sized," and "small" brigades (*dui*). The following excerpt from a memoir by a Tongji student named Chen Yuzong shows how detailed a process this division into brigades became and illustrates the reasoning behind it.[22] It describes decisions made at a strategy meeting that began at 11:00 P.M. on the night of May 29, just after a four-hour emergency session of the campus's Self-Governing Society had ended. Virtually the entire student body of Tongji's Wusong campus (located just outside Shanghai proper) took part in the earlier gathering, but the strategy meeting was a much smaller affair, attended by some 30 activists.

> We decided that the 700 Tongji students at the Wusong campus would form one large brigade. . . . In order to avoid the scrutiny of the police and reach our destination, we decided to break this large brigade into fragments, and then form the fragments into a whole again once everyone was in the Settlement. Thus we divided the *dadui* into sixteen small brigades, with a set of four of these small brigades forming a mid-sized brigade. Different mid-sized brigades would leave Wusong for Shanghai at different hours. Each mid-sized brigade would also take one of four different entry routes, and all four small brigades in a given mid-sized one would split up, the rule being that the small brigades would keep a distance of from 500 to 700 meters between them, neither too close nor too far, so that mishaps [i.e.,

the arrest of one group leading to the arrest of another] would be avoidable, but contact would still be easy to maintain.[23]

Chen describes the different routes the mid-sized brigades were to take and the times they would leave—for example, "the first mid-sized brigade was to go from Wusong to the Tiantongan Station at 8:00 A.M., cross the Suzhou Creek at North Sichuan Road, and go down Nanjing Road to the Bund"—as well as the times and places the mid-sized brigades were to rendezvous with each other. He also provides some details concerning intrabrigade structure, by noting that he was selected to serve as both the general commander of the Tongji large brigade, and the "brigade head [*duizhang*] of the sixteenth small brigade attached to the fourth mid-sized brigade." His group was to bring up the rear, and his second in command was to lead the first small brigade into the ciy.[24]

It is unclear from this account whether in the heat of battle each small brigade followed its assigned route, maintained the prescribed distance from the next closest small brigade, or obeyed the instructions of its brigade head, and so forth. In addition, since this description of student strategy was written forty years after the fact, it may idealize the orderliness and precision of the plans themselves. As Chapter 5 shows, however, contemporary sources frequently described students organizing themselves in similarly careful ways for mass actions throughout the Republican era. And even if we allow for embellishment, Chen's memoir and similar accounts of plans at other schools leave a striking impression of student leaders (and the faculty advisers who played key roles at some schools) approaching the problem of staging a demonstration in the heart of the Settlement as if they were generals mapping out an invasion.[25] Although words would be their only weapons, they conducted themselves much like military strategists, as they organized troops, established chains of command (both at the campus and citywide level), took precautions to minimize casualties, and made elaborate arrangements to keep lines of communication open so that orders could be transmitted within and between brigades.[26]

Not even the most carefully crafted of paramilitary plans, however, could make the students immune from police interference on May 30, and it came as no great surprise when the SMP began arresting student lecturers early in the afternoon. What *was* surprising, at least to Inspector Everson of the SMP, who thought at first that he was dealing with isolated groups of student troublemakers, was the reaction to these arrests, a reaction that indicated the strategizing of the night before had not been in vain. Thanks to staggering the times when different brigades entered the concession and to having lecture teams converge on the central district from different parts of the city, when around 2:30 the SMP finally realized the seriousness of the situation and rang the fire bell to signal a crisis, hundreds of students were preparing to head down Nanjing Road toward the Laozha Station to demand the release of their brethren.

Just after the first arrests were made around 2:00, messengers on bicycles began to spread news of the police actions to the small brigades of various schools. Some schools' teams were still scattered throughout the city giving lectures when they heard of the arrests. Other small brigades had already joined to form mid-sized or large brigades and were marching under flags emblazoned with patriotic slogans such as "Shouwei zujie" (Take back the concessions). Still other small brigades were resting at a girls' middle school in the concession that the students were using as a central base of operations. Upon hearing the news of the initial arrests, however, every brigade headed toward the Laozha Station.

By 3:30 hundreds or perhaps even thousands of students, who had been joined en route by workers and other interested spectators, were converging from all directions upon the harried police at Laozha Station. This created an explosive situation, especially since as Thomas Creamer notes, the police were growing increasingly hostile toward the students at precisely the same time.[27] This change in mood can be traced to two incidents. First, during a scuffle between a group of protesters and a constable on Nanjing Road, members of the crowd tried to take the policeman's gun away from him. Second, by 3:30 the Laozha Station itself was filled with youths who had insisted on accompanying their arrested comrades to the station and then refused to leave until these comrades were freed. It was only with a great deal of trouble that the constables (most of whom were Chinese or Sikh members of the Western-run SMP) succeeded in pushing the bulk of these youths out of the station. No sooner had the police cleared the building, however, than a new contingent of demonstrators appeared on the scene, and a crowd now totaling some several thousand began surging toward the Laozha Station. It was then that the police, fearful and confused, heard their commander order them to shoot, and they turned their guns on the crowd of unarmed protesters and curiosity seekers, killing 11 protesters and wounding some 20 others. According to the official police report, this "had the immediate effect of dispersing the crowd" and allowing traffic patterns to return to "normal."[28]

This return to normality was to prove short-lived, however; the bloodshed of May 30 touched off a series of events that disrupted completely all the "normal" patterns of Shanghai life for weeks to come. The extraordinary events of the very next day gave a clear indication of just how militant a form responses to this violence would take. The following passages from the novel *Ni Huanzhi* by Ye Shengtao, a Shangda professor who was present during the demonstration of May 30 and returned to Nanjing Road on May 31 to retrace the steps of the martyrs, evoke the tension and excitement of the day's events.[29] The first excerpt begins with a young teacher named Ni Huanzhi, the novel's semiautobiographical protagonist, walking along Nanjing Road, where "the forces of evil had given their banquet of blood" the previous day, and finding it filled with angry students and workers.

> Suddenly there was a shrill clamour of bells in the middle of the street as four or five bicycles came dashing through the heavy rain from west to east and flashed past. Small slips of paper scattered from the riders' hands, fluttering in their hundreds amidst the rain, and falling soaked to the ground in their hundreds. This was an order, the order to assemble, the order to take action! At once the groups of people clustered on the pavements sprang into life; from the sidestreets and alleyways students and workers poured into the streets and began distributing leaflets with the slogans "Help the workers," "Help the arrested students," "Take back the Concessions," "Down with the imperialists," and others of the kind, and also sticking them on the shop windows on either side of the street; at every corner and in front of every large store there was someone making a speech to a crowd of citizens who had gathered around to listen; slogans were shouted in one place and taken up all around until the rumbling of the trams was drowned and could only be heard faintly, as if from the bottom of a deep valley; every heart was like a cauldron over a fierce fire, seething and boiling, and in every mind was the same thought.

The SMP used various methods to try to disperse this rapidly growing crowd, including turning fire hoses upon groups of protesters, but these had little effect. According to Ye, the multitude was "in a mood to face even bullets." This battle between the protesters and the police, which ultimately resulted in dozens of injuries and produced new martyrs to add to those killed the previous day, continued for some time. Then around 3:00 P.M., by which time "every shop window" in the area was "covered with slogans and leaflets" and every citizen had heard "at least one or two emergency lectures," the protest entered a new phase as bicyclists once more swept past the crowd. According to Ye's account, their cry this time was "Surround the [Chinese] Chamber of Commerce!" The masses responded by surging northward "like a river in flood" toward the temple grounds that housed this civic body.

> The open-air stage at the temple provided them [the protesters] with an admirable platform. The space in front of the stage was packed tight with an enthusiastic and determined crowd who might have been sitting in a hall for all the notice they took of the rain falling on

their heads. They went up on the stage one by one to express their views and then a debate was held to decide what immediate action to take.

The most effective plan was decided on: they would ask the Chamber of Commerce to declare a strike by the shops and markets; if the Chamber did not agree to this then those present would die rather than withdraw! An enthusiastic burst of applause indicated that this plan was approved wholeheartedly.

The girl students undertook the task of picketing the building and keeping guard over every single entrance; until their demands were met, those involved would be allowed to enter the building but not to leave it.

The leaders of the Chamber of Commerce, who had been meeting to discuss their response to the events of the previous day, agreed to meet with the crowd's representatives. After listening to the protesters' demands, the merchants held an urgent conference among themselves to decide whether a market strike was too drastic an action to take. Eventually, either through patriotism or fear or some combination of the two, the merchants decided that the shops of the Chinese city should close to protest the May 30 bloodshed. When the president of the Chamber of Commerce announced this decision to the crowd, according to Ye, "the waves of cheering almost broke against the sky: 'Shop-strike tomorrow! Shop-strike tomorrow! Shop-strike tomorrow!'"[30] Thus for student protesters the month of May ended on both sorrowful and triumphant notes, with the sound of cheers as well as gunshots ringing in their ears.

STUDENTS AS MARTYRS: JUNE–JULY 1925

Thanks to the bloodshed of May 30 and the response it provoked from all segments of the Chinese population, life would not even begin to return to "normal" in Shanghai until the summer was nearly over. The general strike, which the Chamber of Commerce was cajoled into supporting on May 31, began on June 1, but it was only partially effective at first, since some shopkeepers continued to do business and many workers continued to show up at their jobs. Within days, however, the sanba took hold and began to paralyze the commercial life of the city. More and more shops kept their shutters closed, dockworkers refused to unload ships, and employees of the tramway companies stopped running the trolleys, which Ye Shengdao justifiably refers to as the "life-blood" of the city.[31]

There was never any real question, of course, about whether the students would contribute their share to the sanba; from the moment the shots rang out on May 30, many took it for granted that they would be spending their time on the streets rather than in the classrooms for a while. It came as no surprise, therefore, when thousands of students began devoting the hours they had formerly spent on schoolwork to writing pamphlets, publishing broadsheets, promoting a boycott of British and Japanese goods, pasting up wall posters, and raising money for strike funds. Nor was it surprising (in light of past experience) that some of these youths emerged as leaders of the special Labor-Merchant-Student Union established on June 2 to oversee the sanba. This "triple union" performed a variety of functions: it kept lines of communication open between single-class associations, such as the just-formed General Labor Union (GLU), the newly revitalized Shanghai Student Union, and the "street unions" of the shopkeepers; it made sure that at least some degree of order was maintained during the sanba; and it planned several mass rallies, including the giant citizens' assembly of June 11.[32]

The sanba was such a complex undertaking and students became involved in such a wide array of protest activities that it is impossible to do justice to the events of June and July 1925 in a single chapter, let alone a section of one. Fortunately, other scholars have examined many aspects of this phase of the May 30th Movement. The CCP's role in promoting the sanba, the much-publicized trial of the May 30th "rioters," and the even more widely publicized international investigation held to determine whether the police were justified in firing on the crowd have been treated extensively elsewhere.[33] So too have such subjects as the merchant and worker contributions to the general strike and the diplomatic ramifications of the May 30th Tragedy.[34] Rather than reconstructing a comprehensive picture of the struggles of June and July, therefore, the following pages focus on an aspect of the May 30th Movement that has never been analyzed in the detail it deserves: the special meanings attached to student martyrdom and the impact of martyrdom, both as a phenomenon and as a symbol.

Gu Zhenghong's death is an indication of how powerful martyrs could be as rallying points for mass action, but whereas Gu's death at the hands of an imperialist angered many of his fellow textile workers and some student radicals, it left most of the city's residents untouched. The May 30 killing of unarmed protesters, and unarmed students in particular, by members of a foreign police force was something different. Thanks to long-standing cultural ideals, which placed a high value on education and scholarly pursuits, this shooting of Chinese students had the power to inspire an entire nation rather than merely a part of it.[35] Laborers and civic leaders alike valued students as the flower of China's youth, its greatest hope for the future, and hence they viewed the deaths of these scholars as a cruel form of national humiliation. If, for some, Gu's death epitomized the

way in which capitalism and imperialism were physically grinding down
the Chinese worker, for many more the May 30th Tragedy symbolized the
fact that foreigners were robbing the nation of its greatest treasures and
destroying its very soul. The bullets fired that day had an even deeper significance for students themselves: the deaths of their comrades showed
plainly that imperialism was not merely an abstract concept to be hated,
but a force that could kill them simply for speaking out.

The symbolic power of student martyrdom to inspire Chinese of all
classes helps explain why within days of the May 30th Tragedy the patriotic movement had become something so different, in both quantitative
and qualitative terms, from the struggles of the previous months. Radical
propagandists, who realized immediately that these deaths provided them
with the most effective ammunition they had ever had in their fight to
awaken the nation, took great pains to maximize this power and keep the
image of the May 30th martyrs alive. Student activists—motivated both by
genuine outrage and sorrow at the deaths of their comrades (at least two of
whom had been youth movement leaders) and by a keen awareness of the
way these deaths could serve to inspire apathetic classmates and the public
at large—seized upon the symbolism of martyrdom and sacrifice with a
special vengeance, filling their speeches, posters, and publications with images of the shedding of innocent blood.

This fixation with martyrdom, which the massacre in Guangzhou on
June 23 reinforced, manifested itself clearly in propaganda published in
the special May 30th newspapers that professors and students established.
The most famous and influential of these periodicals, *Rexue ribao* (The
hot-blooded daily), was run by Professor Qu Qiubai and other Shangda
teachers and students. The term *rexue* used in this newspaper's name has
two distinct meanings: a literal one of blood that is warm or hot, and a
metaphoric one of devotion to a righteous cause. The editors of *Rexue
ribao* made it clear in the first sentences of the paper's inaugural issue that
they were aware of this dual meaning. Through a literary device found in
many other writings of the May 30th era, they linked the warm blood
spilled on Nanjing Road to the rising tide of patriotism (a form of *rexue* in
its second sense) manifested by the Chinese masses:

> *Yangnu* [slaves to foreigners], *lengxue* [cold-blooded, i.e., lacking in
> valor]—these are the titles of honor public opinion has generally
> awarded to the people of Shanghai! But now the *rexue* of all the
> people of Shanghai has been heated to the boiling point by foreigners'
> bullets; the *rexue* of our fellow students and workers . . . has already
> washed clean the humiliating stigma of being slavish and *lengxue*.[36]

This opening statement ends with more references to blood and further
plays on the contrast between *re* and *leng* (hot and cold, or warm and cool)

by stressing that although for now only the foreigners possessed weapons, their *lengtie* (cold steel) would ultimately be no match for the *rexue* of patriotic Chinese.

Other protest periodicals, such as the special journals published by various student unions during the May 30th Movement, made use of the same kinds of imagery and literary devices. The opening statement of the inaugural issue of *Shangda wusa tekan* (Shanghai University May 30th special), for example, began by drawing contrasts between images of the Chinese people as people whose "blood is cool" and who are given to "five-minute periods of excitement," and the spirit of patriotic commitment symbolized by the "hot blood" of students and workers that flowed on May 30th.[37] Other pieces in the Shangda journal used similarly sanguinary images. A piece by Gao Erbai entitled "The Causes of the Great Bloodshed of May 30th," for example, was filled with compounds containing the character *xue* (blood). Gao ended his essay by claiming, in fact, that foreign mistreatment of Chinese during the months and years preceding the May 30th killing had made it inevitable that at some point the *rexue* of students, who as a group were so "*xueqi*" (staunch and upright), would come to a boil.[38]

Student propagandists at other schools used blood-related imagery even more directly, by incorporating the character *xue* into the titles of their publications. Thus Tongji students distributed the *Wusaxue tekan* (Blood of May 30th special), members of the Fudan Student Union printed copies of *Huaxue bao* (Chinese blood reports), and their counterparts at Jiaotong published *Wusa xuelei* (The May 30th Tragedy).[39] Youths at less famous Shanghai campuses composed and passed out publications with similar titles, such as *Xuehen* (The stain of blood) and *Qingnian de xue* (The blood of youth).[40] The Shanghai Student Union also published a periodical with the term *xue* in its title (*The Tide of Blood Daily*), as did its counterparts in Guangdong (*Guangdong's Tears of Blood*) and Hunan (*Tears of Blood Special*).[41]

The leading CCP organ of the day, *Xiangdao zhoubao* (The guide weekly), which like *Rexue ribao* contained numerous articles by Shangda professors, also ran many pieces that used sanguinary imagery. One of the least subtle but most revealing of these articles (by an author who took the unsubtle pseudonym of "Chi Fu" or "Mr. Red") was called "The Red Blood of the May 30th Movement and the Reddening of China." Chi Fu argued bluntly that innocent blood spilled by foreign bullets could do more than merely change an apathetic citizenry into a patriotic one—it could literally bolshevize a nation by dyeing its people "red."[42]

Poets and novelists also seized upon the terms *xue* and *rexue*, calling on all "hot-blooded" Chinese to rise up to prove that the martyrs of May 30 had not died in vain. Some of these writers also argued or implied, like Chi

Fu, that the deaths of student protesters at foreign hands was emblematic of national disgrace, and the blood of martyrs was a potent substance with transformative or regenerative powers. Thus, for example, the writer Jiang Guangzi (who was teaching at Shangda at the time of the May 30th Movement) included the following lines in a poem composed just three days after the shooting:

> *The British police have killed and wounded countless numbers of*
> *students.*
> *We honor all you who have served as a sacrificial vanguard!*
> *Oh, the dead,*
> *Oh, the dead,*
> *Glorify these dead! . . .*
> *Your blood will irrigate the soil and bring forth bright red flowers.*[43]

Many of the pieces published in the special July 1925 issue of *Xiaoshuo yuebao* (Short story monthly) dedicated to the May 30th martyrs invoked very similar images. Ye Shengtao even used the exact same metaphor of "flowers of blood" in his contribution, which was a meditation on his feelings as he retraced the steps of the May 30 demonstrators on May 31, a kind of nonfiction version of the section from *Ni Huanzhi* quoted above. Another writer's contribution was called simply "The Song of Blood." According to Vera Schwarcz, phrases containing the word *xue* were used so much in this journal and other literary publications of the time that some intellectuals came close to "fetishizing the blood of 1925."[44]

Schwarcz lists a whole range of sanguinary phrases members of the literati employed at the time—such as "mask of blood," "blood's earth," "blood's eyes" and "blood's hands"—but other than *re* the word probably paired with *xue* the most was *lei* (tears). This was in part simply because the compound *xuelei* can mean "tragedy," as in the name of the Jiaotong newspaper *Wusa xuelei*. Some used the phrase in a more literal sense, however, to mean "tears of blood"; the authors of various wall posters and pamphlets, for example, claimed that tears of this sort filled their eyes as they wrote out their denunciations of imperialism.[45] The powerful term *xuelei* thus fused two tragic images: that of the blood martyrs shed and that of the tears mourners wept when they thought of the death of innocents.

Students and other radical propagandists realized, however, that even the most effective literary images were of only limited use when it came to rallying mass support for the patriotic movement. Hence they continually sought more graphic techniques to keep visions of martyrs' blood and mourners' tears fresh in the popular mind. Dramatic re-enactments of the events of May 30th were one of the most effective of such techniques. Li Jianmin (Li Chien-min), a scholar at the Academia Sinica in Taiwan who has completed the most thorough study of May 30th propaganda to date, lists the titles of 57 different plays and skits dealing with the Nanjing Road shooting and related events, all performed in Shanghai and other cities in 1925.[46] Li notes that more than a quarter of these plays, most of which were put on in the streets by students, have the terms *xue* and/or *lei* in their titles.[47] Thus, for example, the Shanghai Youth Lecturing Society performed a skit entitled simply "Bloodshed," Jiaotong students mounted a production called "The Tears of Patriots," and the pupils of a Huzhou girls school staged the "Tears of the Shanghai River." A British consular official in Ningbo noted that a "most popular" dramatic presentation put on by students in his area was called "The Rising Tide of Blood in the Shanghai Settlements."[48]

Youths did not confine their dramatic efforts to formal presentations, however. At times they also used more innovative forms of "street theater" to invoke images of blood and tears. One of the most interesting involved specially organized troupes of "criers," such as the Kneel and Wail Corps (Guikutuan) of Tianjin. According to Li Jianmin, these troupes devised the only true innovation in the May 30th propaganda campaign. The troupes met regularly to practice wailing and then put this practice to use at gatherings such as mass memorial services, during which they would mount a podium and cry in unison. According to press reports, the largest of these wailing corps, the Human Sympathy Association (Rendaohui), had over a hundred members.*

Students also incorporated sanguinary imagery into their street theater, as a report submitted to the British Foreign Office by the consul-general of Amoy (Xiamen) in June 1925 illustrates. The report noted that youths in that city, not content to use anti-imperialist slogans to remind people of the Shanghai massacre, had taken to smearing blood on the flags they carried when they paraded on local streets.[49] Youths in other cities used similar methods to identify symbolically with the Shanghai martyrs: even in remote Qiongshan, on the island of Hainan, students wore "clothes splashed with red ink to simulate blood," while they collected funds on "streets in which pictures of Chinese corpses [were] posted."[50]

The reference to "pictures of Chinese corpses" brings us to another important technique student propagandists used to reinforce the horror of the Shanghai killings and fan the flames of popular indignation: representations of the martyrs themselves. Virtually everywhere Shanghai residents turned during June and July 1925 their eyes were met by such

---

*Organized weeping groups also played a role in rural unrest. Thus, for example, Elizabeth Perry describes the activities of an organization known as the Mourning Clothes Society, whose members wore white turbans and upon meeting enemies "wept loudly in an effort to unnerve their opponents" (*Rebels and Revolutionaries*, p. 204).

representations, which ranged from crude woodblock caricatures to repro-
ductions of photographs taken at hospitals. The walls near public parks,
where people gathered to read newspapers in ordinary times, were now
covered with simple drawings of protesters (most of whom were shown
wearing the longcoats indicative of members of the intelligentsia) being
killed by foreigners, placed above short anti-imperialist captions.[51] The
pamphlets passed out by the students who swarmed the city's streets were
peppered with woodblock prints and other types of visual representations
of martyrs' bodies. One of the most elaborate of these propaganda tracts,
Wusa xue'an shilu (A true record of the May 30th murders), for instance,
contained a dozen photographs of bullet wounds, as well as a photograph
of the bloodstained clothing a student martyr had been wearing when he
was gunned down by the SMP.[52]

This concern with physical evidence helped bring the reality of the killings home to those who had not actually witnessed the bloodshed, but
propagandists also tried to make the dead seem more than simply deper-
sonalized corpses by devoting attention to the lives of the victims of the
gunfire on Nanjing Road as well as their deaths. The life stories of the
three student martyrs, in particular, were told and retold in speeches,
pamphlets, and newspaper articles. This was in part because, as noted
above, student deaths simply had the most power to move public opinion.
It was also, no doubt, partly because the students and other intellectuals
who gave the speeches and wrote the "martyrs' biographies" (*lieshizhuan*)
identified most closely with the three educated youths and had ready access to information about their lives.[53]

These biographies generally included personal details about the deceased, such as the name of his home town, his age, and school affiliation;
praise of his special virtues; a description of the family members and
others specially affected by his death; and a call for the audience to avenge
his martyrdom. Thus, for example, "Chen Yuqin lieshi chuanlie" (Biographical sketch of the martyr Chen Yuqin), published in the June 7 edition of *Rexue rikan*,[54] begins by stating that the youth was sixteen years old,
was the son of a coconut oil merchant, and had an older brother who was a
star soccer player and a sister who was studying at Datong University. It
goes on to state that Chen was twelve years old when he came to Shanghai
from his Southeast Asian birthplace, that he attended first the primary and
then the middle school affiliated with Jiaotong University, and that he was
the leader of a Cub Scout troop. The piece then ends by listing some of
Chen's virtues (for example, his promise as a scholar and an athlete), the
nature of the injury he received on May 30, the time he died on the following day, and the people who were saddest when they heard the news of his
death (his teachers, his fellow classmates, and the leaders of the Shanghai
Boy Scout Association).[55]

The biographical sketch of Chen's fellow student martyr, Yi Jingyi, which appeared in the same newspaper, is even more hagiographic.[56] The article describes Yi, a twenty-year-old Tongji student, as a youth who was "intelligent and brave," had "lofty ambitions" (*dazhi*), and was ready to lay down his life for his country. It then goes on to detail the events of May 30 itself, noting that Yi was one of the two students who took charge of directing the activities of Tongji students during the demonstration, telling how and when he was wounded, and mentioning that the English police stopped Yi's classmates from taking the martyrs' blood-drenched clothing away with them as a remembrance of their dead comrade.[57] The biography then concludes—after stating that Yi's parents had predeceased him, but that he was survived by his wife and a brother in Qingdao—with the words "this unfortunate sacrifice for his country, oh, what an injury!"

He Bingyi, the third student martyr, also earned a laudatory biographical sketch in *Rexue rikan*,[58] as well as an even more hagiographic eulogy in *Shangda wusa tekan*.[59] The second eulogy praises the twenty-two-year-old Shangda student as someone who was "loyal and brave" and "esteemed by teachers and friends." It also says that even as he lay dying in a pool of blood on Nanjing Road, he continued to shout out patriotic slogans such as "Long live the Republic" and "Down with imperialism."[60] This same anecdote figures prominently in another tribute to He, a handbill Shangda students distributed on the street to commemorate his death.[61] This leaflet, issued in the name of the Shangda Student Union, shows clearly that personal details concerning a martyr could not only help make the fact of death more real but also directly inspire those who survived to rededicate themselves to the cause of patriotism. It reads as follows:

> Oh, He Bingyi, our beloved classmate and patriotic martyr! Even now your dead body is returning to its native place! When your patriotic blood flowed on Nanjing Road, it penetrated into the heart of the nation's citizenry; those three cries of "Long live the Republic" shouted from amid a pool of blood will keep the blood in young men's hearts boiling forever. . . . Beloved compatriots! So that we will not have let this patriotic martyr's blood flow in vain, we must strive to settle accounts with our imperialist enemies. Arise, arise, everyone arise! Our martyr is already dead and buried, while our enemy is still destroying our nation; so fight against imperialism for all you are worth! It is the enemy that massacres China's patriotic young men!

All the themes encountered in the preceding discussion of martyrdom, from a fascination with the imagery of blood to a desire to present the deceased as distinctive and distinctly worthy individuals, came together in a single day's event: the June 30 mass memorial service the leaders of the Labor-Merchant-Student Union organized to mark the one-month anniversary of the heroes' deaths. Press reports of the size of this event vary greatly. The radical *Minguo ribao* claimed that around 200,000 people (most of whom were workers or students) came to the Recreation Ground that day, but the *North China Herald* insisted that only some 20,000– 30,000 took part in the ceremony.[62] Whichever figure is closer to the truth, it is clear that the event far surpassed any of the gatherings held for the laborer Gu Zhenghong and was easily the equal in size of any of the mass meetings of the May 4th era. It was a carefully planned affair, in which representatives from some 150 organizations, including all the major local colleges, took part.[63] Thanks to the efforts of various peacekeepers—ranging from specially assigned troops of Chinese soldiers to Boy Scouts to the two monitors (*jiucha*) each participating organization was ordered to select—it was also an orderly one. The *North China Herald* claimed even "members of the hated foreign press" could pass through the crowds "in perfect safety, though they were assailed with fluent Chinese curses."[64]

The gathering was much like comparable protests of the past, such as the service held in the same grounds six years previously to honor the Beijing student martyr Guo Qinguang. As the *North China Herald* put it, the participants "went through the ordinary Chinese commemorative procedure—bows, periods of silence, shouts, music, etc."[65] There were, however, a couple of extraordinary things about this particular service. One of the most noteworthy was the unusually elaborate way the organizers chose to display physical artifacts and memorabilia associated with martyrdom, both on and around the altar erected in the middle of the park.

This altar itself was an impressive sight, bedecked with multicolored scrolls eulogizing the May 30th martyrs and those who had been killed during the protests of the following days, but the two special booths to either side were even more eye-catching. The booth on the altar's left was a "hall of portraits" (*yixiangting*). Its outer walls were covered by large pictures of the martyrs' faces and giant cloth scrolls filled with information concerning their deaths: its motto was "heroes" (*jiexiong*). To the right of the main altar was the "hall of bloodstained clothes" (*xueyiting*).* This

---

*Bloodstained clothing had special importance during the May 30th Movement, not only as symbols of martyrdom itself but also in some cases as tangible proof that the police lied when they said that they fired only into onrushing crowds. Chinese propagandists claimed, and medical evidence presented at the trial of the May 30th "rioters" supported them, that some youths had been shot in the back. Bullet holes in the backs of bloody shirts were powerful confirmation of this point. This concern with the precise places shots entered the martyrs' bodies also helps account, in part, for the number of photographs of corpses contained in student publications. For more on bloodstained clothing, see Jiaotong University School History Group, *Jiaotong daxue*, p. 767; for the medical evidence on bullet wounds, see the transcript of the trial published as a special supplement to the *North China Herald* in summer 1925.

booth, as its name suggests, was filled with garments the martyrs had been wearing when they were shot, which interested members of the audience could examine at close range: its motto was "tears of blood" (*xuelei*).[66]

The May 30th Movement continued long after this ceremony for the Nanjing Road martyrs, but since the final stages of the struggle have been treated thoroughly by other authors, I will end this narrative of the protests of 1925 here.[67] The memorial service of June 30 is, moreover, a particularly fitting place to conclude a case study of the May 30th Movement. Not only was the rally one of the highlights of the sanba and an impressive spectacle of multi-class national unity, it was also a testament to the central role the imagery of blood and martyrdom played in inspiring Chinese protesters to take action to fight imperialism throughout the spring and summer 1925. We can now return to the topic posed at the beginning of this chapter: the differences between the mass movements of 1919 and 1925.

MAY 4TH AND MAY 30TH

Although much that occurred in May and June 1925 was familiar enough to give those who had watched the May 4th Movement six years previously a strong sense of déjà vu, many features of youth activism had changed during the intervening years. The most obvious was the increased importance of workers as an independent protest force and a component in student strategy. Although Shanghai's May 4th Movement culminated in a sanba involving urbanites of all classes and workers took part in many anti-Japanese mass actions in 1919, the role of labor in the May 30th Movement was qualitatively different. Because this book's main concern is with student protesters, the preceding pages have focused almost exclusively upon the political activities of educated youths in 1925. But because textile strikes were important in triggering the May 30th Movement and some educated youths (such as Liu Hua, who was a working printer, a factory organizer, and a part-time student at Shangda) were part of both the academic and laboring worlds, even this student-centered approach has indicated how crucial worker performances—as strikers and marchers, martyrs and mourners—were to the drama and tragedy of 1925.

The other key difference between the May 4th and May 30th movements concerns the role of political parties. Despite attempts—first by contemporary Japanese observers and more recently by scholars and memoirists in Taiwan—to paint an exaggerated picture of the contributions Sun Zhongshan and his advisers made to the Shanghai student protests of 1919, professional politicians and GMD leaders played a very minor role in the May 4th Movement. It is true that Sun, who was living in

Shanghai at the time, met with some of the national student leaders who gathered in the city in June 1919. It is also true that on occasion youth activists turned to other GMD leaders such as Tang Shaoyi for advice. Nonetheless, on the whole, party politics had little to do with the development of the Shanghai student movement in 1919.

The situation was different in the mid-1920's, since some of the students who assumed leadership roles during the struggles of that era were members of the Socialist Youth League, and many of the most influential professors at Shangda were leading figures in the CCP and/or the GMD. Just how crucial a role the Communists played in determining the course of the May 30th Movement has long been debated. In 1925 propagandists seeking to discredit the struggle spent much energy trying to show that Chinese students and workers were mere pawns in a scheme devised by Russians and implemented by unscrupulous native "bolsheviks." And although at the time (for obvious tactical reasons) CCP writers vehemently decried this accusation as completely unfounded, later Communist historians and memoirists have boasted proudly that the party masterminded the movement. Other writers, both in 1925 and in subsequent years, have argued that this image of the struggle as the brainchild of Communist strategists is partially or wholly inaccurate. Some have gone so far as to claim that if anyone was calling the shots, it was the GMD.[68]

The biases inherent in much of the available evidence make it difficult to come to any firm conclusions regarding this dispute, but several things are clear. First, although the CCP was committed to fostering anti-imperialist sentiments among students and workers throughout the mid-1920's, contemporary propaganda painting May 30th activists as doing the bidding of Russian masters was grossly misleading. The Soviets gave some financial and moral support to the movement, but the CCP does not seem to have been under direct Comintern command at the time. In fact, several sources indicate that local party activists at times caused "considerable embarrassment" to their Russian advisers.*

Second, although many of the leading propagandists and organizers involved in the May 30th Movement were committed Communists, in some cases CCP writers have probably exaggerated the "redness" of important figures in the movement. Thus, for example, although people like Liu Hua and Yang Zhihua had ties to the CCP, Communist claims regarding the ideological leanings and party affiliations of other figures need to be taken with a grain of salt. Gu Zhenghong's alleged conversion to Communism is

---

*The USSR signed an important military agreement with Japan just before the February strike wave broke out. As a result, Soviet advisers wanted Chinese revolutionaries to refrain from anti-Japanese protests. See Rigby, *May 30th Movement*, p. 25.

a case in point. Non-CCP materials provide few personal details of the young laborer's life, suggesting that he was simply an average mill worker, but hagiographic works published in the PRC claim that Gu was a member of the CCP.[69] Richard Rigby notes that there is "no reason to believe this is true," since contemporary Communist sources make no reference to Gu's party affiliation.[70]

Third, although the evidence is strong that plans made in secret meetings of CCP strategists shaped some phases of the movement, in many cases the party was clearly forced to respond to and try to capitalize on events and activities beyond its control. This was true in the case of the February strike wave, and it was as true in May as it had been three months earlier. The May 30th demonstration was a carefully planned event, which students and professors affiliated with the CCP played leading roles in organizing, but the convergence upon the Laozha Station was not. This may have been what a Chinese Communist had in mind some years later when he told the journalist George Sokolsky: "We did not make May 30: it was made for us."[71] Here, as in many instances, it is inaccurate to think of protests in black and white terms, as either purely "spontaneous" or purely "orchestrated" affairs; most of them fall into the large gray area between these poles.

What all of this suggests is that one needs to acknowledge the vital role that individual Communists played in the movement, but should also keep in mind that the struggle had an independent life of its own. Many of the movement's leaders, including some of those who assumed positions of authority in the crucially important Labor-Merchant-Student Union, were members of the CCP or its Youth League, but even their actions cannot be explained as simple attempts to follow a unified set of party directives. They often had to respond to specific situations on the spur of the moment without orders from the Central Committee.[72] It is also worth remembering that Communists were a minority within virtually every major protest organization and hence had to continually make compromises with their allies.

By the time the May 30th Movement ended, however, Communists had become much less of a minority within many campus organizations. Party membership grew approximately tenfold, in fact, from just under 1,000 to around 10,000, during the second half of 1925 alone.[73] As this figure indicates, not only is it fair to say that the May 30th Movement was "made for" the CCP, but one could even say that this struggle "made" the party. Thanks largely to the skillful way radical organizers and propagandists seized the opportunities presented by the bloodshed of Nanjing Road, 1925 was the year the CCP established itself as an influential political entity with a solid popular power base.

The CCP was not, however, the only political party that supported and benefited from nationalist mass actions in 1925; the GMD also played a significant role in the May 30th Movements and gained converts. The available evidence suggests that the GMD had much less influence on Shanghai protesters during 1925 than did the CCP. It is hard to say anything definite about this difference, however, because in 1925 Communists often belonged to both parties. This problem of dual membership means that anyone wishing to sort out the relative importance of the CCP and GMD in shaping the May 30th Movement must deal with the classification problems posed by people like Yun Daiying of Shangda. In the immediate wake of the May 30 shootings, Yun—who was concurrently a member of the CCP, the secretary of the Shanghai GMD's Youth Department, and an influential adviser to leading student activists—went directly from an emergency meeting at GMD headquarters to a gathering of the CCP's Central Committee.[74] Thankfully we do not need to waste time here on trying to figure out whether Yun is best seen as a Communist who happened to be a GMD official or a GMD official who happened to belong to the CCP, but can merely reiterate that political parties played a much more central role in the student movement of 1925 than they had in that of 1919.

The alliance between the CCP and the GMD, though still close enough to accommodate people like Yun, was already marred by intense disputes between left-wing and right-wing groups. This leads us to another major difference between the May 4th and May 30th student movements: the greater importance of factional divisions in shaping the latter. PRC memoirs by former May 4th student activists present a picture of the Shanghai Student Union of 1919 as an organization almost completely free of factional strife, and comparable works published in Taiwan give a similar impression of unity. By contrast, according to May 30th activist Li Qiang, by 1925 the Shanghai Student Union had split into three distinct factions: radicals, rightists, and noncommitted centrists.[75] Whereas the common commitment to patriotism that had united Shanghai's May 4th students continued to bind May 30th youths, by 1925 this unity was tempered and sometimes directly threatened by the increasingly bitter battle between rival factions that were often linked to Communist or anti-Communist groups.[76]

The factional struggles within the student movement, which were matched by intense fights between rival labor organizers and organizations,[77] manifested themselves in fierce debates over such things as tactics. According to Li, left-wing students were in favor of defying the orders of the Shanghai Municipal Council and continuing to hold demonstrations in the International Settlement after May 30, but their right-wing opponents wanted the Shanghai Student Union to confine itself to "legal" activities. The division between leftists and rightists occasionally led to more than mere polite expressions of differing opinions. Li recounts, for example, his anger when a delegate from St. John's University "slandered" Shangda as a bolshevik institution, which "promoted revolution but not education" and probably received outside (i.e., Russian) funding. Sometime later Li and a friend confronted this student and quizzed him about his views. According to Li, "because we were young and had fiery tempers, after a few sentences of the argument, fists started flying." The fight ended with Li's opponent threatening to call the police, after which the St. John's youth "didn't dare come to the Shanghai Student Union."[78]

The growing importance of organized political parties in student politics also helps explain another major difference between May 4th and May 30th students: the greater ideological sophistication of the latter. Both generations of protesters were motivated by a desire to save China from outside exploitation and internal decay. Participants in the events of 1919 did not, however, place this desire for national salvation within a broad intellectual framework, nor did they use it as a basis for a general political program. Although the May 4th *era* was one of China's greatest periods of intellectual ferment and experimentation, the May 4th *protests* remained fairly narrow in focus. Students stuck to limited goals in 1919—getting the "traitorous" officials out of power, making sure that the Chinese delegation did not sign the peace treaty—and their propaganda focused on relatively simple traditional images of outsiders threatening the land with "national extinction" (*wangguo*), a concept discussed in more detail in Chapter 8.

The student protesters of 1925, by contrast, placed their struggle in a broader conceptual framework and had more ambitious goals. Why this was so is easiest to explain in the case of those comparative few who were members of the Socialist Youth League or the CCP; upon conversion to Marxism-Leninism, they acquired a fully elaborated theory of revolution, which included a trenchant analysis of imperialism and a commitment to fighting for comprehensive changes in the status quo. During the years immediately preceding the May 30th Movement, even those students who were not affiliated with any political party had grown familiar with the concepts involved in this "ism." They had also grown familiar with key components of Western Enlightenment thought, such as the notion of individual "rights," which had become central fixtures in Chinese intellectual discourse during the May 4th era. The previous year's anti-Christian movement, whose propaganda attacked missionaries as "cultural imperialists" and demanded "educational rights," gave some May 30th activists firsthand experience with using the new concepts for political purposes.

Thanks to these factors, Shanghai students had the political vocabulary and conceptual ammunition to go beyond simply decrying the Nanjing Road killings as a barbaric act, a blot on national pride. The familiar themes of national humiliation figured prominently in student propaganda pamphlets and magazines of the time, especially those aimed at a wide audience, but these same publications also tried to show that events such as the massacre of May 30 were not isolated occurrences but part of a whole system of exploitation. Missionary control of education, the mistreatment of native laborers by foreign employers, and the Shanghai Municipal Council's direction of a police force empowered to arrest or even kill Chinese who dared to raise their voices in protest—all these, according to May 30th propagandists, were but different faces of a single monster: imperialism.

This view that the city of Shanghai and the Chinese nation as a whole were being threatened by something much more complex than a mere clique of "traitorous" officials had as profound an impact upon May 30th demands as it did on May 30th propaganda. Thus, for example, although some of the famous Thirteen Demands the Labor-Merchant-Student Union issued on June 7 focused on specific issues relating to the massacre—for example, one called for the Shanghai Municipal Council to compensate the families of the May 30th martyrs—others were of a much broader nature: the abolition of extraterritoriality, "absolute freedom of speech" for all Chinese living in the International Settlement, and official recognition of the right for workers to form unions and hold strikes.[79]

This commitment to basic changes in the whole structure of foreign activities in Shanghai, summed up in the popular slogans "Shanghai for the Shanghainese" and "Take back the concessions," helps account for yet another difference between the youth movements of 1919 and 1925: the more lenient attitude of the foreign authorities toward the former. The Shanghai Municipal Council eventually decided that the May 4th protests posed a threat to its authority, but throughout much of the movement it treated student activists with sympathy and restraint. The situation was very different in 1925, in part because British goods as well as Japanese ones were being boycotted, in part because of fears of bolshevik conspiracies, in part because crowds seemed more disposed to violence, but most of all because of a realization that the protesters were challenging a whole way of life.

Whatever the reason, the foreign authorities responded to the protests that followed the killing on Nanjing Road with a repressive campaign unlike anything they had even considered in 1919. On June 1, they issued a proclamation prohibiting "any action that may cause a crowd to collect in the public streets" of the International Concession and ordered the populace to refrain from printing or exhibiting political flags and banners.[80] On June 4 they raided Shangda. By June 6, a total of 22 foreign warships from three Western countries and Japan had anchored in the Shanghai harbor. The May 30th students and workers made it clear in their propaganda that they wanted to wage war against imperialism; the foreign powers responded by turning the International Concession into a war zone, complete with machine-gun posts on many of its main street corners.[81]

Thanks in large part to the might of the enemy and the ambitiousness of the students' demands, the May 30th Movement was in one sense much less "successful" than its predecessor of 1919. Whereas the May 4th Movement's sanba ended on a celebratory note, with victory parades in honor of the dismissal of the three "traitors" in Beijing, the general strike of 1925 ended in disappointment and compromise. The alliance of students, workers, and merchants upon which the strike was based proved no match for the defenders of foreign privilege. This was especially true as the strike wore on and native as well as foreign business began to suffer. However strong their patriotism, Chinese factory owners knew that some propagandists were claiming that both imperialism *and* capitalism were evil, and that in many ways a radicalized work force was a greater danger to their livelihood than was the power of the Shanghai Municipal Council. Similarly, many warlords and Chinese government officials had supported the patriotic protests while the bloodstains on Nanjing Road were fresh, but most turned against the movement before the summer was out because of propaganda that claimed the corruption and weakness of domestic leaders had played a crucial part in reducing China to its present pitiable state.

The May 30th Movement was by no means a failure, however, even though the sanba achieved few of its announced goals. First, the strike led to some short-term changes in the structure of foreign privilege, such as the Shanghai Municipal Council's decision to allow Chinese representatives into its ranks. Much more significantly, by bringing thousands of converts into the CCP and the GMD, the May 30th Movement provided the two parties with the strength to wage their successful Northern Expedition against the warlords in 1926–27.

An additional difference between the May 4th and May 30th movements was the greater interest May 30th students showed in radicalizing and mobilizing workers. Educated youths took some steps to establish alliances with laborers in 1919, and much of their propaganda was directed at the proletariat. May 4th students did not, however, direct nearly as much of their energy toward workers as did their May 30th counterparts. Moreover, whereas in 1919 campus activists were interested almost exclusively in encouraging laborers to take actions that aided multi-class struggles, such as the sanba and the anti-Japanese boycott, in 1925 students were also concerned with helping workers improve working conditions at local factories.

Despite these contrasts, however, the May 30th student protesters had much in common with their predecessors of 1919. Some new factors had begun to shape student political action by the mid-1920's, but the events of 1925 are so clearly recognizable as variations upon May 4th themes that it is fitting to end this chapter with a brief recap of some of the things the two generations of protesters had in common. The most basic point of similarity has to do with motivation: the youths of the May 4th and May 30th movements took to the streets to protest attacks on the dignity of their country and the bodies of their comrades, and both saw themselves as fulfilling a moral role as the conscience of a nation. Once on the streets, moreover, they acted in identical or almost identical ways. The May 30th Movement may have had fewer victory parades, and street fights between protesters and police may have been more common. Nonetheless, the May 4th "repertoire" described in Chapters 2 and 3 remained essentially intact: the student protesters of 1925 relied heavily upon the same basic mix of tightly organized mass rallies, colorful processions, streetside speechmaking drives, boycotts, and the like that their predecessors had turned to in 1919.

In addition, both groups of Shanghai students performed the same set of protest roles, acting as agitators and allies, mourners and martyrs, organization builders and strikers, "law" enforcers and keepers of order.[82] The specific ways these roles were performed varied. In 1925, for example, rather than building a protest league from the ground up, students merely had to reorganize the extant but atrophying Shanghai Student Union.[83] May 30th youths added some new twists to May 4th "law" enforcement roles: along with organizing inspection teams to go from store to store to prevent the sale of boycotted goods, some youths began policing the waterways as well, and in several notorious cases of "piracy" or "customs inspection" (depending on one's point of view), they boarded ships and seized "illegal" cargo.[84] Through these and comparable innovations, the students of 1925 demonstrated their capacity for improvisation. More often than not, however, they found themselves following quite closely in the footsteps of their predecessors, adapting the same kinds of scripts, performing the same kinds of roles, and posing the same kinds of challenges to the established order as their heroes—the student protesters of 1919.

Wall poster that appeared in Beijing during the May 30th Movement of 1925 (*from the Erik Clark Collection, Hoover Institution Archives, Stanford University*)

A march in Beijing protesting the killings in Shanghai on May 30, 1925. Note the English-language slogans and the prominent display, just behind the picture of a martyred protester, of a school flag emblazoned with the name of a local middle school (*from the Erik Clark Collection, Hoover Institution Archives, Stanford University*)

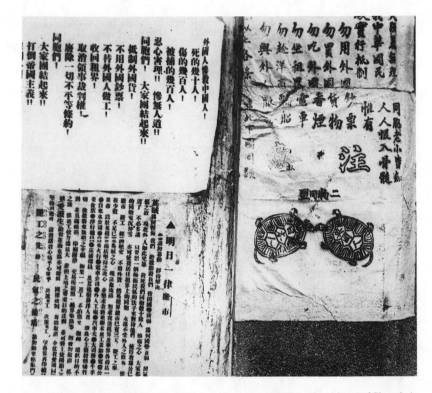

Examples of May 30th propaganda: the handbill on the right urges the citizens of Shanghai, among other things, not to use foreign currency, buy foreign goods, ride on buses operated by the International Settlement, or serve foreigners. The two turtles are labeled "Englishman" and "Japanese"; the caption above them reads "Two things make an alliance." The notice at the top left summarizes the events of May 30 and calls on "brothers" to boycott foreign goods, not to use foreign currency, not to work for foreigners, to recover the International Settlement, to eliminate extraterritoriality, to abrogate all unequal treaties, and to overturn imperialism. The notice at the bottom left calls on Shanghai's citizens to punish the *Yingzei* (British bandits or villains) responsible for the May 30th bloodshed by observing a *bashi* (market strike) the following day and by supporting the ongoing *bagong* (labor strike) *(photo submitted to the U.S. State Department by Consul-General Cunningham; courtesy National Archives)*

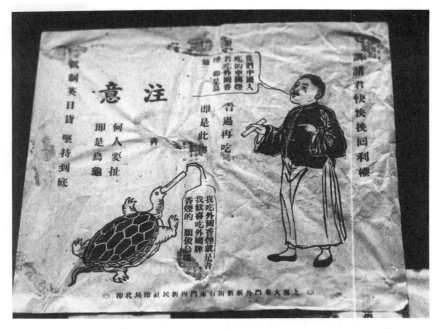

An example of May 30th Movement propaganda: a patriotic citizen smokes only Chinese cigarettes; only turtles smoke foreign brands *(photo submitted to the U.S. State Department by Consul-General Cunningham; courtesy National Archives)*

Bulletin board of the Youth Announcement Group during the May 30th Movement. Among the visible posters are two calling on citizens not to sell food to foreigners and not to work for the English or the Japanese *(photo submitted to the U.S. State Department by Consul-General Cunningham; courtesy National Archives)*

Streetside posters during the May 30th Movement, Shanghai. Depictions of turtles are
visible on two of the posters; the English-language poster calls on the foreign residents of
Shanghai to vote against three proposals that would have restricted Chinese-run businesses
*(photo submitted to the U.S. State Department by Consul-General Cunningham; courtesy National
Archives)*

FIVE

ORGANIZATION
AND MOBILIZATION

ONE OF THE MOST STRIKING FEATURES of all the great Shanghai student movements of the Republican era is the speed and ease with which students were able, in each case, to translate anger over specific events into coherent, sustained, organized outbursts of collective activity. Previous chapters have looked in some detail at two examples of this phenomenon; later incidents triggered a similar pattern of student responses. During the 1930's and 1940's, students would waste no time establishing special protest committees and filling the streets with lecture teams. Within days of the initial incident, each of these youth movements would, like their predecessors of 1919 and 1925, take on a highly bureaucratized form, complete with specialized teams (each with a leader and often a second in command) to plan mass rallies and demonstrations. These mass actions would typically be tightly organized affairs, in which participants would be grouped into big, mid-sized, and small brigades, each commanded by its own brigade head.[1]

Chapter 3 has already shown that one reason students involved in mass actions found coherent, joint actions easy was that their tactics were often variations upon familiar activities. However, the organizational efforts and the mobilization process required to get large numbers of youths out onto the streets in the first place have not been explored. How were brigades formed and brigade heads chosen? Where did campus protest leaders come from, and how did they make contact with their counterparts at other schools? Who made the banners students carried and the leaflets they distributed, and how were the groups placed in charge of such matters formed? These are the kinds of detailed queries this chapter examines, in an effort to shed light on the general question of why students consistently proved so much more effective than members of other urban social groups at mounting highly organized, large-scale protest drives between 1919 and 1949, as well as in more recent decades.[2]

Members of other social groups mobilized themselves (or were mobilized) for large-scale collective action throughout the Republican period, but none did so with the regularity, speed, scope, or combination of apparent spontaneity and tight organization of the students. As earlier chapters have indicated, educated youths often depended on support from workers and shopkeepers to give their protests added clout, and in some cases student-led mass movements evolved out of struggles waged by merchants or laborers. This said, with the exception of the May 30th Movement and other struggles of the mid-1920's, in which laborers either shared the vanguard position with educated youths or took the lead on their own, students played the central role in all the great mass movements of the era. Throughout the Republican era, no other group could match educated youths when it came either to mobilizing large numbers of people for political action or to establishing an organizational network capable of coordinating the activities of these people once mobilized. And, as recent events have illustrated, the same can be said of the Communist era: in 1989 students once again demonstrated their unusual ability to mount highly organized, large-scale mass actions quickly and efficiently.

Many factors help account for this phenomenon. Scholars working on the Republican era, for example, often highlight CCP infiltration of campus organizations and the special anger students felt at the arrest or killing of classmates as key factors in the mobilization process. Although both factors are clearly significant, they do not explain the special features of student mobilization. After all, students were not the only ones with special grievances during the Republican era; laborers suffered a great deal more at the hands of foreigners and native authorities than did educated youths and hence had at least as many reasons to take collective action. Nor were educated youths the only ones in whom CCP organizers were interested; throughout the 1920's and 1930's in particular, the party devoted at least as much attention to politicizing workers. Explanations based on the role of Communist organizers become even more problematic when one remembers the speed and ease with which students mobilized for action in the late 1980's without the help of trained party agitators.

In order to understand why educated youths were consistently more effective than workers at mobilizing for action throughout the Republican era, therefore, one has to look to factors beyond the activities of Communist organizers and the incidents that angered educated youths. The most important of these is the distinctive environment in which students lived and studied. Many features of campus life facilitated the growth of large-scale mass movements, and these features are the main concern of this chapter.

The social world of the Chinese campus was highly organized and structured by a complex network of formal and informal group affiliations that bound students to their classmates and provided a foundation for political mobilization.* Such networks play a central role in student life and student politics in many countries,³ but the literature on European and American campus unrest suggests there was something unusual if not necessarily unique about the role these networks played in the growth of radical student movements in Shanghai and other Chinese cities. Scholars working on Western youth movements have argued that although certain types of pre-existing campus groups and ties between individual students facilitate the growth of radical student movements, "traditional" groups and affiliations tend to hinder the mobilization process, a point I return to below. In contrast, Shanghai student organizers were able to capitalize upon virtually every pre-existing group structure and interpersonal tie.†

I give specific examples of how these pre-existing structures and ties facilitated mass mobilization later in this chapter. Before doing so, however, I first look more closely at the differences between the experience of Shanghai students and that of American and Western European youths and between the social world of the campus and that of the factory. This discussion will help explain the greater frequency of student as opposed to worker leadership of large-scale mass movements. I argue that although workers participated in many types of social organizations and such participation helped facilitate some forms of collective action, the web of interpersonal networks within the factory ultimately proved less useful than

---

*Here and elsewhere in this chapter, I generalize about "campus life" as if there were little difference between one college and another. In reality, institutions of higher learning varied in everything from architecture to the role of religious observances and sporting events, as the detailed discussion in Yeh Wen-hsin, *The Alienated Academy*, pp. 49–166, shows. This chapter presents a composite picture of college life in Republican Shanghai, and the features of the student lifestyle I highlight were part of the experience of most if not all of the city's undergraduates. This picture is based largely on a reading of the memoirs described in the Bibliographic Essay and interviews of graduates of Shanghai institutions during the Republican era.

†Recent work on student unrest in Tsarist Russia describes a similar situation, but there identification with the student community as a corporate entity rather than patriotism seems to have led groups based on traditional ties, *zemliachestva* (regional circles—groups like Chinese native-place associations made up of youths from a common hometown), to play an active role in radical mobilization. For the activities of *zemliachestva*, which in 1896 "began to guide and direct" an "upsurge of student unrest," see James McClelland, *Autocrats and Academics: Education, Culture, and Society in Tsarist Russia* (Chicago: University of Chicago Press, 1979), p. 98.

that within the university when it came to generating sustained, large-scale, pan-class activism.

COMPARATIVE PERSPECTIVES

What do studies of Western youths movements lead the historian interested in mass mobilization to expect of campus organizations? One of the few serious comparative studies of the topic to date, Frank Pinner's influential "Western European Student Movements Through Changing Times,"[4] argues that student organizations can be divided into "socializing" or "traditional" associations (societies that help prepare members "for their future role in society") and "transgressive" associations (groups that "aim to bring about social and political change"). Pinner singles out fraternal organizations with elaborate rituals and codes of behavior, such as the German *Korporationen,* as archetypical examples of "socializing" campus groups; such associations tend to be hierarchical in structure and "conservative in social outlook and behavior." He contrasts these fraternal groups with "transgressive" organizations—in the European case most often socialist or anarchist groups—that attract students "for whom role models are either unavailable or unacceptable" and whose members are linked by ideological as opposed to "traditional" bonds.

Pinner uses this dichotomy to try to account for campus unrest in Western Europe during the 1960's, arguing that a variety of factors led increasing numbers of youths to turn toward "transgressive" as opposed to "socializing" organizations. Comparable studies of American student networks are rare, but anecdotal evidence scattered throughout various sources adds credence to Pinner's basic claim: throughout the twentieth century groups such as fraternities and sports teams (which fit into his "socializing" category) have indeed tended either to remain detached from or to oppose radical mass movements.[5] The leaders of such organizations (and, for that matter, student councils) rarely emerged as the heads of protest leagues during the American youth movements of the 1930's or the 1960's.[6]

The situation on Chinese campuses differed considerably, as the preceding chapters have already shown. For example, many of the youth groups that took part in strike-support work in 1925, such as the Anti-Christian Federation, were clearly transgressive in nature, but others were socializing associations. This is certainly true of the student native-place societies that joined the movement, since such associations performed many of the same functions for Chinese youths during the Republican era that fraternities have performed in the Western context, and membership in these groups was based not on a shared ideology but on a "traditional" tie: a shared hometown. The role the Boy Scouts played in the May 4th Movement (see Chapters 1 and 2) is another case in point. As a hierarchical organization devoted to preparing its members for future roles within society, the Boy Scouts fulfill all of Pinner's requirements for a socializing association, and yet in 1919 ordinary Shanghai scouts played key parts in radical protests, and scoutmasters stepped into a new role as parade monitors. Moreover, these two examples of socializing groups joining radical protests are not atypical. Throughout the Republican era, campus groups founded on traditional affiliations and designed to perform socializing functions routinely provided nascent youth movements with ready-made work groups and trained leaders.

Why does the case of Republican Shanghai differ so markedly from the one Pinner presents? Given the undeveloped state of the comparative literature on student mobilization, a comprehensive answer to this question is impossible. Nonetheless, it is worth highlighting some of the key factors. First, in the Chinese student movement radicalism and nationalism were always intimately entwined. This is important because as studies of late-nineteenth- and early-twentieth-century German campus politics, for example, make clear, although members of European socializing associations may be less likely to join protests that seek to alter the status quo, they are often the readiest to take part in patriotic celebrations and lead nationalistic student movements.[7] Since both dissatisfaction with the actions of domestic authorities and a desire to defend China's sovereignty were factors in all major student movements of the Republican era, these struggles attracted both alienated youths interested in restructuring the political system and socialized ones concerned only with protecting their homeland.[8]

Along with the ties between radicalism and patriotism, elements of China's political and cultural traditions are relevant to understanding the crucial roles seemingly apolitical associations played in mass movements. Two factors stand out as particularly important. First, until the twentieth century, political parties were essentially unknown in China, and imperial edicts explicitly forbade officials from forming cliques or factions (*pai*) for political ends. As a result, dissidents frequently used literary societies, native-place societies, and other kinds of nonpolitical, and hence in imperial eyes legitimate, associations as organizational bases. This trend continued into the Republican era, since China's rulers continued to discourage members of the intelligentsia (including students) from forming overtly political associations. Thus, whereas, throughout the past century, it has been natural for like-minded activist youths in the United States and Western Europe to work through campus branches or equivalents of national political parties, their Chinese counterparts have frequently found it more natural and less dangerous to form literary societies.[9]

Second, Chinese political culture emphasizes group as opposed to individual participation in collective rituals and, by extension, acts of radical political theater. Unlike the Judeo-Christian tradition in which some rituals (such as confession) are essentially individual and others (such as mass) are collective, Chinese religion (in both its popular and elite forms) is based almost exclusively upon rituals that involve clearly articulated groups and group leaders. According to a recent synthesis of anthropological and historical studies, during the imperial era the "basic unit of participation" in most Chinese festivals was "the household, not the individual," and many other rites "celebrated and defined larger groups—'families' of affines and agnates, lineages, native-place associations, temple organizations, occupations." [10]

This emphasis upon group participation in religious rites is relevant here because, as Chapter 3 has shown, events such as festivals and pilgrimages provided students with models or scripts for such key acts of political theater as parades and petition drives. [11] Not surprisingly, therefore, the tendency to base actions on groups as opposed to individuals carried over into the realm of campus unrest. Some student forms of protest are, of course, highly individual: the youths who in 1915 and 1919 bit their fingers to write out patriotic slogans in their own blood, for example, performed very personal acts. Nonetheless, the emphasis upon forms of theater that rely on group affiliations is a striking feature of the Chinese case. Throughout the first half of the twentieth century, petitions to authorities were seldom sent in the name of an individual student, wall posters were frequently signed by groups (for example, literary societies or native-place associations), and marchers consistently organized themselves into units based upon a pre-existing affiliation (usually to a school) and marched under a banner emblazoned with the name of a collective unit. This orientation, which contemporary emphasis upon identification with one's work unit and state rituals centered around groups representing different sectors of society has reinforced, has continued to shape protests of the Communist era. As many observers and commentators concerned with the protests of 1986 and 1989 have noted, the tendency for demonstrators to structure their actions within collective frameworks and identify themselves as parts of larger units remains a distinctive feature of Chinese marches.*

None of these features of student protest is unique to China. Students in other lands have sent petitions in the name of groups and marched under flags identifying the collectivities they belong to. The *degree* to which pro-

---

*For insightful comments on this topic, see Pieke, "Observation"; Strand, "Popular Movements"; idem, "Protest"; and Francis, "Progress."

test is conceived of as performed by groups rather than by collections of individuals does, however, set the Chinese case off from at least the American one. A comparison of photographs of the student demonstrations of the two countries illustrates this. Flags with individual slogans were often the dominant symbols in student marches against the Vietnam War; banners with group names held by either one person or more often two persons leading columns of students from a given city, union, school, or even academic department figure most prominently in the majority of pictures of Chinese protest parades.[12] (For examples of banners of this sort, see the photographic section.)

The emphasis upon group affiliation as a basis for protest participation also came out strongly in my interviews of former activists in Shanghai. One theme the interviewees invariably stressed was the importance of their particular school or people from their native place in the protest movements in which they participated. They were proud of their own acts, but they were equally concerned that the collective units to which they were attached be given credit for leading the struggle. This intramural competitiveness, the concern with showing that one's school was more militant and hence more patriotic than others, also comes out in school histories published in the PRC; most of these argue that the campus in question was the real center of political activism during important movements (for more on school histories, see the Bibliographic Essay).

All these factors help account for the importance of both transgressive and socializing associations in the mobilization process in Republican China. The role of nationalism as a unifying force, the tendency to conceive of protest as a group act, and a competitive dynamic that drove members of a given unit to try to prove that people from their campus or their province were no less patriotic than their counterparts in other schools or associations—all these provide clues to the special features of the Chinese case. For the purposes of this chapter, however, the most important thing is that in times of crisis, the ties established by and the leadership experience gained through membership in a whole spectrum of extracurricular associations—sports teams, school councils, and religious fellowships, as well as Marxist study groups and radical literary societies— provided nascent youth movements with a solid foundation of pre-existing interpersonal connections and organizational structures upon which to build.

CAMPUS LIFE AND FACTORY LIFE

The preceding paragraphs have highlighted one possible reason why Shanghai student organizers could mobilize large groups of people more quickly than their counterparts in the West—they could capitalize upon ties established by both socializing and transgressive groups. These paragraphs have not, however, addressed the main question this chapter seeks to answer: Why in Shanghai did campus activists prove more successful than labor organizers in building mass movements? This question is a key one because it would seem at first glance that workers *should* have been at the center of more Shanghai mass movements than were students, since they were the most oppressed urban group and the one that received most attention from CCP organizers.[13] Differences in lifestyle provide an answer to the question of why educated youths rather than laborers so often took the vanguard position.

One of the many ways in which the world of the factory differed from that of the university was that clubs and associations played a much smaller role in the average worker's daily life than they did in that of the typical student. Workers simply had little time to spend on social or cultural activities, since many worked 60 hours a week or more, and most had families to whom they devoted a large portion of their non-working hours. Students, by contrast, had free time for extracurricular group activities. Finding themselves in a new and alien environment, away from childhood friends and family, students turned to clubs for companionship, a place to exchange ideas, a sense of belonging, and in some cases even a future spouse.* Furthermore, university officials actively encouraged students to form societies and fellowships, which were seen as contributing to the quality of campus life. Factory bosses, although they occasionally promoted anti-radical associations to counter the efforts of radical ones, frequently frowned upon and sometimes forcibly discouraged the formation of clubs in the workplace.[14]

Workers thus generally lacked the extensive network of pre-existing club ties and organizational structures that played so vital a role in the development of student movements, although many were bound together through pledges of "sisterhood" or "brotherhood."[15] These sororal and fraternal associations, which seldom involved more than a dozen people, often worked as teams to protect group members or to achieve collective ends.[16] Sisterhoods and brotherhoods had little potential to form the nuclei for classwide mass movements, however, since "sisters" and "brothers" generally worked at the same factory. Thus, whereas student move-

---

*Even protest leagues could sometimes serve these personal needs, as Zhang Jieren's memoir "'Wusi fuqi': Jiuguo buwang lianai" ("May 4th couple": While saving the nation, don't forget about love), in Lianfu jizhe, *Wo canjiale Wusi yundong*, pp. 25–34, illustrates. Zhang describes how she and her future husband met while working together during the May 4th Movement and how an SSU leader acted as a New Culture equivalent of the traditional go-between in arranging their marriage.

ments could evolve from struggles within a single school to citywide agitations relatively easily thanks to the intercampus communication channels youth associations provided, labor struggles usually remained confined to individual factories because the ties between ordinary workers seldom transcended links to a common workplace.

Native-place associations and gangs, the two most important types of organizations other than unions that connected workers throughout the city, moreover, were less effective than comparable youth groups in helping laborers to generate classwide mass movements. The contrast is particularly striking in the case of native-place associations, since both workers and students belonged to organizations based on hometown affiliation. Native-place ties were if anything even more important to workers than they were to students, since educated youths prided themselves on their ability to think in national and even cosmopolitan terms rather than strictly parochial ones. In spite (or rather in large part *because*) of this difference, native-place connections were more helpful to student activists than they were to labor organizers.

Citywide native-place societies, to which many workers belonged, were essentially benevolent societies established to assist immigrants in Shanghai from a given area of the country.[17] They were a central fixture in the social life of the city throughout the Republican era, because Shanghai's rapid growth had made it a metropolis composed largely of immigrants, who ate distinctive foods, clung to distinctive customs, and spoke mutually unintelligible dialects. Native-place associations helped bring together workers who would not otherwise have been linked, and this kind of bonding could facilitate collective action. Two of Shanghai's most famous nineteenth-century riots, for example, were the work of laborers and merchants from Ningbo, who were angered by the French authorities' attempts to take over land that served as their native-place association's cemetery.[18] Like the ties established by membership in a sworn sisterhood or brotherhood or those formed by laboring side by side in a workshop, native-place connections helped laborers organize strikes by creating small cohesive groups within factories ready to act together to achieve a common goal. In times of widespread worker unrest, such as the mid-1920's, small groups such as these served as key building blocks in the mobilization process.[19]

Although native-place affiliations and societies could bring workers together, they could also undermine class unity. The same particularistic ties established by membership in a native-place association or sisterhood that could help organizers at a given factory bring workers together to stage a strike often hindered the growth of citywide mass movements among laborers. In the absence of other connections, close identification with those from one's native-place in particular undercut the development of class-based solidarity: for every worker from Jiangsu Province who gained support for her mill's strike from Jiangsu silk weavers, there were several Sichuanese factory hands who mistrusted the organizer who came to their plant because he was a "foreigner" from Shandong with a strange way of speaking.[20]

Native-place affiliations had a much less divisive effect within the student community, because university life forced students to participate in what was essentially a national culture. Whatever dialect they spoke at home and whatever customs their families followed, students had to speak the same language, eat the same foods, and generally live the same way as their schoolmates from other regions while at university. This allowed the various single-campus and citywide associations of youths from a given area to act as unifying forces, which aided rather than hindered the growth of classwide movements.[21] The fact that ties to a common birthplace were but one of dozens of links that bound students to each other further minimized the divisive potential of native-place associations; sharing the same hometown could create a special bond among one group of classmates, but the individuals in that group were likely to be just as intimately bound to members of other native-place associations, with whom they attended literary society meetings, religious services, or sporting events.

Like native-place associations, gangs established ties between workers, but again they were problematic when it came to fostering classwide mass actions. The Green Gang, a Mafia-like secret society that was a central fixture of Shanghai society and politics throughout the first half of the twentieth century, was the largest and most important of these illicit organizations.[22] Its members included a large number of workers, and although it devoted more attention to such things as opium smuggling and racketeering than to protest, the Green Gang played an important (though complex) role in the development of the local labor movement.[23] Its influence in the area of labor relations was so great, in fact, that CCP organizers often felt that joining the Green Gang was the best or only way for them to gain a foothold within the world of the Shanghai worker.[24]

This said, ties fostered by common membership in the Green Gang were generally of dubious value for the generation of large-scale mass movements. This was because the gang's leaders (the most important of whom, such as Du Yuesheng, managed to secure powerful positions for themselves within "respectable" society) were most concerned with protecting and maximizing their power within the status quo, and hence viewed with extreme suspicion protest actions that threatened the existing order. These leaders did find labor strikes useful at times, as weapons in factional struggles. Even when they called on their followers to take to the streets, however, they usually took pains to prevent things from getting out of control and giving rise to a genuine mass movement. Du Yuesheng generally found the threat of worker action more useful than actual strikes, and he used his power over laborers to exact a price from the authorities. Thus the Green Gang often functioned as a brake on labor unrest, so that its leader could keep his end of the social unrest "protection racket" bargain he had struck with other members of the Shanghai elite.

A comparison of labor unions and explicitly political student organizations, such as school councils and youth protest leagues, is instructive at this point, since unlike native-place associations and gangs unions were designed to foster precisely the kinds of mass movements of concern here. Explicitly political groups were, however, severely limited in their effectiveness as coordinators of protest actions throughout the period in question. First, they were obvious targets for police suppression during times of social unrest. Second (especially after the GMD came to power in 1927), they frequently fell under direct or indirect governmental control. Once again, however, because of the wider array of clubs and societies found on university campuses, student organizations were less affected by these limitations than were their labor counterparts.

When the police, for example, forced labor unions underground, these worker organizations often became virtually powerless. Outlawed student unions, however, could continue to function by having their members work through other channels, hiding their actions behind the names of nonpolitical youth associations, and holding meetings in halls supplied by religious fellowships or drama societies to which their members belonged.[25] Even complete suppression of a student protest league through mass arrests seldom proved completely effective, since the basic organizational connections out of which a new league could be built remained untouched within the university community. The contrast is just as sharp where governmental control is concerned. When a labor union fell into the hands of the ruling party, workers or agitators wishing to form a new body to coordinate protest actions had to start from scratch; when school councils lost their autonomy because of official interference or infiltration, it was fairly easy for activists to simply form new, unofficial councils. Thanks to their ability to fall back upon a much broader array of pre-existing organizational structures, therefore, explicitly political student groups were consistently able to overcome the inherent obstacles to their success and play vital roles as the core groups responsible for keeping mass movements alive—something labor unions were able to do only rarely.

The contrast between student and worker associations was not always quite so stark, however. The West Shanghai Workers' Club (discussed in Chapter 4) for example, helped link the employees of a number of textile mills, and these connections laid the foundation for the textile strikes of 1925.[26] Recent works by leading scholars of Shanghai labor history have also pointed to the role pre-existing ties and organizations played in facilitating worker mobilization in later years. For example, Emily Honig draws attention to the importance of YWCA activities in forging bonds between ordinary female laborers and radical organizers during the 1940's,[27] and Elizabeth Perry describes the way a Shaoxing opera troupe composed of silk weavers came to "serve as the organizational nucleus" of a 1927 strike.[28] Even so, students were more likely than workers to live within the kind of web of overlapping ties and associations that proves most useful for mobilization on a citywide, as opposed to single institution, scale. And this made the tasks of campus organizers much easier than those of their factory counterparts.

The fact that students were in continual contact with teachers, journalists, and other members of the intelligentsia who played key roles in patriotic upsurges helped extend the web of pre-existing personal connections and organizational structures available to youth movement leaders. Ties established through participation in intelligentsia groups, such as the League of Left-wing Writers (a prominent radical organization founded in the 1930's, which included both student and non-student members) and teachers' unions (whose members were in daily contact with students in the classroom), were crucial for disseminating information on student protests during the 1930's and 1940's.[29] Throughout the Republican era, intelligentsia associations helped students publicize their views and at times even provided nascent youth protest leagues with guidance and meeting halls. Non-student members of these organizations played equally vital roles as everything from advisers to student unions to go-betweens who used their connections to link youth movement leaders from different campuses and even different parts of the country.

THE PHYSICAL ENVIRONMENT OF THE CAMPUS

Other features that set campus daily life off from that of the working world, such as the greater amounts of time that students as opposed to laborers spent together, also had an impact on the youth mobilization process. For most Shanghai students, the campus was an all-encompassing social world. They did not simply study there; they also slept and ate on campus. During the week, they spent nearly all their daytime hours in the company of other students and (less frequently) professors. Evening hours and weekend breaks were also likely to be spent with other students, as youths came together to compete in sporting activities, hold meetings, study, or explore the amusements of Shanghai.

Although workers at a given plant were also likely to spend much of their time with their co-workers, factories tended to be less all-encompassing social worlds than campuses. During working hours, laborers would work side by side and eat in common areas, and some of the larger (and more strike-prone) factories had worker dormitories as well. Nonetheless, outside work, many laborers became part of another social world: that of the family. This had a variety of implications for mass mobilization. Workers were in daily contact with and owed allegiance to two separate groups of people—their fellow laborers and the members of their families—whereas students split neither their time nor their loyalty. Workers had to weigh the effects of protest actions not only on themselves but also on family members, some of whom were dependent children, and to balance this against loyalty to their fellow workers and their anger toward management or a governmental policy. Students also had economic worries, since participation in protest activities could lead their parents or (in the case of students on government scholarships) the authorities to refuse further funding. On the whole, however, students were usually unburdened by outside responsibilities, and all they had to weigh against allegiance to their classmates or a cause was concern for their own comfort and personal safety. Family ties could check student political involvement, both because of economic reasons and (especially in the case of students whose families lived in Shanghai) because of the emotional pressure parents sometimes put on children to stay out of trouble.* In some cases, however, family ties encouraged student militancy by minimizing the risks involved: many leading campus activists were the children of government officials and could feel secure in the knowledge that even if they were arrested, their parents (though disapproving of the youthful transgression) would be able to secure a speedy release.†

---

*This may have been one reason why, according to Zhang Jishun, students from Shanghai were less active participants in many youth movements than their classmates from other areas. Zhang stressed the importance of parental pressure as a check on youth activism both before and after 1949, during a discussion session at the 1988 Symposium on modern Shanghai. Her paper at that conference, "Lun Shanghai zhengzhi yundongzhong de xuesheng qunti, 1925–1927 nian," contains a fascinating treatment of the relative political activism of students from Shanghai and from other parts of the country studying in Shanghai. Zhang focuses primarily upon the social and psychological reasons for the greater militancy of nonnative as opposed to Shanghainese students. One factor she isolates that complements the main theme of the present chapter is the tendency of non-native youths to feel a greater need to establish fraternal mutual-aid societies, such as *tongxianghui*, to overcome their feelings of isolation and inferiority in the alien setting of Shanghai.

†The former campus activists I interviewed in Shanghai in 1986 and 1987 continually alluded to the number of student activists of the 1930's and 1940's whose parents were powerful figures within the local or national political elite and hence were able to pull strings to keep their radical children out of jail. The fact that, for various social and cultural reasons, there was always a greater outcry when police beat up or killed educated youths as opposed to uneducated workers also minimized the risks of student protest. The elite status of students, as children from good families and intellectuals in the making, by no means made them immune to violence, but it often put a check on police brutality.

The all-encompassing nature of university life also gave student activists a major advantage over labor organizers in terms of speed, since they could spread the news of an event or plans for an upcoming protest at any time of the day or night, whereas labor organizers (with the exception of those working at factories with worker dormitories) could depend on finding workers massed together only during working hours. The spatial layout of most Shanghai universities—with common gathering areas, dining halls, and dorms housing large numbers of students—further facilitated swift mobilization. This spatial arrangement made it easy for students or professors to call impromptu assemblies in times of crisis, as well as making informal exchanges of ideas and information across a wide range of members of the university community a natural component of daily life.*

The patriotic upsurge of 1919 provides some of the clearest examples of how the physical layout of universities fostered rapid mobilization. According to memoirs by participants, the May 4th demonstration evolved out of the informal interactions university life fostered. Plans for the event took shape gradually as students at Beijing University (Beijing daxue) met together in clubs and study groups to discuss the Paris Peace Conference, read the wall posters that activists pasted up in common gathering spots, and held ad hoc assemblies in the main campus dining hall to discuss possible ways to express their anger.[30] The entrance of Shanghai students into the May 4th Movement was also facilitated by the physical structure of campus life, since the city's youth first became involved in the struggle after Shao Lizi called an emergency assembly at Fudan on the morning of May 6 simply by ringing the school bell to bring students out of their dorm rooms (see Chapter 2).

The spatial arrangement of campuses proved important in the rise of later movements as well. A memoir by a leader of the struggles of 1925, for example, describes running with a friend from dorm to dorm and dining hall to dining hall to drum up attendance for a mass protest meeting held in the wake of the May 30th shootings.[31] Ringing the school bell would remain a typical means of mobilizing students for action long after the

---

*Many of the comments in the preceding paragraphs apply to universities in many parts of the world as well as those in other Chinese cities. Scranton et al., *Report of the President's Commission on Campus Unrest*, which was commissioned in the wake of the Kent State and Jackson State killings, for example, notes that "the campus is a favorable environment for the growth of commitment and protest because the physical situation of the university makes it relatively easy to mobilize students with common sentiments" (p. 82). And, in a very different context, Samuel Kassow describes the crucial role student dining halls played in the Russian student movements of the late nineteenth century, as "vital centers of protest activity" where information could be exchanged and plans made (*Students, Professors, and the State*, p. 72).

May 4th Movement.* The technique was used to assemble Fudan students in the wake of new crises at least twice during the Anti-Japanese Movement of 1931,[32] and a Tongji University student used his school's bell to call an ad hoc assembly in 1935 that led to his school's entrance into the December 9th Movement.[33] Students at Jiaotong University also used their campus bell to great effect in May 1947: ringing it foiled a late-night attempt by government agents to arrest the school's leading activists by bringing angry youths out of their dorms to protect their classmates.[34]

THE MOBILIZATION PROCESS IN ACTION

Many of the features of college life that facilitated student mobilization outlined above were not unique to Shanghai but rather common to campuses throughout China. As the case of the May 4th Movement's Beijing origins shows, for example, spatial arrangements were a key variable in the capital as well as in Shanghai when it came to organizing educated youths quickly for mass action. In addition, most of my preceding comments concerning the importance of clubs and fellowships in the rise of youth movements hold true for all Chinese cities. This said, the Shanghai student mobilization process was unusual if not unique in at least two ways. First, although colleges in many cities had native-place societies, because of factors alluded to above organizations of this sort played a particularly prominent role in the growth of Shanghai mass movements. Second, the sheer number of local academic institutions (rivaled only by Beijing) affected the way student struggles of the Republican era evolved. The best way to illustrate this point, as well as give a clearer sense of how campus activists took advantage of the leadership training and interpersonal connections provided by participation in student associations and clubs, is to trace the evolution of a relatively minor event: the New Year's Day "anti-U.S. brutality" march of 1947 to protest the alleged rape of a Beijing student by two American soldiers (see Chapter 9 for more on this event). Thanks to a wide range of available materials, including memoirs by participants in the demonstration, it is possible to reconstruct an unusually detailed picture of both the march itself and the flurry of organizational activity that preceded it. The anti-American protest, which took place less than a week after Shanghai students first heard of the incident, involved thousands of students from dozens of local schools, and its excellent organization impressed even Westerners, who tended to be hostile toward all demonstra-

---

*Factories also used bells or whistles to assemble workers, but laborers seldom had access to these means of communication (Elizabeth Perry, pers. comm., Sept. 18, 1989).

tions that attacked foreign privileges or actions.[35] This is hardly surprising—what the students accomplished was indeed impressive. Within a few days they not only selected representatives to speak to the press and agreed upon the main slogans to be shouted and the route to be taken during the parade, but also arranged for special propaganda trucks (including one carrying a mimeograph machine that ran off a "News of the March" bulletin) to lead the demonstrators through the city.[36]

This swift transition from initial anger to a carefully planned demonstration began at Ji'nan University, whose students took the lead in mobilizing Shanghai's youths for action.[37] Ji'nan became a hotbed of protest activity from the moment news of the rape appeared in Shanghai newspapers on December 27. That evening the school's dorm rooms were transformed into impromptu debating halls, as students and progressive professors gathered to argue over how best to express their outrage. Two days later, after posters calling for mass protests had appeared in most common gathering areas, Ji'nan's students took their first major organizational step by convening a special meeting of representatives from all campus clubs and societies. More than a hundred students attended this meeting, which ended with the formation of a special Ji'nan Anti-U.S. Brutality Alliance, a call for a schoolwide strike, and the selection of nineteen people to contact students at other schools and spread news of the strike. This liaison team, working under the direction of a special group leader, quickly established the contacts that would provide a viable basis for citywide mass action. One reason it could accomplish this task so swiftly was that many student associations, such as the New Music Club to which the group singing societies of over a dozen schools belonged, had branches at various campuses.[38]

The students of other Shanghai schools were soon holding emergency meetings of their own, which were generally similar to the one at Ji'nan in terms of end results, although in some cases they differed slightly in form. The assembly at Jiaotong University, for example, was attended by representatives of each department rather than of each club.[39] At Fudan University the Female Students' Association took the lead in organizing the campus for action.[40] All these various meetings, whatever their precise format, ended with angry cries for citywide action. This shared sense of purpose led directly to the establishment of the Anti-U.S. Brutality Alliance, whose inaugural meeting on December 31 was attended by representatives from seventeen local universities and secondary schools. This newly formed alliance, along with calling for a mass demonstration on New Year's Day, divided up responsibility for different aspects of the movement on a school-by-school basis. Several campuses were directed to share overall planning duties; Ji'nan was to handle publicity; the Sports Institute was to supply guards to protect the marchers; and the Shanghai Music Conservatory's students were to teach protest songs to students from other schools.

The preceding sketch suggests how pre-existing connections that shaped campus social life could enable students to stage a carefully orchestrated mass action on short notice. To complete the picture, however, we need to look more closely at the mobilization process within individual campus populations, since in addition to identifying the schools in charge of specific tasks, we must answer even more elementary questions such as How exactly did activists at a given school get their schoolmates out onto the streets? And who made the banners carried at the front of each school's contingent during the march? Some hints regarding these issues can be found in the allusion in the discussion of the Ji'nan meeting to the attendance by heads of student organizations (who presumably mobilized fellow club members to join the school's brigade on New Year's Day). We can cull similar bits and pieces from memoirs by former activists, such as one by a Daxia University alumnus, which describes one of the school's native-place societies preparing banners for the march.[41] Luckily, however, one does not need to rely on such piecemeal methods alone, because a firsthand account that presents a detailed and comprehensive picture of how protest activities were organized at one of Shanghai's major universities exists.[42]

This recently completed memoir by Qin Yishan, a student at Jiaotong University in the mid-1940's, is filled with information concerning the roles pre-existing student associations played in political mobilization. Qin relates, for instance, that during the various protests of 1946 and 1947 (see Chapter 9), responsibility for specific tasks was often assigned collectively to the members of a social club or literary society, and the heads of these associations often doubled as leaders of political task forces. Jiaotong's most politically active student association, the Knowledge and Action Society (Zhixingshe)—a group founded by several students from Hunan Province who shared similarly progressive views as well as the same native-place—usually took charge of overall guidance of protest activities at the school. Two literary societies shared responsibility for publicity work.

Qin, who co-chaired Jiaotong's *jiuchadui* (security task force), provides personal details that help explain how the heads of the various task forces were able to work together so efficiently: many were already linked by associational ties. He, for instance, was a member of the Zhixingshe and had been in an informal study group with the leader of one of the literary societies in charge of publicity work. Thus pre-existing ties linked the heads of three of the main task forces at Jiaotong, and these connections smoothed their efforts to direct the campus student movement. Similar connections, established through membership in other student associations, likewise aided task force leaders in their efforts to recruit volunteers to take part in demonstrations, write pamphlets, make banners, and serve as march monitors.

Extant sources seldom provide as many details concerning student mobilization in other protests of the Republican era. The evidence suggests, however, that the pattern described above for the "anti-U.S. brutality" march is fairly typical, since many features show up in accounts of earlier Shanghai youth protests. As far back as 1919, for instance, the mobilization tended to begin with specially called assemblies of student representatives similar to the meeting of student association leaders at Ji'nan in 1946. More generally, accounts of all modern Chinese youth movements contain numerous examples of student clubs and societies serving as foci for political action, ready-made task forces, and sources of leaders.

The role a Fudan native-place association and sports team played in the December 9th Movement of 1935 illustrates this point clearly. A former student activist from Fudan, in recounting his role in the youth movement, began by mentioning that he was from Guangdong Province.[43] This was important, he said, because one of the most politically active campus groups during the mid-1930's was the school's Guangdong *tongxianghui*, thanks to the fact that one of the few underground CCP organizers on campus was a popular student from that province. Another politically involved group to which the informant belonged was (interestingly enough) the Fudan volleyball team, whose players all happened to hail from Guangdong Province and hence were regularly exposed to progressive ideas at native-place association meetings. When the time came to organize a brigade of march monitors, the informant remembered, the task naturally fell to this physically fit sports team, and the captain of the team just as naturally assumed the role of brigade head. The transformation of both a sports team into a protest task force and its captain into a task force leader fits easily into the mobilization pattern sketched for the "anti-U.S. brutality" agitation and again illustrates the way pre-existing groups and roles helped facilitate student action.

Recently published materials on the history of Shangda, the school that provided the May 30th Movement with so many of its leaders (see Chapters 1 and 4), show that analogous ties and groups played a similar role in the student struggles of the mid-1920's. The information on student activists is particularly interesting in this regard, since it reinforces the image of protest leaders presented in earlier discussions of the May 4th Movement and protest activities at Jiaotong during the 1940's. The students who led the May 30th Movement, like those in charge of political mobilization at

Jiaotong during the Civil War era, were generally neither strangers to one another nor newcomers to leadership roles. On the contrary, many of them were used to working together and acquired group leadership experience well before the May 30th killings, as a brief look at the life histories of three Shangda students, He Bingyi, Liu Hua, and Zhong Fuguang, reveals.

All three students played leading roles in the May 30th Movement: He Bingyi helped direct the speechmaking drive on May 30, serving as a liaison officer and coordinator of Shangda's 38 small brigades, before being shot; Liu Hua presided over the May 24 mass memorial for Gu Zhenghong and was a leading labor organizer; Zhong Fuguang led a special National Student Union propaganda delegation in charge of spreading word of the May 30 shootings to other regions.[44] However, their participation in the May 30th Movement was not all the youths had in common. All three hailed from Sichuan Province and hence were not merely classmates but also members of the same politically active native-place association.[45] Liu Hua was, in fact, the president of this association, as well as being a member of the Shangda student council and a founder of one of the school's leading literary societies.[46] He Bingyi was also prominent in the Sichuan native-place association before the May 30th Movement and served as a keynote speaker at a 1924 memorial service the association sponsored for Huang Ren, the political martyr.[47] Zhong devoted much of her energy to a different campus group—the school's Female Students' Association, in which she was a leading figure—but she, too, took time to attend native-place association meetings; as she put it, "If you did not join an organization [of this sort], you could not get anything done."[48]

These three mini-biographies give a sense of the way political and nonpolitical roles, relationships, and groups overlapped within Shanghai schools in times of crisis; the stories of other Shangda activists reinforce this image. Shangda students formed dozens of literary societies, study groups, and native-place associations during 1923 and 1924, as well as a number of overtly political organizations. Not surprisingly, virtually every youth movement leader the school produced in 1925 came to the struggle equipped with connections and leadership skills gained from participation in one or more of these clubs and societies. Thus, for example, Liu Yiqing (a leading officer of the Shanghai Student Union in 1925), Lin Jun (one of the main speakers at the May 31 siege of the Chamber of Commerce), and Yang Zhihua (a major figure in the "triple union" in charge of the sanba of 1925) had all gained practical experience as organizers well before the May 30 killings, having served together as members of both the Shangda People's Night School Coordinating Committee and the Shangda student council.[49]

Another member of the Night School Coordinating Committee, Zhu Yiquan, helped found and co-edit Shangda's main May 30th periodical, *Shangda wusa tekan*, a journal that attracted student activists from other Shangda circles. Before 1925, the publication's other co-editor, Jia Wei-sheng, for example, had been most active as a leader of the Shangda Zhe-jiang tongxianghui and the treasurer of one of the school's oratory societies.[50] Gao Erbai (whose contribution to *Shangda wusa tekan* is treated in Chapter 4) and Ma Lingshan (a main contributor to the journal throughout summer 1925) linked the editorial staff to still different groups: Gao by virtue of his leadership of the Shanghai Anti-Christian Federation; Ma through his position as a founding member of the Lonely Star Society (Guxingshe) and his connections to the Shangda Shaanxi Native-place Association.[51] Thanks to the plethora of student associations around which extracurricular life at Shandga revolved, the list of overlapping connections between activists—Zhong Fuguang attended native-place association meetings with Liu Hua, who worked closely in labor-related organizations with Yang Zhihua, who in turn knew Zhong Fuguang through the Female Students' Association—goes on and on.

Information about May 30th activists at other Shanghai schools is much harder to find. Available data suggest, however, that there was nothing particularly unusual about the Shangda case in terms of either the range of pre-existing associational ties between activists or the tendency for heads of even the most seemingly innocuous of campus societies to emerge as protest leaders during late spring and summer 1925. A history of Jiaotong University, for example, notes that thanks to the influence of the "May 4th spirit" the students at that school formed dozens of associations during the early 1920's, such as the Economic Society (Jingjixue hui), a music club, and "all kinds of native-place societies."[52] It also mentions in passing that the head of one of the school's study societies, the Academic Research Association (Xueshu yanjiuhui), was a student named Zhang Yonghe, who would go on to serve as one of the four directors of the Jiaotong large brigade on the afternoon of May 30, 1925; the presiding officer at the emergency strategy-planning meeting of Shanghai Student Union representatives held in the immediate aftermath of the day's bloodshed; and one of Shanghai's chief delegates to the important National Student Union coordinating conference the following month.[53]

The preceding paragraphs give ample proof to support the main themes of earlier sections of this chapter. The way organizers of events such as the New Year's Day march of 1947 took advantage of pre-existing ties and group structures, for instance, highlights the importance of many of the differences between the social world of the campus and that of the factory.

The preceding examples of nonpolitical campus groups evolving into march monitor brigades and the like clearly illustrate the inapplicability of Pinner's socializing and transgressive categories in the case of Shanghai youth groups. Members of student associations with certain political orientations were indeed likely to join radical mass movements. Some literary societies were explicitly radical in their orientation; after 1927 (as Chapters 7 and 9 show), certain campus groups opposed all youth activities that threatened the political status quo. As one former student recalled, during the 1940's one could always count on members of certain campus native-place associations siding with the GMD and the members of other such associations opposing the GMD.[54] There was, however, no clear distinction of the sort Pinner describes between different *genres* of student groups in terms of their potential to aid in the political mobilization process.

Memoirs by former underground CCP activists provide additional evidence of the potential for "traditional" groups to become vehicles for transgressive mobilization in times of crisis. These accounts are filled with references to the fact that party members tended to achieve their best results when they worked within the most seemingly innocuous of student associations, such as native-place societies or even Christian fellowships.[55] Underground activists working in factories likewise tried to use pre-existing organizations and ties to their own advantage, for example, by joining and then trying to radicalize brotherhoods, sisterhoods, or even gangs.[56] Their relative failure to instigate large-scale, citywide movements vis-à-vis their campus counterparts had less to do with any lack of talent or ingenuity on their part than with the simple fact that such organizations and ties were fewer and weaker among factory workers. As Communist and non-Communist organizers of the time were well aware, and as this chapter has shown, the social organization of Republican campus life made Shanghai students unusually easy to mobilize for mass action.

II

THE NATIONALIST
PERIOD, 1927–1949

SIX

SHANGHAI AND ITS STUDENTS, 1927–1949

THE POLITICAL REFORMS AND UPHEAVALS of the Nationalist era, which changed the way the city of Shanghai as well as the nation as a whole was governed, also had a profound impact upon the political activities of local students. The unsettled relationship between the GMD and the CCP—who fought each other during the Nanjing Decade (1927–37), joined forces in the Second United Front during the War of Resistance (1937–45), and then squared off in a final struggle for power during the Civil War period (1945–49)—affected campus activists in many ways. So did the attempts of Jiang Jieshi's central government in Nanjing during the late 1920's to turn Shanghai into a "model" municipality and the Japanese invasions of the 1930's and early 1940's that thwarted these reformist efforts and inadvertently sealed the fate of the treaty port system. To place the case studies of student movements of the 1930's and 1940's presented in later chapters in perspective and to provide a general sense of the main continuities and discontinuities between the Warlord and Nationalist eras, it is important to look first at these transformations in local and national politics. This chapter begins by tracing the effects of the Northern Expedition, the undeclared war between China and Japan, and the Japanese surrender of 1945 on the government of Shanghai's three administrative districts. It then analyzes the impact of factional political struggles on the local academic community and the local student movement.

SHANGHAI IN THE NANJING DECADE, 1927–1937

The Nationalist era began in Shanghai in spring 1927, when the participants in the Third Workers' Uprising seized control of the Chinese section of the city and delivered it to the Nationalist Army forces led by Jiang Jieshi. The foreign community in Shanghai watched these events with trepidation, fearing that Jiang would soon try to take possession of the concessions as well. These fears were not unfounded. Jiang had vowed at the start of the Northern Expedition that his ultimate goal was to bring all of China under GMD rule by freeing the nation from warlords and imperialists alike, and earlier in 1927 the Nationalist Army had invaded foreign enclaves in two other Chinese cities. Poised for a showdown, the Western municipal councils placed both concessions under martial law, and in late March some 16,000 foreign troops arrived to help protect the French Concession and the International Settlement. As tensions mounted, Shanghai's foreigners surrounded their enclaves with barbed wire barricades and braced themselves for a battle with the Nationalist Army that never came.

Almost as soon as his forces gained control of Chinese Shanghai, Jiang began to take steps to ease the fears of the foreign community, such as having one of his generals announce that the Nationalists were determined to use diplomatic as opposed to military methods to end the treaty port system. The most important indication that recovering the concessions was not Jiang's top priority came on April 12 when he staged his coup against the radical unions that had spearheaded the Third Workers' Uprising and began a general purge of all "red bandits" and "counter-revolutionaries," general terms that Jiang used to refer to his non-Communist enemies within the GMD as well as to committed members of the CCP. Jiang's actions on April 12 were a clear signal to the West that he now considered his erstwhile leftist allies a greater immediate threat to the nation and his own personal power than he did the imperialists. The meaning of this move against the CCP was not lost on leading foreigners: the Shanghai Municipal Council, which had never before allowed armed Chinese soldiers to march through the International Settlement, gave Jiang permission to have the troops that carried out the April 12 coup travel through the enclave on their way to Zhabei.

The crisis of spring 1927 had some effects on political and social life within Shanghai's foreign concessions. It helped convince the foreign ratepayers of the International Settlement, for example, that they could no longer avoid Chinese representation on the Shanghai Municipal Council. The rising tide of Chinese nationalism also led some members of the ratepayers' association to propose in 1927 the abolition of the rules prohibiting all Chinese other than servants waiting upon foreigners from entering the Settlement's public parks; although the motion was defeated that year, it passed the next. Perhaps the most important change of all, at least in terms of later historical developments, was that some of the

American, British, and Japanese troops that came to protect the foreign community in 1927 remained in the International Settlement to serve as defense forces. Despite these changes, however, the coming of the Nationalist era had little impact on the basic nature of treaty port existence. Although the leaders of the new Nationalist regime continued to talk about regaining control of the enclaves throughout the rest of the Nanjing Decade, it quickly became clear that the new regime was prepared to let Shanghai's concessions continue to function much as they had under the warlords, at least until the Communist threat was destroyed. As a result residents in the foreign enclaves soon settled back into their old patterns of life.

If Jiang's rise to power had little real impact upon political and social life in foreign Shanghai, however, the same cannot be said about the sections of the city under native rule. Jiang's determination to shift economic and political power away from Beijing, which remained under warlord control longer than most other parts of the nation, to the Yangzi Valley region had important implications for the two key cities of the area: Nanjing and Shanghai. In 1928, as a first step in this program, Jiang formally consecrated Nanjing (a city whose name means "Southern Capital" and which had served as the center of imperial power during certain dynasties) as the nation's new capital, by erecting an elaborate memorial to Sun Zhongshan just outside the city and making the metropolis the home of the new central government. Jiang even changed the name Beijing (literally, "northern capital") to Beiping to signify this shift in power. (To avoid confusion, "Beijing" is used in this and later chapters.)

Jiang also had grandiose plans to turn Shanghai into a model urban center. As a result, throughout the late 1920's and early 1930's, the central government introduced a series of reforms aimed at making the Chinese sections of the city, which the GMD renamed the Special Municipality of Greater Shanghai, a fully "modern" metropolis. Under these reforms, Chinese Shanghai was administered by a General Secretariat and ten specialized bureaus for finance, public works, education, public safety (police affairs), land administration, labor, commerce, agricultural affairs, public health, and utilities. At the pinnacle of this administrative structure stood the mayor of Shanghai, who was appointed by and remained directly responsible to the central government in Nanjing and who had the power to appoint the heads of the local government bureaus.[1]

This administrative structure appeared quite straightforward on paper, but one factor made the governance of the Special Municipality much more complicated in practice than it was in theory: the power wielded by the local GMD Dangbu (Party Branch Office). Scholars are only now beginning to provide a nuanced picture of the complex relationships between party and state organizations during the Nanjing Decade. According to important recent studies by Christian Henriot and others, the two types of organizations were supposed to complement each other: the role of Dangbu officers was to provide ideological guidance and oversee the behavior of government bureaus; that of governmental officials was to carry out administrative tasks and implement the central government's policies. In fact, however, as these scholars show, the relationship was often more competitive than cooperative.[2] This was certainly true in Shanghai, where, to use Henriot's phrase, the Dangbu developed into an "autonomous center of power."[3] Fierce power struggles between party and government officials (often allied to different factions within the GMD) were an endemic feature of local and national politics throughout the early years of the Nanjing Decade. Even after 1932 when Dangbu officials began to play a more subordinate role, these struggles hampered the efficiency of Shanghai's "model" bureaucracy.[4]

Bureaucratic infighting was not, however, the most important obstacle the Nanjing regime faced in its efforts to turn Shanghai into a "model" municipality; military factors ultimately played a much greater role in undermining this project. The Japanese invaded and took control of Chinese Shanghai twice during the Nationalist era, in winter 1932 and in summer and fall 1937. The first Japanese occupation lasted only a few months; the League of Nations negotiated a truce between the two sides that restored the status quo ante but left parts of the Chinese municipality a demilitarized zone in which neither country was allowed to station troops. The second invasion was part of an all-out offensive aimed at turning the entire Chinese nation into a colony in a Pan-Asian empire ruled from Tokyo. The Japanese troops who seized control of Chinese Shanghai in 1937 did not withdraw until the Allied forces destroyed this imperialist dream in 1945.

THE OCCUPATION AND ITS AFTERMATH, 1937–1949

Except for a brief period in 1937 when the Japanese military governed the Special Municipality directly, Chinese Shanghai was ruled by native turncoat officials throughout the occupation. For the first years of this period, these puppet administrators were basically independent agents, former bureaucrats who had decided to cast their lot with the foreign invaders. The situation changed in 1940 when Wang Jingwei, one of Jiang Jieshi's longtime rivals for leadership of the GMD, came to an agreement with the Japanese and established a puppet central government in Nanjing, which by then had also fallen to the Japanese army. For the last five years of the war, Shanghai's puppet officials were allied to this new Nanjing regime, a regime that despite its pro-Japanese stance claimed to rule China in the name of the GMD.

The military campaigns of 1932 and 1937 did not directly threaten the foreign concessions, although Chinese airplanes intending to attack a Japanese warship did accidentally drop bombs on the International Settlement in 1937. The Japanese government claimed in both 1932 and 1937 that the invasions were retaliatory forays triggered by attacks upon Japanese nationals and that it had no complaint against Westerners. The foreign consuls and representatives on the municipal councils of the two concessions, for their part, clung to a policy of neutrality. They tried at times to put diplomatic pressure on Japan to withdraw from Chinese territory, but generally they took the position that until Western interests were threatened, the undeclared war between the two nations was not their affair, certainly not something that should lead them to take steps that might risk forcing their home countries to fight Japan. The League of Nations was equally determined not to offend Japan (one justifiable complaint of Chinese patriots throughout this period was that the League never took a strong stance condemning Japanese imperialist actions in China).

The Japanese attitude toward the foreign concessions changed suddenly with the attack on Pearl Harbor in December 1941. On December 8, just after Japan issued its formal declaration of war against the United States and Britain, the Japanese launched an all-out assault on the International Settlement. They sank an English warship stationed in the Huangpu, dropped bombs on the heart of the concession, and sent soldiers onto the Bund and into other parts of the foreign enclave. Within days the Japanese and their puppet allies from the Special Municipality had seized control of virtually all Western businesses within the International Settlement. Their invasion turned the concession into a prison camp for both the Settlement's Chinese nationals (who constituted over 96 percent of the enclave's 1941 population of 1.6 million) and its foreign residents, with the exception of those from Axis countries such as Germany and a variety of "nonenemy" nations ranging from Brazil to the Soviet Union (which had recently signed a special treaty of neutrality with Japan).[5] Since the French Concession was already under the control of the Vichy regime by late 1941, the success of the Japanese invasion meant that by the beginning of 1942 for the first time in nearly a century all of Shanghai was unified under the rule of one group: the Axis powers.

The Japanese invasion of 1941 did more than begin one of the darkest chapters in the city's history; the death blow it dealt to the treaty port system would make post–World War II Shanghai a new kind of city. Chinese diplomats had spent decades trying to negotiate an end to extraterritoriality and to regain control of the Shanghai concessions, but until the start of World War II the main beneficiaries of the treaty port system (Great Britain, France, the United States, and Japan) generally ignored these pleas. The first important signals that the war would alter this intransigence came in July 1940, when both Winston Churchill and U.S. secretary of state Cordell Hull made public statements that their nations were prepared to renegotiate the terms of the unequal treaties forced upon China in the nineteenth century as soon as peace was restored. The United States and Great Britain initially hoped to work out a collective agreement on the treaty port problem with Japan and (eventually) France, but after Pearl Harbor and the fall of Shanghai the two nations decided to take steps to abolish the city's tripartite structure. Thanks to these diplomatic efforts, when the Japanese surrendered and the representatives of the central government of Jiang Jieshi retook control of the city in summer 1945, Chinese officials exercised jurisdiction over the French Concession and International Settlement as well as the former native district.

For the next four years, while the GMD and CCP fought in other parts of China to determine who would rule the nation, the representatives of Jiang's central government administered all of Shanghai much as they had governed the Chinese Special Municipality before 1937. Once again the central government appointed a mayor, who in turn selected the heads of the municipal bureaus. And once again Dangbu officials exerted some influence over local political affairs, although the Party Branch Office does not seem to have been as potent an "autonomous center of power" during the Civil War era as it was in the early years of the Nanjing Decade. In the mid-1940's the GMD did make some efforts to democratize local and national political arrangements by requiring representatives to the National Assembly and municipal officials to stand for election rather than hold their posts by appointment. Corruption and outright rigging was, however, so blatant during these so-called free elections that many Chinese voters and foreigner observers viewed the process as fixed. Even some GMD officials were forced to admit the truth of this claim.

Official corruption and the lack of open elections were two of the main issues critics affiliated with the CCP and the Democratic League (a coalition of non-Communist opposition groups) used to rally popular support for their campaigns against the Nationalist regime throughout the Civil War era. Cries for more "democracy" (*minzhu*) and cleaner government figured prominently in many of the most important urban demonstrations of the period, and the GMD's apparent insensitivity toward these issues, as well as the repressive steps it took to curb manifestations of popular discontent, contributed to the growing alienation of Shanghai's intelligentsia and general citizenry from local and national government representatives (see Chapter 9). In 1945, when the GMD assumed control of Shanghai from the Japanese, the city's Chinese residents greeted the party warmly as a victorious political force that had helped free the nation and the metropolis from foreign control. By 1949, when the GMD was finally forced to cede control of Shanghai and the nation as a whole to the CCP, the Nationalists had completely squandered this initial goodwill. Some of the most radical critics even questioned whether Jiang Jieshi's regime had treated the Chinese citizens of Shanghai any more humanely than had the imperialists.

STUDENT ACTIVISM IN THE NATIONALIST ERA

Chapter 1 presented an overview of the student movements of the pre-1927 period structured around discussions of schools and newspapers that served as "core" groups during early campus protests. The same approach could certainly be used here, since various institutions performed comparable functions in post-1927 struggles. For example, Fudan re-emerged as a leading center for political radicalism in 1931 (see Chapter 7). Newspapers also emerged as core institutions during the post-1927 era: *Qingnian zhishi* (Youth culture) and *Xueshengbao* (Student news) played much the same role in the protests of 1947 that *Minguo ribao* and *Rexue ribao* had played in those of 1919 and 1925.

Focusing on core institutions is, however, ultimately less helpful a device for making sense of the student protests of the Nationalist era than it was in the case of those of the Warlord period. The GMD's rise to power greatly complicated the political dynamics of campus activism by fragmenting the student community. As a result the student movement in the Nationalist era was shaped less by the rise and fall of core institutions than by competition between rival political groups who frequently tried to use student mass actions to further factional ends. As Chapter 4 indicates, the pre-1927 student movement was not completely free of factional strife. Nonetheless, thanks to a shared antipathy toward imperialism and the Warlord regimes, before 1927 campus activists of differing political allegiances were able to unite to fight for common goals. Such cooperation became much more problematic after the GMD's rise to power because, as soon as Jiang Jieshi's central government replaced the Warlord regimes, student activists had one less common enemy; and because Jiang's purge of suspected Communists made CCP organizers understandably suspicious of political activity that involved working with people outside their party.

Jiang Jieshi's rise to power complicated the dynamics of student activism in yet another way. After 1927 factional divisions within the GMD also began to play an increasingly prominent role in campus politics. Thus not only did Communist and non-Communist youths struggle to control the direction of new popular movements, but people affiliated with various Nationalist cliques continually sought to use demonstrations by educated youths to support their own power or to embarrass their political rivals.[6] The case-study chapters that follow provide detailed explanations of how these rivalries affected the most important Shanghai youth movements of the era, but it is worth introducing some of the main divisions within the student community and the way these divisions shaped the development of student activism. In particular, it is worth examining the new roles political parties and factions played vis-à-vis the student movement after 1927, beginning with the way Jiang Jieshi and GMD members loyal to him treated campus unrest during the Nanjing Decade.

JIANG JIESHI AND CAMPUS POLITICS, 1927–1937

The GMD's rise to power presented the party's leaders with a dilemma in regard to mass movements, including student ones. On the one hand, the GMD had a tradition of supporting popular struggles, and mass movements had played a crucial part in making the Northern Expedition a success. On the other hand, once in power Jiang and his supporters had a vested interest in discouraging all threats to the new political status quo. Given the nature of this dilemma, the division in the new ruling party over this issue is not surprising. Some GMD members argued that the party should continue to encourage patriotic youth movements but take active steps to channel youthful militancy to enhance rather than to challenge the power of the new regime. Others argued that popular mobilization was simply too risky a force to encourage. The GMD's top priority should be rooting out all vestiges of Communist influence within the schools, and the new regime should devote itself to convincing educated youths that the best way to serve their country was to study hard and refrain from political activities.

During the first years of his rule, Jiang Jieshi generally sided with those who favored suppression. The Generalissimo personally spearheaded an active campaign against campus radicalism. In a series of speeches to youth groups and educational associations during the first years of the Nanjing Decade, Jiang argued that the Revolution had been completed in 1928 with the Northern Expedition's successful reunification of the country. Student protests thus could no longer help save the nation but would only serve counterrevolutionary purposes. The time for strikes and demonstrations had passed, in other words, and the best thing for patriotic students was to concentrate on their studies and steer clear of all political involvement. "Discipline and obedience," Jessie Lutz concludes in her analysis of these speeches, were the main virtues Jiang emphasized.[7]

Jiang's campaign against campus radicalism was a multifaceted one that used several related techniques to make the educational environment less conducive to the growth of mass movements. The most basic social control technique was to dismiss or execute all students and teachers suspected of being Communists. Less brutal methods were also used, such as making pupils take loyalty oaths and join *baojia*-type cells, in which each student was held responsible for the good behavior of the other members of the group.[8] In addition, the GMD reshaped school curricula so that ideological indoctrination received as much attention as academic subjects and issued edicts calling for school councils and unions to devote themselves exclusively to educational activities. The Nanjing government even made it a crime for students to form new political groups, and GMD cadres went to great lengths to neutralize or gain control over existing student organizations.[9]

The central government continued to rely upon these methods to keep student activism in check throughout the late 1920's and 1930's, but at times circumstances forced Jiang to take a softer or more complex stance toward campus unrest. Such times usually came when Japanese advances into Northeast China provoked popular outrage. These imperialist advances remained a thorn in Jiang's side throughout the Nanjing Decade, because of the Generalissimo's conviction that a divided China could not win a war against its more powerful Asian neighbor. While Jiang felt that fighting internal enemies must therefore remain a higher priority than battling foreign aggressors, he also realized that every sign of weakness toward imperialism provided his rivals within the GMD as well as the CCP with a powerful political weapon against him, since he had staked his claim to political legitimacy on his ability to free the nation from both warlordism *and* outside domination. Thus Jiang walked a thin line throughout the period: his tough statements attacking Japan were a way of proving that he remained a patriotic foe of imperialism and a way of pressuring the Japanese to desist from the most aggressive of their actions, but throughout the Nanjing Decade he consistently stopped short of taking steps that would make all-out war unavoidable.[10]

In order to maintain this balancing act and keep his credibility in the eyes of the populace, Jiang was sometimes forced to side temporarily with those who argued that the GMD should encourage and guide student activism rather than suppress it. For example, after a clash in 1928 between Chinese and Japanese troops in the city of Ji'nan in Shandong Province inspired youths throughout the country to call for a new boycott of all Japanese goods, Jiang's central government briefly lent its support to the popular anti-Japanese movement. At the height of this agitation, GMD representatives called on Shanghai students to "arouse the inhabitants" of the city to fight Japanese imperialism.[11] According to John Israel, Jiang's decision to try to ride out rather than stifle the mass movement of 1928 was motivated by a feeling that, as "potentially dangerous" as patriotic outbursts could be, this one was just "too convenient a diplomatic weapon to dismantle."[12] Both the central government's support for the anti-Japanese agitation of 1928 and the movement itself proved to be surprisingly short-lived: before the end of May, Jiang, who had never lost sight of the fact that the "weapon" of popular unrest could all too easily turn in his hand, was once again taking steps to limit mass protest activities and students were returning to their studies.

Student movements of the 1930's were also double-edged swords from Jiang Jieshi's point of view. The anti-Japanese agitation of 1931 (see Chapter 7) once again forced the Generalissimo to weigh his desire to appear patriotic against his fear that a popular movement might take on an anti-government as well as anti-imperialist dimension. The same can be said of the December 9th Movement of 1935.

The December 9th Movement, like the May 4th Movement before it, is named for the date upon which Beijing police violently disrupted an anti-Japanese protest. Like its predecessor of 1919, this incident inspired educated youths throughout the country to form protest leagues, mount propaganda campaigns, stage school strikes, and promote a boycott of Japanese goods. In 1935, however, the event that triggered the initial demonstration in Beijing was not an international treaty but Japanese plans to turn large parts of North China into "autonomous regions" that would in reality be governed by puppet regimes loyal to Tokyo. As had happened with the protesters of 1919, those of 1935 soon began to attack not only the Japanese but also those native officials who tried to stop the popular movement or seemed too conciliatory toward Japan.[13]

Jiang Jieshi and his followers used a variety of tactics to try to discredit and destroy this movement, such as labeling radical demonstrations Communist plots that had nothing to do with true patriotism and employing force to disperse radical gatherings. The Generalissimo also attempted, however, to steer the movement into a loyalist course so that the enthusiasm of the students could be made to serve rather than undermine the central government. In early 1936, for example, Jiang convened a student "conference" in Nanjing.[14] During the conference—which school administrators, teachers, and carefully screened student "representatives" (but not genuine protesters) from schools throughout China were invited to attend—the central government used the pomp and circumstance of official rituals to convince students that Jiang's party was interested in and willing to listen to their views and that if they would only be patient, the Generalissimo would ultimately free the nation from all forms of imperialist degradation.

Followers of the Generalissimo also tried in several instances to subvert the content of December 9th student demonstrations themselves and introduce a loyalist message into events that looked at first like typical protests. In Shanghai the students who took the lead in trying to steer the local December 9th Movement away from radicalism were members of the Blue Shirt Society (Lanyishe), a fascist (or at least quasi-fascist) secret organization formed in the early 1930's by fervently anti-Communist GMD members who were intensely loyal to Jiang Jieshi.[15] Before 1931 Jiang depended upon his position as Sun Zhongshan's brother-in-law and presumed heir apparent, as well as his ability to use struggles between GMD factions to his own advantage, to secure his hold upon the party and the state. But internal party struggles and the popular upheavals of 1931 convinced the Generalissimo that he needed an organization like the Blue Shirts to protect his position at the helm of the GMD. Founded by friends of Jiang who had served with him as instructors at the Whampoa Military Academy, this organization's leaders used their positions as heads of school military training programs to recruit students into the Lanyishe.

The first mass movement in which the Blue Shirts took an active role was the New Life Movement launched in 1934, which was an attempt by Jiang to use mass mobilization and propaganda techniques like those of the May 4th Movement to serve conservative social and political ends.[16] Whereas students of the May 4th era had lectured the populace on the need to turn away from superstitious beliefs and rituals and to embrace new ideas of "science" and "democracy," participants in the New Life Movement tried to convince their listeners of the need to uphold Confucian values (such as filial piety) and to practice a puritanical style of self-cultivation. And, whereas the May 4th students had decried the warlords as rulers unworthy of respect or popular support, New Life youths urged the people to remain loyal to the Generalissimo and his party. Unlike the May 4th Movement, however, the New Life Movement never succeeded in gaining broad popular support. Even within the academic community in Shanghai and other cities, support for Jiang's campaign remained limited primarily to Blue Shirt members and to the middle-school students who belonged to Boy Scout or Girl Guide troops, which the GMD placed under its direct control after 1927.[17]

The next political campaign in which Blue Shirt members took part, the December 9th Movement of 1935, gained much more widespread support within the local student community. As soon as news of brutal police attempts to break up the December 9 Beijing student demonstration against Japanese aggression reached Shanghai, youths in schools throughout the city began meeting to form protest leagues and plan mass actions. There were sharp splits, however, over whether these mass actions should focus solely on attacking Japanese imperialism or should be used as occasions to criticize the central government as well. Blue Shirt members seem to have played the key role in preventing the local struggle from taking on anti-GMD as well as anti-imperialist overtones.[18]

Thanks in large part to the Blue Shirts' efforts, the earliest mass gatherings of Shanghai students to respond to the December 9th Incident were ambiguous "protests" at best. Throughout mid-December youths gathered at various campuses to hold rallies, after which they often paraded en masse to the Municipal Government Compound to present patriotic petitions to the mayor and other officials. On the surface, these rallies and parades seem like typical Shanghai protest gatherings, since local students had been using similar actions to publicize their grievances for decades. In reality, however, many of these gatherings were designed to defuse rather than incite popular unrest. At the very time that the leaders of Beijing's December 9th Movement were calling on students throughout the nation to fight against GMD oppression as well as Japanese aggression, for example, loyalist youths at Shanghai campus rallies were leading "protesters" in cries of "Long live the Guomindang" and other equally nonmilitant slogans.[19]

The petition parades of December 19 and 20, the first large-scale Shanghai gatherings of the December 9th Movement, provide an even clearer picture of the loyalist implications of some local "protests." Some of these parades evolved into genuine confrontations between angry students and local officials, but in a few instances Blue Shirt activists managed to take control of the events and transform them from radical street theater into rituals of consensus that affirmed rather than challenged the GMD leadership. These loyalist parades may have looked like ordinary protests, but the Blue Shirt students in charge of them took great pains to make sure that the marchers stuck to vague patriotic slogans that did not challenge either Jiang Jieshi or his policies. As the paraders marched from campus to campus, sweeping new groups into their ranks as they went, their most common chants were neutral ones, such as "Welcome to the students of ——— University." As revealing as the slogans the marching youths shouted were the songs they sang: many were GMD party anthems.*

Thanks to these cues, and perhaps even to direct communication between officials and Blue Shirt organizers, the Chinese police did not interfere with these loyalist parades, and local officials greeted the youths as friends rather than opponents. The meetings between these petitioners and the officials followed a ritualized format, in fact, that was wholly devoid of confrontation. First, the mayor or another political figure emerged from his office to greet the "protesters" and listen to their demands. The official then praised them for their patriotism and promised to pass their views on to Nanjing, but ended by encouraging the students to leave foreign policy decisions to the politicians and return to their studies. The students then dispersed happily (sometimes on buses provided by the municipal authorities), shouting slogans such as "Support the central government against Japan."[20]

The Blue Shirts ultimately proved unable to prevent Shanghai's December 9th Movement from evolving into a struggle with genuinely radical aims and slogans. By the end of December, in fact, confrontations between student protesters and officials had become much more common than the consensual gatherings described above. Nonetheless, loyalist youths did succeed for a time at least in keeping Shanghai students from responding to the December 9th Incident in as militant a fashion as the students of other cities such as Beijing and Tianjin. Thus, for example, as late as December 21, while educated youths in these two northern cities were carrying out general classroom strikes, Shanghai papers carried headlines such as "Classes Opening in Various Schools as Usual Today."[21] And although loyalist youths eventually lost control of the local December 9th Movement, they continued to take an active part in mass actions throughout the rest of the Nanjing Decade. For example, after the Xi'an Incident of late 1936, Boy Scouts, Girl Guides, Blue Shirts, and members of other organizations loyal to the Generalissimo participated in rallies and demonstrations to celebrate Jiang Jieshi's release from captivity.†

---

*The use of a party anthem in and of itself does not necessarily mean that an event is a loyalist one; during the protests of 1989 students often sang the "Internationale." Within the context of the mid-1930's, however, and in conjunction with the lack of protest slogans, the selection of such songs is significant.

†The Xi'an Incident began on December 12 when a northern warlord, Zhang Xueliang, kidnapped Jiang Jieshi in order to force the Generalissimo to temporarily suspend his war against the Communists so that all Chinese could unite to fight their common enemy: Japan. During the thirteen days Zhang held Jiang, members of the CCP and other groups held extensive discussions with the Generalissimo on the topic of resisting Japanese imperialism. These discussions proved fruitful; soon after Jiang's release the GMD and CCP formed their Second United Front. For details on the celebrations held in honor of Jiang's release, see *NCH*, Dec. 30, 1936 and Jan. 6, 1937; and SMP reel 31, file no. D7675A.

JIANG'S OPPONENTS AND CAMPUS POLITICS, 1927–1937

The Generalissimo and his followers were by no means the only ones interested in making student outrage and patriotic enthusiasm serve a particular agenda during this period; both rival factions within the GMD and Jiang's Communist foes frequently used demonstrations by educated youths as political weapons. Because of the complexities of the factional alignments and realignments of the era, and because so much of the history of the GMD's internal power struggles remains obscure, I will not try to provide an overview of the way each particular Nationalist clique dealt with the problem of student activism.[22] Instead, I will look briefly at the role one particular faction, the Gaizupai (Reorganizationist Faction), played in local campus politics and then move on to CCP activities.

The Gaizupai stands out as the GMD faction most worthy of attention. First, it was the clique allied to Jiang Jieshi's main rival for leadership of the Nationalist party: Wang Jingwei.[23] Second, Communist writers claim that it was the CCP's chief competitor for control of the Shanghai youth movement during the late 1920's and early 1930's.[24] According to a recent memoir by a former Gaizupai member named Jiang Hao, one reason this clique had so much support within the Shanghai academic community was that many students viewed Wang Jingwei, who had first made a name for himself in 1910 during a youthful attempt to assassinate the last Qing prince regent, as a heroic figure.[25] Thanks to Wang's popularity and the organizational skills of his followers, Jiang Hao claims, by the late 1920's Gaizupai partisans held leadership posts in many local and national student associations. Wang's followers also occupied key positions within the local Dangbu and municipal government, as well as within the administrations of many of the city's principal schools such as Jiang Hao's own university, Jiaotong.

The Reorganizationists used these positions of influence to try to turn each new wave of anti-Japanese sentiment into attacks on the Generalissimo by focusing on his unwillingness to fight the foreign aggressor. The following chapter looks at the way such actions by Wang Jingwei's followers helped force the Generalissimo to resign temporarily from office in 1931. But the youth protests of that year were not the first occasion members of the Gaizupai had used student outrage to further factional aims; they had done so three years previously during the anti-Japanese agitation of 1928 inspired by the Ji'nan Incident. According to Jiang Hao, the administrators at several local schools (including Jiaotong) openly encouraged their students to incorporate criticisms of the Generalissimo into their protests against Japanese imperialism throughout the late 1920's.[26]

The CCP, like the Gaizupai, saw anti-Japanese protests as an effective tool for undermining Jiang Jieshi's new regime. In the first years of the Nanjing Decade, however, the party was in no condition to take full advantage of campus unrest. Jiang's "white terror" succeeded in crippling the Communist organization in Shanghai both physically and psychologically. Many Communist leaders were either killed or forced to go into hiding in the late 1920's. Most of those who managed to survive and remain active in cities such as Shanghai grew intensely skeptical of all activities that smacked of cooperation or collaboration, since these had led to the debacle of 1927. This new mood of skepticism had a profound impact upon the CCP's position vis-à-vis the youth movement. Whereas the party's Youth League had formerly embraced students as a powerful patriotic and progressive force, after 1927 it identified these educated youths as members of the ideologically suspect and generally untrustworthy petit bourgeois class, and began to direct most of its attention toward and put most of its faith in young workers.[27]

CCP organizers never abandoned students altogether. But thanks to the party's new distrust of cooperation with non-Communists or reliance upon members of non-proletarian classes—a distrust party historians have since designated the "leftist errors" of the Li Lisan and Wang Ming lines—these organizers' activities were generally futile and at times even counterproductive. Whereas radical organizers had previously tried to latch onto issues with the widest possible popular appeal and adopt slogans that even patriots who were clearly not Communists could easily support—"Restore educational rights" and "Take back the concessions"—in the late 1920's and early 1930's CCP campus activists showed no interest in working with (or even gaining the sympathy of) people who were not converts to the cause of Marxist revolution. Rather than trying to build broad-based coalitions to fight specific abuses of power by native authorities or specific acts of aggression by foreign powers, Youth League members dissipated their energies in frantic demonstrations on revolutionary holidays, shouting slogans with little appeal for either non-Marxist students or the general public.[28]

The police often violently suppressed CCP-sponsored marches and rallies during the first years of GMD rule, but these acts of repression never elicited the massive outpourings of popular support the mass arrests and killings of earlier times had inspired.[29] The main reason for this was simple: the participants in CCP-led demonstrations did little to endear themselves to the masses. Martyrs shot while shouting out "Long live the soviet areas" and "Prepare for armed revolt" just did not stir the populace at large as had those who died in 1925 with "Shanghai for the Shanghainese" or "Long live the Republic" on their lips.[30] Nor were non-Communist "leftist" students, such as members of the Gaizupai, likely to be moved by the plight of their more radical classmates. The CCP was so set upon repudiating all coalition building that its campus organizers not only refused to try to use factional struggles within the GMD to their own advantage but took pains to attack youths linked to "left-wing" and "right-wing" Nationalist cliques with equal venom, to denounce Wang Jingwei as bitterly as they denounced Jiang Jieshi.[31] Such lack of discrimination on the part of the CCP is not surprising, since by the end of the 1920's the Reorganizationists were almost as rabidly anti-Communist as any of their "right-wing" rivals within the GMD.

The CCP began to show more interest in student organizing and in broadening its base of support within Shanghai's academic community during the early 1930's, although, as Chapter 7 shows, party members continued to take steps guaranteed to alienate uncommitted youths through at least 1932. By the mid-1930's underground Communist organizers, although still few in number, had established a strong presence on many local campuses. When the December 9th Movement spread to Shanghai, these youths squared off against the Blue Shirts for control of the struggle. It is hard to tell on the basis of existing evidence whether, as memoirs by former Communist organizers (not surprisingly) claim, these radical youths ever fully succeeded in gaining control of the local patriotic movement.[32] It is clear, however, that members of the CCP underground played a key role in organizing many of the most militant protests of late 1935 and 1936, protests that ultimately undermined the GMD's attempts to keep the local December 9th Movement from taking on anti-government overtones.[33]

PARTY POLITICS AND CAMPUS POLITICS, 1937–1949

The outbreak of war between China and Japan in July 1937 and the subsequent invasions of Shanghai had a profound unifying effect upon the local student community. Factional divisions within the youth movement did not, however, disappear during these crises. Just as CCP and GMD armies often followed separate battle plans during the Second United Front era (1937–45), radical and anti-radical students continued to compete with each other for control of student groups and promote differing political agendas throughout the late 1930's and early 1940's.[34] Nonetheless, the Japanese occupation gave educated youths of differing political allegiance a new sense of common purpose. Wang Jingwei's decision to form an alliance with the Japanese added to this solidarity by giving patriotic Communist and non-Communist students a common native as well as foreign enemy to oppose.

Although the foreign invasion of 1937 brought Shanghai students together emotionally and ideologically, it divided them geographically, since many educational institutions fled to new locations to escape the Japanese. In some cases the moves were short ones. Jiaotong University, for example, relocated to the French Concession in the late 1930's when its former location in a Chinese part of the city became too dangerous.[35] In other cases, however, students traveled to distant cities such as Kunming and Chongqing, which remained out of reach of the Japanese invaders long after Chinese Shanghai fell.[36] The Japanese occupation of the foreign concessions in December 1941 triggered a further exodus and dispersion of educational institutions and educated youths.[37]

Although the Japanese invasions radically altered the size of the Shanghai academic community, some educators and students either chose or were forced to remain in the city throughout the occupation. Several colleges and many middle schools never relocated at all; other institutions such as Fudan had some of their faculty and students in Chongqing or Kunming and some in Shanghai.[38] Available sources provide little concrete information about the operation of these schools under the puppet regime and the effects of the Japanese occupation on student life. The few memoirs and secondary accounts of the era reveal, for example, that the new government immediately forced students to switch from learning English to learning Japanese and that the puppet regime often replaced previous school administrators and teachers suspected of being too nationalistic with more malleable Chinese or foreign educators.[39] Such details aside, however, the era remains the most obscure chapter in the history of Shanghai academic life.[40] Thanks to the paucity of source materials, the story of student activism of the occupation years is equally obscure.

Other factors inhibit the study of the youth movement of this period, most notably the almost completely covert nature of radical activity during the occupation. The puppet regime was so uncompromisingly repressive of all public expressions of discontent that oppositional demonstrations became exceedingly rare after Japan conquered the foreign concessions. Before 1942, campus activists had had some political space within which to operate; they could generally count on one or another group of powerholders supporting their actions or at least feeling that demonstrations by educated youths should be tolerated as legitimate expressions of public opinion. This political space disappeared under the puppet regime, which had no qualms about dealing swiftly and ruthlessly with protest. As a result, radical students were forced to abandon virtually all public displays of dissatisfaction and had to content themselves with clandestine activities.

The only details that available materials provide about the resistance activities of Shanghai students under the puppet regime concern underground CCP organizers. By definition, members of the Communist underground had always operated secretively; throughout the 1920's and 1930's they had been forced to hide their party affiliation from European and Chinese police forces obsessed with the idea of eradicating the city's "reds."[41] Only during the Japanese occupation, however, did these organizers have to work completely "underground." After 1941 these underground activists had to do more than just disguise their party affiliation: if they wanted to survive—and the Central Committee insisted that members of the CCP underground try to live through the war, so that the Communists would have a chance to take control of the city when the Japanese surrendered—they had to refrain from openly challenging the puppet regime.*

What then did underground student organizers do during the years of the occupation, other than try to ensure that they lived to fight another day? Fragmentary sources suggest that they directed most of their energy toward carrying out political education among their non-Communist classmates by setting up study groups to read radical texts, and winning goodwill by organizing fundraising drives to help impoverished students, setting up religious fellowships, and holding parties.[42] Some underground activists took bolder steps to gain converts. According to a recent chronology of the Shanghai student movement published in the PRC, for example, two young Communists infiltrated and worked their way up to leadership positions in a south Shanghai branch of a youth league established by the puppet regime. This heroic pair then turned the branch headquarters into an active center for socializing and propagandizing; before the occupation ended, they had convinced a dozen or so members of the group to join the CCP.[43] Another group of activists formed a guerrilla theater troupe and performed a play entitled "The Tragedy of the Chinese Traitors" on a downtown street during summer 1942.[44] Such exceptional activities notwithstanding, most CCP underground campus organizers maintained a lower profile, contenting themselves with more modest ef-

---

*The Central Committee's concern with survival was spelled out in a speech by Zhou Enlai calling on underground workers behind enemy lines to work toward the "long-term ambush, gather their strength, await their opportunity," and spend the interim "studying diligently, working diligently, and making friends diligently" (Zhao Shaoquan et al., *Fudan daxuezhi*, p. 151; Wang Min et al., *Dashiji*, pp. 236–37). My discussions of the Communist underground during the 1930's and 1940's have benefited greatly from extensive conversations with Patricia Stranahan and from her works on the topic, such as "Strange Bedfellows."

forts to establish organizational structures and personal contacts, efforts they hoped would help lay the groundwork for a revival of the radical student movement after Japan and its puppets fell.

Underground cadres affiliated with the CCP were not, however, the only people interested in organizing and influencing the political views of Shanghai students during the occupation. Groups loyal to Jiang Jieshi's GMD also maintained underground networks in Shanghai throughout the early 1940's, although readily available sources say little about these networks beyond the fact that they existed.[45] More important than the activities of these underground cadres, at least in terms of the number of students affected, were those of organizers linked to Wang Jingwei's reconstituted, pro-Japanese GMD (hereafter the "Puppet GMD").[46]

Wang Jingwei was determined to present himself as a patriot and the Puppet GMD as the only faction true to the vision of Sun Zhongshan and to the anti-Communist ideals Jiang Jieshi had proclaimed in 1927 but abandoned by forming the Second United Front. A key part of Wang's strategy for proving his regime's legitimacy involved the formation of a new set of loyalist youth groups, such as the Chinese Youth Corps (Zhongguo qingshaonian tuan) and a reconstituted version of the Chinese Boy Scouts (Zhongguo tongzijun). Wang hoped that these youth leagues would perform the same roles for his Puppet GMD that the Blue Shirts and the Boy Scouts had performed for Jiang Jieshi, that is, as training corps for future soldiers and party members, propagandizers of party policies, and participants in mass ceremonials. Wang even called on students to join a New Republic Movement (Xinminguo yundong), whose aims, like those of Jiang's New Life Movement, included increasing the spirit of self-discipline and self-sacrifice among the country's youths and publicizing Sun's Three People's Principles.[47] There was, of course, one major ideological difference between the New Republic and New Life movements: whereas anti-Japanese rhetoric had figured prominently in the latter, participants in the former were taught that Japan was China's most important ally and that they must help the Japanese establish a new East Asian order.[48]

Shanghai's puppet regime took an active role throughout the late 1930's and early 1940's in getting local students to join pro-Japanese youth groups. Along with taking part in propaganda activities associated with the New Republic Movement and military training exercises, these youth groups also participated in officially sponsored demonstrations. On March 12, 1943, for example, some 12,000 members of a local puppet youth corps took part in a rally and parade marking the anniversary of Sun Zhongshan's death.[49] Just over two years later, on the morning of May 5, 1945, 2,000 members of a group the *Shanghai Times* (by then an unabashedly pro-Japanese English-language newspaper) identified as the Shanghai Youth and Juvenile Corps (probably a local version of the Zhongguo qingshaonian tuan) marched in brigades behind bands playing military airs to the city's Grand Theater, where they took part in ceremonies marking Youth Day (a transplanted Japanese holiday).[50] Whereas before the Japanese invasion no year passed without a protest involving youths in Shanghai, the only times students took to the streets in large numbers during the occupation were as part of loyalist marches and rallies such as these, which were always accompanied by speeches praising the puppet regime.[51]

PARTY POLITICS AND CAMPUS POLITICS: THE CIVIL WAR YEARS

If the Japanese invasions brought Shanghai's students together ideologically while dividing them physically, the Japanese surrender had the opposite effect. Almost as soon as the occupation ended, exiled students and teachers began to return to the city from their wartime homes in the south and west of China, and by mid-1946 schools such as Fudan that had been split into Shanghai and non-Shanghai branches during World War II were reconsolidated. While the Shanghai educational community was returning to normal in terms of size and institutional arrangements, the student movement was also returning to normal in terms of factional divisions. As soon as the Japanese threat ended, youth activists of divergent political affiliations stopped being bound by hatred of a common enemy. As a result, the struggles between Communist and anti-Communist students as well as between youths allied to different GMD cliques once again emerged as a central factor in local campus politics.

Only one of the three main groups that battled for control of the local youth movement during the Nanjing Decade played a central role in the student struggles of the Civil War era: the Communist campus underground. This organization, although a connecting thread in the history of Nationalist era student unrest, underwent important quantitative and qualitative changes between the beginning of the Nanjing Decade and the end of the Civil War era. For fairly obvious reasons, hard evidence concerning the underground's numerical strength is impossible to find. The weight of anecdotal evidence presented in memoirs and other materials suggests, however, that the Communist presence on local campuses was much larger during the Civil War years than it had ever been in the 1930's. Complementing this increase in numerical strength was an expansion in the activities permitted members of this underground. Thanks to the CCP's renunciation of earlier "leftist" errors, underground activists were much freer than their predecessors of the early 1930's had been to form temporary alliances with uncommitted youths and to use the "contradictions" within the GMD to serve the cause of revolution.

In contrast to the CCP underground, neither the Blue Shirts nor youth affiliated with the Gaizupai played any part in post-1945 campus struggles. The Blue Shirts disbanded in 1944. The Gaizupai had begun to lose influence before the Japanese occupation, and after 1945 no one with ties to the traitor Wang Jingwei had any hope of playing a role in popular politics. However, two roughly comparable groups arose to compete with the Communists for the allegiance of local students during the Civil War years, and the factional struggles of that era ultimately had much the same feel and complexity as those of the pre-occupation period.

The successor to the Blue Shirts, at least as far as campus politics was concerned, was the Three People's Principles Youth Corps (Sanminzhuyi qingniantuan, or Sanqingtuan for short). This organization, which was founded in 1939 and served as a parent group to the Chinese Boy Scouts, was nominally independent of the GMD.[52] In actual practice, however, party leaders controlled the Sanqingtuan, and the initiation oath required of recruits included a promise to obey Jiang Jieshi's orders and "live up to the tenets of the New Life Movement."[53] Unlike the Blue Shirts, the Sanqingtuan was a public organization rather than a clandestine one and had far fewer links with the GMD secret police. Like the Blue Shirts, however, the Sanqingtuan emphasized loyalty to the Generalissimo and opposition to Communism.

The most crucial similarity between the Blue Shirts and the Sanqingtuan is that GMD leaders used both groups to counteract and undermine the efforts of CCP campus organizers. No scholar has carried out a comprehensive study of how exactly the Sanqingtuan operated on Shanghai campuses, and much about the group's role in the local student movement remains obscure.* In many cases the only readily available sources containing information about the activities of the corps in Shanghai are either works published by the Sanqingtuan's archrivals, the Communist Youth League, or articles that appeared in the loyalist group's own press organs.[54] As problematic as these materials are, it is possible to get at least a rough outline of the general strategies the Sanqingtuan used in its campaign to neutralize the Communist presence on Shanghai campuses. Staging loyalist rallies, disrupting radical gatherings, organizing anti-radical student associations, running for election to school councils—Sanqingtuan mem-

---

*Unfortunately, the most important English-language study of the group, Lloyd Eastman's *Seeds of Destruction*, while revealing much about the Sanqingtuan's ideological orientation and relationship to the Nationalist Party structure, has little to say about what the members of the corps actually did.

bers did all these things during the Civil War era to protect Jiang Jieshi's prestige and gain converts to their cause on local campuses (see Chapter 9 for details).

The post-1945 successor to the Gaizupai, at least in terms of local student politics, was the CC Clique, a GMD faction led by the two Chen brothers. Here again, as in the case of the Blue Shirts and the Sanqing-tuan, the fit is not perfect, since the CC Clique differed from the Reorganization Faction in many ways. Most important, whereas members of the Gaizupai were partisans of Wang Jingwei, both Chen Lifu and Chen Guofu had close personal and political ties to Jiang Jieshi and felt the Generalissimo was the rightful heir to Sun Zhongshan as head of the Nationalist party. Their main goal in factional struggles was not to topple or embarrass Jiang, but to maximize the power of their own group vis-à-vis competing ones, such as the Political Study Clique, whose leaders held key posts in the central government.

Like the leaders of the Gaizupai, however, the heads of the CC Clique believed that the GMD should work to channel rather than to suppress student political energies, and they too tried to use youth movements to embarrass their political enemies within the GMD. Thus throughout the Civil War era, the CC Clique, which had already established a presence on some local campuses in the 1930's, used its influence among Shanghai students, teachers, and school administrators to try to introduce anti–Political Study Clique overtones into each new wave of student unrest. As Chapter 9 shows, CC Clique maneuverings of this sort played a role in both the Anti-Soviet Movement of 1946 and the spring protests of 1947.

The preceding pages give a sense of some of the ways in which student movements of the Nationalist era differed from those of the Warlord period. The increased importance of factional infighting, the rise of Japanese imperialism as a unifying factor and all-consuming issue within the academic community, the GMD's reliance upon loyalist demonstrations to buttress its claim to political legitimacy—these are but a few of the factors this chapter has touched upon that helped transform the nature of the Shanghai student movement. The only way to begin to assess fully the continuities and discontinuities between the youth protests of the Warlord and Nationalist eras, however, is to look in more detail at how a specific post-1927 mass movement evolved in Shanghai. This I do in the following chapter, a case study of the first major student movement in which loyalist "protests," factional struggles, and the like played central roles: the anti-Japanese agitation of 1931.

A 1931 rally in Shanghai protesting Japan's aggression in Manchuria *(from the Alexander Buchman Collection, Hoover Institution Archives, Stanford University)*

兵　士，警察弟兄們：

軍人警察的天職是保衛國家、安定社會。要能夠保護我們的國家，
不讓敵人佔一寸土，才配稱愛國軍人！要能夠保護我們老百姓，不許漢
奸搗亂才配做模範警察！

你們都是愛國愛民的，當然是願意保護國家，保護人民的！

可是，日本帝國主義奪了我們許多地方，要是中國的大小和人的身
體一般大，那麼日本已經斬掉我們兩條大腿──東三省和熱河；現在又
已坎到我們的胸上──華北了！你們愛國的軍人難道不知道麼？漢奸在
日本□了許許多多的漢奸，在各地搗亂。漢奸在天津把政府機關都
佔了。漢奸更在北平扮做警察兵士坎殺學生，漢奸也在南方鬧事，破壞
救國運動，你們「維持治安」「保護人民」的警察能不管麼？

我們知道你們是真正愛國愛民的。因為我們講演的時候，許多警察
都掉下眼淚來；許多兵士不高興打學生。你們不過是服從命令罷了。
但是弟兄們，想一想看，命令重要呢？還是軍人保守士的天職重
要？你們要做一個堂堂的軍人就得保護國家，保護人民。否則，幫助日
本欺負自家人，這是軍人最最坍台的事！

四年前十九路軍已經把日本兵打得落花流水。他們才稱得上模範軍
人。現在，北方也有許多弟兄自動抗日，不肯打自家人，要打我們的仇
人，我們也應該這樣做：

愛國愛民的軍警們：中國人不要打中國人！大家起來，一致對外！

兵士們，要守衛我們的國土，不許敵人佔去一寸地方，把我們的敵
人趕出去，收回失地！

警察們，要維持地方的安全，不許漢奸搗亂，要保護人民不受日本
人和漢奸的欺負，要保護學生愛國運動！

軍人警察和全國人民聯合起來，中國是一切中國人的，大家要救
國！

告軍警書

復旦大學學生救國會啓

A pamphlet printed by the Fudan University National Salvation Association during the December 9th Movement. Entitled "A Proclamation to Soldiers and Policemen," it calls on these two groups to join with students and other patriots to fight the Chinese traitors working with Japanese imperialists to destroy the nation (*from the Nym Wales Collection, Hoover Institution Archives, Stanford University*)

Above: "Begging food from the mouth of cannons"; poster used in anti-Guomindang protests of the Civil War era in Shanghai *(from Chen Lei,* Xiang baokou yao fan chi, *1947)*

Right: Banner reading "Root out the Red Fifth Column" used during a 1947 anti-Communist demonstration organized by Guomindang loyalists in Beijing *(from the Kenneth Lau Collection, Hoover Institution, Stanford University)*

View from the reviewing stand at the February 1946 rally marking Jiang Jieshi's first postwar visit to Shanghai. Held at what was once the racetrack of the International Settlement, an area that would become People's Square, this rally drew representatives from various organizations, each of which carried its own banner. Visible in front are the banners of the Bureau of Education and the Shanghai municipal government *(photo by Arthur Rothstein; courtesy Library of Congress)*

SEVEN

THE STUDENT MOVEMENT OF 1931

IN SEPTEMBER 1931, A WAVE of popular indignation swept Shanghai at the news that Japanese troops had attacked Chinese forces in Manchuria on September 18. Once again, as in 1919 and 1925, the city's educated youths led in spreading the word of this newest imperialist outrage to the populace at large. And, once again, Shanghai students backed up their angry words with deeds—staging strikes and demonstrations, holding parades and rallies, and enforcing the long-standing (but largely ignored) boycott on Japanese goods.[1] They also began an intensive petition campaign to convince the central government to go to war against Japan to protect China's honor and territorial integrity. This campaign began in a typical enough way, with protesters sending the usual telegrams to various government bodies. As the anti-Japanese movement developed, however, students introduced a new twist in their petitioning technique: group trips to Nanjing. The participants demanded and frequently were accorded face-to-face audiences with national political leaders.

As Chapter 6 suggests, such outbursts of patriotic activity presented GMD officials with complex dilemmas. Student agitation against imperialism forced local and national authorities to choose between the Scylla of encouraging a potentially revolutionary force (which could all too easily trigger domestic problems of social control as well as further strain Sino-Japanese relations) and the Charybdis of tarnishing the GMD's image as an anti-imperialist mass party. The central government, by refusing to launch an all-out military campaign against Japan, soon made it clear in 1931 that unconditional support for this particular student movement was out of the question. Jiang Jieshi remained convinced that China could not risk fighting any major foreign power until the nation itself was truly unified. And, although his Nanjing government had nominally been a "national" one for three years, in 1931 various parts of the country were still under the control of either the CCP, the rival GMD regime that Wang Jingwei had established in Guangzhou (Canton) in 1930, or one or another warlord. Therefore, although the Generalissimo and his advisers condemned the September 18th Incident as an intolerable encroachment upon China's national sovereignty, they also stressed the need for patience and the desirability of letting the League of Nations settle the affair. Yes, China must fight for its national integrity, they claimed, but the first step toward achieving this patriotic goal was internal unification—that is, the elimination of all "red bandits" and the reunification of the GMD under Jiang's supreme authority.

The Nanjing government, though unwilling to give in to the students' demand for immediate military action, also realized that it would be foolish (and perhaps even catastrophic) to condemn the nation's youth for protesting so blatant an act of imperialist aggression. Popular indignation was much higher than it had been at any previous point during the Nanjing Decade; the central government knew that it could not afford either to wait out or to take overt action to crush the student movement. Throughout the fall of 1931, therefore, the Nanjing regime tried in various ways to channel student energies into non-threatening directions, an effort in which local representatives of the central government such as Shanghai's mayor played key roles.

The Shanghai branch office of the GMD also took an active interest in the youth movement of 1931 and tried to use the students' patriotic outrage to further its own interests, which, as noted in Chapter 6, did not always parallel those of either the mayor or the central government. Thanks to the fragmented state of Chinese political arrangements and the different agendas of party and government bureaus, there was never a single official policy toward the student movement. Rather, the movement attracted the attention of a wide variety of different officials, who may have agreed on certain points (for example, that Communism was evil) but differed on others (the role of mass movements in the revolution). No wonder, then, that these officials, who were also divided by competing personal and factional loyalties, proved unable to channel the student movement into a loyalist direction. Before we examine this failure in detail, however, let us look at how local and national authorities, beginning with the leaders of the central government, tried to use student unrest to further ideological and factional ends.

CONTROLLING THE STUDENTS:
SEPTEMBER – OCTOBER 1931

The central government first told the press of its intention to shape the student movement into a manageable force exactly one week after the Manchurian invasion. The *China Press* reported this decision in a front-page article in its September 25 issue entitled "Student Feeling to Be Controlled: Ministry of Education Will Direct Outbreak of Passion."[2] The text that followed this headline spelled out the Nanjing regime's vision of such a "controlled" student movement. It would be one without strikes and unruly demonstrations, in which students would "abide by the directions of the school authorities" and teachers, who were instructed to take a leading role in campus political activities.[3] It would be one in which students engaged in patriotic propaganda activities, but never "at the expense of their regular curriculum." And it would also, the Generalissimo and his associates hoped, be one in which GMD-controlled student organizations played the leading role.*

The central government also promoted military training programs to calm student impatience with Jiang's pacific policy toward Japan. One of the first demands youths made when news of the Manchurian invasion reached Shanghai was that they be allowed to form "student armies" (*xueshengjun*) to help defend their country. Participants in earlier mass movements had also talked about, and in some cases even formed, such anti-imperialist armies.[4] The traditional call to arms took on a special urgency, however, now that war seemed a real possibility. Less than one week after news of the Manchurian invasion reached Shanghai, youths from twelve local schools had joined together to establish a student army, and more than 8,000 local students had enrolled in military training programs.[5]

The Nanjing government quickly realized that if it did not satisfy the students' desire to risk their lives for their country, it would never gain control over the youth movement. On September 25, therefore, the offi-

---

*Here the authorities no doubt put most of their hope in the school "self-governing associations" (*zizhihui*), which they had tried for several years to depoliticize and bring under party control. As John Israel (*Student Nationalism*, p. 50) points out, these "ineffectual" organizations soon proved "incapable of containing the flood of nationalism," and students began forming "extralegal groups" to coordinate their protest activities. At first, however, some of these associations played important roles in the anti-Japanese movement, at least in Shanghai. For an interesting document describing one self-governing association's attempt to take charge of the new tide of student activism, see Jiaotong University School History Group, *Jiaotong daxue*, 2:275.

cial Zhongyang (Central) News Agency announced that the "organization of Volunteer Corps by the youth of the country, proposed by various societies following the Japanese atrocities in Manchuria, has obtained the official sanction of the Central Executive Committee." Military exercises would henceforth be part of the "regular daily routine" at all middle schools and colleges.[6] Thus, even though the leaders of the Nanjing regime remained determined to avoid outright war with Japan, they tried to give the impression that war was imminent and that students would soon march into battle.

Another technique of the Generalissimo and his associates to limit and direct youthful militancy without endangering the central government's reputation as a revolutionary patriotic body was to arrange meetings between student petitioners and high officials in Nanjing. Throughout fall 1931 student delegations, some of whom traveled on special trains or with special train passes provided by officials, poured into the capital from all parts of China.[7] Once in Nanjing, those student delegations that proved willing to follow government direction and were not suspected of being Communist were treated to a standard program of ritualized meetings and diversions. John Israel describes the main features of a typical visit.

> After a group had been fed and lodged under close surveillance, its leaders would be summoned to the Kuomintang's [Guomindang's] Ministry of Propaganda for an intimate talk about government plans to resist Japan, and secret party resolutions would be produced as evidence of sincerity. High-level party and government officials would speak to the assembled students, who would afterward be shepherded to the government offices to present their petition; Chiang Kai-shek [Jiang Jieshi] would usually appear to say a few words. If they behaved very well, they might be treated to a pilgrimage to Sun Yat-sen's [Sun Zhongshan's] tomb before being escorted to a train waiting to take them home.[8]

Many delegations, especially those granted an audience with the Generalissimo himself, left for home with a feeling of great accomplishment. Although the country's policy toward Japan may not have changed as a result of their petition, they went away convinced that the Nanjing regime took their opinions seriously. Why else would the authorities have provided them with transportation to the capital and accepted their petitions? Jiang's reassurance that he was doing all he could to keep imperialism at bay and his advice that educated youth could best aid their country by studying hard to prepare for future leadership roles were not exactly what many petitioners had set out to hear. Nonetheless, the Generalissimo's words and the accompanying pomp and circumstance helped allay many students' fears by restoring their faith in the ruling party and convincing them that the central government would make good on its promises to fight Japan in due time. Thus one former petitioner, whom John Israel talked with decades later, gave his interviewer the impression that his group had left Nanjing feeling that their "trip had been a success; they had been well fed, they had seen the capital, and Chairman Chiang [Jiang] had spoken to them in person."[9]

While the leaders of the Nanjing regime were busy entertaining student petitioners and drafting policies to establish volunteer corps, local officials in Shanghai were taking steps of their own to decrease the intensity of student unrest and channel its direction. The Chinese governors of Shanghai Special Municipality kept a very low profile during September and seem to have been concerned most with trying to limit student activism. These local officials made some attempts to demonstrate their sympathy with the anti-Japanese movement, such as lowering the flags on all government buildings to half-mast on September 24, which the central government had declared a day of national humiliation, and helping enforce Nanjing's order that all places of amusement remain closed on that date.[10] For the most part, however, because of fears that untoward incidents between protesters and Japanese citizens would lead to reprisals by Japanese marines stationed in the city, local government officials contented themselves with trying to contain rather than fan the flames of student enthusiasm. The city's mayor, Zhang Qun, does not seem to have made an official statement condemning the Manchurian invasion until September 22, and even then he showed most interest in counseling the Chinese populace not to overreact to Japan's aggression. Zhang and Xu Peihuang, the head of the municipal Education Bureau, did hold several meetings with college presidents during September and October to discuss the political situation and student participation in the popular movement. Their main goal in these gatherings, however, was to convince campus officials of the need to prevent disruptive student strikes, not to give the administrators advice on how to guide the student movement.[11]

In contrast, the cadres of the local Dangbu took an active role in popular anti-Japanese activities from the start of the popular movement and focused on controlling and channeling rather than stifling student activism.[12] The most important steps of local GMD branch activists centered around the formation of "resist Japan to save the nation societies" (*kangri jiuguohui*—hereafter *kangrihui*). According to official GMD policy, student kangrihui were by definition extralegal organizations, since the party's Third National Congress had ruled that the only political associations students could legally form were "self-governing societies" (*zizhihui*) devoted exclusively to campus internal affairs. Nonetheless, in the words of one recent student of the anti-Japanese movements of the 1930's, during the days immediately following the Manchurian invasion single-school kangrihui sprung up "like bamboo shoots after a spring rain" in Shanghai and other major cities.[13]

These single-school groups soon joined together to form citywide leagues to coordinate anti-Japanese activities at different schools and generally supervise the local student movement. On September 22, for example, representatives from over 30 local universities gathered at the Shanghai Baptist College to form the Alliance of Resist Japan to Save the Nation Societies of All Shanghai Colleges (hereafter College Resistance Alliance). This group's first actions were to organize propaganda teams to drum up support for the patriotic movement in the city's outlying areas and neighboring cities such as Suzhou and to make plans to send a delegation to Nanjing to petition the central government.[14] Middle-school and vocational school students were not far behind in forming their own protest league. Just two days after the founding of the College Resistance Alliance, representatives from 37 secondary schools met to form an umbrella group of their own, which immediately called on its members to devote the last three days of the month to a "stop classes to propagandize" drive to publicize the September 18th Incident.[15]

Official GMD policy notwithstanding, the leaders of the Shanghai Dangbu did not attempt to prevent such "extralegal" student organizations from functioning; instead they did all they could to gain control over the new youth leagues. The Dangbu's ultimate goal was to incorporate all such student groups into the recently established citywide kangrihui, a semi-official alliance of resistance associations run by party leaders and members of elite organizations such as the Chinese Chamber of Commerce.[16] It is difficult to gauge just how successful the Shanghai Dangbu was in its efforts to bring student kangrihui under its wing. Branch office cadres do seem to have gained enough influence over both the Middle-School Resistance Alliance and the College Resistance Alliance to keep these groups from turning into centers of anti-GMD as well as anti-Japanese agitation during the early months of the 1931 movement. According to John Israel, in Shanghai as elsewhere, secondary school students proved more amenable to party control than did college-age youths. He notes, for example, that during an early meeting of the Middle-School Resistance Alliance, one of the league's leaders went so far as to call on his comrades to "honor the principles of party government, guard against machinations of the 'reactionary clique,' and keep anti-Japanese activities from interfering with studies."[17] However, even though university students proved less docile than their middle-school counterparts, Dangbu cadres did manage at times to get members of the College Resistance Alliance to participate in mass rallies that attacked Japanese imperialism, but in a way that supported rather than challenged GMD party rule.[18]

Supervising the enforcement of the anti-Japanese boycott and organizing rallies in support of the boycott, which were partly anti-imperialist "protests" and partly loyalist displays, were the two main preoccupations of the GMD-controlled citywide kangrihui. Local GMD leaders realized that the only way to keep popular activism, by students or by members of other social groups, from taking on an anti-party hue was to provide acceptable outlets for popular outrage. Nothing served this purpose better than carefully orchestrated events, such as the giant Municipal Citizens' Assembly (Shimin dahui) held at the Recreation Ground near Shanghai's West Gate on September 26. During this event kangrihui leaders encouraged the audience to shout anti-imperialist slogans; they also stressed that the only hope for true national salvation lay in remaining loyal to Jiang Jieshi and the GMD.* This meeting drew an enormous crowd of somewhere between 30,000 and 100,000 students, workers, and other citizens, thanks in part to the fact that employers at several of Shanghai's main Chinese concerns made the day a special holiday so that their employees could attend the rally.[19]

The Municipal Citizens' Assembly began with a series of impassioned political speeches, in which GMD spokesmen and other civic leaders denounced Japanese aggression while "admonish[ing] against hasty action." Many of these orators also called upon Wang Jingwei's Guangzhou regime to reunite with Jiang Jieshi's Nanjing government to form a united front against the foreign foe.[†] After the speeches ended, the crowd shouted slogans and approved the text of a telegram to be sent to Nanjing, in the name of the Shanghai kangrihui, calling on the central government to take a firmer stand against Japanese aggression. The day's excitement then ended with a colorful parade complete with the traditional banners and pennants. According to a September 27 *Shen bao* report, the march was led by a brigade from the postal workers' union, who were flanked on one side by representatives of the Dangbu and on the other by a brigade of women

---

*Along with staging mass rallies, Shanghai Dangbu activists also sponsored an "exhibition of anti-Japanese compositions written by school children" and anti-Japanese student "oration contests" (see *NCH*, Nov. 3, 1931, p. 101). Officials in other cities also organized anti-Japanese events, in an effort to prevent the CCP from cornering the market on patriotic protest displays. For GMD-sponsored rallies in Beijing similar to the Shanghai Citizens' Assembly, see Israel, *Student Nationalism*, p. 51.

†In 1931 phrases such as "united front" and "work together against outsiders" (*yizhi duiwai*) generally referred to healing breaches within the GMD. This is in sharp contrast to the situation several years later; after further Japanese encroachments upon Chinese territory, some began to argue that the GMD and CCP should work together to resist Japan. Neither the CCP nor any of the major factions within the GMD was interested in forming this kind of true "united front" in 1931.

(presumably members of the newly formed Shanghai women's kangrihui).[20] This vanguard group was followed by "students, workers, merchants, agriculturalists and finally Boy Scouts." [21] On the whole, therefore, the *Shen bao* account—which praises the orderliness of the affair and comments on the "intense" mood of the marchers, who shouted anti-Japanese slogans and distributed anti-Japanese pamphlets as they walked along Shanghai's streets—makes the September 26 parade sound like a typical Shanghai demonstration. A memoir by a Communist organizer, who participated in an unsuccessful CCP attempt to disrupt the Municipal Citizens' Assembly and turn it into a forum for anti-GMD agitation, does note one unusual feature about this particular "protest": the marchers who paraded under kangrihui banners met with no obstruction from the police.[22]

STUDENTS OUT OF CONTROL: SEPTEMBER–NOVEMBER 1931

Despite these efforts by local and national party and government officials to channel student anger and energy into acceptable forms of expression, the authorities ultimately proved unable to keep the student movement from developing into an independent and threatening force. Events outside these officials' immediate control played an important role in this failure. If Japan had withdrawn on its own accord, or at least refrained from advancing farther into northeast China, Jiang may well have been able to contain youth activism. Unfortunately, Japanese troops continued to threaten Manchuria throughout the fall of 1931. The growing militancy of the student movement, which (as later pages show) took on a decidedly radical hue in early December, can therefore be traced in part to the simple fact that Nanjing's reassurances became harder and harder to believe as months went by and Japanese encroachments continued to outstrip Chinese war preparations.

Long before the dramatic events of early December, however, there were already indications that official attempts to harness the national student movement were in trouble and that Shanghai youths were likely to prove particularly troublesome in this regard, in part because of tensions between local party and government officials. The Shanghai Dangbu seems to have been relatively unconcerned about the problem of student strikes, for example, and to have at least indirectly encouraged them. This was true even after the central government expressly condemned such actions and the head of the municipal Education Bureau began to take steps to keep students in their classrooms.[23] The day after the Nanjing regime forbade all classroom strikes, an estimated 4,000 local college students suspended their studies to devote all their time to anti-Japanese protest activities.[24] They were joined by a large contingent of middle-school students the following day, which, according to a *China Press* report, brought the total number of strikers to 45,000.[25] From the start, therefore, Shanghai students showed that although they were willing to follow some official directives—for example, in late September student lecture teams from various campuses cleared their plans with school authorities before taking to the streets[26]—they would not bow to all of Nanjing's dictates, especially if they received mixed signals from the local authorities.

More ominous omens of future student troubles appeared on September 28, when youths in Nanjing and Shanghai vented their anger in ways that went far beyond the limits of a "controlled" student movement. In Nanjing, over 4,000 students marched through the morning rain to the GMD party headquarters to present petitions. They listened to speeches urging patience and loyalty by the head of the Control Ministry and Jiang Jieshi himself, lectures effective enough to inspire some pro-GMD slogans. The official speeches were not soothing enough, however, to satisfy a group of students from the Central University (Zhongyang daxue) who marched to the Foreign Ministry, where they beat Foreign Minister Wang Zhengting within an inch of his life. Thanks to rumors that Wang was secretly pro-Japanese, that he had failed to heed advance warnings of the Japanese invasion, that he had gone on vacation to Hangzhou when he should have been taking steps to prevent the fall of Shenyang, these youths labeled Wang a "traitor" and viewed him as the one responsible for the national crisis. When they stormed into his office, therefore, they were improvising upon one of the more violent May 4th scripts, since in 1919 Beijing youths had ransacked the home of a "traitorous" official in much the same way.[27]

At the same time, equally dramatic developments were taking place in Shanghai, where a petition brigade of some 3,000 students was hurriedly making plans to travel to Nanjing to add its voice to the clamor for war.[28] This brigade was to be the third Shanghai delegation to set off for the capital since the September 18th Incident. The first delegation, organized by the College Resistance Alliance, had been a small one of 51 representatives from 24 different schools. This group, whose petition drive had received the express approval of local GMD leaders, had left on September 25. Its leaders had vowed that if the central government did not respond satisfactorily to the Alliance's demand for immediate military mobilization, they would send word back to Shanghai for the organization's members to come to the capital en masse. The delegation succeeded in gaining an audience with representatives of the central government two days later, but the group's leaders telegraphed their Shanghai constituents that same day to say that they were dissatisfied with the reception given their petition and had therefore decided to stay on in the capital.[29]

Alliance members in Shanghai immediately called an emergency meeting to organize a mass petition drive, in which all students and teachers from member-schools would be invited to participate.[30] Before plans for this multi-campus protest drive could be finalized, however, a second delegation of 600 to 800 Fudan students set out for Nanjing on the night of September 27.[31] It is unclear whether this Fudan delegation sought or received official permission to travel to Nanjing, but school authorities clearly knew of the students' plans in advance, since they assigned four teachers as chaperones.[32] Like the College Resistance Alliance delegation, the Fudan delegation encountered no difficulties in securing passage to Nanjing for its members. Nor did the Fudan students have trouble gaining an audience with Jiang Jieshi himself: just hours after they arrived in Nanjing, many of these Shanghai youths were listening to the same speech the Central University petitioners had heard just before the Nanjing youths set out to attack the "traitorous" foreign minister.

The third contingent of Shanghai petitioners had a much rougher time getting to the capital. It ran into trouble, in fact, as soon as its members began converging on Shanghai's North Station on the night of September 28. According to a report in the following day's edition of the *China Press*—which appeared under the provocative headline "Shanghai Students Mob Railway Station When Denied Nanjing Passage: Terminus Officials Flee Before Wrath of 3,000 Angered Youths"—this trouble almost led to a violent rampage like that earlier in the day in Nanjing.[33] Initially the railway authorities were willing enough to sell the youths tickets for the night express. Soon after the sale was completed, however, Colonel Chen Xizeng, the head of the Shanghai Public Security Bureau (the department in charge of policing the Special Municipality), who had no doubt just received word of the attack on the foreign minister, called to tell the stationmaster that no more students should be permitted to travel to the capital. Upon hearing that the students had already bought tickets, Colonel Chen and other local officials rushed to the station to try to persuade the youths to call off the petition drive. These efforts only annoyed the crowd of protestors, who shouted that they would travel to the capital no matter what obstacles officials put in their path.

Colonel Chen, realizing that the situation was hopeless, rushed back to his office to persuade Nanjing to change its mind. A little later he phoned North Station to tell the railway authorities that Jiang Jieshi had given permission for the youths to travel to Nanjing, as long as they arrived at a specified time. According to the *China Press*, when the railway authorities passed this message on to the students, who had spent the period between Chen's departure and his phone call "roam[ing] around the terminus seeking the station master and other officials upon whom to vent their anger," this diffused a potentially explosive situation.[34]

Han Jiemei, a participant in the petition drive, gives a similar account of the evening's events. Where the *China Press* correspondent saw a wrathful student mob, however, Han saw a band of frustrated patriots. "Although the railway guards tried to prevent us," Han writes, "we shouted out slogans and charged into the station." Once inside the station, Han continues,

> full of youthful energy and moving swiftly, some climbed up into freight cars, some forced their way into passenger cars, some crawled up on top of the trains, and suddenly all was chaos. The station authorities, realizing the situation was hopeless, had to issue [us] seven or eight freight cars, and only then did the situation calm down. When the cars left the station, the send-off party was quite large, with patriots of all social classes shouting out slogans.[35]

The Nanjing and Shanghai outbursts of September 28 highlight the limited effectiveness of the central government's main technique for keeping youthful fervor in check: orchestrated meetings between student petitioners and political leaders. When students agreed to play by Nanjing's rules and treat these events as rites of supplication—through which powerholders showed their benevolence by deigning to listen to their subjects' views, and these subjects proved their loyalty by being satisfied with whatever the officials said—the meetings indeed helped legitimate Jiang's image as a popular ruler. But students were not always prepared to be so passive. They were not always willing to let a local or national official decide such things as the response a petition deserved or when youths could travel to Nanjing.

Memoirs and newspaper accounts concerning the Shanghai petition drives of September and November show, in fact, that student protesters often viewed their trips to the capital less as deferential pilgrimages than as quasi-military campaigns. The martial quality of these trips to Nanjing is not surprising, since in 1931 students were obsessed with the idea of going to war for their country. Official plans for volunteer corps and programs of military instruction in the schools—though never comprehensively implemented on a national scale—were enough to satisfy the desire of some youths to prove their patriotism through physical struggle. Others fulfilled this need by joining semiofficial anti-Japanese training corps.[36] Still others went further and enlisted in special youth brigades, some of which set off for Manchuria on their own accord to assist General Ma Zhanshan, whose attempts to engage the Japanese in battle in November transformed him instantly into a national hero.[37]

Many more students, however, quenched their thirst for battle by bringing a martial attitude and military discipline to other anti-Japanese activities, such as marching and petitioning. Youth armies had been formed during earlier protest movements, and the tendency of the students of 1931 to think in martial terms was by no means novel. The May 4th students, for example, created a disciplined, barracks-like atmosphere on campus (see Chapter 2), and the organizers of the May 30th demonstration of 1925 planned their "invasion" of the International Settlement as if they were generals (see Chapter 4). Never before, however, had student protesters so consistently treated their protests as a form of or a substitute for open warfare.

The September 28 attacks on Foreign Minister Wang and Shanghai's North Station were the first important events in the anti-Japanese movement to take the form of physical skirmishes. But two contemporary first-hand reports by Wu Youyi and Shi Cun, participants in the Fudan petition brigade that left Shanghai on September 27, suggest that students viewed their actions in martial terms even before any actual violence broke out.[38] Both reports' detailed accounts of the logistical preparation required for petition drives involving hundreds of youths rely heavily upon martial images and metaphors.

Wu's report devotes much attention to the internal structure of the Fudan petition brigade, which adhered to many of the same hierarchical and organizational principles examined in Chapters 2, 3, and 5. The author claims, for example, that because 600–700 youths obviously "could not set out on a journey like a loose sheet of sand," they immediately established a general command bureau and a general service department to organize and direct the trip to Nanjing. The former, which took control of general planning and strategy, was headed by a general commander and two vice-commanders. These three leaders passed on orders directly to the heads of large brigades composed of a hundred or so students, and each of these unit chiefs in turn supervised the actions of ten small subordinate brigades. The general service department supervised the work of special teams in charge of propaganda work, transportation, communications, business affairs, and so forth. It also oversaw the operations of two first-aid brigades, one for male students, the other for female ones. There is nothing unusual about this general organizational structure; participants in other movements paid equally close attention to bureaucratic principles and established comparably elaborate chains of command. Wu's final comment on the system, however, reveals that the special spirit of Fudan youths in 1931. "I think that in terms of militarized discipline [*jilu jun-duihua*] and taking absolute obedience as one's principle," he writes, "our organization is a model worth examining."

Shi Cun's account of the Fudan petition drive evokes the quasi-military spirit of the time even better. On the night of September 27, for example, Shi and his classmates were so excited by the idea of committing their lives to saving the nation that they were unable to sleep and spent the train ride composing a poem entitled "Ye xingjun" (Troops of the night).[39] This image of themselves as an army was reinforced soon after the youths arrived in the capital, when many of them put on military uniforms and hats lent them by Nanjing students. Shi's account of the group's activities in Nanjing plays up the physical hardships the youths had to endure, particularly the lack of food and the incessant rain of September 28. When the youths were finally given a giant meal of "3,000 loaves of bread and several dozen tons of gruel" the next afternoon, after a morning spent petitioning at GMD headquarters for the second day in a row, according to Shi, "just like soldiers on the battlefield obtaining these kinds of food, everyone viewed them as if they were delicacies and devoured them with wolfish tongues and tiger's mouths to the point of exhaustion."*

These two reports show that even in September some students were already thinking of trips to Nanjing as analogous to military campaigns. The quasi-military air of these early protests was no match, however, for that which accompanied the great petition drive of November 24, in which somewhere between 7,000 and 10,000 youths took part.[40] Shanghai student protesters took a break from petitioning during October and the first part of November, devoting their time instead to enforcing the anti-Japanese boycott, staging parades and demonstrations, writing and distributing pamphlets, pasting up anti-Japanese posters, and carrying out massive fund-raising campaigns to aid General Ma.[41] When by late November the central government had still made no move to change its policy of avoiding war with Japan, Shanghai youths decided to try once again to bring their case to the nation's leaders. This time they were prepared, however, to do more than simply ask Jiang Jieshi to mobilize the nation's troops: the College Resistance Alliance announced that if Jiang remained unwilling to go to war with Japan, its delegation would call on the Generalissimo to resign.[42]

To match the increased militancy of student demands, the November 24 petition drive was also a more tightly organized affair than the September 28 drive, as well as the first one in which Shanghai youths dressed from the start in military uniforms. The city's residents were thus treated to an unusual sight on the morning and early afternoon of November 24, as thousands of petitioner-soldiers donned battle garb, divided up into school troops, and marched along Shanghai's streets, keeping time to the music of campus bands and carrying flags bearing slogans such as "Calling on the

---

*Shi, for his part, had been lucky enough to secure a good meal the previous evening; a friend who lived in Nanjing provided him with a chicken dinner. This did not, however, prevent Shi from eating "four loaves of bread and four bowls of gruel" on the afternoon of September 29.

government to regain the lost territories."[43] "Strict order was obeyed" by the youths, according to the *China Press*; petitioners listened only to the "commanders of their respective schools," and these youths, in turn, obeyed the orders of the Ji'nan University student who served as the march's overall commander-in-chief.[44] One reason the students established such a careful chain of command was no doubt their fear that the authorities would once again try to prevent their brigade from setting off for Nanjing. As it was, the authorities had little choice in the matter: the petitioner-soldiers simply took over the station, forcing their way onto scheduled trains and commandeering extra cars until all the troops were bound for Nanjing.[45]

STUDENTS IN CONTROL: EARLY DECEMBER 1931

This train-commandeering incident was the first of a series of militant student protests during late November and early December in which educated youths quite literally took the law into their own hands and usurped official prerogatives. The headlines in Shanghai's English-language newspapers give a good sense of the excitement of the time. Foreign reporters occasionally sensationalized their account of student unrest, as in the *China Press* headline "Shanghai-Nanking Tracks Opened for Commandeered Express in Mad Race to Shanghai, Students at Throttle—Miracle Saves Trainload of Undergrads from Catastrophe."[46] There was, however, a solid basis in fact for this and many other colorful headlines, such as "Kuomintang Headquarters Wrecked," "Educational Crisis Looming," "Government Structure Threatened," "Students Amok," and "City Government 'Captured': Demand for Arrest of Police Officials: Mayor Resigns," all of which appeared in the December 15 issue of the weekly *North China Herald*.

The incident to which the last two headlines allude, the Popular Tribunal (*Minzhong fating*) affair of December 9–10, is worth looking at in some detail for two main reasons. First, it was the most dramatic event in Shanghai during the entire anti-Japanese upsurge of 1931. And, second, it illustrates more clearly than any other single event one of the central claims of this book: that a key to the power of student protest is the ability of educated youths to undercut the legitimacy of established authorities by literally or symbolically turning the tables on governmental officials. Previous discussions of the May 4th and May 30th movements have shown that long before 1931 Shanghai's students had begun to challenge foreign and native authorities by stepping into roles ordinarily reserved for power-holders. This tendency toward usurpation was never quite so blatant in earlier decades, however, as it was in December 1931, when according to a reporter for the *China Press*: "Youth, drawing deep from its reserve of vibrant energy and overwhelming numbers, turned Dictator in Greater Shanghai."[47]

The Popular Tribunal affair grew out of a fairly routine protest meeting on December 9, at which some hundred representatives of campus groups gathered to hear two student leaders from Beijing University and Nanjing's Central University. These two youths had come to Shanghai to galvanize support for resistance to the Nanjing authorities' increasingly draconian measures to silence student demonstrators in the capital. The Nanjing Garrison Command, which had initially treated petitioners with kid gloves, had begun to crack down on more radical student protesters in early December. The most famous case of police repression involved 180 members of the Beijing University Demonstration Corps. The members of this group, which John Israel claims was the "most potent pro-Communist student group in China at the time," had traveled to Nanjing to demand not only a change in foreign policy but also a change in government.[48] The Nanjing Garrison Command arrested the Beijing youths on December 5 as the students marched through the capital shouting such inflammatory slogans as "Oppressed masses organize and rise!" Later that same night, after Central University students mounted a sympathy demonstration to protest these arrests, the Beijing revolutionaries were "roped together, herded aboard a special train, and sent to Peiping [Beiping] under armed escort."[49]

The first response in Shanghai to the arrests came on December 7, when 15,000 local students held an "indignation parade" to call on the GMD to stop oppressing the youth movement.[50] Student leaders called the December 9 meeting to plan additional protest activities along the same lines. Before they could finalize their plans, however, 20–30 plainclothes special agents and hired thugs broke into the meeting, seized the guest speakers, and tried to spirit the two youths off in a black sedan.[51] The students in the audience rose up to prevent the arrests, and although their efforts were unsuccessful, the protesters did manage to take a prisoner of their own: a worker named Wang Fusheng, who had been part of the raiding party.

Those who witnessed the abduction immediately began rallying their classmates for action, and within an hour or so a large group of enraged youths descended upon the local GMD party headquarters. As the *China Press* colorfully put it, however, this "student army" was unable to gain any satisfaction at the Dangbu offices, which were inhabited only by "coolies with brooms and mops," and the youths had to content themselves with "transform[ing] the place into a potpourri of broken desks, chairs and splintered window panes."[52] The students, who now numbered around

3,000, then moved on to the Municipal Government Compound, in the hope of finding Mayor Zhang Qun and convincing him to help them secure the release of Xu Xiuchen, the student representative from Beijing.[53] (Xu's Nanjing counterpart had managed to slip away from his captors before being incarcerated, though not without sustaining injuries that required his hospitalization.)

The mayor was at his office when the "student army" arrived, and the youths immediately took control of the compound to ensure that he would stay there until their demands were met. By early evening student sentries, some of whom had managed to secure arms, had cut all outside phone lines and stationed detachments at every entrance.[54] And if the presence of these guards was not enough to deter escape attempts by the mayor and his associates, beyond the student sentries stood an angry crowd of 5,000 youths. Nor could the bureaucrats count on the glass and steel of their private automobiles to protect them from the mob's fury: as an additional security measure, the protesters seized all cars belonging to officials.

Despite this attempt to hold the mayor and his staff hostage, the students did not hold Zhang Qun personally responsible for the arrests earlier in the day; rather they sought to use him to wreak revenge on those they blamed for the outrage. The main villain the students singled out for censure was Colonel Chen of the Public Security Bureau, under whose orders they (correctly) assumed the raiding party had been operating. The youths also criticized Dangbu leaders, whom they blamed for working with Chen to subvert and suppress the student movement, and whose absence from party headquarters earlier in the day the students resented. When student representatives met with the mayor, in a series of negotiations that lasted straight from mid-afternoon until the morning of December 10, they put forth five main demands: that Xu be released; Colonel Chen be executed; key members of the Dangbu be dismissed; Wang Fusheng and the other thugs involved in the disruption of the December 9 meeting be punished; and future student gatherings be free from outside interference.

The mayor balked at some of these demands—particularly the call for Chen's execution, which he rightfully pointed out only a court could order—but he almost immediately agreed to the others. By the middle of the night, not only had he agreed to try to secure Xu's release and to take steps to ensure that similar outrages would not occur in the future, but he had even told the youths that he would place the colonel on suspension, pending investigation of the students' charges that the Public Security Bureau had gone too far in its zeal to prevent disorder. He also swore to work to bring the perpetrators of the December 9 assault to justice. The mayor's willingness to compromise, a result perhaps of the fact that he and Colonel

Chen belonged to rival cliques within the GMD,[55] was encouraging to the students. The youths refused to disperse, however, until they saw Xu Xiuchen with their own eyes. Zhang's first requests to the Public Security Bureau to release Xu from custody proved fruitless, and the mayor remained a prisoner within his own office for hours after he had acceded to most of the students' demands.

It was during this period, while the students were waiting for Xu to be released, that the protesters convened the Popular Tribunal. Emboldened by their successes, which convinced them that taking measures into their own hands was the only way to guarantee results, the students agreed "unanimously" (according to the *North China Herald*) to set up a "special court" to try the prisoner Wang Fusheng for crimes against the youth movement.[56] The assembly chose a law student as the chief magistrate and selected five more student delegates (at least one of whom was also majoring in law) from local universities as well as two representatives of the municipal government to serve as his assistants. (Zhang Qun declined the students' request that he act as one of the judges, but it is interesting that he did allow two lesser officials to participate in his stead.) In addition to this board of eight "magistrates," the students chose a Daxia University youth to serve as court reporter and appointed some twenty members of various schools' volunteer corps to act as bailiffs.[57]

The Popular Tribunal's initial order of business, at its first and only formal session in a special hall within the government compound, which began around 10:00 A.M. on December 10, was to interrogate Wang Fusheng. This interrogation—during which (at least according to one source) student investigators used bamboo sticks to prod the defendant's memory—soon brought important results.[58] The prisoner confessed to taking part in the disruption of the December 9 meeting. He also admitted that both the Public Security Bureau and the Dangbu had sanctioned the raid and gave the court the names and addresses of three men who had been part of the plot to seize Xu. The Tribunal then issued "warrants" for these three men and dispatched a group of students to carry out the necessary "arrests" in the court's name. When Wang, continuing his confession, claimed that Xu (of whose precise whereabouts the mayor had claimed to have no knowledge) was probably being held at the Public Security Bureau itself, the students began to shout "Execute Chen Xizeng."

The court then drafted one final document: in a supreme act of usurpation, it issued a warrant for the arrest of the head of the city's main Chinese police force, Chen Xizeng himself. It also dispatched a delegation, which included both a municipal government secretary and a number of students, to the Public Security Bureau to demand that Xu be released immediately.[59] According to the *North China Herald*, tensions ran high during the next quarter of an hour or so, as members of the "gathering held their breath in waiting, while the mayor walked to and fro in the hall." The tension finally broke at 10:37 when Xu himself arrived, "to the accompaniment of wild cheers," and gave the assembled crowd an account of his detainment, which had included a night incarcerated on a boat anchored off the Bund.[60] The students continued to hold meetings and pass resolutions at the Municipal Government Compound until 2:00 in the afternoon, when they finally dispersed and allowed the mayor to go home to rest.

REACTIONS, COUNTERATTACKS, FRAGMENTATION: DECEMBER 10–JANUARY 28

Xu's triumphant return and the students' subsequent dispersal marked the end of a tense confrontation, but the effects of the two-day mini-uprising would continue for weeks. The struggles of December 9 and 10 precipitated important changes in Shanghai's governing elite, as various school administrators and municipal government officials including Mayor Zhang tendered their resignations to apologize for their inability to control student actions.[61] The Popular Tribunal affair also had a major impact upon the activities of student protesters; the experience emboldened some militants but simultaneously exacerbated latent ideological and factional rifts within the anti-Japanese movement.

The first indication of a new boldness on the part of the most radical student protesters came on December 11, the anniversary of the abortive Communist-backed Canton Commune of 1927. Open praise for Marxist doctrines and explicit denunciation of the GMD as a party, as opposed to criticism of specific governmental policies, had been rare during the preceding months of student activism. According to a *China Press* article entitled "Students Active in Celebrating Communist Day," however, at various times on December 11 bands of students gathered in public areas (including the vicinity of the Municipal Government Compound) to brazenly wave red flags and give speeches calling for the overthrow of GMD rule.[62] A further sign that some students at least saw the usurpation of December 10 as but the first step toward a general insurrection came five days later, when the "student court" cosponsored an advertisement in local newspapers offering rewards of $3,000 and $2,000 respectively for the arrest of Colonel Chen and a leading member of the Dangbu.[63]

Although (and in large part precisely because) the Popular Tribunal affair strengthened the resolve of Communist youths and encouraged them to come out into the open, however, the events of December 9 and 10 ultimately served to weaken anti-Japanese forces in Shanghai. The emergence of openly "red" protesters destabilized the consensus of opinion that had previously united patriotic students of differing political ideologies. This consensus had been based upon a shared assumption that forcing a change in national foreign policy toward Japan was a higher priority than forcing a change in either the basic personnel of the central government or its overall ideological orientation. The Popular Tribunal challenged much more than a specific policy, however, for it called into question both the character of political leaders and the legitimacy of existing political institutions and bureaus. This and comparable events in other cities in early December—for example, on December 8, students in Nanjing had "arrested" several plainclothes policemen for spying on a youth group meeting[64]—alarmed not only the authorities, but also more moderate elements within the popular movement itself.

Extant sources make it difficult to reconstruct and document the precise dynamics of ideological and factional splits within the Shanghai student movement at this time, or to chart the relationship between youth activists and members of other social groups. Fragmentary evidence suggests, however, that the Popular Tribunal was one of the last great moments of unified student action in 1931. During the days and weeks that followed, "radical" and "moderate" students increasingly pulled apart. Tensions between youth groups and labor organizations also intensified during this period, and by mid- to late December only the most optimistic of Communist organizers continued to entertain hopes for a multi-class general strike of the type seen in 1919 and 1925.

Some of the most intriguing, though tantalizingly fragmentary, evidence on this question comes from the *China Press*. A December 11 article notes, for example, that as early as the afternoon of December 10 splits began to develop between student representatives from colleges and those from middle schools during a mass meeting held at Jiaotong University to discuss the future of the movement. The *China Press* report contradicts itself as to whether the younger students were more "moderate" than the older ones or vice versa.* The article clearly states, however, that the meeting was marked by sharp divisions over both the issue of the sincerity of the Nanjing authorities and the question of how much say middle-school and college students respectively should have in determining the course of the local patriotic movement.

A report in the following day's issue of the same paper, entitled "Stu-

---

*"Moderates" in this case were those willing to accept at face value the central government's vague promises—issued in response to a student telegram of December 9—that the authorities would be more resolute in resisting Japanese aggression and protecting the youth movement.

dents Call off Nanking Trip to Counter Labor's Move Here," is even more intriguing. This piece claims that "fear of a serious clash with laborers" led student representatives to suspend plans to "send 30,000 students to Nanking" to protest both Xu's arrest and the League of Nations' proposals concerning Manchuria, which Chinese patriots viewed as unacceptably pro-Japanese. According to the *China Press* report, relations "between students and laborers" had "been much strained" as a result of the Popular Tribunal, because the prisoner Wang Fusheng was a worker employed by the Shanghai Arsenal. It is hard to believe that this fact alone accounted for tensions between students and laborers, which became so high that some believed "general hostility" between the two groups could "break out at any time." A more plausible (though unverifiable) supposition is that Dangbu leaders may have begun to stir up anti-student feeling within the local "yellow unions" and labor kangrihui under their control, in an effort to counterbalance the Popular Tribunal.

GMD leaders, in addition to using party-controlled labor organizations as a check on student militancy, also took steps to reassert their authority within youth leagues. Dangbu officials tried, for example, to reorganize the city's College Resistance Alliance and to establish a party-led National Students Federation. The *North China Herald* labeled such reorganization attempts, and meetings at which Dangbu leaders stressed that "the Party had never suppressed or oppressed any patriotic movement," GMD "countermoves" aimed at combating the actions of the Popular Tribunal.[65]

This determination on the part of the authorities to bring pre-existing student organizations back into line was also a response to the recent attempts of Communist organizers to establish a new anti-Japanese coalition group to compete with the GMD's citywide kangrihui. The CCP's drive to undercut the position of the kangrihui predated the founding of the Popular Tribunal, but it picked up steam only after December 10. This drive was led by members of the Association of Returned Students from Japan (Liuri huiguo xueshenghui, hereafter Association of Returned Students), an organization that several dozen radical Chinese youths—who had recently left their studies in Tokyo to demonstrate their anger over the September 18 Incident—formed in late November 1931 with help from two special agents of the CCP. Available sources say little about one of these Communist agents, but the other, Wu Chixiang, has written a detailed memoir about his role in the Association of Returned Students.[66] According to this memoir, Wu had studied in Tokyo from 1928 until he was arrested by the Japanese authorities in 1930 for his activities as editor of a radical political journal. Upon regaining his freedom later that year, Wu returned to Shanghai, where he was recruited into the Communist Youth League. Shortly thereafter he became a member of the CCP itself and took an active part in the party's West Shanghai division. When the

Central Committee decided to infiltrate the delegation of returned students, Wu was an obvious choice. His mission was to lay the groundwork for an organization to replace the CCP-led Great Alliance of Anti-imperialists, an earlier front group that the GMD had driven underground.

Wu saw the founding of the Association of Returned Students as a first step toward this goal. The members of this group immediately began trying to establish a citywide patriotic alliance by convening and presiding over two public meetings, which they invited representatives from dozens of local patriotic groups to attend. At the second of these two meetings, on December 6, the new coalition formally adopted the name Shanghai People's Anti-Japanese National Salvation Alliance (Shanghai minzhong fanri jiuguo lianhehui, or Minfan for short). The group's decision to use the stronger term "oppose" (*fan*) instead of "resist" (*kang*) in its name was an explicit effort to distinguish itself from the citywide kangrihui, which the Minfan condemned as an association "controlled by bureaucrats."[67]

Although formally established before the Popular Tribunal affair, the Minfan did not become an important public force until December 11 when it tried to capitalize on the crisis of the previous day by announcing an anti-Japanese citizens' asssembly two days hence.[68] This December 13 assembly, which according to one estimate drew close to 10,000 people (including representatives from over 50 patriotic organizations),[69] was similar in format to the one the kangrihui had sponsored on September 26. Like the earlier GMD-sponsored event, the Minfan gathering of December 13 took place at the Recreation Ground outside the West Gate and included emotional speeches about the situation in northeastern China.[70] After listening to these speeches by representatives of native-place, youth, and worker groups, the participants passed several resolutions and then formed ranks to march through the city.

Although similar in basic format to the earlier assembly, the December 13 demonstration differed both in terms of content and in terms of its treatment by officials and the official press. The best way to get a sense of these contrasts is to compare the descriptions of the two assemblies in the *Shen bao*, one of Shanghai's leading newspapers and one that by 1931 was firmly controlled by GMD censors.[71] Whereas the *Shen bao*, as noted above, highlighted the enthusiasm and orderliness of the September 26 rally, its portrayal of the December 13 gathering was much less sympathetic. The headline introducing the *Shen bao* report on the Minfan rally, "*Baotu* [thugs or agitators] Create Disturbances and Destroy More Than Ten Tramcars During Yesterday's Municipal Citizens' Assembly," is indicative of the difference in tone and emphasis.[72] It is difficult to determine why the tramcars were destroyed and whether the *baotu* allegedly involved in the incident were radicals who got carried away or outside agitators hired by the Minfan's enemies to discredit the demonstration. It *is* clear, however, that the *Shen bao*'s focus on this violence placed the December 13 citizens' assembly in a much less favorable light than the September 26 one.

Physical violence was not the only negative aspect of the event to which the *Shen bao* drew attention. The newspaper also pointed out that some marchers "seized the opportunity" to "distribute reactionary pamphlets and shout revolutionary slogans." The report used the same derogatory term, *baotu*, to refer to these marchers as it used to describe those who destroyed the tramcars. But here there was no ambiguity regarding the meaning of this term: just as in the official press all rural Communists were vilified as "red bandits," all tracts that attacked the "revolutionary" GMD were routinely described as "counter-revolutionary" or "reactionary" (*fandong*) publications and the CCP members or sympathizers who distributed such materials were automatically labeled *baotu*.

The Minfan continued to achieve some success in organizing public gatherings similar to the December 13 assembly throughout late December and early January, but the organization never accomplished its ultimate goal of spearheading a general strike of the type seen in 1919 and 1925. The popular movement, which had begun to fragment into radical and moderate camps in early December, continued to fall apart during the weeks that followed, particularly after Jiang Jieshi announced his resignation from all governmental posts on December 15. Jiang's decision to step down was in large part due to the embarrassment caused by the protests of the preceding months, an embarrassment that Wang Jingwei and his supporters within the GMD had used to their own advantage by claiming that Wang would gladly join Jiang in forming a united front against Japan if the Generalissimo relinquished some of his power within the party.

Just how important a role backstage machinations by Wang Jingwei (who spent much of fall 1931 in Shanghai) and his supporters played in spurring students on to action in late November and early December is hard to determine from published documentary sources. However, both British consular dispatches and a recent study by Donald Jordan suggest that such machinations were absolutely crucial in shaping the course of political events in early December.[73] Jordan notes, for example, that Japanese naval attaché Kitaoka claimed, in a secret message sent to Tokyo just after the Popular Tribunal Incident, that student followers of Wang Jingwei as well as Communists figured prominently in the attack on the mayor's office.[74] Jordan also cites comments by political leaders such as He Yingqin (a former Chinese minister of war), whom he interviewed in Taibei, and British consular reports to support his claim that Wang Jingwei's faction, identified at times with the Guangdong regime, provided much of the financial support for student anti-Japanese activities and played a key role in manipulating them.[75] In any case, whatever financial and logistical support the Generalissimo's rivals had given to the youth movement before Jiang's resignation stopped abruptly when a new set of leaders took power in Nanjing in mid-December, and (in part at least as a testament to just how important this support had been to the movement in its earlier stages) the anti-Japanese struggle began to degenerate almost immediately thereafter.[76]

Clear proof of the popular movement's loss of momentum came with the December 17th Incident, or rather with the failure of this violent episode to provoke a massive popular response. Some thousand Shanghai youths traveled to the capital to take part in the December 17 demonstration, which ended with the police arresting and beating scores of students. One local student, Yang Tongheng, even died as a result of injuries he received. By late December, however, internal divisions and external pressure had so crippled the Shanghai student movement that not even the power of martyrdom could bring it back to life. Just days after the Nanjing bloodshed, the reorganized College Resistance Alliance called on its members to resume their studies, and close to half of the pupils at local middle schools had returned to the classroom.[77]

The anti-Japanese agitation continued long after students called off their classroom strike, which at its height in early December had paralyzed virtually all local institutions of higher education. If not actually marking the end of the youth movement, however, the resumption of classes was certainly the beginning of the end. In late December and early January, students would continue to publicize and enforce the boycott and raise money to support the fight for national salvation.[78] Some youths would also take part in rallies and marches during this period, such as the Min-fan-sponsored memorial procession of January 10, in which marchers followed the martyr Yang Tongheng's coffin through the streets of Shanghai.[79] But there was no question that the popular movement was starting to wind down well before the Japanese invaded Shanghai on January 28.

THE 1931 STRUGGLE: FIASCO OR PROTOTYPE?

Historians have not treated the student movement protesting the Japanese invasion of Manchuria kindly: they have tended either to ignore the upsurge completely or to present it as a case study in failure,* especially when

---

*Few Western scholars include the 1931 struggle among the great student movements of modern Chinese history, and the one historian who treats the upsurge in detail, John Israel, subtitles the final section of his chapter on the event "Evaluation: A Fiasco" (*Student Nationalism*, p. 83). Chinese Communist writers played down the importance of the 1931 upsurge even before 1949. On May 23, 1947, for example, the CCP's official Xinhua News Agency described the Anti-Hunger, Anti–Civil War Movement then in progress as following in the footsteps of three (not four) earlier heroic student struggles: those of 1919, 1925, and 1935. Post-1949 CCP treatments of 1931 are discussed below and in the Bibliographic Essay.

contrasted to the "successful" struggles of 1919 and 1925. The anti-Japanese agitation of 1931 did not precipitate a general strike of the type that paralyzed Shanghai during both the May 4th and the May 30th movements. Even though youths throughout the country protested the Japanese invasion of 1931, the student movement never became a truly national one led by an umbrella group capable of coordinating concurrent protest activities in different cities. Finally, at just the moment when the movement should have entered its climactic phase and gained a groundswell of popular support—when the police used violence to suppress the Nanjing demonstration of December 17—it began to collapse.

Writers affiliated with the CCP in particular have tended to ignore the demonstrations of 1931 or emphasize their shortcomings and have published fewer historical materials concerning these events as opposed to those of 1925 and 1935. Party historians have usually viewed the anti-Japanese protests of the early 1930's as an embarrassing chapter in the development of the Chinese student movement, a time of missed opportunities and CCP errors in judgment. In traditional party historiography, the evolution of the post–May 4th student movement is a simple tale of popular struggles against imperialist aggressors and domestic oppressors, in which underground Communist organizers play heroic roles in shaping and leading mass actions. The actual picture is more complex in each case than the starkly black-and-white CCP versions suggest. It is much easier, however, to fit struggles such as the May 30th Movement or the antiwar protests of the late 1940's into this narrative framework than it is to turn the story of the 1931 struggles into a tale glorifying the efforts of CCP organizers. Such organizers were not, after all, key players in much of this drama, nor were they particularly successful when they were at center stage.

Finally, and perhaps most important in terms of understanding the way Communist historians treat the student movement of 1931, the first half of the Nanjing Decade was a period of intense turmoil and re-evaluation within the CCP itself. Devastated by Jiang Jieshi's catastrophic purge of 1927, the CCP vacillated from one "erroneous line" to another. Thus party theorists classify 1931 as a year when the "leftist errors" of the Wang Ming line exerted a harmful influence upon all aspects of party policy. Histories and memoirs alike blame these "leftist" tendencies for many of the failures of the student movement of the day, arguing that adherence to the Wang Ming line led those few underground organizers who had survived party purges and police bullets to alienate themselves from the masses. Most works that criticize the "leftist errors" of the time, especially those published before the late 1980's, are fairly vague about the precise nature of the "mistakes" of CCP activists and content themselves with pointing to several general problems: Communist organizers of the early

1930's were not willing enough to form united fronts; they did not try hard enough to use the enemy's "contradictions" to the CCP's advantage; they used inappropriate slogans (such as "Uphold the soviets") at a time when general anti-imperialist rallying cries would have been more effective; and they failed to realize that "legal" tactics (such as petitions) were as useful as "extralegal" techniques (such as seizures of government buildings) in furthering the Communist cause.[80]

Some recently published memoirs give a more concrete sense of the problems "leftist errors" could create. Two reminiscences by Wen Jizhe, a former Communist Youth League leader who went on to become dean of graduate studies at the Chinese Academy of Social Sciences, are particularly valuable in this regard.[81] For example, in late September 1931 Wen asked his superior within the Youth League, "Little Zhu," if he should join a protest trip to Nanjing with some of his classmates from the Fudan Middle School. Zhu replied that petitioning was a "petit-bourgeois" activity, and Wen decided not to go to the capital. Two months later Wen, now head of the propaganda department of the Fudan kangrihui, asked Zhu about participation in the second big petitioning campaign. If he did not take part, Wen pointed out, he would risk becoming "cut off from the masses." Zhu responded that Wen could go to Nanjing if he did so "not in his capacity as a Communist Youth League member, but only as an individual." Wen found this distinction "laughable," since "of course I did not publicly announce that I was a member of the League," an identification that could all too easily result in imprisonment or death. Wen's memoirs contain details of a number of similarly ludicrous incidents, such as the time a radical speaker scared off most of the members of a large audience during a lecture at Fudan by peppering his speech with calls to protect the Chinese soviet areas and support the Red Army.

Despite this scholarly neglect of the anti-Japanese protests of 1931, the mass movement of that year deserves a place alongside the more celebrated struggles of 1919 and 1935. Undeniably, as John Israel points out, the mass movement of 1931 did not measure up to either the May 4th or the December 9th Movement in terms of precipitating a change in the government's foreign policy, nor did the political events of 1931 bring any "major literary or intellectual movements" in their wake, as did those of 1919 and 1935.[82] It is also clear that 1931 was indeed a time of missed opportunities for Communist and non-Communist organizers alike. Nonetheless, the youth movement of 1931 had a major impact upon local and national affairs. For all their shortcomings, the student protesters of 1931 mounted a series of impressive collective protests, ranging from rallies and streetside lecturing campaigns to petition drives to Nanjing, which helped to bring both the Japanese actions in Manchuria and the central government's weak response to the attention of a large portion of China's urban populace.

One can even claim that, where Shanghai is concerned, the youth movement triggered by the September 18th Incident played a more important role in the development of the student protest tradition than its much better known successor—the December 9th Movement of 1935. The year 1931 stands out, in fact, as one of the two or three main turning points in the history of the city's student movement. Just as the May 4th Movement set the tone for much that would follow during the Warlord period, many themes that dominate the history of mass movements of the GMD era first appeared during the anti-Japanese movement of 1931. In addition, in terms of the evolution of the student protest repertoire, 1931 is probably second in importance only to 1919: mass petition drives, train commandeerings, and other activities that were novel in 1931 became fairly typical parts of Shanghai student movements. Chapter 9 provides examples of the tactical debt student protesters of the Civil War era owed to their predecessors of the early 1930's; here I look briefly at some ways in which the December 9th Movement of 1935 in Shanghai was shaped by events that took place four years previously.

1931 AND 1935: TOWARD A NEW REPERTOIRE

The railway confrontation that began on December 23, 1935, when a thousand youths, mostly from Fudan University, paraded to Shanghai's North Station to demand free passage to Nanjing, provides the clearest illustration of the strength of the continuities between 1931 and 1935. This late December confrontation between protesters and officials, the dramatic highpoint of Shanghai's December 9th Movement, bore a strong resemblance to the clashes of four years earlier. For example, on December 23, when the student petitioners stormed aboard a train bound for Nanjing, the railway authorities tried to prevent the youths from proceeding to the capital by uncoupling the train's engine. The student response to this interference completes the parallels between the 1935 confrontation and its predecessor: the protesters refused to leave the cars and insisted that they would get themselves to Nanjing one way or another, even if it meant driving the train themselves.[83]

Negotiations between protesters and officials continued throughout December 23 and 24, as more and more students made their way to the station to join the petitioners on the train. The total number of participants grew from 1,000 to 2,500 by the afternoon of the second day, with female students making up a fifth of the total.[84] Leading figures in local cultural and intellectual circles—such as Hu Ziying, who had recently helped establish the Shanghai Women's National Salvation Association—came to the station to join the vigil. Supporters from various classes kept student morale up by praising the youths for their patriotism, and the bread and other supplies these supporters brought helped the students maintain their stamina.

The deadlock ended on December 24 when the train set off for Nanjing, although just how this action was accomplished varies from account to account. According to some versions, the students victoriously overcame all obstacles and set off for Nanjing driving the train themselves, with help from patriotic railway workers. According to other versions, the authorities realized that the only way to defuse the situation was to get the youths out of the station. They therefore hooked an engine to the train and let it start heading west, but planned from the start to prevent the delegation from getting close to Nanjing. Whichever account one follows, the ending of the story is the same: the students did not reach the capital. The authorities stopped the train en route, forced the youths to disembark, then herded the protesters back to Shanghai in special buses. Evaluations of the overall success of the protest also differ: some see the incident as an example of officials' skillfully managing to defuse a potentially explosive situation; others claim that even though aborted, the petition drive played a crucial role in radicalizing, publicizing, and solidifying student commitment to the patriotic movement. Each interpretation clearly contains a grain of truth.

The confrontation at the North Station was not the only incident of the December 9th Movement that might have given observers of the 1931 protests a feeling of déjà vu. Even the most seemingly singular of 1931 events, the Popular Tribunal affair, had counterparts of sorts during the December 9th Movement. No single occurrence that combined all the elements of drama and usurpation seen at the Municipal Government Compound in early December 1931 took place in 1935 or 1936, but there were clear echoes of the Popular Tribunal in several student actions during the December 9th Movement. For example, the headline "Public Safety Bureau Wrecked in Mob Attack," which appeared in an English-language newspaper in January 1936, illustrates that Shanghai students of the mid-1930's were as ready as their predecessors of 1931 to use militant methods to contest the authorities' enforcement of the law.[85] The March 25th Incident of 1936 illustrates this point as well. The Public Security Bureau's decision to force its way into Fudan University to arrest all students suspected of being "reds" led to a raid that left dozens of students and teachers wounded and one police officer dead. Campus militants took revenge by holding several of the raiding police officers hostage and refusing to release them until the authorities assured them that no additional raids would be carried out in the future.[86]

In another incident in 1936, there was actually talk of forming a new "popular tribunal." On January 25 in the nearby town of Kunshan, students from Shanghai were mistreated by the local police. The students had come to Kunshan as part of one of the famous December 9th propaganda drives, which campus activists in cities throughout China organized at the beginning of 1936. These campaigns were devised to spread the word of the patriotic movement to China's rural masses and to maintain student morale during the winter vacation. Urban protest leagues sent large groups of students to march or ride their bicycles to neighboring towns and villages. There the youths held demonstrations, gave speeches, staged patriotic plays, and encouraged the local populace to form anti-Japanese societies.

Shanghai students involved in the Kunshan incident had already been on the road for several days. Up to this point the propagandists had met little resistance, at least according to a contemporary firsthand account.[87] In one town, the author of this report claims, members of the local Public Security Bureau not only tolerated the students' activities but actually treated the marchers "very well," in large part because most of the police officers were from Manchuria and hence had a special reason to hate the Japanese imperialists. The situation in Kunshan was very different, however. The head of the local Public Security Bureau there "treated us very rudely and put red caps on us" (that is, insisted that they were Communists and thus undesirable elements). This infuriated the students, who proceeded to make plans to bring the police chief before a popular tribunal to pay for his insults; in the end they settled for holding a demonstration outside the Public Security Bureau's headquarters.

This chapter has argued that 1931 marked a major transition in the history of the Shanghai student movement, whose significance is second only to those of 1919 and 1949. The differences between the student struggles of the Warlord era and those that took place after the GMD assumed power—differences that have also been suggested in Chapter 6 and will become even clearer in Chapter 9—are crucial for assessing the mass movements of the Republican era as a whole. Some of the most important differences relate to tactics: for example, mass petition drives to the capital were virtually unknown before 1931, but a key part of the protest repertoire over the next eighteen years. Another major difference is the strategies the authorities used to combat student unrest. No important government-sponsored "protests" of the type examined in this chapter (and in Chapter 9) took place in Shanghai before 1927—the Warlords did not make the efforts their GMD successors did to infiltrate and control campus organizations.

This said, long-term continuities are also worth remembering. Although the student movement of 1931 had novel features, in many ways it stuck closely to pre-established patterns and models. For every innovation, such as the formation of the Popular Tribunal, there were many repetitions. The use of petitions, streetside lectures, marches structured around large and small brigades, memorial parades for martyrs, and calls for general strikes—all these post-1927 student protest actions followed Warlord-era precedents. And, as other chapters illustrate, there were also important continuities between the periods before and after the GMD's rise to power in terms of the kinds of protest leagues youths formed and the techniques members of these leagues used to publicize their causes. In the 1930's, therefore, one sees a new generation of students responding to a new set of challenges in distinctive ways. But this change is less a departure from earlier patterns than an elaboration of them. The GMD's rise to power, in other words, while transforming the May 4th model of political engagement, did not make this model obsolete.

EIGHT

THE LANGUAGES OF
STUDENT PROTEST

EARLIER CHAPTERS HAVE REFERRED to student propaganda drives
and lecture campaigns, but so far little has been said about how exactly
educated youths went about publicizing their patriotic movements and
trying to gain converts. What themes did protesters stress in streetside
speeches? What role did pictorial representations play in student *xuanchuan* (propaganda or public relations) efforts? Did protesters use different
rhetorical techniques and strategies to reach different audiences? Earlier
chapters have shed some light on these and similar questions, but it is time
now to examine the topic of student xuanchuan in closer detail and look at
the various texts activists used to try to gain support. Understanding the
communicative strategies embedded in and embodied by these texts is crucial; if the slogans student protesters shouted and the speeches they gave
had not moved their intended audience, it would have been impossible for
these youths to gain the amount of popular support they did.

The plural "languages" is used in the title of this chapter to draw attention to the wide range of media and idioms Shanghai student propagandists employed. These youths used so many different techniques to communicate with one another and with outsiders that it becomes impossible
to speak of a single "language" of political protest. Protest languages were
by no means limited to verbal and written speech, furthermore, since students also relied upon ritualized acts (such as kneeling when presenting
petitions) and material objects (such as bloody shirts and coffins) to get
their messages across to spectators. It is possible to delineate many non-
verbal languages or "codes," beginning with this grammar of gestures and
rhetoric of relics, which supplemented student literary creations. As ear-

lier chapters have shown, even such mundane choices as the clothes educated youths wore could help them communicate with their audience; both the caps of May 4th protesters and the military uniforms students donned in the early 1930's became powerful, immediately recognizable symbols of patriotic outrage.

Even if one limits a discussion of student languages to speeches, leaflets, and wall posters—the main types of texts examined in this chapter—it is still misleading to think in terms of a single language of protest.* Students varied their communicative strategies to fit specific audiences. The words protesters used to alert passersby to the dangers of imperialism were often quite different from those they used to plead with governmental authorities; the pictures they used to decorate wall posters pasted in public places were not those they used in publications intended for on-campus circulation. Sometimes these differences in propaganda styles were so subtle that we can describe them as shifts from one "dialect" to another, since they involved nothing more than an alteration in emphasis or a slight change of format. At other points, however, students felt that the intended audiences were so disparate that the only way to communicate a message effectively to these groups was to package it in completely different ways.

The most obvious examples of student publicists using wholly dissimilar languages to communicate the same message involve attempts to gain foreign support. Because of the importance of foreign opinion in determining the outcome of Chinese power struggles, student protesters in all major cities issued some propaganda in English during every major Republican protest movement (see photographic section for examples). Thanks to the peculiar nature of local politics, Shanghai youths made even more frequent use of foreign-language propaganda than did their counterparts in non–treaty port cities.[1] Sometimes they even placed native and foreign versions of the same statement or slogan side by side on a pamphlet or banner.[2]

Western audiences were not, however, the only ones for whom students felt they needed to translate their ideas. Educated youths frequently thought that a great deal of "translation" was required to make their mes-

---

*My use of the term "languages" to refer to distinctive modes of discourse, as well as to formally recognized linguistic systems such as Chinese and English, follows that of Mikhail Bakhtin in *The Dialogic Imagination*. According to Bakhtin, "At any given moment . . . a language is stratified not only into [phonetic] dialects . . . but into languages that are socio-ideological: languages belonging to professions, to genres, languages peculiar to particular generations, etc." (p. xix). Some of the best discussions by sinologists of the kinds of problems of language and audience at issue in this chapter can be found in David Johnson et al., *Popular Culture in Late Imperial China*; see esp. D. Johnson, "Communication, Class, and Consciousness in Late Imperial China" (pp. 34–72); and Evelyn Rawski, "Problems and Prospects" (pp. 399–417).

sage intelligible to the *laobaixing* (literally "hundred names," a traditional term for the common people or the masses). Students often quite self-consciously used two totally different vocabularies and types of texts to address educated and uneducated members of the native population, as the charter of a Jiaotong University protest league founded in 1931 illustrates. One of the most interesting sections of this charter is a special appendix that details the working plan of the league's "propaganda bureau" (*xuanchuan zu*). Section 3 of this appendix, which lists the topics propaganda workers should stress and the methods they should use, is divided into two subsections with very different emphases: the first deals with attempts to reach audiences consisting of members of the "knowledgeable" or "educated" (*youzhishi*) classes, the second with publicity work directed at members of the "ignorant" or "uneducated" (*wuzhishi*) classes.[3]

No single chapter can provide a comprehensive introduction to all the student languages alluded to above and in addition analyze the main messages students set out to communicate. The goals of this chapter, therefore, are more modest and selective: to highlight the main rhetorical strategies students used to reach members of different social and cultural groups, and to elucidate a few of the dominant themes and enduring motifs in the propaganda drives of the Republican era. The logical place to begin is the efforts of student publicists to reach their most important intended audience—the common workers and peasants who constituted the laobaixing. I begin by discussing the obstacles students encountered in trying to influence the uneducated masses and gain their support, and the strategies educated youths used to overcome these hurdles. After treating these two subjects, I conclude with a much briefer look at how students communicated with members of the "educated" (*zhishi*) world.

SPEAKING TO THE MASSES: THE PROBLEM

The need for an effective way to reach the laobaixing, and the difficulties inherent in communicating political messages to ordinary laborers and peasants, is a key thread running through nearly all student discussions of propaganda work. This concern took on a special significance after the CCP became an important factor in the youth movement in the mid-1920's. Communist theorists claimed that China's only hope for salvation lay in a social revolution led by workers and peasants. Student members of the CCP and its associated youth leagues naturally placed enormous emphasis upon developing propaganda techniques to bring ordinary workers, coolies, and peasants into their patriotic movements.

The tendency of student propagandists to single out the laobaixing as a specially important target audience, however, predates the 1921 founding of the CCP by several years. May 4th youths were intensely concerned with convincing the uneducated masses to join their movement. But even the great demonstrations of spring and summer 1919 cannot be singled out as the point at which intelligentsia protesters first turned their attention to the laobaixing: politically minded students and teachers had already become convinced, several years before the fight against the Treaty of Versailles even began, that China could be saved only if intellectuals found some way to awaken and enlighten the nation's masses.

One outgrowth of this concern was the "plain speech" (*baihua*) movement. Generally considered to have begun in 1917 with Hu Shi's famous call in *Xinqingnian* (New youth) for intellectuals to abandon "classical" or "literary" Chinese (*wenyan*) and compose poems and stories in the vernacular, this movement was a manifestation of the desire of young intellectuals to bridge the cultural gap that separated them from uneducated members of society.[4] The same desire also helped inspire the formation of the "speechmaking corps" students organized in winter and spring 1919 (see Chapter 2), whose goal was to spread new (and in most cases imported) scientific and political ideas to the general populace.*

The precise connections between cultural struggles such as the baihua and popular speechmaking campaigns and the anti-Japanese mass movement of 1919 are intimate and complex, as Chapter 2 suggests. On the one hand, the discussions that followed Hu Shi's call for the development of a vernacular literature and the meetings that preceded popular lecture campaigns helped lay the ideological and organizational groundwork for the political struggles that followed. On the other hand, once the anti-Japanese agitation began, students began to confront new problems that forced them to re-examine their treatment of the problem of communicating with the laobaixing.

Before the May 4th demonstrations, even those New Culture intellectuals most convinced that the move away from wenyan could do as much to revive Chinese culture as the move from Latin to the vernacular had done for Europe continued to treat "the people" in abstract terms. For all their talk of using baihua, these New Culture intellectuals had little contact with a truly "popular" audience before the spring of 1919, and they continued to write poems, stories, and essays that only a tiny fraction of the laobaixing could read and understand with ease. Perry Link makes a

---

*This interest in bridging the gap between China's educated elite and the untutored masses was not always conceived as a simple matter of finding a way to edify the laobaixing. One strain in New Culture thought romanticized the simplicity and purity of village life and argued that intellectuals had much to learn from the uncorrupted "folk" who lived there. The most important exponents of this view were the participants in the folk-literature movement, which is treated thoroughly in Hung, *Going to the People.*

clear case for this lack of contact between New Culture intellectuals and non-intellectual readers in his study of the popular "Mandarin duck and butterfly" romances, which were written in a more genuinely vernacular style derived from the traditional art of storytelling, but which baihua writers despised as backward and vulgar. According to Link, the baihua "vernacular" that New Culture writers used was so heavily influenced by wenyan patterns of composition and Western literary techniques and concepts that, to typical members of the popular audience, practitioners of the new style "seemed as far removed from the mainstream of popular culture as the advocates of the eight-legged essays [the New Culture Movement] sought to overthrow." Link notes that even the title of the most famous New Culture magazine, *Xin qingnian*, "had elite overtones to the popular ear, since the term *ch'ing-nien* [*qingnian*] had traditionally been used only in reference to young males of upper-class households." [5]

Between 1915 and 1919, therefore, the champions of the baihua movement had much less impact upon the popular audience than did the authors of "butterfly" romances. Young, classically educated writers such as Hu Shi, many of whom had studied in America or Japan, created a genuinely new literature. It was not, however, one that appealed to the people as a whole, but only to intellectuals like themselves. There were exceptions to the general lack of contact between intellectuals and laobaixing during the early stages of the New Culture Movement. For example, some educated youths made attempts during the anti-Japanese agitation of 1915 to develop propaganda that even the semiliterate could understand. In addition, as noted in Chapter 2, many future leaders of the May 4th political movement gained important experience as public speakers in late 1918 and early 1919 by forming or joining popular lecture corps. Until May 1919, however, most intellectuals continued to be concerned more with the theoretical issues involved in communicating with the masses than with the practical side of the problem.

This changed dramatically when the provisions of the Treaty of Versailles became known and the May 4th arrests occurred. Determined to demonstrate that the Chinese people as a whole were unwilling to see their nation humiliated by traitorous officials, students in Shanghai and other cities began to view an ability to address and influence the laobaixing as a pragmatic necessity as well as an abstract good. This need, not the earlier articles in "obscure" newspapers by Hu Shi and Chen Duxiu calling for literary reform, inspired the first real flowering of baihua writing. This at least is the contention of Stanley High, who was in China at the time and later wrote about the events he witnessed in *The Revolt of Youth*.[6] High claims that the May 4th demonstrations provided the impetus for intellectuals to develop a writing style that ordinary people could understand, and he argues that the first important exercises in baihua writing were the masses of political pamphlets and broadsheets that appeared in the late spring, summer, and fall of 1919.[7]

The problem of developing a truly vernacular style of writing did not disappear as soon as May 4th protesters discovered that popular support could help them achieve their goals. Later generations of student activists continued to wrestle with the difficulty of composing pamphlets that spoke to a popular audience.* One of the most common self-criticisms of student protesters throughout the Republican era was that they had been unable to communicate effectively with non-intellectuals, that their language had remained too literary and too lofty for their intended audience. Some of the propaganda failures students attributed to shortcomings of this sort were probably due to another kind of problem: at times, members of the laobaixing understood the students' messages quite well but simply disagreed with them. References to stylistic failures were more than just a convenient excuse, however; student reliance on traditional literati patterns of speech and writing did indeed continue to hinder mass propaganda work.

Moreover, the problems involved in communicating with the laobaixing went far beyond the tendencies of educated youths to slip into classical patterns of sentence construction and to fill their works with alien terms and obscure allusions. Student propagandists were well aware that no matter how successful they were at simplifying and enlivening their literary styles, written works in and of themselves would never have much impact upon the laobaixing as a whole. Many workers and peasants could recognize no more than a few dozen characters at most and hence gained little from even the liveliest and most colloquial of written leaflets. Students realized that, to achieve mass support, they needed to supplement their essays with streetcorner speeches, their proclamations with cartoons. Even when they turned to non-literary media, however, educated youths occasionally had problems communicating with "uneducated" audiences.

Differences of dialect were one obvious source of trouble. According to Zhong Fuguang, who led a traveling propaganda brigade up the Yangzi River to spread news of the May 30th Movement, the students and townspeople of Anhui Province had no problem understanding her and another member of the brigade named Ceng Kejia. They could make no sense,

---

*An illustration of the awareness among educated youths of this issue can be found in the apologetic remarks Jiaotong University students appended to a June 1947 protest pamphlet entitled "Xin wuyue yanyi" (The significance of the New May), which is held at the Shanghai Municipal Library. The authors conclude their pamphlet, which is discussed later in this chapter, by apologizing for the work's poor literary style: their goal throughout was to "write a piece that all laobaixing could read and understand" (p. 12).

however, out of what the third member of the group, Wang Delin, said. Wang was unable to speak anything but his native Shanghai-style Wu dialect. As a result, Wang was placed in charge of keeping track of "the various kinds of propaganda materials, the daily expenses and so forth," leaving Zhong and Ceng to do the talking.[8]

Other kinds of cultural differences could also prove troublesome. Even when ordinary citizens could understand every word of a student lecturer, for example, the gap between the intelligentsia and non-intelligentsia worlds was so great that the intended message did not always come through. An anecdote by Zhang Guotao, an early CCP leader who was a student in Beijing during the May 4th Movement, illustrates the nature of this problem. Zhang and a group of his classmates formed a streetside lecture team in the wake of the May 4th demonstration to publicize the villainy of the "three traitorous officials." One day, after they had given a series of speeches to passersby, a preacher (presumably a Chinese Christian as opposed to a foreign missionary, although Zhang does not specify) came up to the youths and told them how deeply their words had moved him. The preacher pointed out, however, that the speeches the students gave were "not colloquial enough" and had probably meant little to the average worker or peasant in the audience. He then proceeded to give them pointers on how to reach the typical spectator based upon his own experiences in proselytizing.[9]

Despite these obstacles, student propagandists were amazingly successful at influencing popular audiences, as the sheer number of ordinary workers, peddlers, and coolies who joined student-initiated mass movements indicates. How were educated youths able to bridge the various linguistic and cultural gaps separating them from the laobaixing? To answer this question, it is necessary to look closely at several specific aspects of student propaganda work, beginning with the various media, art forms, literary devices, and technologies educated youths used to publicize their causes.

SPEAKING TO THE MASSES: TECHNIQUES

Mention has been made in earlier chapters of the media students used to communicate with the laobaixing—drawings pasted on walls, streetside speeches, theatrical performances. It is time now to give a more systematic account of these various propaganda methods, because the nature and sheer variety of student publicity techniques goes a long way toward explaining the surprising ability of educated youths to influence and gain support from a broad cross section of Chinese society.

The specific techniques students used to communicate with popular audiences varied from movement to movement, and propagandists grew increasingly inventive as the Republican era wore on. Since much of the propaganda repertoire was already in place as early as 1925, however, Li Jianmin's comprehensive analysis of May 30th publicity campaigns provides a useful starting point for the present discussion.[10] In a section devoted to "methods of propaganda," Li identifies and describes no less than eighteen distinctive devices protesters used to publicize the May 30th Movement and gain converts. Not all these methods were used by students alone, nor were all of them specifically geared toward reaching a popular audience. A quick rundown of Li's list of techniques—which can be divided into the four general categories of oral communications, written works, pictorial representations, and physical reminders—can nonetheless help give a sense of the diverse methods student publicists used to speak to the laobaixing.

Li lists five distinct types of oral propaganda: seated talks, lectures, theatrical productions, musical performances, and crying displays (see Chapter 4). All of these except the first, which generally involved student representatives discussing political issues over tea with officials or members of civic groups, have relevance for the topic at hand. Lectures were often directed at ordinary passersby and typical members of urban and rural communities; the same was true of theatrical and musical performances, which used drama, rhythm, and melody to bridge the cultural gaps between students and the laobaixing. Crying displays used the universal language of tears to accomplish this same purpose.

Li notes that written forms of propaganda were intended primarily for educated audiences. Literary techniques are not, however, without interest here; as noted above, student propagandists often tried (though in some cases unsuccessfully) to write in a way that even semiliterate readers could understand. Because of the nature of the Chinese written language, such readers constituted an important segment of the urban population: the Chinese system of using characters as opposed to letters to represent words makes full literacy extremely difficult to achieve, but it makes partial literacy (recognition of some written terms) comparatively easy.[11] According to the most thorough recent estimate, even in late imperial times some 30–45 percent of Chinese men and 2–10 percent of Chinese women were able to recognize at least "a few hundred characters," and evidence suggests that rates of both full and partial literacy rose markedly in Republican times.[12] Olga Lang found, for example, in her famous survey of working-class families in Beijing during the 1930's that no less than 32 of the 58 households surveyed included men who could and did read newspapers.[13] In addition, even those who could not recognize more than a handful of characters could be affected by written forms of propaganda, since literate spectators often read proclamations and the captions to pictures aloud to nonliterate friends and acquaintances.*

Thus many laobaixing were exposed in one way or another to all the types of written propaganda Li identifies, such as magazine and newspaper articles, telegrams of protest, proclamations and general statements issued by associations, the testaments of protest known as "records written in blood" (*xueshu*), leaflets, and wall posters. These last two categories of written propaganda were particularly important in influencing the laobaixing, for many were distributed or posted in public gathering places. Written with partially literate readers in mind, they relied upon repetition of a few emotionally charged slogans or key words as opposed to extended argumentation.

Li catalogues six distinctive types of pictorial representations, beginning with drawings and cartoons that either stood on their own or appeared as illustrations in written texts (see photographic section for examples). The May 30th propagandists supplemented these drawings—which were often crude but effective portrayals of armed foreigners attacking unarmed Chinese victims—with photographs, portraits, postcards, movies, and slide shows. These forms of nonliterary propaganda were no match for essays when it came to explaining complex issues, such as the meaning of extraterritoriality. Pictures could be much more useful than words, however, in bringing the horror of the slaughter home to the general public. And there was no more effective way to remind one's audience that the protesters and spectators killed by the imperialists were once living individuals than to show pictures of the martyrs' faces.[14]

Protesters also used a wide variety of "material objects" (*shiwu*) to remind people of the "national humiliation" of May 30th. Armbands, bloodied clothing, flags flown at half-mast—all could have a propaganda value. Such objects had little persuasive power in and of themselves, but in conjunction with the other types of propaganda methods described above, they could play an important part in keeping a movement alive. Specially produced items, such as May 30th writing pads, May 30th soap, "national humiliation" towels, May 30th memorial wash basins, and May 30th watches, served as daily reminders of the Nanjing Road shootings.

---

*The same was true of newspapers, according to Andrew Nathan and Leo Ou-fan Lee ("Mass Culture," p. 372). They cite a remark of an American visitor to Yangzi River villages in the 1920's that whenever a new issue of a newspaper published in a neighboring city arrived in a local village there would be "gatherings at which a good reader [would read] in a very dignified manner, to an audience" of ordinary townspeople. Many other examples of texts being read aloud to nonliterate audiences are described in other chapters in David Johnson et al., *Popular Culture in Late Imperial China*.

Li's discussion of these various publicity techniques is easily the most comprehensive work on May 30th propaganda methods to date. Even he admits, however, that it is less than completely exhaustive. Li notes, for example, that protesters and patriotic businessmen produced such a "kaleidoscopic" array of May 30th memorial objects that it was impossible for him to discuss them all in a single chapter. Among the most interesting items he does not mention are handpainted fans bearing patriotic inscriptions and drawings, which one English-language weekly claimed students gave away "in large quantities" at theatrical performances in August 1925.[15] Nor does he refer to the May 30th seals or handkerchiefs pictured in a recently published collection of documents on the movement.[16]

Some types of oral and written propaganda do not fit cleanly into Li's categories. The suit of clothes covered with slogans one Beijing protester wore in 1925, which turned the man into a kind of walking wall poster, is a case in point.[17] So, too, is the interesting fund-raiser put on by students at a Shanghai middle school after the May 30th shootings, which is described in an article entitled "The Light Side of the Strike" that appeared in the English-language newspaper *Celestial Empire* of August 1, 1925. Some 300 people paid a dollar or so each to attend this affair. The day began with students giving speeches on political topics and calling on the crowd to uphold the boycott on foreign goods. The performance then ended with "a programme of boxing, singing, dancing, and one-act plays."*

Despite these minor caveats, Li's overview of propaganda methods remains a valuable résumé of the main techniques participants in the May 30th Movement used to communicate their ideas to the masses.[18] It also serves as a useful introduction to the general topic of student propagandizing during the Republican era. Some of the techniques Li describes seem to have been peculiar to the May 30th Movement. No other struggle appears to have inspired quite as many types of nationalist memorabilia, for instance, and crying brigades did not play a major role in any other movement.[19] But most of Li's eighteen methods are by no means unique to the

---

*The newspaper report gives a number of other interesting details. For example, Chinese Boy Scouts and members of the local Chinese volunteer corps helped maintain order during the performances. The main gist of the speeches made by the student orators was that "all the good which had been done in China by foreign missionaries and raised the prestige of foreigners in China had been undone by the incidents of May 30th." The report is silent, however, about the precise content of the performances. One is left wondering whether student dancers played out scenes depicting the events of May 30th, making that part of the performance an early forerunner of the political ballets of later decades. The dance routines, boxing displays, and the like might just as easily have been presented solely for their entertainment value, as a means of drawing a larger crowd than speeches alone would bring. CCP rural organizer Peng Pai found apolitical magic tricks a useful way of luring peasants to meetings in Haifeng in the early 1920's; see his *Seeds of Peasant Revolution*, p. 26.

upheavals of 1925. All but a few of the techniques (for example, cinematic portrayals of political events) are mentioned in standard works on the May 4th Movement,[20] and some techniques, such as the drafting of petitions, have lineages that stretch back well into imperial times (see Chapter 3). Moreover, nearly all eighteen methods reappeared after 1925 as basic elements of later student propaganda campaigns.[21]

Participants in later movements did, however, give special twists to the time-tested publicity techniques used during the May 30th Movement. Every generation of student propagandists may have relied upon the same basic methods, but significant stylistic modifications and changes in emphasis did occur over time. Students were continually inventing new types of visual aids to get their messages across to the people, as well as finding new venues in which to give speeches and place posters.

Some of the best examples of such improvisations relate to slogan writing. During 1925 students generally contented themselves with pasting sheets of paper or cloth emblazoned with slogans on walls, but during the following decades students would develop new methods for ensuring that as many people as possible were exposed to patriotic slogans. The following quotation from a 1936 North China Daily News article, which is subtitled "An Innovation Shown by Troublemakers," describes one technique participants in the December 9th Movement used to supplement the traditional stationary wall posters: "An innovation in tactics was shown by demonstrators [yesterday] in that they chalked their slogans—anti-Government, anti-smuggling, and anti-Japanese—on rickshaws and motorcars which they encountered in the streets. It is believed some of these slogans unwittingly were carried to far corners of the [International] Settlement by these vehicles."*

After World War II, Shanghai's protesters would go even further in their efforts to make sure that as many people as possible read their slogans. Press reports on the mass peace demonstration of June 23, 1946, and the marches against American brutality some six months later (see Chapter 9 for details) show this clearly. For example, one account of the June 23 gathering, which was held to celebrate the departure for Nanjing of a petition delegation and drew a crowd of 50,000–60,000 students and other citizens, contains a lively description of the scene at the "normally

---

*August 10, reproduced in SMP files, reel 27, no. 7108. In fact the propaganda method this article labels an "innovation" was a revival and updating of a technique used at least as early as 1919, which had perhaps fallen into disuse during subsequent mass movements. In an article entitled "Striking Students Active in the Boycott," China Press, May 29, 1919, pp. 1 and 3, a journalist covering the May 4th Movement wrote that "as usual, police officers were engaged yesterday in . . . tearing down inciting handbills and posters and cleaning chalk-marked rickshaws."

drab North Station" on that day: "Today [the station] wore five-colored clothes, with red and green posters and slogans written in multi-colored chalk everywhere on the walls, the posts, the cars and the ground."[22] Six months later the students participating in the anti-American brutality agitation would go to equally great lengths to ensure that their message reached a wide audience, as graphically illustrated by a picture on the front page of the *North China Daily News* showing a Jiaotong University school bus plastered with anti-American slogans. The caption notes that the protesting youths similarly decorated trams and "local buildings in the downtown area" as well.[23]

Noteworthy among other major post-1925 innovations is the increasingly important role of group singing as a propaganda technique during the 1930's. There are references to protesters singing patriotic songs as part of mass gatherings as far back as the anti-Russian agitation of 1903, and bands accompanied many May 4th Movement marches. Nonetheless, musical performances took on a special prominence during the anti-Japanese struggles of the December 9th era, when students and members of other social groups began to form "mass choral groups." The aim of these associations was to help save the nation by bringing large groups of people together to learn and then perform the powerful new patriotic compositions composed by Nie Er and other songwriters to criticize Japanese imperialism.[24]

The first such national salvation choral societies were formed in Shanghai in late 1935 and early 1936 as modest experiments in a new form of cultural activity. Within two years, these associations had become the nucleus of a movement of giant proportions. According to the newspaper *Li bao* of April 25, 1937, Shanghai already had more than 60 group singing clubs by April 1937, with over 120,000 members from all ranks of society.[25] The performances of these associations were as impressive as their membership statistics.

An extravaganza the Shanghai YMCA Popular Singing Association held at the Public Recreation Ground on June 7, 1936, is typical. According to a press account in a Chinese-language Hong Kong daily, a crowd of "over five thousand" people made up of "male and female movie stars, students, workers, storekeepers, and soldiers" came to hear the members of the association sing.[26] The day's program began with all 700 members of the YMCA group singing a series of songs, many of which had such nationalistic titles as "The January 28th Remembrance Song." Smaller sets of singers then contributed special numbers, such as "Who Says We're Too Young," which was performed by a group of children. By the end of the day's program, the whole crowd of 5,000 spectators had joined the members of the YMCA group in rousing renditions of the popular patriotic hymns "Save China" and "The March of the Volunteers," an experience the reporter found deeply moving.

Students were by no means the only (or even the main) participants in this multi-class group singing movement, but this new form of musical performance had profound implications for youth movement propagandists. National salvation songs provided a valuable medium for spreading ideas and embedding slogans in the mind of the general population, and collective singing became an important way of expressing national and/or class solidarity. Student propagandists, like other proponents of the national salvation movement of the late 1930's, were quick to see the potential of this technique, and singing began to play an increasingly prominent part in political gatherings like the memorial services held each year on May 4, 9, and 30.[27]

Collective singing continued to play this central role in student propaganda drives and political mass gatherings throughout the Republican era. If memoirs by former participants are to be believed, no march of the Civil War years was complete without a mass rendition of "Unity is Strength," a popular anthem sung to the tune of "Solidarity Forever." [28] "The March of the Volunteers" and other songs from the War of Resistance remained popular during the late 1940's, and special words were sometimes fitted to these and other familiar tunes to suit specific post–World War II incidents.[29] Thus, for example, during a train-commandeering incident in May 1947 (see Chapter 9), one resourceful member of a school mass choral society taught a group of protesters a revised version of "Frere Jacques." [30]

The spring of 1947, which witnessed a wide range of protests stemming from many grievances, stands out as a particularly creative time for other propaganda media as well. This at least is the contention of a July 1947 article "The Artistic Creations of the Anti-Hunger, Anti–Civil War Movement," which appeared in *Xuesheng bao* (Student news), Shanghai's leading underground student newspaper.[31] This article begins its discussion of recent advances in propaganda with the following comments on student slogans:

> We have already moved past the old "Down with such and such" and "Up with such and such" types [of chants] and have now begun to shout out these lively and specific new slogans "Our stomachs are empty!" and "We are begging food from the mouths of guns!" The style of chanting has also advanced in a new direction: formerly there was always one person leading everybody in chants, and sentences were shouted intermittently. But now people have created linked chants in which sentences are joined together. There are also question and answer refrains, making for livelier chants.

The article gives two examples of these new types of chants, both developed by youths at Jiaotong University. The first, which emphasized that the hyperinflation of the time was causing police officers as well as students and other citizens to suffer, went as follows: "Policeman, what is your salary?" "Several tens of thousands." "Is that enough?" "No, no!" "Why is that?" "Because of the Civil War."[32] The second chant—also aimed at convincing those in charge of putting down student demonstrations that protesters were not the real enemy—took the form of a series of linked sentences: "Soldiers, policemen, and students are all part of one family"; "People don't beat up on their own kin"; "Establish democracy and seek peace."

This *Xuesheng bao* article also notes important new advances in written forms of propaganda, particularly banners, both in terms of content and technique during the Anti-Hunger, Anti–Civil War Movement of the previous spring. Several of the liveliest banners carried during the Shanghai marches of May 1947 spoke to widely shared grievances over inflation, the disruption caused by the Civil War, and official corruption. One such banner, which focused on the last of these issues, read: "You raise a pig to eat its meat, you raise a dog to keep your house safe, and you raise a cat so he'll catch rats. But we ask you: What do we get from feeding all these bureaucrats?" The article then describes new types of banners such as "living posters" in which "each person on the street carries one word" and the whole message becomes clear only "when they are linked up."[33] The article goes on to give the titles of various songs students adapted to fit the needs of the movement, lists several plays protesters performed, and describes some interesting political woodcuts. It concludes by saying that the pictorial pamphlets "May 20th" and "The Tragic History of May," produced by Nanjing's Central University and the Shanghai Student Union respectively, will "be of use to historians" someday.[34]

Other contemporary documents as well as archival materials and memoirs reinforce the impression that the propaganda accompanying the Anti-Hunger, Anti–Civil War Movement was unusually varied and creative. Descriptions and pictures of the giant march held on May 19, in particular, present a vivid picture of this creativity and the scale of student propaganda efforts.[35] According to a recent memoir by several former Ji'nan University students who took part in the demonstration, student propagandists spent the march "lecturing, singing, putting on plays," and distributing leaflets. All told, this source estimates that the marchers passed out over 20,000 copies of a leaflet entitled "Gao tongbao shu" (Announcement to our brethren) that spelled out the aims of the protest.[36]

The same memoir presents a detailed description of the activities of a band of students known as the Ji'nan Food Bowl Group, whose performances during the march received more attention from spectators than those of any other propaganda team. The Food Bowl Group combined acting techniques, symbolic physical objects, songs, and banners to get its message across to the masses. The members of the group dressed in "shabby" clothes and "carried broken food bowls in their hands." Each bowl had a different character written on it, and when the marchers walked together, they created a living poster saying "We want to eat our fill." [37] According to contemporary press accounts and memoirs alike, the group was an impressive sight as its members marched through the city's streets waving flags and beating time on their broken bowls with chopsticks, while singing songs protesting the misery caused by the economic hardships of the Civil War and governmental oppression. [38]

This overview of propaganda methods illustrates the range of media and techniques students used to publicize their message. Educated youths were continually looking for new ways to reach the illiterate and semiliterate as well as the literate. This eclecticism and creativity goes a long way toward explaining the success of student propaganda drives. Other factors also have to be examined, however, to complete the picture. First, we must place the publicity work that accompanied youth movements within the context of other attempts to bridge the gap between the zhishi and wuzhishi cultural worlds. These other efforts are important because they could serve as models for student attempts to propagandize the masses and also because they helped prepare the laobaixing to receive and decode the messages embedded in student texts.

SPEAKING TO THE PEOPLE: PRECEDENTS

As wide as the gulf that separated educated youths from ordinary workers, shopkeepers, clerks, coolies, and peasants was, recent work by many scholars has convincingly demonstrated that it is inaccurate to conceive of traditional Chinese society as split between completely unconnected "elite" and "popular" cultural realms. The traditional image of Chinese culture as sharply bifurcated into "high" and "low," or "great" and "little," traditions is seriously flawed; a wide range of people and texts served as intermediaries between the zhishi and wuzhishi cultural spheres. [39] The ability to read and write wenyan—the language of imperial edicts, petitions, and other official documents, as well as that of classical poetry, the civil service examinations, and scholarly treatises—established a boundary between the educated elite and the uneducated masses. [40] But this line was by no means a clearly distinct one even in imperial times: there were always clerics, popular authors, failed examination candidates, and others who had some familiarity with wenyan and wrote texts that are hard to classify as either "high" or "low" creations; and there were always songs, religious works, operas, story cycles, and the like familiar to both "elite" and "popular" audiences.[41]

The New Culture intellectuals of the late 1910's were by no means either the first or the last members of an elite group to produce persuasive texts aimed at wuzhishi audiences. Imperial officials and preachers had shown an interest in speaking to the laobaixing long before the May 4th students were born. In addition, throughout the twentieth century the very governments challenged by Shanghai student protesters continued to develop techniques of their own for bridging the gap between the zhishi and wuzhishi realms. Sometimes this officially sponsored propaganda was aimed explicitly at undercutting the efficacy of radical movements. In other cases, such as the New Life campaigns of the 1930's, this anti-radical purpose merged with reformist goals, such as promoting mass literacy or ridding the people of superstitious practices.

The existence of bridges between the zhishi and wuzhishi worlds meant that even in 1919, when May 4th propagandists first set out to spread patriotic ideas among the masses, what they were doing would not have seemed completely alien either to themselves or to members of their audience. There was much that was novel about their general project and about the specific types of vernacular texts they produced, but neither was wholly without precedent. There was nothing new about members of elite groups trying to propagandize among the masses, and thanks to events such as the mass literacy and public morality campaigns of the Guomindang years, this kind of publicity work became increasingly commonplace as the Republican era progressed. Nor was trying to write in the vernacular or produce texts that make sense to both fully educated and semi-literate audiences an unprecedented act in 1919. Hu Shi freely admitted that his ideas concerning baihua were inspired in large part by an early exposure to and love of traditional heroic epics, which were written in a style that mimicked colloquial patterns of speech, and newspapers were already beginning to experiment with vernacular news reporting in late Qing times. To return to the metaphor used in Chapter 3 to describe tactical choices, student propagandists benefited from a wide range of pre-existing xuanchuan "scripts" upon which to improvise.

What were these "scripts" and where did they come from? Memoirs by student activists rarely single out specific activities and texts as models for their propaganda work, and other sources such as press reports are equally short on hard evidence. The following discussion thus does not try to prove that student propagandists self-consciously drew inspiration from one or another text or activity. Instead, it sketches some of the written works and social practices likely to have influenced youth movement publications, dramas, and speeches, and/or to have shaped the way the laobaixing received these communications.

Once again, as with collective action scripts, many of the potential models for student propaganda work had little or nothing to do with protest activities. The activities and publications analyzed in Victor Mair's "Language and Ideology in the Written Popularizations of the *Sacred Edict*" are a case in point. Mair's study focuses upon various methods officials used to inculcate the Kangxi emperor's famous *Sacred Edict* of 1670, which was "widely recognized as the most concise and authoritative statement of Confucian ideology," among the general populace. The most important of these methods were vernacular commentaries on and explications of the sixteen basic maxims that made up Kangxi's famous work and public lectures, which sometimes took on a highly ritualized form, whose goal was to explain the meaning of the *Sacred Edict* to ordinary citizens.

The written popularizations of Kangxi's short classic, like comparable vernacular explications of official texts written in pre-Qing times, used a variety of literary and pictorial devices to embed the imperial wisdom in the minds of the laobaixing. By mixing citations of the original wenyan maxims themselves with commentaries and stories written in a fully vernacular or semiclassical style, and then supplementing these with dozens (or in some cases even hundreds) of illustrations accompanied by easily understood captions, the authors of such works created texts at least partially accessible to all strata. These popularizations were not intended to be read solely by individuals in private settings. Instead their authors hoped that government officials, village elders, and tutors would read them aloud and explicate the texts in collective settings, so that all the laobaixing would be able to understand the moral precepts of filial piety and obedience stressed in the *Sacred Edict*. In some cases they even included songs for these instructors to sing or to teach to the common people.

The imperial court gave a boost to these popularizers during the mid-eighteenth century by requiring local officials to read out the Kangxi emperor's maxims to the people twice a month as part of the "village lecture" (*xiangyue*) system.[42] These officials were told, furthermore, to supplement these readings from the *Sacred Edict* by arranging for orators to provide colloquial speeches on Confucian morality.[43] Most scholars agree, however, that during the last decades of the Qing era the xiangyue gatherings, which were supposed to serve as powerful rites symbolizing and reinforcing communal solidarity, had degenerated into mere formalities that only a small portion of the population even bothered to attend.[44]

Confucian tenets continued to be spread, nonetheless, through less formal types of performances. Ad hoc lectures using music and storytelling techniques to draw and reach popular audiences, for example, were common in many towns and villages. The impact of these kinds of lectures-cum-performances upon future student activists, as well as upon their future audiences, was vividly illustrated by one of the May 4th Movement's most famous participants: the dramatist, scholar, and sometime propagandist Guo Moruo. In his memoir *Shaonian shidai* (The time of my youth), Guo describes growing up in a village whose inhabitants were mesmerized by the lecturers on the *Sacred Edict* who came from time to time to tell them "stories about loyalty, filial piety, and fidelity from the morality books [*shanshu*]." These lecturers—some of whom would "accompany themselves with bells, fish-shaped woodblocks, bamboo clappers, and the like"—would use tables to set up makeshift daises on street corners and chant maxims, sing songs, and tell stories. The best of them "could make the listeners weep," according to Guo, by putting so much feeling into their recitations that the events became theatrical performances. Almost all of them could keep a crowd enthralled for "two or three hours" with this kind of "entertainment."[45]

These late imperial Confucian proselytizing techniques, from the production of chapbooks to the popular performances Guo and his contemporaries witnessed in their youth, are relevant here because student propagandists produced counterparts to all of them during their xuanchuan drives. The pamphlets Republican-era students distributed among the laobaixing were often quite similar in basic format to popularizations of the *Sacred Edict*, with the same mixture of repeated catchphrases, evocative illustrations, easily remembered couplets, and simply written explications of key terms. Twentieth-century protesters simply substituted anti-imperialist cartoons for pictures demonstrating proper forms of ritual behavior and replaced Confucian maxims such as "Esteem most highly filial piety" with patriotic ones like "If you unite together, no one can oppress you."[46] And, like their Confucian predecessors, student propagandists used public performances—ranging from informal performances on hastily erected platforms that used music and popular storytelling techniques to more formal and ritualized lectures in temples or guild halls—to further embed key slogans in the minds of the laobaixing.[47]

Written popularizations of the *Sacred Edict* and village lectures on moral topics were by no means the only kinds of texts and activities that provided scripts for student publicists and helped prepare the laobaixing to receive youth movement propaganda; nor were they the only ones to rely upon the stylistic devices described above. Buddhist sutras written in the vernacular and filled with tales of heroes as well as theological arguments,

publications by rebel groups, popular almanacs, and picture books condemning religious heresies—these are but a few types of traditional texts
that used a mixture of captioned drawings, colloquial stories, and re-
petitive slogans in an effort to influence the laobaixing.[48] In the realm
of orally transmitted texts, such things as sermons by itinerant Daoist
preachers or Christian missionaries and the operatic performances that
accompanied village festivals also set important precedents for student attempts to bridge the gap between the zhishi and the wuzhishi realms.[49]
In addition, contemporary texts and activities, such as the lectures and
publications that accompanied government-sponsored mass literacy campaigns and the GMD's New Life Movement, are also worth remembering
when trying to trace the genesis of student protesters' publicity scripts.
These sporadic official xuanchuan campaigns, which relied upon the same
written and oral propaganda techniques discussed above,[50] were important
because they kept ordinary people familiar with zhishi communication
styles during the periods between radical youth movements.

The precise connections between these various forms of xuanchuan and
student propaganda work are difficult to trace, but in the case of certain
activities such as Christian proselytizing some interesting links can be
found. Zhang Guotao's account of a Christian pastor's lesson in rhetoric
(see above) is but one case in point. Other May 4th student activists, many
of whom studied at missionary schools and hence were regularly exposed
to Christian services, also learned public speaking techniques from ministers and priests. It is not surprising, therefore, that English-language
newspapers sometimes referred to student speechmakers as "preaching"
to the masses.[51] Later generations of student activists also "learned"
xuanchuan skills from watching missionaries. In at least one post–May 4th
struggle, a preacher even intentionally assumed the position of role model.
In 1947 the Reverend James G. Endicott applied his considerable gifts as a
public speaker to the cause of protest, giving speeches on political issues to
student activists at St. John's University, speeches that inspired some of
these youths to devote themselves to the fight against the Civil War and
left many members of the crowd in tears.[52] But even when foreign priests
and ministers were overtly hostile to a student cause, as for obvious reasons they often tended to be in the 1920's, this did not stop students from
adapting missionary techniques to the cause of patriotic protest. The anti-
Christian propaganda work of the early 1920's had more than a passing
similarity to missionary publicity efforts: in 1924 student activists matched
the Christmas week festivities of the Christians with an anti-Christian
propaganda week of their own, during which they distributed mock Christmas cards and gave anti-religious sermons outside churches (see Chapter 1).

Missionaries were not the only ones who served simultaneously as the targets of and the role models for student propagandists—Chinese officials often found themselves in the same position. Educated youths frequently issued proclamations that resembled those routinely issued by local police chiefs and other authorities. Such orders, which appeared on walls and poles in all major cities, were a form of elite communication to which ordinary laobaixing were frequently exposed. All Shanghai citizens, from members of the literati to rickshaw pullers, were used to seeing and heeding these official broadsheets, which were often intentionally written in the simplest of vernacular forms to reach as lowly an audience as possible. Often they contained little more than a list of basic rules and regulations followed by descriptions of the punishments for specific types of misbehavior.[53]

For several reasons students probably found the idea of preparing posters similar in style to official orders and pasting them in spots usually reserved for authorized communications an appealing one. First, it was easy to do, since the models were so familiar and omnipresent. Second, just as holding mass actions that resemble government ceremonies can raise questions regarding the legitimacy of the way power is wielded within a society (a point examined at length in Chapter 10), this kind of propaganda work implicitly challenged the idea that only designated officials had the right to instruct the populace on proper behavior. And third, official-looking posters were almost certain to attract the attention of passersby, who would be afraid not to read the notices—or have the orders read to them—in case the new rules and regulations applied to them.

It is impossible to determine the precise role each of these factors played in leading Shanghai students to produce posters that looked like official communications, and extant sources also leave doubts as to how often the mimicry was self-conscious. What *is* clear, even from the most cursory examination of photographic and textual evidence, is the strange parallelism between official and protest communications. It was often hard to tell at first glance what "authority"—an official one such as the head of the police force or an unofficial one such as the president of the Shanghai Student Union—was responsible for a given proclamation. Only when passersby came close enough to read the text could they discover whether the "rules and regulations" in question were those of a patriotic movement or the official establishment. Some of these posters contained injunctions to refrain from breaking the laws, others injunctions to boycott foreign goods; some described how lawbreakers would be punished, others the fate of China if the rules of the boycott were not enforced. As different as they could be in content, however, in terms of style, wording, and placement, the two types of communications were often almost indistinguishable. The implications of this were understood by at least some contemporary observers. A *China Press* article on May 4th propaganda describes a number of different techniques activists were using to promote the boycott of 1919 and points to the "clever" way in which "some of the handbills pasted on Japanese shop doors were so arranged as to make them look like official sealing orders issued by Chinese yamens."[54]

So far this section has looked almost exclusively at how non- or anti-revolutionary writers provided students with propaganda scripts or models. Students also learned many techniques from a group of revolutionary authors: professional propagandists affiliated with the CCP. Both Qu Qiubai and Chen Duxiu, for example, two of the party's top theorists and publicists, were on the faculty of Shanghai University during the May 30th Movement and helped teach many student propagandists the tricks of the trade. Nor was 1925 the only year Communist propagandists were in a position to help mold student movement publicity work to serve party ends. In the 1930's many of the intellectuals to whom student activists looked for guidance were CCP members of the League of Left-wing Writers. In the 1940's many of the journals, such as *Qingnian zhishi* (Youth culture), that provided student protesters with data to use in their pamphlets—and at times even with the slogans they placed on their banners—were underground CCP organs.

The preceding pages have not exhausted the topic of the models and scripts that facilitated student movement propaganda work, but they should give a sense of the range of oral and literary traditions that student publicists were able to borrow from in their work—traditions that simultaneously helped prepare the laobaixing to receive and decode these new elite messages. Whether the specific traditions in question were used to convey "conservative" or "radical" messages was largely irrelevant, since students sometimes improvised upon forms that had traditionally been used to maintain orthodoxy and stifle rebellion. What mattered was that the traditions promoted effective communication between the zhishi and wuzhishi worlds and thereby helped students achieve a remarkable degree of success in gaining the support of ordinary peasants, workers, soldiers, and coolies.

Speaking to the Masses:
Key Words and Symbols

So far this chapter has focused upon the technological and stylistic aspects of student communication with the laobaixing, but has said little about the content of student protest messages and the images and themes student propagandists employed to gain support. An examination of these images and themes is crucial, because no matter how wide a range of techniques youth activists had at their disposal, and no matter how many traditions they could tap to aid their publicity efforts, their efforts would have proved in vain if their basic message did not move the members of their intended audience. The task of making the laobaixing feel that all Chinese (not just students) had a tangible stake in the movements in question was not always easy, since the specific grievances that motivated educated youths might easily seem irrelevant or overly abstract to members of the wuzhishi world. Missionary control of colleges, extraterritoriality, censorship, lack of political freedom, crackdowns on dissident intellectuals, and rising tuition costs—all of which at one time or another inspired Shanghai students to take collective action—had little meaning for mill workers, rickshaw pullers, prostitutes, or vegetable sellers, whose main concern was making enough money to feed themselves and their families.

How then did educated youths manage so often to convince members of less privileged social groups to support student-led mass movements? How did they so often succeed in making abstract causes tangible to people obsessed with the practical problems of existence? Student propagandists accomplished these tasks by finding and exploiting a set of easily recognizable, emotionally charged ideas and symbols with broad popular appeal. As abstract as the ideals that motivated the students may have been at times, the publicists for each of Shanghai's great student-led mass movements managed to boil a complex message down to a simple form that could be expressed easily in a few short catchphrases or evoked by physical objects or pictorial representations. Moreover, in each case the essential message student propagandists stressed was one with as much relevance for members of the laobaixing as for members of the zhishi world.

Joseph Chen's analysis of the May 4th activists' exploitation of popular fears of *wangguo* (national extinction) is an excellent illustration of the process of condensation.[55] Chen argues that students and other intellectuals involved in the patriotic struggles of 1919 quickly realized that the only way to gain mass support was to find an image that all Chinese would understand. Although these intellectuals may have been concerned with the intricacies of international treaties, they knew that the laobaixing would not find abstract diplomatic grievances equally compelling. Thus, in their propaganda, they continually played upon the idea that a Japanese takeover of Shandong Province would be the first step in the extinction of the Chinese nation as an independent entity, the beginning of the end of the entire Chinese cultural universe.

Chen delineates several factors that made the concept of wangguo reso-
nate strongly among Chinese of all classes. He notes, for example, that the
recent fate of Korea, which propagandists used as an example of what
could befall China, offered clear proof that Japan was capable of "ex-
tinguishing" any nation that fell under its control.[56] More important, he
shows that thanks to China's own history of suffering at the hands of foreign conquerors, by the early twentieth century wangguo had become a
"popular political myth." Fears of national extinction had been so thoroughly "inculcated into the minds of the Chinese all through the ages via
the writings and sayings of literary men, through novels, folklore, legends,
plays, operas, and other mass media," that utterance of the phrase wangguo struck fear into the hearts of everyone from the highest official to the
lowliest coolie.

May 4th publicists also made much use of the term *maiguo* (traitor),
another emotionally charged word with deep resonances. The traitorous
official, willing to risk endangering the nation in order to protect his own
position or gain additional power, is a stock figure in innumerable Chinese
stories, legends, operas, folksongs, and popular novels. By using this term
repeatedly to refer to pro-Japanese officials and then extending its meaning to include all those who opposed the students or even all those who
transgressed the rules of the boycott, May 4th propagandists presented the
movement in a way that made it easy for even the least educated members
of their audience to tell the heroes from the villains.

Educated youths and other intellectuals used symbolic acts and pictures
of objects with powerful folk resonances to further reinforce the idea that
students were bravely protecting the nation from evil foreign powers and
domestic traitors. When young protesters wrote "Save our Shandong"
with their own blood, they were transmitting an easily decoded message
that they were willing to die to prevent China's wangguo. And when protesters used representations of tortoises (animals associated with cuck-
oldry, lack of filiality, and other negative traits in Chinese folklore) to illustrate injunctions against buying Japanese goods, they were sending an
equally clear message to the populace at large: those who help the enemy
are not only not true Chinese, they are not even fully human.[57]

May 30th propagandists similarly made use of easy to understand, emotionally charged terms and images. Several May 30th symbols are treated
at some length in Chapter 4—bloodstained clothes, pictures of bullet
wounds, martyrs' corpses. And we have also examined some of the slogans,
such as "Shanghai for the Shanghainese," which propagandists of the
mid-1920's used to give their cause broad popular appeal. Before we move
on to propaganda of the 1930's, however, it is worth looking briefly at another kind of symbolism participants in the May 30th Movement used to

make their message immediately accessible to even the least literate members of the popular audience: animal imagery.

One of the animals that appeared most frequently on May 30th posters and broadsides was the tortoise, which once again served to vilify and dehumanize those who dealt with foreigners. A set of eleven photographs of "anti-foreign posters," which Edwin S. Cunningham, the American consul-general in Shanghai, submitted to the secretary of state on June 12, 1925, provides clear evidence of the popularity of tortoise imagery.[58] Several of the posters in this fascinating collection have pictures of tortoises and/or captions that refer to the animals. In one picture tortoises are labeled with the Chinese characters for "Japanese person" and "English person." In other cases, however, the people designated as tortoises are Chinese who help foreigners and hence forfeit their claim to be patriots or even people. The caption of one poster implies that any Chinese who smokes a foreign-made cigarette is no better than a tortoise; another broadside says that anyone who dares to tear down patriotic posters is a tortoise. (See photographic section for sample shots from Cunningham's collection.)

The tortoise was by no means the only animal May 30th propagandists used to influence the masses. Many pamphlets of the time aimed at winning the support of workers, for example, claimed that Japanese employers treated native workers as "cattle" (*niuma*). Innumerable articles and leaflets applied the epithet "running dog" (*zougou*) to all Chinese who opposed the popular movement.[59] According to a police report published in the Shanghai Municipal Council's official organ, *The Municipal Gazette*, in at least one case protesters used theatrical as well as textual methods to get this particular animal identification across. A group of workers who suspected one of their fellows of being a spy for the Japanese "imprisoned" this man "for over 24 hours" and then "compelled" him to suffer "the indignity of being photographed while branded with a paper notice bearing the words 'I am a dog.'"[60] In an overview of the "comprehensive and absolutely unscrupulous" propaganda campaign that accompanied the May 30th Movement, the same report refers to a number of comparable ways protesters denigrated and dehumanized their enemies. The report claims that "notices vilifying foreigners as desperadoes, murderers and monsters, and denouncing all Chinese who worked for them as slaves, dogs, cuckolds and reptiles" became a common sight in the International Settlement in June 1925.[61]

Propagandists of the 1930's similarly used a core set of concrete images and symbols to make their message accessible and meaningful to ordinary citizens. As in 1919, the idea that the Chinese nation was in danger of becoming a colony of Japan was a central theme in much student publicity work, although in the 1930's the dominant catchphrase was *jiuguo* (save the nation) rather than wangguo.[62] Chants, slogans, songs, banners, and organization names—throughout the decade the term *jiuguo* continually figured in all of these. Whenever student propagandists tried to convince their listeners or readers of the need to support a boycott or to take part in a rally, the main reason they gave was always that doing so would aid the cause of national salvation, a cause they hoped all Chinese would understand and consider worthy.

Educated youths used various symbols to convince the populace that the only way to save the nation was to persuade the central government to take stronger steps to protect China from Japanese aggression. Graphic pictures of Chinese civilians killed by foreign troops were one powerful and easily grasped reminder of the urgency of the political situation.[63] Other types of pictorial representations—such as maps that highlighted the amount of Chinese territory already under Japanese control—were also effective tools for making this point.[64] Perhaps the most effective propaganda technique, however, for convincing ordinary citizens that students were more devoted to saving the nation than was the central government involved neither written nor illustrated texts. The protesters' constant invocations of martial images through gestures and clothing—described in the previous chapter—probably did more than words or pictures to persuade the laobaixing that educated youths were ready to lay down their lives for the cause of jiuguo.

Throughout the 1910's, 1920's, and 1930's, therefore, symbols and slogans that appealed to a basic sense of nationalism were at the center of student attempts to speak to the laobaixing. Educated youths found that the most effective way to present themselves as being on the side of ordinary citizens was to emphasize the threat foreigners and domestic traitors posed to all patriotic Chinese. By painting a crude, black-and-white picture of political events as a struggle between the friends and the foes of China, in which those who sided with the enemy were vilified as monsters or beasts, students were able to reach members of the laobaixing at a basic emotional level. The specific symbols used might change from movement to movement, but whether students used pictures of tortoises or dogs, whether they shouted "Shanghai for the Shanghainese" or "Chinese people do not beat up Chinese people," the implication was the same: "we" (all Chinese who have not forfeited their claim to Chineseness or indeed humanity by collaborating with the enemy) must band together to fight "them" (the foreigners and traitors who are killing our nation).[65]

Students used this same kind of emotional nationalistic propaganda during the Civil War years to bridge the gap between the zhishi and wuzhishi worlds. Thus, for example, in late 1946 and early 1947 during the protests triggered by the alleged rape of a female college student by American marines, educated youths tried to stir up anti-American feeling among the masses by calling attention to instances in which U.S. military personnel had mistreated Chinese of various classes, ranging from rickshaw pullers to the children of officials.[66] During a 1948 movement protesting American plans to rearm Japan, students issued pamphlets filled with grotesque caricatures of foreign soldiers and reminders of how much all Chinese had suffered at the hands of the Japanese devils during World War II.[67] As in earlier decades, the students involved in these protest movements emphasized that Chinese officials who cooperated with the imperialists were as bad or worse than the foreign aggressors themselves, and that the same was true of those who interfered with patriotic movements. The implication of "Chinese people do not beat up Chinese people," which became an even more common slogan in the Civil War years than it had been in the 1930's, was that the Chinese police officers and secret agents (*tewu*) who routinely used violent means to suppress protests had forfeited their right to be considered Chinese.[68]

During the Anti-Hunger, Anti–Civil War Movement of 1947, however, student propagandists did not depend solely (or even primarily) upon symbols and slogans that appealed to patriotism and xenophobia. As earlier comments on propaganda techniques and texts from this struggle suggest, the youths relied most heavily upon economic themes to win the laobaixing's support. Patriotism played a part in the publicity drives of spring 1947 and students often shouted slogans such as "Chinese people do not beat up Chinese people." Nonetheless, in most of their key chants, songs, performances, and posters, students used the shared experience of economic hardship rather than ethnic or national commonalities to build bridges between themselves and the uneducated masses. If the main thrust of most earlier propaganda drives had been "students and laobaixing must band together to fight a common diplomatic and military threat," the central message in 1947 was "students and laobaixing must band together to fight the common economic peril of starvation."

The specific symbols and slogans students used to convey this message—broken rice bowls, banners emblazoned with the phrase "We want to eat our fill," leaflets full of anecdotes concerning students and workers suffering from the lack of money and food—carried an unambiguous message to members of both the zhishi and the wuzhishi worlds. The cry "We are begging for food from the mouths of guns" conjured up particularly powerful images. This sentence drew attention to the economic distress imperiling students and workers alike and placed the blame for this suffering on the central government's insistence that military funding take precedence over all other types of spending. Even more arresting than this chant was a poster Tongji students carried during the demonstrations of May 1947, which used the phrase as a caption for a picture of an emaciated youth holding a bowl up to the mouths of two smoking cannons.[69]

Another food-related propaganda image was the *youtiao*. The term literally means "oily strip," and a youtiao is a deep-fried confection sold by Shanghai street vendors, similar in taste to an unusually greasy and bland doughnut, although it is long and thin instead of round in shape. It is hard to imagine a less likely candidate for enshrinement as a political emblem than the common youtiao, generally considered the cheapest and lowliest form of Shanghai street-food. During the demonstrations of spring 1947, however, the youtiao became one of the central symbols of student propaganda, particularly that aimed at the laobaixing.

The youtiao's value as a symbol lay in its ability to communicate economic realities in a meaningful manner to those unacquainted with budgetary statistics and other abstractions. When student propagandists tried to persuade their fellow students or other intellectuals that the GMD was not allocating enough money to fund schools and provide students with living stipends, they often contrasted the percentage of the national budget allocated to education (3.6) with that allocated to the military (80).[70] But when they wanted to make the same point to ordinary workers and coolies, educated youths were more likely to simply claim that a student receiving a government scholarship could afford to eat only two or three youtiao a day, a diet no Shanghai resident would have considered sufficient. This claim is stated in one way or another in nearly all the leaflets from the movement that survive in Shanghai archives.[71] The most interesting piece of youtiao propaganda was not a simple written text, however, but an unusual flag. One of the most evocative photographs of the great Anti-Hunger, Anti–Civil War demonstration of May 19, 1947, shows a student holding up a flag with the words "One day's food allowance is not even enough to buy" and two greasy doughnuts hanging below it suspended by what appear to be pieces of string.[72]

The common thread running through all student attempts to gain the support of the laobaixing, whether Japanese-made straw hats cut in the shape of turtles or youtiao suspended from flags, was a desire to show that members of the zhishi and wuzhishi worlds were threatened by common foes. Most frequently the enemies attacked in the caricatures, songs, plays, slogans, and posters students used to reach semiliterate and illiterate citizens were well-known figures from popular lore: the foreign aggressor and the corrupt native powerholder. Even when external threats were less critical than internal ones, however, as was the case during the Civil War years, educated youths still managed to find symbols such as broken rice bowls that transcended class boundaries. Time and again, by employing the broadest possible array of communicative techniques, packaging their messages in forms easily comprehended by all strata of society, and exploiting symbols with powerful emotional resonances for the laobaixing, educated youths succeeded in convincing large segments of their audiences that the youth movement was serving the interests of the nation as a whole rather than merely the interests of the educated elite.

SPEAKING TO ELITES: PROPAGANDA AS DIALOGUE

Student propaganda aimed at members of the zhishi world relied upon many of the themes examined in the preceding sections of this chapter. This is not surprising. Students were aware, after all, that teachers, journalists, and merchants shared some if not all of the concerns relating to imperialism, domestic corruption, inflation, and the like that troubled the uneducated masses. In addition, some student texts were clearly designed to speak simultaneously to members of the zhishi and wuzhishi worlds. Youth movement activists knew, for example, that the slogans they chanted during marches and the songs they sang at rallies would be heard by businessmen as well as dockworkers, uncommitted classmates as well as streetside vendors, and hence if possible should play upon broadly shared ideals and fears.

This said, there were often important differences between the way student propagandists spoke to educated as opposed to uneducated audiences. There were stylistic differences; for example, when writing specifically for Chinese elites, students often wrote in wenyan as opposed to baihua and used more classical allusions. There were also differences in the types of arguments authors used to gain support for a cause. For example, when writing primarily for their classmates, young propagandists often made chauvinistic references to the special patriotism of students, which would have been out of place in communications intended for members of other social groups.[73] The differences between propaganda texts created to influence educated audiences and those aimed at the laobaixing are so varied and complex that it is impossible to do justice to all of them. One general contrast between the two types of texts stands out, however. To an unusual extent, texts for elite audiences tended to be shaped by (and at times explicitly framed as responses to) things members of their intended audiences said and wrote themselves. Put bluntly, student communications with the laobaixing generally took the form of "monologues" in which educated youths imparted information to and tried to change the viewpoints of the masses; student communications with members of the zhishi world more frequently took the form of "dialogues."

In light of Mikhail Bakhtin's arguments on the "dialogic" quality of novels, as well as recent studies in audience-centered literary criticism, it is dangerous to refer to any text as purely "monologic." As critics like Bakhtin stress, acts of speech and pieces of writing are always part of and shaped by intra- or intertextual dialogues: even seemingly straightforward communications are usually, in part at least, responses to previously created works; and all authors are influenced by the ideas and beliefs of the audience for whom they are writing, or at least by what they imagine the members of their intended audience think and feel.[74] Although there was, therefore, a "dialogue" of sorts between student propagandists and their laobaixing audiences, in the sense that educated youths were intensely concerned with trying to find the themes with the strongest popular resonances, members of the wuzhishi world were usually accorded such a passive role that the term "monologue" still seems appropriate. Student propagandists might decide to emphasize certain themes and play down others because of the reaction of their wuzhishi listeners or readers, but the relationship between student speakers and writers and laobaixing audiences was almost never an egalitarian one. Streetside lectures in which students placed themselves physically above their listeners and seldom solicited comments from them were not interchanges between equal partners. And because members of the laobaixing almost never produced written texts challenging student claims, student authors did not generally engage in fully realized, explicit dialogues with members of the wuzhishi world.

In propaganda work directed at foreigners and domestic elites, however, students tended to adopt more interactive modes of communication. One reason for this shift from monologue to dialogue was simple snobbery. For all of their populist rhetoric, many students considered themselves the social superiors of the laobaixing and hence were comfortable in adopting one-way modes of communication when speaking to popular audiences.[75] But students had no such sense of superiority vis-à-vis Chinese officials and foreign consuls, and this had a profound effect upon the way they addressed members of these elite groups. Besides the obvious difference of adopting a more formal manner of speaking and writing when communicating with people they considered their social and intellectual equals, student propagandists abandoned the pose of being instructors and presented themselves as participants in a mutually beneficial exchange of ideas and opinions.

In some cases, students even adopted forms of speech and gestures that placed them in inferior positions to members of the elite audience they sought to persuade. The clearest example of this was the bended-knee petition, in which students used the same ritual gestures that officials traditionally adopted when remonstrating with emperors. Some students of the

Republican era objected to this form of remonstrance, claiming that to beseech representatives of the Warlord or GMD regimes to act benevolently was to grant too much legitimacy to the existing political status quo. Similarly, when a group of students knelt on the steps outside the Great Hall of the People in 1989 to present a petition to representatives of the CCP, some participants in the People's Movement objected to this action as an overly submissive one. Such criticisms aside, the different postures students adopted when speaking to officials as opposed to members of the laobaixing have been striking throughout the twentieth century. Wuer Kaixi's dramatic interruptions of Li Peng during a nationally televised meeting notwithstanding, China's most recent generation of protesters have once again tended to instruct or admonish ordinary citizens but ask for or demand "dialogues" with officials.[76]

Another important factor behind the move from monologue to dialogue was the number of texts attacking student protest produced by foreigners and members of domestic elite groups. Thanks to their high level of literacy and their feeling of frequently being directly threatened by protest activities, conservative members of the zhishi world produced a steady stream of anti–youth movement propaganda throughout the Republican era. Student activists realized that the only way to counteract this negative propaganda was to answer their critics directly; youth movement propagandists were forced, in other words, to engage in an indirect dialogue with their opponents by producing texts that countered attacks on the youth movement.

Here I am using the term *dialogue* more metaphorically, since student protesters only occasionally composed texts explicitly designed as responses to works by their opponents. When reading through the propaganda and counter-propaganda of the time, however, one is often struck by a strong sense of interaction between the texts written by friends and foes of each mass movement. Even when authors do not allude directly to the claims of their opponents, it is clear that each side is locating its arguments within common reference points, that each is continually being influenced by the symbols used and the charges leveled by the other.

English-language publications written with Western readers in mind illustrate this point. Participants in Republican student movements (particularly those in cosmopolitan cities such as Shanghai) were interested in gaining support for their cause from members of Shanghai's expatriate communities, famous European and American intellectuals, foreign diplomats, and the ordinary citizens of Western countries. Student protesters realized from the start, however, that to win the sympathy of these groups they had to do more than simply translate their standard propaganda materials into English or some other Western language, since many of the arguments and symbols with the greatest appeal to Chinese audiences would at best have no resonances for foreigners and at worst would alienate them. Students knew, for example, that wangguo imagery had almost no emotional power for Western readers and that some of the animal imagery so useful for appealing to the laobaixing would offend foreigners. Students were well aware, in other words, of the special problems in making their cause seem worthy to an audience with ideals, values, and points of reference quite different from those of most Chinese.

These problems were not terribly difficult for Shanghai students to overcome, however, since Western values and ideals were not wholly alien to most of them. Many had either studied abroad or been exposed to foreign teachers and foreign ideas in local schools. In addition, articles defending student protests by sympathetic foreign journalists provided students with models for their own appeals to non-Chinese audiences; in a couple of important cases foreign writers even served as advisers to student protest leagues.[77] Finally, and perhaps most important, the antagonistic propaganda written by defenders of foreign privilege to discredit Chinese protests gave students clear indications of the themes and issues that Western readers found most compelling.

The influence of this kind of antagonistic propaganda on student writings is clearest in the case of the May 30th Movement. This is largely because Shanghai's most widely read English-language weekly newspaper, the *North China Herald*, waged a virulent and extensive publicity campaign to discredit the mass movements of the mid- to late 1920's. The pro-British publishers and editors of this newspaper seldom had kind words for any Republican protest, but they viewed the May 30th Movement as particularly dangerous because of the threat it posed to the semicolonial concession system of which the *North China Herald* was part. Determined to show all actions that challenged this system in as negative a light as possible, these defenders of foreign privilege filled the pages of the *North China Herald* and its daily counterpart, the *North China Daily News*, with articles describing all supposedly "patriotic" or "nationalist" protests as the work of xenophobic mobs manipulated by hidden Soviet hands.

The *North China Herald* did more, however, than merely print such stories. Both the daily and the weekly organ also printed provocative cartoons that played upon Western fears of "anti-foreignism" and Soviet machinations.[78] These cartoons struck a resonant chord with at least a section of the foreign community; according to Arthur Ransome's perceptive essay "The Shanghai Mind," the twin bogeys of "bolshevik" conspiracies and "Boxer" violence were at the heart of the contemporary treaty-port mentality.[79] The *North China Herald* played upon these paired fears by popularizing the phrase "red Boxerism" as an epithet for all anti-imperialist activities. Special propaganda pamphlets, such as "A Bolshevised China: The World's Greatest Peril," were filled with reprints of newspaper articles with sensationalist headlines such as "Anti-Christ Campaign a la Russe." The main goal of these pamphlets is summed up neatly on the first page of a *North China Herald* tract entitled "China in Chaos"; the editors state that their aim is "to demonstrate that 'Nationalism' is not a spontaneous Chinese patriotic movement but is a new form of Boxerism with much Russian inspiration behind it." [80]

Shanghai student protesters were well aware of the arguments the *North China Herald* and other opponents of the May 30th Movement were using to discredit their protests, as even a brief survey of the English-language pieces the students wrote to defend the popular movement indicates. These defenses almost always contain explicit attempts to refute the two main charges of the *North China Herald* campaign—that the protests were xenophobic and bolshevik—by arguing that the participants in the May 30th Movement were patriots acting spontaneously to protect their nation. Whenever students and non-student intellectuals—who also devoted much energy during summer 1925 to appealing for foreign support [81]— wrote letters and pamphlets in English, they tended to emphasize two themes. First, most protesters involved in the May 30th Movement were not "reds" at all, but ordinary citizens whose only concern was China's fate. Second, the protesters were not xenophobes, but simply people angered by specific infringements upon Chinese territory and specific acts of violence committed by foreigners.

A letter students of the Shanghai Baptist College submitted to the English-language newspaper *Min Pao* in June 1925 is but one of many contemporary propaganda pieces that stressed these two themes. The titles of two of the letter's subsections, "Tools of Red" and "Anti-foreign," reveal the authors' concern with the main charges leveled against the movement by *North China Herald* writers and others of that ilk. [82] It is absurd, the authors argued, "to stamp the students as tools of Bolshevism," and they derided foreigners "so ignorant as to be frightened away by the mere mention of Bolshevism in connection with anything." Although condemned by Western writers as "anti-foreign," in fact the students are merely "anti-injustice."

The authors of this letter then proceed to do something common in student publications aimed at foreign audiences: they appeal to the values and ideals Westerners claim to hold most dear. In the case of the May 30th Tragedy, the students of Shanghai Baptist College argue, the Chinese students were merely fighting for their "rights" and the "rights" of the workers; if anyone stood in the way of justice and incited "racial hatred," it was the British-run police force, which engaged in "wanton murder of peacefully demonstrating students." This notion that the self-proclaimed representatives of "civilization" rather than the supposedly "backward" Chinese were the ones committing "barbaric" acts was a favorite motif in pro–May 30th Movement propaganda directed at foreign readers.[*] This motif figures prominently, for example, in an article entitled "Did the Boxer Uprising Recur in 1925?" This piece, printed in a journal published by Chinese students studying in America, argues that if anyone acted like a "Boxer" (that is, in an irrationally violent, anti-foreign manner) in 1925, it was the members of the Shanghai Municipal Police. Although foreign policemen claimed to be "gentlemen," these Westerners were nonetheless ready to "shoot to kill" into a crowd of unarmed students and workers.[†]

Participants in every Republican mass movement of the 1930's and 1940's had to face similarly negative images created by foreign critics. The Western press would never again mount as elaborate a propaganda campaign to discredit student protests as that the *North China Herald* mounted in the mid-1920's. Nevertheless, from the May 30th Movement until 1949, new generations of students were continually drawn into dialogues with foreign critics determined to present Chinese protesters as uncivilized anti-foreign rioters manipulated by political parties or unscrupulous foreign hands. As a result, throughout the 1930's and 1940's, defenders of youth movements pleaded with Western readers to understand that Chinese student protesters were not xenophobic, but were simply trying to fight specific threats to China's national sovereignty. And, time and again, in open letters to English-language newspapers and foreign consuls, students and sympathetic teachers argued that campus unrest was the product

---

[*]Reels 137–39 of the U.S. Department of States document series on Chinese affairs, USDS, "1910–1929," contain numerous other examples of appeals for foreign support and understanding written by students and by non-student intellectuals, many of which similarly appeal to notions of "rights" and "justice," stress the theme of civilized versus barbaric behavior, and devote much space to denying claims that Chinese protesters were xenophobic and being manipulated by bolsheviks. See, e.g., "The Tragedy in Shanghai—May 30th and Our Point of View," by students at Jinling University; reel 138, 893.5040/185. Chinese Christians studying at missionary-run schools in Shanghai and other cities seem to have been particularly active in this type of propaganda work; see Creamer, "Hsueh-yun," pp. 34–37.

[†]This piece, by a writer who signs himself I Hu, appeared in the *Chinese Students' Monthly*, 21, no. 3 (1926). The idea that foreigners had now become the "Boxers" also figures in Chinese-language materials. For example, the magazine *Guowen zhoubao* (The national weekly) ran an article entitled "Duiyu yang Yihetuan zhi suogan" (Reaction to the foreign Boxers) in its June 28, 1925, issue. One week later, a cartoon in the same mainstream journal showed a giant foreign policeman bayoneting tiny Chinese protesters; the caption read "Who is the Boxer?" Not all pro–May 30th Movement propagandists, however, accepted the idea that "Boxerism" was by definition a tag to be avoided. By 1925 some Chinese Marxist polemicists had begun to argue that the Boxer Uprising of 1900 had been an early attempt to free the nation from the shackles of imperialist oppression. Thus, these writers claimed, despite the insurrection's excesses, the original boxers had in fact been heroes rather than villains. See Wasserstrom, "'Civilization' and Its Discontents," for examples of this revisionist approach to the Boxers.

of spontaneous, patriotic indignation rather than something agents of the CCP and the Soviet Union created to serve their own ends.

Some defenders of the student movements of the 1930's and 1940's contented themselves with simply presenting the facts as they saw them to Western readers and then asking for sympathy. They would say, for instance, that claims their movement was anti-foreign and/or "red" were lies invented by groups, such as the GMD or the representatives of an imperialist power, whose unjust acts students were protesting. After stressing that they were members of no political party and were willing to treat any nation that behaved justly toward China as a friend, these writers would list specific grievances—such as the Japanese invasion of Manchuria in 1931 or the beating up of student protesters in 1947—and appeal to their Western readers' sense of justice and fair play.*

Not all pro–youth movement propagandists were content to simply state their case in this straightforward fashion. As in 1925, some defenders of post–May 30th student movements also found it useful at times to try to turn the tables on the propaganda criticizing their actions in the English-language press. A particularly striking example of this technique in action is found in one of the many letters calling for the immediate withdrawal of U.S. troops from Chinese soil that the *China Weekly Review* published in 1947. Most of Shanghai's English-language press, with the notable exception of the *China Weekly Review*, had been quick to label all the protests of 1946 and 1947 directed against a continued American military presence in China "anti-foreign" agitation, a synonym for uncivilized behavior to those possessing a treaty-port mentality. The authors of this letter, however, stood this kind of accusation on its head by taunting the United States for calling itself a "civilized nation" and yet being unable to keep its soldiers from "committing such a brutal act" as the raping of a Chinese student. The authors of the letter then went on to use biblical imagery learned from Western missionaries to attack the American actions, saying that soldiers had come from the West in "sheep's skin with

---

*Some of the best examples of these types of pieces can be found in the "Letters from the People" section of the *China Weekly Review* throughout the Civil War years. See, e.g., the various pieces by teacher and student groups defending the Anti-Hunger, Anti–Civil War Movement in the June 7, 1947, issue (pp. 5–8). A typical one is entitled "Special Students" and begins: "I am a student of the National Fuh Tan University [Fudan], and am surely not Communist-inspired nor a subversive element, as [the] government [claims]. As a human being I can keep silent no longer. I appeal to you." The writer then says that all students "who stand for justice and right are agitated by the increasing number of tragic incidents" and describes a particularly brutal encounter in which the police stood by as GMD agents attacked ordinary student protesters with "iron rods and wooden sticks." The youth, after stating that incidents such as this one (in which "30 students were wounded, three of them seriously") are becoming all too common, ends with "We hope anxiously that public opinion will support us and assist us to maintain justice and right."

the alleged purpose of [promoting] peace and stability," but had soon proved they were no better than "wolves."[83]

The dialogues between student protesters and their foreign critics that accompanied the May 4th Movement were similar to those of the 1920's, 1930's, and 1940's in many ways. There was, however, one important basic difference: the issue of bolshevik conspiracies, which was so central in propaganda battles of later years, did not play a significant role in the discourse of 1919.[84] Because China still lacked an organized Communist party, no full-scale "red scare" developed in 1919, even though this was the year when anti-bolshevik propaganda reached its first peak in the United States.

Despite the absence of "bolshevik conspiracy" theories in 1919, May 4th propagandists still had to defend their actions from charges of outside manipulation. Although Japanese propagandists were unable to exploit the fears of "red conspiracies" their English counterparts used to such effect in 1925, they cast doubt on the "patriotism" of the anti-Japanese boycott of 1919 by arguing that it had been engineered by Westerners to serve the ends of American and European interests. Claims that Westerners and unscrupulous Chinese politicians had tricked the student class into leading the battle against Japanese products and had sown anti-Japanese feeling among the Chinese populace as well filled the pages of publications aimed at Japanese residents of Chinese cities.[85] Similar arguments appeared in various Chinese and English-language newspapers controlled by Japanese interests. Thus, for example, the May 30, 1919, issue of the Chinese-language edition of the Qingdao newspaper Seitō shimpō ran an article entitled "Missionaries as Political Agitators," which claimed that the United States was "using China as her tool in order to increase her own power" in the East.[86] Pro-Japanese English-language newspapers steered clear of blaming May 4th activities on Western missionaries, preferring to attribute the unrest to the machinations of a different set of outside agitators—scheming Chinese politicians. An editorial in the pro-Japanese Shanghai Times claimed, for instance, that whether Chinese students knew it or not, the youths were allowing themselves to be "utilized by a certain faction of their own countrymen, who are much more concerned regarding power passing into their own hands and out of the hands of the present Chinese Government than of anything else."[87]

These Japanese attempts to create conspiracy theories notwithstanding, May 4th propagandists were much less troubled by talk of "hidden hands" than were their successors. There is little evidence that anyone (except perhaps the Japanese themselves) gave much credence to claims that the students involved in the anti-Japanese boycott of 1919 were acting as the puppets of either foreign missionaries or opportunistic native politicians.

Although the May 4th students occasionally found it useful to stress the "spontaneous" quality of their protests in English-language propaganda pieces,[88] they did not spend much energy denying claims that they were mere pawns of foreign agents or domestic factions.

The same cannot be said, however, about the charge of xenophobia. The specter of Boxerism did not hang as heavily over the May 4th Movement as it would over the May 30th Movement six years later.[89] Nonetheless, Western as well as Japanese opponents of the 1919 struggle routinely condemned the protests as anti-foreign acts. May 4th students, who prided themselves on their cosmopolitanism and drew much of their ideological inspiration from recently introduced Western notions of science and democracy, were deeply offended by the idea that foreigners attributed their behavior to an irrational xenophobia. Because of this and their pragmatic understanding that foreigners could not be expected to sympathize with an anti-foreign movement, students went to great lengths in 1919 to prove to Westerners that they were enlightened patriots and not backward xenophobes.

One of their main techniques was to remind Westerners that they had no quarrel with any foreign country other than Japan. May 4th propagandists continually mentioned that the only products Chinese were boycotting were those made in Japan and that China's citizens had friendly feelings toward the people of countries such as England and the United States, even though the Western allies had strained this goodwill by supporting Japan's claims at the Paris Peace Conference. During the course of the movement, groups representing all points on the social spectrum issued statements in English affirming their class's lack of enmity toward Western countries and stating that their quarrel was with the Japanese and with domestic traitors. For example, Chinese employees of the French Tramway Company began an open letter to the *North China Herald* by claiming that their "resentment" was "directed against a certain nation" but that they remained "on good terms with the others."[90] In a general statement to the foreign community at large, the Shanghai Commercial Federation emphasized that the main reason Chinese merchants were joining the mass movement was a desire to find solutions for "internal political questions"; they besought China's "foreign friends" to "understand our patriotic motive and be in sympathy with us."[91]

The group that spent the most energy trying to convince foreign readers that May 4th activists had no enmity toward the West, however, was the Shanghai Student Union (SSU). Throughout summer 1919 the SSU issued a series of English-language communications whose sole purpose was to refute the charges of Western journalists that the SSU was an "anti-foreign" organization and was promoting social disorder. SSU leaders used a variety of media to refute these charges. They wrote letters to Shanghai's foreign community at large and to key Western-run institutions, such as the Shanghai Municipal Council, filled with polite references to the SSU's desire to "be of service" to its "foreign friends" and with reminders to these "friends" that the Union was "using all [its] influence to warn the students to maintain peace and order." [92] Representatives of the SSU stressed similar themes in meetings with reporters from local English-language newspapers. In a meeting with a reporter from the pro-Japanese *Shanghai Times*, the union's secretary went beyond claiming that the May 4th Movement was not an "anti-foreign agitation" and that the SSU had explicitly instructed its members "not to molest Japanese or any foreigners." He stated that the SSU was taking an active role in preventing members of other classes from committing anti-foreign acts by sending "a great number of students to advise the illiterate and loafer classes not to create any trouble with foreigners whatsoever, as that would be injuring our cause." [93] In addition, the SSU prepared and distributed at least one special English-language leaflet that harped on similar themes in an effort to win the support of Shanghai's Western community. Entitled "An Appeal to Our Foreign Friends," the handbill read as follows:

> The present movements in Shanghai are pure PATRIOTIC DEMONSTRA-
> TION [sic] and will do *no harm* to our FOREIGN FRIENDS.
> We can ensure the preservation of peace and order even such [sic]
> has to continue and we feel sure that nothing at present will entertain
> your *interference*, but on the contrary we sincerely and earnestly re-
> quest your *sympathy* with us. [94] (emphasis in original)

Shanghai students interested in gaining Western support for the May 4th Movement did not always content themselves with simply stating their grievances and denying that they were anti-foreign troublemakers. At times the youths used slightly more elaborate persuasive devices to appeal to the sympathies and predispositions of foreign readers: students seem to have viewed drawing analogies between Chinese struggles for independence and comparable European and American events as a particularly effective way of winning Western support. Thus in a lengthy *China Press* article, "Students' Explanation of the Strike," a May 4th activist explicitly equated the Chinese struggle against Japan with the Allies' fight against Germany in World War I. After labeling the Japanese the "Huns of the East," the student wrote:

> Your statesmen are at this moment sitting in Paris trying to mete out
> justice to the nations of the world. Your sons, your brothers are lying
> on the fields of France and Belgium, in the hills of Italy, in the distant

snows of Russia to preserve democracy and justice. You have established the principle that militarism shall not prevail. You have given of
all of your strength to destroy imperialism.

Will you not sympathise with China when she is trying to do in her
way what you have done in Europe?[95]

This article was by no means the only propaganda piece to present the
May 4th Movement as a fight for goals championed by the West. Other
defenses of the student movement also played upon the image of the Japanese as the "Huns of the East." For instance, in a letter to the editor of the
Shanghai Times, an angry Chinese reader criticized the newspaper's antagonistic attitude toward the recent protests and called the May 4th Movement a fight against "Japan's Kaiser worshippers."[96] The SSU made use of
similar imagery in a letter to Shanghai's foreign consuls, which stressed
that China's present fight against "Asian Imperialism" was "no different"
from the battle the Allies had waged against German imperialism.[97] In addition to linking the fight against Japan with the recent war, students presented their struggle as a battle for the same rights Westerners had fought
to win for themselves in earlier centuries. One student publication aimed
at foreign residents in China combined both of these themes: "Friends of
Great Britain, America and France! You have your Magna Carta, your
Declaration of Independence, your French Revolution . . . can you see our
nation destroyed by autocracy, by corruption, by debauchery, and not wish
to help us? . . . We are fighting your battles as much as our own, for what
you have done on the Atlantic, we must do on the Pacific."[98]

This chapter has examined the media, themes, and symbols through
which student protesters communicated with those whose support they
sought. It has shown how educated youths varied the tone and style of
their propaganda to fit the levels of literacy, cultural backgrounds, prejudices, and predispositions of specific audiences—how in fact they developed different "languages" to speak to different social groups. It has also
drawn special attention to the disparate ways in which students spoke to
the laobaixing, on the one hand, and educated Chinese and Westerners, on
the other. Whereas youth movement propagandists generally used instructive modes to communicate with the former, they often entered into
more egalitarian forms of discourse with the latter.

The distinction between propaganda "monologues" and "dialogues" is
a crucial one, but it is important to note that student communications
aimed at the laobaixing were by no means created in a discursive vacuum.
For example, popular audiences played an indirect but nonetheless important role in shaping youth movement propaganda texts. Unlike educated

opponents of mass movements, the laobaixing influenced student propagandists not by creating their own set of propaganda texts to which the
youths then had to respond, but by responding more enthusiastically to
certain themes and slogans (which students would then repeat in later
communications) than to others (which students would then abandon).

In addition, student propaganda directed at the masses was frequently
influenced by counter-propaganda of a different sort: that of domestic and
foreign conservatives determined to keep youth movements from gaining
popular support. Throughout the years of GMD rule, for example, student protesters were continually trying to counteract the impact of official
propaganda campaigns such as the New Life Movement, all of which were
aimed at persuading the laobaixing to work together with the ruling
authorities to unify China by ridding it of the "reds." Foreigners also
produced texts aimed at the masses, to which student movement propagandists had to respond. During the May 30th Movement, for instance,
along with producing English-language attacks on "red Boxerism," Western defenders of foreign privilege affiliated with the *North China Herald*
printed and distributed a Chinese-language daily entitled *Chengyan* (True
words). Written in simple Chinese, *Chengyan* was filled with stories denouncing the leaders of the May 30th Movement as people concerned not
with the Chinese people but with filling their own pockets with silver and
serving their Russian masters.[99]

To understand the meaning of the propagandizing radical students did
among the masses, therefore, we must place these efforts within the context of an ongoing contest for the loyalty of the laobaixing. What makes
the intertextual dialogues that accompanied this contest particularly interesting is the similarity of the two sides' efforts in terms of themes and
techniques. Virtually all radical and anti-radical propaganda drives of the
Republican era, for example, attempted to convince the general populace
that China was threatened by imperialists and domestic traitors willing to
do the bidding of foreign masters. The specific villains varied from CCP
members working hand in glove with Soviet agents to GMD officials
taking bribes from the Japanese, depending upon the political orientation
of the person telling the story to the masses, but the basic plot was much
the same in either case.

Perhaps the most striking similarities, however, relate not to propaganda content or themes but to the communicative techniques used to
bridge the gap between the zhishi and wuzhishi worlds. Virtually all the
methods student propagandists employed in their efforts to reach the
masses—organized speechmaking drives, group singing, slogan shouting,
the distribution of pamphlets and primers in colloquial Chinese, the pasting up of wall posters and so forth—were used by anti-radical publicists to

discredit youth activism in the eyes of ordinary citizens. Moreover, it is often almost impossible to tell, until one looks carefully at the content of a propaganda text or performance, whether the message being communicated is an attack on the established order or a defense of it. For example, in terms of style and composition, anti-radical pamphlets such as the *Taochi xunbao* (Reports on red suppression) series—which were printed during the Northern Expedition—looked much like popular tracts advocating social revolution, and both types of texts used similar mixtures of anecdotes, poems, and illustrations to make their messages accessible to the laobaixing.[100] If texts with different ideological viewpoints often looked identical at first sight, so too did propaganda performances, since the lecturers who took part in GMD-sponsored publicity campaigns tended to come from the same ranks as those who gave speeches attacking the status quo.[101]

The striking similarities between loyalist and oppositional propaganda drives, although they may seem odd at first, are in fact only to be expected. Since their organizers and participants generally came from comparable backgrounds and shared common assumptions about how to speak to the laobaixing, it is hardly surprising that they produced similar texts. In a sense these similarities merely suggest that one of the main points about "scripts" stressed in Chapter 3, and again in this chapter's discussion of the use student propagandists made of the xiangyue tradition, needs to be carried one step further. Both of these earlier discussions highlighted ways in which student protesters were able to improvise upon their enemies' scripts to further radical ends. Opponents of the established order were not the only ones who could improvise in this fashion, however; as the Republican era wore on, loyalists often found it useful to turn the tables on student protesters and adapt propaganda techniques invented to further radical ends to serve conservative purposes. In the end, it becomes impossible in most cases to tell who was borrowing from whom. Both sides drew from and in the process modified a common communicative repertoire. And, as the next chapter shows, what was true for propaganda also held true for demonstrations.

NINE

STUDENT STRUGGLES
OF THE MID-1940'S

THE CAMPUS UNREST OF the Civil War years does not lend itself easily to the kind of analysis used in previous case-study chapters, which focus primarily on the student response to a specific triggering event, such as the May 4th Incident or the Japanese invasion of 1931. New "incidents" of various sorts, such as the Beijing rape case of 1946, did occur throughout the Civil War years, and Shanghai's educated youths responded to these outrages in familiar ways—by organizing streetside lecture campaigns, staging classroom strikes, and holding marches. There was, however, a distinctive rhythm to the student struggles that followed World War II: in looking at the 1940's as opposed to earlier decades, it is generally much harder to figure out where one movement ends and the next one begins.

Links between successive waves of campus unrest prior to 1945 are noted in passing in earlier sections. For example, Chapter 1 drew attention to the role of the anti-Christian movement of 1924 in laying the groundwork for the May 30th Movement of the following year. Nonetheless, in the great student struggles of the 1910's, 1920's, and 1930's, one or two key events figured centrally in the birth of the new movement. But this is not true of the most important student struggle of the 1940's, the Anti-Hunger, Anti–Civil War Movement. This movement evolved so gradually out of a long series of smaller struggles that one can make a strong case for tracing its roots back to May 1947 or to December 1946 or even to spring 1946.

Another factor that gives the protests of the Civil War era a unique feel is the extreme polarization between loyalist and radical youths during this period and the battles members of the two groups waged to show that they alone spoke for the student community as a whole. There was nothing new about student activists of differing political allegiances competing with each other; as Chapters 6 and 7 show, such competition played a key part in campus protests of the Nanjing Decade. No matter how fragmented the academic community became during the 1930's, however, it was always possible to talk of the Shanghai youth movement as a single entity. Student activists of the most divergent points of view shared a common commitment to at least one basic principle: the need to save China from Japanese imperialism. Young partisans of the Blue Shirts, Reorganizationist Faction, and Communist party might disagree how best to carry out this task or which national leaders to attack, but a common ground still united these student activists.

This common ground disappeared when Japan surrendered in 1945. From that point on, radical and loyalist youths began to disagree not only about tactical issues and the virtues of specific political figures and parties but also about the foreign power posing the most serious threat to China's sovereignty: opponents of the GMD tended to criticize the United States; students loyal to the ruling party directed their anger against the "red imperialism" of the Soviet Union. Divisions within the academic community grew so wide during the Civil War era that the local student movement ceased to exist as a single entity. After 1945 there were always two student movements, which for the sake of convenience are referred to here as "pro-government" and "anti-government" or "loyalist" and "radical."

Not all Shanghai students identified completely with either the pro-CCP or the pro-GMD camp. In fact, until at least 1947 the vast majority adamantly claimed that they were not supporters of either side but only neutral critics of both the parties fighting the Civil War. Many viewed the leaders of *both* the GMD and the CCP as partially responsible for China's problems; many felt that the nation needed to be protected from *both* the Soviets and the Americans.[1] The same cannot be said, however, of the campus activists who sought the allegiance of middle-of-the-road youths. Within months of Japan's surrender, pro- and anti-radical students and teachers were hard at work laying the groundwork for competing youth movements, each of which was designed to bring uncommitted youths out onto the streets, each of which sought to prove to the city and the world that these youths subscribed to a particular formula for national salvation, and each of which relied (as we will see) upon a common repertoire of May 4th–style tactics.

The competition between pro- and anti-government campus activists was so fierce between 1945 and 1947 that the story of Shanghai student protest during these years becomes a tale of pitched battles for control of the city's streets. These battles were for the most part nonviolent, as the two sides tried to outdo each other's public displays or outshout each other's speakers at campus meetings. In some cases, however, the struggles turned violent, and members of opposing camps engaged in physical combat. Whatever form the battles took, however, the same prize was always at stake: the ability to show, for a time at least, that one's own youth movement represented student opinion and that the other side was a mere fabrication of outside agents.

THE FIRST SKIRMISHES: DECEMBER 1945 – FEBRUARY 1946

The first major Shanghai street battle between radical and anti-radical students of the Civil War era took place on December 20, 1945, the day General George C. Marshall arrived in Shanghai en route to Chongqing to begin his famous "mission" to negotiate an end to the Civil War between the GMD and CCP. Local officials greeted the general with a great deal of pomp and circumstance, as a way of showing Marshall that the GMD was committed to the peace process and that the Chinese people had nothing but goodwill toward Generalissimo Jiang's most important ally, the United States. The day's ceremonies began with a personal representative of the Generalissimo meeting Marshall at the airport; they ended with a welcoming banquet at one of the city's finest hotels, at which Chinese politicians and generals toasted the special envoy and Sino-American friendship. The day's most spectacular event was a welcoming parade that began at the Shanghai airfield, a parade in which disciplined lines of GMD Youth Troops marched behind Chinese and American flags, while military bands played the national anthems of the two countries.[2]

These official activities were not, however, the only ones to take place on December 20. That evening radical students staged an alternative welcoming ceremony. Like the official ceremony, one general aim of this alternative gathering was simply to applaud the special envoy for coming to China to work to end the Civil War. Just as the GMD designed its ceremony to bolster the party's public and international image, however, radical students had an additional agenda in mind when they organized their gathering. Thus, whereas some of the slogans students shouted were innocuous statements of welcome, others had a stronger political content. Shouts of "Welcome to Special Envoy Marshall" and "Long live the Chinese republic" mingled with calls for the withdrawal of American troops, an end to the Civil War, and an increase in freedom of speech and publication.

The two welcoming ceremonies were strikingly similar in form. March-

ing youths played a crucial role in both the official and unofficial ceremonies. Patriotic music also figured in both ceremonies, although radical
demonstrators marched to songs from the War of Resistance against Japan
rather than to national anthems. The protesters even marched behind
standard-bearers carrying American and Chinese flags. Finally, whereas the
authorities had greeted Marshall with carefully worded official speeches,
radical students composed an equally carefully worded letter to the special
envoy outlining their own views on the contemporary political situation,
which they planned to present to him after they had marched to their final
destination: the hotel in which the official welcoming banquet was being held.[3]

The participants in the alternative welcoming ceremony never reached
the hotel, however; almost as soon as their demonstration began, a group
of anti-radical youths disrupted the gathering. CCP documents assert that
these youths were members of the Sanqingtuan. Communist journals of
the time and recent PRC memoirs alike tend to attribute all disruptions of
radical youth protests to Sanqingtuan interference and to stress the number of violent acts members of the corps committed. Because of the paucity of other sources dealing with the events in question, it is often hard to
judge the validity of these claims. At least one non-Communist source,
however, confirms the CCP's claim that members of the GMD-sponsored
youth league did indeed beat up participants in the alternative welcoming
ceremony and prevent the march from reaching its planned destination.[4]

Two kinds of battles between pro- and anti-government forces took
place on the day Marshall arrived in Shanghai. The first was a symbolic
struggle: the rival parades and welcoming ceremonies presented competing images of China's youth as loyal followers of the GMD or patriotic
critics of the government. The second was the physical struggle that took
place during the protest parade itself, when members of the anti-radical
Sanqingtuan attacked participants in the radical youth movement's first
post–World War II mass action. These battles typify two of the main
types of skirmishes between pro- and anti-government forces of the period. Throughout the following years, radical students would continue to
use demonstrations and mock official ceremonies to undercut the efficacy
of displays by loyalist youths, and members of anti-radical groups would
continue to try to prevent these demonstrations and mock ceremonies.

LOYALIST "PROTESTS": JANUARY–FEBRUARY 1946

Pro-government youths did not, however, limit their political activities to
disrupting radical marches and taking part in explicitly loyalist displays. If
they had, it would have been hard for even the most nimble rhetorician to

present groups such as the Sanqingtuan as carrying on the "May 4th Tradition." What then did pro-GMD students do to stake their claim as heirs
to this tradition? Their most important action was to stage events that
looked essentially like traditional patriotic protests but had distinctively
loyalist overtones. These pseudo-protests were comparable in many ways
to events of the 1930's, such as the Blue Shirt–engineered "protest" of the
December 9th era (see Chapter 6) and the Dangbu-sponsored loyalist
rallies of 1931 (Chapter 7). In contrast to the 1930's, when both radical and
anti-radical "protests" tended to focus on Japanese aggression, after 1945
students with differing political views and allegiances stressed different
grievances and singled out different foreign countries for criticism.

The events of January and February 1946 illustrate this tendency of
radical and loyalist students to mobilize around disparate causes. A comparison of the activities of January 13 and 14 is particularly revealing in
this regard and illustrates just how similar in form loyalist "protests" could
be to their anti-government counterparts. At first glance, the student
parades on these days look like mirror images. Closer inspection reveals,
however, that despite their stylistic similarities the two events focused
upon different issues and served opposite purposes.

The first parade was part of an elaborate mourning ceremony held to
honor four martyrs killed in Kunming on December 1, 1945: a music
teacher named Yu Zai and three students, all of whom were shot by "special agents" (tewu) carrying out reprisals for protests against the Civil
War.[5] Students were not the only ones involved in the January 13 service at
Shanghai's Jade Buddha Temple; many of those in attendance were workers, and leading educational and cultural figures including Song Qingling
helped plan the event.[6] Educated youths did, however, play a key role in
the memorial service and dominated the march that followed, as this quote
from a radical press account indicates.

> Most of those who joined the march were students: male and female
> college students, middle-school students, elementary school stu-
> dents—some of all of these were there, the youngest no more than
> eleven or twelve sui [ten or eleven years] old. The most spirited
> [protesters] were also the students; at the memorial service they were
> the ones crying, they were the ones whose hearts were fired by the
> people's speeches, and it was they who called out slogans until their
> throats were hoarse during the demonstration.[7]

In addition, the band that led the parade as the participants marched
through the city chanting, singing, and chalking slogans on walls, tele-
phone poles, and sidewalks was a student one: the Female Secondary
School Students Band.[8]

The specific goal of this march was to pressure the government into punishing the perpetrators of the Kunming killings, whom many believed to be GMD agents, but the protesters used the occasion to voice other concerns. The demonstrators, who marched behind two giant flags emblazoned with the phrases "Long live democracy" (*Minzhu wansui*) and "Remember the students and teachers killed in Kunming," shouted out a series of slogans on a wide range of issues as they passed buildings associated with the GMD. Thus, for example, when the marchers reached their first target destination, the Municipal Government Compound, they criticized the GMD's Communist eradication drive by calling on China's ruling party to "hurry up and establish a cooperative government" with the CCP. At their second target destination, the city's police headquarters, the marchers turned to a new slogan: "Policemen shouldn't act as the running dogs of the special agents!" When the marchers arrived at the offices of the most important official press organ, *Zhongyang ribao* (Central daily), they began chanting slogans that expressed their anger over the way official newspapers had censored and distorted facts relating to recent Kunming events. One of the main slogans here was "Reporters, show that you have hearts!" In addition to these specialized slogans, shaped to fit specific venues, the protesters also used the occasion to call for the immediate withdrawal of all U.S. troops from Chinese soil.

The day after this demonstration, youths were once again marching through the city of Shanghai. This parade was staged to protest the local French consulate's decision to send a French national alleged to be a Nazi collaborator to Saigon for trial rather than prosecuting him in China.[9] Many teachers and students viewed this decision, which the consulate made without informing the GMD authorities, as an infringement of China's sovereignty. Since similar infringements had routinely triggered student protests throughout the previous three decades, there was nothing unusual about the cause of this parade. Nor was the form of the demonstration surprising, since it was almost identical to that of the previous day: a large group of youths once again marched in ranks, this time behind the Boy Scout Band, writing with chalk on poles and walls, singing and shouting out slogans. A visit to the Municipal Government Compound was also part of the itinerary, although for obvious reasons the first stop was the French Consulate.

The march of January 14, although it resembles a typical May 4th–type student protest, had some unusual features, features that, when taken together, make it hard to consider the event a simple "protest." First, although the "protesters" sang and shouted out slogans as they marched, the song they sang was the national anthem rather than an air with radical connotations, and none of their slogans attacked the central government or its basic policies. Admittedly some of these slogans, such as "Down with imperialism" and even the nonpartisan patriotic cry of "Long live the Republic," were typically used by participants in radical protests such as those of the previous day and the Marshall visit. Whereas, however, on both of these earlier dates students had also shouted slogans critical of domestic powerholders, the January 14 marchers stuck primarily to loyalist chants such as "Long live the national government," "Long live Chairman Jiang" and "Long live the Three People's Principles." [10] An even more important difference between the events of January 13 and 14 is the reception the two groups of marchers received at the Municipal Government Compound. On January 13, local police tried to prevent students from carrying out their demonstration, and the mayor refused to address the crowd outside his office; on January 14, police interference was conspicuous by its absence, and the mayor was equally conspicuous by his presence and the praise he accorded the "protesters."

The January 14 march is thus a difficult one to classify. On the one hand, it looked much like a typical patriotic student protest. On the other hand, the slogans participants shouted had no relation to those of the main youth protest movement of the time, the December 1st Movement, and in terms of general intent the event had much in common with the loyalist marches of youths that the GMD staged to mark revolutionary anniversaries, such as October 10 and the birthdays of Sun Zhongshan and Jiang Jieshi.[11] Spectators of the anti-French parade on January 14 who had observed the radical protests of the previous day may well have thought that the two events were part of a single movement, as they listened to cries of "Down with imperialism" coming from the mouths of marching youths a second day in a row. Those who watched and listened carefully and stayed with the marchers until the end, however, might have had a sense that things had somehow been turned topsy-turvy. How else would they have made sense of hearing the mayor praise the anti-French students for their patriotism? How else would they have accounted for the "protest" of January 14 ended with what one paper called a "thunderous cry" of "Protect the mayor, leader of youth"?[12]

Perhaps the best way to make sense of events such as the January 14 parade is to return to the concept of collective action scripts. If, as Chapter 3 argues, many protests can be understood as inverted renditions of official ceremonies, then the best way to interpret the January 14 demonstration is as a similar kind of theatrical turning of the tables. The main difference is simply that in mid-January 1946 one sees loyalists improvising upon a radical script rather than vice versa. In this particular case, it is hard to tell whether the loyalist students involved were aware of their debt to the radical street-theater repertoire. The student demonstrations that accom-

panied the loyalist Anti-Soviet Movement of the following month, however, were so similar to those radical students traditionally staged that
there seems little doubt that the organizers of these "protests" were trying
quite self-consciously to transform subversive forms of street theater into
pro-GMD dramas.[13]

The main pretext for the anti-Russian demonstrations in Shanghai of
February 23–26, as well as for those in other Chinese cities, was the continued presence of Soviet troops in Manchuria.[14] In addition to resenting
the presence of Russian soldiers on Chinese soil, participants in the movement also held these soldiers responsible for the recent death of a young
Chinese engineer, Zhang Xinfu, who had been killed in mysterious circumstances while traveling through a part of north China under Soviet
control. The two central demands of the movement—that a foreign power
withdraw its troops and that a martyr be avenged—thus mirrored those
behind the radical protests of December 20 and January 13, respectively.
And just as specific grievances had spilled over into a general cry for democracy in these anti-GMD demonstrations, it quickly became clear that
the February marches were intended as an attack on communism itself
rather than simply on Soviet troops. These parallels in demands and aims
were less striking, however, than the parallels in tactics.

The Shanghai Anti-Soviet Movement began much like the protest campaign to welcome General Marshall. As in late December, one of the first
things student activists did was to form a special patriotic association, the
Shanghai Students Sovereignty Protection Committee, to plan mass actions, formulate slogans, issue manifestos, and so forth; and, as in December, the first public event this anti-Soviet group sponsored was a disruption of an official ceremony. In this case the official gathering in question
was not one sponsored by the GMD, however, but a reception honoring
the twenty-eighth anniversary of the establishment of the Russian Red
Army, held at Shanghai's Soviet Consulate on February 23. In contrast to
their radical predecessors of December 20, the anti-radical students involved in this disruption met with little interference. Even though a number of local notables—ranging from Western diplomats to the mayor of
Shanghai himself—attended the celebration at the Soviet Consulate, neither the police nor ruffians tried to prevent the anti-Russian youths from
marching to the outer walls of the consulate, where they spent the evening
shouting anti-Russian slogans and singing patriotic songs.[15]

The Anti-Soviet Movement may have begun like the alternative campaign to welcome General Marshall, but its final phases were much more
reminiscent of the January 13 march in honor of the Kunming martyrs.
The last major event of the movement was a mass memorial service for
Zhang Xinfu. An estimated 30,000 students and members of other social

groups attended the service to honor the Anti-Soviet Movement's only martyr, which was held on February 26 at Aurora University. The memorial service was followed by a parade through the streets of downtown Shanghai, which closely mirrored the January 13 demonstration honoring the Kunming martyrs. Contemporary observers claimed that one unusual feature of the January 13 demonstration was the way in which protesters marched to three separate target destinations and shouted different slogans at each one.[16] But even at this level of detail one finds parallels in the February 26 anti-Soviet demonstration: the February marchers singled out the Soviet Consulate, the Municipal Government Compound, and the building that housed *Shidai ribao* (the Contemporary daily, a Russian-owned newspaper) as targets and shouted out different slogans at each place.

This brief sketch of the first and last mass gatherings of the Anti-Soviet Movement does not exhaust the topic of its similarities to May 4th–type patriotic student struggles. In between these two events, for example, anti-Soviet students carried out a streetside speechmaking campaign to spread news of the Manchurian situation to the laobaixing. The participants in the struggle also formed the same kind of unofficial police force to maintain order during demonstrations that radical protesters had routinely established ever since 1919, even though in the case of the Anti-Soviet Movement the official police proved perfectly willing to protect all marchers.[17] Some participants and supporters even took pains to reinforce the impact of the similarities between the struggle and earlier patriotic mass movements by issuing statements and slogans aimed at convincing their audience that the fight against the Soviets was part of the May 4th tradition of youth activism. This was clearly the intent of one proclamation the Shanghai Students Sovereignty Protection Committee issued. It explicitly stated that in 1946 the Soviets were doing in Manchuria what the Japanese had done in 1931, and it told students to rally around the slogan "We are unwilling to see another September 18."[18] A pro-GMD magazine used an even more direct rhetorical device to locate the anti-Soviet struggle within the tradition dating back to 1919: it published a photograph of a group of senior professors taking part in a Nanjing demonstration against Russian imperialism beside a caption identifying the intellectuals as former May 4th student activists who were once again marching to save their nation from a foreign aggressor.[19]

The demonstrations that accompanied the Anti-Soviet Movement are hard to classify, since they had aspects in common with both official ceremonials and protests. Comtemporary press accounts do not simplify this classificatory problem, since newspapers of the time presented two completely contradictory images of the movement. Loyalist news organs portrayed the struggle as a spontaneous outpouring of patriotic outrage which many GMD leaders may have sympathized with but played no role in directing.[20] The radical press presented the events of late February as completely contrived actions, which the GMD engineered itself to offset the impact of "truly popular" events such as the January 13 march, divert criticism from government policies, and give Chinese and foreign observers the impression that the nation's students were fervently anti-Communist.[21] According to this interpretation, the Anti-Soviet Movement was just a series of government-sponsored rallies, which students joined because school officials pressured them to attend or because they were lured by promises of free loaves of bread.[22]

The problems involved in assessing these claims of outside manipulation, which each side leveled at the other side's mass actions throughout the period, is discussed in more detail later in this chapter. For the moment three comments should suffice. First, there is probably a good deal of truth behind some CCP assertions. GMD officials and administrators certainly played a key role in stirring up anti-Soviet sentiment on some Shanghai campuses, in some cases officials and administrators probably even used coercive tactics to bolster attendance at anti-Russian demonstrations, and many student leaders of the Anti-Soviet Movement were cadres of the GMD-run Sanqingtuan.[23] Second, local law enforcement agencies clearly dealt more leniently with anti-Soviet "protest" activities than with the earlier anti-American ones.[24] Third, despite these first two points, the rallies and demonstrations of late February were more than simply government-run rallies. Many students were genuinely displeased by the continued presence of Soviet troops in northern China, and a desire to vent this displeasure inspired at least some youths to take to the streets. In addition, the anti-Russian demonstrators of 1946 were not unambiguously loyalist; some student participants criticized the government for not taking a stronger stance against the Soviet Union.

Interestingly, some sources indicate that Shanghai's anti-Soviet demonstrators tended to hold the Political Study Clique of the GMD specially responsible for the central government's weak stance toward the USSR. They also singled out individual members of this clique for criticism during their rallies.[25] This makes it tempting to type the anti-Soviet demonstrations simply as right-wing protests engineered by the leaders of the CC Clique—the hard-line archrivals of the more conciliatory Political Study Clique—in a simultaneous effort to discredit the CCP and to embarrass their enemies within the GMD. This explanation is especially appealing because the CC Clique's leaders would use similar tactics against their rivals in 1947.[26]

This explanation (even if it could be proved) would not in and of itself solve the problem of typology, however. Showing that intra-GMD factional struggles played a part in shaping the Anti-Soviet Movement does not necessarily prove that the demonstrations are best treated as protests rather than as officially sanctioned spectacles. Factional conflict was so rife in Shanghai (and all of China) during this era that even the most seemingly straightforward of loyalist displays, which had no protest connotations whatsoever, often became a vehicle for intraparty struggles.[27] Thus, for example, a rally held on February 15, 1946, to celebrate Jiang Jieshi's first visit to Shanghai since the Japanese surrender was, according to a recent memoir by two former officials, so shaped by factional rivalries that in its final form the event became an expression of the contemporary balance of power between cliques.[28] Members of different groups fought over who should introduce Jiang, and the decision to place some local officials on the stage and force others to sit in the audience reflected the relative political strength of competing factions.

In the end, the best way to classify events such as the anti-Soviet marches is to simply consider them part official ceremonies and part genuine protests. The existence of such ambiguous events helped make the drama that unfolded on the streets of Shanghai between December 1945 and February 1946, in which bands of marching youths played the leading roles, a strange and confusing one. Foreign observers and ordinary citizens—the main audiences for the performances—were forced to make sense of a bewildering array of look-alike events. These ranged from the straightforward youth-based official spectacles that the GMD arranged to welcome General Marshall in December and Generalissimo Jiang a month-and-a-half later to equally unambiguous protest actions such as the January 13 martyrs' memorial march. But it also included events that are difficult to classify, such as the Anti-Soviet demonstrations of February 1946 and street brawls between competing student groups. Since many of these various genres of mass action were almost identical in form if not in substance, it was no easy feat for the casual observer to know what to make of the confusing mixture of inversions and counter-inversions that radicals and their opponents used to show they alone spoke in the name of Shanghai's youth and the May 4th tradition.

THE WOMEN'S DAY MARCHES

The situation during the months that followed the Anti-Soviet Movement remained just as confusing. Throughout this period, pro- and anti-government forces continued to improvise upon each other's scripts, and each side continued to mount spectacles aimed at least in part at undermining the impact of the other side's actions. As in January and February 1946, not all of these later spectacles were strictly speaking "student demonstrations," since members of other classes took part in many of the street battles of March through June, just as workers and other non-students had participated in earlier gatherings such as the parade honoring the Kunming martyrs. Nonetheless, during these months educated youths continued to play a highly visible role in most pro- and anti-government rallies alike and youth brigades were almost always at the forefront in multi-class marches. In a final continuation of the pattern set in the period December 1945 to February 1946, from March through June 1946 radicals and loyalists consistently staged mass actions at the same (or nearly the same) times, thus adding further to the difficulty of distinguishing between pro- and anti-government displays.

Shanghai students waited less than two weeks after the end of the Anti-Soviet Movement before taking to the streets again in large numbers. When they did so, it was as part of not one demonstration but two wholly separate events, both of which were held to honor International Women's Day on March 8, a holiday that the GMD and the CCP alike considered a "revolutionary" and hence worthy one.[29] Participants in both celebrations claimed to be concerned with furthering the cause of Shanghai women, although they differed greatly over the question of whether this was best done by supporting the GMD status quo or by working for radical change. The similarities between the two mass actions go much further, however, than their temporal coincidence and their espousal of a common goal. Both events began with rallies centering around speeches by leading civic and cultural figures: the pro-GMD assembly was held at the Grand Theater and drew a crowd of approximately 2,000 women and girls, many of them students; the protest rally was held at Fuxing Park and may have been attended by as many as 30,000 people, again almost exclusively women and female students. The two events followed familiar "scripts" after the speeches ended, as participants in both gatherings formed ranks and marched through the city.

Despite these basic similarities, the two affairs were quite different in content and meaning. The speakers, for example, advanced very different viewpoints. The mayor of Shanghai and other speakers at the pro-GMD gathering celebrated the GMD's accomplishments in the realm of social programs and stressed the need for Chinese women to aid the country by playing traditional roles. Xu Guangping, the main speaker at the protest gathering, had taken part in the May 30th Movement in her youth, was a leader of the Shanghai women's and peace movements throughout the Civil War era, and held a special place within intellectual and radical circles as the widow of the heroic social critic and author Lu Xun.[30] Her fiery speech called on Shanghai women to fight for peace, democracy, and their own liberation.

The marches that followed the rallies also seem to have differed in terms of size and effectiveness, at least according to pro-CCP accounts, which unfortunately are the only readily available ones that provide detailed information on the day's activities.* These admittedly biased sources give little information on the women who took part in the GMD-organized Women's Day parade. However, since non-Communist and Communist press accounts note that members of the Sanqingtuan and its junior organization, the Girl Scouts, figured prominently in the GMD's celebration of March 8, we can assume that many of the participants in the loyalist march were female students.[31] CCP sources, though vague about the backgrounds of the women in the pro-GMD demonstration, are clear about the total number of participants: even though officials offered free snacks to attract participants to the affair, only a "few hundred" women took part; as a result the procession had little impact upon the citizenry as a whole. This contrasts with the much more impressive and effective radical Women's Day celebration, in which thousands of female students and workers marched under banners emblazoned with slogans such as "We won't act as slaves again."[32]

Communist accounts of the radical march describe it as a stirring and dramatic event. As in the January 13 parade honoring the Kunming martyrs, members of the Female Secondary School Students Band led the participants in the anti-government Women's Day demonstration through the city and provided the musical accompaniment for such tunes as "The Sisters' Marching Song." The attempts of government special agents to disrupt the parade proved unsuccessful, thanks in part to the efforts of male students and workers who formed a special security force for the march. Overall, according to these radical accounts, the march was a resounding success. First, it helped revive the city's long-dormant women's movement and raised popular awareness of women's issues through chants such as "Female workers and male workers should get equal pay!" Second, it helped counteract the negative influence of the Anti-Soviet Movement,

---

*The imbalance between radical and non-radical sources relating to the Women's Day events stems from the fact that the official press often tried to minimize the impact of the opposition's protests by pretending that they had not taken place. Thus although CCP works such as Bao Renyu's memoir "Sanwan jiemei," and SCYL, *1945–1949*, pp. 31–33, as well as accounts in the radical press such as Wu Hua, "Quan Shanghai funü" (Wu may not have been a member of the CCP, but he or she was definitely a fervent critic of the GMD) explicitly compare and contrast the radical and loyalist celebrations of March 8, loyalist sources such as *Zhengyanbao* (March 9, 1946, p. 3) provide information only on the Grand Theater rally and subsequent march sponsored by the GMD.

by showing once again that radical organizers could mount large-scale mass actions as well as their opponents.

THE JUNE PEACE MARCHES

Radical and anti-radical students took part in a variety of political activities during April and May 1946.[33] The next major battle for control of the streets did not come, however, until late June, when once again the two camps staged a pair of related demonstrations similar in form but completely different in intent: the Anti–Civil Disturbance march, which loyalist youths held on June 21; and the Anti–Civil War demonstration, which radicals staged on June 23.[34] The participants in both events claimed to be working toward national stability and peace, but they had diametrically opposed visions of how these ends could be attained. The loyalists placed all blame for the Civil War on the CCP; for them the only way to stabilize the nation was to destroy the Communists. The leaders of the radical demonstration, which was held to celebrate the departure for Nanjing of the representatives of a Peace Petition Brigade, by contrast, felt that the GMD bore most of the responsibility for the Civil War; for them the key to peace lay in convincing Jiang Jieshi to work with the CCP rather than try to annihilate it; the need for compromise was the main theme of the Brigade's petition. Despite their differing visions, the loyalist and radical demonstrations can be understood only when viewed as a pair, since the Anti–Civil Disturbance and Anti–Civil War movements of June were each in an important sense reactions to the other.

Even though the highpoint of the radical movement took place after the highpoint of the loyalist one, the best place to begin this account of the June battles is with the formation of the Peace Petition Brigade. This brigade was sponsored jointly by two groups, the Alliance of Shanghai Popular Organizations (Shanghai renmin tuanti lianhehui) and the Alliance of Shanghai Students Fighting for Peace (Shanghai xuesheng zhengque heping lianhehui). The first was established on May 5 by the leaders of 52 different opposition groups, ranging from women's federations to merchants' associations, an umbrella organization to coordinate their antiwar efforts. The student alliance was not founded until June 19, when representatives from 72 local educational institutions decided they needed a league to perform a similar function for school protest associations, which had multiplied quickly after students at Jiaotong formed an antiwar committee on June 13.[35]

The establishment of these alliances was a response to growing popular disillusionment with the escalating war between the GMD and the CCP.

Thanks largely to General Marshall's intervention, representatives of the two parties had signed a temporary truce on January 10. This truce soon proved almost completely ineffectual, however, and hostilities continued throughout the spring. By early June a full-scale war was under way. Many critics of the war considered both the GMD and the CCP at least partially responsible for this situation and therefore did not direct their criticism solely at the government. On June 8, for example, Xu Guangping and 163 other leading cultural and intellectual figures addressed an open letter to General Marshall, Jiang Jieshi, the CCP, and other political parties calling on all those who cared for the fate of the Chinese nation to work to establish peace.[36]

By late June, however, antiwar efforts began to take on definite anti-GMD and by extension anti-American overtones. Many protesters felt by then that Jiang Jieshi was in a better position than anyone else to end the hostilities by agreeing to form a joint government with the CCP. Popular antagonism toward the United States increased because, even though Marshall claimed to be working to keep the two antagonists negotiating, American funds were underwriting Jiang's continuing crusade against the Communist base areas. By the time the Peace Petition Brigade was formed, therefore, antiwar activists were directing most of their criticism toward the central government and the United States.[37]

Government officials and leaders of pro-GMD groups attempted to curtail the growth and counteract the efforts of the new and increasingly radicalized antiwar groups in a variety of ways. Not surprisingly, given the importance of Shanghai campuses as foci for protest activities, many of these measures were directed at the student population. Four examples of loyalist activities on local campuses in June 1946, all taken from a recent textbook on the Shanghai youth movement of the Civil War era, illustrate the range of methods GMD supporters used to undercut the influence of campus radicals.[38] This textbook is hardly a neutral source, since it was written by historians affiliated with the Shanghai branch of the Communist Youth League and is based largely on memoirs by former CCP organizers. Nonetheless, in light of what other materials tell us about the general context of campus politics of the time, the book's descriptions of loyalist interference at four local schools seem plausible enough to warrant repeating here.

The Youth League textbook gives only the briefest sketch of anti-radical activities at Jiaotong University and the North City Middle School. It claims that students affiliated with the Sanqingtuan led an attempt to undermine antiwar agitation at Jiaotong by "spreading rumors and scandal." Arguing that all antiwar agitation was a Communist plot to subvert public order, these Sanqingtuan members allegedly warned their classmates not to "let themselves be used by a political party"—the CCP—by joining the school's antiwar association. The anti-radical drive at the North China Middle School was quite different. This campaign was led not by anti-radical students but by the school's principal, who tore down posters calling for an end to the war and expelled student activists.

The Youth League textbook provides a more detailed description of anti-radical interference at Datong University and its affiliated middle school. Its picture of the dramatic events at these schools on June 21 and 22 is somewhat sensationalized. Nonetheless, occasional exaggerations and perhaps even a few manufactured details aside, the basic chain of events presented in the Youth League publication remains a believable one in light of other evidence; the following paragraphs present its version of events without further caveats or editorial comments.

The two Datong schools emerged as leading centers of protest activity on June 20, when campus leaders announced the beginning of a seven-day boycott of classes, during which all students were to devote themselves to antiwar propaganda work. This propaganda week officially began the next day with an Anti–Civil War, Fight for Peace Mass Rally, which some 2,000 Datong students attended. One reason for this high turnout, which brought middle-school and college students alike to the rally, was the high reputation of the two scheduled speakers: the beloved educator Tao Xingzhi and the historian Wu Han. Members of the Datong Sanqingtuan, dismayed by the size of the crowd, tried their best to prevent these two prominent opposition figures from speaking to the assembled students. First, the anti-radical youths cut the rally's supply of electricity. Then Sanqingtuan members stormed to the front of the crowd and started chanting "Don't let outsiders come to lecture at our school." The student chairing the assembly soon put an end to this attempted disruption by calling for a show of hands from the student body as a whole as to whether they wanted to hear Tao and Wu speak. Sanqingtuan members were outnumbered some 1,900 to 3 in this show of hands. The anti-radical youths, seeing themselves defeated, slunk away to the accompaniment of the crowd's laughter, and Tao and Wu began their speeches.

The jubilation of Datong's anti-government forces proved short-lived, however, for their opponents came back in much greater force on the second day of the strike, backed by no less a personage than the city's mayor, K. C. Wu. Wu had come to the Datong campus on the afternoon of the first day of the strike and issued a statement personally guaranteeing that "no force would be used to suppress the student movement." All he asked in return was that Datong's pupils show that they were willing to "put primary emphasis upon their educational work" by ending the strike and turning out for their examinations the following day. This request proved to demand more than the students were willing to give.

Wu was infuriated when, upon returning to the campus on the morning of June 22 to oversee the tests, he found only a handful of students in the classrooms. He marched to the campus sports field, where the bulk of the student body had already congregated for another protest rally, and addressed Datong's pupils for a second time. The crowd had made him "lose face" by ignoring his plea of the preceding day, he claimed, and forfeited its right to governmental protection. By refusing to take their exams, he continued, the students had proved that they were willing to be used to further the ends of outsiders. He concluded by saying that "those who don't take tests are troublemakers" and that "troublemakers must be punished severely!"

Protest leaders responded by trying to convince the mayor that their actions were just. The head of the Datong Self-governing Association defended the decision to continue the strike by crying out: "Exams can be delayed; we can't wait for peace." Chen Chenzhong, one of two youths chosen as student representatives in the Peace Petition Brigade that set out for Nanjing on June 23, then refuted the charge of outside manipulation. "The reason we students oppose the war is solely because we are patriots," he said. Mayor Wu was not convinced, however, and cursed Chen as a "troublemaker." Just then over 200 policemen in "full battle gear" raided the meeting. Aided by the Sanqingtuan members and "special agent students" (tewu xuesheng) already in the crowd and armed with knives, the officers broke up the meeting by arresting a number of protest leaders and beating up other radicals.

Loyalists realized, however, that they could not compete with radicals simply by using disruptive tactics. GMD supporters were keenly aware of the unpopularity of the Civil War. They knew the power that images of peace and stability could have for Chinese intellectuals and ordinary citizens, who had suffered through the protracted eight-year War of Resistance against Japan only to be plunged into a new military struggle. They also knew that radicals were swiftly monopolizing the imagery of peace, and that the people were beginning to think of the phrase "Oppose the Civil War" (fan neizhan) as a synonym for opposition to the GMD. In the quest for positive as well as negative methods to undermine this monopoly, loyalists began rallying around their own peace slogan, "Oppose domestic turmoil" (fan neiluan), a phrase they tried to instill with clear anti-Communist overtones.

Extant sources tell much less about the highpoint of the loyalist Anti–Civil Disturbance demonstration, the march supporters held on June 21, than they do about equivalent events staged by the opposition. The scholar interested in radical protests of the Civil War years can sometimes piece together a nuanced picture of a mass action, thanks to the existence of a range of memoirs and other primary materials. By contrast, virtually the only materials on the June 21 loyalist march are descriptions of the parade in contemporary newspapers or in general histories of the youth movement of the period. To add to the problem of historical reconstruction, the biases inherent in the two main types of available sources—newspapers controlled by the GMD and pro-CCP materials published in the PRC— are so great that any account of what took place must be pieced together from descriptions that contradict each other at every turn.

This last problem is not unique to loyalist marches, of course; pro- and anti-GMD sources often present widely differing pictures of radical demonstrations. In the case of events that challenged as opposed to supported the status quo, however, a third set of sources usually steers a middle course between the exaggerations of the two Chinese camps: accounts written by Western journalists and diplomats. Unfortunately for the historian, these foreign observers tended to be much less interested in loyalist displays than they were in radical ones, in large part simply because opposition demonstrations much more frequently attacked one or another Western power as well as the Chinese authorities. The contrast was clear in the case of the events of June 1946: whereas Western journalists and diplomats had much to say about the Peace Petition Brigade demonstration of June 23, during which anti-American as well as anti-GMD slogans figured prominently, they had almost nothing to say about the Anti–Civil Disturbance agitation of June 21.

This silence on the part of Western observers creates special difficulties for the historian. The divergence between pro- and anti-GMD accounts is so great that it becomes virtually impossible to make even the simplest statements about events such as the loyalist parade with any conviction. The issue of calculating how many people took part in the march illustrates this point. Estimates of crowd size depend largely upon the source's view of the cause in question, and this is true of virtually all the events treated in this chapter. In the case of many of these actions, however, the historian can still come up with a fairly good ballpark figure simply by comparing the estimates in sympathetic and antagonistic Chinese sources with those provided by Western sources. In the case of the Anti–Civil Disturbance march, however, a pro-GMD source estimates the crowd at 20,000 and a pro-CCP one puts it at fewer than a thousand.[39]

This said, several things are worth noting about this march. First, both sympathetic and unsympathetic accounts agree that the demonstration was organized by and proceeded under the flag of a group known as the

Alliance of Shanghai Students Opposed to Civil Disturbance. Second, these sources also agree that most marchers were middle-school students and their slogans specifically identified the CCP as the main cause of domestic unrest. Third, it seems safe to assume that anti-GMD sources are right in claiming that the Sanqingtuan had much to do with mobilizing youths to take part in the march. Pro-GMD sources tend to be silent on this point, but the claim seems extremely plausible in light of the context and is supported by evidence in a rare Western comment on Anti–Civil Disturbance activities in the *Shanghai Evening Post and Mercury*.[40] Finally, there seems little reason to doubt three other details provided only in pro-GMD accounts of the parade: many of the participants wore military uniforms of some sort, the Middle-School Students Military Band led the parade, and the youths sang "anti–civil disturbance songs" as they marched through the city.

These sketchy details reveal that this parade, like the anti-French and anti-Soviet demonstrations earlier in the year, was a hybrid event that had features in common with both government-sponsored street displays and genuine protests. There were strong similarities in form between the June 21 march and official ceremonies, such as those the GMD had staged the previous May 5 to mark the return of the central government to Nanjing from its wartime base in Chongqing, in terms of the part played by uniformed marchers of middle-school age (under twenty).[41] In some ways, however, the June 21 demonstration unfolded more like a protest than an official celebration. Forming a student alliance around a topical issue and then marching behind a flag emblazoned with this alliance's name while shouting patriotic slogans are two of the most basic steps in the classic student movement mobilization pattern (see Chapter 5). Even the donning of military uniforms can be seen as part of the traditional protest repertoire; whereas this was done by anti-GMD students in 1931 to show their determination to fight Japanese invaders (see Chapter 7), participants in the 1946 loyalist "protest" did so to show their commitment to fighting Soviet forces and CCP "bandits" in North China.

In many ways, in short, the June 21 march was similar to the Anti-Soviet Movement of February 1946. In one crucial way, however, this demonstration was even less like a traditional student protest than the marches against "red imperialism." Unlike participants in the parades of four months before, the loyalist youths who joined the June 21 march posed no challenge to the GMD, since they did not call for any changes in specific policies or criticize individual party leaders. The sole aims of the June 21 march seem, therefore, to have been to increase support for the authorities and undercut the position of the radical peace movement by shifting attention from GMD warmongering to CCP rebellion.

The leaders of the opposition waited just two days before striking back with an impressive parade of their own. This parade, which followed a rally at the North Station in honor of the departure of the Peace Petition Brigade, dwarfed the march of June 21. The GMD-controlled *Dagongbao* estimated that some 50,000 people took part in the June 23 event; the radical press claimed twice as many participants.[42] Even the lower figure would make this march the largest radical protest in Shanghai in over a decade.

This difference in size notwithstanding, however, the June 23 peace march had much in common with the protest parade to greet General Marshall. Once again the protesters demanded greater democracy and the immediate withdrawal of American troops. Once again, the protest closely resembled an official ceremony, with those participating performing parts normally reserved for powerholders. Furthermore, just as the official welcoming ceremony on the same day had given added punch to the December 20 protest action, recent political events gave special meaning to the selection of the Peace Petition Brigade in June. In April Shanghai's citizens had taken part in their first "free" elections, elections the GMD trumpeted as proof that it was leading China on the path toward true democracy. This plan backfired, however, when Chinese opposition figures and foreign observers alike pointed to a wide range of improprieties—ranging from intimidation of voters to outright fraud—charges that even some officials were forced to admit were valid.[43] The GMD's position was further compromised when the opening of the first postwar National Assembly (originally scheduled for May 5) was delayed until November.[44] In this context of rigged elections and delays in the convening of the country's "representative" body, the selection of a petition brigade (which protesters claimed would "truly" represent the popular will) became a particularly significant gesture.

Mimicry and usurpation went far beyond this, however. The form of the June 23 demonstration showed striking similarities to recent official spectacles, such as the February rally (a picture of which appears in the photographic section) honoring Jiang Jieshi's first postwar visit to Shanghai.[45] The same festive air that had accompanied Jiang's rally prevailed at the train station where the protesters gathered to send off the Peace Petition Brigade, with brightly colored banners, mass singing, and firecrackers enlivening the scene in both cases. At Jiang's rally carefully selected representatives of various official bureaus, military units, and party branches addressed the crowd; the June 23 opposition rally centered around speeches by representatives of each of the main cultural, student, and worker groups involved. The militaristic parades by uniformed youths, a constant feature of many official ceremonies as well as of the June 21 march, were duplicated in the march that followed the Peace Petition Brigade's departure for Nanjing. No formal "troops" were involved in the June 23 march, but three specially chosen "commanders" (*zong zhihui*) led the June march, and a team of St. John's University students, marching in the vanguard behind a banner emblazoned "Alliance of Students Fighting for Peace," provided an equivalent in the area of youth.[46]

Finally, as in many protests of both this and other eras, during the June march some demonstrators mirrored the actions, and temporarily usurped the roles, of their traditional enemies: the police. A special brigade of march monitors, drawn from the ranks of the protesters, accompanied the procession as it traveled from the train station to Fuxing Park, where a final rally was held. These march monitors were supposed to simply keep order among the demonstrators, but their potential function as a shadow law enforcement agency was clear. When the monitors saw "reactionary" pamphlets and objects hurled at demonstrators' heads from the upper windows of the Great World Building, they rushed into this amusement center and apprehended three of those responsible. Then, as some had no doubt seen their official counterparts do to protesters in past demonstrations, the monitors searched the troublemakers for identification and found a piece of paper linking the men to a branch of the Sanqingtuan. The monitors then took the men into "custody" and escorted them to Fuxing Park, where they were displayed to the crowd, along with another self-admitted Sanqingtuan member other monitors had "arrested" earlier for slapping a female marcher on the ear. What exactly these shadow police planned to do to the "criminals" next is unclear, since they were forced almost immediately to hand the four men over to the official police, a large contingent of whom had surrounded the park and demanded that the Sanqingtuan members be handed over to be punished according to the law.[47]

The events of June 21 and 23 show how completely entwined the loyalist and radical traditions of mass action had become by 1946. It is still possible to isolate instances in which one side borrowed a technique associated with the other to undercut the opponent: for example, loyalist students' formation of the Alliance of Shanghai Students Opposed to Civil Disturbance to serve as a counterweight to the Alliance of Shanghai Students Fighting for Peace radical students had established just days previously; or the radicals' selection of "popular" delegates just days after Shanghai's first official post–World War II elections. For the most part, however, by 1946 it made no sense to try to figure out who was imitating whom when it came to staging mass actions. Both sides were simply combining and recombining the same props and movements and improvising from the same scripts, in a constant give-and-take. Symbolic of this push and pull between radicals and loyalists was the fate of some anti-

Communist slogans loyalist students had chalked on walls during the June 21 demonstration. In some cases radicals following the same march route two days later rubbed out the one word "turmoil" (*luan*) in the phrase "oppose domestic turmoil" (*fan neiluan*) and substituted the character for "war" (*zhan*), thereby turning an anti-CCP slogan into an anti-GMD one.

AGAINST U.S. BRUTALITY: DECEMBER 1946–JANUARY 1947

The next important public struggles between loyalist and radical youths began six months after the June parades, when local students called for a new round of protests against the continued presence of U.S. troops in China and the alleged rape of a Beijing student by two American marines. Earlier chapters examine the evolution of the New Year's Day march that capped this agitation (see Chapter 5), as well as the themes stressed in anti-American propaganda pieces of the time (see Chapter 8). Here, I look briefly at the attempts loyalist students at Ji'nan University—the school whose students took the lead in organizing the New Year's Day demonstration—made to counteract protest activities in late 1946.

Memoirs and other materials published in the PRC present these loyalist activities by Ji'nan students as following a by-now familiar pattern of officially sponsored intimidation.[48] According to these sources, when Mayor K. C. Wu heard in late December that students at Ji'nan University had launched a classroom strike and begun to distribute anti-American propaganda, he angrily telephoned Zhang Wangwen, a top administrator at the school, to talk about strategies to keep the nascent movement from growing. Following this talk, Zhang called several dozen of the school's "special students" and Sanqingtuan members together and directed them to form an anti-strike group to counter the efforts of the main campus group promoting the strike, the Anti-brutality Committee (Kangbaohui).

Communist sources claim that this group took its first steps to undercut the school strike on the morning of December 31, when its members disrupted a protest meeting by shouting "We want to go to class!" and other similar cries and trying to bully students into joining their cause. According to PRC sources, progressive students quickly exposed the loyalist special students for the troublemakers they were by pointing out that in ordinary times the members of the anti-strike group rarely wanted to attend classes, and the vast majority of the school's pupils voiced their continued commitment to the strike. Frustrated by this turn of events, Dan Jiarui, leader of the anti-strike group and a notorious "special agent student" whose past abusive behavior had earned him the nickname Ji'nan Wolf (*Ji'nan zhi lang*), pulled out a knife and attacked one of the youths running the meeting. This action set off a brawl during which Dan and two other youths were injured.

Not surprisingly, the English-language press organs *China Press* and *China Daily Tribune*, both of which by this point were controlled by the GMD, give different versions of these events. According to the *Daily Tribune*, the fight at Ji'nan began after "a group of students broke into a classroom to urge other students attending class at the time to go on strike" and take part in a parade against American imperialism. When the youths attending class refused, "the hot-heads [i.e., the radicals] started to argue and reproach the body of saner and more level-headed students. The battle of tongues soon developed into fight [sic] on the open ground outside the classroom resulting in three students being injured. It is said one of the demonstrators used a dagger as a weapon." [49]

The *China Press* article on the day's events gives a more neutral, less detailed account of the scuffle, saying only that a "free-for-all occurred" at Ji'nan "when students favoring a protest strike and students insisting on attending classes argued with each other and finally got into a fight on campus." This article also contains an interesting paragraph concerning a propaganda battle preceding the verbal and physical fights. "It was learned that early in the morning [of December 31] notices of a student strike posted in Chinan [Ji'nan] campus were torn down by some students and replaced with those demanding continuation of classes. Later these replaced notices were again torn down and the original ones put up." [50]

Struggles between pro- and anti-strike student factions continued during the following two weeks. Throughout early January newly constituted radical and loyalist youth groups, both claiming to speak for the majority view within the student community, continually issued opposing statements to the press concerning the U.S. military presence in China and the way the authorities should handle the Beijing rape case. [51] There were no repeats of the violence seen at Ji'nan on December 31, however, and loyalist youths did not even try to disrupt the New Year's Day anti-American demonstration. This demonstration, in fact, was much freer from outside disturbance than virtually any other anti-American protest of the era, in large part because the local authorities, realizing how much genuine popular anger the Beijing rape had generated, took the unusual step of providing the marchers with police protection. [52]

Although anti-radical students and GMD officials did not try to disrupt the New Year's Day demonstration against American imperialism, the first day of 1947 was not completely free of competition between loyalists and radicals for control of the street. Just one hour after participants in the anti-American parade began marching westward from the Bund up Nanjing Road toward the old French Park, members of the Sanqingtuan and other participants in a loyalist procession honoring the adoption of a new Chinese constitution began working their way eastward along Nanjing Road toward the Bund. It is unclear from extant sources just where the two sets of paraders passed each other—this too occurred without incident—and it is also unclear whether either side planned its parade to counteract the effects of the other's. The fact remains that spectators in downtown Shanghai were treated to an interesting collection of competing images on New Year's Day, as they watched the two processions (one led by propaganda trucks covered with posters challenging GMD policies, and the other by colorful floats bedecked with GMD flags and loyalist banners) pass by.[53]

AGAINST WAR AND HUNGER: MAY 4–MAY 20

Loyalist and radical youths were involved in so many mass actions and factional struggles during the months that followed the New Year's Day parades that an entire chapter would be needed to do them justice; as a result only a few highpoints can be treated here. The April confrontations at Shanghai Baptist College between students who favored a strike to protest the school's grading system and youths who opposed this classroom boycott; the fierce electoral campaign members of loyalist and progressive student groups waged for control of the Fudan student council throughout the spring of 1947; and the mass petition drive middle-school students organized in early May to fight a GMD plan to introduce a new standardized test for all graduating seniors—these are but a few of the campus struggles that will be passed over.[54] Instead the following pages focus on a month-long series of interrelated student political actions that began on the twenty-eighth anniversary of the May 4th Movement.

The different ways loyalist and radical students celebrated this holiday, which all agreed was the most important day in the history of the nation's youth movement, illustrates how fragmented this movement had become by 1947. Some students spent the day attending the official commemoration and heard Mayor K. C. Wu and other officials speak about the meaning of the May 4th Movement (in which Wu reminded the audience he had taken part as a youth), and assure them that the GMD remained committed to the ideals of 1919. Other students chose to show their allegiance to these same ideals by devoting the day to anti-American propaganda work. While their loyalist counterparts listened to speeches extolling the GMD, these radical youths covered the city with posters attacking the party's most important ally, an act for which the police arrested two students from Shanghai Law School (Faxueyuan).[55]

These arrests breathed new life into the city's radical student movement by giving local youths an incident of official repression around which to rally. The student body at the Law School immediately launched a strike to protest the arrests, dubbed the "Shanghai Law School's May 4th Incident," and demanded that the police release their classmates. The struggle turned into a citywide one on May 8 when the Anti-brutality Alliance, which youths had formed the previous December to coordinate anti-American protest activities, established a special committee to take charge of the movement to free the arrested students. On May 9, this committee brought together more than 500 representatives from various Shanghai schools to go in person to the Municipal Government Compound to petition the authorities to release the imprisoned students. The petition was granted almost immediately.[56]

A number of other events during the first half of May, both in Shanghai and other cities, added to the growing momentum of the radical student movement. Two of the most important took place on May 10, when students at Shanghai's Jiaotong University began a "save the school" strike and youths at Nanjing's Central University announced plans to launch an anti-hunger classroom boycott on May 13. The Jiaotong strike was a complex affair, in which factional politics (the school was a CC Clique stronghold) as well as genuine grievances played central parts.[57] The strike began when Minister of Education Zhu Jiahua, a foe of the CC Clique, announced plans to reduce funding for Jiaotong, abolish two of its departments, and change its name.[58] Viewing Zhu's move as an attack upon one of their faction's main Shanghai power bases, Jiaotong students affiliated with the CC Clique (with the support of some key professors and school administrators) immediately set about mobilizing support for a popular counterattack among their classmates around the slogans "Save our school" and "Long live Jiaotong."

Three factors helped this movement evolve quickly into a militant effort that virtually every Jiaotong student supported. First, students of all political persuasions and factional affiliations had pride in their alma mater. Second, for reasons explained below, in 1947 many members of the academic community were growing increasingly disillusioned with GMD educational policies. Third, underground Communist organizers at Jiaotong decided that they could best serve the cause of revolution by using the GMD's internal contradictions to their own advantage by supporting the movement and trying to radicalize it from the inside. After the initial classroom strike failed to force Zhu to change his plans, leaders of the Jiaotong struggle were then able to mobilize close to 3,000 students on May 13 to take their case directly to the capital.

This Jiaotong mass petition drive was strikingly similar to some of the events examined in Chapter 7. The Jiaotong youths, like their predecessors of the 1930's, began by marching to the North Station and attempting to board trains for Nanjing. Authorities at the North Station tried (as officials had often tried in the previous decade) to prevent the student petitioners from traveling to the capital. And, in a final parallel to the events of 1931 and 1935, these efforts failed, as students boarded the trains over the objections of the railway authorities and set off for Nanjing. But the outcome was different in 1947: whereas student petitioners of the 1930's had seldom won major concessions from the authorities, Minister Zhu agreed to the Jiaotong students' demands soon after the student-driven train had left the North Station.

The anti-hunger strike by the students of Nanjing's Central University differed somewhat from the one at Jiaotong. Factional tensions seem to have played a less central role in the Nanjing struggle, and the goals of the Central University students were much broader than those of their counterparts at Jiaotong.[59] The students at Central University launched their strike to show support for an unsuccessful petition drive the school's professors had staged in late April to pressure the central government to increase funding for education. The youths also wanted to focus attention on the way runaway inflation and the GMD's policy of allotting less than 5 percent of the national budget to fund state educational institutions (while using some 80 percent of the budget for military expenses) were hurting the nation's students and teachers. In addition to trying to convince their classmates to boycott class, the leaders of the Central University strike sent representatives to meet with educated youths in other parts of the city and the country to turn the fight against hunger and militarism into a nationwide student effort.

The Central University struggle struck a resonant chord with students throughout China, especially those studying at the approximately two-thirds of the nation's colleges and universities run by the state.[60] Even youths from wealthy families attending private colleges were feeling the effects of the hyperinflation by early 1947. The price of some basic foods doubled between February and late April and then rose by another 20 percent during the first ten days of May alone.[61] Nevertheless, the price increases hit the students (many of whom were on fixed government stipends) and professors (who were on fixed government salaries) at public institutions much harder, and these people were affected more directly by the GMD's skewed budgetary policies than were their counterparts at private schools. Not surprisingly, therefore, students at institutions dependent upon state funds responded most energetically to the efforts of Central University students to turn the fight against inflation and the GMD's budgetary policies into a nationwide mass movement. Youths at public colleges and universities led the fight to rally the nation behind the slogans of "Resolve the educational crisis" (*Qiangjiu jiaoyu weiji*) and "Oppose hunger, oppose civil war" (*Fan ji'e, fan neizhan*), and their professors offered the strongest adult support for the new youth movement.[62]

This meant that in Shanghai the students who led in mobilizing support for the new Anti-Hunger, Anti–Civil War Movement in mid-May were those from state schools such as Fudan, Tongji, Ji'nan, and the Shanghai Law School. On May 14, pupils from these four schools went on strike to demand an increase in funding for education and student stipends; youths from other state schools, including the Jiaotong students who had just returned to classes after the successful conclusion of their petition campaign, also began to boycott their classes that same day.[63] Three days after the strike began, students from all the striking schools formed an Alliance of Shanghai National Universities.

In one of their first acts, the leaders of this new organization announced on May 17 that a delegation of 37 representatives would leave for Nanjing on May 19 to present a petition of protest to the central government.[64] The colorful parade, complete with marchers carrying broken rice bowls, that the Alliance staged on May 19 to send this delegation on its way (see Chapter 8) was one of the largest student-run protest events of the period, involving some 7,000 youths from fifteen local schools. When the Shanghai delegation arrived in the capital on May 19, it joined with student representatives from Hangzhou, Suzhou, and Nanjing in issuing a joint declaration of aims. This joint declaration marks one of the major turning points in the evolution of the fight against war and hunger from a collection of localized struggles to a truly national mass movement.

The parade held in the capital the following day, in which the visiting petitioners and students from various Nanjing universities took part, helped complete this evolutionary process. When the central government sent hundreds of policemen and soldiers (including some armed with machine guns) to block the march route, they gave students throughout the nation, at public and private institutions alike, a new incident to protest: the May 20th Tragedy. As soon as word spread that the police had arrested more than 50 marchers and used clubs, leather belts, and fire hoses against other protesters, students across China began to rally around the triple cry of "Fight hunger, fight civil war, fight oppression."

REACTIONS TO THE NANJING TRAGEDY: MAY 20–JUNE 2

The May 20th Tragedy triggered an outburst of organizational activity within the student community. Youths in various cities formed special associations to publicize the Nanjing events and coordinate new protests against the ongoing problems of inflation, war, and lack of freedom of speech.[65] Student leaders from different parts of China met in Nanjing in late May to lay the groundwork for a national protest league to take charge of planning a one-day multi-city protest against the Civil War. Scheduled for June 2, this one-day nationwide event was to be more than just a student affair: it was to take the form of a general strike in which workers and merchants would also take part, a sanba of the sort that had paralyzed Shanghai in June 1919 and 1925.[66]

This decision to attempt a sanba required students to bring people outside the academic community into the mass movement, and as a result propaganda work became the top priority of Shanghai students in the final days of May. The city's educated youths used familiar methods to gain the support of the populace for the fight against hunger, war, and oppression: they declared a classroom strike so that they could devote themselves to propaganda work and spent their time composing, printing, and distributing handbills and filling the city with teams of streetside lecturers.[67]

The GMD authorities in Shanghai and other cities took several steps to undermine the radical student movement in late May and early June. Some of these steps were attempts to control public knowledge and perception of the recent Nanjing tragedy. Thus, for example, the authorities suspended all newspapers that presented the youth protests in a positive light. In Shanghai this meant the closure of three popular news organs, *Wenhuibao*, *Lianhebao*, and *Xinmin wanbao*, all of which had been critical of government policies in the past but had not been viewed as openly subversive or dangerous until late May 1947.[68] Officials also issued press statements of their own to counteract the "false" claims protesters made. In these statements, GMD leaders called on students to refrain from further illegal activities—such as taking part in unauthorized mass gatherings and distributing "counter-revolutionary" (anti-GMD) propaganda—and told youths not to let themselves be used by unscrupulous Communist agitators.[69]

The authorities, realizing that limiting the flow of information and making statements would not be sufficient in themselves to prevent further demonstrations, used physical force to back up their words. During the last ten days of May, the police and special agents in Shanghai and other cities arrested at least several hundred and perhaps as many as several thousand students for propaganda work relating to the May 20th Tragedy and the upcoming Anti–Civil War Day.[70] The police also seized and held many other students on unspecified charges or on suspicion of Communist sympathies. Many arrests occurred without incident, with law enforcement agents simply detaining individual youths on the streets, but in some cases dozens of policemen or special agents raided protest league meetings or laid siege to entire campuses to try to root out student leaders who had managed to avoid arrest.[71]

Along with legal measures of this sort, officials and supporters of the GMD also launched a campaign of extralegal terror against campus radicals. In a series of violent incidents in late May and early June, special agents, anti-radical youths, and hired thugs attacked students suspected of Communist leanings.* In one such incident near the Fudan campus on May 26, a band of thugs armed with "wolf's teeth clubs" (wooden planks studded with nails) beat up a group of students returning to their dorms after attending an evening meeting celebrating the release of some of their classmates from jail.[72] The line between "legal" arrests and outright terror was not always clear. For example, after police carried out a raid on one Wuhan campus to seize suspected radicals, as a parting gesture they fired several rounds of dumdum bullets into a dormitory, killing three youths and seriously wounding five others.[73]

In addition to verbal and physical methods of undermining the radical student movement, officials turned to the by-now familiar technique of mobilizing loyalist youths to rally behind the GMD. Just as pupils at various Shanghai schools had established an Anti–Civil Disturbance Alliance the previous June to match the efforts of antiwar campus groups, in late May and early June 1947 pro-government students formed "anti-strike committees" to counteract the influence of radical "May 20th support committees."[74] Loyalist students even founded an equivalent to the new radical National Student Alliance established in Nanjing. Called the All-China Student Association for National Salvation and School Protection, this pro-government youth league's stated purpose was to organize the youth of the country into a "gigantic stabilizing force."[75]

As part of this effort, the group sent a special ten-man delegation to Shanghai, which held a press conference at the local New Life Club on June 1. According to a report on this conference carried in the GMD-controlled English-language *China Daily Tribune*, the members of the delegation insisted that 80 percent of the nation's student body was in favor of "the peaceful and uninterrupted pursuit of their studies" and resented being "dragged into the political maelstrom." The loyalist youth league's main immediate aim, therefore, was "to seek an early end to the present chaotic situation in universities and schools and to restore peace and order in society."[76]

---

*As in the case of arrests, the most comprehensive information regarding attacks of this sort can be found in Communist sources, which obviously have an interest in playing up the level of violence and present the events in a one-sided light. There is enough evidence in non-Communist sources to show that although CCP sources may exaggerate at times, they are justified in claiming that a campaign of terror took place. See, e.g., the AP report carried in *China Mail*, May 29, 1947, p. 1, which provides details of late May attacks that occurred at Fudan—"students were knocked unconscious and many others suffered severe injuries"— and Datong University—"eleven were injured . . . [one] student's eye was pulled out by a hook."

The GMD's campaign to use loyalist youths to discredit and raise doubts about the popularity of the radical student movement went beyond the sponsorship of anti-strike committees: in late May party leaders and officials in Shanghai called on these youths to take part in an anti-Communist rally scheduled for June 2.[77] Ostensibly, the GMD chose this particular date because it was Youth Reconversion Day, the first anniversary of the demobilization of the Chinese Youth Army. The Generalissimo had established this Youth Army—crack troops composed of selected volunteers from middle schools and colleges—during the final months of the war against Japan, and the organization's former members remained intensely loyal to the GMD cause throughout the mid-1940's, playing leading roles in some of the assaults on radical students alluded to above.[78] The decision to hold a loyalist spectacle on June 2 had a broader significance: radical students had proclaimed this to be Anti–Civil War Day and planned massive demonstrations throughout the nation on this date.

On June 2, it was immediately clear that loyalist youths had won this newest battle for control of Shanghai's streets, in large part because of the enormous toll of the GMD's recent campaign of repression. This campaign had convinced less politicized students that they were likely to pay a high price for participating in anti-government protests. It also robbed the radical youth movement of its leaders: few of these students had managed to elude both policemen and special agents, and most of those lucky enough to stay out of jail and out of the hospital had fled to Hong Kong. As a result, none of the mass demonstrations against war and repression scheduled for June 2 took place in Shanghai or other cities, and the general strike called by student leaders failed to materialize.

Observers of Shanghai street politics were surprised to see, in fact, that the only banners referring to "strikes" they saw in the hands of youths on June 2 were those emblazoned with anti-radical slogans, such as "We want to study" and "The sanba is a Communist plot." These banners were carried by participants in the Youth Reconversion Day demonstration, which took place exactly as planned despite recently issued regulations prohibiting all mass gatherings.* This demonstration was similar in many ways to those during the Anti-Soviet Movement of 1946. Once again there was a

---

*The CCP made much of the hypocrisy of the GMD's willingness to allow this anti-Communist event to take place at a time when all gatherings of dissenters were considered breaches of martial law and were being violently suppressed. For example, one of the articles on the June 2 loyalist march in a local radical magazine carried the title "Who Is Breaking the Law?" ("Shishei pohuai faming?" *Qingnian zhishi*, 13 [1947]: 2). The same issue of this journal also included a translated excerpt from an unspecified English-language periodical describing a Western journalist's surprise on June 2: first, at seeing a parade taking place without police interference, just after the authorities had prohibited any gathering of more than ten people; and, second, at discovering that the slogans shouted by the marchers were not "Oppose the civil war, oppose hunger," but calls for the suppression of the CCP.

hint of "protest" in the marchers' slogans, some of which called for an end to "bureaucratic capitalism."[79] Once again the demonstration unfolded much like a May 4th–style political event: it began with a mass rally in a park, during which youths formed a patriotic league (in this case one devoted to "the promotion of national reconstruction") and ended with lines of youth marching through the city's main streets waving banners and shouting slogans. Once again, however, as in the case of the anti-Soviet demonstrations, it was ultimately clear that the overall intent of the June 2 march was to support rather than to challenge the status quo. There were many signs of this: local officials played a prominent role in the day's events (Mayor Wu himself reviewed former Youth Army troops at the start of the rally); far from interfering with the parade, the police seized at least one bystander for jeering; and the symbols and banners used in the day's march emphasized Communist failings (one parade float representing the sufferings of ordinary Chinese in Communist base areas showed a life-size dummy strung up on a giant cross labeled "liberated regions").[80]

REACTIONS TO THE 1947 PROTESTS

Although anti-radical youths succeeded in winning the battle for control of the streets on June 2, by mid-1947 loyalist forces were already well on their way toward losing the larger war for public opinion. As Suzanne Pepper argues persuasively, the first half of 1947 marked a major turning point in the way students and members of the intelligentsia as a whole viewed the GMD.[81] The continuation of the Civil War, official insensitivity toward student grievances relating to the Beijing rape case, the authorities' continual attempts to label all manifestations of discontent "red" protests, and above all the mass arrests and beatings of the spring—each of these contributed to the intellectual community's alienation from the GMD. The repressive measures that kept anti-GMD demonstrators off the streets on June 2 backfired in the long run and ultimately strengthened the radical student movement by hardening the resolve of committed campus activists, bringing new student converts into the movement, and convincing formerly uncommitted or apathetic professors to join the opposition.[82]

The protests of the first half of 1947 and the repressive tactics the authorities used to suppress these events also had a profound impact upon people outside the academic community. Extant sources make it difficult to assess the claim, made in virtually all Communist accounts, that the protests of May in particular and the campaign of terror that followed showed the "masses" the GMD's true face.[83] Although there is good reason to view such accounts with skepticism, there is truth to the claim that student struggles against war and hunger enjoyed broad popular support. If officials had not genuinely feared a June 2 sanba, they would have had no reason to use draconian measures to prevent its occurrence. Even reports in GMD-controlled newspapers occasionally admitted that people outside the intelligentsia (including even some policemen) were in sympathy with the protests of May.[84]

If solid data concerning the impact the events of May and June had on Shanghai's masses are lacking, there is much evidence concerning the effect student protests and GMD repression had on two other non-academic groups: foreign journalists and Western consular officials. Given the GMD's reliance upon American aid and its general concern with foreign opinion, both student activists and officials took the views of these two sets of observers seriously, since statements by foreign reporters, editors, and diplomats stationed in China shaped the views of the Western public and Western governments. Even a cursory survey of 1946 and 1947 wire service reports, the articles and editorials in the major English-language Hong Kong and Shanghai newspapers, and consular dispatches shows that the events of May and June triggered a definite shift in the way foreign observers felt about and treated Chinese student protests.

The shift was clearest in the case of the English-language press. Throughout 1946, Western journalists and editors tended to present all radical protests, such as the peace march of June 23, in a negative light and to stress the "anti-foreign," "riotous" side of the events and accept GMD talk of "Communist manipulation" at face value.[85] Many foreign journalists continued to portray the first major protests of 1947 in the same fashion, as the headlines "Hysterical Students Still Parading" (which appeared in boldface capital letters on the front page of the Hong Kong–based *China Mail* just after the Anti–U.S. Brutality marches of January) and "Riotous Students" (which topped a UP report on the first protests of May) indicate.[86]

The English-language press's coverage of the radical student movement began to change dramatically in the middle of May.[87] Instead of accepting official statements attributing all domestic unrest to "red" agents, wire service reporters began to refer to "alleged" Communist conspiracies. They also began to put more emphasis upon the severity of police repression and less upon the "lawlessness" and "riotousness" of the students.[88] By early June, even newspapers such as the *Shanghai Evening Post* and Hong Kong's *South China Morning Post*, which had seldom had kind words for radical protesters in the past, began to admit that student demonstrators had legitimate grievances. Editorials in these papers criticized the GMD for using violent methods to suppress domestic dissent and refusing to see that genuine discontent as well as Communist agitation were involved in the popular fight against war, hunger, and oppression. For example, the *South China Morning Post*'s editorial of June 5, "Peace by Repression," read in part:

> It cannot be said that the abandonment of Monday's [Anti–Civil War Day's] demonstrations added to the prestige of the governments, national or provincial. The arrests of students and newspaper writers have been carried out with heavy hands . . . the authorities should by now have realised the stupidity of trying to destroy "dangerous thoughts." . . . This long discredited policy is precisely what, in the opinion of all enlightened people is wrong with countries like China and Russia. It confirms the accusations of party dictatorships, and it alienates sympathy.[89]

There were several reasons for this change in the English-language newspapers' treatment of radical protests in mid-May 1947. The Anti-Hunger, Anti–Civil War Movement was the first postwar struggle in which radicals made almost no use of anti-imperialist (in Western eyes "anti-foreign" and hence objectionable) slogans of any sort.[90] Another factor was the qualitative change in the severity of the methods the authorities used to suppress popular unrest. Last, and most important, the sheer number of students who continued to protest, even after the bloodshed of May 20 had made it clear how risky such behavior could be, seems to have convinced many foreign journalists that there was genuine popular dissatisfaction with the GMD within the academic community. Thus in late May and June 1947, Western journalists who had formerly dismissed radical student demonstrations and strikes as events orchestrated by a small handful of Communist agitators began to see these protests as spontaneous expressions of discontent and to wonder if the loyalist youths working to end the Anti-Hunger, Anti–Civil War Movement were in fact the outside agitators serving the ends of a political party.*

The events of mid-1947 also won the sympathy of at least some leading foreign diplomats and helped convince them that the radical student movement had become a more genuine expression of popular opinion than its loyalist counterpart. This comes out clearly in a May 27 telegram from Leo Lamb of the British embassy in Nanjing to George Kitson of the London Foreign Office.[91] Lamb writes that his first reaction to the protests of May was to dismiss them as orchestrated events. Believing them to be masterminded by a C.C. Clique intent upon embarrassing factional rivals, he viewed them "as just another of those well organised 'spontaneous' agitations which have of recent years become a regular rou-

---

*One sign of this shift in attitude toward anti-radical youths is that wire services began to refer to people agitating against strikes as "special students." By contrast, during the anti-Soviet demonstrations of 1946, these press services used neutral terms such as "students" to refer to loyalist youth activists; see, e.g., the AP report in *China Mail*, Feb. 26, 1946, p. 1.

tine." Lamb claims, however, that a new spirit of resistance entered into the movement in mid-May. He admits that this shift was due in part to the efforts of Communist agents, who had been "fishing in these alluring troubled waters" the C.C. Clique created, but goes on to say that there is "more to this well-synchronised movement than that." Lamb concludes that the Anti-Hunger, Anti–Civil War Movement "is in fact a manifestation, albeit in many ways half-baked, of the nearest approach to public opinion which can exist in this country, against Kuomintang fascism, which . . . has not hesitated to use its secret police and hired ruffians to wreak vengeance on collegiate liberalism."

Lamb was not the only foreigner to express this view of the 1947 protests; U.S. ambassador John Leighton Stuart made similar points in the memos he sent to the American secretary of state in late May and early June. Stuart began a June 4 memo, for example, by criticizing the attempts of Jiang Jieshi and other officials to "explain away the student and other agitations as incited by Communists."[92] The ambassador admitted that there certainly were "Communist agents planted in colleges" who were "instigating disturbances and inflaming the grievances of students," but went on to say that "if ever there could be an unmistakable manifestation of the people's will," it was "in the present and widespread swelling demand for peace." In a similar vein, in a May 30 memo dealing with the student protests against the Civil War, Stuart had included the rhetorical question: "Will the Government leaders regard the will of the people, now at last articulate, as a mandate to be carried out in the spirit of new republican principles?"[93]

Since (as the preceding paragraphs suggest) the sympathy observers feel toward mass actions often has much to do with whether they consider the events to be orchestrated by outside agitators, it is worth concluding this section with some comments on the relative spontaneity of loyalist and radical student demonstrations of the mid-1940's. This issue is a complex one, since both sides consistently claimed that their own displays were true manifestations of popular feeling, but that their opponents' were put-up jobs. Thus many contemporary accounts of specific events cancel each other out. The only thing that is clear from the conflicting evidence is that none of the events examined thus far should be typed as either wholly "spontaneous" or wholly "manipulated."* Outside agitators played some

---

*There is a tendency in the literature on popular unrest to think in terms of a clear distinction between the actions of spontaneous "crowds" and manipulated "mobs." Both scholarly discussions of the topic, such as Rudé's influential *The Crowd in History*, and firsthand descriptions of mass actions tend to divide events according to this dichotomy. In order to grasp the historical reality, however, it is more useful to think in terms of a continuum; most Shanghai demonstrations fall in the gray area between the completely orchestrated rally and the completely spontaneous crowd action.

role in even the most "genuine" expressions of popular anger, but many participants in even the most "orchestrated" events truly believed in the slogans they were shouting.*

This said, there is reason to believe that, on the whole, the radical youth movement enjoyed a broader base of popularity than the loyalist one, especially after the campaign against American brutality began in late December 1946. Diplomatic communications such as those cited above are one important indicator of this, since British and American diplomats were allies of the Generalissimo and shared his concern with the problem of Communist manipulation. Despite their support of the GMD and suspicion of the CCP, these diplomats were openly skeptical about the "spontaneity" of loyalist displays such as the anti-Soviet marches, yet they admitted that radical marches were true expressions of widely held student grievances in which the machinations of Communist agents played a secondary part at best.

Another important sign that the radical youth movement was more popular within the student community was that loyalists seemed to grow less interested in staging May 4th–style mass actions between mid-1946 and mid-1947. Pro-GMD students never completely abandoned their efforts to use such "protests" to attack the CCP and factional rivals during this period, as the C.C. Clique's role in the Jiaotong School Protection Campaign illustrates. Loyalist mass actions involving youths did grow much less frequent after the Anti–Civil Disturbance demonstration of June 1946, and in some of those that did take place (such as the Youth Reconversion Day parade) the organizers tried hard to disguise the fact that these events were orchestrated loyalist spectacles rather than protest marches.

One can stress several interrelated factors in explaining this decreasing interest on the part of loyalists. One can argue, for example, that student

---

*The claims that Communist agitators were the main agents behind much protest activity, first made in GMD-controlled press organs and more recently resurrected in PRC memoirs and histories, greatly overestimate the power of these few activists, though underground CCP organizers did indeed play some role in many radical marches. Conversely, although there may be truth to radical claims that events such as the anti-Soviet "protests" were engineered by the GMD, this does not negate the fact that these loyalist displays capitalized on genuine patriotic outrage. For example, in a recent memoir, former CCP underground member Wu Cengliang claims that the GMD masterminded the loyalist marches of February 1946, but then admits that anti-Soviet feeling was so strong that Communist organizers (like himself) had to join the marches or risk alienating themselves from the masses, although once involved in the movement they tried to keep it from turning into an all-out attack on communism per se. Interestingly, Wu's discussion of the Anti-Soviet Movement, which appears in an unpublished 1981 reminiscence entitled "Huiyi Jiaoda xuesheng yundong de jige duanpian" (A few remembered fragments concerning the Jiaotong University student movement; copy in my possession), is not included in the otherwise almost identical published version of his memoir, "Kangzhan shengli qianhou Jiaoda xuesheng yundong duanpian."

supporters of the GMD simply decided that there were more efficient ways to serve their cause than to take to the streets. One can also argue, however, that the anti-radical demonstrations of 1946 were too patently phony to have an effect upon the academic community, foreign observers, or the population at large; as soon as GMD leaders realized this, they began to spend less energy on building a loyalist youth movement. Finally, one can argue that the tactical shift away from May 4th–style actions had less to do with the intent of loyalist students than with their inability to convince ordinary students to take part in such events as the period progressed.

There is probably some truth in each explanation, but since virtually no memoirs by former leaders of the loyalist youth movement have come to light, it is difficult to say much more about the first two, except that Communist sources support the second argument. Less biased sources do, however, add some credence to the suggestion that anti-radical students grew less able to mobilize their classmates as time went on. For example, English-language press accounts show that loyalist youths tried to drum up support for a renewed series of anti-Soviet protests during March 1947. But, in spite of covering city walls with posters decrying Soviet interference in Chinese domestic affairs and announcing plans for classroom strikes and marches in late March, anti-radical students do not seem to have succeeded in staging a single mass action during this month.[94]

Whatever the reason for the loyalist retreat, from mid-1947 until the Communist takeover of 1949 the radical student movement had a virtual monopoly on the staging of mass actions. Loyalist youths never surrendered the streets completely to their radical competitors; some student mass actions that either supported the GMD or were at least equivocal in their political significance did occur during the last two years of the Republican era. But the great majority of student demonstrations after June 1947, such as the large anti–U.S. imperialism bonfire rally at Jiaotong University the following May 4, had an unmistakably radical intent.[95]

Radicals occasionally boasted that their control of the streets during the second half of the Civil War era was a sign that the GMD had lost its mandate to rule. This point of view is put most forcefully in a pamphlet student protesters distributed on Sun Zhongshan's birthday in November 1947. Entitled "The Shanghai Student Alliance's Announcement to All Its Compatriots in Remembrance of the President's Birthday," this leaflet cited the fact that the previous month the GMD had not "dared" to "celebrate" the anniversary of the 1911 Revolution and now did not "dare to hold a large-scale memorial for the president's birthday"; this fear of public ceremonies was proof that Jiang's "evil designs" had alienated the masses from the ruling party.[96]

The full implications of the indictment of the GMD contained in this leaflet can be understood only within the context of China's distinctive political culture. Throughout Chinese history, every emperor was expected to prove that he was a true "son of Heaven" and hence deserved the Heavenly Mandate by performing appropriate sacrifices on specific holy dates (to keep the cosmos in harmony with the earth) and by treating the people benevolently (as Mencius said, although Heaven alone could grant or withdraw its Mandate, Heaven always "sees with the eyes and hears with the ears of the people"). In such a context, the GMD's failure to mark the holiest days in its own revolutionary calendar, the anniversary of the 1911 Revolution and the birthday of the party's founder, in an appropriately grand fashion was easy to read as an ominous sign. If, as the radical handbill implied, this failure resulted from the fear that any public event involving large groups of people would take on anti-government overtones, then the GMD's grip on the Mandate of Heaven was indeed slipping fast. In the end, it would be troops from the countryside rather than students who would deliver Shanghai to the Communists in 1949, but by upstaging official ceremonies with acts of subversive street theater throughout the Civil War era radical youths played a key role in making this finale possible.

 TEN

THE POWER OF
STUDENT PROTEST

CHAPTERS SUCH AS THE PRECEDING ONE provide clear proof that Shanghai student demonstrations could be, and often were perceived as, powerful acts. Protests led by educated youths effected changes in official policies, and at times they precipitated the downfall of local and even national leaders. But perhaps the most telling indication of the power students had in Republican Shanghai is the energy those who governed the city devoted to suppressing, containing, or diverting the political activities of educated youths. The severe measures the Shanghai Municipal Council used to try to stop anti-imperialist protests of the Warlord era is a clear sign that the leaders of the International Settlement viewed student-led demonstrations as serious events that posed tangible threats to the treaty port system of foreign privilege. After taking power in 1927, the GMD soon began to share this image of youth movements as dangerous. This was clearest in 1947 when the GMD proved itself willing to risk alienating Western observers and losing the goodwill of Chinese intellectuals rather than to allow student political activities to go unchecked. What gave student protesters their power? Why did the authorities so often view the acts of unarmed youths—whose demonstrations rarely posed discernible physical or economic threats to the running of the city or the state—with so much alarm? These are the questions, to which the June Massacre of 1989 has given new relevance, this chapter attempts to answer.

COMPARATIVE PERSPECTIVES

In dealing with questions of this sort, it is important to remember that student protests in differing cultural and historical contexts have had widely varying results.[1] There are other countries besides China (for example, Burma) where the actions of educated youths have helped topple regimes; there are also many nations (including most Western European ones) in which intensive outbursts of student activism have at best succeeded only in calling the legitimacy of particular policies, institutions, or individual powerholders into question.[2] Although student protests have played an integral role in virtually every phase of China's twentieth-century political transformation, demonstrations led by educated youths have been much more peripheral to other comparable events, such as the Russian Revolution of 1917.[3] The elites that educated youths in various nations have threatened have also viewed and responded to campus unrest in different ways: some (such as those of South Korea) have, like their Chinese counterparts, taken all large-scale student demonstrations seriously and at times used sustained campaigns of violence and intimidation to end such manifestations of discontent; others have tried to dismiss youth movements as unimportant events occurring on the fringe of "real" politics and have reacted more mildly toward even those protests that involved large numbers of students. One goal of this chapter, therefore, is to go beyond the specifics of the Shanghai case and explore some key variables that account for the relative power or powerlessness of different groups of educated youths and the relative seriousness or lack of seriousness of official responses to student demonstrations. It tries to provide some insights, in other words, into why the role of student protesters in Chinese politics is so different from that of their counterparts in other nations, including the United States.

The American campus unrest of the 1960's and 1970's and the wider Civil Rights and Antiwar movements in which students played important roles undeniably had a profound impact upon American politics.[4] In addition, as the Kent State and Jackson State killings of 1970 illustrated, officials sometimes used harsh repressive measures, including guns and tear gas, against American students. Nonetheless, as the events of 1970 also show, American student protesters have generally had a much more limited power than their Chinese counterparts. The student strikes that followed the Kent State and Jackson State shootings were the biggest the United States had ever seen and involved more students than even the largest of China's Republican-era youth movements.[5] Unlike the protests that followed comparable Chinese confrontations between law enforcers and educated youths, however, these American protests did not trigger general strikes by workers, lead to the resignation of top governmental officials, or provoke the government to launch a sustained campaign of mass arrests and violence. Although this chapter does not try to give a definitive answer to the question of why the Chinese and American cases differ, it tries to draw attention to and illuminate the central issues such an answer would need to address.

STUDENTS AND THEIR ALLIES

Several overlapping factors account for the power of student movements in Republican Shanghai, beginning with the ability of educated youths to gain the support of members of other classes and work with them. Although students may have lacked economic clout, throughout the Republican era they continually proved able to win sympathy and support from other social groups, whose actions could in turn have an impact upon municipal, national, and in some cases even international markets. This ability of student protesters to influence financial affairs meant that the authorities had at least one pragmatic reason to fear youth movements. It is easy to see why, for example, representatives of foreign business interests considered the youthful leaders of the mass movements of 1919 and 1925 dangerous, since students played key roles in organizing, mobilizing support for, and enforcing the terms of the multi-class boycotts and general strikes of those years.

In addition, even though comparable sanba did not occur in 1931 or 1947, economic fears also had an impact on the way the authorities treated the youth movements of these two years. Students involved in the protests of the early 1930's and mid-1940's continually called on Chinese of all classes to join them in their fight to save the nation and at times proposed the launching of new general strikes. The Nationalist government thus had good cause to worry that youth movements would lead to recurrences of the multi-class protests seen during the Warlord era. This was especially true in late May 1947, since a series of rice riots and worker protests against inflation had occurred in Shanghai and other cities in late April and early May, just before students had begun agitating for a June 2 sanba.[6]

This ability of Shanghai's educated youths to find allies among members of other classes, particularly workers, sets them apart from student protesters in other contexts. One of the main reasons that the student protests throughout Western Europe and the United States in the 1960's and early 1970's rarely achieved the same order of results as the Shanghai struggles of the Republican era was the failure of militant educated youth to forge comparable alliances outside the intelligentsia. When, as happened in France in May 1968, worker and student agendas did converge, the results were dramatic.[7] Such convergences were, however, the exception rather than the rule. For example, at the same time that French workers were joining students on the streets, their West German counterparts were viewing university unrest in their own country in an increasingly negative light,[8] and efforts by American students to expand the university protests of spring 1970 into a general strike involving workers à la Paris events of 1968 failed.[9] Because of a combination of cultural and political factors (dealt with below) large segments of the Shanghai population frequently viewed student demonstrators as heroes worthy of support. In contrast, according to public opinion polls, during the 1960's and 1970's high percentages of Americans felt that campus activists had no business in politics and viewed student protests unfavorably.[10]

REPUBLICAN CHINA AS A DEVELOPING NATION

Another factor that helps explain the potency of youth movements in Republican Shanghai is the special status of students as a presumptive elite. Evidence from comparative case studies of student unrest suggests a strong negative correlation between the percentage of youths in a given country able to attend college and the likelihood that even relatively small student protests can have profound political consequences. Thus, Philip Altbach argues in a recent essay, student protesters have had more impact in developing nations (an admittedly vague category, but one that Republican China surely fits), where college students form a small and cohesive elite group, than they have had in most of the industrialized nations of Western Europe and North America, where much larger numbers of people generally have access to institutions of higher education.[11]

The reasons for this difference are complex and relate to the kinds of issues that lead students in developing nations as opposed to industrialized states to take to the streets, as well as to the sheer size of student populations. Most important, independence struggles and resistance directed at foreign colonial or imperial powers have provided the context for many of the strongest youth movements. In developing nations, the role of educated youths in such struggles has frequently had implications for future campus activism: in some cases participation in independence movements has helped students earn a reputation as selfless patriots among segments of the general population, who, even after foreign threats have disappeared, continue to allow such youths to speak in the name of the people as a whole. Thus, in many Latin American nations, as in China, students have come to be "considered repositories of the ideals of their nation and spokesmen for their people."[12]

As important as images of patriotism are, the simple fact that comparatively small numbers of people are generally able to attend institutions of higher learning in developing nations remains perhaps the main reason for the authorities' fear of even relatively small students movements in those lands. In 1970, when 5,000 or even 10,000 students out of a population of 7 million college students staged a demonstration in the United States,[13] it was easy for the authorities to dismiss such an action as simply rash behavior on the part of a group of young men and women. Those who govern even the largest of developing nations do not have this luxury; they are forced to take student protests seriously and view them as indications that a significant part of the nation's pool of future officials is growing disaffected with the regime and hence may be unwilling to serve it. The central government in Nanjing certainly did not have the luxury of disregarding a demonstration of 10,000 college students during China's Civil War era, since this number represented more than 10 percent of the entire college population of GMD-controlled China.[14]

TRADITIONAL ROLES OF THE INTELLIGENTSIA

Because of the high status accorded intellectuals in Chinese culture and the long-standing links between education and political power in Chinese society, student disaffection had an additional meaning within the Republican context, a meaning that added further to the potential power of student protesters. Long before the May 4th Movement, a tradition of viewing scholars and examination candidates as the conscience of the nation was well established. Imperial rulers had not always treated their learned critics kindly, of course, as the tragic life histories of the Song Dynasty scholar Chen Dong (see Chapter 3) and many others illustrate. Within the official ideology, however, it was accepted that intellectuals (including students) had a duty to speak out when the nation was threatened by corrupt officials or foreign aggressors and that rulers should listen to what these dissenters said. Even those intellectuals who sacrificed their lives while fulfilling their roles as critics of the state helped reinforce these ideals, since the authors of official dynastic histories elevated Chen Dong and others like him to the status of heroic martyrs. This image of the patriotic scholar-official as noble critic was enshrined in operatic performances and popular lore as well as official records: for example, Qu Yuan, the hero honored each year during the Dragon Boat Festival, one of the most important celebrations in the folk calendar, was a loyal minister who had committed suicide after proving unable to convince his sovereign to take his advice.

The facts that Shanghai's student protesters belonged to a culture with a long history of treating education as a legitimate route to political power and that even in 1919 these youths considered themselves (and were viewed as being) part of an ongoing tradition of intelligentsia dissent had important implications for the potency of their acts. Unlike their counterparts in nations, such as Tsarist Russia, in which education was not the main traditional route to the top echelons of the bureaucracy, Chinese students did not have to strive to create a political role for themselves, but could as intellectuals claim a right to participate in the affairs of the state.[15] History and tradition also made it easier for educated youths to bring workers into their mass movements: ordinary citizens were used to taking political cues from scholars and hence did not need special persuasion to treat student streetside lectures as serious forms of discourse.

Conversely, history and tradition made it difficult for China's native rulers to dismiss the claims of educated youths out of hand by saying that students had no business taking part in politics. Foreign observers of Republican student protests *did* frequently advance this viewpoint: English-language press accounts and diplomatic dispatches are filled with statements saying in effect, "we would never allow youths to meddle in important affairs in this way." But although Warlords and GMD officials occasionally issued statements calling on students to stick to their books and leave the governance of the country to those in power, it was hard for them to back up these claims with appeals to tradition.

History and tradition, finally, played a crucial role in giving student protesters self-confidence. Here the similarities and contrasts with the Russian case are of interest. Samuel Kassow's work on Russian campus unrest argues that the student movement of late Tsarist times was plagued by identity crises and self-doubts; participants engaged in an "unending argument" about the movement's "nature and purpose," and educated youths "asked themselves whether they were politically important." An awareness of the smallness of their numbers and arguments by revolutionaries that only workers could lead the nation out of autocracy diminished the self-confidence of Russian activists. By the beginning of the twentieth century, these factors could be offset somewhat by invoking memories of the great student strike of 1899 and other historic events. Even if a new coterie of educated youths felt that their own protests fell short of these earlier struggles, they could at least place their actions within the context of an ongoing tradition of protest, and an attachment to this tradition of *studentchestvo* heroism helped inspire new generations of students to take to the streets.[16] Nonetheless, feelings of marginality and doubts concerning the ultimate value of student protests continued to plague the Russian student movement up until 1917.

Shanghai students had fewer causes for insecurity regarding their political role and indeed exhibited less. Shanghai's twentieth-century students have always been able to locate their actions within an ongoing heroic tradition of political engagement stretching back for millennia. After the student protests of 1919 succeeded in triggering a sanba and bringing about the downfall of three of the nation's leading officials, students had little reason to doubt the efficacy of their actions. As with their counterparts in Latin America (where student-led university reform movements in several countries achieved important victories during the first decades of this century and campus activism has continued to be a central factor in governance)[17] and Korea (where student demonstrations brought down the regime of Syngman Rhee in 1960 and have since become an endemic part of national politics),[18] early victories provided subsequent generations of Chinese students both a sense of purpose and the self-confidence to take collective action. Success in this case clearly bred success.

STUDENT PROTEST AS SUBVERSION

As significant as the three factors discussed above are, they alone are not enough to account for the efficacy of Republican student movements. The knack Chinese students had for inspiring members of other classes to take political action, the special status they had as people being groomed to join the governmental elite, and their ability to place their protests within a long-standing tradition of intelligentsia dissent—all these were unquestionably important. However, to answer the question posed earlier of why China's foreign and native rulers viewed youth movements with such alarm throughout the Republican era, another factor must be worked into the equation: the ability of student protesters to appropriate and subvert the meaning of official rhetoric, forms of action, and organizational techniques.

A dominant theme in many of the preceding chapters is that there was a close, though complex, symbiotic relationship between the behavior of student protesters and that of the powerholders they challenged. For example, Chapter 2 drew attention to the bureaucratic principles May 4th activists followed in forming the Shanghai Student Union; Chapter 8 argued that radical youths and their opponents used similar persuasive techniques to try to influence the political views of the untutored laobaixing; and several different sections highlighted the ties between student mass actions and official ceremonies and procedures, such as courtroom trials (Chapter 7) and government-sponsored holiday celebrations (Chapter 3). In sum, the preceding pages are filled with examples of students' performing various acts of usurpation, appropriating roles, rituals, and modes of discourse ordinarily reserved for officials, policemen, judges, and other people in positions of authority. These acts of usurpation deserve special attention here because it was through them that student protesters gained their greatest power—the power to create a subversive street theater that challenged and undermined the legitimacy of policies, institutions, political figures, and at times even entire regimes.

RITUAL, THEATER, AND CHARISMA

To understand fully the subversive power of Shanghai student protesters, we must ask how the powerholders these youths challenged legitimated their own position. How did those who ruled Shanghai and the Chinese nation assert hegemony? What modes of discourse and forms of action did they use to show that they alone had the right to make certain decisions and perform certain political acts? How, in short, did they cultivate an aura of charisma, so that at least some of those they governed accepted the power they exercised as something other than illegitimate brute force?

Clifford Geertz provides perhaps the best methodology for answering these sorts of questions, in a recent essay entitled "Centers, Kings, and Charisma: Reflections on the Symbolics of Power." Taking Max Weber's ideas concerning "charismatic authority" as his starting point, Geertz argues that charisma is the key to explaining how governing elites justify their power.[19] He notes, however, that Weber was vague about the precise mechanisms through which elites perpetuate their charisma and that, with a few notable exceptions, later scholars have done little to clarify this issue. Geertz attempts to rectify this by tracing the way rulers in three different cultural and historical settings—Elizabethan England, fourteenth-century Java, and nineteenth-century Morocco—used royal processionals to enhance their charisma. He ends by parting company with Weber on one crucial point: Weber claimed (and later Weberians have continued to argue) that modern societies become "deritualized" as they grow more "rational" and hence their governors become less dependent upon ceremonial forms; Geertz stresses that *all* elites use rituals to give their actions an aura of charisma.[20] To illustrate this point, Geertz looks at the role of personal appearances by candidates in contemporary American presidential campaigns, claiming that here we see the royal progress recast in a quintessentially "modern" idiom.

In Geertz's view, the important thing about processions, and by extension other official ceremonies as well, is that they link governing elites with symbols and values that a particular society considers in some way "sacred," a linkage that gives political power a numinous air.

> At the political center of any complex society . . . there is both a governing elite and a set of symbolic forms expressing the fact that they are indeed governing. No matter how democratically the members of

the elite are chosen (usually not very) or how deeply divided among themselves (usually much more than outsiders imagine), they justify their existence and order their actions in terms of a collection of stories, ceremonies, insignia, formalities, and appurtenances that they have either inherited or, in more revolutionary situations, invented. It is these—crowns and coronations, limousines and conferences—that mark the center as center and give what goes on there its aura of being not merely important but in some odd fashion connected with the way the world is built.[21]

Geertz's essay is problematic in one crucial way: it treats the definition and possession of the center as an almost purely consensual process.[22] By admitting that "in more revolutionary situations" elites invent symbolic forms to justify their power, Geertz admits the possibility of conflicting images of the center. But even in non-revolutionary times, when elites rely upon inherited rather than invented ceremonial forms, and even when there is a fair degree of consensus concerning the ideals and symbols members of a polity consider sacred, the right of those in power to represent and speak from the center is often disputed. Geertz's vision of the political center has much in common with Gramsci's concept of hegemony: both seek to explain how rulers use means other than domination to rule. Gramsci, however, emphasizes that elites must continually *reimpose* their worldview upon the rest of the population and *reclaim* their rights to charismatic symbols; simply asserting their authority is not enough. Even though Geertz's main arguments remain valid, therefore, it is worth remembering that elites must actively defend as well as simply reside at the center. In the words of British cultural theorist Stuart Hall: "Hegemonizing is hard work."[23]

This caveat aside, Geertz's depiction of powerholders as dependent upon stories and political rituals to assert their right to reside at and speak from the political "center" has much relevance for the study of popular protests.[24] This is particularly true of demonstrations that mimic official forms and procedures, since this kind of political theater represents a symbolic attempt to subvert or take control of the ceremonies and stories elites use to justify their rule. To put it differently, this form of theater can strip a governing elite of its "charisma" either by raising doubts about the centrality of the symbols and values stressed in official rites or more frequently by implying that the present rulers do not truly represent or speak from the political center.*

---

*My argument here is influenced heavily by Lukes, "Political Ritual," which argues that both official ceremonies (such as coronations) and popular demonstrations seeking to change the status quo should be seen as "political rituals," which Lukes defines as "symbolic strategies" that "different groups [use] to defend or to attain power vis-à-vis other groups." I prefer,

The concepts of "center" and "countertheater" help to put the youth movements of the Republican era in perspective. If Geertz's claims regarding the importance of charisma are correct—and his arguments are persuasive—officials' alarm at the political activities of educated youths is easily understood. Powerholders could not ignore student statements that looked like official edicts, shadow police forces, or mock trials. By their very nature these acts subverted the "stories, ceremonies, insignia, formalities, and appurtenances" the authorities used to legitimate their position at the political center. And no ruling elite's grip on Republican Shanghai was so secure that it could afford to take such subversion in this political center lightly.

STUDENT CHALLENGES TO FOREIGN PRIVILEGE

One might object that whereas native officials may have been concerned about protecting their position at the center from student threats, notions of legitimacy have little relevance for explaining the behavior of foreign authorities, whose distrust of student protests usually stemmed from fears that youth movements would result in anti-foreign riots. This objection is only half-true. There is no question that thanks in large part to the specter of Boxerism, the rulers of Shanghai's concessions tended to be more concerned than native powerholders with the problem of anti-foreign violence. But foreign authorities were also troubled by the potential of students protests to undermine the legitimacy of their position, for even semicolonial elites depend upon "stories" (which they tell both to those they govern and to audiences in their home countries) and "ceremonies" to justify their rule.

The events of June 1919 provide the clearest example of a case in which Western authorities moved to suppress a youth movement for reasons that had less to do with fears of a new "Boxerism" than with notions of legitimacy. During the May 4th Movement, the activities that most concerned the Shanghai Municipal Council were those carried out by student secu-

---

however, to describe demonstrations as acts of theater rather than as "rituals" for several reasons. First, the Chinese term for ritual, *li*, refers exclusively to orthodox acts. Second, in ritual performances all those present are participants of a sort, whereas in theatrical events there is a clearer (though by no means always definite) distinction between actors and audience. Third, participants in rituals generally think it essential to follow inherited scripts. Indeed they often see the efficacy of their acts as dependent upon replication of an earlier performance. In contrast, participants in the improvisational political theater of demonstrations (though often taking many lines and their blocking from earlier performances) do not feel the need to stay within preset limits. For a more comprehensive discussion of the distinctions and overlaps between ritual and theater, see Schechner, *Ritual, Play, and Performance*, pp. 196–222; for further comments on this topic with specific reference to the Chinese case, see Esherick and Wasserstrom, "Acting Out Democracy."

rity forces and inspection teams. Western critics claimed that these students were "usurping" roles reserved for "duly constituted authorities," that is, for the British-run Shanghai Municipal Police. What made this particular usurpation so powerful was that, as Frederic Wakeman's work on Shanghai police forces shows, one of the main "stories" foreigners told to justify the concession system was that the Chinese were unable to maintain order among themselves.[25] When Boy Scouts and other youths proved capable of keeping the peace during mass actions, this undermined the validity of the foreigners' story of Chinese incapacity. In addition, since these youths wore badges and uniforms similar to those used by the official police, they challenged the foreign governing elite's monopoly over the distribution of one kind of charismatic insignia; this explains why the Municipal Council's June proclamation specifically forbade Chinese from wearing such items.[26]

The Boy Scouts and members of shadow security forces were not the only protesters whose actions posed implicit or explicit threats to the legitimacy of the concession system. For example, when student inspection teams enforced the boycotts of 1919, 1925, and 1931, they usurped another role claimed by foreigners: that of regulating international trade and controlling China's customs system. The propaganda distributed by educated youths also challenged the presumptions and undermined the authority of Shanghai's foreign governing elites. One of the main foreign defenses of the concession system—a theme that encompasses the argument that foreigners were better able to maintain order in the city than were the Chinese authorities—was that groups such as the Shanghai Municipal Council were part of an effort to civilize China by introducing Western ideals and methods to a savage people. Student propagandists of the Republican era (and those of 1925 in particular) used a variety of methods to undercut this story of Chinese barbarity and backwardness and to show that it was often foreigners who were guilty of uncivilized behavior. Students even used cartoons and posters that portrayed foreigners as animals to make their point. This kind of bestial symbolism had a strong impact, in part at least because so many of the "stories" foreigners used to defend their privileged position in China assumed that the Chinese were somehow less rational, more childlike, less fully human than Westerners.*

---

*The preceding paragraphs have highlighted some of the "stories" foreigners used to legitimate the concession system, but have said nothing about the "ceremonies" upon which Western powerholders depended. As far as I know, no work has been done to date on the political rituals foreigners in Shanghai used to justify their authority. Even a casual survey of the pages of the *North China Herald* shows, however, that throughout the last decades of the nineteenth century and the first decades of the twentieth they used a rich variety of public spectacles (public reviews staged by foreign volunteer corps and members of the Shanghai Municipal Police, celebrations of Empire Day, dedications of buildings and statues) to reinforce the legitimating stories alluded to above.

STUDENTS AND THE GMD CENTER

Whereas youth movements of the 1910's and 1920's challenged the legitimacy of concession authorities, student protests of later decades posed much greater problems for the GMD. Unlike the defenders of foreign privilege, the GMD based its claim to political legitimacy on much more than an ability to administer justice and maintain order. Although some party rituals and ceremonies stressed these familiar themes, the GMD depended upon presentations of itself as a popular, patriotic party of the masses to justify its right to rule. The GMD's attempt to define the political center in this fashion, as an arena marked by symbols of national renewal as well as of stability, had important implications for protesters. It meant that specific acts of usurpation—for example, the "popular tribunals" of the 1930's, the selection of "people's delegates" in 1946 following the GMD elections for the National Assembly—were not the only events that challenged the legitimacy of the GMD. Any patriotic mass action that was not part of an officially sanctioned mass movement threatened the party's hold on the political center, since by its very nature such an act raised doubts about the party's claim that it alone spoke for "the people" and the cause of national salvation.

When the protesters were students, the implication was even more troubling for the GMD. The party emphasized images of newness and youth in its rhetoric and rituals. Jiang Jieshi and his followers filled their speeches with calls to work to build a "new" China, and their words and actions made it clear that they expected educated youths to serve as the vanguard corps and standard-bearers for this effort. Jiang's attempts to mobilize student cadres to lead the New Life Movement and his organization of the Youth Army at the end of World War II are but two of the most obvious ways the Generalissimo used the symbolism of youth and newness to try to bolster his personal power. His concern with this kind of symbolism was shared by other party leaders, as the prominent role marching youths played in virtually every major GMD ceremonial occasion of the 1930's and 1940's attests. Even Wang Jingwei's pro-Japanese GMD and the puppet regimes in Shanghai and other cities felt the need to organize "patriotic" student movements of their own and to launch drives such as the New Republic Movement. These are clear signs of just how entrenched at the political center images of newness and youth had become by the latter half of the Republican era.

Another reason radical protests by educated youths were particularly vexing to the GMD relates to the special role students and scholars played in the revolutionary process that culminated in the Northern Expedition.

Educated youths figured centrally in the GMD's rise to power. Many of the party's original members had been radicalized while studying in Japan. Many of the cadres responsible for the GMD victories of the mid-1920's joined the party after participating in the student-led mass movements of 1919 and 1925. Struggles such as the May 4th and May 30th movements also contributed to the success of the Northern Expedition in other ways; they not only familiarized the population at large with protest techniques but also helped give resonance to the anti-imperialist rhetoric the GMD subsequently used to such effect.

Perhaps as important as these various tangible contributions of students to the Northern Expedition, however, was the symbolic role patriotic scholars played in the GMD's "myth of origin." Such myths—tales that explain how and why a governing elite rose to power and that link it to positive symbols from the past—are among the most important stories a ruling group tells about itself to justify its rule.* In the case of the post-1927 GMD, the dominant figure in these myths was Sun Zhongshan, a man deified as the father of the Revolution as well as the party, whose memory was invoked rhetorically or ritualistically (for example, through visits to his tomb and readings of his will) on almost all major occasions of state. Symbols associated with Sun were not, however, the only images from the past in the GMD's myths of origin. Party leaders also presented themselves as part of two other traditions: militant Confucian loyalism (as exemplified by scholar heroes such as Zeng Guofan, the suppressor of the Taiping Uprising, with whom Jiang Jieshi in particular identified); and the May 4th cultural renaissance.[27]

The three traditions exemplified by Sun Zhongshan, Zeng Guofan, and the May 4th students are in many senses at odds. Sun lived most of his life as a rebel who founded and collaborated with secret societies; Zeng spent much of his suppressing disorder; one of the main intellectual inspirations behind the May 4th Movement was an iconoclastic desire to destroy the very rituals and moral prescriptions Confucian scholars celebrated. Despite these apparent contradictions, GMD stories and ceremonies presented the party as rooted in all three traditions, that is, as a force that was morally conservative yet politically revolutionary, fervently nationalistic

---

*The tendency for such stories to use positive symbols from the past holds true even for elites that explicitly claim to be creating a wholly new political center. Among the best examples of this are the French revolutionaries of the late eighteenth century. While repudiating virtually all political symbols identified with the Old Regime, these revolutionaries relied heavily upon representations of figures associated with classical Greece and Rome to legitimate their new order. See Hunt, *Politics, Culture, and Class*, pp. 20, 28; and Ozouf, *Festivals and the French Revolution*, which illustrates the way in which revolutionaries incorporated traditional symbols, motifs, and icons into these new rituals celebrating the birth of a wholly "new" France.

yet intent upon bringing China into the modern age by learning from the West.

The GMD's desire to present itself in this fashion required that its political rituals draw somewhat selectively from each of the three traditions. Thus, for example, the anti-Confucian iconoclasm of May 4th activists was largely ignored in GMD celebrations of the anniversary of the 1919 youth movement, and Sun's identification with bandit heroes of the past was downplayed in rites honoring the Guofu (Father of the Nation).[28] Indeed, one of the most interesting things about GMD political rituals is their eclectic, idiosyncratic blending of images and ideas from clashing traditions. Nowhere was the peculiar nature of the resulting mix revealed more clearly than in the New Life Movement, whose participants used May 4th propaganda techniques to spread moral precepts drawn from the Confucian tradition as well as the political ideals embodied in Sun's Three People's Principles.

The main significance of the GMD's myths of origin for understanding the power of student protest is that two of the three historical traditions with which party leaders identified were scholarly ones. The GMD never claimed to be the party of a specific class; rather, its leaders tended to criticize the whole idea of class interest and class conflict as Communist notions that contradicted the basic national and cultural unity of all Chinese. After the Nationalists came to power, however, and the CCP began to identify itself with the worker and peasant masses, the GMD (in part simply by default) began to identify itself with the scholar-official class. The GMD claimed, however, to be run by a distinctly new breed of scholar-officials committed to revolutionary change and modern ideas as well as to traditional moral values, whose characters had been formed by apprenticeships to Sun Zhongshan (in the case of leaders like Jiang) or participation in the May 4th Movement (in the case of officials such as Hu Shi).

The GMD's identification with the scholar-official class and the student protest tradition gave educated youths the power to delegitimize the party. Student protests on the anniversary of the May 4th Movement that criticized the government of Jiang Jieshi, such as those held in Shanghai in 1947 and 1948, explicitly challenged one of the most sacred stories the GMD used to legitimate its rule, by implying that party leaders were not true to the May 4th spirit. Other student actions posed similar threats to GMD myths of origins. When radical youths lectured the masses in the time-honored fashion of Confucian officials and "preachers," when student protesters distributed anti-GMD pamphlets on the anniversary of Sun Zhongshan's birth that denounced Jiang Jieshi for perverting the true meaning of the Founding Father's principles, they undermined the GMD's image of itself as a revolutionary party that represented the most educated, modern sector of society, the intelligentsia, and had the right to speak in the name of the people as a whole.

STUDENT PROTESTS AS SUBVERSIVE THEATER

One of the keys to the power of Shanghai students during the Republican period, therefore, was their ability to create a theater of public display that undermined the hegemony of foreign and native powerholders by appropriating, parodying, and otherwise subverting official discourse and forms of action. To return to the martial metaphors used at the beginning of this book, student theater became a crucial part of an ongoing battle not for territory but for possession of symbolic high ground: the political center. Through words and actions that attacked legitimating stories and ceremonies, student protesters helped dislodge first the defenders of foreign privilege and then the GMD from this central position. By challenging foreign pretensions of civility and undermining the GMD's claim that it alone spoke for national rejuvenation, revolution, youth, popular patriotism, and intellectual traditions, participants in youth movements established a position for themselves as key figures in the struggle to determine how and by whom their nation should be ruled.

This tendency to appropriate and subvert official rhetoric, symbols, and forms of action is not unique to China's educated youth; students in widely different historical and cultural contexts have engaged in similar kinds of street theater. In one of the most colorful scenes of the American antiwar strikes of 1935, for example, a group of University of Washington students drove a truck covered with loyalist placards in a Seattle Army Day parade and then reversed these placards as soon as the parade reached the center of Seattle to reveal the appeal "Fight Against War."[29] During the American campus struggles of the 1960's, the public burning of draft cards served as a counterculture equivalent to official rituals of enlistment and undermined their meaning; in teach-ins educated youths often assumed roles ordinarily reserved for professors; and in marches against the U.S. involvement in Vietnam, protesters mocked symbols (such as the flag) that the ruling elite routinely used in legitimating rites.[30]

There is also nothing uniquely Chinese about the fact that student protesters of the Republican era gained much of their power from the way their demonstrations undermined hegemonic myths. Samuel Kassow argues, for example, that Russian students posed a significant threat to the state simply because the Tsarist autocracy prided itself on its ability to maintain order. Periodic demonstrations by angry educated youths in

"Russia's large urban centers" had a "corrosive effect on the legitimacy" of this elite, because such a political theater "destroyed any illusion that the system had complete control."[31] Many writers interested in Western European and American student protests have similarly drawn attention to the threats student protests pose to the hegemony of institutions (including the liberal university itself) and ideologies.[32]

What then was special about the Chinese case? More generally, if student demonstrations so frequently constitute a subversive form of political theater that challenges official stories and ceremonies, why do performances of this sort have more power in some places than in others? Some answers to these questions have already been suggested. Audience response is crucial in interpreting all genres of theater, for example, and earlier comments concerning worker reactions to student protests are relevant here. Whereas Shanghai's rickshaw pullers, mill workers, and peddlers frequently showed their support for student usurpations by staging sympathy strikes, joining the youths on the streets, or providing marchers with free food and drink, American laborers more often felt offended or confused by the street theater on and around university campuses in the United States between 1964 and 1974.[33]

There is, however, one important factor that has not been dealt with yet: the varying roles of public displays in different contexts. Geertz is certainly right in stressing that all elites, "no matter how democratically" chosen, rely upon rituals to legitimate their rule. Not all elites, however, are equally dependent upon such rites. In addition, some elites must maintain a monopoly over all forms of political performance in order to maintain their power; others do not. The efficacy of street theater depends in large part on the precise role of political rituals within a given society.

Most generally, as events in Eastern Europe in the late 1980's showed, the symbolism of popular demonstrations is particularly threatening in one-party states. In pluralistic systems, in which competitive forms of street theater such as parades for candidates and election night rallies are considered an ordinary and legitimate part of politics, a popular demonstration is seen as just one more of many such expressions of public opinion. As such, the usurpations involved in radical exhibitions of street theater that mock official forms need not be seen as serious threats in and of themselves, since members of the elites in such systems depend upon the election process itself as well as the consensual public rituals (inaugurations, convocations of parliament, state of the union addresses) to enshrine their rule within a charismatic aura.

In one-party states, on the other hand, there is no room for competitive street theater in normal politics. Public rituals are among the only signs that the ruling elite truly speaks for the people, and hence the party must monopolize performances of this type. These elites do not have the luxury of dismissing popular expressions of dissatisfaction as unimportant. If they have the strength and will to maintain their power, their only choices are to deflect the impact of the unrest by diverting it in a loyalist direction (and hence sustain their hegemony) or to use brute force to stop the performance (and abandon hegemony for domination).

This was precisely the dilemma Jiang Jieshi faced during the student movements of 1931, 1947, and other years. Having never stood for election, his claim to rule in the name of the people was based almost exclusively upon the image of popularity and charisma he cultivated through loyalist marches on anniversary dates and other comparable political rituals. The political theater of student demonstrations and petition drives, whose participants also claimed to speak for the people, posed a potent threat to this charismatic image. Jiang and his followers tried in each case to counter this threat by mounting performances of their own aimed at demonstrating that the GMD leaders were in fact still the leaders rather than the targets of the popular movement. When these efforts failed, Jiang had no choice but to step aside, as he did in 1931, or to abandon all attempts to reimpose his hegemony and turn to what Gramsci justly considers a much weaker form of rule—force and domination.

The power of Shanghai's student protesters came from many sources. Their ability to inspire and mobilize members of the laobaixing and to gain the sympathy of foreign observers empowered their acts. So too did the ease with which they could present themselves as heirs to traditions of patriotic political engagement. In the end, however, their greatest source of strength lay in their ability to undermine the myths and rituals upon which the defenders of foreign privilege and GMD rule relied. Throughout the Republican era, speaking in the name of the people and determined to save the nation, Shanghai's students continually took to the streets to challenge the legitimacy of those who lay claim to the political center. These challenges helped change the course of Chinese history.

EPILOGUE

THE MAY 4TH TRADITION
IN THE 1980'S

WHEN I SET OFF FOR SHANGHAI in August 1986 to research the events treated in the preceding chapters, youth movements comparable to those of 1919 and 1947 seemed a thing of the past. Student demonstrations had occurred periodically after the founding of the People's Republic in 1949. In the early 1950's, for example, students had marched to call for an end to American involvement in Korea, and later in the same decade educated youths had participated in the Hundred Flowers Campaign. In 1966–67, students had played key roles in the Red Guard Movement that launched the Great Proletarian Cultural Revolution, and in 1976 they had taken part in the April 5th Movement that helped signal the end of that "revolution." More recently still, students had joined other dissident intellectuals and workers in writing posters and giving streetside speeches criticizing the government during the Democracy Wall Movement of the late 1970's, and protests involving educated youths had taken place in Chinese cities throughout the first half of the 1980's. In 1980, for example, 87 students in the city of Changsha in Hunan Province staged a hunger strike to protest the government's attempt to keep a non-CCP member from running for local office. And just one year before I arrived in China, youths in Beijing and several other cities had staged a series of anti-Japanese demonstrations. But, although all these post-1949 events shared some features with the great student-led mass movements of the Republican era, none qualified as bona fide successors to struggles such as the May 4th Movement.

The students who took part in the anti-American demonstrations of the early 1950's, for example, though angered by the imperialist actions of a foreign power, had a relationship to China's own rulers very different from that of their predecessors of 1919. May 4th activists had opposed native oppression and corruption as well as foreign aggression, but the anti-imperialist student movement of the early 1950's was directly sponsored by the new CCP regime.[1] Since there was no anti-government dimension to these anti-American marches, they had more in common with the GMD-engineered anti-Soviet "protests" of the 1940's than with the marches of 1919.

The Red Guard Movement, a much more complex and important struggle, also had a loyalist dimension that made it fundamentally different from May 4th–style struggles. Students involved in the Cultural Revolution employed many of the same tactics as their pre-1949 predecessors: they too wrote wall posters to express their grievances, surrounded municipal buildings to gain the attention of political leaders, and demanded free passage on trains bound for the capital. In addition, since the Red Guards were as concerned with influencing the laobaixing as earlier generations of educated youths had been, they relied upon many of the same stylistic devices in their propaganda—such as using drawings of tortoises and other kinds of animal imagery to vilify their opponents.[2] Such similarities aside, however, because of their general rejection and hatred of Western culture as well as foreign imperialism, their anti-intellectualism, and their intense personal loyalty to Mao Zedong, the Red Guards need to be placed outside the May 4th tradition. They themselves acknowledged this by singling out the Boxers rather than the student protesters of 1919 and 1935 as the heroes from the past with whom they identified most closely.[3]

The student activism that accompanied the Hundred Flowers Campaign and the campus struggles of the late 1970's and early 1980's, by contrast, did involve youths who thought of and presented themselves as inheritors of the May 4th tradition. In some cases protesters involved in these events even spoke of their efforts as part of a "new May 4th Movement," and in all cases they showed a fondness for many of the tactics examined in earlier chapters, such as staging mass actions on holidays and days of national humiliation (the first anti-Japanese protests of 1985 took place on the anniversary of the September 18th Incident of 1931), turning funeral marches into events that criticized the government (the April 5th Movement began with ceremonies marking Zhou Enlai's death), and using streetside lectures to spread their ideas (such lectures were common during the Democracy Wall Movement).[4] Such similarities and continuities aside, however, neither the Hundred Flowers Campaign nor the student protests of the 1970's and early 1980's evolved into full-fledged equivalents to the movements examined in earlier case-study chapters. The April 5th Movement of 1976, the Changsha protest of 1980, and the anti-Japanese agitation of 1985 all proved short-lived. And although the Democracy Wall Movement lasted a good deal longer, like the Hundred Flowers Campaign of the 1950's, it never developed into a broad-based mass movement.

THE REBIRTH OF THE MAY 4TH TRADITION

My image of May 4th–style popular struggles as a thing of the past was shattered in December 1986, for in that month a new student movement strikingly like those of the Republican era swept the nation.* I first heard about this new movement in the second week of December, when foreign teachers at Fudan University (where I was living) began to hear rumors that youths at the University of Science and Technology (Keji daxue) in Anhui Province (whose vice-chancellor at the time was the dissident Fang Lizhi) had staged two protests calling for more democracy. Foreign newspapers such as the Hong Kong–based *South China Morning Post*, which was available for sale in local hotels, soon confirmed that protests had taken place on December 5 and on the anniversary of the December 9th Movement. These papers also carried reports of other early December protests in Wuhan and Shenzhen, although the main issue in Shenzhen had not been democracy but a proposed tuition increase.[5]

Fudan itself remained fairly quiet until December 18, even though (as I would learn later) this was not true of other local campuses. Well before December 18, students at East China Normal University (Huadong shifan daxue) had marched around their campus protesting compulsory morning exercises, poor living conditions in the dorms, and the quality of cafeteria food. During this same period, their counterparts at Tongji and Jiaotong began to put up wall posters calling for increased political reforms and complaining about campus living conditions. Tongji's and Jiaotong's position in the vanguard of Shanghai's pro-democracy struggle was no accident. Fang Lizhi had given guest lectures at these two schools earlier in the fall of 1986, and (in part because of these lectures) students at Tongji and Jiaotong had established informal study groups before the Anhui protests to discuss methods for bringing about political change.

Unaware of these developments in other parts of the city, I spent the

---

*My discussion of the 1986–87 protests is based primarily upon firsthand observation of events in Shanghai, discussions with Chinese and Western participants and observers, and newspaper reports. Western wire service reports and translations of relevant Chinese-language press accounts can be found in the December 1986–January 1987 issues of Foreign Broadcast and Information Service (FBIS), *Daily Report: China*. A lively narrative of the protests can be found in Schell, *Discos and Democracy*, pp. 211–44.

morning of December 18 in the Fudan library scanning newspaper reports on the campus unrest of the 1940's and wondering whether Shanghai students would take to the streets to show their support for the new movement. I got my answer around noon when a Chinese friend told me that, given my scholarly interests, I might want to investigate what was happening at Fudan's front gate. Arriving at the gate, I saw a column of some 200–300 youths marching through the campus. Most of their banners simply identified the marchers as students from nearby Tongji University, but some of the placards carried political slogans such as "Long live democracy" (*Minzhu wansui*), "Down with bureaucratism" (*Fandui guanliaozhuyi*), and "Democracy, freedom, equality" (*Minzhu, ziyou, pingdeng*).

Most of the crowd that had gathered seemed as surprised by the march as I was. In fact, since the Chinese press had not carried any reports on the protests in Anhui and Wuhan, I was better prepared for an event like this than some onlookers, although by December 18 many Fudan students and professors had heard about the other protests through Voice of America or BBC radio broadcasts, foreign newspapers, or word of mouth. The best informed of the observers told me that the Tongji students had come to the campus to chide Fudan students for being so slow to join the new student movement and to publicize a citywide march planned for the following day.

I spent the next morning at Tongji University reading the student wall posters, which by then completely covered all the bulletin boards in the center of the campus ordinarily reserved for official announcements (see photographic section). These posters were a varied lot. Some bore poems celebrating "democracy" (*minzhu*), a term whose meaning was seldom defined clearly; others were filled with factual accounts of recent student protests, such as the Anhui demonstration of December 9. Still others contained allusions to youth movements of the Republican era and calls for contemporary students to show as much bravery and patriotism as the heroes of 1919 and 1935. Many challenged Shanghai students to prove that they were as concerned with the fate of the nation as their counterparts in Anhui by staging demonstrations in the center of the city.

Later that same day I watched the first of these demonstrations. Early in the afternoon a large crowd of protesters converged on the headquarters of the Shanghai municipal government, a building that stands on a section of the Bund once part of the International Settlement. Many of the protesters, perhaps 2,000–3,000, had marched together for several miles from the Tongji and Fudan campuses north of the city in order to reach this destination. Other members of the crowd had come from campuses east of downtown Shanghai, such as Jiaotong and Huadong; still others were not students at all but curious passersby. Many demonstrators carried placards, some of which were nothing more than crude banners made of sheets or dish towels, bearing school names or simple slogans celebrating democracy. There was little chanting and, aside from abortive attempts at choruses of the "Internationale," to which few people appeared to know all of the words, little singing either.

The marchers had no clear sense of purpose once they reached the municipal government headquarters. After standing in front of the building for a half-hour or so and calling on the mayor to come out and speak to them, they tried to march down Nanjing Road. This plan was thwarted, however, by a police blockade. Since the demonstrators had no desire for a physical confrontation with the police officers—who for their part looked on the protesters with bemused expressions and seemed uninterested in interfering with the event as long as it kept within certain limits—the marchers headed up Fuzhou Road instead, a narrower street without the same symbolic resonances or commercial importance as Nanjing Road (see photographic section).

The column of demonstrators snaked along Fuzhou Road until it reached People's Square, a space in the center of the city where the Shanghai Race Course once stood and the headquarters of the local Communist party now stands. There the crowd broke up into groups of a few dozen to a few hundred people each, who clustered around youths giving speeches from atop makeshift platforms. A large contingent of police also gathered at People's Square as these speeches began, but rather than try to disrupt the rally, the officers contented themselves with cordoning off the area so that workers and other ordinary citizens would not be able to join the crowd. The only dramatic event that took place during this protest before I left to return to Fudan late in the afternoon came when one youth scaled the fence separating the party headquarters from the public part of the square. He was subsequently taken away by the police stationed in front of the official building.

I heard widely conflicting stories about how the protest ended later that evening and what took place during the early hours of the following morning, and it remains difficult to sort out truth from rumor. According to all accounts, some students went back to their schools directly from the People's Square rally, but others formed a column and marched back to the Bund. The main point of disagreement relates to what happened after these last protesters reached the Bund. Some wall posters and oral reports claimed that a core group of youths remained on the Bund quite late on the night of December 19, and that the police eventually moved in to force them to return to their schools. According to the most extreme of these accounts, the police arrested or beat up several dozen students. I never found any solid confirmation of beatings or formal arrests. Trustworthy sources did agree, however, that police officers forced some students who did not want to leave the Bund to accept offers of free transportation (on buses supplied by the local authorities) back to their campuses.

Whatever actually occurred, the important thing in terms of the development of the movement was that most students believed that incidents of police brutality had taken place. This gave activists a stronger basis for organizing mass actions and a clearer focus when it came to articulating their goals and formulating demands. Prior to what wall posters at Fudan and other campuses dubbed (in time-honored fashion) the "December 19th Incident," local youths had nothing approaching a developed political agenda and were united only by a vague feeling of discontent arising from a variety of disparate grievances, ranging from the poor quality of campus food, to the CCP leadership's tardiness in introducing meaningful political reform, to the fact that Chinese security guards had roughed up a Tongji graduate student for dancing in the aisles during a recent concert by the Western pop group Jan and Dean. As news of the alleged beatings spread after December 19, however, issues of free speech and assembly came to the forefront and the student movement gained a clearer sense of direction.

The Fudan wall posters I read after December 19 were as varied as those at Tongji in terms of style and substance. I saw everything from poems to a lengthy essay comparing the current "December 19th Movement" to the great youth struggles of 1919 and 1935 to a translation of a *Far Eastern Economic Review* article on the Anhui protests of early December. The one element common to most if not all of these posters was the idea that the main goal of the present movement should be to fight for the right to protest itself. Thus, for example, posters that described the December 19th Incident invariably ended with demands that the police stop interfering with the nonviolent protests of patriotic students, which were legal acts according to the nation's constitution. Posters that focused on the official press's silence about the student demonstrations in Shanghai and elsewhere had a similar thrust; they generally ended by calling on the press to tell the people what was really going on. This and a related call for the official media to allow protesters air time to state the reasons behind the current unrest became two of the core demands of the student movement. A third was that local officials should engage in a meaningful dialogue with student leaders.

Not content with simply putting up wall posters condemning the December 19th Incident, Shanghai's students staged additional demonstrations in the center of the city on each of the next several days. These protests generally resembled the December 19 one: they usually began at the Bund and ended with rallies at either People's Square or back at the waterfront. There were some differences, however. First, at least on the two days immediately following the initial demonstration, each new march drew a larger crowd than the last; by Sunday, December 21, according to estimates by some reporters, 20,000–30,000 people were on the streets.[6] This was in part because the number of schools involved in the movement grew steadily: genuinely angered by the same grievances and intent that their alma mater not appear any less patriotic than its counterparts, on each successive day students from several new schools would journey downtown, waving school banners to show which institution they represented.

Another difference was that the later protests were more coherent, less anarchic affairs than the first. This was in part because the December 19th Incident gave students a clearer focus. It was also because students got better organized and more experienced at demonstrating as time went on. During the initial march and rally on December 19, students spent much of their time milling about aimlessly, chatting happily among themselves, and waiting for someone else to do something. There was more organized chanting during later marches and (thanks to the appearance of wall posters with the words to the "Internationale") more effective singing. Students also succeeded in marching up Nanjing Road during some of their later demonstrations, a symbolic victory in their battle with the police, who remained remarkably restrained in their behavior toward the protesters during the days that followed the alleged incidents of brutality.

The demonstrations in the heart of the city were the highpoint of the Shanghai movement, but students either planned or carried out several other mass actions as well. A visit by Shanghai mayor Jiang Zemin (the man promoted to the post of CCP general secretary in 1989 after Zhao Ziyang's fall) to Jiaotong University to try to convince students at his alma mater to refrain from political activities, for example, turned into a protest gathering of sorts when students heckled the mayor for spouting empty platitudes and challenged him with difficult questions that he obviously did not want to answer. Student activists at Fudan and other schools also engaged in shouting matches with members of official student bodies, which protesters claimed were unrepresentative organizations filled with "running dogs" handpicked by the authorities. Then, finally, wall posters appeared throughout the city calling on youths to stage a general classroom strike on Monday, December 22, to complement the ongoing series of demonstrations.

This ambitious strike never took place, however. As the new week started, the Shanghai movement began to wind down instead of intensify. One reason for the movement's decline was that the authorities' patience with the protests was clearly running out. One thing that had emboldened youths in Shanghai and other cities was a feeling that powerful figures within the CCP leadership might look favorably upon pro-democracy activities. Students had attributed a great deal of significance to the fact that in November the leading official newspaper, *Renmin ribao* (People's daily), had published a number of articles praising Anhui's University of Science and Technology (whose administrators were experimenting with running that institution along more democratic lines). The youths viewed articles such as these, as well as the restraint the authorities showed in dealing with the early December protests, as signs that a faction within the ruling elite (that might even include Deng Xiaoping) was as frustrated as the students were with the slow pace of political reform. The youths who marched on December 19 did not feel, therefore, that they were taking any great risk by protesting. Nor did they think that CCP leaders had any cause for concern, since the protests were intended not to attack either the party or its basic policies, but simply to help speed up the implementation of reforms that were supposed to be in the works. By the time the citywide student strike was set to start in Shanghai, however, school administrators and party officials had begun to send clear signals that participants in further, more militant protests would be risking their futures.

The authorities relied primarily upon propaganda rather than force to convince Shanghai's students to return to classes and stay off the streets. The Public Security Bureau pasted official notices on bulletin boards near protesters' wall posters that warned students not to be misled by a "small group of malcontents" trying to stir up trouble on local campuses. Radio broadcasts and newspapers criticized the city's educated youths for creating traffic problems and preventing laborers from going to and from work. School administrators and official student organizations took part in this propaganda campaign as well, by pasting up posters of their own that expressed sympathy for the protesters' goals but cautioned that further demonstrations would hinder rather than help the cause of reform. To back up this point, a few of these posters noted that derogatory comments about leading reformists within the party had been heard during some protests. Official propaganda pieces also used the specter of the Cultural Revolution to denigrate the new protests by claiming that the "democracy" for which the students were clamoring seemed the same as the "great democracy" that the Red Guards had favored, and by reminding readers and listeners that the young activists of the 1960's had also used anonymous wall posters.

These references to Red Guardism were effective, despite the fact that many of the most active protesters in 1986 were freshmen and sophomores of nineteen or twenty, and hence too young to remember much about the excesses of the Cultural Revolution firsthand. Even the youngest protesters had heard horror stories about those dark years from relatives, however, and the idea that they had anything in common with the anti-foreign Red Guards was appalling to many students in 1986, since these youths wanted the authorities to widen, not close, the new "open door." The idea that pro-democracy protests might inadvertently strengthen the hand of opponents of reform within the party also worried students, for they remained convinced that leaders such as Deng Xiaoping (then still considered an ardent reformer) had recently put China on the right path. One indication of this concern was that as soon as official notices condemning the protests as hurting the reforms began to appear, students (who until then had tended not to mention specific political leaders in their writings) began to insert praise for Deng in some of their wall posters and banners.

Pragmatic fears about their own futures also played a role in making students abandon their plans for more militant protests. The case of the disputed events of December 19 aside, the police do not seem to have resorted to strong-arm tactics in Shanghai in 1986. Nonetheless, as soon as the official propaganda campaign against the movement began, youths were well aware that new actions would involve serious risks. Rumors that the party was compiling a blacklist of protesters and that student activists might face imprisonment or at the very least jeopardize their chances of being assigned to a good job after graduation were heard everywhere. Whether such written blacklists existed was irrelevant, because from December 19 on video cameras had routinely scanned the crowds that gathered outside the municipal government building, and students knew that the authorities could use these visual records to identify protesters. The youths, though supportive of Deng Xiaoping, also remembered his treatment of the last protesters he had criticized for going too far: "If you want to know what democracy means," some student banners read, "ask Wei Jingsheng" (a leader of the Democracy Wall Movement incarcerated at the end of that struggle who remained a political prisoner in 1986).

A mixture of factors thus contributed to the decline of the Shanghai protest movement in 1986. Concern that the struggle was hurting the cause it sought to help, worries about the form repression might take, political inexperience, lack of direction, and insufficient organization within the movement all played some part in getting students to return to their campuses. By Christmas, the demonstrations in Shanghai had stopped and—thanks to the efforts of special janitorial brigades—the bulletin boards of all local campuses once again displayed only officially approved notices. But although Shanghai had emerged as the main center for student activity on December 19 and was the site of the largest demonstrations of the year, the 1986 democracy movement did not end when that city's youths stopped marching. Students in Nanjing, who had been fairly quiescent during the first weeks of the month, staged a number of demonstrations in late December.[7] The educated youths of Beijing, who had also been comparatively slow to join the movement, continued to participate in dramatic protests—including a New Year's Day march to Tiananmen Square and public burnings of official newspapers that had criticized the student struggle—up through the first days of 1987.[8] Nonetheless, by mid-January the last of the campus protests had ceased.

Aftershocks from the movement continued to be felt for some time, however. As soon as the demonstrations stopped, the party leadership instigated a purge of several prominent reformist figures and launched a general campaign against "bourgeois liberalization," the trend official propagandists blamed for filling students' heads with incorrect ideas. The highest-ranking victim of this campaign was CCP general secretary Hu Yaobang, a leading proponent of reform whom the party's elder statesmen held responsible for the pro-democracy protests, even though he had issued no public statements supporting the demonstrations and few student wall posters or banners had praised him. Party propagandists never spelled out the precise nature of Hu's supposed role in the movement; instead they contented themselves with blaming the former general secretary for creating the unhealthy ideological atmosphere that made the protests possible and for failing to suppress the demonstrations once the troubles began. The official press also attacked several leading dissident figures within the intelligentsia, including the astrophysicist Fang Lizhi and the journalist Liu Binyan, for helping to stir up discontent.

Whereas these prominent intellectuals were expelled from the party and deprived of some of their posts, few student leaders were punished directly for their actions. A small number of workers were jailed for committing acts of violence—in most cases helping to overturn cars or other vehicles—during specific demonstrations. The police seem to have spent much less energy tracking down student protesters; most of the educated youths arrested or brought in for questioning during or after the movement were released from custody after at most a few hours. The only repercussions most students suffered, in fact, was that they had to spend part of summer 1987 doing community service in rural areas as part of a government program aimed at instilling their generation with a new spirit of self-sacrifice.

THE 1986–1987 "DEMOCRACY" PROTESTS IN PERSPECTIVE

The protests of late 1986 and early 1987 were important because they were the first sustained series of student demonstrations in the People's Republic not directly sponsored or explicitly encouraged by top party officials. As such, they were a throwback of sorts to pre-1949 mass movements. The students who took part in Shanghai's December 19th Movement borrowed some of their rhetoric from the Democracy Wall Movement of the previous decade. In addition, although they vehemently denied any similarities between themselves and the Red Guards, the demonstrations of the late 1960's, as well as those that accompanied the April 5th Movement of 1976 and various struggles of the early 1980's, provided the students of 1986 and 1987 with important scripts from which to improvise.* Nonetheless, though indebted in many ways to various events of the Communist era, the December 19th Movement had most in common with student struggles of the Republican period, particularly those of the Civil War years.

The events of late 1986–87 resembled most closely those of 1947, for the Anti-Hunger, Anti–Civil War Movement of that year also evolved gradually out of a series of sporadic protests triggered by disparate causes. In both the late 1940's and the late 1980's, poor living conditions and inflation played a prominent role in stirring up student discontent, but demands for more free speech and complaints about police brutality ended up at the center of the struggle. In addition, in both spring 1947 and fall 1986 student protesters staged one of their first important protests on a politically charged date (May 4 in one case and December 9 in the other) that the party in power reserved for official celebrations of a revolutionary anniversary. Some of the slogans participants in the two movements

---

*The connections between the Red Guard Movement and the protests of the late 1980's, including those of 1989, are difficult to assess at this time. Any speculation inevitably leads to controversy, because of the way in which official propagandists tried in both 1986 and 1989 to discredit student activism by conjuring up images of the "ten years of chaos" of the Cultural Revolution (see below). The contrasting implications of four facts indicate the complexity of the issue. (1) Many participants in the 1986 and 1989 protests were convinced that their actions and ideas were in no way comparable to those of the Red Guards. (2) Protesters can be influenced in subtle ways even by past movements from which they wish to dissociate themselves; this was clearly the case in 1986 and 1989. (3) Some of the recent actions that looked most like resurrections of Cultural Revolution symbolism were in fact infused with new, quite different meanings: for example, whereas Red Guards carried pictures of Chairman Mao to prove their devotional loyalty to the Great Helmsman, in 1989 similar representations (though often of a younger, pre–Cultural Revolution Mao and sometimes showing Mao alongside other deceased party leaders such as Zhou Enlai and even Liu Shaoqi) were used largely to suggest that current powerholders were falling short of the ideals of earlier leaders of the CCP (see Esherick and Wasserstrom, "Acting out Democracy"). (4) Some of the older graduate students and younger teachers who marched alongside and advised undergraduate protesters during the late 1980's were former Red Guards, as were some of the intellectuals who supported the movement from the sidelines (for a case in point, see Human Rights in China, *Children of the Dragon*, pp. 43–46). For interesting, though at times conflicting, discussion of supposed and real tactical and ideological similarities between the Red Guards and the protesters of the late 1980's, see Yi Mu and Thompson, *Crisis at Tiananmen*, esp. p. 28; A. Chan and Unger, "Voices from the Protest Movement"; and Schwarcz, "Memory, Commemoration, and the Plight of China's Intellectuals."

shouted were even similar or identical—"Long live democracy" figured prominently in the protests of 1947 and 1986 alike—as were many of the tactics they used and the march routes they followed. Virtually all the older Chinese in any kind of official capacity with whom I spoke during and immediately after the December 19th Movement echoed the official party line that protests of the Communist era differed in all respects from those that had helped bring the CCP to power. The similarities to past events were so clear in 1986, however, that men and women who had taken part in the Anti-Hunger, Anti–Civil War Movement as youths usually admitted informally that what students were doing in the era of Deng Xiaoping was indeed strikingly like what they themselves had done in the time of Jiang Jieshi.

Despite these and other points of similarity, the December 19th Movement differed from the Anti-Hunger, Anti–Civil War Movement (and indeed from all the great student struggles of the Republican era) in certain basic ways. Most important, the students of 1986 did not make concerted efforts to mobilize workers to support their cause. Although a large number of individuals not connected with academic institutions joined the marches in Shanghai and other cities in 1986, students not only seemed uninterested in trying to capitalize upon labor discontent but also sometimes actively discouraged workers from joining their movement. For example, one reliable source told me of instances in which workers went to People's Square in Shanghai and, standing just outside the police cordon, called out "We support you, younger brothers" to the youthful protesters. Instead of responding happily to these calls, the students told the workers to go home.

There were several reasons for this lack of interest in worker support. One was elitism on the part of some student protesters. As educated youths, proud of their status as intellectuals, many protesters simply viewed their movement as too high-minded a concern to interest workers. Although on the surface their calls for more "democracy" would appear to have been broad-based appeals for support without any kind of class basis, many student propagandists invested this term with distinctly elitist connotations. Although the most commonly used and best English-language translation for the Chinese term *minzhu* is "democracy," as used in many wall posters the term had little or nothing to do with things such as universal suffrage or political pluralism. Instead, the authors of these posters often implied (as did Fang Lizhi in some of his 1986 speeches) that the most important step the CCP could take to make China more "democratic" was to grant the intelligentsia a stronger voice in political affairs.[9]

But there was another reason besides elitism that made educated youths refrain from trying to mobilize workers in 1986: many students still thought that Deng Xiaoping's regime was essentially on the right track and feared that if workers became involved, the movement would take on an anti-reform hue. They knew that the best way to appeal to laborers was to emphasize issues such as inflation and the new price hikes scheduled for 1987. It would have been easy for students to focus on these topics, since intellectuals like workers in state enterprises were on fixed salaries and hence among those most vulnerable to the hardships caused by price increases. Nonetheless, although all the students I talked with admitted that cost of living problems had played a role in fostering discontent on their campuses, educated youths consistently steered away from making inflation or the price hikes central issues. They feared that any such move would imply criticism of the recent economic experiments with free markets and hence aid the anti-reform camp within the CCP leadership, the very people students claimed were standing in the way of democratization.

One other basic difference between the protests of late 1986 and the great pre-1949 mass movements was that neither anti-imperialist nor anti-foreign sentiment played a major role in the December 19th Movement. Incidents involving foreign powers were a direct cause of the student struggles of 1919, 1925, and 1931, and even though the Anti-Hunger, Anti–Civil War Movement was triggered primarily by domestic incidents, student anger over the behavior of U.S. troops stationed in China and the GMD's reliance on Western aid helped lay the groundwork for the protests of spring 1947. In 1986, by contrast, student protesters were not critical of any foreign power. Anti-foreign feelings have never disappeared completely as an influence on the behavior of Chinese students, as the anti-Japanese protests of 1985 and the anti-African incidents of December 1988 show all too clearly.[10] Nonetheless, in the 1986 protests, as far as I could tell, anti-foreignism was not a factor: if the students referred to foreign powers at all, it was to praise those that were more "democratic" than China.

The comparatively limited scope and effectiveness of the December 19th Movement also differentiated it from the great student struggles of the Republican era. Although demonstrations occurred in cities throughout China in 1986 and early 1987, the fight for democracy did not evolve into a true national movement. Students in different parts of the country did not come together, as their predecessors of 1919 and other years had, to form an umbrella union capable of coordinating nationwide protest activities. Nor did youths in individual cities establish sophisticated, highly bureaucratized local protest leagues. Even in Shanghai, where the December 19th Movement reached its peak, protest actions were generally carried out in an ad hoc fashion throughout the struggle. In part because of their lack of organizational structures, the protesters of 1986–87 also proved unable to carry through any sustained mass actions other than marches and rallies. Thus no equivalents to the dramatic train commandeerings of the 1930's and 1940's or the long-term classroom boycotts of the Warlord era took place at this time.

A final contrast has to do with the comparative ease with which the authorities were able to end the December 19th Movement. The student movements examined earlier never ended until either the participants felt they had won important concessions from the authorities (as happened with the dismissal of the "three traitorous officials" in 1919) or those authorities had used mass arrests and violence to cripple the struggle (as happened in 1947). In 1986 and 1987, however, the CCP leadership was able to end the student unrest without making major concessions to the protesters or using force to crush the movement. In sum, although the democracy protests of the mid-1980's marked a revival of the May 4th protest tradition, the movement that emerged was a relatively minor affair compared to the great student struggles of 1919, 1925, 1931, and 1947.

THE PEOPLE'S MOVEMENT OF 1989

If the events of 1986 proved that May 4th–style student activism was alive and well in the China of Deng Xiaoping, those of 1989 showed that educated youths were still capable of leading major as well as minor mass movements.* The People's Movement of 1989, which began in April and ended soon after the Beijing Massacre of June 4, was in one sense a continuation of the December 19th Movement. The student protesters of 1989 rallied around the same watchword of *minzhu*, a term that they too tended to either define in the elitist fashion outlined above, or use in an all-encompassing sense to connote a loosening of political and cultural constraints.[11] The protesters of both years also shared many of the same specific complaints: in 1989, as in 1986, the slow pace of political reform and the poor quality of campus living conditions helped inspire youths to take to the streets. Moreover, the connections between the democracy struggles of 1986 and 1989 go far beyond the goals and grievances participants shared: there were also important continuities in personnel. Many

---

*Here and elsewhere in this section, my information comes largely from discussions with Chinese and Western observers of and participants in the student protests of 1989. In order to protect the anonymity of Chinese informants, I never give specific names to refer to information they have provided, although I credit Western informants where appropriate. In addition, in both cases, wherever possible I provide citations to relevant document collections, articles, and the like. The Bibliographic essay provides an overview of these sources, but I should mention here that my basic understanding of the struggles has been shaped most profoundly by the following four essays, all of which are by scholars who were in China in spring 1989: Pieke, "Observations"; Esherick, "Xi'an Spring"; Saich, "When Worlds Collide"; and Yasheng Huang, "Origins."

campus activists of 1989, including some of the struggle's leaders, such as Liu Gang, received their initiation into the world of street politics during the December 19th Movement.

As strong as these similarities and connections between the two movements were, however, the events of 1989 were quite unlike those of 1986 and 1987 in terms of the militancy of student demands and the effectiveness of student actions. One reason for this difference was the students' greater disenchantment with the political situation as a whole. As a result the participants in the People's Movement were less wary of bringing economic as well as political issues to the fore and of looking for popular support outside the confines of the campus. A number of events during the years since 1986 had alienated the already disenchanted academic community still further from China's rulers. Rumors and verified reports of high-level corruption and nepotism increased markedly in the late 1980's, for example, and just before the spring protests began, the party announced that it would abandon its recent experiments with allowing college graduates some freedom in job selection and that henceforth the state would once again assign them to posts as it saw fit. Even in April 1989 few student protesters felt that the party should be displaced as the nation's ruling party, although by the end of the movement this situation began to change dramatically. From the very start of the 1989 protests, however, student protesters had a much stronger sense than had the participants in the December 19th Movement that China's problems stemmed from deep-rooted causes rather than one or two specific policy decisions.

There was still a good deal of elitism within the student movement when the new round of protests began in April 1989. Throughout the spring, many educated youths were ambivalent at best about bringing workers out onto the streets; during some early demonstrations educated youths even roped their brigades off from the general populace to prevent members of the population at large from joining their marches.[12] Nonetheless, on the whole, the campus activists of 1989 were more interested than their predecessors of 1986–87 in gaining the support of non-students. During May and early June in particular, students frequently called on teachers, journalists, and even policemen and soldiers to join them on the streets. In a move reminiscent of the May 30th Movement, some student lecture teams descended on factories to try to bring workers into the movement as well. And support from all these and other social groups was forthcoming: spectators cheered when student demonstrators passed, journalists marched for a free press, donations of food and drink poured into Tiananmen Square during the student occupation, and workers in various cities formed independent labor unions.[13]

In addition to growing out of a more deeply rooted sense of discontent and evolving into a more broadly based mass movement, the People's Movement soon began to outstrip its predecessor in many ways. The student organizations of 1989 were much more sophisticated than those of 1986–87, in part simply because campus activists had spent the intervening years meeting together informally in dorm rooms and cafeterias to talk about political issues and establish the personal ties so vital to the formation of effective campus leagues. The "democracy salons" that evolved out of these informal gatherings were crucial to the growth of the 1989 movements: just as May 4th activists had honed their organizational and oratorical skills in speechmaking corps during the early spring of 1919, key figures in the People's Movement—Wang Dan, Wuer Kaixi, and Shen Tong—were active participants in or leaders of campus study societies before they emerged as heads of student protest leagues.[14]

The student movement of 1989 also differed from its immediate predecessor in terms of the range of mass actions the participants staged, the attention the world press accorded the protests, and of course the severity of the suppression. In terms of its overall impact and importance, in fact, the People's Movement had most in common with the great youth movements of the Republican era, although it differed from these struggles in several important ways. Anti-imperialism, for example, though a constant feature in pre-1949 student unrest, had no more significance in getting students out onto the streets in 1989 than it had in 1986, and in contrast to the May 30th Movement and the student struggles of the 1930's and 1940's, during the People's Movement there was no organized opposition party with a significant presence on Chinese campuses to fan the flames of campus unrest.

There were differences as well between past and present relating to student tactics and propaganda. Hunger strikes of the sort students staged in 1989, though not without precedent in Chinese history, were not a central part of the Republican-era student protest repertoire.* The students' fa-

---

*As other scholars have noted, stories of heroes denying themselves food in order to draw attention to political or social injustice can be found in dynastic histories more than 2,000 years old (Watson, "Renegotiation of Chinese Cultural Identity"), and Chinese Buddhists have a long tradition of using fasting as a protest technique (Pieke, "Ritualized Rebellion"). Closer to the present, Shanghai silk weavers used a hunger strike as a collective bargaining tactic during a Republican-era labor dispute (Elizabeth Perry, pers. comm.). Such precedents aside, the tactic became an integral part of the Chinese *student* protest repertoire only recently, with the Hunan strike of 1980 being the pivotal event in this process (Yi Mu and Thompson, *Crisis at Tiananmen*, pp. 42–44), and even in 1989 educated youths still frequently described their fasts as an adaptation of the methods of Gandhi and other foreign practitioners of nonviolent resistance. This said, the novelty of the hunger strike even as a student tactic should not be overstressed; throughout the twentieth century educated youths have turned frequently to related techniques that carried similar symbolic connotations of self-sacrifice and commitment, such as swearing oaths to persevere until death to achieve a goal and committing suicide to draw attention to oppression. For further discussion of this point and relevant citations, see Esherick and Wasserstrom, "Acting out Democracy."

mous Goddess of Democracy statue was also a novelty, as was the use participants in the movement made of recently coined foreign terms ("glasnost" and "people power" appeared on some banners) and recently developed communication technologies (such as fax machines and television broadcasts), and the prominent roles that Wuer Kaixi and other members of national minority groups assumed in student protest leagues.[15] The sustained student occupation of Tiananmen Square itself, furthermore, had no real Republican-era precedent. The festive atmosphere that accompanied some stages of this occupation—the rock music, dancing, and jubilant behavior of students in May led foreign journalists to speak of a "Chinese Woodstock" and an "almost millenarian sense" among protesters[16]—also set the act apart from the typical May 4th–style mass gathering.

There were, finally, basic quantitative differences between the 1989 movement and its Republican-era equivalents. Although some pre-1949 student-led marches had involved tens of thousands of educated youths, professors, and ordinary citizens, these demonstrations were no match for the biggest mass actions of 1989: reporters estimated that no less than one million people took part in some Beijing protests, and the largest demonstrations in provincial cities such as Wuhan, Chengdu, and Shanghai attracted crowds in the hundreds of thousands.[17] If the size of the protesting crowds exceeded anything seen before 1949, the numbers of people affected by the state-sponsored violence that followed these marches was also unlike anything seen during previous May 4th–style mass movements. As earlier chapters have shown, Chinese and foreign powerholders used violent methods to suppress student struggles throughout the Republican period. Between May 1925 and March 1926 scores of unarmed demonstrators were killed when first members of foreign-run police and defense forces and then later soldiers and guards in Chinese-run units turned their guns upon protesting crowds, and in 1947 the GMD launched a sustained campaign of mass arrests and intimidation to terrorize dissidents. The sheer level of carnage seen in the June 4 Massacre and related events in Chengdu was, however, unprecedented in the annals of Chinese student movements.*

---

*As a participant in public forums and seminars on the People's Movement, I have heard panelists and members of the audience compare the bloodshed of 1989 to a variety of other events, including the GMD's Party Purification drive of 1927 and violent suppression of dissent on Taiwan in 1947; the CCP's Anti-Rightist Campaign of the 1950's and Cultural Revolution purges; and the massacres of Korean and Burmese students in the 1980's. All of these events, some of which involved higher death tolls than the massacres of June 1989, are indeed analogous in one way or another to the violent repression of the People's Movement. Nonetheless, if we limit discussion to May 4th–style protests that ended in bloodshed, the March 18 Tragedy of 1926, in which the death toll was high but clearly not comparable to that of June 4, remains the event closest to the massacres of 1989. For a discussion of similarities

These and other contrasts and novelties notwithstanding, the similarities between the 1989 struggle and the mass movements examined in earlier chapters are more striking than the differences. This is especially true of student tactics, since the youths of 1989 relied heavily upon many traditional May 4th protest forms. Like their counterparts of 1919 and other years, these youths held mass rallies, marched through city streets waving banners emblazoned with the name of their school, petitioned the authorities, and gave streetside lectures to publicize their cause.

The continuities between past and present are also evident in patterns of organization and mobilization. During their dramatic occupation of Beijing's Tiananmen Square, for example, educated youths formed a shadow bureaucracy much like those their predecessors had established to coordinate pre-1949 mass actions (see Chapters 2, 4, and 5). In 1989, as so often before, students set up a sophisticated protest league complete with specialized bureaus to oversee tasks such as sending representatives to speak to foreign reporters, preventing unauthorized personnel from interfering with strategy meetings by student leaders, and supplying medical aid to sick or injured protesters.[18] As in the past, students even took on the roles of police officers at times, directing traffic near the Square and apprehending several people for splattering ink on a giant portrait of Chairman Mao.[19] In addition, although little concrete information has come to light thus far concerning the way in which protest leagues evolved and student leaders were selected, preliminary evidence suggests that the pre-existing ties and experiences described in Chapter 5 as key factors in Republican-era mobilization may have played equally important roles in 1989.*

---

between the violence of March 18 and June 4, see Barmé, "Blood Offering." For a clear account of what exactly took place on June 4, 1989, which rightly takes pains to dispel some of the incorrect impressions left by the initial media coverage—for example, it emphasizes that most of those killed were not students but members of the laobaixing and that most of the violence took place near, but not in, Tiananmen Square—see Munro, "Who Died in Beijing, and Why."

*Craig Calhoun's "Beijing Spring" is one of the firsthand accounts that addresses issues of this sort most directly. Calhoun argues (p. 442) that much organizing in 1989 "came through the borrowing of templates from other settings" and that class monitors often evolved into key figures in the mobilization process, since they were "as prepared to organize food for hunger strikers" as they ordinarily were to supervise the "circulation of course materials." Francis, "Progress of Protest," notes in a similar vein that the highly organized nature of official campus life ironically served to prepare educated youths for new protest roles. The political experience Shen Tong, Wang Dan, and Wuer Kaixi had gained through participation in study societies and democracy salons in early 1989 has already been noted above, but it is worth pointing out that at least one of these youths, Wuer, had also honed his leadership skills in another setting: his high school's student council (Yu Mok Chiu and Harrison, *Voices from Tiananmen*, p. 155). Heads of provincial protest groups were also frequently youths used to playing leadership roles. To give but one example, a female student leader of the People's

There are strong similarities as well between the propaganda techniques youths used in 1989 and those examined in Chapter 8. Protesters once again used a variety of different "languages" to communicate with different audiences, and once again not all of these languages were verbal. The students used animal imagery in their propaganda (see, for example, the Shanghai wall poster portraying Li Peng as a gorilla included in the photographic section); they smashed small bottles to show their displeasure with Deng Xiaoping, whose given name is a homophone for small bottle; and they wore distinctive clothing—headbands covered with slogans and "Science and Democracy" T-shirts—that announced their political views.

Once again, student texts intended for the laobaixing focused on key words and readily accessible symbols with relevance and emotive power for Chinese of all classes. After June 4, for example, blood-related imagery reminiscent of that propagandists had turned to following the massacres of the mid-1920's figured prominently in student publicity drives. In Nanjing, students covered wall posters with the character *xue* written in red ink to symbolize the blood of martyrs.[20] In Beijing, youths displayed bloody shirts taken from the backs of victims of the June 4 Massacre. And, in Shanghai, students at Fudan turned the entire front gate of their university into a call for mourning and revenge. First, they placed a mourning band on the national flag flying above the gate to symbolize the death of China. Then, quoting from Lu Xun's famous essay on the March 18th Massacre of 1926, "More Roses Without Blooms," they wrote the slogan "blood debts must be repaid in kind" in bold letters across the top of the gate.[21]

As in the past, student communications with the laobaixing also stressed nationalist themes. Even though anti-foreign and anti-imperialist slogans were absent this time, educated youths continued to define their struggle as a patriotic one, an effort to "save the nation" (*jiuguo*) from corrupt officials. Students made this point through a variety of means, ranging from pasting up posters detailing specific acts of corruption committed by officials and their children to joining with teachers and actors to perform comic cross-talk dialogues mocking CCP leaders.*

In still another parallel to past propaganda activities, students turned to different techniques and stressed different themes when trying to reach foreign audiences as opposed to the laobaixing. In an effort to gain the

---

Movement in Qufu had been a department representative (a post similar to a classroom monitor, but with a higher status and wider responsibilities) before the struggle started.

*One of the most interesting of these propaganda performances used comic cross-talk and operatic techniques to satirize Li Peng (who was portrayed as a conniving prostitute currying the favor of an old man) and Deng Xiaoping (as the elderly patron). I am grateful to Henry Rosemont, Jr., who witnessed the display, for describing this performance.

support of the world community, the students of 1989 wrote some of the slogans on their banners in English and—especially at the time of Gorbachev's visits to Beijing and Shanghai—Russian, as well as other foreign languages, and they tended to downplay "patriotic" concerns in these communications and emphasize the democratic aspect of their movement. They also used other techniques to make their struggle seem comparable to those of earlier protesters in other lands, from wearing shirts covered with slogans such as "We shall overcome" to citing parallels between their use of hunger strikes and those of dissidents in foreign nations to covering their banners with quotes such as "Give me liberty or give me death."[22]

The specific foreign analogies and symbols protesters invoked in 1989 were often recent ones, but there was nothing new about Chinese students using allusions to non-Chinese events to make sense of their own actions and to gain the support of foreign observers. As Chapter 8 has shown, as early as 1919 Chinese students were invoking images of the Magna Carta and other Western icons and comparing their fight against Japan to the Allies' fight against Germany to gain foreign understanding of and support for the May 4th Movement. When Shanghai students carried an effigy of the Statue of Liberty during several mid-May parades (see photographic section), and when youths in Beijing erected their famous Goddess of Democracy in Tiananmen Square later that same month, they were following a time-honored tradition of incorporating Western symbols into their propaganda campaigns.

These statues were more complex icons than this last comment suggests, however, for while they evoked one set of images for foreign observers, they evoked others for Chinese citizens. The Goddess of Democracy, for example, was not an exact copy of the Statue of Liberty, although Western press accounts often implied that this was the case. The Goddess combined elements borrowed from that sculpture with motifs reminiscent of effigies of Chinese popular deities and was similar in other ways to the Socialist-Realist representations of Communist heroes and heroines that grace PRC monuments. The Shanghai Statue of Liberty was a faithful copy of the work that stands in New York's harbor, but its use as the centerpiece of a parade gave it special connotations in the Chinese context, since representations of gods were traditionally carried in a similar fashion, and during the Cultural Revolution large white effigies of Chairman Mao were used in the same way during National Day spectacles. Thus, as in the past, not only did the students of 1989 produce separate texts to appeal to different audiences, they also created texts whose resonances depended on the cultural background of the observer, just as the references to "national extinction" and representations of tortoises that filled Shanghai student propaganda of the Warlord era had different connotations for native and foreign citizens of Shanghai.*

As for official responses, the parallels between the events of 1989 and those of the Republican era remain strong, for virtually everything the CCP did had some kind of pre-1949 equivalent. The official call for public meetings with specially selected student "leaders" in April was reminiscent of Jiang Jieshi's effort over a half-century before to undermine the December 9th Movement by convening an equally contrived national student conference. When China's Communist rulers issued statements dismissing the popular protests of 1989 as the creation of a handful of troublemakers beholden to a foreign power, imposed martial law to try to keep people off the streets, and organized obviously phony pro-government rallies to bolster support for their regime, they were also using measures to which their pre-1949 counterparts had turned to suppress earlier expressions of discontent.[23] Even the "big lie" propaganda campaign after June 4, during which officials claimed that no massacre had taken place and that soldiers rather than protesters had been the main victims of violence, was not completely unprecedented: in 1925 and 1926, the authorities had tried in a similar fashion to keep people from knowing how many demonstrators had been killed in confrontations and to claim that soldiers and policemen involved in these events had acted only to protect themselves.[24]

Ironically, many of the top CCP officials conducting the repression of the People's Movement and the accompanying campaign of misinformation began their own political careers as student protesters and radical propagandists. Both Qiao Shi (the national minister of security) and Jiang Zemin (who was Shanghai party secretary during the protests and CCP general secretary during the campaign to discredit the movement that followed the June 4 Massacre), for example, were active in the Shanghai youth movement during the Civil War years. Yao Yilin (a senior vice-premier and a member of the Politburo's Standing Committee) was a leading figure in the December 9th Movement of 1935, and Deng Xiaoping's involvement with underground newspapers, during the time he spent in France as a student and organizer, earned him the title of "Dr. Mimeograph." Even this irony of former protesters taking charge of suppress-

---

*For the construction and meaning of the Chinese statues of "liberty" and "democracy," see Yi Mu and Thompson, *Crisis at Tiananmen*, p. 72; Human Rights in China, *Children of the Dragon*, pp. 116–23; and Gladney, "Bodily Positions and Social Dispositions." Gladney highlights the similarity between these statues and the effigies of Mao carried during parades of the Cultural Revolution era, and notes that the protesters had recently been reminded of these parades by clips in the influential film *He Shang* (River elegy), which was openly shown in early 1989 before being banned as subversive. For pictures of the white Mao statues in question, see *China Reconstructs*, Dec. 1966, p. 3; and *Beijing Review*, Oct. 3, 1969, p. 7.

ing and discrediting renewed outbreaks of student unrest was nothing new, however; the same thing had occurred during the Nationalist era. Shao Lizi, a participant in one of the earliest Shanghai campus strikes in 1905 and a key adviser to the student activists of 1919 and 1925 (see Chapters 1, 2, and 4), is but one of the most famous cases in point. By the 1930's both Shao and his longtime comrade in arms Yu Youren had risen to prominent positions within the Nationalist regime; these and other former activists played a part in the GMD's campaigns to contain campus unrest during the 1930's and 1940's.

Another point of continuity between past and present has to do with the importance of factional splits within the ruling party. Many details about the intraparty divisions, alignments, and realignments within the CCP during spring 1989 remain obscure. It is clear, however, that disagreements within the Chinese leadership over how best to deal with the earliest student protests profoundly influenced the development of the movement. Whether the result of genuine ideological divisions, personal rivalries between individuals and cliques loyal to specific leaders, or (most likely) a combination of both, these disagreements were responsible for much of the hesitancy and inconsistency that characterized the party's initial official responses to the protests of April and early May. These disagreements helped the movement expand: as in 1986, the lack of clear signals made protesters feel that at least some people in high positions supported their calls for swifter reforms, a belief that later events—for example, Zhao Ziyang's tearful meeting with students at Tiananmen before his fall from power—indicate may have been well founded. Here again, the parallels with events of the Nationalist era are striking, for (as Chapters 6, 7, and 9 have shown) factional divisions within the GMD played comparable roles in the growth of pre-1949 student movements, such as the anti-Japanese struggle of 1931 and the Anti-Hunger, Anti–Civil War Movement.

MAY 4TH STREET THEATER IN 1989

It was by no means clear at the outset that the protests of 1989 would evolve into a struggle comparable to the great student movements of the Republican era. Some similarities and continuities between past and present began to emerge, however, from the moment the first mass actions took place in mid-April. The students who took part in these gatherings improvised upon one of the most deeply entrenched scripts in the May 4th repertoire, which had been revived and given additional meaning during the April 5th Movement of 1976: the funeral march of protest. Students marched to honor Hu Yaobang, whose stature within the academic community—as a symbol more than as a person—had risen so dramatically after his purge in 1987 that upon his death from a heart attack in 1989 students treated him up as a "martyr" for the cause of *minzhu*. The long-dormant democracy movement had begun to show some signs of revival earlier in the year. Fang Lizhi and other dissidents had, for example, already launched a petition campaign aimed at persuading Deng Xiaoping to release Wei Jingsheng and other political prisoners.[25] In addition, student activists at various campuses had begun to discuss ways to use the seventieth anniversary of the May 4th Movement to draw attention to China's current problems.[26] Hu's death in April was nonetheless crucial for the development of the new movement, since it gave students a specific issue around which to rally.

If the echoes of the past were loud as soon as students held their initial marches of mourning, however, they became a roar during the weeks that followed. When student groups formed teams of bicyclists to spread news of protest events and official reprisals from one part of the capital to another, they were reviving a tactic used in Shanghai during the May 30th Movement. When students in various cities converged on railway stations to secure passage to Beijing to present their demands in person to representatives of the CCP, they were following closely in the footsteps of many past generations of protesters. When student propagandists, angered by official attempts to use memories of the Cultural Revolution to discredit the People's Movement, distributed handbills claiming that members of the current regime were responsible for creating "turmoil,"[27] these youths were using the same technique to turn the tables on their detractors that publicists for the May 30th Movement had when accused of Boxerism (see Chapter 8). And when the student leader Chai Ling bit her finger and used her own blood to write out a placard criticizing Premier Li Peng for his opposition to the student struggle, she was turning to a method of protest that her predecessors of 1915 and 1919 had also used.[28]

The loudest echoes of the past, however, probably came one month before the massacre, on the seventieth anniversary of the May 4th Movement. The party had planned to commemorate this day with much pomp and circumstance, since official histories credit the May 4th Movement with paving the way for the founding of the CCP and the fall of the warlords. As a key event in the party's own myth of origins, and an event that symbolizes many of the values of patriotism, self-sacrifice, newness, youth, and revolutionary ardor that constitute the political "center" in Communist China, the anniversary of the May 4th Movement has always been a time for official rituals intended to reassert the CCP's legitimacy. Traditionally, the main feature of these rituals has been speeches (sometimes by May 4th veterans) recounting the events of 1919 and calling upon contemporary students to emulate the spirit of patriotism of the heroes who fought warlordism and imperialism. Such speeches have always ended, however, with reminders that since the CCP is now in power the best way to live up to the May 4th spirit is to study hard to help the party build socialism or (in recent years) achieve the Four Modernizations, not to stage new protests. The commemoration festivities the CCP leadership had planned for 1989 were presumably much like those of past years, the only difference being that since this was the seventieth anniversary of the event the scale would be grander.

Student protesters upstaged these official festivities, however, just as their predecessors of the Civil War era had upstaged GMD anniversary commemorations, by presenting an alternative May 4th street theater celebration of their own at Tiananmen Square. By carrying banners that criticized the current regime's failure to live up to the democratic ideals championed by the youths who fought the warlords, the student participants demonstrated that their ideas and those of the CCP's leaders concerning the contemporary relevance of the May 4th Movement differed considerably. The students' choice of Tiananmen Square for this alternative celebration in 1989 had a double meaning: this was the square to which the original protesters of 1919 had come; and this was the square where the party's most important official ceremonies are traditionally held. By choosing to hold their rally at Tiananmen Square, the students of 1989 made two clear statements: that they, not the party elders, were the true inheritors of the May 4th legacy; and that the struggle against oppression begun in 1919 had not ended in 1949.

The student performance on the May 4th anniversary had crucial symbolic implications: it was nothing less than a theatrical attack on the CCP's hegemony. By laying claim to the most sacred political location in the nation's capital and by disputing the party's interpretation of one of the key episodes in its own story of the Revolution, students challenged the CCP leadership's claim to reside at the political center and to represent the nation's core values. Throughout the weeks that followed, participants in the 1989 struggle continued to press this attack with new forms of subversive street theater that reinforced the idea that they, rather than the party leaders, were the true successors to the heroes of May 4th. As in the case of the May 4th anniversary protest itself, the locations students chose for their protest contributed to the efficacy of this symbolic attack: perhaps their most inspired decision was to set up headquarters on and around the Monument to the People's Heroes in the heart of Tiananmen Square, since this memorial sculpture is covered on all sides by marble friezes of key events from the Chinese Revolution and includes one panel devoted exclusively to the events of 1919 (see photographic section).

Fuzhou Road, Shanghai, December 19, 1986. The slogan on the banner in the center reads "Down with bureaucratic authoritarian rule; Fight for freedom and democracy." The smaller characters to the right identify the banner as the work of Tongji students *(photo courtesy Anne E. Bock)*

Bulletin board at Tongji University, December 18, 1986. The wall posters range from slogans demanding more political openness to detailed accounts of protests in other cities. Students read them avidly, and some even recited the contents of selected posters into cassette recorders. Campus security guards discouraged foreigners from reading the posters, and one asked me to leave soon after I took this photograph.

Demonstration in Shanghai, late May–early June 1989 *(photo courtesy Deborah Pellow)*

Police cordon trying to contain a demonstration in Shanghai, late May–early June 1989 *(photo courtesy Deborah Pellow)*

Protesters use buses to bring Shanghai to a standstill, late May–early June 1989 *(photo courtesy Deborah Pellow)*

A student poster that appeared in Shanghai in spring 1989. The poster, which purports to be a copy of an official news release, says that a "monstrous cold-blooded beast," which goes by the name of Peng and can assume human form, escaped from the Beijing Zoo on May 19 (the date that Li Peng gave a speech harshly criticizing the student movement as an act of "turmoil"). The poster calls on the whole nation to watch for this "man-eating" demon, which is known for creating "turmoil." The picture on the right shows the monster's original form; those to the left, the human form the beast has assumed. A brief note at the bottom admonishes authorities at the Shanghai Zoo to keep watch over "Chicken Jiang," a reference to Jiang Zemin, then head of the Shanghai CCP *(from the Charles L. and Lois Smith Collection on Contemporary China, Harvard-Yenching Library)*

Fudan University students returning from a demonstration in May 1989. The flag they carry is inscribed with the name of their department (electrical engineering?) as well as of their school *(from the Charles L. and Lois Smith Collection on Contemporary China, Harvard-Yenching Library)*

One of several marble friezes on the Monument to the People's Heroes in central Beijing, this sculpture depicts the patriotic activism of students during the May 4th Movement. The students of 1989, who presented themselves as inheritors of the May 4th tradition, used the Monument as a central gathering place during their occupation of Tiananmen Square *(photo courtesy Anne E. Bock)*

As important as the symbolic possession of the May 4th tradition was for students, they also pressed their attack by using drama to challenge other kinds of official myths and to parody or lay claim to other symbols and values sacred to the Communist order. The hunger strike, for example, was, among other things, a powerful challenge to the CCP's image of itself as a party committed to ideals of self-sacrifice and selflessness. By publicly refusing to eat, in some cases to the point of courting death, the hunger strikers showed that Communist "saints" such as Lei Feng were not the only youths willing to die for the good of the country. The uses students made of the Goddess of Democracy and Statue of Liberty were likewise dramatic challenges to the party's ability to control the creation and use of sacred icons.

A series of additional student attacks on the CCP's hegemony occurred during Mikhail Gorbachev's visit to China in mid-May. The CCP had planned to make as much symbolic capital as possible out of Gorbachev's visit, the first by a top Soviet leader in nearly thirty years, by holding a number of public reviews and meetings. The general theme China's top officials hoped to stress was that the leaders of the PRC and the Soviet Union were once again on the same track toward progress, since both groups were now interested in experimenting with political reforms and economic restructuring without abandoning either Marxism or one-party rule. The fact that China's move toward reform predated glasnost and perestroika by several years made this theme especially appealing, since it implied a reversal of precedent in which the CCP was now serving as a role model for the Soviets.

Deng Xiaoping's plans for Gorbachev's visit were knocked off kilter by the student movement, which continued to grow and gain support from journalists, workers, and other non-students throughout early May. Since students and their supporters had effectively taken over Tiananmen by the time Gorbachev arrived, the party scrapped its plans for outdoor ceremonies on the square. Adding to the loss of face the party suffered from the inconvenience this caused, students carried banners and wrote group letters to Gorbachev whose main thrust was that China was no longer leading the Soviet Union in terms of reform, but had in fact fallen behind. Throughout Gorbachev's stay, students continued to embarrass the CCP leadership by holding demonstrations that competed with official events— including a march in Shanghai that drew attention away from the Soviet leader's visit to that city—and by implying that Deng had much to learn from his Russian counterpart when it came to democratization.

The various attempts of students to undercut the effectiveness and subvert the meaning of official ceremonies in 1989 is reminiscent of the events of the Civil War era described in Chapter 9. In the 1940's, as in the 1980's, youths often staged protests on anniversary dates and revolutionary holidays (such as Women's Day, May Day, and May 4th) that the ruling party itself was trying to use to bolster its legitimacy, and marked the arrival of a foreign dignitary with calls for more democracy.

Other aspects of the protests of 1989, besides this tendency to subvert official ceremonies, were reminiscent of the Civil War era. When groups of student lecturers tried to convince soldiers to join rather than suppress the popular movement and called out slogans such as "Chinese people do not beat up Chinese people," for instance, they used arguments and appeals to patriotism much like those that participants in the Anti-Hunger, Anti–Civil War Movement had once used to sway GMD policemen. In some cases the student protesters of 1989 even sang the exact same tunes their predecessors had sung: the most bizarre example of this is that, just as their counterparts of 1947 had once done, contemporary youths turned "Frere Jacques" into a protest song by putting new words to the traditional French air.[29] The students' concern with bureaucratic corruption, their anger at the government's attempts to use official youth groups to control campus life, and their indignation at the distorted reports on popular protest carried in official news organs—these too were reminiscent of the 1940's.

Shanghai Scenes

What role did Shanghai's students play in the People's Movement? During the first weeks of the struggle, Shanghai students essentially followed the lead of Beijing protesters.[30] Like their counterparts in the capital, as well as educated youths in cities throughout China, they too took to the street to mourn Hu Yaobang in April.[31] They too had filled their city's streets and squares with throngs of demonstrators (see photographic section) and groups of hunger strikers in May.[32] And they too had covered the walls of their campuses with defiant posters attacking corruption and calling for free speech—a theme that took on special meaning in Shanghai thanks to the government's suppression of a leading local reformist newspaper whose editor, Qin Benli, was accused of fostering discontent and presenting the People's Movement too favorably.[33] Local observers were treated to impressive sights and sounds throughout April and May. A memoir by a foreign teacher describes, for example, "stunning scenes" such as "seeing the conductor of the Shanghai Symphony Orchestra carrying a bouquet, preceded by two motorcycles, walking ahead of the brass section of the orchestra playing 'The Internationale' while hundreds of thousands [of protesters and spectators] roared approval."[34]

Despite the drama of such events, until June 4 Tiananmen Square remained the heart and soul of the People's Movement. It was only after the

Massacre, when further protests in the capital began to seem little more than attempts at group suicide, that students in cities far from Tiananmen, particularly those in provincial industrial centers such as Shanghai and Wuhan, became of central importance. In the aftermath of June 4, Shanghai's educated youths, acting (at least according to some sources) on orders from Beijing-based student organizations,[35] tried to bring business and transportation in their city to a standstill by using buses as barricades to block all major thoroughfares (see photographic section), a task that members of local radical labor unions helped them accomplish. Students and workers also gathered en masse at the city's North Station, the site of so many protests of the 1930's and 1940's, to obstruct railway traffic and thus make the blockade of the city complete.

The organizers of these actions, which were similar to those taking place simultaneously in Wuhan,[36] saw them as the first step toward a general strike, whose goal would be to pressure the government to ease its policy of repression and perhaps even convince one or another party leader to come out in support of the People's Movement. There was, however, another more practical reason for erecting barricades in the streets and blocking the tracks: doing so could help prevent a local replication of the massacre in central Beijing.

Whatever the inspiration for the blockade, by June 5 Shanghai was at a standstill. The situation grew tense during the following days. Protesters, in some cases calling themselves members of "dare to die" squads (a name taken from anti-imperialist struggles of the past), squared off against the worker militias the party had organized hastily and assigned the task of clearing the streets.[37] Confrontations between protesters and their foes sometimes turned violent, especially after a train plowed into a crowd near the North Station, killing several people and injuring many more.[38] And, despite the efforts of worker militias, protesters kept their barricades in place through June 7.

The de facto general strike imposed by the barricades never evolved into a full-fledged sanba of the type seen in 1919 and 1925, however. Although many citizens were angered by the violence in Beijing and the local bloodshed at the North Station, many were also scared of the reprisals that sustained militance could bring. When Shanghai's mayor gave a carefully worded speech on June 8—which could be interpreted either as a defense or guarded condemnation of the June 4 Massacre and contained a promise not to use force locally—and then dispatched additional teams of militia, the protesters abandoned their attempt to paralyze the city. The local People's Movement ended the following day, as it had begun, with marches of mourning. The difference was that now instead of demonstrating in honor of a dead official, the several thousand protesters who gathered on June 9 came to pay homage to the martyrs killed in and around Tiananmen Square.

THE LEGACY OF 1989

As this is being written in September 1990, the long-term impact of the People's Movement remains uncertain. The parallels with earlier periods are so close that it is tempting to look to the past for clues concerning China's future course. It is tempting to compare, for example, the CCP of today with the GMD of 1947. In both cases we see ruling parties struggling to retain or regain their hold on the Mandate of Heaven after rounds of popular protests. In both cases we see parties that have tarnished their images at home and abroad through campaigns of repression aimed at preventing new outbursts of urban unrest. And in both cases we see parties so afraid that any mass gatherings will turn into a protest that they are unable to carry out even their most sacred rituals in a public fashion. Just as the GMD toned down its celebrations of the Double Ten holiday and Sun Zhongshan's birthday in 1947, in the aftermath of the June 4 Massacre, the CCP abandoned its plans to mark the fortieth anniversary of the founding of the People's Republic with lavish spectacles. On October 1, 1989, instead of being filled as in past years with enormous crowds representing all strata of society, Tiananmen Square was surrounded by armed guards who allowed only members of the People's Liberation Army and carefully screened civilians to enter the plaza and take part in the ceremonies.[39] And to match this loss of control of a key sacred space, in late 1989 the CCP was so scared of symbols associated in any way with the People's Movement that it banned all impromptu singing of one of the party's most revered songs: the "Internationale."[40]

The analogy between 1947 and the present is problematic, however, in two key regards. First, there is at present no civil war in China's countryside, nor even clear signs that a majority of Chinese peasants are dissatisfied with the ruling regime.[41] Second, there is no opposition party comparable to the CCP of the 1940's capable of capitalizing on urban disaffection. Despite the similarities between the Civil War era and the present, therefore, history does not provide any definite answers to the question of whether the CCP will be able to resolve its legitimacy crisis through internal reform or suffer the fate of its predecessor.

One thing that *is* clear from the events of 1989 is that campus activism will continue to play a role in shaping China's future. (A new round of student protests, possibly triggered by an anniversary celebration or the death of a hated or beloved figure, may well have already taken place by the time these words appear in print.) Despite seventy years of cultural transformation and political upheaval, students have retained their ability to challenge the legitimacy of ruling elites by appropriating or undermining hegemonic rituals, myths, and ideas. The May 4th tradition, in sum, remains very much alive, with its repertoire of action and symbolic power very much intact.

China's future will be determined in part, therefore, by how successful new generations of students are at keeping this tradition alive and making it serve their goals. It is important to remember, however, that these youths will inherit a complex tradition, which is fraught with internal contradictions and ambiguities as well as with power. This is easy to forget, because throughout the past seven decades writers, activists, and propagandists have continually set about transforming the flesh-and-blood student protesters of history into mythic heroes. In the process, these mythmakers have often oversimplified both the protesters themselves and the meaning of key events.

1989 AS MYTH AND HISTORY

The May 4th Movement provides the clearest example of this mythmaking process. As already noted, CCP propagandists have invested the events of 1919 with sacred significance. For them the May 4th Movement serves as a prologue to the Revolution; they present it as the first national struggle in which members of all classes joined together to fight imperialism and as the event that led to the formation of the Communist Party. Other writers in China and abroad have created a competing image of the May 4th Movement as China's road not taken. For them, the anti-imperialist protests of 1919 and the accompanying New Culture Movement represent China's great flirtation with cosmopolitan ideals of science and democracy, and the years 1917–22 stand out as a brief period when enlightened intellectuals committed to nonviolent change took center stage. Both these images of the May 4th Movement also stress the cultural iconoclasm of the struggle and claim that its participants were dedicated to breaking away from the restrictions of an authoritarian Confucian tradition that placed too much emphasis upon hierarchical relationships and constricting social roles, thus hampering individual freedom and egalitarian modes of behavior. In both these images, student protesters are presented as having been opposite in every way to the unpatriotic, traditionalist, and authoritarian officials they attacked.

There is a factual foundation for both of these heroic images of May 4th; if this were not true, neither image would be effective as a historical myth.[42] As earlier chapters show, however, it is hard to fit the actual events of 1919 into either framework without distorting the historical reality. The elitism of Chinese students toward non-intellectuals that shows through in comments by student union leaders on the violent tendencies of the loafer class (see Chapter 8), for example, contradicts the vision of multi-class solidarity in the CCP May 4th myth. The poison scare and attacks on Japanese nationals alluded to in Chapter 2, on the other hand, are hard to reconcile with the image of May 4th activists as cosmopolitan figures that is a central part of the non-Communist myth. Finally, the hierarchical and bureaucratic nature of student associations and groups of ten, which were so similar in form to Confucian systems of social control (see Chapter 2), makes attempts to portray May 4th iconoclasts as breaking free from traditional patterns of behavior extremely problematic.

A similar, and similarly problematic, mythmaking process, to which Chinese dissidents as well as Western journalists and scholars have contributed, has already begun for the People's Movement. Like their predecessors of 1919, the students of 1989 have been heroicized in accounts that present them as unselfish men and women, whose egalitarian ideals, commitment to democracy, nonviolent actions, and disdain for corruption, bureaucratism, and authoritarian traditions (this time in Communist as opposed to Confucian guise) make them the complete antithesis of rulers such as Li Peng and Deng Xiaoping. Once again, student protesters have come to represent China's road not taken, its chance to break away from entrenched problems and start anew. Once again, historical complexity is in danger of being reduced to a handful of slogans ("Long live democracy"), icons (the Goddess of Democracy), and images (the lone protester confronting the tanks near Tiananmen Square).

As with the May 4th myths, this representation of the People's Movement has a solid basis in fact. Many students acted bravely with little or no regard for their own safety. Many protesters wrote posters that demonstrated a passionate desire to create a freer society. Many educated youths insisted on the importance of nonviolent resistance even after the state showed its readiness to use guns. And there were certainly participants in the struggle who were committed to paying whatever price was necessary to save their nation from the perils of corruption and nepotism.

The image of the People's Movement as a purely democratic and non-violent one, and of the students of 1989 as heroes capable of creating a wholly new enlightened and egalitarian society, is, nonetheless, seriously flawed. Although official reports invariably exaggerated attacks on soldiers and the like, participants in the People's Movement, including in some cases students, did turn to violence at various points in 1989. Some looting did take place, crowds did set fire to armored vehicles, and some soldiers were killed by angry citizens. It is also clear that not all campus activists were fully committed to egalitarian ideals in 1989, and indeed that some felt disdain toward the laobaixing. Two foreigners who were teaching in China have reported, for example, that some of their pupils were horrified by the thought that introducing democratic reforms would mean that un-educated peasants as well as intellectuals would be allowed to vote.[43] The tendency of many educated youths to go along with one part of the official line regarding the random acts of violence that accompanied some early demonstrations and to attribute all rowdy behavior to "bad elements" and "workers" who had infiltrated student ranks is another indication of elitism of this sort.[44]

Students were also not completely committed to democratic practices and egalitarian principles when it came to the operation of protest leagues. Some journalists and scholars drew attention to this fact during the People's Movement,[45] and later reports on the organizational activities of dissident leaders outside China since June 4 add weight to these comments. Recent reports, often by writers generally sympathetic toward Chinese dissident groups, have criticized such things as misappropriations of funds by protest leaders, the insensitivity of student organizers toward the needs of worker groups, and the appeal that ideas associated with the "new authoritarianism" have for student activists and their mentors.[46]

These kinds of criticisms remind us of several things. First, the activists involved in the People's Movement were flesh-and-blood individuals not mythic heroes, and as a result their ideals and their actions were not always in perfect accord. Second, we need to go beyond simply calling the protests part of a "democracy" movement and explore the question of what exactly the term *minzhu* meant to Chinese activists in 1989. It is ethnocentric to assume that Chinese are incapable of instituting democratic practices or to hold Beijing's protesters to unrealistically high standards of behavior and claim that they should be viewed as democratic only if some ideal form of transparently open politics took place on Tiananmen Square. It is equally ethnocentric, however, to assume without close investigation of student texts and actions that the term *minzhu* as used in 1989 was ex-actly analagous to what Westerners mean by democracy.[47]

Perhaps more important than either of these points, the kinds of problems alluded to above remind us that the dominant political culture will leave its imprint upon even the most radical of struggles and most mille-narian movements, simply by making certain patterns of behavior and modes of discourse seem a natural part of the landscape. Throughout the preceding chapters I have highlighted the similarities between the words and deeds of May 4th–style protesters and those of the ruling elites they challenged. I have emphasized that an ability to usurp, appropriate, and adapt official modes of communication and ceremonial forms helped to empower student movements. I have also stressed the importance of patterns of daily life in facilitating campus mobilization and coherent mass action. As the events of 1989 remind us, however, the tendency of protesters to improvise from familiar social and cultural scripts is a double-edged sword: it can lend power to a struggle but can also lead protesters to (often unintentionally) reproduce inequities embedded in the status quo within their own movements.

The hierarchical and highly bureaucratized nature of the organizations students formed during both the Republican and Communist eras is perhaps the best illustration of this point. This phenomenon should not be seen as proof that educated youths were somehow insincere in their concern with democracy or their criticisms of official bureaucratism. Rather, it should be interpreted as an indication of just how entrenched certain patterns of organization have been throughout modern Chinese history.

I do not mean to argue, as Lucian Pye does in a recent essay, that Chinese political culture is an immutable force that will continually frustrate all those who seek genuine reform or radical change.[48] As I have tried to show throughout the preceding pages, political culture needs to be understood as a fluid entity rather than as a static one. Hegemonic forms of practice may change slowly, but they do change, and protests, though shaped by these forms, can also play a role in transforming them.

I also do not mean to imply that the occupation of Tiananmen Square was a simple reproduction of the CCP regime in miniature. Students broke away from official political and cultural patterns in a variety of ways. There was a great deal more freedom of expression in the Square than in government-run parts of China, and ordinary students had a greater say in the decisions of protest leagues than ordinary citizens have in Central Committee policy formation. The very fact that youths took on leadership roles in the Square had radical implications in a society governed by a small band of elders. In addition, the power exercised by women such as Chai Ling, whose status within the movement was higher than that of any female official within the CCP regime, also marked a break from the dominant order, a break that was matched in symbolic terms when students used "goddess" statues in ways reminiscent of official uses of icons celebrating deified male heroes such as Mao.[49]

This said, it *is* true that student forces *did* reproduce many features of the CCP regime during their occupation of Tiananmen Square, and this is a reminder of the staying power of some hegemonic forms. Here again, the case of female activists is instructive. As important as individual women assuming top leadership roles was, it is worth remembering that most of the heads of protest organizations were male.[50] The fierce factional infighting in Tiananmen Square, during which protesters resurrected old Cultural Revolution labels such as "renegade" and "traitor" to attack their enemies, is another example of the persistence of entrenched political habits.[51]

What does all of this mean for historians interested in disentangling myth from history, a task that is always at best problematic and in the case of events such as the People's Movement especially so? Most basically, it means that we should be suspicious of simple explanations and unambiguous interpretations. Rather than focus on a few key images and slogans that seem to sum up the "crisis of 1989," we should highlight the diversity of the symbols and street theater performances that made the People's Movement such a powerful and dramatic event. Rather than tell a tale of a few specific heroes and heroines, we should try to gain some insight into the background and activities of as wide a variety of the participants as possible, the followers and compromisers as well as the leaders and martyrs. We should try, in short, to shed light on the complexity and contradictions as well as the bravery and horror of 1989. Above all, we should continually remind ourselves of, and try to understand, the influence that inherited traditions of mass action and contemporary patterns of politics and daily life, as well as new ideas, had upon the fight to start China toward a new future in 1989.

 REFERENCE
MATTER

 **NOTES**

For complete authors' names, titles, and publication data for the works cited here in short form, see the Bibliography, pp. 391–412. The following abbreviations are used in the Notes and Bibliography:

CASS	Chinese Academy of Social Sciences
CCP	Chinese Communist Party
CPR	*China Press Review*
CWR	*China Weekly Review*
CWR: Monthly	*China Weekly Review: Monthly Report*
CYL	Communist Youth League
F.O.	Foreign Office (U.K.)
GMD	Guomindang
NCH	*North China Herald*
SASS	Shanghai Academy of Social Sciences
SCYL	Shanghai branch of the Communist Youth League
SCYL, *Pictorial*	SCYL, *Shanghai qingnian yundongshi tupianji*
SMA	Shanghai Municipal Archive
SML	Shanghai Municipal Library
SQY	*Shanghai qingyunshi yanjiu* (Researches on Shanghai youth movement history)
SQZ	*Shanghai qingyunshi ziliao* (Materials on Shanghai youth movement history)
USDS, "1919–1929"	U.S. Department of State, "Department of State Records Relating to the Internal Affairs of China, 1919–1929" (microfilm)
WS	SASS, ed., *Wusi yundong zai Shanghai shiliao xuanji*
WY	CASS, ed., *Wusi aiguo yundong*

INTRODUCTION

1. See Strand, *Rickshaw Beijing*, esp. pp. 285–89, for effective use of both kinds of imagery to deal with related topics.

2. See, e.g., the discussion of "wars of movement" and "wars of position," in Gramsci, *Prison Notebooks*, esp. pp. 229–39; and, with specific relation to student movements, the discussion of the American "civil war" of the 1960's in Miles, *Radical Probe*, pp. 44–62.

3. Quoted in Wang Min et al., *Dashiji*, p. 274.

4. The following paragraphs are a truncated version of the more comprehensive discussion of Chinese protests as political theater presented in Esherick and Wasserstrom, "Acting out Democracy."

5. For a particularly elaborate example of such analyses, see White's treatment of the 1968 Chicago Democratic Convention in *Making of the President, 1968*, pp. 257–313.

6. Hermassi, *Polity and Theatre*.

7. Turner, *From Ritual to Theater*; and idem, "Social Drama."

8. Geertz, *Negara*.

9. For an analysis of this theater by one of its "stars," see Abbie Hoffman, *Soon to Be a Major Motion Picture* (New York: Putnam, 1980).

10. Brewer, *Party Ideology and Popular Politics*, esp. pp. 156–57, 181–91; Rogers, "Popular Protest."

11. Thompson, "Patrician Society"; idem, "Eighteenth Century English Society."

12. N. Davis, *Society and Culture*, p. 123. Some studies of American parades also stress this dual potential of street theater; see S. Davis, *Parades and Power*.

13. For a good general discussion of the differences and connections between these and other performance genres, see Schechner, *Performance Theory*.

14. For a useful discussion of this topic, see Schwartz, *World of Thought*, esp. pp. 67–75.

15. Hayes, "Specialists and Written Materials," esp. p. 107; other contributions to D. Johnson et al., *Popular Culture*, touch upon this theme.

16. MacKerras, *Chinese Theatre*, esp. pp. 202–3; Leo Orleans, ed., *Chinese Approaches to Family Planning* (Armonk, N.Y.: M. E. Sharpe, 1979); and *Beijing Review*, Oct. 3, 1969, p. 7, which contains a photograph and description of a particularly elaborate spectacle staged to mark the twentieth anniversary of the founding of the People's Republic.

17. Evelyn Rawski and Susan Naquin, *Chinese Society in the Eighteenth Century* (New Haven: Yale University Press, 1987), pp. 61–62.

18. Esherick, *Boxer Uprising*, esp. pp. 63–67.

19. See MacKerras, *Chinese Theatre*, pp. 48–49, for the period leading up to the 1911 Revolution, and pp. 155–56, for the use of plays as a "propaganda weapon against the Japanese" during the War of Resistance.

20. For a description of a play attacking Deng Xiaoping, popular in Shanghai theaters in spring 1989, see Warner, "Shanghai's Response."

21. Yeh, *Alienated Academy*, pp. 281–85; China, Bureau of Education, Statistical Section, *Quanguo gaodeng jiaoyu tongji*.

22. Israel, *Student Nationalism*, p. 6.

23. Some exceptions are Wu Mu et al., *Zhongguo qingnian yundongshi*; Bao Zunpeng, *Zhongguo qingnian yundongshi*; and Israel, "Reflections."

24. See, e.g., Chow, *May 4th Movement*; Creamer, "Hsueh-yun"; Israel, *Student Nationalism*; and Pepper, "The Student Anti-War Movement," in her *Civil War*, pp. 42–94.

25. See, e.g., Wu Mu et al., *Zhongguo qingnian yundongshi*; and Bao Zunpeng, *Zhongguo gongchandang qingnian yundongshi*.

26. Dirlik, "Ideology and Organization."

27. Among the works on these topics that have influenced me most are Hobsbawm, *Primitive Rebels*; Rudé, *The Crowd in History*; Tilly, *From Mobilization to Revolution*; Perrot, *Workers on Strike*; N. Davis, *Society and Culture*; and Thompson, *English Working Class*.

28. For useful overviews of this approach, see the introductory and concluding chapters of Pye and Verba, *Political Culture and Development*.

29. See, e.g., Pye, *Spirit of Chinese Politics*; and Solomon, *Mao's Revolution*.

30. Hunt, *Politics, Culture, and Class*, pp. 10–11; Baker, *French Revolution*, pp. xi–xxiv.

31. Thompson, "Eighteenth Century English Society," p. 164.

32. Various contributors to Kwang-Ching Liu, *Orthodoxy*; D. Johnson et al., *Popular Culture*; and Watson and Rawski, *Death Ritual*, address this issue. See also the important discussion in Duara, *Culture, Power, and the State*, esp. pp. 262–63; and Elizabeth Perry's work on the influence of rural protest patterns on the activities of Shanghai workers in *Shanghai on Strike*.

33. Comments in various memoirs by leading intellectuals who came of age during the first decades of the century draw attention to the extent to which even the children of elite families were exposed to popular culture performances. See, e.g., the early chapters of Chiang Mon-lin, *Tides from the West*; and Guo, "Shaonian shidai."

34. For example, Tilly, *The Contentious French*; Thompson, "Eighteenth Century English Society"; and N. Davis, *Society and Culture*.

35. Ozouf, *Festivals*; Schechner, *Performance Theory*; see also various contributions to Schechner and Schuman, *Ritual, Play, and Performance*.

36. This is my way of overcoming some of the problems eloquently described by Prasenjit Duara in "The Methodological Limbo of Social History," in *Culture, Power, and the State*, pp. 261–65, such as that of merging diachronic and synchronic approaches to a particular problem and utilizing both narrative and analytic tools.

37. Geertz, "Centers, Kings, and Charisma."

38. The following paragraphs are based largely on Israel, *Student Nationalism*, pp. 1–9; E-tu Zen Sun, "Academic Community"; and various general works on Chinese education discussed in the Bibliographic Essay. According to Israel (p. 5): "In 1932, between 75 and 88 percent of all college students were men, and 69 percent were in the 21–25 age bracket."

39. The best single source for information on the social backgrounds of Shanghai college students is Yeh, *Alienated Academy*, esp. pp. 65–69, 114–15, a work that also includes a wealth of detail concerning the evolution of specific local institutions such as St. John's and Fudan, the rituals and rhythms of campus life, and the

differences between missionary schools, state institutions and private colleges. For additional works that treat related issues, see the Bibliographic Essay.

40. Israel, *Student Nationalism*, p. 5.

41. See Altbach, "Student Political Activism." As Altbach notes, the situation in China is similar to that in Latin American and various Third World Asian countries; see also the various contributions to Emerson, *Students and Politics*.

42. A. Chan and Unger, "China After Tiananmen," surveys some of the ways that the "police and the courts in China" continue to "observe class distinctions." Along these same lines, after police beat up a student at a rock concert in Shanghai in 1986—an incident that helped trigger the campus unrest of that year—the authorities apologized for this incident, claiming that the youth had been mistaken for a worker (Elizabeth Perry, pers. comm., Sept. 18, 1989).

43. The contrast between Chinese and Russian students is revealing in this regard; see Kassow, *Students, Professors, and the State*, esp. pp. 48–87. The American and European student movements of the 1960's can also be seen to a large extent as attempts to create a new political role *for*, rather than reassert a traditional one *of*, students; see the general discussions in Altbach, "Student Political Activism"; and Statera, *Death of a Utopia*, esp. p. 49.

44. On the Berkeley Free Speech Movement, see Heirich, *The Beginning*; for an analysis of another American student struggle that remained primarily an on-campus one, see Friedland and Edwards, "Confrontation at Cornell."

Chapter 1

1. For a Chinese account of the British invasion of Shanghai, see the diary excerpts translated in Arthur Waley, *The Opium War Through Chinese Eyes* (Stanford: Stanford University Press, 1968), pp. 186–96.

2. Useful general popular and scholarly accounts of Shanghai's evolution into a cosmopolitan center include Darwent, *Shanghai*; Potts, *Short History of Shanghai*; W. Johnson, *Shanghai Problem*; Liu Huiwu, *Shanghai jindaishi*, vol. 1; and B. Wei, *Shanghai*.

3. According to W. Johnson, *Shanghai Problem*, pp. 45, 98, the International Settlement had 31,000 feet of water frontage compared to the French Concession's 3,800, and this was one key reason the former became the "commercial and financial center of Shanghai."

4. Ibid., pp. 45, 99, 118: as of the mid-1930's, the International Settlement contained 8.3 square miles, the French Concession 3.9, and the Chinese municipality 320. Boundaries had remained fairly static during the previous two decades, although the International Settlement authorities had waged on ongoing struggle with the Chinese authorities over who should police some of the roads that extended out from the Settlement (ibid., pp. 213–25).

5. B. Wei, *Shanghai*, p. 74. British interests were so powerful in the International Settlement that Chinese residents frequently referred to the area as the *Ying zujie* (English Concession); see Clifford, "The Western Powers."

6. For a good analysis of the complex issue of Chinese representation on the foreign councils, see Clifford, "The Western Powers."

7. Kotenev, *Shanghai: Its Mixed Court*; W. Johnson, *Shanghai Problem*, pp. 128–58.

8. B. Wei, *Shanghai*, p. 17.

9. Ibid., p. 17; and W. Johnson, *Shanghai Problem*, pp. 114–15. For a colorful description of the activities and headquarters of the Shanghai magistrate circa 1916, see Gamewell, *Gateway*, pp. 151–53; for a list of the officials who served as daotai for the Shanghai area, see Liu Huiwu, *Shanghai jindaishi*, 1: 417–18.

10. B. Wei, *Shanghai*, pp. 176–77; Elvin, "Gentry Democracy in Shanghai"; idem, "The Administration of Shanghai."

11. Darwent, *Shanghai*, pp. 176–77. According to Clifford, "The Western Powers," pp. 2, 20, by 1925 Japanese nationals made up well over a third (14,000) of Shanghai's entire foreign population (37,600), and only a quarter of the foreigners eligible to vote in the French Concession were actually French.

12. B. Wei, *Shanghai*, pp. 119–20.

13. Jones, "The Ningbo *Pang*." My thinking on the role of native-place ties and guilds in Shanghai life has been influenced by the various discussions on the topic that took place during the September 1988 International Symposium on Modern Shanghai (hereafter "Shanghai Symposium") and by the papers presented at that conference by Emily Honig and Bryna Goodman in particular. See Chapter 5 for more about *tongxianghui*.

14. Gamewell, *Gateway*, pp. 246–47.

15. For sample faculty rosters, see Lamberton, *St. John's University*, pp. 66–68; the student enrollment figure is from Gamewell, *Gateway*, p. 247.

16. Two of the most important sources for general information on Shanghai's institutions of higher education during the first half of the twentieth century are the essays and memoirs gathered in a special issue of the Shanghai *Wenshiziliao* (Materials on culture and history) entitled *Jiefangqian Shanghai de xuexiao* (Shanghai's pre-Liberation schools), 59 (1987); and Li Chunkang, "Shanghai de gaodeng jiaoyu." The following paragraphs draw heavily upon these works; see also the individual school histories discussed in the Bibliographic Essay.

17. Gamewell, *Gateway*, pp. 243–52.

18. Rankin, *Early Chinese Revolutionaries*, pp. 69–81.

19. My notion of "core" institutions is based in part on arguments in unpublished papers by, and discussions with, Liu Xinyong.

20. Wang Min, "Wusi xuqu." For specific background on the *Subao* and the Patriotic Academy and the connections between them, see Yao, "Shanghai xinshi xuetang," esp. pp. 36–38; and Zhang Dachun, "Qingmo xuechao."

21. Zhang Dachun, "Qingmo xuechao"; Rankin, *Early Chinese Revolutionaries*, pp. 61–64; Shi Weixiang et al., *Jiaotong daxue*, pp. 45–47; "A 'Strike' at the Imperial Nanyang College," *NCH*, Nov. 19, 1902, p. 1075.

22. For strikes of the period, see the firsthand account in Chiang Monlin, *Tides from the West*, esp. p. 48; Rankin, *Early Chinese Revolutionaries*, p. 71; Wang Min, "Wusi xuqu," p. 7; and above all Borthwick, *Education*, pp. 140–45.

23. Yue, "Shanghai ju'e yundong."

24. Ibid., p. 59.

25. "The First Stadium in Shanghai," in Shanghai Cultural Publishing House, *Anecdotes*, pp. 154–56.

26. "Zhang Yuan Garden and the 1911 Revolution," in Shanghai Cultural Publishing House, *Anecdotes*, pp. 159–63; see also "The Need of a Public Hall for Chinese Residents," *NCH*, May 7, 1903, p. 885.

27. For relevant citations of *Subao* articles, see Yue, "Shanghai ju'e yundong."

28. See ibid.; and Liu Huiwu, *Shanghai jindaishi*, 1: 300–301.

29. See Liu Huiwu, *Shanghai jindaishi*, 1: 300–301; and *NCH*, May 7, 1903, p. 885. Both sources emphasize the role of the Patriotic Academy in these events. The *NCH* notes, for example, that the representatives of the "fair sex" attending the meeting were from two local schools for girls, one of which was that affiliated with the Patriotic Academy. It also claims that a "third of the gathering was composed of students of the Ai Kuo [Aiguo] ('Lovers of Country') and Yo Ts'ai [Yu Cai] ('Nursery of Talents') Academies." See *NCH*, Apr. 30, 1903, p. 832, for a description of an earlier rally, during which most of the speakers were either teachers or students from "local schools and colleges where the English language and modern science are taught."

30. Yue, "Shanghai ju'e yundong"; Yao, "Shanghai xinshu xuetang," pp. 37–38; and Liu Huiwu, *Shanghai jindaishi*, 1: 301.

31. Liu Huiwu, *Shanghai jindaishi*, 1: 301.

32. For Ma's life and Zhendan's early days, see Zhao et al., *Fudan daxuezhi*, 1: 27–57; and Hayhoe, "Chinese University Ethos."

33. Kikuchi, *Chūgoku minzoku undō*, pp. 11–56; and Remer, *Chinese Boycotts*, pp. 29–39.

34. For local anti-American boycott activities, see Liu Huiwu, *Shanghai jindaishi*, 1: 310–18; for the role of students, see also Wang Min, "Wusi xuqu," p. 8. For Ma's role in the 1905 boycott, see the Aug. 8, 1905, dispatch by British consul-general Pelham Warren in F.O. 228/2155, which also stresses the part students (with whom Ma was a particularly popular speaker) played in this struggle.

35. Zhao et al., *Fudan daxuezhi*, pp. 30–31, 47–48; Hayhoe, "Chinese University Ethos," pp. 331–33; Zhang Dachun, "Qingmo xuechao," pp. 124–25.

36. For background on these papers and others like them, see Wang Pengnian et al., "Shanghai guoren zibande Zhongwen ribao."

37. Zhao et al., *Fudan daxuezhi*; see also Joseph Chen, *May 4th Movement*, p. 80*n*; Hayhoe, "Chinese University Ethos."

38. *Jiefangqian Shanghai de xuexiao* (see note 16 to this chapter), p. 55.

39. Rankin, *Early Chinese Revolutionaries*, p. 206.

40. Zhao et al., *Fudan daxuezhi*, p. 62; *NCH*, June 28, 1913, p. 973.

41. Kikuchi, *Chūgoku minzoku undō*, pp. 163–72; and Remer, *Chinese Boycotts*, pp. 46–54. For a sense of the kinds of mass actions students and others used to publicize and gain support for the boycott, see the Mar. 18 rally described in *NCH*, Mar. 27, 1915, p. 921. According to an International Settlement police report (SMP Files, reel 65, document no. 6691), of the several thousand people who attended this event, "the majority were either returned students from Japan or were attached to various colleges in and around Shanghai."

42. Cheng, "Ligong ci sinian"; July 1917 issues of *Minguo ribao*.

43. Hu Hou, "Ji wusi yundong qianhou liuri xuesheng de aiguo yundong" (A record of the patriotic activities of Chinese students studying in Tokyo before and after the May 4th Movement), in CASS, *Wusi yundong huiyilu*, 3: 457–59; Xu

Deheng, "Wusi qiande Beida"; *NCH*, June 1, 1918, p. 512; Wang Min, "Wusi xuqu," p. 10; and Chow, *May 4th Movement*, pp. 79–80. For a more comprehensive treatment of the Jiugoutuan's formation and the 1918 protest marches, see Jeffrey Wasserstrom, "Taking It to the Streets," chap. 1.

44. *Minguo ribao*, June 4, June 7, July 5, 1918, and other late spring and summer issues contain reports on the political activities of returned students from Japan.

45. See Xu Deheng, "Wusi qiande Beida," p. 231; idem, "Huiyi Guomin zazhishe" (Memories of the National Magazine Society), in Zhang Yunhou et al., *Wusi shiqi de shetuan*, 2: 37–40; and *Minguo ribao*, July 24, 26, and 27, 1918, p. 12, in which the bylaws of the organization are reproduced.

46. Zhang Yi, "Fudan shisheng."

47. Zhao et al., *Fudan daxuezhi*, p. 112.

48. Cai Xiyao and Wang Jiagui, *Shanghai daxue*, pp. 3–4; Huang Meizhen et al., *Shanghai daxue shiliao*.

49. The best overall treatments of the anti-Christian movement are Lutz, *Christian Colleges*, pp. 204–46; idem, *Chinese Politics*; Yip, *Chinese Students*; and Liu Xinyong, "Fei jidujiao yundong."

50. For more on these interim political activities, see Wang Min et al., *Dashiji*, pp. 34–62.

51. See *NCH*, Apr. 15, 1922, p. 175, for a description of the major Shanghai event of this sort, an attempt by some 50 members of a local anti-Christian federation to disrupt a YMCA meeting.

52. Lutz, *Christian Colleges*, pp. 220–21, for example, translates and analyzes a 1922 piece that speaks of missionaries as the "assault column" of the capitalist forces seeking to "invade China . . . cut her to pieces and exploit her economically."

53. For the evidence from police files and other sources concerning the role CCP-affiliated youth groups played in the anti-Christian agitation of 1922, see Wasserstrom, "Taking It to the Streets," chap. 3. For background on the Shanghai branch of the Shehuizhuyi qingniantuan, see Liu Xinyong and Wang Min, "Shanghai Shehuizhuyi qingniantuan."

54. See the memoirs in Cai Xiyao and Wang Jiagui, *Shanghai daxue*, such as "Gao Erbai tongzhide huiyi" (Reminiscences by Comrade Gao Erbai), pp. 86–91.

55. For background on the "flag episode" of June 2, 1925, which triggered the St. John's strike, see Yeh, *Alienated Academy*; and Lamberton, *St. John's University*, pp. 101–2. Strikes during 1924 at missionary schools outside Shanghai are treated in Yip, *Chinese Students*, pp. 38–39; and Lutz, *Chinese Politics*, pp. 139–46.

56. See, e.g., the Christmas Day, 1924, edition of *Minguo ribao*, which is devoted to the anti-Christian movement.

57. Jiang Zhichan, "Shanghai xuelian."

58. See Wieger, *Chine moderne*, 6: 146.

59. The following comments on Shangda's role are based on data provided in Cai Xiyao and Wang Jiagui, *Shanghai daxue*, pp. 22–24; for more details on the centrality of Shangda within the 1924 anti-Christian movement, see Lutz, *Chinese Politics*, pp. 103–4.

60. The table of contents of an issue of *Fei jidujiao* (which was published as a supplement to *Minguo ribao*) is reproduced in Yip, *Chinese Students*, p. 44; for more

information on the journal, see the chapter devoted to it in *Wusi de shiqi qikan jieshao* (An introduction to periodicals of the May 4th era) (Beijing: Renmin chubanshe, 1959), 3: 61–76.

61. For information on Guanghua, see *Jiefangqian Shanghai de xuexiao* (see note 16 to this chapter), pp. 159–66; for details concerning the radicalism of Southern University, see the police reports cited in note 5 to Chapter 4.

62. For Gao's keynote article, "Wusa liuxue de dongyin" (The causes of the bloodshed of May 30th), see Huang Meizhen et al., *Shanghai daxue shiliao*, pp. 213–23.

63. Cai Xiyao and Wang Jiagui, *Shanghai daxue*, p. 36. For additional examples of the continuities in personnel between the anti-Christian struggle of 1924 and the May 30th Movement of 1925, see Wasserstrom, "Taking It to the Streets," chap. 3.

64. Kotenev, *Shanghai: Its Municipality*, p. 124; Huang Meizhen et al., *Shanghai daxue shiliao*, pp. 130–32.

65. On Shangda's closure and relocation, see Cai Xiyao and Wang Jiagui, *Shanghai daxue*, pp. 38–44; and the documents in Huang Meizhen et al., *Shanghai daxue shiliao*, pp. 150–60.

66. "Tuan Shanghai diwei xueshengbu guanyu xuesheng yundong qingkuangde baogao" (A report on the student movement situation by the student bureau of the CYL's Shanghai office), *Dang'an yu lishi*, 1986, no. 4, pp. 11–14.

67. For basic information on these and related protests of late 1925 and early 1926, see Wang Min et al., *Dashiji*, pp. 78–87. For general information on the revival of anti-Christian activities in late 1926, see Lutz, *Chinese Politics*, pp. 192–97; and for details on Shanghai agitation, which again peaked around Christmas, see *NCH*, Dec. 26, 1925, p. 565, which singles out students from Shangda and a few other campuses as the leading propagandists involved. Some relevant documents concerning the activities of Shangda's students during this time are also provided in Huang Meizhen et al., *Shanghai daxue shiliao*; see, e.g., the anti-Christian diatribe published in the Shangda Middle School newspaper reprinted on pp. 162–63. For citations to additional relevant sources, and a more comprehensive treatment of Shanghai student protest activities in the wake of the March 18th Tragedy in particular, see Wasserstrom, "Taking It to the Streets," chap. 5.

68. For narratives of these uprisings, see Zhou Shangwen and Jia Shiyou, *Shanghai gongren sanci wuzhuang qiyishi*; and Chesneaux, *Chinese Labor Movement*.

69. Liu Ding, "Xuesheng yundong"; Wang Guichang, "Shanghai gongren sanci wuzhuang qiyi"; and Cai Xiyao and Wang Jiagui, *Shanghai daxue*, pp. 43–49.

CHAPTER 2

1. Schwarcz, *Chinese Enlightenment*; and Hu Shih, *Chinese Renaissance*; Schwartz, *Reflections*.

2. Hu Sheng, *Cong yapian zhanzheng*, 2: 964–65.

3. For a typical pro-GMD assessment of the May 4th Movement, which stresses the role of Sun Zhongshan as a patron of early student protest groups, see Bao Zunpeng, *Zhongguo qingnian yundongshi*.

4. Two of the best accounts of this demonstration and the events leading

up to it are Chow, *May 4th Movement*; and Peng Ming, *Wusi yundongshi*, esp. pp. 263–90.

5. Charlotte Furth's "May Fourth in History," which looks for precursors of May 4th actions and ideas in the period 1898–1912, makes a convincing case for the need to place the May 4th Movement within a longer time frame than is usually done. The page she devotes to mass actions, as opposed to the intellectual trends that are her main concern, gives a good sense of what was *not* novel about the agitation of 1919.

6. The May 4th Movement as a whole is unusually well documented; see the Bibliographic Essay for details. For events in Shanghai in particular, one of the most important sources is the collection of newspaper reports and other documents published in *WS*. For national events, the most important document collection is *WY*.

7. For an insightful discussion of the development and symbolic importance of such assemblies, see Strand, *Rickshaw Beijing*, pp. 177–78.

8. Joseph Chen, *May 4th Movement*, pp. 75–76; Zhu Zhonghua, "Wusi yundong"; Zhang Tingjing, "Canjia wusi yundong"; and Li Yuji, "Shanghai xuesheng" (dates in this account are, however, inaccurate). For the text of the telegram Shao received, see *WS*, p. 171.

9. For details of one such meeting, see the memoir by Wei Xuzheng, "'Wusi' yundong zai Aiguo nüxiao," p. 7. See also *Minguo ribao*, May 7, 1919, p. 11.

10. For the text, see *WS*, pp. 171–72.

11. *WS*, pp. 178–85.

12. *Xiaoshi tongxun* (Fudan), 1984; Joseph Chen (*May 4th Movement*, p. 76) claims that in 1919 people went so far as to call Fudan "the Peita [Beida] of Shanghai," in honor of its activism.

13. Xin et al., "Wusi shiqi." Shao Lizi was a member of this organization; so was Cao Rulin (one of the three traitorous officials), until May 12, 1919, when he was stripped of his membership.

14. See Joseph Chen, *May 4th Movement*, pp. 73, 79–80.

15. See Peng Ming, *Wusi yundongshi*, esp. pp. 325–26.

16. SMP file I.D. no. 6691, reel 65.

17. *Shanghai Times*, May 8, 1919, p. 7; *China Press*, May 8, 1919, p. 2. See also *WY*, 1: 267–68, for a school-by-school breakdown of march participants.

18. *China Press*, May 8, 1919, p. 2.

19. Quanguo fulian fuyunshi yanjiushi, "Wusi yundong," mentions three female teachers involved in the "day-to-day" running of the SSU. Zhu Zhonghua, "Wusi yundong," p. 267, touches on the role of school principals in the organization.

20. Zhu Zhonghua, "Wusi yundong," p. 267.

21. Li Yuji, "Shanghai xuesheng," p. 61.

22. This breakdown follows that in Joseph Chen, *May 4th Movement*, esp. p. 74, quite closely.

23. Along with Joseph Chen, *May 4th Movement*, see Wang Min et al., *Dashiji*, which gives a very clear chronology of relevant events. For a comprehensive chronology of the movement in different parts of the country, complete with lengthy quotations from the contemporary press, see *WY*, 2: 487–561. At a still greater

level of detail, Yu Heng's "Fudan daxue dashiji" is a chronology of May 4th activities on a single campus.

24. See *WS*, pp. 195–96.

25. Along with previously cited memoirs, virtually all of which were written by former SSU members, see Ye Ruyin, "Ji 'wusi.'"

26. See *WY*, pp. 193–94, which lists all the schools represented, and Yu Heng, "Fudan daxue dashiji," pp. 17–18. The same figures also appeared in a *Minguo ribao* article of May 10, 1919 (reprinted in *WS*, pp. 191–92).

27. Joseph Chen, *May 4th Movement*, p. 83.

28. Ye Ruyin, "Ji 'wusi,'" p. 141, mentions that each college was allowed to select five representatives, and each middle school four.

29. Zhu Zhonghua, "Nanwang de suiyue"; Cheng, "Ligong ci sinian," p. 25.

30. Zhu Zhonghua, "Nanwang de suiyue," p. 33; and other pieces in *Xiaoshi tongxun*, 8 (1984).

31. Yu Heng, "Fudan daxue dashiji," p. 15; a sample speech, delivered by Cheng Tianfang (then known as Cheng Xueyu), is given in *Minguo ribao*, Apr. 14, 1919, p. 8, which identifies Cheng as part of the Fudan University Traveling Lecture Corps.

32. For an insightful discussion of the Speech Corps and its role in the May 4th Movement, which complements the argument presented here, see Dirlik, "Ideology and Organization."

33. See the entries for Mar. 30, May 9, and May 15 in Yu Heng, "Fudan daxue dashiji," pp. 15, 18, 19.

34. For an example of a school association assigning students to represent it on specific committees, see ibid., p. 19.

35. Wu Daoyi, "Yiming xiaochuna" (A little cashier), in Lianfu jizhe, *Wo canjiale wusi yundong*, pp. 9–11.

36. A number of these branches are listed in the school-by-school breakdown of protest activity found in *WY*, 1: 197–98.

37. Yu Heng, "Fudan daxue dashiji," p. 19; Shi Weixiang, *Jiaotong daxue xiaoshi*, p. 116; and Tu Tingxiang et al., *Tongji daxue xuesheng yundongshi*, p. 4. Wei Xuzheng, "'Wusi' yundong zai Aiguo nüxiao," p. 7, simply refers to her school protest coordinating committee as the Student Association (Xueshenghui).

38. The transmission of policy from the central union to branch offices was eased by the fact that some activists held key positions in both the SSU and their school's own protest association; see Tu Tingxiang et al., *Tongji daxue xuesheng yundongshi*, p. 4; and Yu Heng, "Fudan daxue dashiji," p. 19.

39. Yu Heng, "Fudan daxue dashiji," p. 19.

40. Shi Weixiang, *Jiaotong daxue xiaoshi*, p. 116. See also Wei Xuzheng, "'Wusi' yundong zai Aiguo nüxiao," p. 7, which describes a similarly bureaucratized middle-school branch union.

41. Shi Weixiang, *Jiaotong daxue xiaoshi*, p. 116.

42. *WS*, pp. 198–99; Yu Heng, "Fudan daxue dashiji," p. 23.

43. Yu Heng, "Fudan daxue dashiji," p. 20; see Chapter 4 for information on similarly elaborate bureaucratic structures and chains of command in later student movements.

44. Samuel G. Inman, "The Rising Student Tide in Latin America," in High, *Revolt of Youth*, pp. 147–70.

45. My use of the term "thick description" is taken from Clifford Geertz's essay by that name in *Interpretation of Cultures*, pp. 3–30.

46. See, e.g., the statement by one youth at the first SSU planning meeting criticizing the technique of sending telegrams, as reported in the *Shanghai Times*, May 9, 1919, p. 7. The student's complaint was that telegrams are effective only if they are read; Yuan Shikai had proved how futile this protest tactic could be by simply refusing to open any of the thousands he received when he announced his intention to become emperor.

47. One-day strikes were called at a number of campuses, most notably on the May 9 Humiliation Day, so that students could devote more time to propaganda work; see *WS*, pp. 186–88, which also lists the businesses that closed down to honor the anniversary and show support for the Beijing students.

48. The lower estimate appears in *China Press*, May 27, 1919, p. 1, and *Minguo ribao*, May 26, 1919; cited in Tu Tingxiang et al., *Tongji daxue xuesheng yundongshi*, p. 5. The SSU claimed to represent more than 20,000 youths, and this total was accepted in some local Chinese-language press accounts, such as the May 27 *Shen bao* report (reprinted in *WS*, pp. 256–57).

49. Joseph Chen, *May 4th Movement*, pp. 90–91. Chen's overall treatment of the May 26 events is hard to improve upon, and I have followed his account quite closely in this paragraph. For more details, such as the names of all the schools represented, see *China Press*, May 27, 1919, p. 1; *WS*, pp. 256–57; or *NCH*, May 31, 1919, p. 578.

50. The 52 schools involved in this event were soon joined by a number of others until, according to the *China Press* (May 30, 1919, p. 1), "all the schools of the middle grade and above [were] registered with the Students' Union," and hence were part of the strike.

51. This distinguishes the May 4th strikes from those that accompanied certain American events, such as the Free Speech Movement, in which university officials themselves were among the prime targets of student anger. See Wallerstein and Starr, *University in Crisis*, for cases in point.

52. *China Press*, May 27, 1919, p. 1, claimed that "perfect order prevailed" throughout the day.

53. *Minguo ribao*, May 30, 1919, as cited in Yu Heng, "Fudan daxue dashiji," p. 23.

54. For an account of these activities by a student at Fudan Middle School, see Zhang Tingjing, "Canjia wusi yundong," pp. 30–31.

55. *WY*, 1: 195.

56. Joseph Chen, *May 4th Movement*, pp. 101–3; *NCH*, June 7, 1919, p. 623; *WY*, 2: 265–66; and *WS*, pp. 273–77.

57. The Shanghai memorial service was but one of many to honor Guo; according to *WY*, 2: 255–56, 262, similar services had taken place in Beijing and Guangzhou earlier.

58. For the rules adopted by the students of two schools, Jiaotong University and Pudong Middle School, see *WS*, pp. 257–60.

59. See *China Press*, May 31, 1919, p. 3, for a detailed account of how the students of a middle school for girls run by missionaries, who were among the last to join the strike, justified their action to the institution's patrons by emphasizing

their patriotic motives and their intention to keep up with educational activities while on strike.

60. See Tu Tingxiang et al., *Tongji daxue xuesheng yundongshi*, p. 6; and *WS*, pp. 258–60.

61. This schedule was adopted by the Jiaotong branch union; it was published in *Shen bao*, May 28, 1919, and reprinted in *WS*, p. 258.

62. *China Press*, May 31, 1919, p. 3; Shanghai Nihon Shōkō Kaigisho, *Santō mondai*, p. 175.

63. *WS*, pp. 257–58.

64. Ibid.

65. Cheng "Ligong ci sinian," p. 26.

66. *China Press*, May 29, p. 1.

67. For a clear, brief summary of the *baojia* system, in which households were grouped together in units of 10, 100, and 1,000, see Wakeman, *Strangers at the Gate*, p. 24n; see also Franz Shurmann, *Ideology and Organization in Communist China*, enl. 2nd ed. (Berkeley: University of California Press, 1970), pp. 368–76, 409–12.

68. My discussion of these groups is based on the discussion in Joseph Chen, *May 4th Movement*; Chow, *May 4th Movement*; *Far Eastern Review*, 15, no. 6 (June 1919): 441; *China Press*, May 13 and 14, 1919; *WY*, 2: 247–48; *Shen bao*, May 12, 1919, p. 10; *NCH*, May 17, 1919, pp. 415–16; and Paul Jones, "The Students' Revolt in China," *Independent*, Sept. 20, 1919, p. 399. Although I limit my discussion to Shanghai, groups of ten were formed in many cities: a May 29 consular dispatch from Ningbo (F.O. 371/3695, p. 105755), mentions ten-man groups in that city; Shanghai Nihon Shōkō Kaigisho, *Santō mondai*, pp. 177–78, describes "groups of ten" in Chefoo (Yantai); and Chesneaux, *Chinese Labor Movement*, p. 152, claims that in Hunan "nearly four hundred such groups [of ten] combined to form a provincial federation."

69. Non-student groups of ten did, however, continue to form throughout the movement, both in Shanghai and in other cities. In the end the organizational structure caught on among everyone from Boy Scouts to ordinary laborers to prostitutes; see Chesneaux, *Chinese Labor Movement*, p. 152; and *WY*, 2: 195.

70. For a sample case, in which a group of ten exposed a company for selling Japanese goods, see *Shen bao*, May 17, 1919.

71. For detailed day-to-day accounts of the strike, see *WY*, 2: 1–298; and Joseph Chen, *May 4th Movement*, pp. 11–177. For additional details on merchant participation, see Bergère, *L'âge d'or*, pp. 218–22; and Fewsmith, *Party, State, and Local Elites*. For the role of workers, see Chesneaux, *Chinese Labor Movement*, pp. 151–56.

72. Various sources reprinted in *WY*, vol. 2, portray students as "exhorting" and "convincing" the commercial class to put and then keep their shutters down. For less sympathetic accounts, which claim that students intimidated merchants into joining the strike, see early June issues of *NCH* and the *Shanghai Times*.

73. Educated youths were at least in part responsible, for example, for the rash of attacks on people caught wearing Japanese-made straw hats, which occurred early in the movement in various cities; see *Shanghai Times*, May 20, p. 7, and Hankow (Hankou) dispatch no. 75, June 9, 1919, from W. R. Brown (F.O. 371/3695).

74. *Celestial Empire*, June 14, 1919, p. 518; see also SMP file I.D. no. 6691, reel 65, which notes that the police were willing to allow youths to assist them "for the first day or two" of the strike.

75. Fascinating sidelights on the foreign community's reaction to the strike, including its concerns regarding fresh vegetables and drivers, are provided in the "Notes of Strike" section run by *China Press* during early June; see, e.g., June 10, p. 4.

76. See *NCH*, June 14, 1919, p. 685; and *Celestial Empire*, June 14, 1919, p. 518.

77. The *Shanghai Times*, a pro-Japanese newspaper, consistently emphasizes (and probably overstates) the level of violence in its June 6–13 issues; see, e.g., June 7, 1919, p. 9. But even the *China Press*, which was consistently sympathetic toward the students' cause, cites violent incidents that it saw as justifying the presence of foreign volunteers; see, e.g., June 6, 1919, p. 1.

78. *NCH*, June 14, 1919, p. 718.

79. See dispatch no. 236, June 21, 1919 (F.O. 371/3695).

80. See Joseph Chen, *May 4th Movement*, esp. p. 122, for sample SSU pronouncements aimed at allaying foreign fears; for more about student appeals to Western audiences in 1919 and other years, see Chapter 7.

81. See dispatch no. 236, June 21, 1919 (F.O. 371/3695).

82. See *China Press*, June 13, 1919, pp. 1–2; and dispatch no. 238, June 21, 1919 (F.O. 371/3695). Unfortunately, the festivities were marred by a clash between some marchers and the police, which ended in injuries and arrests.

83. Chang Kuo-t'ao, *Chinese Communist Party*, 1: 64–65; *WY*, 1: 472–74.

CHAPTER 3

1. The extensive bibliography to Phillips, *Student Protest*, esp. pp. 359–84, is filled with examples of works that try to isolate the reasons only some students become activists. See also Lipset, *Rebellion*, pp. 80–123, for a survey of approaches to what he calls "protest-proneness."

2. This is true to a greater or lesser degree of all standard works on the topic; see, e.g., Israel, *Student Nationalism*; Pepper, *Civil War*, pp. 42–94; Wu Mu et al., *Zhongguo qingnian yundongshi*; and Bao Zunpeng, *Zhongguo qingnian yundongshi*.

3. Yip, *Chinese Students*.

4. Saitō, "Neizhan shiqi Shanghai xuesheng."

5. Bao Zunpeng, *Zhongguo qingnian yundongshi*; Yu Xueren, *Zhongguo xiandai xuesheng yundongshi*.

6. SMP Files, reel 65, I.D. no. 6691; *San Francisco Chronicle*, June 5, 1989, p. A15. For general background on the tactics of Western youths during the 1960's, see Friedland and Horowitz, *Knowledge Factory*, pp. 68–88; and Katsiaficas, *Imagination of the New Left*.

7. Walter, *Student Politics in Argentina*, pp. 44–45.

8. Brower, *Training the Nihilists*, p. 135.

9. For a 1989 example of such a kneeling protest in Beijing, see Yi Mu and Thompson, *Crisis at Tiananmen*, p. 18.

10. See, e.g., Bao Zunpeng, *Zhongguo qingnian yundongshi*, pp. 165–66; and

idem, *Zhongguo gongchandang qingnian yundong shilun.* The pro-CCP version of this explanation appears in countless works published in the People's Republic, including Wu Mu et al., *Zhongguo qingnian yundongshi* and virtually every issue of *SQZ.*

11. See, e.g., Wu Cengliang, "Jiaoda xuesheng yundong," pp. 44–54.

12. Tilly, *From Mobilization to Revolution,* pp. 151–59.

13. Schechner, "From Ritual to Theatre and Back," in Schechner and Schuman, *Ritual, Play, and Performance,* pp. 196–222, esp. p. 222.

14. Gitlin, *The Sixties,* esp. pp. 250, 263.

15. Kassow, *Students, Professors, and the State,* pp. 54–56.

16. Brower, *Training the Nihilists,* p. 124.

17. Tilly, *The Contentious French,* pp. 116–18.

18. N. Davis, *Society and Culture;* Rogers, "Popular Protest"; Brewer, *Party Ideology and Popular Politics,* esp. pp. 182–86; Thompson, "Patrician Society, Plebeian Culture."

19. For good accounts of the events, see *WS,* pp. 256–57; and *Minguo ribao,* May 27, 1919, p. 10; press estimates of attendance ranged from 12,000 (*China Press,* May 27, 1919, p. 1) to 25,000 (*Shen bao,* May 27, 1919).

20. For background on sports meets of the pre–May 4th period, as well as an illustration of one such gathering, see Borthwick, *Education,* pp. 139–40; descriptions of sports meets and Boy Scout reviews that Shanghai's May 4th activists themselves took part in just before the outbreak of the movement can be found peppered throughout the 1918 and 1919 issues of *Minguo ribao.* The prevalence of school banners in protest marches is clear from the pictures in SCYL, *Pictorial.* The use of the Recreation Ground for sports meets is mentioned in Shanghai Cultural Publishing House, *Anecdotes,* p. 154.

21. Lo, *Three Kingdoms,* p. 9.

22. Perry, "Shanghai on Strike."

23. *Shanghai Times,* May 24, 1919, p. 7.

24. *Minguo ribao,* June 1 and 2, 1918; *NCH,* June 8, 1918.

25. For the rituals of school life, see Borthwick, *Education,* esp. pp. 29–30, 135–36.

26. This point is brought out most explicitly in Tilly, *The Contentious French,* pp. 116–17: N. Davis, *Society and Culture,* pp. 161–64; and Brewer, *Party Ideology and Popular Politics,* pp. 182–86. See also Thompson, "Patrician Society, Plebeian Culture"; and idem, "Moral Economy"; and Rogers, "Popular Protest."

27. *NCH,* Nov. 24, 1917, pp. 467–68; Gu Jiegang describes and analyzes both Sheng's funeral and that of another Shanghai notable in "Funeral Processions," trans. in Patricia B. Ebrey, ed., *Chinese Civilization and Society: A Sourcebook* (New York: Free Press, 1981), pp. 289–93.

28. For the service for Guo, see *WS,* pp. 272–78; and *WY,* 2: 265–66.

29. The best general source on Chinese funeral practices is Watson and Rawski, *Death Ritual.*

30. Borthwick, *Education,* p. 135; Shu, *Wo he jiaoyu,* pp. 57–58.

31. Joseph Chen, *May 4th Movement,* p. 166.

32. *Shanghai Times,* Nov. 20 and 25, 1918; *Shen bao,* Nov. 23, 1918.

33. *NCH,* June 14, 1919, p. 725; *Shanghai Times,* June 13, 1919, p. 7; *WY,*

pp. 286–87; and the June 21 report (dossier no. 238) from Mr. Phillips, Shanghai's acting counsul-general, F.O. file no. 371/3695.

34. Kemp, "Boy Scouts"; *NCH*, Nov. 24, 1917, p. 469, and Mar. 15, 1919, p. 712. The estimate of 500 scouts comes from Gamewell, *Gateway*, p. 248; for an excellent photograph of a Scout review, see Gamewell, p. 234.

35. Kemp, "Boy Scouts."

36. This phenomenon was not limited to Shanghai, since other Chinese cities also had Boy Scout troops. See the news clippings in the dispatches from Tianjin (Sept. 1, 1919) and Hankou (Dec. 17, 1919) in F.O. 228/3527, for examples of Scout activities outside of Shanghai.

37. For a description of Chinese Boy Scout drills, see *NCH*, Nov. 24, 1917, p. 469.

38. For examples of Boy Scouts playing these peacekeeping roles, see Joseph Chen, *May 4th Movement*, pp. 118, 127–28; *WY*, 2: 136, 167, 215, and 242, as well as the pictures before p. 207.

39. See *NCH*, Mar. 15, 1919, p. 712.

40. Foreigners played important roles in "teaching" youths how to carry out anti-imperialist struggles before 1919 as well. An *NCH* editorial of Aug. 11, 1905, p. 332, called attention to this irony by remarking that the anti-American agitation of that year was being conducted in a "characteristically American manner." According to this article, the Shanghai protestors of 1905 learned most of their techniques from American missionaries, and Americans should "feel gratified with the aptitude manifested by their pupils, even if they are perhaps the first victims of the weapons they have placed in [these pupils'] hands."

41. See "Chinese Cadets at Drill," *NCH*, June 2, 1917, pp. 505–6, for a description of the military training program at one local college just before the May 4th Movement.

42. There is a rapidly growing literature on the connections between festivals and protest in various contexts; see, e.g., N. Davis, *Society and Culture*; Perrot, *Workers on Strike*; Hershatter, *The Workers of Tianjin*; and Esherick, *Boxer Uprising*.

43. On the lecture teams, see *WS*, esp. pp. 294–297, 399; *Xiaoshi tongxun* (Fudan), 8 (1984), esp. p. 19.

44. See *China Weekly Review*, June 1, 1918, p. 29, for a description of a typical school pageant of the era; and Joseph Chen, *May 4th Movement*, p. 65, for a discussion of May 4th Movement dramatic performances.

45. Cheng, "Ligong ci sinian."

46. And in turn, members of other social groups would adapt May 4th student scripts to suit their own ends in later years, as David Strand's insightful discussion of 1925 guild worker protests in Beijing shows (see *Rickshaw Beijing*, p. 187).

47. See Remer, *Chinese Boycotts*.

48. For basic background on pre-twentieth-century student movements, see Huang Xianfan, *Songdai taixuesheng*; Lin Yutang, *Press and Public Opinion*; and Bao Zunpeng, *Zhongguo qingnian yundongshi*.

49. Chang Kuo-t'ao (*Chinese Communist Party*), e.g., notes that he took part in both of these earlier anti-Japanese struggles before becoming a leader of the May 4th Movement in Beijing.

50. The May 4th protest in Beijing itself was similar in form and location to two

earlier events: the protest that capped the anti-Japanese agitation of 1918 (see Chapter 1) and the 1895 mass petition drive that intellectual reformers organized to criticize the Qing government's capitulation to Japan after the Sino-Japanese war, which is described in Nathan, *Chinese Democracy*, p. 8. Chang Kuo-t'ao, *Chinese Communist Party*, also discusses the connections between the anti-Japanese protest of 1918 and the May 4th demonstration of the following year and compares the 1918 march with its predecessor of 1895.

51. On pre-twentieth-century intelligentsia activism and loyalism, see Bao Zunpeng, *Zhongguo qingnian yundongshi*; Lin Yutang, *Press and Public Opinion*, esp. pp. 28–39, 46–57; Lee, *Government Education*, pp. 186–96; and Wakeman, *The Great Enterprise*. Israel, "Reflections," provides a good discussion of the basic differences between the political activities of examination candidates and those of twentieth-century students.

52. For the text of Duan's speech, see *WY*, 1: 473; for an account of Chen's life, which includes translated excerpts from the dynastic history itself, see Lin Yutang, *Press and Public Opinion*, pp. 48–50.

53. According to Lin Yutang, *Press and Public Opinion*, Chinese scholars began to send petitions at least as early as A.D. 153.

54. Tsing, "Urban Riots and Disturbances," p. 301. The attack on the house of one of the "three traitorous officials" that followed the Beijing demonstration of May 4 also had historical precedent. According to Frederic Wakeman (*The Great Enterprise*, p. 383), in the mid-seventeenth-century, "mobs—often led by students—attacked" people alleged to be traitors "or their homes" on various occasions.

55. For a sense of the tactical similarities between Shanghai students and those in other cities, see Strand, *Rickshaw Beijing*, pp. 173–77; and the comments on Shandong protests in David Buck, *Urban Change in China* (Madison: University of Wisconsin Press, 1978), pp. 116–17. The role of the May 4th model in shaping later protests in Beijing is stressed in Strand, "Popular Movements" and "Protest"; work in progress on Nanjing mass movements by Sebastian Heilmann, as well as John Israel's discussions of demonstrations in various cities during the 1920's and 1930's, further confirm the national scope of the May 4th repertoire.

56. For more details and citations concerning these petitions, see Chapter 7.

57. For descriptions of pilgrimages, see Yang, *Religion in Chinese Society*, pp. 87–88; and Naquin and Rawski, *Chinese Society*, pp. 85–86. For the role of petitioning in Chinese religion, see also Ahern, *Chinese Ritual and Politics*; and the contributions to Kwang-Ching Liu, *Orthodoxy*; and to Wolf, *Religion and Ritual in Chinese Society*.

58. Naquin and Rawski, *Chinese Society*, p. 85.

59. See the firsthand accounts in *Shenghuo*, 6, no. 43 (Nov. 17, 1931): 793–96; and *Fanri jiuguo* (Resist Japan and save the nation), 2 (1931): 12–16.

60. See Israel, *Student Nationalism*, pp. 47–79.

61. For relevant documentary citations of this event, see Chapter 9; and Jeffrey Wasserstrom, "Popular Protest."

62. On American teach-ins, see Menashe and Radosh, *Teach-ins*.

63. Kassow, *Students, Professors, and the State*, esp. pp. 90–92. As Kassow shows, the connections between brawls and student movements was at times a close one, since the nation's first nationwide student strike was triggered by a confrontation

between educated youths and police on the anniversary of the founding of St. Petersburg University.

64. Tilly, *The Contentious French*, pp. 116–18.

65. Zhou Peiyuan, "Zai jiaohui xuejiao de aiguo douzheng."

66. Full citations concerning the 1989 protests can be found in the Epilogue; all the events described in this paragraph are treated in Yi Mu and Thompson, *Crisis at Tiananmen*.

67. Thompson, "Moral Economy," pp. 77–78.

CHAPTER 4

1. For a comprehensive analysis of Chinese campus unrest during the early 1920's, see Jiaoyu zazhi, *Xuexiao fengchao*; for Shanghai events in particular, see Wang Min et al., *Dashiji*, pp. 34–70.

2. Two sample anniversary gatherings are described in Wang Min et al., *Dashiji*, pp. 50, 56.

3. For details of these activities, see the memoirs and newspaper reports in SASS, *Wusa*, 1: 270–97.

4. For one such early people's night school, established at Jiaotong during the May 4th period, see Jiaotong University School History Group, *Jiaotong daxue*, pp. 187–89. Tsi C. Wang, *Youth Movement in China*, pp. 216–20, contains a general discussion of youth popular education drives of the time.

5. Chesneaux, *Chinese Labor Movement*, pp. 254–56; Rigby, *May 30th Movement*, pp. 23–28; *NCH*, Feb. 14 and 21, 1925. For useful newspaper reports, protest pamphlets, and other materials, see SASS, *Wusa*, 1: 297–450; see also the SMP reports in reel 65, file no. I.O. 6023; and reel 67, file no. C.I.D. 10381.

6. *NCH*, Feb. 21, 1925.

7. Praise predominates in memoirs and textbooks published in the PRC dealing with the May 30th Movement (see the Bibliographic Essay); for classic examples of condemnation, see contemporary pieces in *NCH*.

8. *NCH*, Feb. 14, 1925; *Shishi xinbao*, Feb. 22, 1925; reprinted in SASS, *Wusa*, 1: 430–32.

9. Liu became such a powerful force in labor relations by the end of the strike that employers would come to him during the following months to find out what to offer their workers in order to prevent new walkouts (Chesneaux, *Chinese Labor Movement*, p. 256).

10. For Mao Dun's reminiscences of the May 30th Movement, see Huang Meizhen et al., *Shanghai daxue shiliao*, p. 134.

11. SMP files, reel 67, file no. C.I.D. 10381.

12. *Minguo ribao*, Feb. 13 and 16, 1925; reprinted in SASS, *Wusa*, 1: 408–11; for reports from less sympathetic newspapers, see ibid., 1: 422–33.

13. The role of native-place societies is discussed at length in Chapter 5.

14. The image of Chinese workers being treated as *niuma* (cows and horses) was a common theme in much contemporary propaganda; see, e.g., the leaflet reprinted in SASS, *Wusa*, 1: 338.

15. See the report in ibid., 1: 570–71.

16. Ibid., 1: 571–78.

17. Ibid., 1: 574.

18. For this memoir, which was originally written in 1938 and then revised by the author in 1965, see ibid., 1: 574–78.

19. Wang Min et al., *Dashiji*, p. 75; Cai Xiyao and Wang Jiagui, *Shanghai daxue*, p. 34.

20. *Minguo ribao* report; reprinted in Huang Meizhen et al., *Shanghai daxue shiliao*, pp. 137–38.

21. Wang Min et al., *Dashiji*, p. 75; Rigby, *May 30th Movement*, p. 31.

22. Chen Yuzong's memoir, "Canjia wusa fandi douzheng huiyi" (Memories of taking part in the May 30th anti-imperialist fight), was written in 1965 and is printed in SASS, *Wusa*, 1: 672–80.

23. Ibid., p. 675.

24. Ibid., p. 676.

25. For more details on the planning that went into the May 30th demonstration and the organization of brigades in particular, see SASS, *Wusa*, 1: 650; various materials in Cai Xiyao and Wang Jiagui, *Shanghai daxue*, such as the interview with Zhou Wenzai, in which the former student activist mentions that he "was the leader of one of the Shangda Middle School *xiaodui*" (p. 101); and Xu Deliang, "Wusa yundong." See also the documents in Jiaotong University School History Group, *Jiaotong daxue*, pp. 765–77, and Huang Meizhen et al., *Shanghai daxue shiliao*, pp. 138–40. Faculty members seem to have played a particularly important role at Shangda; the two chief commanders of the Shangda brigades, Yun Daiying and Hou Zhaoyi, were professors.

26. One of the most interesting methods the protesters devised for passing messages—in which special "communication officers" proved their identity by wearing adhesive plasters on their left hands—is described in Xu Deliang, "Wusa yundong," p. 58.

27. See Creamer, "Hsueh-yun," pp. 22–26, for a good reconstruction of the day's events.

28. Quoted in Rigby, *May 30th Movement*, p. 36.

29. The quoted passages are taken from A. C. Barnes's English-language translation, published under the title *Schoolmaster Ni Huan-chih* (Beijing: Foreign Language Press, 1958), pp. 243–49; for other works of fiction dealing with the May 30th Movement, see Rigby, *May 30th Movement*, pp. 255–58.

30. Much of Ye's account is confirmed in other sources, such as the memoirs and contemporary press accounts in SASS, *Wusa*, 1: 729–54; and the SMP report in USDS, "1919–1929," reel 137, 893.5045/122. Ye does, however, make some minor factual mistakes: e.g., according to Rigby, *May 30th Movement*, p. 38, the business leader who announced the Chamber of Commerce's acceptance of the crowd's demands was only the acting chairman. There are also, of course, some differences of opinion regarding issues such as the unanimity of the crowd: e.g., the SMP report claims that many of those gathered outside the Chamber of Commerce building were opposed to the idea of a general strike but were afraid to make their views known.

31. Ye Shengtao, *Schoolmaster Ni Huan-chih*, p. 256.

32. For the founding of the "triple union," see SASS, *Wusa*, 2: 273–77.

33. Along with previously cited works, see Clifford, *Shanghai, 1925*; Ren and

Zhang, *Wusa yundong jianshi*; Li Jianmin, *Wusa can'an*; Hua, *Zhongguo dagemingshi*; and Kotenev, *Shanghai: Its Municipality.*

34. See, e.g., Borg, *American Policy.*

35. See Rigby, *May 30th Movement*, pp. 72–74, which includes a reference to Deng Zhongxia's conviction that if only workers' blood had been spilled the country "wouldn't have given a damn" (*mobu guanxin, yipi bufang*).

36. This first issue appeared on June 4, 1925; the whole run of *Rexue ribao* was reprinted by Renmin chubanshe in 1980.

37. For selected articles from and an index to this journal, see Huang Meizhen et al., *Shanghai daxue shiliao*, pp. 211–44; see also Cai Xiyao and Wang Jiagui, *Shanghai daxue*, pp. 152–200.

38. This piece is reprinted in Huang Meizhen et al., *Shanghai daxue shiliao*, pp. 213–23.

39. All these titles are mentioned in Li Jianmin, *Wusa can'an*, pp. 60–62, which contains an exceptionally comprehensive list of the names of May 30th pamphlets and journals. Copies of most of these campus publications are extremely rare, but some excerpts from *Wusaxue tekan* are reprinted in SASS, *Wusa*, 2: 119; and Jiaotong University School History Group, *Jiaotong daxue*, pp. 761–63.

40. See Li Jianmin, *Wusa can'an*, p. 60, which also contains the names of several other school publications containing the term *xue.*

41. See ibid., pp. 60, 63, where Li draws attention to the fact that 15 of the 67 May 30th publications he found mentioned in newspapers, consular reports, and other such sources contained the word *xue* in their title. For a sample article from the SSU paper, *Xuechao rikan*, see SASS, *Wusa*, 1: 692–98.

42. Chi Fu's "Wusa zhi chixue yu Zhongguo zhi chihua" appeared in 1926, but *Xiangdao zhoubao*'s 1925 issues are filled with articles that make similar points in subtler ways.

43. Jiang Guangzi, *Shiwen xuanji*, pp. 59–61.

44. Schwarcz, *Chinese Enlightenment*, p. 155; Schwarcz's section "The Exhilaration of Blood: 1925–1926" (pp. 153–63) is a fascinating discussion of the impact of student martyrdom on radical intellectuals of the 1920's.

45. For examples, see the pamphlet and posters translated in USDS, "1919–1929," reel 137, file 893.5045/123.

46. See Li Jianmin, *Wusa can'an*, pp. 57–60. Li's list is based mostly on materials found in Chinese newspapers, although he has examined other materials, such as consular dispatches to the British Foreign Office. Both his list of play titles and his list of publications referred to in notes 38–40 above are *extensive* but are unlikely to be *comprehensive*, since many pamphlets and skits probably never earned a mention in major newspapers such as *Shen bao* and *Dagongbao.*

47. Ibid., p. 63.

48. The titles of all these plays can be found in ibid., pp. 57–58; the Ningbo consul-general's comments are from his dispatch no. 19 of June 26, 1925, in F.O. 228/3143.

49. Amoy (Xiamen) dispatch of June 9, 1925, in F.O. 228/3142.

50. Kiungchow (Qiongshan) dispatch of June 25, 1925, in F.O. 228/3144.

51. See, e.g., the picture of a giant hand strangling a man in a long coat reproduced in USDS, "1910–1929," reel 137, file 893.5045/123.

52. This pamphlet was published in August 1925 by the SSU.

53. For several *lieshi zhuan*, see SASS, *Wusa*, 1: 722–26. These pages include two biographies of martyred workers who died from injuries received on May 30, but one is a reconstructed life history compiled long after the fact rather than an actual piece of 1925 propaganda.

54. Reprinted in ibid., p. 724.

55. For a much more elaborate eulogy, with a fuller account of both Chen's life history and his virtues, see the article from a 1925 issue of a Jiaotong school news-paper (no exact date given) reproduced in Jiaotong University School History Group, *Jiaotong daxue*, pp. 771–73.

56. Reproduced in SASS, *Wusa*, 1: 723–24.

57. For more details on Yi's leadership role in planning and implementing the May 30 demonstration, see the memoir by Tongji's other main student leader, Chen Yuzong, "Canjia wusa fandi douzheng."

58. See the June 6, 1925 issue.

59. This article is reproduced in both SASS, *Wusa*, 1: 722–23; and Huang Meizhen et al., *Shanghai daxue shiliao*, pp. 149–50.

60. He Bingyi was not the only martyr whose last words figured in hagiogra-phies: Chen Yuqin was said to have uttered "fuchou" (revenge) just before he died; see SCYL, *Pictorial*, p. 20.

61. Reproduced in SASS, *Wusa*, 1: 723.

62. *Minguo ribao* report, July 1, 1925, reprinted in SASS, *Wusa*, 2: 497–500; *NCH*, July 4, 1925, p. 504.

63. For additional information on the planning of this event, see *Minguo ribao*, June 30, 1925.

64. *NCH*, July 4, 1925, p. 504.

65. Ibid.

66. SASS, *Wusa*, 2: 497; photographs of the altar and the two booths can be found in the opening pictorial section of this same work. For a much clearer pic-ture in the "hall of bloodstained clothes," see SCYL, *Pictorial*, p. 21.

67. For later events, see Rigby, *May 30th Movement*; and Clifford, *Shanghai, 1925*.

68. See, e.g., Ma et al., *Zhongguo laogong yundongshi*. Ma, a member of the right-wing of the GMD at the time, claimed a great deal of the credit for leading the May 30th Movement for himself and other non-Communists, including the gang-ster Du Yuesheng; see Rigby, *May 30th Movement*, pp. 31, 208, for details and fur-ther citations.

69. See, e.g., the life history given in SASS, *Wusa*, 1: 560–61.

70. See Rigby, *May 30th Movement*, p. 206n62; note in this regard that the "im-portant essays" on the May 30th Movement published before 1949, which are gathered together in the first section of SASS, *Wusa*, vol. 1, refer to Gu simply as a "worker."

71. Sokolsky, *Tinderbox*, p. 36.

72. At times, these organizers even found themselves carrying out Central Committee plans in highly individual ways. The most notable example of this re-lates to the May 30 demonstration itself. According to one memoir, on May 29, while most party representatives were telling youths at various campuses that the event would begin in the early afternoon, the CCP's leading organizer, Li Lisan,

was informing students at Jiaotong, the Fudan Middle School, and one other school in the Xujiahui section of Shanghai that the protest was scheduled for the next morning. Thus on May 30, "before the other shools had left, before their pamphlets had even been printed," the Xujiahui students had already set out; Huang Meizhen et al., *Shanghai daxue shiliao*, p. 139.

73. Rigby, *May 30th Movement*, p. 171; the sources for figures on CCP membership are analyzed in a detailed note in ibid., p. 234.

74. Chang Kuo-t'ao, *Chinese Communist Party*, p. 426.

75. Li Qiang, "Wusa qianhou."

76. Strand, *Rickshaw Beijing*, p. 182, notes that "factional conflicts" were also rife within Beijing's student community just before the May 30th slaying.

77. Chesneaux, *Chinese Labor Movement*, esp. pp. 255–56.

78. See Li Qiang, "Wusa qianhou."

79. See Rigby, *May 30th Movement*, pp. 45–46, for a translation of the full list of demands.

80. *British Chamber of Commerce Journal* (Shanghai), June-Aug. 1925, p. 173.

81. Rigby, *May 30th Movement*, p. 40.

82. In regard to this last role, Qu Qiubai went so far as to claim in a *Xinqingnian* article (Mar. 25, 1926), that the triple union of laborers, students, and merchants formed to oversee the sanba of 1925 functioned as a kind of "local government"; cited in Clifford, *Shanghai, 1925*, p. 23.

83. For a memoir and several newspaper reports concerning this "reorganization" of the SSU and comparable efforts to inject new life into campus branch unions, see SASS, *Wusa*, 2: 134–45. See also the SSU's pamphlet *Wusahou zhi Shanghai xuesheng*, pp. 15–18.

84. See "Student [*sic*] in the Role of Pirates," *NCH*, Aug. 8, 1925, p. 123.

CHAPTER 5

1. For post-1925 examples, see Wu Youyi, "Fujing qingyuan"; Tu Tingquan and Liu Zuomin, "Yi'erjiu yundong"; and Qin, "Jiaoda."

2. My thinking on the issues explored in this chapter has been influenced significantly by discussions with and unpublished papers by Liu Xinyong of Fudan University. Some of the ideas explored in this chapter were first aired in Wasserstrom and Liu, "Student Protest."

3. Altbach, "Students and Politics," pp. 82–89.

4. In Lipset and Altbach, *Students in Revolt*, pp. 60–95.

5. See, e.g., the discussion of Cornell fraternities in Friedland and Edwards, "Confrontation at Cornell," p. 325; and the treatment of anti-radical vigilante squads in R. Cohen, "Revolt of the Depression Generation," pp. 156–57, 316–18.

6. Horowitz, *Campus Life*, esp. pp. 169, 239. Of course, some athletes did emerge as protest leaders in the 1960's and in at least one case "a leading fraternity man" chaired a strike meeting in 1935 (Wechsler, "Revolt," p. 286). For additional examples of leaders of "socializing" organizations taking active roles in protests of the 1930's, see R. Cohen, "Revolt of the Depression Generation," p. 309. Cohen's detailed study makes clear, however, that such occurrences were the exception, not the rule.

7. Jarausch, *Students, Society, and Politics*, esp. p. 402.

8. This discussion suggests that the distinction between transgressive and so-cializing associations is likely to be of little value in situations in which students fought imperialism and colonial rule.

9. For insightful discussions of the restrictions on forming factions and parties, the political importance of study societies in late imperial China, and related issues, see Wakeman, "Price of Autonomy"; and idem, *The Great Enterprise*, pp. 934–42.

10. Naquin and Rawski, *Chinese Society*, p. 86.

11. The contrasts between Western and Chinese ritual traditions and their im-plications for political theater are explored in more detail in Esherick and Wasserstrom, "Acting out Democracy."

12. Compare, e.g., SCYL, *Pictorial*, cover photo, and pp. 6, 7, 34, 68, with the illustrations in DeBenedetti, *American Ordeal*, following pp. 78, 138. The pre-dominance of group banners in the 1989 marches and rallies is clear from a two-page color photograph of Tiananmen Square in the *New York Times Magazine*, June 4, 1989, pp. 6–7.

13. For general background on Shanghai's working class and CCP attempts to mobilize it for action, see Chesneaux, *Chinese Labor Movement*; Honig, *Sisters and Strangers*; Hammond, "Organized Labor in Shanghai"; and Zhu Bangxing et al., *Shanghai chanye*. The following discussion is based on information provided by these works, and on the findings that will be presented by Elizabeth Perry in her forthcoming *Shanghai on Strike* and have already been presented in "Shanghai on Strike: Work and Politics"; and in an unpublished paper "Strikes Among Shanghai Silk Weavers." Perry's unpublished works are all cited with the author's permission.

14. Emily Honig, pers. comm., May 11, 1988. Occasionally, as in the case of Archibald Rose—a general manager at the British American Tobacco Company, who thought that workers' clubs and even unions could serve a useful social and moral function for laborers uprooted from traditional village support networks—bosses saw worker organizations as positive rather than inherently dangerous asso-ciations (Elizabeth Perry, pers. comm., Sept. 18, 1989).

15. Sisterhoods are treated at length in Honig, *Sisters and Strangers*, esp. pp. 209–17; the best general English-language analysis of brotherhoods is Hershatter, *Workers of Tianjin*, esp. pp. 169–70.

16. In addition to the two sources cited in the previous note, see Perry, "Strikes Among Shanghai Silk Weavers," p. 16, which describes a twelve-man brotherhood that became the head security team during a strike.

17. For general background on these associations, which are referred to as ei-ther *tongxianghui* (native-place associations), *huiguan* (guilds), or *bang* (groups), see Jones, "The Ningbo *Pang*"; and Negishi, *Shanhai no girudo*.

18. Jones, "The Ningbo *Pang*."

19. This concept of fragmented units serving as building blocks for mobiliza-tion comes from Perry, *Shanghai on Strike*, which contains numerous illustrations of the process in action.

20. Zhu Bangxing et al., *Shanghai chanye*, provides a number of illustrations of the divisive potential of native-place affiliations and associations; see esp. pp. 264–65, 625. This source is admittedly biased against native-place ties, since it was written by CCP members who viewed such affiliations as "feudal" and back-

ward. Nonetheless, although it overstates the issue, it does provide important examples of such ties inhibiting worker solidarity within key industries. The same issue is treated well in Honig, *Sisters and Strangers*, pp. 4–5, 75–76, 246.

21. Some examples of citywide youth groups based on place of origin, such as the Association of Anhui Students Sojourning in Shanghai, are mentioned in SASS, *Wusa*, 1: 408–17. Most native-place societies drew members from more than one class: the general *huiguan* that workers joined often included at least some merchant and student members; and campus *tongxianghui* were often open to teachers as well as students.

22. For general background on the Green Gang, see *Wenshi ziliao* (Shanghai series), 54 (1986), which is devoted entirely to the gangs of old Shanghai; Isaacs, *Five Years of KMT Reaction*; and Martin, "Tu Yueh-sheng." Cai Shaoqing, "Secret Societies," is a good general discussion, by a leading PRC historian, of the problems native-place societies and gangs posed for radical labor organizers.

23. Information on this role can be found in the sources listed in the previous note and also in Zhu Bangxing et al., *Shanghai chanye*, esp. pp. 263–64, 625–26. See also Hershatter, *Workers of Tianjin*, pp. 167–75, for a good discussion of the similarly complex role this organization played in the lives of workers in another Chinese city.

24. This phenomenon is discussed in some detail in Perry, "Shanghai on Strike."

25. This point was brought out in several interviews I conducted with former student activists in Shanghai in 1986 and 1987; see also the discussion of the situation at Fudan University in 1946 found in Fu Yilan, "Kanglian huodong zai Jida."

26. Chesneaux, *Chinese Labor Movement*, pp. 254–56, has a good brief account of the strike; for further citations and details on the role of the West Shanghai Workers Club, see Chapter 4.

27. Honig, *Sister and Strangers*, pp. 217–24.

28. Perry, "Strikes Among Shanghai Silk Weavers," p. 11.

29. Some comments on the role of individual non-student intellectuals and intelligentsia groups in these later youth movements can be found in Chapters 6 and 7; for additional information, see SASS Teachers' Movement History Group, *Shanghai jiaoshi yundong*.

30. Peng Ming, *Wusi yundongshi*, pp. 221–41, 263–72. See also the memoirs in CASS, *Wusi yundong huiyilu*, such as Kuang Husheng, "Wusi yundong jishi" (A Factual record of May 4th), 1: 302–17. Many of these writings by former members of student associations contain valuable information on the role such groups played in the Beijing youth movement of 1919. These materials and Dirlik's "Ideology and Organization" show that in Beijing, like Shanghai, pre-existing ties and associations played a crucial role in the youth mobilization process.

31. Chen Yuzong, "Canjia wusa fandi douzheng."

32. See Zhu Qichao, "Zai nuhou zhong qianjin" (Advancing amid tears), *Fudan*, Nov. 13, 1984, p. 4.

33. Tu Tingquan and Liu Zuomin, "Yi'erjiu yundong."

34. SCYL Youth Movement Research Group, *1945–1949*, pp. 106–7.

35. The *North China Daily News*, which seldom had kind words for protesters of any sort, for example, referred to the event as "spectacular" (Jan. 4, 1947).

36. For the bulletin and a description of the march as a whole, see Wang Ping,

"Ji Shanghai xuesheng kangbao dayouxing" (Remembering Shanghai's great march against brutality), *Wen cui*, 2, no. 4 (1947): 27–29.

37. The following paragraph is based primarily upon an interview I conducted in Shanghai during 1987 with a former Ji'nan student leader; and upon Fei and Zhu, "Jianku douzheng"; and Fu Yilan, "Kanglian huodong zai Jida." See also SCYL Youth Movement Research Group, *1945–1949*, pp. 67–68; Wang Jieshi and Wang Ping, "Cong 'kangbaolian' dao 'yingjihui.'"

38. Chen Liang, "Fengbao zhige."

39. Hao and Shao, *Zhongguo xuesheng yundong*, p. 269.

40. Zhao et al., *Fudan daxuezhi*, p. 185.

41. Liu Yusong, "Daxia daxue Liangguang tongxianghui."

42. Qin, "Jiaoda."

43. Interviewed in Shanghai in April 1987.

44. Cai Xiyao and Wang Jiagui, *Shanghai daxue*, pp. 107–8.

45. Ibid., p. 17; for basic biographical information on He, Liu, and Zhong, see ibid., pp. 54, 56, 106–8, respectively.

46. Ibid., pp. 12, 15, 17.

47. Ibid., p. 127; Huang Meizhen et al., *Shanghai daxue shiliao*, pp. 121–28.

48. For Zhong's memoir, see Cai Xiyao and Wang Jiagui, *Shanghai daxue*, pp. 106–8; for additional information concerning Shangda student associations, see Huang Meizhen et al., *Shanghai daxue shiliao*, pp. 88–164.

49. See Cai Xiyao and Wang Jiagui, *Shanghai daxue*, pp. 21, 34, 36–37.

50. See ibid., pp. 67–68; and Huang Meizhen et al., *Shanghai daxue shiliao*, p. 105.

51. Gao's lengthy *Shangda wusa tekan* article and a sample contribution by Ma are reprinted in Huang Meizhen et al., *Shanghai daxue shiliao*, pp. 213–27; for a complete index to the journal, see ibid., pp. 239–44. For details on Gao's political activities, see Cai Xiyao and Wang Jiagui, *Shanghai daxue*, pp. 23, 35, and 86–91. On Ma's role in the Guxingshe and general background on this multifaceted society, see ibid., pp. 104, 187–97. I have found no explicit reference to Ma's membership in the Shaanxi Native-place Association; however, because he contributed an article to the special "Sun Zhongshan Remembrance Issue" of the association's journal, I think it safe to assume that he was active in this group (ibid., p. 202).

52. Shi Weixiang et al., *Jiaotong daxue xiaoshi*, pp. 184–99.

53. Ibid., pp. 198, 207–8.

54. A former St. John's student told me of this dichotomy between pro- and anti-GMD *tongxianghui* during an interview conducted in Shanghai in 1987.

55. In addition to previously cited memoirs, see Pan et al., "Jiefang zhanzheng shiqi"; and the various remembrances of underground work gathered in Wang Min, *Chuntian de yaolan*. Several of my informants mentioned CCP activists' uses of religious fellowships during the student movements of the late Republican period. This theme is also treated at length in Xie Shengzhi, "Fangwen Chen Zhenzhong tongzhi tanhua jilu" (A record of an interview with Comrade Chen Zhenzhong), manuscript held in the SCYL archive.

56. Honig, *Sisters and Strangers*, pp. 224–34; Perry, "Shanghai on Strike"; SASS, *Wusa*, 1: 142–48.

CHAPTER 6

1. Zheng Zuan, "A Study of the Municipal Administration of the Greater Shanghai of the Guomindang" (Paper presented at the 1988 Shanghai Symposium); W. Johnson, *Shanghai Problem*, pp. 117–27; Henriot "Le gouvernement municipal."

2. Henriot's argument, which focuses on Shanghai political struggles, is presented in great detail in "Le gouvernement municipal," and in much condensed form in Henriot, "Municipal Power and Local Elites." The kind of competitive situation he describes and analyzes was by no means unique to Shanghai: disputes between party and government officials were endemic in much of the nation during the late 1920's and early 1930's, as Wang Ke-wen, "Kuomintang in Transition," pp. 177–207, clearly indicates.

3. Henriot, "Le gouvernement municipal," p. 99.

4. For a useful general overview of GMD factionalism, see Eastman, *Abortive Revolution*.

5. B. Wei, *Shanghai*, pp. 248–51.

6. Campus factional struggles of the period, during which youths allied with such GMD cliques as the Western Hills and Nationalism (Guojiazhuyi) groups and the Reorganizationist Faction (Gaizupai) struggled with each other and with the CCP for control of school councils and citywide protest leagues, were extremely intricate. Like those within the broader political community that the campus struggles replicated in microcosm, their secretive nature also makes them hard to chart. One can, however, get a sense of the divisive quality of factional splits by looking at memoirs by former student activists, such as Wu Shaowen, "Huiyi yi-jiusaner nian." For a good general examination of GMD factional disputes of the early 1930's, see Wang Ke-wen, "Kuomintang in Transition."

7. Lutz, *Christian Colleges*, p. 267.

8. For a discussion of *baojia*-type social control systems, which were also adopted to aid in rather than to inhibit the growth of student movements, see Chapter 2.

9. Israel, *Student Nationalism*, pp. 16–17.

10. For good discussions of Jiang's dilemma and the steps he took to overcome it, see Coble, "Chiang Kai-shek"; and Cavendish, "Anti-Imperialism."

11. *Zhongyang ribao* (Central daily), May 7, 1928; quoted in Israel, *Student Nationalism*, pp. 18–19. For details on Shanghai student activities prompted by the Ji'nan crisis, which included the usual mix of streetside lecturing drives and demonstrations, see Wang Min et al., *Dashiji*, pp. 103–5.

12. Israel, *Student Nationalism*, p. 19.

13. Ibid., pp. 111–56; CCP, Central Party History Research Group, *Yi'erjiu yundong*; Lutz, "December 9, 1935"; Israel and Klein, *Rebels and Bureaucrats*, pp. 283–84; Snow, *Notes*; Chiang Nan-hsiang, *Roar of a Nation*.

14. Israel, *Student Nationalism*, pp. 138–41; for more details and a contemporary view, see *China Critic*, Jan. 23, 1936, pp. 78–79.

15. For background on the Blue Shirts, and diametrically opposed arguments concerning whether the group should be considered a Chinese equivalent to Nazi youth leagues, see Eastman, "Fascism"; and M. H. Chang, *The Chinese Blue Shirts*.

16. Eastman, "Fascism," contains both a useful introduction to the New Life Movement and some information on the Blue Shirts' role in the campaign.

17. Israel, *Student Nationalism*, pp. 94–97; for information on the activities and control of the Boy Scouts during the Nationalist era, see GMD, *Zhongguo jiaoyu nianjian*, pp. 1334–37.

18. The only detailed descriptions I have found of the Blue Shirt role in Shanghai's December 9th Movement have been in memoirs published in the PRC; see especially Jiang Zonglu, "'Yi'erjiu' yundong"; and the various reminiscences on the December 9th period in Ji'nan University Overseas Chinese Research Group, *Ji'nan xiaoshi*, vol. 2. Much evidence supports the basic claims made in these memoirs regarding factional splits within the local student movement; see, e.g., the lengthy report on the December 9th Movement in the Shanghai Municipal Police files, reel 27, file no. 7081. Although the SMP report does not specifically identify right-wing student activists as Blue Shirts, it does reinforce the idea that loyalist youths actively tried to keep the struggle from turning into a challenge to Jiang Jieshi, especially in the movement's earliest stages. For further citations and a much fuller discussion of the December 9th Movement in Shanghai, see Wasserstrom, "Taking It to the Streets," chap. 5.

19. See the Dec. 21, 1935, report in SMP files, reel 27, no. 7081, pp. 4–5.

20. The preceding paragraph is based on bits and pieces from a variety of sources including memoirs in Ji'nan University Overseas Chinese Research Group, *Ji'nan xiaoshi*; articles in *North China Daily News*, Dec. 21, 1935, p. 9; *China Press*, Dec. 20 and 21, 1935, p. 1; and mid-December issues of *Le journal de Shanghai*; SMP, reel 27, file no. 7081.

21. See the translated news reports in SMP files, reel 27, no. 7081.

22. For good discussions of GMD factionalism, see Eastman, *Abortive Revolution*; and Wang Ke-wen, "Kuomintang in Transition."

23. For background on the Gaizupai, see Wang Ke-wen, "Kuomintang in Transition."

24. See, e.g., Li Huaming et al., "Jiuyiba."

25. Jiang Hao, "Guomindang Gaizupai."

26. Ibid.

27. See Israel, *Student Nationalism*, p. 15, on the party's shift in its attitude toward students after 1927; see also contemporary articles in CYL organs such as *Liening qingnian* (Leninist youth), many of which are reproduced in the multi-volume document series "Zhongguo qingnian yundong shiliao" (Beijing: CYL, 1950's).

28. For descriptions of some of these protests, see Wang Min et al., *Dashiji*, pp. 117, 123–24, 127.

29. One of the most violent incidents took place on Apr. 8, 1930, when police fired into a crowd of more than a thousand workers and students attending a CCP-sponsored meeting. Liu Yiqing, an important student leader of the May 30th Movement (see Chapter 5 for details of his activities), was killed, and more than ten people were seriously wounded (ibid., p. 121).

30. For examples of the kinds of slogans Communist marchers favored, see ibid., pp. 118, 124, 126; various translations of CCP materials on propaganda work in the Jay Calvin Huston Collection (Hoover Institution) Box 3, Package II, Part

III, folder 4a; and Jiaotong University School History Group, *Jiaotong daxue*, 2: 271.

31. During a Dec. 15, 1929, rally, for example, the crowd alternated between slogans such as "Down with the Reorganizationists" (*Dadao Gaizupai*), the more generic "Down with the GMD" (*Dadao Guomindang*), and "Oppose attacks on the Soviet Union" (*Fandui jingong Sulian*)—a reference to the Nanjing government's recent treatment of members of the Soviet consulate in Harbin; see Wang Min et al., *Dashiji*, p. 113 (for a brief account of the Harbin incident) and p. 118 (for details on the Dec. 15 rally). See also the CCP handbill distributed on July 16, 1930—translated as item no. 18 in the Huston Collection, Box 3, Package II, Part III, folder 4a—which attacks both the Reorganizationist "running dogs" and Jiang Jieshi's Nanjing government.

32. The various contributors to SCYL Youth Movement Research Group, *Yi'erjiu yundong*, stress the guiding role underground CCP members eventually played in the local December 9th Movement.

33. For later protests, see Wang Min et al., *Dashiji*, pp. 188–98.

34. Ku, "Disputes."

35. Shi Weixiang et al., *Jiaotong daxue xiaoshi*, pp. 323–25.

36. Tu Tingxiang et al., *Tongji daxue*, pp. 81–90.

37. See *Jiefangqian Shanghai de xuexiao* (Shanghai schools before liberation), *Wenshi ziliao* (Shanghai series), 59 (1988) for specifics; see China, Ministry of Information, *China*, pp. 181–90, for a useful overview of the forced migrations of students throughout China during the late 1930's and early 1940's.

38. For Fudan's fate, see Zhao et al., *Fudan daxuezhi*, pp. 151–62.

39. For some rare data on the fate of three schools that continued to function in Shanghai after 1941, see *Jiefangqian Shanghai de xuexiao*, pp. 164–65, 192, 256 (cited in note 37 to this chapter).

40. Although not specifically dealing with students or student protest, an important study of intellectual life during the Japanese occupation period is Fu Po-shek, "Passivity, Resistance, and Collaboration." This work contains information on such related themes as the anti-Japanese propaganda work carried out by members of "resistance theatre" companies, some of whom taught at local universities; see esp. pp. 106–7.

41. For this obsession with "reds," see Wakeman, "Shanghai Public Security Bureau."

42. Lin Xinchin, "Gudao xueyun"; and Zhao et al., *Fudan daxuezhi*, p. 158.

43. Wang Min et al., *Dashiji*, p. 243.

44. Ibid., p. 239.

45. Zhao et al., *Fudan daxuezhi*, p. 158, for example, mentions in passing that GMD underground groups maintained a presence at Fudan after 1941. For interesting comments on the activities of one underground GMD youth group, the Sanqingtuan (Three People's Principles Youth Corps), in occupied sections of Shanghai before December 1941, see Yu Ying, "Shanghai diqu." More is said about the Sanqingtuan later in this chapter.

46. The following paragraphs are based largely on information in Yu Ying, "Shanghai diqu"; and Yu Zidao et al., *Wang Jingwei*, esp. pp. 228, 240–41.

47. The best general discussion of propaganda projects such as this carried out

by Wang and other members of the puppet GMD is Iriye, "Toward a New Cultural Order," which stresses the importance attached to educated youths.

48. For a sense of the way in which Wang's regime merged the symbolism of Sun's Three People's Principles and the ideal of patriotic self-cultivation with images of a Japanese-led East Asian order, see Yu Ying, "Shanghai diqu," p. 78.

49. For details, see *Shanghai Times*, Mar. 12, 1943.

50. Ibid., May 5, 1945.

51. For another example of a student mass action engineered by the puppet regime, see Lin Xinchun, "Gudao xueyun," p. 13.

52. For background on the Sanqingtuan, see Chinese Ministry of Information, *China*, pp. 214–16; and Eastman, *Seeds of Destruction*, pp. 89–107.

53. For a translation of the oath, see China, Ministry of Information, *China*, p. 215.

54. For citations of specific memoirs and other works that contain negative portrayals of Sanqingtuan activities, many of which either were written by former CYL activists or have been published under CYL auspices, see notes to Chapter 9. The main Sanqingtuan newspaper with information on its activities in Shanghai, *Zhengyanbao* (Sincere words daily), is also cited extensively in that chapter.

CHAPTER 7

1. Israel, *Student Nationalism*, pp. 47–86; Li Guocheng, "Kangri zhanzheng qian," Li Huaming et al., "Jiuyiba."

2. See also *Shen bao*, Sept. 25, 1931.

3. For the role of teachers in the government's policy, see Israel, *Student Nationalism*, p. 49; and Kawai, *Kokumintō Shina*, pp. 166–68.

4. See Chapter 1; *WS*, pp. 258–60; and SASS, *Wusa*, 2: 138–41.

5. Wang Min et al., *Dashiji*, p. 134.

6. Translated in *China Press*, Sept. 26, 1931, p. 2. The government was already committed in principle to military training in the schools before September 1931, but this program had never been fully implemented; see Israel, *Student Nationalism*, p. 54; and Li Guocheng, "Kangri zhanzheng qian," pp. 85–88.

7. Li Guocheng, "Kangri zhanzheng qian," pp. 94–142.

8. Israel, *Student Nationalism*, p. 60.

9. Ibid., p. 61.

10. *NCH*, Sept. 29, 1931, p. 444.

11. My interpretation of the Shanghai municipal government's role in the 1931 agitation follows closely that in Henriot, "Le gouvernement municipal," esp. p. 94.

12. Here again I am following ibid., pp. 98–99. Dangbu in various other parts of the country also tended to be more interested in reviving or carrying through mass movements than were their local government counterparts, at least according to Wang Ke-wen, "Kuomintang in Transition," pp. 189–93.

13. Li Guocheng, "Kangri zhanzheng qian," pp. 75–76; for comprehensive information concerning the various kangrihui students and members of other social groups founded in Shanghai, see SASS, *Jiuyiba*, pp. 112–73, esp. pp. 150–57.

14. Li Guocheng, "Kangri zhanzheng qian," p. 96; Wang Min et al., *Dashiji*, p. 132; *Xinwenbao*, Sept. 24, 1931, reprinted in SASS, *Jiuyiba*, pp. 42–43.

15. *Xinwenbao*, Sept. 25, 1931, reprinted in SASS, *Jiuyiba*, pp. 44–46; Wang Min et al., *Dashiji*, p. 133. Similar protest leagues were formed at roughly the same time in many other cities and provinces, although in some cases both middle-school and college students joined one organization; see Li Guocheng, "Kangri zhanzheng qian," pp. 76–77.

16. See Henriot, "Le gouvernement municipal," p. 99; Henriot notes that the president of the citywide kangrihui, Tao Baichuan, was also the director of the propaganda department of the Shanghai GMD. The fact that leading party representatives were among the main speakers at the September 26 anti-Japanese rally sponsored by the kangrihui—described below—is an additional indication of the party's active role in this organization. The links between the local GMD branch office and the special workers' kangrihui, established in early October, were also close: according to the *NCH* (Oct. 6, 1931, p. 11), this labor group held its founding meeting at GMD headquarters. For full details concerning the citywide kangrihui's leadership, see the newspaper reports about the group reprinted in SASS, *Jiuyiba*, pp. 19–25; several of Shanghai's most prominent capitalists—including Yu Xiaqing—are listed as members of the association's governing board.

17. Israel, *Student Nationalism*, p. 50.

18. Henriot, "Le gouvernement municipal," p. 99.

19. For varying attendance estimates, see *China Press*, Sept. 27, 1931, p. 1 (30,000); *NCH*, Sept. 29, 1931, p. 441 (50,000); and Sha, *Manhua jiuguohui*, p. 1 (100,000+). For some of the employers who gave their laborers a special holiday, see *China Press*, Sept. 26, 1931, p. 1.

20. Most of this *Shen bao* report is reprinted in SASS, *Jiuyiba*, pp. 23–25; for the founding of a postal workers' and a women's kangrihui, see ibid., pp. 150, 152.

21. The Boy Scouts was a quite different organization in 1931 than it had been during the May 4th and May 30th eras. In 1928 the GMD had taken full control of this association as part of its general effort to limit the autonomy of student organizations of all sorts. See GMD, *Zhongguo jiaoyu nianjian*, pp. 1334–37, for information on the role of the Boy Scouts in GMD China.

22. Zhang Yabing, "Quanzhang zhongxue he Daxia daxue xuesheng geming huodong jiankuang" (A sketch of student revolutionary activities at Quanzhang Middle School and Daxia University), *Dangshi ziliao* (Shanghai), 20 (1984): 74–80.

23. Henriot, "Le gouvernement municipal," p. 99.

24. *China Press*, Sept. 26, 1931, p. 1.

25. Ibid., Sept. 27, 1931, p. 1.

26. Ibid., Sept. 28, 1931, p. 4.

27. For a lively account of the attack on Wang, see Israel, *Student Nationalism*, pp. 52–53.

28. Li Guocheng, "Kangri zhanzheng qian," p. 101.

29. Israel, *Student Nationalism*, pp. 51–52.

30. Wang Min et al., *Dashiji*, p. 135.

31. Shi Cun, "Fujing qingyuan"; and Wu Youyi, "Fujing qingyuan."

32. Wu Youyi, "Fujing qingyuan."

33. *China Press*, Sept. 29, 1931, p. 1.

34. Ibid.

35. Han Jiemei, "Banshijieqian de huiyi." For still another version of the night's events, see Li Goucheng, "Kangri zhanzheng qian," p. 101.

36. *Le journal de Shanghai*, Nov. 1, 1931, p. 12, describes one such corps of 3,000 officers and men, which had 108 instructors, most of whom came from the famous Whampoa Academy.

37. See Wang Min et al., *Dashiji*, p. 140, for one such volunteer brigade.

38. Wu Youyi, "Fujing qingyuan"; Shi Cun, "Fujing qingyuan."

39. For the complete text of this poem, see *Kangri jiuguo* (Fudan), 3 (Nov. 7, 1931): 16.

40. *China Press*, Nov. 25, 1931, p. 1; Tu Tingxiang et al., *Tongji daxue*, p. 59.

41. For details on these interim activities, which occasionally led to violent clashes between protesters and police and Japanese marines, see Wang Min et al., *Dashiji*, pp. 137–40; *Le journal de Shanghai*, Oct. 6, p. 6, Nov. 1, p. 6, Nov. 11, p. 6, Nov. 20, p. 6, Nov. 22, p. 12; and *NCH*, Oct. 6, pp. 11–12, Oct. 13, p. 50, Oct. 20, p. 98, Nov. 3, p. 103. The mid-November fund-raising drive organized to support General Ma was probably the highlight of the interim period in terms of student mass action. According to *Le journal de Shanghai* (Nov. 20, 1931, p. 6), during this drive some "15,000 male and female students from various Shanghai universities," who had all "decided to stop their studies to devote themselves to three days of propagandizing," flooded the streets of the concessions to solicit contributions from pedestrians and people in passing cars.

42. *China Press*, Nov. 25, 1931, p. 1.

43. See Tu Tingxiang et al., *Tongji daxue*, p. 59, and *China Press*, Nov. 25, 1931, p. 1, for descriptions of this demonstration.

44. China Press, Nov. 25, 1931, p. 1; see also Ren, "Jiuyiba," which calls attention to the greater "militarization" (*junduihua*) of the November petition drive.

45. In addition to the previously cited accounts, see Huang Lin, "Wo zai Shanghai dixia."

46. *China Press*, Dec. 8, 1931, p. 1.

47. *China Press*, Dec. 10, 1931, p. 1.

48. Israel, *Student Nationalism*, p. 68.

49. Ibid., p. 69.

50. See Wang Min et al., *Dashiji*, p. 143; and *China Press*, Dec. 7, 1931, p. 1, for details.

51. My reconstruction of the events of December 9 and 10 is based on Wen, "Sanshi niandai chu"; SASS, *Jiuyiba*, pp. 66–74; Henriot, "Le gouvernement municipal," pp. 103–5; *China Press*, Dec. 10 and 11, 1931; *NCH*, Dec. 15, 1931; *Le journal de Shanghai*, Dec. 11, 1931, p. 4; and U.S. Department of State, "Department of State Records Relating to the Internal Affairs of China, 1930–1939" (microfilm), 893.00 PR Shanghai/43, "Shanghai Political Report for December 1931," pp. 5–9; and Israel, *Student Nationalism*, p. 72.

52. *China Press*, Dec. 10, 1931, p. 1. Nanjing students had been similarly frustrated the previous day, when they surrounded the garrison headquarters in the capital, only to find out after five hours that the building was deserted; see *China Press*, Dec. 9, 1931, p. 2.

53. Here and elsewhere different reports give slightly divergent chronologies: thus, for example, *NCH* (Dec. 15, 1931) says that the attack on the GMD headquarters occurred *after* the main body of student protesters had arrived at the municipal government buildings. The same report mentions destroyed furniture

and broken glass and claims that the youths who stormed the party offices "desecrat[ed] the portrait of Sun Yat-sen."

54. Wen "Sanshi niandai chu," claims that some students obtained weapons by taking the guns of the military police who guarded the Municipal Government Compound's gates, and other youthful sentries armed themselves with clubs.

55. Sun Sibai, "Jiuyiba."

56. *NCH*, Dec. 15, 1931.

57. *Shen bao*, Dec. 11, 1931, reprinted in SASS, *Jiuyiba*, pp. 71–74; Wen, "Sanshi niandai chu."

58. See *NCH*, Dec. 15, 1931, for the use of bamboo, to which the paper claims the municipal government representatives objected.

59. For more details on Wang's confession, see SASS, *Jiuyiba*, pp. 72–73, which contains what seems to be a verbatim account printed the day after the trial in *Shen bao*. According to this account, the court first asked Wang some basic informational questions and then called on a student witness to testify that he had seen the accused strike the Beijing University student representative during the December 9 meeting. After this identification, Wang confessed his role in the skirmish and described how he had gotten involved in the affair. One interesting point in the testimony is Wang's answer to the question of whether the participants in the raid were paid: he replied that there was no need to offer them money, since the assailants "were all party [GMD] members" (who presumably felt that beating up a suspected Communist was a natural expression of party loyalty).

60. *NCH*, Dec. 15, 1931.

61. *China Press*, Dec. 11, 1931, pp. 1–2.

62. Ibid., Dec. 12, 1931, p. 3.

63. *NCH*, Dec. 22, 1931, p. 411; lesser amounts were offered to anyone who turned in either "criminal" dead rather than alive.

64. *China Press*, Dec. 9, 1931, p. 2; according to this report "only the counsel of more moderate students prevented [the Nanjing police officers from] being lynched."

65. *NCH*, Dec. 22, 1931, p. 411.

66. Wu Chixiang, "Shanghai minzhong"; this memoir is reprinted in SASS, *Jiuyiba*, pp. 457–65.

67. For details concerning the Minfan's founding meetings and reprints of the group's early proclamations, see SASS, *Jiuyiba*, pp. 32–38.

68. Ibid., p. 35.

69. Wang Min et al., *Dashiji*, p. 144.

70. SASS, *Jiuyiba*, p. 36.

71. These two *Shen bao* reports are reprinted in SASS, *Jiuyiba*, pp. 23–25 and 35–37, respectively.

72. The headline for the *Shen bao*'s report on the earlier rally, by contrast, was an essentially neutral one: "Over Eight Hundred Organizations Hold a Resist Japan and Save the Nation Citizens' Assembly."

73. Jordan, "Shifts"; F.O. 676/104, especially Consul-General Brenan's dispatch no. 14 from Shanghai, Jan. 14, 1931, and Sir Miles Lampson's dispatch no. 96, Jan. 16, 1931.

74. Jordan, "Shifts," pp. 209–210.

75. Factional alignments were so complex and protean during this period that these terms can be misleading; Wang Jingwei was at times intimately connected with the Guangdong regime, but at other times at odds with it; see Wang Ke-wen, "Kuomintang in Transition," pp. 276–320.

76. Sir Miles Lampson's dispatch no. 96, Jan. 16, 1931, in F.O. 676/104.

77. *NCH*, Dec. 22, 1931, p. 411.

78. On student protest activities in late December 1931 and the first weeks of 1932, see Wang Min et al., *Dashiji*, pp. 144–50; and *NCH*, Dec. 29, 1931.

79. Wu Chixiang, "Shanghai minzhong."

80. Wu Mu et al., *Zhongguo qingnian yundongshi*, pp. 116–22; Jiang Zhichan, "Wang Ming."

81. Wen, "Sanshi niandai chu"; and idem, "Jiuyiba."

82. Israel, *Student Nationalism*, pp. 83–84.

83. *China Press*, Dec. 24, 1935, p. 1; Zhao, "Yi'erjiu yundong zai Fudan," in SCYL Youth Movement Research Group, *Yi'erjiu yundong*, pp. 7–11; SASS, *Yi'erjiu*, pp. 21–35.

84. *China Press*, Dec. 25, 1935, p. 1.

85. Ibid., Jan. 27, 1936.

86. See Zhao et al., *Fudan daxuezhi*, pp. 114–15, for a detailed account of this incident. My reconstruction is also based on my interview of a former Fudan student activist in spring 1987. According to this informant, the Fudan standoff was not settled until Du Yuesheng—the Green Gang leader whose combination of close connections with various local officials and membership on Fudan's governing council put him in an ideal position to negotiate a settlement—agreed to serve as a mediator. The person I interviewed, who is now an emeritus professor at Fudan, was one of the students who visited Du to request his aid. For interesting comments on press coverage of the March 25th Incident, see Lin Yutang, *Press and Popular Opinion*, pp. 136–37.

87. See Lu, "Shanghai xuesheng de minjian xuanchuan" (Shanghai students propagandize the people), a 1936 *Dazhong shenghuo* (Life of the masses) article written by a participant in the protest; reprinted in CCP, Shanghai Party History Documentation Group, *Yi'erjiu*, pp. 46–52.

CHAPTER 8

1. Li Jianmin, *Wusa can'an*, p. 33, notes that May 30th protesters issued propaganda materials in Japanese, French, German, Russian, English, Mongolian, Uighur, Manchu, and even Esperanto.

2. For a picture of one such banner from the mid-1940's, see SCYL, *Pictorial*, p. 75.

3. This document is reproduced in full in Jiaotong University School History Group, *Jiaotong daxue*, 2: 279–88. The protest league in question was open to faculty members and staff personnel as well as to students and seems to have been an officially sponsored or at least a semiofficial association. The idea that a special language was needed to communicate with the laobaixing also appears in texts by unambiguously radical authors writing specifically about student propaganda

work. See, e.g., "Women zenyang xiang laobaixing xuanchuan" (How are we to propagandize among the common people?), *Qingnian zhishi*, 13 (1947): 23–24.

4. DeFrancis, *Chinese Language*, pp. 243–44; Chow, *May 4th Movement*, pp. 28–29.

5. Link, *Mandarin Ducks*, p. 18. Link says that baihua writers "created a style which appeared to most readers as a strange new language strongly associated with the West and with the new Westernized elite" (p. 19), a point echoed in DeFrancis, *Nationalism*, see esp. pp. 10–12.

6. High, *Revolt of Youth*, pp. 184–85.

7. Hu Shi himself admitted this when he wrote that "after 1919, vernacular literature spread as though it wore eight-league boots"; quoted in Chow, *May 4th Movement*, p. 279.

8. Zhong Fuguang, "Wo zai wusa douzhengzhong de xuanchuan huodong" (My propagandizing activities during the May 30th struggle), in Shanghai zonggonghui, *Wusa yundong*, pp. 131–33.

9. Chang Kuo-t'ao, *Chinese Communist Party*, 1: 60.

10. Li Jianmin, *Wusa can'an*, pp. 30–37.

11. See DeFrancis, *Chinese Language*, pp. 204–8. DeFrancis himself seems to favor what he calls a "demanding definition" of literacy: "the ability to accomplish such relatively elementary tasks as corresponding about family matters and reading newspapers and instructions in various matters." He admits, however, that if "knowing only a few hundred characters" qualifies a person as being "literate," then China has probably had a fairly high literacy rate for some time.

12. Rawski, *Education*, p. 140; Nathan and Lee, "Mass Culture."

13. Cited in Nathan and Lee, "Mass Culture," p. 374.

14. The Shanghai Student Union printed 28 different postcards with pictures of the faces of martyred and wounded protesters and bystanders (Li Jianmin, *Wusa can'an*, p. 36). For a discussion of a May 30th propaganda film, see SASS, *Wusa*, 1: 682–85.

15. "Students Organize Entertainment in Aid of Strikers," *Celestial Empire*, Aug. 8, 1925, p. 72. According to this report, one fan contained the simple phrases "The Ninth of May and the Thirtieth of May. Oh, you patriots! What are you doing to remove the disgrace?" Another fan had "an appeal for a continuance of the boycott on one side" and a "picture showing Chinese being harassed by foreign wolves" on the other.

16. SASS, *Wusa*, vol. 1, introductory pictorial section.

17. For a picture of this man, see Shanghai zonggonghui, *Wusa yundong*, p. 72; and Strand, *Rickshaw Beijing*.

18. As works published in the PRC in particular stress, intellectuals were not the only participants in the xuanchuan work Li analyzes. See, e.g., the memoirs by laborers who gave streetside lectures and distributed leaflets during the May 30th Movement in SASS, *Wusa*, 1: 661–72; and Shanghai zonggonghui, *Wusa yundong*, pp. 128–30.

19. Some forms of memorabilia, such as commemorative seals, were used in other years; see, e.g., the photo of a May 4th–era seal in the pictorial section of *WY*, vol. 1.

20. SCYL, *Pictorial*, pp. 6–13.

21. See, e.g., Freyn, *Prelude to War*, pp. 41–42; and various police reports contained in the SMP files, reels 27 and 28, such as D. 7333, which describes, among other things, a play commemorating the eleventh anniversary of the May 30th Tragedy.

22. Qin Fangshao, "Wode gegong" (My song), *Zhou bao*, 43 (June 29, 1946): 10–12.

23. *North China Daily News*, Jan. 1, 1947, p. 1. The caption refers to the bus in the picture as a PUB (Public Utility Bureau) vehicle, but "Guoli Jiaotong daxue xiaoche" (National Jiaotong University school vehicle) is clearly painted on the side of the bus.

24. Shanghai Party History Documentation Group, "*Yi'erjiu*," pp. 235–45, 431–33.

25. Reproduced in ibid., p. 236.

26. Ibid., pp. 237–39.

27. Ibid., pp. 241–43.

28. See Si, "Jishouge," for a discussion of this song and some sample lyrics.

29. For an example of the continuing popularity of "The March of the Volunteers" among demonstrators, see *Dagongbao*, Feb. 25, 1946, p. 3; for an example of a writer putting new words to an old tune, see Si, "Jishouge," p. 12.

30. Chen Liang, "Fengbao zhi ge."

31. *Xuesheng bao*, n.s., 11 (July 10, 1947): 3.

32. For an almost identical question and answer chant, see "Ji Jiaoda 'Wusa can'an'" (Remembering Jiaotong University's "May 30th Tragedy"), *Qingnian zhishi*, 13 (June 8, 1947): 16.

33. "Living posters" had been used in Kunming a year earlier; see Steve Thorpe's photographs of the December 1st Movement (Hoover Institution Archive, 81068-10. A-V).

34. Unfortunately, this historian was unable to locate copies of either of these two pamphlets, though I was able to find similar student works from the time.

35. For several interesting photographs of this march, see SCYL, *Pictorial*, p. 78.

36. Wang Ping et al., "Xiang baokou yao chifan." For several comparable and similarly titled handbills distributed during marches in 1947, see SMA, A4 208.

37. Wang Ping et al., "Xiang baokou yao chifan," pp. 24–25.

38. See *Dagongbao*, May 20, 1947, p. 4, for a contemporary description of the Food Bowl Group.

39. This point is stressed in various essays in D. Johnson et al., *Popular Culture*; and Kwang-Ching Liu, *Orthodoxy*. I use the terms *zhishi* (educated) and *wuzhishi* (uneducated) instead of comparable pairs such as "elite" and "popular" wherever possible. As noted above, this was a dichotomy student protesters themselves made.

40. Wenyan can in a sense be seen not only as the language of high culture but also as the language of power and authority, as Evelyn Rawski ("Problems and Prospects," p. 400) suggests.

41. For a useful model for looking at these intermediaries, see D. Johnson, "Communication, Class, and Consciousness."

42. For background on the xiangyue system, see Hsiao, *Rural China*, pp. 184–258; and Cheek, "Contracts and Ideological Control."

43. Mair, "Language and Ideology," pp. 349–52.

44. Ibid., pp. 353–54; Cheek, "Contracts and Ideology." For a detailed and un-flattering description of a Shanghai lecture on the *Sacred Edict*, see the letter in *Chinese Repository*, 17 (1848): 586–88, which is quoted at length in Mair.

45. These comments on and quotations from Guo's piece are taken from Mair, "Language and Ideology," pp. 354–55.

46. Various versions of this maxim appear in many student movement propa-ganda texts; see, e.g., Freyn, *Prelude to War*, p. 42. For examples of student leaflets from Republican-era movements, see *WS*, and SASS, *Wusa*. In addition, a number of original copies of revealing Civil War–era handbills are held at SMA and SML; for descriptions and information concerning several such pieces, see Wasserstrom, "Taking It to the Streets," chap. 7.

47. Freyn, *Prelude to War*, written by a foreign student who accompanied Bei-jing youths on a propaganda campaign through the countryside in the aftermath of the December 9th Incident, provides some of the most detailed descriptions of such performances.

48. Some of these genres are dealt with in more detail below. For a useful over-view of the varieties of written texts available to members of the wuzhishi world in imperial times, see Hayes, "Specialists and Written Materials." For a good intro-duction to and comments on popular Buddhist texts, see Daniel Overmyer, "Val-ues in Chinese Sectarian Literature"; and Susan Naquin, "The Transmission of White Lotus Sectarianism in Late Imperial China," in D. Johnson et al., *Popular Culture*, pp. 219–54 and 255–91. For an insightful analysis of a set of nineteenth-century elite texts, written at least in part for a laobaixing audience, that used many of the same rhetorical and pictorial strategies found both in popularizations of the *Sacred Edict* and student protest pamphlets to attack a religious heresy (Christian-ity), see P. Cohen, *China and Christianity*.

49. Once again various contributions to D. Johnson et al., *Popular Culture*, pro-vide important background information on these kinds of activities. In addition to Johnson, "Communication, Class, and Consciousness," see James Hayes's com-ments on entertainers in his "Written Materials," pp. 75–111; Tanaka Issei, "The Social and Historical Context of Ming-Ch'ing Local Drama," pp. 143–60; and Barbara Ward, "Regional Operas and Their Audiences: Evidence From Hong Kong," pp. 161–87.

50. "My Gramophone's Solo," in Sherman Cochran, Andrew Hsieh, and Janis Cochran, eds., *One Day in China: May 21, 1936* (New Haven: Yale University Press, 1983), pp. 76–79, provides a revealing glimpse of one such official counter-part to post–May 4th radical, mass-movement propaganda work. Part of a GMD anti-Communist propaganda performance, the lecture described in this piece was strikingly like an updated xiangyue lecture: the only difference was that the text that the speaker was required to explicate was not the Kangxi emperor's *Sacred Edict*, but a newer defense of orthodoxy by a state leader: Jiang Jieshi's "Letter to the People of Shanxi Province Regarding the Extermination of Communists."

51. For example, an account in the *China Press* (May 13, 1919, p. 1), describes "Y.M.C.A. Middle School students" continuing "their open air preaching."

52. Endicott, *James G. Endicott*, p. 242; 1988 interview with John W. Powell, editor and publisher of *China Weekly Review* during the mid- to late 1940's.

53. For a description of a typical "vernacular handbill" the head of the Shanghai Public Security Bureau ordered his men to paste "on walls along the Bund in

1930," see Wakeman, "Shanghai Public Security Bureau." For a translation of a fairly typical official proclamation of this sort condemning certain types of protest activities, see the article "Intimidators Are Special Target of New Proclamation," *Shanghai Times*, July 14, 1925, reprinted in USDS, "1910–1929," 893.5045/176.

54. *China Press*, May 17, 1919, p. 2.

55. See Joseph Chen, *May 4th Movement*, pp. 28–32.

56. For a typical mention of the Korean case, see *WS*, p. 190; see also *China Press*, May 25, 1919, p. 5, which notes that banners reading simply "Look at Korea" were carried during one May 4th demonstration.

57. A good example of the use May 4th propagandists made of tortoise imagery can be found in a British consular dispatch from Kiukiang (Jiujiang; no. 32, June 5, 1919, in F.O. 371/3695 section 1113000). "Sidelights of the Boycott," *China Weekly Review*, June 14, 1919, p. 58, attests to the popularity of comparable propaganda in Shanghai, where in the "native city practically every electric light pole was decorated with Japanese straw hats cut in the shape of turtles." For the folkloristic connotations of turtles, who are also sometimes said to be animals incapable of feeling shame, see Eberhard, *Chinese Symbols*, pp. 294–96.

58. These photographs and translations of their captions are reproduced in USDS, "1910–1929," reel 137, 893.5045/123.

59. For examples of *zougou* imagery, as well as other interesting propagandistic uses of animal imagery—e.g., a cartoon that presents the British as a chicken that Chinese must drive out of Shanghai—see the file labeled "Youguan *Chengyan* baofu ziliao" (Materials relating to *True Words*) in SMA.

60. "Police Report for June," *Municipal Gazette*, Aug. 6, 1925, p. 244.

61. Ibid., p. 245. For specific examples of the materials upon which this police report is based, see the SMA file cited in note 59 to this chapter.

62. There were, however, still references to "national extinction" in many chants of the mid-1930's; see, e.g., the slogans listed in Li Xin, "Yi'erjiu."

63. For photographs of posters bearing this type of illustration, see *Le journal de Shanghai*, Nov. 12, 1931.

64. See, e.g., those described in a secret SMP report dated Feb. 10, 1936, file D7108, reel 27.

65. The slogan "Chinese people do not beat up Chinese people" (*Zhongguoren buda Zhongguoren*) is mentioned in various December 9th memoirs, such as Li Xin, "Yi'erjiu."

66. *Meijun zaihua baoxinglu* (A true record of atrocities committed by American troops in China) (Shanghai: n.p., 1946; copy held at SML), which was distributed by Ji'nan University students during late 1946 and early 1947, is filled with examples of American abuses in China.

67. See, e.g., the pamphlet *Bazuguo tuixiang: Duli ziyou jiefang* (For the advancement of the homeland: Independence, freedom, liberation) (Shanghai: St. John's University Student Association, 1948).

68. For an example of a use of "Chinese people do not beat up Chinese people" in a post–World War II demonstration, see Yi Sheng, "Shanghaishi dazhong xuesheng."

69. For a picture of this frequently reproduced poster, which appears to be made from a woodcut, see SCYL, *Pictorial*, p. 78.

70. For an example of a contemporary leaflet explicitly aimed at students that uses this contrast, see "Wei Nanjing qingyuan xue'an gao quanguo tongxueshu" (A proclamation to all the nation's students concerning the bloody suppression of the Nanjing petitioners) (Shanghai, n.d., probably late May 1947; copy at SMA, A4 208: 1-1226).

71. See, e.g., "Gao zhigongjie tongbaoshu" (Proclamation to our working brothers) (Shanghai: n.p., 1947; copy at SMA, A4 208: 1-1264.

72. SCYL, *Pictorial*, p. 78.

73. For example, the ending lines of the leaflet "Wei Nanjing qingyuan xue'an gao quanguo tongxueshu" (see note 70 to this chapter) were "If we are still *qingnian* [youths], if we are still students, if we are still patriots, we will not remain silent."

74. For Bakhtin's arguments, see *Dialogic Imagination*; for a good introduction to audience-centered approaches to literary criticism, see Suleiman and Crosman, *Reader in the Text*.

75. For a clear illustration of this elitism, see the comments by a May 4th youth movement leader on the need for students to "advise the illiterate and loafer classes" in *Shanghai Times*, June 6, 1919, p. 7.

76. For Wuer's exchange with Li Peng and subsequent comments that perhaps the premier should have shown *him* deference, see Yu Mok Chiu and Harrison, *Voices from Tiananmen*, p. 151; for reactions to the bended-knee position, see Lianhebao, *Tiananmen yijiubajiu*, pp. 60–61; and for general discussions of the role of remonstrance in imperial China and modern mass movements, see Strand, "Protest"; and Solinger, "Democracy with Chinese Characteristics." My comments on criticisms of petitioning postures as overly submissive are based on interviews.

77. The most famous examples are Edgar and Helen Foster Snow, whose role as advisers to and propagandists for December 9th Movement activists in Beijing is detailed in Snow, *Notes*.

78. See, e.g., the cartoon on the front page of *NCH*, Jan. 29, 1927.

79. Ransome's essay is printed in his *Chinese Puzzle*, pp. 29–32. Some citations of the *North China Herald*'s fear-mongering and the steps protesters took to counteract this type of propaganda are given below; for much more detailed discussions of and additional citations regarding "red" and "Boxer" imagery in the polemics of the 1920's, see Wasserstrom, "First Chinese Red Scare?"; and idem, "'Civilization' and Its Discontents."

80. Both "A Bolshevised China" and "China in Chaos" were published in Shanghai in 1927 by the *North China Herald*.

81. For several defenses of the May 30th Movement by non-students, see Rigby, *May 30th Movement*, pp. 98–107. Various examples of such texts are included in USDS, "1910–1929," reels 137–39.

82. Part of the June 27, 1925, issue of *Min pao* containing this letter is reprinted in USDS, "1910–1929," reel 138, 893.5040/195.

83. See "Kunming Protests," *CWR*, Jan. 18, 1947, p. 183; see also the "Letters from the People" section of *CWR*, Jan. 11, 1947.

84. There were a few references to bolshevism even in 1919; see, e.g., F.O. 228/3527, Hankow (Hankou) dispatch no. 96, Aug. 29, 1919; and the editorial in *NCH*, June 14, 1919, p. 685.

85. For an extreme example of this type of argument, see "A Truthful Explanation of the Student Disorders," in the May 29, 1919, issue of the Japanese-language edition of the Qingdao newspaper *Seitō shimpō*, translated in F.O. 371/3695, Tsingtao (Qingdao) dispatch no. 25, June 5, 1919, enclosure 2. This article blames American missionaries for having "compelled" Beijing students "to revolt and boycott Japan." For a much more comprehensive presentation of Japanese anti–May 4th arguments, see Shanhai Nihon Shōkō Kaigisho, *Santō mondai*.

86. For a translation of this article, see F.O. 371/3695, Tsingtao (Qingdao) dispatch no. 25, June 5, 1919, enclosure 4. For another interesting example of Chinese-language propaganda attacking the May 4th Movement, see the article translated in F.O. 228/3527, Tsinan (Ji'nan) dispatch no. 53, Sept. 20, 1919. Most of this propaganda emanated from cites in North China under Japanese control, but similar arguments appeared in Japanese-run Chinese-language papers in other parts of China as well. See, e.g., the translation of a Fujian newspaper article in F.O. 371/3695, Amoy (Xiamen) dispatch no. 39, June 9, 1919. This piece claims students in that area were content to be Western puppets: "When the foreigner orders them to deliver anti-Japanese speeches, they delightedly obey."

87. "The Students' Demonstrations," *Shanghai Times*, June 7, 1919. For further examples of English-language propaganda attacking the May 4th Movement from a pro-Japanese perspective, see other issues of the *Shanghai Times* and the clippings from the *North China Star* and the *North China Daily Mail* in F.O. 228/3527, pp. 10529–31. The *North China Daily Mail* piece is particularly interesting, since it places much of the blame for May 4th activities in North China on two institutions with close ties to the West: the Chinese Boy Scouts Association and the YMCA.

88. See, e.g., the letter from the SSU to foreign consuls in Shanghai reproduced in Joseph Chen, *May 4th Movement*, p. 129; and "Students' Explanation of the Strike," *China Press*, June 10, 1919, p. 8.

89. The Japanese did make some efforts to conjure up fears of a new Boxerism in 1919, and Xu Guoliang, chief of police in Shanghai's Chinese city, referred to student protesters as "second-time Boxers" at one point; see Joseph Chen, *May 4th Movement*, p. 119.

90. *NCH*, June 14, 1919, p. 724, quoted in Joseph Chen, *May 4th Movement*, pp. 158–59.

91. *NCH*, June 14, 1919, p. 713, quoted in Joseph Chen, *May 4th Movement*, p. 127.

92. See, e.g., He Baoren's letter to the Shanghai Municipal Council, printed in *NCH*, June 7, 1919, p. 650, and quoted in Joseph Chen, *May 4th Movement*, p. 118.

93. "Interview with Union's Secretary," *Shanghai Times*, June 6, 1919, p. 7.

94. Joseph Chen, *May 4th Movement*, p. 135.

95. *China Press*, June 10, 1919, p. 8. The author of this article goes on, interestingly, to play upon foreign self-interest by pointing out that the Japanese had already forced Western missionaries out of areas of northeast China under their control and that Western businessmen would be the next to suffer.

96. *Shanghai Times*, June 9, 1919, p. 9.

97. Joseph Chen, *May 4th Movement*, p. 129. For a more extreme example of this kind of English-language propaganda, see the pamphlet entitled "See Eastern Germany," enclosed in F.O. 228/3527, Foochow (Fuzhou) dispatch no. 2, Jan. 15,

1920. This fascinating, rabidly anti-Japanese pamphlet vilifies the Japanese as "a bunch of savages" who must be fought to "keep the world safe for democracy."

98. Quoted and translated in Tsi C. Wang, *Youth Movement in China*, p. 183.

99. Copies of issues of *Chengyan* are held at SMA.

100. For further bibliographic and textual information on *Taochi xunbao*, see Wasserstrom, "First Chinese Red Scare."

101. For example, the piece "My Gramophone's Solo" (see note 50 to this chapter) was written by an elementary school teacher in charge of anti-Communist propaganda lectures in a Shanxi village.

CHAPTER 9

1. Suzanne Pepper makes a persuasive case for the prevalence of this view among Chinese students (*Civil War*, pp. 42–94).

2. *Wenhuibao* Dec. 21, 1945, p. 1; "Welcome Marshall!" *Newsweek*, 26 (Dec. 31, 1945), p. 44; *Shanghai Evening Post and Mercury*, Dec. 17, 1945.

3. "Gao shizhang tongxue yu shehui renshi shu" (Proclamation to our teachers, fellow students, and the citizens of society), *Renren kanzhou* (The people's magazine), 2, no. 2 (1946): 2–3; Yi Sheng, "Shanghaishi dazhong xuesheng"; SCYL Youth Movement Research Group, *1945–1949*.

4. "Youth Corps Attacks Local Student Parade," *CWR*, Dec. 29, 1945, pp. 79–80.

5. Pepper, *Civil War*, pp. 44–52; for a review of recent Chinese work on the topic, see Israel, "Sources."

6. For Song Qingling's role in the service, see SCYL Youth Movement Research Group, *1945–1949*, p. 24.

7. Shen, "Renmin busi!"

8. My description of the parade is based on ibid.; Miu, "Gongji Yu Zai"; and Y. F. Chao, "Shanghai Students Stage Day-long Demonstration," *CWR*, Jan. 19, 1946, pp. 136–37. Most details in these sources, all of which are either pro-CCP or independent, are verified in reports in the Jan. 14 issues of the government-controlled papers *China Press* and *Dagongbao*.

9. *Zhengyanbao*, Jan. 15, 1946, p. 3; *Dagongbao*, Jan. 15, 1946, p. 3; *North China Daily News*, Jan. 15, 1946, p. 1; and *CWR*, Jan. 19, 1946, p. 129, and Jan. 26, 1946, p. 145. The *Zhengyanbao*, an organ of the Sanqingtuan, not surprisingly gives the most glowing account of the event, saying that 30,000 students took part; the more moderate *Dagongbao* says that only 2,000 youths marched.

10. See *Zhengyanbao*, Jan. 15, 1946.

11. For descriptions of two such loyalist displays, see *Wenhuibao*, Oct. 11, 1945, p. 1, and Oct. 31, 1945, p. 2. Members of the Sanqingtuan and the Boy Scouts figured prominently in virtually all loyalist displays of this type during the mid-1940's.

12. *Zhengyanbao*, Jan. 15, 1946.

13. My account of the anti-Soviet demonstrations is based on *Zhengyanbao*, Feb. 24–28, 1946; *China Press*, Feb. 24–26, 1946; *North China Daily News*, Feb. 24–27, 1946; *CWR*, Mar. 9, 1946, pp. 37–38; "Xinwen jicui," *Wen cui*, 20 (1946): 6; and various articles in *Shidai xuesheng*, 1, no. 9/10 (Mar. 1946). See also SCYL Youth

Movement Research Group, *1945–1949*, pp. 27–31; and Wu Mu et al., *Zhongguo qingnian yundongshi*, pp. 232–36.

14. For protests in other cities, see "News of the Week," *CWR*, Mar. 2, 1946, p. 15; *China Press*, Feb. 24, 1946; p. 1; and Wu Mu et al., *Zhongguo qingnian yundongshi*, pp. 27–31; for general background, see Pepper, *Civil War*, pp. 212–15.

15. "Party Marks Red Army Day Holiday," *China Press*, Feb. 24, 1946, p. 1.

16. Shen, "Renmin busi!"

17. *North China Daily News*, Feb. 27, 1946, p. 1.

18. Some anti-Soviet propaganda also compared the Russian threat to that posed in 1915 by Japan's Twenty-one Demands; see ibid.

19. *Xinwen tiandi* (News of the world), 11 (1946): 6.

20. See late February issues of *Zhengyanbao*, for variations on this theme.

21. "Xinwen jicui," *Wen cui*, 20 (1946): 6; see also the articles in *Shidai xuesheng*, 1, no. 9/10 (Mar. 1946).

22. For a modern reworking of this interpretation, see SCYL Youth Movement Research Group, *1945–1949*, pp. 27–31.

23. Radical claims of Sanqingtuan involvement are backed up by at least one far from radical press report; see *North China Daily News*, Feb. 25, 1946, p. 1.

24. An editorial entitled "The Young Idea" (*North China Daily News*, Feb. 25, 1946, p. 5), contrasts the authorities' suppression of anti-American actions and tolerance of anti-Soviet ones. For an unpersuasive dissenting view, which claims that all talk of official sponsorship of anti-Soviet activities is "slanderous," see *Zhengyanbao*, Feb. 28, 1946, p. 2.

25. See the articles in *Shidai xuesheng*, 1, no. 9/10 (Mar. 1946).

26. Lamb's May 27, 1947, letter, F.O. 371/63324; Pepper, *Civil War*, p. 59.

27. For background on GMD factional divisions, see Tien, *Government and Politics*, pp. 45–72; and Eastman, *Seeds of Destruction*. For specifics on the Shanghai situation, see Mao and Jiang, "Kangzheng shengli hou."

28. Mao and Jiang, "Kangzheng shengli hou," pp. 180–81; note, however, that the authors remember the date of the rally incorrectly, claiming that it took place in late 1945.

29. The following comments on the Women's Day demonstrations are based on SCYL Youth Movement Research Group, *1945–1949*, pp. 31–33; Bao Renyu, "Sanwan jiemei"; Wu Hua, "Quan Shanghai funü"; "Women's Festival Observed Here," *North China Daily News*, Mar. 9, 1946, p. 5; and *Zhengyanbao*, Mar. 9, 1946, p. 3.

30. For Xu's participation in Beijing protests of the mid-1920's, see Spence, *Gate of Heavenly Peace*, pp. 184–85; for her participation in protests of the mid-1940's, see SCYL Youth Movement Research Group, *1945–1949*, pp. 24, 48.

31. For the role of the Sanqingtuan, see *North China Daily News*, Mar. 9, 1946, p. 5; for the role of the Girl Guides, see *Zhengyanbao*, Mar. 9, 1946, p. 3.

32. SCYL Youth Movement Research Group, *1945–1949*, pp. 31–33; Bao Renyu, "Sanwan jiemei."

33. For details, see SCYL Youth Movement Research Group, *1945–1949*, pp. 44–46.

34. Newspaper reports are virtually the only sources of information for the Anti–Civil Disturbance march, but the Anti–Civil War demonstration is dealt with in detail in You, "Liuyue"; SCYL Youth Movement Research Group, *1945–*

1949; Chen Zhenzhong, "'Liu'ersan' yundong pianduan huiyi"; and Miu, "Fan neizhan."

35. SCYL Youth Movement Research Group, *1945–1949*, pp. 47–49.

36. Ibid., p. 48.

37. For more on the growth of anti-American sentiment, see Griggs, *Americans in China.*

38. SCYL Youth Movement Research Group, *1945–1949*, pp. 49–51.

39. *Dagongbao*, June 22, 1946; p. 4; SCYL Youth Movement Research Group, *1945–1949*, p. 51.

40. *Shanghai Evening Post and Mercury*, June 24, 1946, p. 1.

41. For descriptions on the May 5 parade, in which uniformed Boy Scouts figured prominently, see *Dagongbao*, May 6, 1946, p. 4.

42. Ibid., June 24, 1946; You, "Liuyue," estimates 100,000 protesters.

43. The 1946 issues of *CWR* are filled with articles and editorials dealing with the Shanghai elections and comparable ones in other cities: see, e.g., "Democratic Elections?" Mar. 16, 1946, pp. 48–49; Charles J. Canning, "Scandal in Yunnan: Bribery Quite Common in 'Elections,' Paper Openly Declares," Apr. 27, 1946, pp. 184–85; "Officials Held on Ballot Box Stuffing Charge," May 11, 1946, p. 235. See also "Wild West Election in Shanghai," *Shanghai Evening Post and Mercury*, Apr. 30, 1946: 8, which says that political bosses "had recourse to every old trick in the bag, starting with violence and intimidation and ending with the stuffing of ballot boxes," and that the "amount of general skullduggery manifested on this occasion seems excessive even by liberal Shanghai standards."

44. "News of the Week," *CWR*, May 11, 1946, p. 235.

45. For descriptions of this rally, see *Dagongbao* and *Zhengyanbao*, Feb. 15, 1946; and *Shanghai Herald*, Feb. 14, 1946, p. 2.

46. See Miu, "Fan neizhan"; Miu was one of the three "commanders."

47. SCYL Youth Movement Research Group, *1945–1949*, pp. 55–56. Because of the tendency of the authors of this work to paint the Sanqingtuan (whose members were, after all, always the arch-enemies of the Communist Youth League) as blackly as possible, this source's version needs to be taken with a grain of salt. Possible exaggeration notwithstanding, however, there seems little reason to doubt that something like this indeed happened, especially in light of the report in *CWR*, June 29, 1946, p. 102, of a man being "seized by the demonstrators, led through the streets and exhibited as a provocateur."

48. The following paragraphs are based upon the group memoir by Wang Ping et al., "Dou 'lang' suoyi"; SCYL Youth Movement Research Group, *1945–1949*, pp. 66–67; and an interview with a former student activist from Ji'nan University conducted in Shanghai in 1986. Although these accounts agree on most points, there are some discrepancies concerning precise details such as dates; where these exist, I have based my reconstruction on the most plausible version.

49. *China Daily Tribune*, Jan. 1, 1947, p. 2.

50. *China Press*, Jan. 1, 1947, p. 5.

51. For such statements to the press, see the January issues of *China Press Review*, (Shanghai).

52. *North China Daily News*, Jan. 3, 1947, p. 3.

53. For a good description of the parade supporting the new constitution, see *North China Daily News*, Jan. 3, 1947, p. 3; a picture of a parade float appears on the

front page of the same issue. One further structural similarity between the radical and loyalist marches, besides those cited in the text, was that each was preceded and followed by rallies of some sort. For photographs of the protest march, see SCYL, *Pictorial*, pp. 74–75.

54. For these and other struggles of the period, see Wang Gangjun et al., "Hujiang daxue"; Zhao et al., *Fudan daxuezhi*, pp. 186–88; SCYL Youth Movement Research Group, *1945–1949*, pp. 78–81; and Wang Min et al., *Dashiji*, pp. 264–67.

55. For details on the day's events, see the May 5, 1947, issues of *Wenhuibao*, *Xinwenbao*, *China Press*, and *North China Daily News*.

56. Wang Min et al., *Dashiji*, p. 268.

57. The following reconstruction of the Jiaotong protests is basd upon early May issues of *North China Daily News*, *China Press*, and the Chinese newspapers translated in *CPR*; Pepper, *Civil War*, p. 60; SCYL Youth Movement Research Group, *1945–1949*, pp. 81–89; the group memoir by Zhou Fenwu et al., "'Jiaoda wansui'"; Qin, "Jiaoda"; and, especially, "Political Report," *CWR: Monthly*, May 31, 1947, p. 5.

58. According to SCYL Youth Movement Research Group, *1945–1949*, p. 81, one reason Zhu was so interested in Jiaotong was that he had been trying for some time, unsuccessfully, to wrest control of the school from members of the CC Clique and place it in the hands of one of his relatives, an administrator at the university.

59. I have found no convincing direct evidence that factional struggles played any role at all in the Central University strike. Some sources do, however, suggest that members of the CC Clique encouraged school disturbances of all sorts in early May in order to embarrass Zhu Jiahua; see "Political Report," *CWR: Monthly*, May 31, 1947, p. 5.

60. For the precise breakdown of state versus private schools, see *Dagongbao* (Tianjin), July 10, 1947, cited in Pepper, *Civil War*, p. 59.

61. Pepper, *Civil War*, p. 58. CCP sources generally claim that inflation was even more severe in early 1947; see Wu Mu et al., *Zhongguo qingnian yundongshi*, p. 253, which states (unfortunately without documentary reference of any sort) that prices quadrupled between February and May.

62. For the national evolution of this struggle, see Pepper, *Civil War*, pp. 58–61; Wu Mu et al., *Zhongguo qingnian yundongshi*, pp. 253–55; and Xu Renhua and Li Lu, *Wu'erling*.

63. Wang, *Dashiji*, p. 269.

64. Ibid., pp. 269–70.

65. Xu Renhua and Li Lu, *Wu'erling*, 1: 431–50 and 2: 1–398; on Shanghai reactions in particular, see Cao Shiqun, "Qu Nanjing qingyuan" (Going to Nanjing to petition), *Shanghai dangshi ziliao tongxun*, 19 (Sept. 1984): 26–32.

66. *CWR*, May 24, 1947, p. 359, mentions plans for the involvement of workers and members of other classes and notes that students hoped the June 2 Anti–Civil War Day would mark the start of a new May 4th Movement.

67. Wang Min et al., *Dashiji*, pp. 271–74; SCYL Youth Movement Research Group, *1945–1949*, pp. 99–113.

68. The papers were suspended on May 24; for a translation of the official notice issued by the Shanghai Garrison Command explaining the rationale behind this act, see the opening editorial, "Freedoms Restricted," in *CWR*, May 31, 1947.

69. For translations of such statements, see the late May issues of *CPR*; and "News of the Week," *CWR*, May 24, 1947, p. 359.

70. The opening editorial in *CWR*, May 31, 1947, claims that 85 Shanghai students were arrested for making speeches on the streets in a single day; Xu Renhua and Li Lu (*Wu'erling*, 2: 119–21) provide a list of the names and school affiliations of more than 200 Shanghai students arrested during the month of May.

71. Communist narratives and memoirs are filled with descriptions of the mass arrests and of the efforts of protesters at some schools to prevent their leaders from being taken. See, e.g., SCYL Youth Movement Research Group, *1945–1949*, pp. 105–13. Several non-Communist periodicals covered the arrests extensively; see late May and early June issues of *CWR*, *Guancha* (The observer), and the Tianjin edition of *Dagongbao*.

72. For details on this event, see Wang Min et al., *Dashiji*, p. 273; and the letter "Special Students" signed "A Student of Fuh Tan" in *CWR*, June 7, 1947, p. 7. The term "wolf's teeth clubs" comes from an interview I conducted in Shanghai in 1986 with a victim of the attack.

73. Pepper, *Civil War*, p. 65.

74. See late May and early June issues of *CPR*.

75. *China Daily Tribune*, June 2, 1947, p. 2.

76. Ibid.

77. For descriptions of this event, see the June 3, 1947, issues of *North China Daily News*, *Zhengyanbao*, and, especially, *China Daily Tribune*.

78. Pepper, *Civil War*, p. 61.

79. *Zhengyanbao*, June 3, 1947, p. 4. Like earlier attacks on the central government's "softness" toward the Soviet Union, this was probably largely an outgrowth of factional rivalries.

80. See the photographs carried on the front pages of the June 3, 1947, issues of *North China Daily News* and *China Daily Tribune*.

81. Pepper, *Civil War*, pp. 52–70.

82. For relevant comments on this shift in public opinion, see Ambassador Stuart's June 4 dispatch to the American secretary of State, in U.S. Department of State, *Foreign Relations*, pp. 159–60.

83. See, e.g., Wu Mu et al., *Zhongguo qingnian yundongshi*, p. 255.

84. See, e.g., the report on the May 19 Shanghai march in *Dagongbao* (Shanghai), May 20, 1947.

85. The most important exception to this tendency was *China Weekly Review*, which took a more complex stance toward Chinese protests and Chinese politics generally than any other English-language paper: its writers often criticized the GMD harshly and had kind words for opposition protests, but its editorials also attacked the CCP at times and claimed that Jiang Jieshi was still the only man to lead the nation. For more on *China Weekly Review*'s editorial stance, as well as the general topic of foreign reporters' treatment of student protests of the mid-1940's, see Wasserstrom, "Waiguo jizhe."

86. *China Mail*, Jan. 4, 1947, p. 1; the UPI report appears in *South China Morning Post*, May 16, 1947.

87. Here again there are exceptions; not surprisingly, the GMD's English-language press organs, such as *China Press* and *China Daily Tribune*, continued to portray radical protests in a negative light throughout the period.

88. My statements concerning wire service coverage of Chinese protests is based upon a survey of AP, UPI, and Reuters reports carried by *China Mail* and *South China Morning Post*.

89. *South China Morning Post*, June 5, 1947, p. 6; see also the same issue's editorial "China's Students."

90. For a good sense of the hostility foreign reporters of the mid-1940's felt toward manifestations of "anti-foreignism," see "Hysterical Students Still Parading," *China Mail*, Jan. 4, 1947, p. 1.

91. F.O. 371/63324, file 76.

92. U.S. State Department, *Foreign Relations*, pp. 161–62.

93. Ibid., pp. 154–55.

94. On the abortive Anti-Soviet Movement, see *North China Daily News*, Mar. 17, 1947, p. 1, which contains photographs of students carrying out propaganda work.

95. For details concerning this and other protests of the last two years of the Civil War era, see SCYL Youth Movement Research Group, *1945–1949*; Wang Min et al., *Dashiji*; and Wang Min, *Chuntian de yaolan*, pp. 285–91.

96. This leaflet, whose Chinese title is "Shanghai shi xuelian wei jinian zongli zhengchen gao ge jie tongbao shu," is held at SMA.

CHAPTER 10

1. For a sense of the range of possible outcomes, see the overview of 1968 youth activism across the globe in Katsiaficas, *Imagination of the New Left*, pp. 37–57; and the contributions to Lipset and Altbach, *Students in Revolt*, and DeConde, *Student Activism*.

2. Altbach, "Student Political Activism," pp. 41–43; a note on page 43 lists fifteen countries other than China—including Bolivia, Iran, Nigeria and Bangladesh—as among those in which student protests either toppled a regime or had "significant political results."

3. Kassow, *Students, Professors, and the State*, esp. pp. 404–5, the most comprehensive English-language study of the topic to date, shows that students were an important force in some phases of the Russian Revolution: their strikes of 1899, 1901, and 1911 called the legitimacy of autocratic rule into question, and they played a central role in the upheavals of 1905. However, they did not fulfill the same kind of vanguard role in multi-class mass movements as Chinese students, and, Kassow notes, the political importance of the student movement declined during the years immediately preceding 1917.

4. For contrasting assessments of that role, see Miles, *Radical Probe*; Scranton et al., *Report of the President's Commission*; Gitlin, *The Sixties*; Miller, *Democracy Is in the Streets*; and DeBenedetti, *American Ordeal*.

5. Gitlin (*The Sixties*, p. 410) claims that there were "strikes at about 30 percent of the nation's twenty-five hundred campuses," and that "at least a million students probably demonstrated for the first times in their lives during that month of May." Similar figures appear in Scranton et al., *Report of the President's Commission*, pp. 45–46.

6. On the rice riots of 1947; see the May 1–10 issues of *CPR* (Shanghai and other cities), *North China Daily News*, and *Dagongbao* (Shanghai and Tianjin).

These same newspapers also provide information on worker protests of the period. See also Perry, "Shanghai on Strike"; and Zhang Chi, "Liangzhong jinian" (Two kinds of anniversaries), *Wen cui*, 6 (May 30, 1947): 43–46, which contains a detailed account of how radical workers tried to turn officially sponsored celebrations of May Day into anti-GMD protests.

7. Statera, *Death of a Utopia*, pp. 120–41; Katsiaficas, *Imagination of the New Left*, pp. 87–116.

8. Statera, *Death of a Utopia*, pp. 114–20.

9. Katsiaficas (*Imagination of the New Left*, pp. 130–39) argues against the prevailing image of the working class as a conservative force in 1970, but even he is forced to concede that reaction to student protest and the antiwar movements as a whole was mixed at best among blue-collar workers.

10. See, e.g., DeBenedetti, *American Ordeal*, p. 243.

11. Altbach, "Student Political Activism," pp. 43–46. See also Seymour Lipset, "University Students and Politics in Underdeveloped Countries," in idem, *Student Politics*, pp. 3–53; and various essays in Lipset and Altbach, *Students in Revolt*; as well as the contributions to Donald Emerson, ed., *Students and Politics in Developing Nations* (New York: Praeger, 1968).

12. Francis Donahue, "Students in Latin-American Politics," in DeConde, *Student Activism*, p. 254.

13. Scranton et al., *Report of the President's Commission*, p. 43.

14. Pepper (*Civil War*, p. 56) says that in late 1946 only 80,646 youths attended college in GMD-controlled regions.

15. For attempts by Russian students to create a political role for themselves, see Kassow, *Students, Professors, and the State*.

16. Ibid., pp. 399, 400, 403.

17. Kenneth Walker, "A Comparison of the University Reform Movements in Argentina and Colombia," in Lipset, *Student Politics*, pp. 293–317.

18. Sungjoo Han, "Student Activism: A Comparison Between the 1960 Uprising and the 1971 Protest Movement," in Chong Lim Kim, et., *Political Participation in Korea* (Oxford: Clio Books, 1980), pp. 143–64.

19. For Weber's conceptualization of "charisma," see Gerth and Mills, *Max Weber*, esp. pp. 245–52, 262–64; see also Eisenstadt, *Max Weber*, esp. pp. ix.—lvi.

20. For further discussions and critiques of Weberian ideas concerning "de-ritualization," see Lukes, "Political Ritual"; and MacKenzie, *Politics*, p. 212.

21. Geertz, "Centers, Kings, and Charisma," p. 15.

22. In this regard, Geertz is open to some of the same critiques that Lukes ("Political Ritual") uses to attack "neo-Durkheimian" studies of ceremonies and parades.

23. Cited in Lipsitz, "Struggle for Hegemony," p. 146.

24. Scholars have already demonstrated that the framework Geertz proposes is useful for making sense of political behavior in a wide variety of cultural and historical contexts. See, e.g., Hunt, *Politics, Culture, and Class*; and the essays in Wilentz, *Rites of Power*.

25. See Wakeman, "Shanghai Public Security Bureau," pts. I ("Law and Order"), II (The New Police System), and IV (Police Sovereignty), in particular. As the *CWR* (Jan. 5, 1929; cited in ibid.) put it: "One of the publicly announced reasons for maintaining the present foreign regime is that the place would quickly

go to ruin if the Chinese were running it." Realizing the importance of this argument, one of the main things Sun Chuanfang and his GMD successors set out to
prove when they began reforming the policing systems and general administrative
procedures within the native city in the 1920's was that Chinese authorities could
indeed maintain order. This, according to Wakeman, was a key part of their effort
to "prove to the world that the Chinese deserved to recover control over the foreign settlements" (see ibid., pt. I, for this statement and relevant citations of Chinese works).

26. For the text of this proclamation, see *North China Herald*, June 14, 1919,
p. 718.

27. For a provocative discussion of the general symbolic changes that accompanied the GMD's shift from a party of rebellion to a party of order and the
meaning of Jiang Jieshi's growing identification with Zeng Guofan after 1926 in
particular, see M. C. Wright, *Last Stand*, pp. 300–12. But see also Paul Cohen's
"Post-Mao Reforms" for a critique of Wright's dismissal of the GMD's policies of
the Nanjing Decade as "little more than a rerun of Tongzhi Restoration." Cohen's
arguments concerning the need to place GMD reforms in a more balanced perspective, as policies with a definite forward-looking aspect, are persuasive and build
upon several recent, well-documented case studies of Nationalist activities. At the
level of political ritual and symbolism, however, Wright's analysis of the Confu-
cianization of the party remains convincing.

28. For GMD interpretations and celebrations of the May 4th Movement, see
Schwarcz, *Chinese Enlightenment*; for Sun's identification with bandit heroes, including the Taiping leaders Zeng Guofan opposed, see M. C. Wright, *Last Stand*,
p. 301. Wang Jingwei's puppet GMD of the late 1930's and early 1940's—which
staked its claim to legitimacy on the idea that Jiang Jieshi had diverted the party
from Sun Zhongshan's original course and which hence remained committed to
the same myths of origin—had to be even more selective in its use of some historic
symbols, particularly those linked to the anti-imperialist May 4th tradition. Interestingly, the puppet regime did issue statements praising the student protesters of
1919 on at least one occasion. On May 4, 1945, the puppet GMD marked the anniversary of two important events: the beginning of the patriotic student struggle of
1919; and the birth of one of the nation's great heroes, the recently deceased Wang
Jingwei. In honoring the May 4th Movement, however, the puppet authorities
were careful to ignore the struggle's anti-Confucian aspect and to gloss over the
fact that the students of 1919 protested Japanese imperialism and the acts of pro-
Japanese native officials. Rather than presenting the May 4th Movement as a fight
against imperialism, leaders of the puppet GMD treated it as a struggle against
warlords "whose misgovernment of the country was leading [China] to increasing
chaos and disunity." See "China's Youth Urged to Follow in Steps of Late Leader;
Struggle Lauded," *Shanghai Times*, May 5, 1945, p. 1.

29. Wechsler, "Campus Revolt," p. 289.

30. DeBenedetti, *American Ordeal*, pp. 107–9, 128–30, 395.

31. Kassow, *Students, Professors, and the State*, p. 405.

32. See, e.g., Katsiaficas, *Imagination of the New Left*, esp. pp. 127–30; this is also
an underlying theme in Statera, *Death of a Utopia*; and Miles, *Radical Probe*.

33. See DeBenedetti, *American Ordeal*, pp. 395–96.

Epilogue

1. W. C. Chen, *Chinese Communist Anti-Americanism.*

2. For Red Guard activities in Shanghai, see Walder, *Chang Ch'un-ch'iao*; and Hunter, *Shanghai Journal.*

3. For examples, see Wasserstrom, "'Civilization' and Its Discontents."

4. For a sample contemporary reference to the Hundred Flowers Campaign as a "new May 4th Movement," as well as a comment by a student activist calling on Beijing University youths to carry on in the May 4th tradition, see Doolin, *Communist China*, p. 18; this book contains a useful overview of and translations of documents concerning campus protest activities of the late 1950's. For general background on the April 5th Movement, see Yan and Gao, *"Wenhua da geming" shinianshi*, pp. 586–640. For information on the Beijing Democracy Wall Movement, see Nathan, *Chinese Democracy*; for related Shanghai student protest activities, see MacLaren, "Educated Youth Return." For analyses of the 1985 protests in North China, see Pepper, *Deng Xiaoping's Political and Economic Reforms*; and G. H. Chang, "Student Protests." One additional point of interest in terms of continuity between protests of the post–Cultural Revolution era and their predecessors, which scholars have tended to overlook, is that the term "Democracy Wall" goes back at least as far as 1946 and was used during the Hundred Flowers Campaign as well; see the photograph in *Xinwen tiandi* (News of heaven and earth), 11 (Mar. 31, 1946): 7, and Doolin, *Communist China*, p. 15.

5. See, e.g., Foreign Broadcast and Information Service, *Daily Report: China*, Dec. 12, 1986, pp. P1–3.

6. *New York Times* (national ed.), Dec. 12, 1986, p. 1.

7. Foreign Broadcast and Information Service, *Daily Report: China* Dec. 24, 1986, pp. K2–3.

8. *New York Times*, Jan. 2, 1987, p. 1; Jan. 6, 1987, p. 3.

9. For an illuminating analysis of Fang Lizhi's 1986 speeches and vision of democracy, see Kraus, "Fang Lizhi."

10. *New York Times*, Jan. 4. 1989, p. 3.

11. For more developed discussions of the meanings of "democracy" in 1989, see Esherick and Wasserstrom, "Acting out Democracy"; and Solinger, "Democracy with Chinese Characteristics."

12. Niming, "Learning How to Protest"; Forster, "Impressions."

13. Pieke, "Observations," provides an illuminating account of the significance of audience response during various stages of the People's Movement. One of the best treatments of worker participation in the events of 1989 is Walder, "Political Sociology."

14. Chong, "Petitioners, Popperians, and Hunger Strikers," p. 115. See also Shen Tong's own comments in Human Rights in China, *Children of the Dragon*, pp. 46–48, which highlights the contact provincial student activists had with Beijing organizers such as himself during the months preceding the start of the People's Movement.

15. For a provocative discussion of the implications of this last phenomenon, as well as comments on the role minority-related issues played in Xi'an protests, see

Dru Gladney, "The Peoples of the People's Republic: Finally in the Vanguard?" *Fletcher Forum of World Affairs*, 12, no. 1 (1990): 62–76.

16. See Human Rights in China, *Children of the Dragon*, for comments by Orville Schell on the millenarian mood during the occupation (p. 12) and photographs of a joyous dancing couple (p. 8) and a rock-and-roll party on May 25 (p. 102), which give a good sense of this festive atmosphere.

17. Information on 1989 events in provincial cities is hard to find. Three of the most important sources for events outside of Beijing are eyewitness reports in the special sections on provincial unrest in the *Australian Journal of Chinese Affairs*, 23 and 24 (1990); and Wu Mouren et al., *Bajiu*. Along with these sources, for comments on Shanghai events I have relied upon Pellow, "Choreography of Dissent"; the careful reconstruction of events in Maier, "'Tian'anmen 1989,'" which makes use of Chinese press reports and a CCP *neibu* (internal circulation only) report that details protest activities throughout the country; and personal communications with Patricia Stranahan and Nicholas Clifford.

18. See *Newsweek*, May 29, 1989, p. 21, for the protection accorded student leaders. Francis, "Progress of Protest"; Niming, "Learning How to Protest"; and Strand, "Protest," draw attention to the highly organized nature of the 1989 struggle as a whole.

19. Wakeman, "June Fourth Movement"; *Washington Post*, May 24, 1989, p. 20.

20. I am grateful to Chris Borstel and Julie Strauss for information on Nanjing events.

21. I am grateful to Deborah Pellow for showing me a photograph of this scene and to Jonathan Spence for drawing my attention to the various ways in which dissidents continue to use quotes from Lu Xun, whom the CCP regime still exalts as a sacred figure, to attack the contemporary political status quo. For a translation of the relevant section of Lu Xun's essay, see Schwarcz, *Chinese Enlightenment*, p. 159.

22. Calhoun, "Beijing Spring," p. 441; *San Francisco Chronicle*, May 14, 1989, p. 11.

23. For a description of loyalist demonstrations, see *Los Angeles Times*, June 1, 1989, p. 13.

24. On the massacres of the mid-1920's, see Schwarcz, *Chinese Enlightenment*, esp. pp. 156–57; for an introduction to the "big lie" campaign of 1989, see Munro, "Who Died in Beijing, and Why."

25. Chong, "Petitioners, Popperians, and Hunger Strikers."

26. There had also been a series of short-lived, small-scale campus protests in Beijing between 1987 and 1989; see Francis, "Progress of Protest."

27. Han Minzhu, *Cries for Democracy*, pp. 269–71. For examples of other kinds of student refutations of the Cultural Revolution analogy, see ibid., pp. 112–14; and Yu Mok Chiu and Harrison, *Voices from Tiananmen*, pp. 91–93.

28. *San Francisco Chronicle*, June 5, 1989, p. 15.

29. Associated Press report, in *San Francisco Chronicle*, Apr. 28, 1989. "Frere Jacques" has been used for political purposes on a variety of other occasions in China as well: the tune was used by the GMD in the late 1920's (John Israel, pers. comm.), and during the Cultural Revolution the air was used as the basis for dozens of political songs (Carma Hinton, pers. comm.).

30. The following reconstruction of local events is based on Forward, "Letter from Shanghai"; Warner, "Shanghai's Response"; K. Wright, "Political Fortunes"; and the works cited in note 17 above.

31. Wu Mouren, *Bajiu*, pp. 10–11.

32. For examples, see ibid., pp. 229–30, 258–59, 287, and 408–9.

33. For details, see K. Wright, "Political Fortunes."

34. Pellow, "Choreography of Dissent," pp. 10–11.

35. Warner, "Shanghai's Response," p. 302.

36. According to ibid., p. 302, Beijing students also sent a directive to Wuhan youths to shut down their city; for information on Wuhan events, I am grateful to Eddie Yuan.

37. A photograph showing the banner of one Shanghai "dare to die" squad is held in the Smith Collection at Harvard's Yenching Library.

38. Warner, "Shanghai's Response," pp. 309–10.

39. For a lively and ironic description of Tiananmen on Oct. 1, 1989, see "A Tourist-Eye View of 'Happy Normality,'" in the Hong Kong magazine *China Review*, Nov. 1989, pp. 44–45. Not surprisingly, China's official media denied that there was anything unusual about the 1989 National Day celebrations, just as in 1947 GMD news releases claimed that the small-scale ceremonies held on key dates were due solely to a new "austerity" campaign; see, e.g., *China Press*, Oct. 10, 1947, p. 1.

40. Forward, "Letter from Shanghai," p. 297.

41. David Zweig, "Peasants and Politics," *World Policy Journal*, Fall 1989, pp. 633–45.

42. Here and below, my thoughts on the relationship between myth and history have been influenced by conversations with Paul Cohen.

43. Mary Erbaugh and Richard Kraus, "The 1989 Democracy Movement in Fujian and Its Consequences," *Australian Journal of Chinese Affairs*, 23 (1990): 153. For related comments, see other pieces in the same issue, such as Forster, "Popular Protest in Hangzhou."

44. Conversations with Eddie Yuan and Kristen Parris have influenced my thinking on these points. It is also important to remember that not all members of the laobaixing sympathized with or trusted the students; even after the June 4 Massacre, some looked upon educated youths as spoiled troublemakers.

45. One of the most insightful and important of these is Lubman, "Myth."

46. For sample critiques, see A. Chan and Unger, "China After Tiananmen"; Chan and Kwong, "Trashing the Hopes of Tiananmen"; and Rosemont, "China: The Mourning After."

47. For further discussion of this point and relevant citations, see Esherick and Wasserstrom, "Acting out Democracy."

48. Pye, "Tiananmen."

49. For further discussion on this second point, see Gladney, "Bodily Positions and Social Dispositions."

50. Han Minzhu, *Cries for Democracy*, p. 171.

51. Schwarcz, "Memory," p. 127.

 **BIBLIOGRAPHIC ESSAY**

BECAUSE OF REPUBLICAN SHANGHAI's status as an international city, important sources for the study of events such as the May 4th Movement are housed in archives and libraries on three continents and in close to a dozen countries. Since special collections of materials relating to the Chinese protests of 1989 are located in Australia, North America, Europe, and Hong Kong, the evidence concerning post-1949 events is scattered even more widely. Significant secondary studies of twentieth-century protests have been completed by scholars working in various Western countries, China, Taiwan, Hong Kong, and Japan. Given the amount of material and its wide geographic diffusion, a short essay such as this cannot cover all the relevant literature. Instead, I will content myself with selectively surveying some of the most important collections, compilations, and secondary analyses that shed light on Shanghai student protests of the first half of the twentieth century and with making some general comments on the reliability and usefulness of certain kinds of sources. I conclude with brief remarks on materials for the study of the protests of 1989.

PRIMARY SOURCES: REPUBLICAN CHINA

Archives, Libraries, and Document Collections: Shanghai

The most important archives and libraries for study of this topic are, not surprisingly, those in Shanghai itself. Among those I visited in 1986–87 were the Shanghai Municipal Archive, the Shanghai Municipal Library, the Fudan University Library, and the Shanghai Communist Youth League Youth Movement History Group Archive. I also gained access to materials in informal historical archives

---

For complete authors' names, titles, and publication data for the works cited here in short form, see the Bibliography, pp. 391–412.

of these events, whereas those treating comparable protests of the mid-1920's present these marches in a much more positive light. Second, one reason memoirs are published is to glorify the role of the CCP in leading the Chinese people to "liberation," and reminiscences that appear in journals and books tend to over-emphasize the role underground Communist organizers played in student move-ments. Even unpublished reminiscences frequently fall victim to the same bias, be-cause the authors and interviewees are concerned with presenting a politically correct interpretation.

My strategy for compensating for the inherent biases in these accounts has been a simple one: wherever possible, I have cross-checked descriptions of student pro-tests in PRC memoirs and interviews against accounts in sources written by people with different political orientations and prejudices. Thus, for example, in the case of the May 4th Movement, I have compared analyses in PRC reminiscences with those in English-language newspapers; memoirs published in Taiwan, such as those gathered in *Wo canjiale wusi yundong* (compiled by Lianfu jizhe); and the Japanese sources in *Santō mondai ni kansuru Nikka haiseki no eikyō* (compiled by Shanhai Nihon Shōkō Kaigisho). In the case of student protests of the Civil War era, I have played information from PRC memoirs off accounts in contemporary newspapers and periodicals, ranging from the American *China Weekly Review* (which tended to be fairly sympathetic toward student protests) to the British *North China Daily News* (hostile toward popular demonstrations of any sort) to various news organs controlled by the GMD or factions within the Nationalist camp, such as *Zhengyanbao*, *China Daily Tribune*, and *Dagongbao*.

Each of these non-PRC sources has biases of its own, of course. For example, memoirs concerning the events of 1919 published in Taiwan tend to highlight Sun Zhongshan's role in inspiring May 4th students, and foreign reporters frequently viewed student protests largely in terms of their probable impact on Sino-Western relations. Nonetheless, since the biases in these and other sources—such as the reports members of the Shanghai Municipal Police or British consular officials made concerning protests of the 1920's and 1930's—are not the same as those in PRC reminiscences, they can be used to test the veracity of firsthand accounts of student protests in CCP-sponsored publications such as the *Wenshi ziliao* series or the reminiscences of student activists studying in Shanghai in the 1940's in *Chun-tian de yaolan* (edited by Wang Min et al.).

It has not always been possible to check every piece of information found in PRC memoirs against other sources, since the value of the reminscences lies pre-cisely in the details they provide concerning specific student organizations, per-sonalities, and campuses. Where it has been possible to cross-check accounts in memoirs against those in other sources, the reminiscences have proved extremely trustworthy, with the exception of information concerning the role of the CCP in youth movements. As a result, there seems little reason to doubt the descriptions in these memoirs of such things as the march routes students followed on a specific date or the number and types of literary societies that existed on a given campus in a given year. Although one must remain skeptical about claims of success and the extent of underground CCP leadership, much of the information in PRC memoirs can be used with no more than the usual amount of skepticism historians bring to bear on any source.

Several useful English-language memoirs by Chinese and foreign writers also exist. Of the works by Chinese authors, the most important are *The Rise of the Chinese Communist Party* by Chang Kuo-t'ao (Zhang Guotao—a former CCP leader who left China after a falling-out with Mao), which contains information on both the May 4th and May 30th struggles; and Chiang Mon-lin's *Tides from the West*, a valuable source for understanding student life and student protest during the first decades of the twentieth century. Of those by foreign writers, Helen Foster Snow's *Notes on the Chinese Student Movement* and *My China Years* contain reminiscences of the December 9th Movement in Beijing during which she and her husband taught and served as advisers to student activists. Hubert Freyn's *Prelude to War* is also a useful source. Freyn was studying in Beijing in the mid-1930's and accompanied some Chinese classmates to do propaganda work in the countryside in the aftermath of the December 9th Incident. And, finally, John and Alice Dewey's *Letters from China and Japan*, though more about events in Beijing, provides insights into the May 4th Movement. John Dewey also wrote a number of articles on Chinese events for American magazines during 1919 and 1920; a listing of these as well as of a wide range of other Chinese-, Japanese-, and English-language materials on the May 4th Movement can be found in Chow Tse-tsung's *Research Guide to the May 4th Movement*.

Secondary Works: Republican China

Campus Histories

During the past decade or so, virtually every major Shanghai school with roots in the Republican era has sponsored the publication of a campus history. These have taken a variety of forms, ranging from the fairly straightforward narrative of Shi Weixiang et al., *Jiaotong daxue xiaoshi, 1896–1949*, to the more scholarly Zhao Shaoquan et al., *Fudan daxuezhi, 1905–1949* (which contains documents as well as descriptive chapters). All these school histories highlight the part students from a particular campus played in various youth movements, and some such as Tu Tingxiang et al., *Tongji daxue xuesheng yundongshi, 1919–1949*, are devoted entirely to this topic.

In addition to narrative histories, several collections of documents and/or memoirs deal with specific schools. The Jiaotong University School History Group, for example, compiled a two-volume collection of materials on the history of that university, *Jiaotong daxue xiaoshi ziliao*, and a 1984 issue of Fudan's campus history journal, *Xiaoshi tongxun*, was devoted almost exclusively to materials on that school's role in the May 4th Movement. Shanghai daxue, a school that no longer exists, has also been the subject of two school histories, which combine narrative with documents and memoirs: Cai Xiyao and Wang Jiagui, eds., *Shanghai daxue*; and Huang Meizhen et al., eds., *Shanghai daxue shiliao*. In 1988 a special issue in the Shanghai *Wenshi ziliao* series (vol. 59, *Jiefangqian Shanghai de xuexiao*) was devoted to brief campus histories and memoirs of school life before 1949.

Foreign scholars have also written a number of useful works focusing on particular Chinese schools. There are several full-length campus histories, such as Mary Lamberton's *St. John's University, Shanghai, 1879–1951*, and Philip West's *Yenching* rectly with Shanghai events; the great exception is the Shanghai Youth League's *Yi'erjiu yundong zai Shanghai*. John Israel has written a useful general survey of the way PRC historians tended to approach the national movement before the Cultural Revolution, "The December 9th Movement: A Case Study in Chinese Communist Historiography," and as the recent history edited by Zhonggong, Zhongyang dangxiao, Dangshi yanjiuban, *Yi'erjiu yundong shiyao*, illustrates, the themes he stresses are still present in much work being done in China. Whereas PRC approaches play up the positive role of Communist organizers in the December 9th Movement, a very different perspective is offered in Li Guocheng, "Zhongguo kangri zhanzheng qian de xuesheng yundong (1931–1936)," which contains interesting comparisons of the youth struggles of 1931 and 1935.

Student protests that occurred during the War of Resistance have received little attention, and in fact there is little information on local educated youths between 1937 and 1945. Hu Kuo-tai's "Disputes on the Question of Wartime Education and the Formation of an Educational Policy for the Guomindang in the War," sheds some light on the use the CCP and GMD hoped to make of educated youths during the Second United Front. A rare discussion of student activities in Shanghai during the War of Resistance is Tang Shibai and Wen Xiaoyi, "Shilun gudao shiqi Shanghai xuesheng yundong de jige tedian."

Protests of the Civil War era have received a good deal more attention, especially from Chinese scholars. The best English-language work on the subject is Suzanne Pepper's *Civil War in China*, a chapter of which is devoted to the student antiwar movement. Jessie Lutz's essay "The Chinese Student Movement of 1945–1949" also provides a useful overview of the key events. As for Chinese-language publications, nearly every issue of *Shanghai qingyunshi ziliao* and *Shanghai qingyunshi yanjiu* contains at least one article or memoir relating to the Civil War era, and the Shanghai Communist Youth League's Youth Movement Research Group has produced a valuable general narrative of local events, *1945–1949 Shanghai xuesheng yundongshi*.

The Student Protests of 1989

As this is being written in September 1990, an enormous amount has already appeared about the occupation of Tiananmen Square and its bloody aftermath. Close to a hundred books, ranging from document compilations to eyewitness accounts to narrative histories to photographic essays, have been published on the subject; articles on the Chinese crisis of 1989 have appeared in scores of academic journals, some of which have devoted whole issues to the topic; and many more scholarly and popular publication projects dealing with the events in Beijing, and in a few cases the provinces as well, are forthcoming. In addition, archives devoted to the Chinese democracy movement have been established or are in the process of being set up at, among other places, Harvard, Yale, the University of Toronto, the University of Hawaii, Australia National University, and the International Institute of Social History, Amsterdam.

The flood of activity connected with documenting and analyzing the protests of 1989 makes it impossible to do more here than describe some of the works that I have found most useful. A much more thorough overview of early works on these protests can be found in Tony Saich and Nancy Hearst's "Bibliographic Note," in

Tony Saich, ed., *The Chinese People's Movement*, a book that also includes a valuable appendix by Stefan Landsberger providing a chronology of events in Beijing, as well as important essays on various topics by Kathleen Hartford ("The Political Economy Behind Beijing Spring"), Frank Niming ("Learning How to Protest"), Woei Lien Chong ("Petitioners, Popperians, and Hunger Strikers"), Lawrence Sullivan ("The Emergence of Civil Society in China, Spring 1989"), Seth Faison ("The Changing Role of the Chinese Media"), and Saich himself ("When Worlds Collide: The Beijing People's Movement of 1989"). Because Saich and Hearst do such a good job of describing and highlighting the value of the works mentioned in their bibliographic note, I generally limit myself here to studies they do not discuss.

To begin with general works, one of the best narratives of the 1989 protests is Yi Mu and Mark Thompson's *Crisis at Tiananmen*, which combines description and analysis of key events with translations of several important documents. A number of other works that either mix narrative and translations of wall posters, interviews with student leaders, official interpretations of the protests, and the like, or are devoted exclusively to document reproduction are cited in Saich and Hearst's bibliographic note. The most important of these for my purposes are Human Rights in China, *Children of the Dragon*; Han Minzhu, *Cries for Democracy*; and Wu Mouren et al., eds., *Bajiu Zhongguo minyun jishi*, which provides a detailed chronology of the events of spring 1989 in Shanghai and other provincial locations as well as in Beijing and reproduces newspaper accounts dealing with these events. One document collection that Saich and Hearst do not mention is Mok Chiu Yu and J. Frank Harrison, eds., *Voices from Tiananmen Square: Beijing Spring and the Democracy Movement*, which contains translations of several interesting pamphlets and wall posters. One of the best collections of photographs is Peter and David Turnley's *Beijing Spring*.

Several articles and conference papers that touch most directly upon the kinds of historical and symbolic themes dealt with in this book deserve special mention. Three important and provocative essays on symbolic questions by anthropologists interested in the events of 1989 are Dru Gladney's "Bodily Positions and Social Dispositions: Sexuality, Nationality and Tiananmen"; Frank Pieke's "Observations During the People's Movement in Beijing, Spring 1989"; and James Watson's "The Renegotiation of Chinese Cultural Identity in the Post-Mao Era: An Anthropological Perspective." Although nearly all discussions of the events of 1989 refer to historical precedents, relatively few authors have looked in any detail at the connections between these events and earlier protests. Some exceptions to this tendency are Jonathan Spence's concluding chapter in *The Search for Modern China*, which analyzes contemporary struggles for democracy in terms of ongoing themes in Chinese history from the imperial era through the revolutionary one; Andrew Nathan's "Chinese Democracy in 1989: Continuity and Change"; Corrina-Barbara Francis's "Progress of Protest in China," which looks in some detail at the debt the students of 1989 owed their predecessors of three years before; and David Strand's excellent analysis of continuities in Beijing protests over the last seventy years, which has appeared in two slightly different versions.

Compared with the wealth of materials available to the scholar interested in Beijing, relatively little has been published on events in the provinces. Press reports in American, Chinese, and Hong Kong newspapers and magazines do, however, provide important information on Shanghai events. So do the following insightful firsthand accounts: Ray Forward, "Letter from Shanghai"; Deborah Pellow, "A Choreography of Dissent: Shanghai 1989" (unpublished); Kate Wright, "The Political Fortunes of Shanghai's *World Economic Herald*"; and Shelley Warner, "Shanghai's Response to the Deluge." John Maier's "'Tian'anmen 1989': The View from Shanghai" is a careful reconstruction of local events based largely on Chinese documents.

 **BIBLIOGRAPHY**

For a list of abbreviations used in the Bibliography, see p. 331.

ARCHIVES AND GOVERNMENT DOCUMENT COLLECTIONS CONSULTED

China

Fudan University Campus History Archive, Shanghai.
SCYL Youth Movement History Group, Shanghai.
Shanghai Municipal Archives, Shanghai.

Europe

British Public Record Office, Foreign Office Papers, London.
International Labor Organization Archive, Geneva.
YMCA International Archive, Geneva.

United States

Hoover Institution Archive, Stanford.
Shanghai Municipal Police Files, 1919–41, Berkeley, Calif. (microfilm).
U.S. Department of State Records Relating to Internal Affairs of China, 1919–49, Berkeley, Calif. (microfilm).

PERIODICALS SURVEYED

The locations of relatively unaccessible periodicals are given in brackets at the end of each entry using the following codes:

H   Hoover Institution
SML   Shanghai Municipal Library
F   Fudan University Library
B   University of California, Berkeley
UL   University of London, School of Oriental and African Studies
P   Libraries of the Centre de Recherches et de Documentation sur la Chine
         Contemporaine and the Ecole des Langues Orientales, Paris.

An asterisk indicates a Chinese periodical classified as *neibu* or "for internal circulation only" and hence difficult or impossible to find outside of China.

Celestial Empire. Shanghai, 1918–19 [UL].
China Critic. Shanghai, 1935–36.
China Daily Tribune. Shanghai, 1946–47 [H].
China Mail. Hong Kong, 1945–47.
China Press. Shanghai, 1918–41, 1945–49 (some years unavailable) [H].
China Press Review. Shanghai, 1945–47 [B].
China Weekly Review. Shanghai, 1919–41, 1945–49.
China Weekly Review: Monthly Reports. Shanghai, 1946–47 [H].
Dagongbao (L'impartiale). Shanghai and Tianjin (separate editions), 1945–49.
*Dangshi ziliao (Materials on party history). Shanghai, 1980–87 [F].
Dazhong shenghuo (Life of the masses). Shanghai, 1935–36.
Dongfang zazhi (Eastern miscellany). Shanghai, 1918–25.
Geming wenxian (Documents on the revolution). Taibei, 1951–70.
Kangri jiuguo (Resist Japan, save the nation). Shanghai (Fudan), 1931 [F].
Le journal de Shanghai. Shanghai, 1931–36 [P].
Minguo ribao (Republican daily news). Shanghai, 1918–25 [F].
North China Daily News. Shanghai, 1919–41, 1945–49 [H].
North China Herald. Shanghai, 1919–41.
Qingnian zhishi (Youth culture). Shanghai, 1947 [F].
Rexue ribao (Bloodshed daily). Shanghai, 1925 [B].
*Shanghai dangshi ziliao tongxun (Communications and materials on Shanghai party
         history). Shanghai, 1981–88 (selected issues) [SML].
Shanghai Evening Post and Mercury. Shanghai, 1945–47 [H].
Shanghai Herald. Shanghai, 1945–46 (some issues unavailable) [H].
*Shanghai qingyunshi yanjiu (Researches on Shanghai youth movement history—
         continuation of *Shanghai qingyunshi ziliao*). Shanghai, 1987–88 [F].
*Shanghai qingyunshi ziliao (Materials on Shanghai youth movement history).
         Shanghai, 1981–86 [F].
Shanghai Times. Shanghai, 1918–19, 1943–45 (some years and issues unavailable)
         [1943–45: H].
Shen bao (Shanghai news). Shanghai, 1918–49 (selected issues).
Shenghuo (Life). Shanghai, 1931–32.
Shidai xuesheng (Contemporary students) [SML].
South China Morning Post. Hong Kong, 1945–47.
Taochi xunbao (Reports on Red suppression). Hong Kong, 1926 [B].
Wen cui (Articles digest). Shanghai, 1946–47 [F].

Xiangdao zhoubao (The guide). Shanghai, 1925–27.

Xin qingnian (New youth). Shanghai, 1919–25.

Xinwenbao (The news). Shanghai, 1946–47 [F].

Xinwen tiandi (News of heaven and earth). Chongqing and Nanjing, 1946–47.

Xueshengbao (Student news). Shanghai, 1947 [F].

Zhengyanbao (Sincere words). Shanghai, 1946–47 [F].

Zhongyang ribao (Central news). Nanjing, Chongqing, Shanghai, 1931–47 (selected issues) [F, SML].

BOOKS AND ARTICLES

Adamson, Walter L. *Hegemony and Revolution.* Berkeley: University of California Press, 1980.

Ahern, Emily. *Chinese Ritual and Politics.* New York: Cambridge University Press, 1981.

Altbach, Philip. "Student Political Activism: China in Comparative Perspective." *Issues and Studies*, 26, no. 1 (1990): 23–46.

———. "Students and Politics." In Lipset, *Student Politics*, pp. 74–96.

Baker, Keith. ed. *The French Revolution and the Creation of Modern Political Culture*, Vol. 1, *The Political Culture of the Old Regime.* New York: Pergamon, 1987.

Bakhtin, M. M. *The Dialogic Imagination: Four Essays.* Ed. Michael Holquist. Trans. Caryl Emerson and Michael Holquist. Austin: University of Texas Press, 1981.

Bao Renyu. "Sanwan jiemei yitiaoxin" (30,000 sisters with one heart). In Wang Min, *Chuntian de yaolan*, pp. 144–48.

Bao Zunpeng. *Zhongguo gongchandang qingnian yundongshi de pipan* (A critique of the CCP's history of the Chinese youth movement). Nanjing: Haijun zongsi-ling, Zhenggongchu, 1948.

———. *Zhongguo gongchandang qingnian yundong shilun* (A discussion of the history of the CCP's youth movement). Nanjing, 1947.

———. *Zhongguo qingnian yundongshi* (A history of the Chinese youth movement). Taibei: Zhengzhong shudian, 1954.

Barmé, Geremie. "Blood Offering." *Far Eastern Economic Review*, June 22, 1989, p. 37.

Bastid, Marrianne. *Educational Reform in Early Twentieth Century China.* Trans. Paul J. Bailey. Ann Arbor: University of Michigan, Center for Chinese Studies, 1988.

Beijing University School History Group, eds. *Beijing daxue xuesheng yundongshi, 1919–1949* (A history of the Beijing University student movement, 1919–1949). Rev. ed. Beijing: Beijing chubanshe, 1988.

Bergère, Marie-Claire. *L'âge d'or de la bourgeoisie chinoise, 1911–1937.* Paris: Flammarion, 1986.

Borg, Dorothy. *American Policy and the Chinese Revolution of 1925–1928.* New York: Macmillan, 1947.

Borthwick, Sally. "Changing Concepts of the Role of Women from the Late Qing to the May Fourth Period." In David Pong and Edmund Fung, eds., *Ideal and*

Reality: Social and Political Change in Modern China. New York: University Press of America, 1985, pp. 63–92.

―――. *Education and Social Change in China: The Beginnings of the Modern Era.* Stanford: Hoover Institution Press, 1983.

Brewer, John. *Party Ideology and Popular Politics at the Accession of George III.* New York: Cambridge University Press, 1976.

Brower, Daniel. *Training the Nihilists.* Ithaca, N.Y.: Cornell University Press, 1975.

Cai Shaoqing. "Secret Societies and Labor Organizations in the Early History of the Chinese Communist Party." *Duke Working Papers in Asian/Pacific Studies,* n.d.

Cai Xiyao and Wang Jiagui, eds. *Shanghai daxue* (Shanghai University). Shanghai: SASS, 1986.

Calhoun, Craig. "The Beijing Spring, 1989." *Dissent,* Fall 1989, pp. 435–47.

Cao Shiqun. "Qu Nanjing qingyuan" (Going to Nanjing to petition). *Shanghai dangshi ziliao tongxun* (Communications on party history materials), 19 (1984, no. 9): 26–32.

CASS. *Wusi aiguo yundong* (The patriotic May 4th Movement). 2 vols. Beijing: Zhongguo shehui kexueyuan, 1979.

―――. *Wusi yundong huiyilu* (Remembrances of the May 4th Movement). 3 vols. Beijing: Zhongguo shehui kexueyuan, 1979.

Cavendish, Patrick. "Anti-imperialism in the Kuomintang, 1923–1928." In Jerome Chen and Nicholas Tarling, eds., *Studies in the Social History of China and South-east Asia.* Cambridge, Eng.: Cambridge University Press, 1970, pp. 23–56.

CCP. Central Party History Research Group, ed. *Yi'erjiu yundong shiyao* (A basic history of the December 9th Movement). Beijing: Zhonggong, Zhongyang, Dangxiao chubanshe, 1986.

―――. Shanghai Party History Documentation Group, ed. *"Yi'erjiu" yihou Shanghai Jiuguohui shiliao xuanzhi* (Selected historical materials on the post–December 9th Shanghai National Salvation Association). Shanghai: SASS, 1987.

Chan, Anita, and Jonathan Unger. "China After Tiananmen: It's a Whole New Class Struggle." *Nation,* Jan. 22, 1990, pp. 79–81.

―――. "Voices from the Protest Movement, Chongqing, Sichuan." *Australian Journal of Chinese Affairs,* 24 (1990): 259–79.

Chan, Yuan Ying, and Peter Kwang. "Trashing the Hopes of Tiananmen." *Nation,* Apr. 23, 1990, pp. 545, 560–64.

Chang, Gordon H. "A Report on Student Protests at Beijing University." *Bulletin of Concerned Asian Scholars,* 18, no. 3 (1986): 29–31.

Chang Kuo-t'ao. *The Rise of the Chinese Communist Party.* 2 vol. Lawrence: University of Kansas Press, 1971.

Chang, Maria Hsia. *The Chinese Blue Shirts: Fascism and Developmental Nationalism.* Berkeley: University of California, Institute of East Asian Studies, 1985.

Cheek, Timothy. "Contracts and Ideological Control in Village Administration: Tensions in the 'Village Covenant' System in Late Imperial China." Paper presented at the Annual Meeting of the Association for Asian Studies, Washington, D.C., 1984, cited with the author's permission.

Chen, Joseph. *The May 4th Movement in Shanghai.* Leiden: E. J. Brill, 1971.

Chen Liang. "Fengbao zhi ge" (Songs from the tempest). *SQZ*, 9 (1983): 26–34.

Chen Shaoting, ed. *Wusi yundong de huiyi* (Memories of the May 4th Movement). Taibei: Bajie chubanshe, 1979.

Chen, Wen-hui C. *Chinese Communist Anti-Americanism and the Resist-America Aid-Korea Campaign*. Lackland, Tex.: Air Force Personnel and Training Research Center, 1955.

Chen Yuzong. "Canjia wusa fandi douzheng" (My participation in the May 30th anti-imperialist struggle). In SASS, *Wusa*, 1: 672–80.

Chen Zhenzhong. "'Liu'ersan' yundong pianduan huiyi" (Fragments remembered about the June 23rd Movement). In Wang Min, *Chuntian de yaolan*, pp. 149–57.

Cheng Tianfang. "Ligong ci sinian" (Four years at the Li Temple; English title: "My Student Life in Futan University"). *Chuanji wenxue*, 1, no. 7 (1962): 24–27.

Chesneaux, Jean. *The Chinese Labor Movement, 1919–1927*. Stanford: Stanford University Press, 1968.

Chi Fu. "Wusa zhi chixue yu Zhongguo zhi chihua" (The red blood of May 30th and the reddening of China). *Xiangdao zhoubao*, 155 (1926): 1496–98.

Chiang Monlin. *Tides from the West: A Chinese Autobiography*. New Haven: Yale University Press, 1947.

Chiang Nan-hsiang, ed. *The Roar of a Nation: Reminiscences of the December 9th Student Movement*. Beijing: Foreign Languages Press, 1963.

China. Bureau of Education. Statistical Section, ed. *Quanguo gaodeng jiaoyu tongji* (National statistics on higher education). Nanjing: Bureau of Education, 1936.

———. Ministry of Information. *China After Five Years of War*. New York: Chinese Press Service, 1943.

Chong, Woei Lian. "Petitioners, Popperians, and Hunger Strikers: The Uncoordinated Efforts of the 1989 Chinese Democratic Movement." In Saich, *Chinese People's Movement*, pp. 106–25.

Chow Tse-tsung. *The May 4th Movement*. Cambridge, Mass.: Harvard University Press, 1960.

———. *Research Guide to the May 4th Movement*. Cambridge, Mass.: Harvard University Press, 1963.

Cleverley, John. *The Schooling of China*. Boston: George Allen & Unwin, 1985.

Clifford, Nicholas. *Shanghai, 1925: In Defense of Foreign Privilege*. Ann Arbor: University of Michigan Press, 1980.

———. "The Western Powers and the 'Shanghai Question' in the National Revolution of the 1920s." Paper presented at the International Symposium on Modern Shanghai held at SASS, Sept. 1988.

Coble, Parks. "Chiang Kai-shek and the Anti-Japanese Movement in China: Zou Tao-fen and the National Salvation Association, 1931–1937." *Journal of Asian Studies*, 44, no. 2 (1985): 293–310.

Cochran, Sherman, and Andrew Hsieh, with Janis Cochran, eds. and trans. *One Day in China: May 21, 1936*. New Haven: Yale University Press, 1983.

Cohen, Paul. *China and Christianity*. Cambridge, Mass.: Harvard University Press, 1963.

———. "The Post-Mao Reforms in Historical Perspective." *Journal of Asian Studies*, 47, no. 3 (1988): 518–40.

Cohen, Robert P. "Revolt of the Depression Generation: America's First Mass

Student Protest Movement, 1929–1940." Ph.D. dissertation, University of California, Berkeley, 1987.

Creamer, Thomas. "Hsueh-yun: Shanghai's Students and the May 30th Movement." Master's thesis, University of Virginia, 1975.

CYL Youth Movment Research Group, eds. *Diyici guogong hezuo shiqi de Gongqingtuan zhuantilun wenji* (Collected essays on special issues concerning the Communist Youth League of the time of the First United Front). Beijing: CYL, 1985.

———. *Zhongguo qingnian yundong shiliao* (Historical materials on the Chinese youth movement). 10 vols. Beijing: CYL, 1957.

———. *Zhongguo Shehuizhuyi qingniantuan chuangjian wenti taolun wenji* (Collected articles on questions relating to the founding of the Chinese Socialist Youth League). Beijing: CYL, 1984.

Darwent, C. E. *Shanghai: A Handbook for Travellers and Residents*. Shanghai: Kelly & Walsh, 1920.

Davis, Natalie. *Society and Culture in Early Modern France*. Stanford: Stanford University Press, 1975.

Davis, Susan. *Parades and Power: Street Theatre in Nineteenth Century Philadelphia*. Philadelphia: Temple University Press, 1986.

DeBenedetti, Charles. *An American Ordeal: The Antiwar Movement of the Vietnam Era*. Syracuse, N.Y.: Syracuse University Press, 1990.

DeConde, Alexander, ed. *Student Activism: Town and Gown in Historical Perspective*. New York: Scribner's, 1971.

DeFrancis, John. *The Chinese Language: Fact and Fantasy*. Honolulu: University of Hawaii Press, 1984.

———. *Nationalism and Language Reform in China*. Princeton: Princeton University Press, 1950.

Dewey, John, and Alice Chapman Dewey. *Letters from China and Japan*. Ed. Evelyn Dewey. New York: E. P. Dutton, 1920.

Dirlik, Arif. "Ideology and Organization in the May 4th Movement." *Republican China*, 12, no. 1 (1986): 3–19.

Doolin, Dennis, J. *Communist China: The Politics of Student Opposition*. Stanford: Hoover Instutition, 1964.

Duara, Prasenjit. *Culture, Power, and the State: Rural North China, 1900–1942*. Stanford: Stanford University Press, 1988.

Eastman, Lloyd. *The Abortive Revolution*. Cambridge, Mass.: Harvard University Press, 1974.

———. "Fascism in Kuomintang China: The Blue Shirts." *China Quarterly*, 49 (1972): 1–31.

———. *Seeds of Destruction*. Stanford: Stanford University Press, 1984.

Eberhard, Wolfram. *A Dictionary of Chinese Symbols*. New York: Routledge, 1986.

Eisenstadt, S. N., ed. *Max Weber on Charisma and Institution Building*. Chicago: University of Chicago Press, 1968.

Elvin, Mark. "The Administration of Shanghai, 1905–14." In idem and G. William Skinner, eds., *The Chinese City Between Two Worlds*. Stanford: Stanford University Press, 1974, pp. 239–62.

———. "The Gentry Democracy in Shanghai, 1905–14." In Jack Grey, ed., *Modern China's Search for a Political Form*. London: Oxford University Press, 1969, pp. 41–65.

Emerson, Donald, ed. *Students and Politics*. New York: Praeger, 1968.

Endicott, Stephen. *James G. Endicott: Rebel Out of China*. Toronto: University of Toronto Press, 1980.

Esherick, Joseph. *The Origins of the Boxer Uprising*. Berkeley: University of California Press, 1987.

———. "Xi'an Spring." *Australian Journal of Chinese Affairs*, 24 (July 1990): 209–35.

Esherick, Joseph, and Jeffrey N. Wasserstrom, "Acting out Democracy: Political Theater in Modern China," *Journal of Asian Studies*, 49, no. 4 (1990): 835–65.

Fei Zhirong and Zhu Hongxing. "Jianku douzheng, yingjie jiefang" (Struggling hard to usher in liberation). Manuscript, SCYL archive.

Feuer, Lewis. *The Conflict of Generations*. New York: Basic Books, 1969.

Fewsmith, Joseph. *Party, State, and Local Elites in Republican China: Merchant Organizations and Politics in Shanghai, 1890–1930*. Honolulu: University of Hawaii Press, 1985.

Forster, Keith. "Impressions of the Popular Movement in Hangzhou, April/June 1989." *Australian Journal of Chinese Affairs*, 23 (1990): 97–120.

Forward, Roy. "Letter from Shanghai." *Australian Journal of Chinese Affairs*, 24 (1990): 281–98.

Francis, Corrina-Barbara. "The Progress of Protest in China: The Student Movement of the Spring of 1989." *Asian Survey*, 29, no. 9 (1990): 898–915.

Freyn, Hubert. *Prelude to War: The Chinese Student Rebellion of 1935–1936*. Shanghai: China Journal, 1939.

Friedland, William, and Harry Edwards. "Confrontation at Cornell." In DeConde, *Student Activism*, pp. 318–36.

Friedland, William, and Irving Horowitz. *The Knowledge Factory*. Chicago: Aldine, 1970.

Fu Po-shek. "Passivity, Resistance, and Collaboration: Intellectual Choices in Occupied Shanghai, 1937–1945." Ph.D. dissertation, Stanford University, 1989.

Fu Yilan. "Kanglian huodong zai Jida: Youguan riji zailu" (The Protest Alliance's activities at Ji'nan University: notes from my diary). Manuscript, SCYL archive.

Furet, François. *Interpreting the French Revolution*. Cambridge, Eng.: Cambridge University Press, 1978.

Furth, Charlotte. "May Fourth in History." In Benjamin Schwartz, ed., *Reflections on the May 4th Movement*. Cambridge, Mass.: Harvard University Press, 1981, pp. 59–68.

Gamewell, Mary. *The Gateway to China: Pictures of Shanghai*. New York: Revell, 1916.

Geertz, Clifford. "Centers, Kings, and Charisma: Reflections on the Symbolics of Power." In Sean Wilentz, ed., *The Rites of Power*. Philadelphia: University of Pennsylvania Press, 1985, pp. 13–38.

———. *The Interpretation of Cultures*. New York: Basic Books, 1973.

———. *Negara: The Theatre State in Nineteenth Century Bali*. Princeton: Princeton University Press, 1980.

Gerth, H. H., and C. Wright Mills, eds. *From Max Weber: Essays in Sociology*. New York: Oxford University Press, 1946.

Gitlin, Todd. *The Sixties: Years of Hope, Days of Rage*. New York: Bantam, 1987.

Gladney, Dru. "Bodily Positions and Social Dispositions: Sexuality, Nationality and Tiananmen." Paper presented at the Institute for Advanced Study, Princeton, Apr. 26, 1990, cited with the author's permission.

GMD. Bureau of Education. *Zhongguo jiaoyu nianjian* (Chinese educational yearbook). Nanjing: Central Government, 1948.

Gramsci, Antonio. *Selections from the Prison Notebooks.* Ed. and trans. Quintin Hoare and Geoffrey Nowell Smith. New York: International, 1971.

Griggs, Thurston. *Americans in China: Some Chinese Views.* Washington, D.C.: Foundation for Foreign Affairs, 1948.

Guo Moruo. "Shaonian shidai" (Childhood). In idem, *Moruo wenji* (Collected works of Guo Moruo). Shanghai: Xinwenyi, 1955, pp. 29–30.

Hammond, Edward. "Organized Labor in Shanghai, 1927–1937." Ph.D. dissertation, University of California, Berkeley, 1978.

Han Jiemei. "Banshijieqian de huiyi" (Memories of a half-century ago). *Wenshi ziliao* (Shanghai series), 51 (1985): 274–79.

Han Minzhu, ed. *Cries for Democracy: Writing and Speeches from the 1989 Chinese Democracy Movement.* Princeton: Princeton University Press, 1990.

Hao Yingde and Shao Pengwen. *Zhongguo xuesheng yundong jianshi, 1919–1949* (A basic history of the Chinese student movement, 1919–1949). Hebei: Hebei renmin chubanshe, 1985.

Hayes, James. "Specialists and Written Materials in the Village World." In D. Johnson et al., *Popular Culture*, pp. 75–111.

Hayhoe, Ruth. "Towards the Forging of a Chinese University Ethos: Zhendan and Fudan, 1903–1919," *China Quarterly*, 94 (1983): 323–41.

Hayhoe, Ruth, and Marrianne Bastid, eds. *China's Education and the Industrialized World.* Armonk, N.Y.: M. E. Sharpe, 1987.

Heirich, Max. *The Beginning: Berkeley 1964.* New York: Columbia University Press, 1970.

Henriot, Christian. "Le gouvernement municipal de Shanghai, 1927–1937." Ph.D. dissertation, Sorbonne, Paris, 1983.

———. "Municipal Power and Local Elites." *Republican China*, 11, no. 2 (1986): 1–21.

Hermassi, Karen. *Polity and Theatre in Historical Perspective.* Berkeley: University of California Press, 1977.

Hershatter, Gail. *The Workers of Tianjin.* Stanford: Stanford University Press, 1986.

High, Stanley, ed. *The Revolt of Youth.* New York: Abingdon Press, 1923.

Hobsbawm, Eric J. *Primitive Rebels.* Manchester: Manchester University Press, 1959.

Honig, Emily. *Sisters and Strangers: Women in the Shanghai Cotton Mills, 1919–1949.* Stanford: Stanford University Press, 1986.

Horowitz, Helen Lefkowitz. *Campus Life: Undergraduate Cultures from the End of the Eighteenth Century to the Present.* New York: Knopf, 1987.

Hsiao Kung-chuan. *Rural China: Imperial Control in the Late 19th Century.* Seattle: University of Washington Press, 1967.

Hu Kuo-tai. "Disputes on the Question of Wartime Education and the Formation of an Educational Policy for the Guomindang in the War." *Republican China*, 14, no. 1 (1988): 30–56.

Hu Sheng. *Cong yapian zhanzheng dao wusi yundong* (From the Opium War to the May 4th Movement). 2 vols. Beijing: Renmin chubanshe, 1981.

Hu Shih. *The Chinese Renaissance*. 1933. Reprinted—New York: Paragon, 1963.

Hu Xiaqing. "'Yi'erjiu' yundong zhong de Ji'nan daxue" (Ji'nan University during the December 9th Movement). *Dangshi ziliao*, 12 (1982): 36–39.

Hua Gang. *Zhongguo dagemingshi* (The history of China's Great Revolution). Shanghai: Chungeng shudian, 1932.

Huang Lin. "Wo zai Shanghai dixia douzheng shenghuo de duanpian" (Fragments on my life fighting with the Shanghai underground). *Shanghai dangshi ziliao tongxun* (Reports on Shanghai party history materials), 1986, no. 9, pp. 14–22.

Huang Meizhen et al., eds. *Shanghai daxue shiliao* (Historical materials on Shanghai University). Shanghai: Fudan, 1984.

Huang Xianfang. *Songdai taixuesheng jiuguo yundong* (The national salvation movement of Song Dynasty students). Shanghai: Shangwu yinshu guan, 1936.

Huang, Yasheng. "The Origins of China's Pro-Democracy Movement and the Government's Response: A Tale of Two Reforms." *Fletcher Forum of World Affairs*, Winter 1990, pp. 30–39.

Human Rights in China. *Children of the Dragon: The Story of Tiananmen Square*. New York: Macmillan, 1990.

Hung Chang-tai. *Going to the People*. Cambridge, Mass.: Harvard University Press, 1985.

Hunt, Lynn. *Politics, Culture, and Class in the French Revolution*. Berkeley: University of California Press, 1984.

Hunter, Neale. *Shanghai Journal: An Eyewitness Account of the Cultural Revolution*. New York: Praeger, 1969.

Iriye, Akira. "Toward a New Cultural Order: The Hsin-min Hui." In idem, ed., *The Chinese and the Japanese*. Princeton: Princeton University Press, 1980, pp. 254–74.

Isaacs, Harold. *Five Years of KMT Reaction: Gang Rule in Shanghai*. Shanghai: China Forum, 1932.

Israel, John. *The Chinese Student Movement, 1927–1937: A Bibliographic Essay Based on the Resources of the Hoover Institution*. Stanford: Hoover Institution, 1959.

———. "The December 9th Movement: A Case Study in Chinese Communist Historiography." *China Quarterly*, 23 (1965): 140–69.

———. "Reflections on the Modern Chinese Student Movement." In Seymour Lipset and Philip Altbach, eds., *Students in Revolt*. Boston: Houghton Mifflin, 1969, pp. 310–33.

———. "Sources in Institutional History: A Review of Essays on the December First Movement." *CCP Research Newsletter*, 1 (1988): 35–38.

———. *Student Nationalism in China, 1927–1937*. Stanford: Stanford University Press, 1966.

Israel, John, and Donald Klein. *Rebels and Bureaucrats: China's December 9ers*. Berkeley: University of California Press, 1976.

Jarausch, Konrad H. *Students, Society, and Politics in Imperial Germany*. Princeton: Princeton University Press, 1982.

Jiang Guangzi. *Jiang Guangzi shiwen xuanji* (Selected prose and poetry of Jiang Guangzi). Beijing: Renmin chubanshe, 1955.

Jiang Hao. "Guomindang Gaizupai zai Shanghai de huodong" (The activities of the GMD's Reorganizationist Faction in Shanghai). *Shanghai difangshi ziliao*, 1 (1982): 197–205.

Jiang Zhichan. "Dageming shiqi de Shanghai xuelian" (The Shanghai Student Union during the Great Revolution). In CYL Youth Movement Research Group, *Gongqingtuan*, pp. 96–120.

———. "Wang Ming 'zuoqing' luxian dui xuesheng jiuwang yundong yingxiang" (The influence of Wang Ming's "leftist" line on the students' salvation movement). *SQY*, 22 (1988): 81–88.

Jiang Zonglu. "'Yi'erjiu' yundong zhong de Shanghai Fudan" (Shanghai's Fudan University during the December 9th Movement). *Geming huiyilu* (Remembering the Revolution), 20 (1986): 62–84.

Jiaotong University School History Group, ed. *Jiaotong daxue xiaoshi ziliao* (Materials on the history of Jiaotong University). 2 vols. Shanghai: Jiaotong daxue, 1986.

Jiaoyu zazhi. *Xuexiao fengchao de yanjiu* (English title: The Study of School Storms). Shanghai: Commercial Press, 1922.

Ji'nan University Overseas Chinese Research Group, ed. *Ji'nan xiaoshi, 1906–1949, ziliao xuanquan* (Selected materials on the history of Ji'nan University, 1906–1949). 2 vols. Guangzhou: Ji'nan daxue, 1983.

Johnson, David. "Communication, Class, and Consciousness." In idem et al., *Popular Culture*, pp. 34–72.

Johnson, David, Andrew Nathan, and Evelyn Rawski, eds. *Popular Culture in Late Imperial China*. Berkeley: University of California Press, 1985.

Johnson, William C., Jr. *The Shanghai Problem*. Westport, Conn.: Hyperion, 1973 [1937].

Jones, Susan Mann. "The Ningbo *Pang* and Financial Power in Shanghai." In Mark Elvin and William Skinner, eds., *The Chinese City Between Two Worlds*. Stanford: Stanford University Press, 1974, pp. 73–96.

Jordan, Donald. "Shifts in Wang Jingwei's Japan Policy During the Kuomintang Factional Struggle of 1931–1932." *Asian Profile*, 12, no. 3 (1984): 199–214.

Kassow, Samuel D. *Students, Professors, and the State in Tsarist Russia*. Berkeley: University of California Press, 1989.

Katsiaficas, George. *The Imagination of the New Left*. Boston: South End, 1987.

Kawai Shingo. *Kokumintō Shina no kyōiku seisaku* (Guomindang China's educational policy). Tokyo: Tōa Kenkyūjo, 1941.

Keenan, Barry. *The Dewey Experiment in China: Educational Reform and Political Power in the Early Republic*. Cambridge, Mass.: Harvard University Press, 1977.

Kemp, G. S. F. "Boy Scouts Association of China." *Xin qingnian* (New youth), 2, no. 5 (1917): 455–57.

Kiang Wen-han. *The Chinese Student Movement*. New York: King's Crown Press, 1948.

Kikuchi Takaharu. *Chūgoku minzoku undō no kihon kōzō: Taigai boikotto no kenkyū* (The structure and base of Chinese nationalist movements: Researches on anti-foreign boycotts). Tokyo: Dainan, 1966.

Kotenev, A. E. *Shanghai: Its Mixed Court and Council*. Shanghai: North China Daily News & Herald, 1925.

————. *Shanghai: Its Municipality and the Chinese.* Shanghai: North China Herald, 1927.

Kraus, Richard. "The Lament of Astrophysicist Fang Lizhi." In Arif Dirlik and Maurice Meisner, eds., *Marxism and the Chinese Experience.* Armonk, N.Y.: M. E. Sharpe, 1989, pp. 294–315.

Ku Kuo-tai. "Disputes on the Question of Wartime Education and the Formation of an Educational Policy for the Guomindang in the War." *Republican China*, 14, no. 1 (1988): 30–56.

Kuhn, Philip. *Rebellion and Its Enemies in Late Imperial China.* Cambridge, Mass.: Harvard University Press, 1971.

Lamberton, Mary. *St. John's University, Shanghai, 1879–1951.* New York: United Board for Christian Colleges in China, 1955.

Lears, T. Jackson. "The Concept of Cultural Hegemony: Problems and Possibilities." *American Historical Review*, 90 (1985): 567–93.

Le Bon, Gustave. *The Crowd: A Study of the Popular Mind.* 1895. Reprinted—New York: Putnam, 1980.

————. *The Psychology of Revolution.* New York: Putnam, 1913.

Lee, Thomas H. C. *Government Education and Examinations in Sung China.* New York: St. Martin's, 1985.

Lestz, Michael. "The Meaning of Revival: The Kuomintang 'New Right' and Party Building in Republican China, 1925–1936." Ph.D. dissertation, Yale University, 1982.

Levin, Molly, and John Spiegel. "Point and Counterpoint in the Literature on Student Unrest." In Donald Light, Jr., and John Spiegel, eds., *The Dynamics of University Protest.* Chicago: Nelson Hall, 1977, pp. 23–50.

Li Chunkang. "Shanghai de gaodeng jiaoyu" (Higher education in Shanghai). *Shanghaishi tongzhiguan qikan*, 2, no. 1 (1934): 603–68.

Li Guocheng. "Zhongguo kangri zhanzheng qian de xuesheng yundong (1931–1936)" (The Chinese student movement up to the War of Resistance [1931–1936]). Ph.D. dissertation, Zhongguo wenhua xueyuan, Taiwan, 1974.

Li Huaming et al. "'Jiuyiba' he 'yi'erba' shiqi de Shanghai xuesheng yundong" (The Shanghai student movement during the era of the September 18 and January 28 [Incidents]). *Shehui kexue*, 1984, no. 1, pp. 85–86, 90.

Li Jianmin. *Wusa can'an houde fanying yundong* (The anti-British movement after the May 30th Incident). Taibei: Academia Sinica, 1986.

Li Qiang. "Wusa qianhou de Shanghai xuesheng yundong" (The Shanghai student movement before and after the May 30th Movement). In Shanghai zonggonghui, *Wusa yundong*, pp. 5–11.

Li Xin. "Yi'erjiu zai Tongji daxue" (The December 9th Movement at Tongji University). *SQZ*, 13 (1984, no. 3): 13—18.

Li Yuji. "Shanghai xuesheng xiangying wusi aiguo yundong de jingguo" (Experiences while Shanghai students responded to the patriotic May 4th Movement). *Chuanji wenxue*, 30, no. 5 (1977): 59–62.

Lianfu jizhe (Alliances of Associated Editors), eds. *Wo canjiale wusi yundong* (I joined the May 4th Movement). Taibei: Lianhebao, 1979.

Lianhebao, ed. *Tiananmen yijiubajiu* (Tiananmen, 1989). Taibei: Lianjing chuban, 1989.

Lin Xinqin. "Gudao xueyun shigang" (An outline history of the student movement of the lonely island period). *SQZ*, 17 (1986): 5–14.

Lin Yutang. *A History of the Press and Public Opinion in China*. 1936. Reprinted— New York: Greenwood, 1968.

Link, Perry. *Mandarin Ducks and Butterflies: Popular Fiction in Early Twentieth Century Chinese Cities*. Berkeley: University of California Press, 1981.

Lipset, Seymour. *Rebellion in the University*. Chicago: University of Chicago Press, 1976.

———, ed. *Student Politics*. New York: Basic Books, 1967.

Lipset, Seymour, and Philip Altbach, eds. *Students in Revolt*. Boston: Houghton Mifflin, 1969.

Lipsitz, George. "The Struggle for Hegemony." *Journal of American History*, 75, no. 1 (1988): 146–50.

Liu Ding. "Xuesheng yundong yu Shanghai gongren wuzhuang qiyi" (The student movement and Shanghai's armed workers' uprisings). *Dang'an yu lishi*, 1987, no. 2, pp. 65–68.

Liu Huiwu, ed. *Shanghai jindaishi* (The modern history of Shanghai), vol. 1. Shanghai: Huadong shifan daxue, 1985.

Liu Kwang-Ching, ed. *Orthodoxy in Late Imperial China*. Berkeley: University of California Press, 1990.

Liu Xinyong. "Diyici guonei geming zhanzheng shiqi de fei jidujiao yundong" (The Anti-Christian Movement during the First Revolutionary Civil War). *SQZ*, 19 (1986): 1–8.

Liu Xinyong and Wang Min. "Shanghai Shehuizhuyi qingniantuan chuangjian de chutan" (A preliminary exploration of the establishment of the Socialist Youth League in Shanghai). In CYL Youth Movement Research Group, *Zhongguo Shehuizhuyi qingniantuan*, pp. 40–54.

Liu Yusong. "Yi Daxia daxue Liangguang tongxianghui huodong pianduan" (Fragmentary recollections of the activities of the Two Guangs [Guangxi and Guangdong] Native-Place Association at Daxia University). Manuscript, SCYL archive.

Lo Kuan-chung. *Three Kingdoms*. Trans. and ed. Moss Roberts. New York: Pantheon, 1976.

Lubman, Sarah. "The Myth of Tiananmen Square: The Students Talked Democracy, But They Didn't Practice It." *Washington Post*, July 30, 1989.

Lukes, Stephen. "Political Ritual and Social Integration." *Sociology*, 9, no. 2(1975): 289–308.

Lutz, Jessie. *China and the Christian Colleges, 1850–1950*. Ithaca, N.Y.: Cornell University Press, 1971.

———. *Chinese Politics and Christian Missions: The Anti-Christian Movements of 1920–1928*. Notre Dame, Ind.: Cross Cultural Publications, 1988.

———. "The Chinese Student Movement of 1945–1949." *Journal of Asian Studies*, 31, no. 1 (1971): 89–110.

———. "December 9, 1935: Student Nationalism and the Chinese Christian Colleges." *Journal of Asian Studies*, 26, no. 4 (1965): 627–48.

Ma Chaojun et al., eds. *Zhongguo laogong yundongshi* (A history of the Chinese labor movement). Taibei: Zhongguo laogong yundong shi bianzuan weiyuanhui, 1959.

MacKenzie, W. J. M. *Politics and Social Science*. Hammondsworth, Eng.: Penguin, 1967.

MacKerras, Colin. *The Chinese Theatre in Modern Times*. Amherst: University of Massachusetts Press, 1975.

———. "Education in the Guomindang Period." In David Pong and Edmund Fung, eds., *Ideal and Reality: Social and Political Change in Modern China*. New York: University Press of America, 1985, pp. 153–84.

MacLaren, Anne. "Educated Youth Return: The Poster Campaign in Shanghai from November 1978 to March 1979." *Australian Journal of Chinese Affairs*, 4 (1979): 1–20.

Maier, John H. "'Tian'anmen 1989': The View from Shanghai." *China Information*, 5, no. 1 (1990): 1–3.

Mao Zipei and Jiang Menglin. "Kangzheng shengli hou Shanghai Guomindang neibu de paixi douzheng" (GMD intra-party factional struggles following the winning of the War of Resistance). *Wenshi ziliao* (Shanghai series), 1975, no. 5, pp. 175–84.

Martin, Brian. "Tu Yueh-sheng and Labor Control in Shanghai." *Papers in Far Eastern History*, 32 (1985): 99–138.

Masi, Edoarda. *China Winter: Workers, Mandarins, and the Purge of the Gang of Four*. Trans. Adrienne Foulke. New York: E. P. Dutton, 1982.

Menashe, Louis, and Ronald Radosh, eds. *Teach-ins: U.S.A.—Reports, Opinions, Documents*. New York: Praeger, 1967.

Miles, Michael W. *The Radical Probe: The Logic of Student Rebellion*. New York: Atheneum, 1971.

Miller, James. *Democracy Is in the Streets*. New York: Simon & Schuster, 1987.

Miu Pengniao. "Fan neizhan douzheng de liangge duanpian" (A couple of fragments concerning the anti–Civil War struggle). *Wenshi ziliao* (Shanghai series), 1979, no. 3, pp. 66–71.

———. "Gongji Yu Zai" (The public memorial service for Yu Zai). *SQZ*, 4, (1982): 39–42.

Munro, Robin. "Political Reform, Student Demonstrations and the Conservative Backlash." In Robert Benewick and Paul Wingrove, eds., *Reforming the Revolution: China in Transition*. Chicago: Dorsey, 1988, pp. 63–80.

———. "Who Died in Beijing, and Why." *Nation*, June 11, 1990, pp. 811–22.

Naquin, Susan, and Evelyn Rawski. *Chinese Society in the Eighteenth Century*. New Haven: Yale, 1987.

Nathan, Andrew. *Chinese Democracy*. New York: Knopf, 1985.

———. "Chinese Democracy in 1989: Continuity and Change." *Problems of Communism*, Sept.–Oct. 1989, pp. 16–29.

Nathan, Andrew, and Leo Ou-fan Lee. "The Beginnings of Mass Culture: Journalism and Fiction in the Late Ch'ing [Qing] and Beyond." In D. Johnson et al., *Popular Culture*, pp. 360–95.

Negishi Tadashi. *Shanhai no girudo* (The guilds of Shanghai). Tokyo, 1951.

Niming, Frank. "Learning How to Protest." In Saich, *Chinese People's Movement*, pp. 82–104.

Ono Kazuko. *Chinese Women in a Century of Revolution, 1850–1950*. Ed. Joshua Fogel. Stanford: Stanford University Press, 1989.

Ozouf, Mona. *Festivals and the French Revolution.* Trans. Alan Sheridan. Cambridge, Mass.: Harvard University Press, 1988.

Pan Wenzheng et al. "Jiefang zhanzheng shiqi Shanghai Xuewei nanzhong quwei de gongzuo" (Work in the male secondary school students' division of the Shanghai Student Affairs Bureau during the War of Liberation). *Shanghai dangshi ziliao tongxun*, 6 (1986): 4–31.

Pellow, Deborah. "A Choreography of Dissent: Shanghai 1989." Unpublished memoir, cited with author's permission.

Peng Ming. *Wusi yundongshi* (A history of the May 4th Movement). Beijing: Renmin chubanshe, 1984.

Peng Pai. *Seeds of Peasant Revolution: Report on the Haifeng Peasant Movement.* Trans. Donald Holoch. Ithaca, N.Y.: Cornell University East Asia Papers, 1973.

Pepper, Suzanne. *Civil War in China: The Political Struggle, 1945–1949.* Berkeley: University of California Press, 1978.

———. *Deng Xiaoping's Political and Economic Reforms and the Chinese Student Protests.* Indianapolis: Universities Field Staff Services Reports, 1986.

———. "Education for the New Order." In John K. Fairbank and Roderick MacFarquhar, eds., *The Cambridge History of China*, Vol. 14, *The People's Republic of China, Part I.* Cambridge, Eng.: Cambridge University Press, 1987, pp. 185–217.

Perrot, Michelle. *Workers on Strike: France, 1870–1891.* Trans. Chris Turner. New Haven: Yale University Press, 1987.

Perry, Elizabeth. *Rebels and Revolutionaries in North China, 1845–1945.* Stanford: Stanford University Press, 1980.

———. "Shanghai on Strike." Paper presented at the International Symposium on Modern Shanghai held at SASS, Sept. 1988, cited with author's permission.

———. *Shanghai on Strike: The Politics of Chinese Labor.* Stanford University Press, forthcoming.

———. "Shanghai on Strike: Work and Politics in the Making of a Chinese Proletariat." Paper presented at the Annual Meeting of the Association for Asian Studies, San Francisco, 1988, cited with author's permission.

———. "Strikes Among Shanghai Silk Weavers, 1927–1937: The Awakening of a Labor Aristocracy." Unpublished paper, 1987, cited with author's permission.

Phillips, Donald. *Student Protest, 1960–1970.* New York: University Press of America, 1985.

Pieke, Frank. "Observations During the People's Movement in Beijing, Spring 1989." Paper presented at the International Institute of Social History, Amsterdam, July 7, 1989, cited with author's permission.

———. "A Ritualized Rebellion: Beijing, Spring 1989." Unpublished paper, cited with author's permission.

Potts, Francis L. H. *A Short History of Shanghai.* Shanghai: Kelly & Walsh, 1928.

Pye, Lucien. *The Spirit of Chinese Politics.* Cambridge, Mass.: MIT Press, 1968.

———. "Tiananmen and Chinese Political Culture: The Escalation of Confrontation from Moralizing to Revenge." *Asian Survey*, 30, no. 4 (1990): 331–47.

Pye, Lucien, and Sydney Verba, eds. *Political Culture and Development.* Princeton: Princeton University Press, 1965.

Qin Yishan. "Guanyu Jiaoda (46–47 nian) xuesheng yundong de yixie duanpian"

(Several fragments concerning the student movement at Jiaotong University). Manuscript, SCYL archive.

Quanguo fulian fuyunshi yanjiushe. "Wusi yundong yu Shanghai funü" (The May 4th Movement and Shanghai women). *Wenshi ziliao* (Shanghai series), 27 (1979): 10–19.

Rankin, Mary. *Early Chinese Revolutionaries: Radical Intellectuals in Shanghai and Chekiang, 1902–1922*. Cambridge, Mass.: Harvard University Press, 1971.

Ransome, Arthur. *The Chinese Puzzle*. London, Unwin, 1927.

Rawski, Evelyn. *Education and Popular Literacy in Ch'ing China*. Ann Arbor: University of Michigan Press, 1979.

———. "Problems and Prospects." In D. Johnson et al., *Popular Culture*, pp. 399–417.

Remer, C. F. *A Study of Chinese Boycotts*. Baltimore: Johns Hopkins, 1933.

Ren Jianshu. "'Jiuyiba' shibian hou de Shanghai xuesheng yundong" (The Shanghai student movement after the September 18th affair). *SQZ*, 1982, no. 4, pp. 6–11.

Ren Jianshu and Zhang Quan. *Wusa yundong jianshi* (A basic history of the May 30th Movement). Shanghai: Shanghai renmin chubanshe, 1985.

Rigby, Richard. *The May 30th Movement*. Canberra: Griffin, 1980.

Rogers, Nicholas. "Popular Protest in Early Hanoverian London." *Past and Present*, 79 (1978): 70–100.

Rosemont, Henry, Jr. "China: The Mourning After." *Z Magazine*, Mar. 1990, pp. 85–96.

Rudé, George. *The Crowd in History*. London: Wiley & Sons, 1964.

Saich, Tony. "When Worlds Collide: The Beijing People's Movement of 1989." In idem, *Chinese People's Movement*, pp. 25–49.

———, ed. *The Chinese People's Movement: Perspectives on Spring 1989*. Armonk, N.Y.: M. E. Sharpe, 1990.

Saitō Tetsurō. "Neizhan shiqi Shanghai xuesheng de yishi, shenghuo he yundong" (The ideology, lives, and activities of Shanghai students during the Civil War). *Fudan xuebao*, 1986, no. 6, pp. 89–95.

SASS. *"Jiuyiba"–"Yi'erba" Shanghai junmin kangri yundong shiliao* (Historical materials on the Shanghai resist-Japan movement of the military and the people from "September 18" to "January 28"). Shanghai: SASS, 1986.

———. *Wusa yundong shiliao* (Historical materials on the May 30th Movement). 2 vols. Shanghai: SASS, 1981, 1987.

———. *Wusi yundong zai Shanghai shiliao xuanji* (Selected historical materials on the May 4th Movement in Shanghai). Shanghai: SASS, 1960.

SASS Teachers' Movement History Group, eds. *Shanghai jiaoshi yundong huiyilu* (Memoirs of the Shanghai teachers' movement). Shanghai: Shanghai renmin chubanshe, 1985.

Sassoon, Anne Showstack, ed. *Approaches to Gramsci*. London: Writers & Readers, 1982.

Schechner, Richard. *Performance Theory*. Rev. ed. New York: Routledge, 1988.

Schechner, Richard, and Mady Schuman, eds. *Ritual, Play and Performance*. New York: Seabury Press, 1976.

Schell, Orville. *Discos and Democracy: China in the Throes of Reform*. New York: Pantheon, 1988.

Schwarcz, Vera. *The Chinese Enlightenment*. Berkeley: University of California Press, 1986.

———. "Memory, Commemoration, and the Plight of China's Intellectuals." *Wilson Quarterly*, Autumn 1989, pp. 120–29.

Schwartz, Benjamin. *The World of Thought in Ancient China*. Cambridge, Mass.: Harvard University Press, 1985.

———, ed. *Reflections on the May 4th Movement: A Symposium*. Cambridge, Mass.: Harvard University Press, 1972.

Scranton, William, et al. *The Report of the President's Commission on Campus Unrest*. New York: Avon, 1981.

SCYL, comp. *Shanghai qingnian yundongshi tupianji* (Collected pictures dealing with the history of the Shanghai youth movement—referred to in notes as SCYL, *Pictorial*). Shanghai: Shanghai renmin meishu chubanshe, 1987.

SCYL Youth Movement Research Group, ed. *Yi'erjiu yundong zai Shanghai* (The December 9th Movement in Shanghai). Shanghai: SCYL, 1985.

———. *1945–1949 Shanghai xuesheng yundongshi* (A history of the Shanghai student movement, 1945–1949). Shanghai: Shanghai renmin chubanshe, 1983.

Sha Qianli. *Manhua jiuguohui* (An informal account of the National Salvation Association). Beijing: Wenshi ziliao chubanshe, 1983.

Shanghai Cultural Publishing House. *Anecdotes of Old Shanghai*. Shanghai: Shanghai wenhua chubanshe, 1985.

Shanghai Party History Documentation Group, ed. *"Yi'erjiu" yihou Shanghai Jiuguohui shiliao xuanzhi* (Selected historical materials on the post–December 9th Shanghai National Salvation Association). Shanghai: SASS, 1987.

Shanghai Student Union. *Wusahou zhi Shanghai xuesheng* (Shanghai students since May 30th). Shanghai: Shanghai xuesheng lianhehui, 1925.

Shanghai zonggonghui. Gongren yundong shiliao weiyuanhui, ed. *Wusa yundong liushi zhounian jinian ji* (Materials collected for the sixtieth anniversary of the May 30th Movement). Shanghai: Shanghai zonggonghui, 1985.

Shanhai Nihon Shōkō Kaigisho, ed. *Santō mondai ni kansuru Nikka haiseki no eikyō* (The effects of the boycott of Japanese products connected with the Shandong question). Shanghai, 1919.

Shen You. "Renmin busi! Ji 'yi'eryi' Shanghai renmin da youxing" (The people are not dead! Remembering the big December 1 demonstration of the people of Shanghai). *Wen cui*, 15 (1946): 25–26.

Shi Cun. "Fujing qingyuan de qianqian houhou: Jielu Shi Cun riji." (Before and after petitioning the capital: Extracts from Shi Cun's diary). *Kangri jiuguo*, 2 (1931): 12–16.

Shi Weixiang et al. *Jiaotong daxue xiaoshi, 1896–1949* (A school history of Jiaotong University, 1896–1949). Shanghai: Jiaoyu chubanshe, 1986.

Shurmann, Franz. *Ideology and Organization in Communist China*. Enl. 2nd ed. Berkeley: University of California Press, 1970.

Si Tuhan. "Jishouge yinqi de huiyi" (Memories of inspiring songs). In Wang Min, *Chuntian de yaolan*, pp. 9–23.

Snow, Helen Foster. *My China Years*. New York: William Morrow, 1984.

——— [Nym Wales]. *Notes on the Chinese Student Movement, 1935–1936*. 1959. Reprinted—Madison, Conn.: Scholarly Press, 1973.

Sokolsky, George. *The Tinderbox of Asia*. New York: Doubleday, 1932.

Solinger, Dorothy. "Democracy with Chinese Characteristics." *World Policy Journal*, Fall 1989, pp. 621–32.

Solomon, Richard. *Mao's Revolution and Chinese Political Culture*. Berkeley: University of California Press, 1971.

Spence, Jonathan, *The Gate of Heavenly Peace*. New York: Viking, 1981.

———. *The Search for Modern China*. New York: Norton, 1990.

Statera, Gianni. *Death of a Utopia: The Development and Decline of Student Movements in Europe*. New York: Oxford University Press, 1975.

Stranahan, Patricia. "Strange Bedfellows: The Communist Party and Shanghai's Elite in the National Salvation Movement." Paper presented at the International Symposium on Modern Shanghai held at SASS, Sept. 1988.

Strand, David. "'Civil Society' and Public Sphere in Modern China: A Perspective on Popular Movements in Beijing, 1919–1989." *Duke Working Papers in Asian/Pacific Studies*, 90-01 (1990).

———. "Protest in Beijing." *Problems of Communism*, 39 (1990): 1–19.

———. *Rickshaw Beijing: City People and Politics in the 1920s*. Berkeley: University of California Press, 1989.

Suleiman, Susan, and Inge Crosman, eds. *The Reader in the Text: Essays on Audience and Interpretation*. Princeton: Princeton University Press, 1980.

Sun, E-tu Zen. "The Growth of the Academic Community, 1912–1949." In John K. Fairbank and Albert Feuerwerker, eds., *The Cambridge History of China*, Vol. 13, *Republican China, 1912–1949, Part 2*. Cambridge, Cambridge University Press, 1986, pp. 361–420.

Sun Sibai. "'Jiuyiba' yu 'Yi'erjiu' xuesheng yundong bijiao yanjiu" (Comparative researches on the September 18th and December 9th student movements). *Lishi yanjiu*, 178 (1985, no. 6): 119–36.

Tang Shibai and Wen Xiaoyi. "Shilun gudao shiqi Shanghai xuesheng yundong de jige tedian" (An exploration of several points relating to the Shanghai student movement of the lonely island period), *SQY*, 1987, nos. 3–4, pp. 74–82.

Thompson, E. P. "Eighteenth Century English Society: Class Struggle Without Class?" *Social History*, 3, no. 2 (1978): 133–65.

———. *The Making of the English Working Class*. New York: Vintage, 1966.

———. "The Moral Economy of the English Crowd in the 18th Century." *Past and Present*, 50 (1971): 76–136.

———. "Patrician Society, Plebeian Culture." *Journal of Social History*, 7, no. 4 (1974): 382–405.

Tien Hung-mao. *Government and Politics in Kuomintang China, 1927–1937*. Stanford: Stanford University Press, 1972.

Tilly, Charles. *From Mobilization to Revolution*. Reading, Mass.: Addison-Wesley, 1978.

———. *The Contentious French*. Cambridge, Mass.: Harvard University Press, 1986.

Time Magazine, ed. *Massacre in Beijing: China's Struggle for Democracy*. New York: Warner Books, 1989.

Tsing Yuan. "Urban Riots and Disturbances." In Jonathan Spence and John Wills, eds., *From Ming to Ch'ing*. New Haven: Yale University Press, 1979, pp. 271–320.

Tu Tingquan and Liu Zuomin. "Yi'erjiu yundong zai Tongji" (The December 9th

Movement at Tongji University). In SCYL Youth Movement Research Group, *Yi'erjiu yundong*, pp. 19–23.

Tu Tingxiang et al. *Tongji daxue xuesheng yundongshi, 1919–1949* (A history of the student movement at Tongji University, 1919–1949). Shanghai: Tongji, 1985.

Turner, Victor. *From Ritual to Theatre*. New York: Performing Arts Journal Press, 1982.

———. "Social Drama and Ritual Metaphors." In Schechner and Schuman, *Ritual, Play, and Performance*, pp. 97–122.

Turnley, Peter, and David Turnley. *Beijing Spring*. New York: Stewart, Tabori & Chang, 1989.

United States. Department of State. "Department of State Records Relating to the Internal Affairs of China, 1919–1929." Microfilm.

———. ———. *Foreign Relations of the United States, 1947*, Vol. 7, *China*. Washington, D.C.: U.S. Government Printing Office, 1972.

Wakeman, Frederic, E. Jr. *The Great Enterprise*. Berkeley: University of California Press, 1985.

———. "The June Fourth Movement in China." *Items*, 43, no. 4 (1989): 57–64.

———. "The Price of Autonomy: Intellectuals in Ming and Ch'ing [Qing] Politics." *Daedalus*, 101 (Spring 1972): 35–70.

———. "The Shanghai Public Security Bureau, 1927–1932." Unpublished manuscript, cited with the author's permission.

———. *Strangers at the Gate*. Berkeley: University of California Press, 1966.

Walder, Andrew G. *Chang Ch'un-Ch'iao and Shanghai's January Revolution*. Ann Arbor: University of Michigan, Center for Chinese Studies, 1978.

———. "The Political Sociology of the Beijing Upheaval of 1989." *Problems of Communism*, Sept.–Oct. 1989, pp. 30–40.

Wallerstein, Immanuel, and Paul Starr, eds. *The University in Crisis Reader*, Vol. 2, *Confrontation and Counterattack*. New York: Random House, 1971.

Walter, Richard. *Student Politics in Argentina*. Boston: Basic Books, 1968.

Wang Gangjun et al. "Hujiang daxue de fan 'jidianzhi' douzheng" (The fight against the "old grade system" at Shanghai University). *SQZ*, 1982, no. 1, pp. 63–68.

Wang Guichang. "Shanghai gongren sanci wuzhuang qiyi zhongde xuesheng" (Students in Shanghai's Three Workers' Uprisings). In CYL Youth Movement Research Group, *Gongqingtuan*, pp. 274–82.

Wang Jieshi and Wang Ping. "Cong 'kangbaolian' dao 'yingjihui'" (From the Anti–U.S. Brutality Alliance to the Rescue Association). In Ji'nan University Overseas Chinese Research Group, *Ji'nan xiaoshi*, 2: 127–60.

Wang Ke-wen. "The Kuomintang in Transition: Ideology and Factionalism in the 'National Revolution,' 1924–1932." Ph.D. dissertation, Stanford University, 1985.

Wang Min. "Wusi xuqu: Zhongguo de caoqi xuesheng yundong" (May 4th overture: The early period of the Chinese student movement). In idem et al., eds. *Shanghai xuesheng yundong dashiji*, pp. 1–17. Shanghai: Xuelin, 1981.

———, ed. *Chuntian de yaolan* (The cradle of spring). Beijing: CYL, 1982.

Wang Min et al., eds. *Shanghai xuesheng yundong dashiji* (Major events in the Shanghai student movement). Shanghai: Xuelin, 1981.

Wang Pengnian et al. "Shanghai guoren zibande Zhongwen ribao" (Shanghai's Chinese-run Chinese-language newspapers). *Shanghai difangshi ziliao*, 5 (1986): 11–20.

Wang Ping et al. "Dou 'lang' suoyi" (Trivial memories of the fight with a wolf). In Wang Min, *Chuntian de yaolan*, pp. 162–67.

———. "Xiang baokou yao chifan: 'Wu'erling' yundong zhong de Ji'nan daxue" (Begging for food from the mouths of guns: Ji'nan University during the May 20th Movement). *SQZ*, 1982, no. 3, pp. 22–26.

Wang, Tsi C. *The Youth Movement in China*. New York: New Republic, 1927.

Warner, Shelley. "Shanghai's Response to the Deluge." *Australian Journal of Chinese Affairs*, 24 (1990): 299–314.

Wasserstrom, Jeffrey, "'Civilization' and Its Discontents: The Boxers and Luddites as Heroes and Villains." *Theory and Society*, 16 (1987): 675–707.

———. "The First Chinese Red Scare? 'Fanchi' Propaganda and 'Pro-red' Responses During the Northern Expedition." *Republican China*, 11, no. 1 (1985): 32–51.

———. "Popular Protest and Political Spectacle in Post–World War II Shanghai." Paper presented at the Annual Meeting of the Association for Asian Studies, San Francisco, 1988.

———. "Taking It to the Streets: Shanghai Students and Political Protests, 1919–1949." Ph.D. dissertation, University of California, Berkeley, 1989.

——— [Hua Zhijian]. "Waiguo jizhe he 1946–1947 nian de Shanghai xuesheng yundong (Foreign journalists and the Shanghai student movement of 1946–47). *SQY*, 22 (1987): 29–39.

Wasserstrom, Jeffrey, and Liu Xinyong. "Student Protest and Student Life: Shanghai, 1919–1949." *Social History*, 14, no. 1 (1989): 1–30.

Watson, James. "The Renegotiation of Chinese Cultural Identity in the Post-Mao Era: An Anthropological Perspective." Paper presented at the Four Anniversaries China Conference, Annapolis, Md., Sept. 1989, cited with author's permission.

Watson, James, and Evelyn Rawski, eds. *Death Ritual in Late Imperial and Modern China*. Berkeley: University of California Press, 1988.

Wechsler, James. "Revolt on the Campus, April 13, 1934–April 12, 1935." In De-Conde, *Student Activism*, pp. 280–94.

Wei, Betty Peh-T'i. *Shanghai: Crucible of Modern China*. Oxford: Oxford University Press, 1987.

Wei Xuzheng. "'Wusi' yundong zai Aiguo nüxiao" (The May 4th Movement at the Patriotic School for Girls). *Aiguo zhongxue xiaoqing tekan* (The Patriotic Middle School's special anniversary magazine), Dec. 2, 1981, p. 7.

Wen Jizhe. "'Jiuyiba' yihou Shanghai xuesheng yundong yiji 'Gong wutai shijian'" (The Shanghai student movement after September 18th and the Public Arena Incident). *SQZ*, 1985, no. 15, pp. 9–12.

———. "Sanshi niandai chu 'zuo' ying cuowu dui Shanghai xueyun de yingxiang" (The influence of "leftist" errors on the Shanghai student movement of the early 1930's). *SQZ*, 1983, no. 10, pp. 7–10.

West, Philip. *Yenching University and Sino-Western Relations, 1916–1952*. Cambridge, Mass.: Harvard University Press, 1976.

White, Theodore. *The Making of the President, 1968*. New York: Atheneum, 1969.

Wieger, Léon, ed. and trans. *Chine moderne*. 10 vols. Hsien Hsien, Hebei: n.p., 1920–32.

Wilentz, Sean, ed. *The Rites of Power*. Philadelphia: University of Pennsylvania Press, 1985.

Williams, Raymond. *Marxism and Literature*. New York: Oxford University Press, 1977.

Wolf, Arthur, ed. *Religion and Ritual in Chinese Society*. Stanford: Stanford University Press, 1974.

Wright, Kate. "The Political Fortunes of Shanghai's 'World Economic Herald.'" *Australian Journal of Chinese Affairs*, 23 (1990): 121–32.

Wright, Mary C. *The Last Stand of Chinese Conservatism*. Stanford: Stanford University Press, 1972.

Wu Cengliang. "Kangzhan shengli qianhou Jiaoda xuesheng yundong duanpian" (Fragments on the student movement at Jiaotong University before and after the victory in the War of Resistance). *Dangshi ziliao*, 15 (1983): 44–54.

Wu Chixiang. "Shanghai minzhong fanri jiuguo lianhehui de chengli he huodong qingkuang" (Circumstances relating to the establishment and activities of the Minfan). *Dangshi ziliao*, 9 (1984): 69–76. Reprinted–SASS, *Jiuyiba*, pp. 457–65.

Wu Hua. "Quan Shanghai funü zhan qilaile" (All the women of Shanghai rose up). *Shidai xuesheng*, 1, no. 9/10 (1946): 16–17.

Wu Mouren et al., eds. *Bajiu Zhongguo minyun jishi* (English title: *Daily Reports on the Movement for Democracy in China*). New York: privately published, 1989.

Wu Mu et al. *Zhongguo qingnian yundongshi* (A history of the Chinese youth movement). Beijing: Zhongguo qingnian chubanshe, 1984.

Wu Shaowen. "Huiyi yijiusaner nian Shanghai Ji'nan daxue Gongqingtuan de huodong" (Remembering the activities of the Ji'nan University branch of the CYL in 1932). *SQZ*, 1985, no. 15, pp. 13–15.

Wu Youyi. "Fujing qingyuan de jingguo" (The experience of petitioning in the capital). *Shenghuo*, 6, no. 43 (1931): 793–96.

Xin Honglin et al. "Wusi shiqi de Huanqiu Zhongguo xueshenghui" (The Chinese World Students Association at the time of the May 4th Movement). *SQZ*, 1984, no. 12, pp. 91–95.

Xu Deheng. "Wusi qiande Beida" (Beida before May 4th). In *WY*, 1: 228–33.

Xu Deliang. "Wusa yundong yu Shanghai daxue" (The May 30th Movement and Shanghai University). *Wenshi ziliao* (Shanghai series), 22 (1978): 53–62.

Xu Renhua and Li Lu, eds. *Wu'erling yundong ziliao* (Materials on the May 20th Movement). 2 vols. Beijing: Renmin chubanshe, 1985, 1987.

Yan Jiaqi and Gao Gao. *"Wenhua da geming" shinianshi* (A ten-year history of the "Cultural Revolution"). Tianjin: Tianjin renmin chubanshe, 1986.

Yang, C. K. *Religion in Chinese Society*. Berkeley: University of California Press, 1961.

Yao Minghui. "Shanghai caoqi de xinshi xuetang" (Shanghai's early new-style schools). *Shanghai difangshi ziliao*, 4 (1986): 27–46.

Ye Ruyin. "Ji 'wusi' Shanghai xuesheng lianhehui" (Remembering the May 4th Shanghai Student Union). In Chen Shaoting, *Wusi yundong de huiyi*, pp. 141–50.

Ye Shengtao. *Schoolmaster Ni Huan-chih*. Trans. A. C. Barnes. Beijing: Foreign Languages Press, 1958.

Yeh Wen-hsin. *The Alienated Academy: Culture and Politics in Republican China, 1919–1937*. Cambridge, Mass.: Harvard University Press, 1990.

Yi Mu and Mark V. Thompson. *Crisis at Tiananmen: Reform and Reality in Modern China*. San Francisco: China Books, 1989.

Yi Sheng. "Shanghaishi dazhong xuesheng huanying Maershi teshi shimo" (The full story of the welcome for special envoy Marshall by Shanghai middle-school and college students). *Minzhu*, 12 (1946, New Year's ed.): 289–91.

Yip, Ka-che. *Religion, Nationalism and Chinese Students: The Anti-Christian Movement of 1922–1927*. Bellingham, Wash.: Western Washington University, 1980.

You Han. "Liuyue ershisan natian" (That day, June 23). *Zhou bao*, 43 (June 29, 1946): 8–10.

Yu Heng. "'Wusi' shiqi Fudan daxue dashiji" (Major May 4th events at Fudan University). *Xiaoshi tongxun* (Fudan), 8 (1984): 14–31.

Yu Mok Chiu and J. Frank Harrison, eds. *Voices from Tiananmen Square: Beijing Spring and the Democracy Movement*. New York: Black Rose, 1990.

Yu Xueren. *Zhongguo xiandai xuesheng yundongshi changbian* (An extended history of modern Chinese student movements). Jilin: Huabei shifan daxue chubanshe, 1988.

Yu Ying. "Shanghai diqu riwei qingnian tuanzu zhi yange gaishu" (An outline of the evolution of Shanghai youth leagues under the Japanese puppets). *SQY*, 25 (1988, no. 1): 74–80.

Yu Zidao et al., eds. *Wang Jingwei hanjian zhengquan de xingwang* (The rise and fall of the political power of the traitor Wang Jingwei). Shanghai: Fudan, 1987.

Yue Zhi. "Shanghai ju'e yundong shulun" (On the Resist Russia Movement in Shanghai). *Dang'an yu lishi*, 1986, no. 1, pp. 58–64.

Zhang Dachun. "Qingmo Shanghai liangda xuechao" (Shanghai's two big late Qing student storms). *Shanghai difangshi ziliao*, 4 (1986): 118–27.

Zhang Jishun. "Lun Shanghai zhengzhi yundongzhong de xuesheng qunti, 1925–1927 nian" (A discussion of student groups in Shanghai political movements, 1925–1927). Paper presented at the International Symposium on Modern Shanghai held at SASS, Sept. 1988.

Zhang Quan and Ren Jianshu. *Wusa yundong jianshi* (A basic history of the May 30th Movement). Shanghai: Shanghai renmin chubanshe, 1985.

Zhang Tingjing. "Canjia wusi yundong de huiyi" (Memories of taking part in the May 4th Movement). *Wenshi ziliao* (Shanghai series), 27 (1979): 28–32.

Zhang Yabing. "Quanzhang zhongxue he Daxia daxue xuesheng geming huodong jiankuang" (A sketch of revolutionary activities at Quanzhang Middle School and Daxia College). *Dangshi ziliao*, 20 (1984): 74–80.

Zhang Yi. "Fudan shisheng zai 'wusi' yundong zhong de zuoyong" (The role of Fudan's teachers and students in the May 4th Movement). *Xiaoshi tongxun* (Fudan), 8 (1984): 39–41.

Zhang Yunhou et al., eds. *Wusi shiqi de shetuan* (May 4th–era social organizations). 3 vols. Beijing: Sanlian shudian, 1972.

Zhao Shaoquan et al., eds. *Fudan daxuezhi, 1905–1949* (The Fudan University gazetteer, 1905–1949). Shanghai: Fudan, 1985.

Zhou Fenwu et al., "'Jiaoda wansui'" ("Long live Jiaotong University"). In Wang Min, *Chuntian de yaolan*, pp. 180–98.

Zhou Peiyuan. "Zai jiaohui xuejiao de aiguo douzheng" (Patriotic struggles at a missionary school). In CASS, *Wusi yundong huiyilu*, 2: 639–44.

Zhou Shangwen and Jia Shiyou. *Shanghai gongren sanci wuzhuang qiyishi* (A history of Shanghai's Three Workers' Uprisings). Shanghai: Shanghai renmin chubanshe, 1987.

Zhu Bangxing et al., eds. *Shanghai chanye yu Shanghai zhigong* (Shanghai industries and Shanghai workers). 1939. Reprinted–Shanghai: Shanghai renmin chubanshe, 1984.

Zhu Zhonghua. "Nanwang de suiyue: Wusi yundong zai Shanghai zayi" (An unforgettable time: Assorted memories of the Shanghai May 4th Movement). *Xiaoshi tongxun* (Fudan), 8 (1984): 32–38.

———. "Wusi yundong zai Shanghai" (The May 4th Movement in Shanghai). In CASS, *Huiyilu*, 3: 265–73.

CHINESE CHARACTER LIST

Gongtong jiuguohui	共同救國會	Liuri huiguo xueshenghui	留日回國學生會
Guanghua daxue	光華大學	Liuri xuesheng jiuguotuan	留日學生救國團
Guikutuan	跪哭團		
guofu	國父	luan	亂
Guoli Jiaotong daxue xiaoche	國立交通大學校車	maiguo	賣國
		minfan	民反
guomin dahui	國民大會	*Minguo ribao*	民國日報
Guomindang	國民黨	*Minli bao*	民力報
Guominjun	國民軍	Minzhong fating	民眾法庭
Guxingshe	孤星社	minzhu	民主
houtai	後台	"Minzhu wansui"	民主萬歲
Huadong shifan daxue	華東師範大學	"Minzhu, ziyou, pingdeng"	民主,自由,平等
Huanqiu Zhongguo xueshenghui	寰球中國學生會	"Mobu guanxin, yipi bufang"	莫不關心,一屁不放
		Nanfang daxue	南方大學
Huaxue bao	華血報	neibu	內部
huiguan	會館	nengyan shandao	能言善道
Jiaotong daxue	交通大學	*Ni Huanzhi*	倪煥之
jiexiong	傑雄	niuma	牛馬
jilu junduihua	紀律軍隊化	pai	派
Ji'nan daxue	暨南大學	"Qingjiu jiaoyu weiji"	搶救教育危機
Ji'nan zhi lang	暨南之狼		
Jingjixue hui	經濟學會	qingnian	青年
jiucha	糾察	*Qingnian de xue*	青年的血
jiuchabu	糾察部	*Qingnian zhishi*	青年智試
jiuchadui	糾察隊	Quanguo xuelian	全國學聯
jiuguo	救國	re	熱
Juiguotuan	救國團	Rendaohui	仁悼會
junduihua	軍隊化	*Renmin ribao*	人民日報
kaimushi	開幕式	rexue	熱血
kang	抗	*Rexue ribao*	熱血日報
kangbaohui	抗暴會	sanba	三罷
kangri hui	抗日會	Sanminzhuyi qingniantuan	三民主義青年團
kangri jiuguo hui	抗日救國會		
Keji daxue	科技大學	Sanqingtuan	三青團
Kexue daxue	科學大學	*Shangda wusa tekan*	上大五卅特刊
Lanyishe	藍衣社		
laobaixing	老百姓	Shangda Zhejiang tongxianghui	上大浙江同鄉會
lei	淚		
leng	冷	Shanghai daxue	上海大學
lengtie	冷鐵	Shanghai minzhong fanri jiuguo lianhehui	上海民眾反日救國聯合會
lengxue	冷血		
li	禮		
Lianhebao	聯合報	Shanghai renmin tuanti lianhehui	上海人民團體聯合會
lieshizhuan	列士傳		

Shanghai xuesheng zhengque heping lianhehui	上海學生爭確和平聯合會	*Xuehen*	血痕
		xuelei	血淚
		xueqi	血氣
shanshu	善書	*Xueshengbao*	學生報
Shaonian shidai	少年時代	xueshu	血書
Shehuizhuyi qingniantuan	社會主義青年團	Xueshu yanjiuhui	學術研究會
		xueyiting	血衣庭
Shidai ribao	時代日報	yangcheng gong	養成工
shirentuan	十人團	yangnu	洋奴
Shishi xinbao	時事新報	yanjiang	演講
shiwu	實物	"Ye xing jun"	夜行軍
"Shouwei zujie"	守維組界	Ying zujie	英租界
Subao	蘇報	yizhi duiwai	一致對外
sui	歲	yixiangting	遺像庭
tai	台	youzhishi	有智識
Taochi xunbao	討赤詢報	zhan	戰
tewu	特務	Zhendan daxue	震旦大學
tewu xuesheng	特務學生	zheng heping	爭和平
Tongji daxue	同濟大學	*Zhengyan bao*	正言報
Tongmenghui	同盟會	zhihui	指揮
Tongwen shuyuan	同文書院	zhishi	智識
tongxianghui	同鄉會	Zhixingshe	知行社
wangguo	亡國	Zhongguo guomin gonghui	中國國民公會
Wenhuibao	文滙報	Zhongguo qingshaonian tuan	中國青少年團
wenyan	文言		
Wusa xue'an shilu	五卅血案實錄	"Zhongguoren buda Zhongguoren"	中國人不打中國人
Wusa xuelei	五卅血淚		
Wusaxue tekan	五卅血特刊	Zhongguo tongzijun	中國童子軍
wuzhishi	無智識		
Xiangdao zhoubao	嚮導週報	Zhongguo xuesheng tongmenghui	中國學生同盟會
xiangyue	鄉約		
xiaodui	小隊		
Xiaoshuo yuebao	小說月報	Zhongyang daxue	中央大學
xiatai	下台	Zijuehui	自覺會
Xinmin wanbao	新民晚報	zixiu	自修
Xinqingnian	新青年	zizhihui	自治會
xuanchuan	宣傳	zong zhihui	總指揮
xuanchuan zu	宣傳組	zougou	走狗
xue	血		
xuechao	學潮		
Xuechao rikan	血潮日報		

INDEX

In this index an "f" after a number indicates a separate reference on the next page, and an "ff" indicates separate references on the next two pages. A continuous discussion over two or more pages is indicated by a span of page numbers, e.g., "57–59." *Passim* is used for a cluster of references in close but not consecutive sequence.

Library of Congress Cataloging-in-Publication Data

Wasserstrom, Jeffrey N.
  Student protests in twentieth-century China : the view from
Shanghai / Jeffrey N. Wasserstrom.
      p. cm.
  Includes bibliographical references and index.
  ISBN 0-8047-1881-4 (alk. paper) :
  1. Student movements—China—Shanghai—History—20th century.
2. Students—China—Shanghai—Political activity—History—20th
century.   I. Title.
LA1134.S4W37 1991
378.1'981—dc20   90-22307
                                                        CIP

⊗ This book is printed on acid-free paper